The Classic Tales

THE CLASSIC TALES

4,000 YEARS
OF JEWISH LORE

Ellen Frankel

JASON ARONSON INC.
Northvale, New Jersey
London

First Softcover Edition—1993

10 9 8

Library of Congress Cataloging-in-Publication Data

Frankel, Ellen.
The classic tales
  Bibliography : p.
  Includes index.
  1. Legends, Jewish.   2. Jewish folk literature.
3. Bible. O.T.–Legends. 4. Talmud–Legends.
5. Hasidim–Legends.   I. Title.
BM530.F68 1989   296.1'9   88-35119
ISBN 0-87668-904-7 (hb)
ISBN 1-56821-038-8 (pb)

Manufactured in the United States of America. Jason Aronson Inc. offers books and cassettes. For information and catalog write to Jason Aronson Inc., 230 Livingston Street, Northvale, New Jersey 07647.

In memory of my beloved teacher

Hershel Jonah Matt, ז״ל

Contents

PART II.   FROM UR TO EGYPT—THE FIRST FOUR GENERATIONS

PART III.   FROM SLAVERY TO FREEDOM

Section 2. Love

Section 3.   Reward and Punishment

Section 4.   Figures in History

Section 5.   Israel among the Nations

Section 6.   Fools

Section 7.   The Fantastic

Section 8.   Fox Fables

Acknowledgments

Making my way through four thousand years of stories has been no easy task. Many people have guided me along the way, foremost among them my editor Arthur Kurzweil, whose encouraging words and unflagging faith heartened me when I tired and gave me courage when I became overwhelmed by the magnitude of the undertaking. His commitment to publishing new works of Judaica for our generation of readers and writers has been an inspiration to many.

I would also like to thank my production editor, Dorothy Erstling, whose enthusiasm and professionalism made the final phase of the project as rewarding as the first.

Many people helped me track down the often elusive origins of the tales. Yitzhak Buxbaum, a marvelous maggid and scholar of the Jewish tale tradition, provided me with many sources, including the oral teachings of his teacher, Rabbi Shlomo Carlebach. Rabbi Carlebach, too, lent me words of encouragement and guidance.

In addition, I would like to thank my friend Norman Shore, whose emendations of the manuscript saved me later embarrassment and whose mastery of the midrashic tradition inspired me to do my homework well.

I am also grateful to Dr. Arthur Lesley, Director of the Joseph Meyerhoff Library at the Baltimore Hebrew University; Dr. Arthur Green; Rabbi Nehemiah Polen; Annette and Eugene Labovitz; Jerry Schwarzbard, Reference Librarian at the Jewish Theological Seminary Library; and Ruth Clements, for their help in researching sources.

For assistance in finding suitable artwork to illustrate the stories, I am indebted to the staff at Art Resources; and Evelyn Cohen and Debby Newman Camin, curators of graphics at the Jewish Theological Seminary.

I would like to thank Art Waskow for his linguistic inventiveness in recasting midrash in an American idiom, particularly for the pun "humus" and "human" in the Eden account and "God-wrestling" in the story of Jacob and the angel.

Every story-teller needs an audience. I am grateful to Mitch and Wally Chefitz and the Havurah of South Florida for being my first listeners. Their enthusiastic response was a welcome antidote to the mute acquiescence of my computer. And I also wish to thank my class at the 1988 National Havurah Institute for "field-testing" the tales with their hearts and heads.

I owe a special debt of gratitude to my two writer friends, Charlotte Weaver-Gelzer and Sarah White, whose patient listening and thoughtful commentary helped carry me through the many months of research and writing. As newcomers to the Jewish narrative tradition, they were able to bring to the project fresh eyes and a wider perspective, which enhanced my own appreciation of the tales.

Finally, I wish to thank my husband Herb Levine and my children, Sarah Pearl and Les, for their unwavering support and enthusiasm. As a result of my writing this book, we have become a family of story-tellers. Each night as I sat down to dinner after a day of reading and writing,

Sarah and Les would ask me to tell them the story I had discovered that day; months later when I repeated that tale, they would stop me in the middle and finish it. Their joy in hearing and telling stories has confirmed for me the power of the folk tradition in transmitting Jewish history and values.

To Herbie I wish to give a special measure of thanks. He has been my partner, my loyal fan, my listener, and my friend. Without his faith and company, I could not have told my tales.

Introduction

What is a tale?

By itself, rather a humble thing, a brief entertainment, the occasion for a tear, a smile, a sigh, an understanding nod. To a child drifting toward the shoals of sleep, it shines a reassuring beacon; to a soul beset with care, it momentarily unknits the brow. A good tale will repolish old truths that have lost their shine, reminding us of what we always knew. While in the tale's thrall, we temporarily forget the stalking Dark Angel and regain our lost youth. But all this magic is short-lived. Once the tale releases us, we deny our enchantment.

But something else happens when tales join their voices together into a great chorus of stories echoing down through the generations. Taken collectively, a people's tales gain uncommon strength. They never let their listeners out of their thrall.

So it is with Jewish tales. In their presence, we become *listeners*, heeding an ancient call: Hear, O Israel! Indeed, our very lives become part of the Tale; we see design where others see accident, consummation where others see only death. We learn to *interpret* history, not only to record it, turning over each event in our minds until we determine its rightful place in the sacred scroll, the weathered skin of our collective experience.

For a people's tales are its memory, its conscience, its channel to the divine imagination. In them are embedded the formative experiences of the nation, the primal sensibilities that first shaped and even now continue to shape a particular people's vision of the world. A national body of tales is just that: a collective mind imbued with centuries of wisdom and an infinite recall, legs sinewed by a thousand odysseys, fingers flexed to recapture treasures glimpsed and lost, a heart pressed and steeled by the vise of fate, blood and bile and breath stirred up and cooled in the service of an inventive God.

What precisely makes our body of tales *Jewish*? Not language, since we have told stories in so many—Hebrew, Aramaic, Greek, Latin, Arabic, Ladino, Yiddish, Romance languages, English. Not place, since we have wandered the whole earth, borrowing landscapes and climates and even fantasied realms from every people we have met. Not characters, since we have played—or played at—them all: merchant, sage, servant, harlot, king, princess, artist, fool.

What, then, characterizes us as *Jewish* storytellers? Are our stories indeed any different from the Arabian Nights, the Indian Panchatantra, or the Brothers Grimm? Have we in our stories, if nowhere else, attained the early Zionists' dream: to be a nation like all other nations, to tell the same stories?

But we are not like other nations. Our stories, taken as a whole, are different in the same way that our way of life is different. And that is because our task is different. Adam and Eve were told to conquer the earth, subdue it, and fill it with their progeny. Noah received the same commission later on. But with Abraham and Sarah it was different. They were told to "go forth," to leave home and go on a quest as any hero must, but not to seek treasure

or fame or beauty or power, but to seek God in themselves and among strangers. And so we have continued to
this day. And wherever we have gone, we have told
stories about our journey.

Perhaps Abraham became the first Jew because he
loved to tell certain kinds of stories, stories about all
things being connected, about unity and pattern and
purpose, about a single spirit infusing the world with
meaning. It was not that he was the first storyteller—no,
his world already abounded with tales, of the Mesopo-
tamian gods Marduk and Tiamat, of Utnapishtim the
ark-builder and Gilgamesh the wanderer, of floods and
heavenly strife and human strivings—but Abraham saw a
different world than his neighbors. Where they saw cruel
gods and capricious fate, he saw design. Where they saw
the rule of power, he saw covenant and accountability.
Where they saw the wheel of fortune, he saw history.

And he told stories that reflected that vision: the
creation and its majestic order. The Tree of Knowledge
and its challenge to humanity. The Flood and its promise
for the future. The tales he told were new to his neighbors' ears. Perhaps they seemed laughable or even threat-
ening. What folly to have faith in such intangible divinity!
A God of happy endings, fairy tales whose plots humanity helps shape. Absurd! Dangerous!

But Abraham and Sarah had faith nonetheless and
continued to tell stories. And Abraham told Ishmael the
stories, but somehow they made no sense to him. For
Ishmael was a man of action, a hunter, a wild ass of a man
who preferred to read the lessons the land taught him
instead of the lessons of an invisible God. So Abraham
told his tales to Isaac. And this son listened and promised
to pass them on.

So was born history—*toldot* in Hebrew, literally,
"generations." Stories transmitted from parent to child. A
different kind of history than we moderns understand.
Yet every bit as true as the stories of Herodotus and
Gibbon. Perhaps even truer.

We are Jews today because of those stories. Though

life often seems to lack meaning, we make up stories to wrest meaning out of the absurd and unjust vicissitudes of our lot. That is the basic impulse of the Jewish tale: to make sense out of the things that happen to us, as individuals and as a people. And to tell these stories takes as much faith as to believe in one God. For they are essentially the same thing.

It has often been said that the number of plots available to a storyteller is limited. But oh, the infinite permutations to these plots!

It is precisely these permutations that make a national body of tales unique. Although the human condition is universal, each people has to weave its own national costume out of the tangled skein of its particular experiences. And although we Jews have lived almost everywhere and have spoken almost every tongue, we have our own distinct voice that resonates in our tales, sometimes only faintly, sometimes with the clarity of a shofar blast.

Often it is an old voice that speaks in a Jewish tale. These ancient echoes are brought back to life through the device of *proof-texts*, words and phrases quoted from previous speakers, usually biblical, who lend their sacred authority to a new teller's words and so make listeners more willing to lend an ear. Proof-texts do more than lend authority, however; they also lend pattern to a tale, bringing it into the Golden Chain, *shalshelet* in Hebrew, *goldeneh keyt* in Yiddish, the unbroken strand stretching between the generations.

But there are new voices, too. In fact, our written and oral traditions are nothing more—or less—than an interminable conversation among the generations. The Prophets consulted their elders, centuries dead, for guidance about the new generations who had forgotten the old stories. And they invented new tales, some horrific, others consoling, to address the new challenges facing their people.

The Rabbis of the Talmud also talked among themselves and with their predecessors, embellishing the old stories to teach or to prove or to persuade or simply to delight each other and future listeners. These embellishments constitute a genre of storytelling called *midrash*, from the Hebrew verb "to search out," a process of reading between the lines of the biblical text to fill in the missing stories. The Rabbis never asked themselves *why* a particular story might have been left out; they simply assumed that the earlier tellers deliberately left room for future stories, the way a prudent gardener will leave room between new seedlings for future growth.

And so, the rabbinic sages "invented" the story of Abraham smashing his father's idols, a tale not found anywhere in the biblical text. Why? Because they perceived that the Bible began Abraham's story too late, with God's command to leave Ur: "Go forth from your native land and your father's house to the land that I will show you." Why, asked these later readers, did Abraham have to leave his home? What did he do to merit such an uprooting? To answer these questions, they imagined a young man in the throes of religious doubt, challenging his entire culture with the revolutionary idea of a single, invisible God. They imagined him at home, the child of an idol maker, caught between filial devotion and the undeniable call of faith. Out of this imaginative reconstruction came the tale of a rebellion, a conversion—his entire family's as well as many strangers'—and a voluntary exile from all he knew. Did the Rabbis make this story up out of whole cloth? Yes. But also no. The seeds were there; they grew from roots firmly planted in the sacred text.

Many of the tales so familiar to us derive from this midrashic process: the baby Moses choosing a burning coal over Pharaoh's crown and certain death; God unsuccessfully peddling the Torah to the other nations until Israel finally accepts it; David's life spared by a spider and a wasp; Solomon flying on his magic carpet in search of new and greater wisdom. Ask most Jewish children to tell you a Bible story and chances are that many of them will tell you the *midrash* about Abraham and his clever trick with his father's idols. They know—as many adult Bible scholars do not—that all these stories are an inseparable part of the Torah, whether they were given at Sinai or at Yavneh or in the study houses of Europe. As our tradition teaches, the Torah is a tree of life to all who hold fast to it—the healthy trees must grow and bear fruit.

Besides the creative technique of *midrash*, the Rabbis also bequeathed to us the principle of *"Ein me'ukhar ve'ein mukdam ba-torah"* —"There is no before and after in the Torah." *Torah* here means the entire body of sacred literature. Chronology is simply not a constraint to the Jewish storyteller. Of course, to a modern historian such a principle is simply preposterous. Imagine Plato sitting down to tea with Galileo Galilei! But then, imagine it!

The rabbis saw the entire tradition as a unity, just as modern physicists see cosmic space as curving back on itself. Why not seat Isaac in a talmudic academy or Moses in Rabbi Akiva's classroom? After all, the generations have much to teach each other, and if they cannot physically meet in this life, why not in the world of the tale, perhaps as close as we can come to the gates of Eden while we still draw breath? Luckily for us, the rabbinic sages were not hampered by modern strictures about chronology and dates. They freely roamed the plains of time, watering their fancies at any well they chanced upon. Had they stayed home, fretting about the proprieties of history, how much the poorer we would be!

After the talmudic sages finished their five-hundred-year conversation and lapsed into silence, others took up the thread, spinning new *midrashim* and borrowing freely from the tales of other peoples: the Panchatantra of India, the Kalila and Dimna of Persia, Aesop's Fables, the 1001 Arabian Nights, the Christian Gesta Romanorum, local folktales. Wherever we wandered, mostly as traders, scribes, and interpreters, we collected tales and transmitted them, often translating them into new languages to peddle with our wares. In large measure, the classic fairy tales of the Brothers Grimm entered Europe through Jewish mouths. Some of these stories changed their voices and assumed foreign tongues; others stayed within our family and still speak to us today.

And new voices continue to add their savor to the stew: Hasidic voices telling of wonder-working rabbis buttonholing God; oriental voices from Morocco, Yemen, Iraq, and Tunisia, sometimes still carrying echoes of ancient enchantments, at other times smelling of the bazaar and apricot groves; women's voices filling in the spaces left for them by three thousand years of silence, resurrecting old ghosts, discovering hidden treasures, bringing new energies to tired tongues. And each of our own voices, retelling all of these stories and making them our own, participating in *toldot*, the history of generations listening.

And of what do our stories tell?

The first ones naturally speak of origins—how the world began, the creation of monsters and miracles, the alphabet and humankind; then of families—their quarrels and reconciliations, their births, marriages, and deaths; then of national matters—how a people is forged by slavery and tempered by the wilderness, how a nation takes possession of its land and negotiates its covenant with God.

These early tales are familiar to most peoples. Every national folklore begins at the beginning and introduces its ancestors to later generations. Such first heroes always stand larger than life, even if some have feet of clay. They are our models and our goads, the golden molds to our tin coins. They contend with giants and spirits, maintain a special relationship with the heavens, die gloriously.

But something happens to Jewish heroes in the wake of national exile, first at the hand of Babylonia in 586 B.C.E. and then again in 70 C.E. at the hand of Rome. No longer do our stories glorify our own power, for we have become powerless. No longer do we people our tales with Jewish kings, for we are now the subjects of other crowns. No longer do our heroes talk directly to God, for the heavens have barred their gates, at least the front ones. Now they must take the long way around.

And so beginning with talmudic tales set in the period following the Roman conquest, Jewish stories take on a different cast. The vision embodied within them is now profoundly religious and moral, addressing the problem most challenging to all religious systems: theodicy—God's justice in the world. With rare exception these tales vindicate God's role in human affairs, arguing for the triumph of good over evil, for the ultimate just recompense of sinner and saint, for the redemptive power of charity. Instead of stating their message explicitly, they *dramatize* the value system embodied in the Jewish tradition: study, worship, and deeds of loving kindness. The heroes in these tales are spiritual giants; their adversaries, the monsters called Lust and Greed and Vanity and Moral Arrogance. And there are small nameless heroes, too, those whose deeds might save only a single soul, perhaps only themselves. But as the tradition teaches: One who saves a single life is to be regarded as having saved the whole world.

Perhaps the most significant feature in these later tales, which span two thousand years and dozens of countries, is their sense of irony. In the days of the Bible, God was a partner in every plot, if not the main actor. If Moses triumphed over Pharaoh, it was only because God orchestrated the grand opera of the Exodus. If Joshua or Deborah or David or Elijah mastered their enemies, it was only because God fulfilled their prophecies.

But what of Rabbi Akiva emerging from the mystical orchard unscathed, or Yohanan smuggled to Vespasian in a coffin and bargaining for Yavneh, or the Maharal of Prague outwitting Israel's enemies with an automaton fashioned out of mud and magic? Although God is obviously behind these scenes, it is now human wisdom and cunning that take center stage. For without a land, without the covenant bound up with the land, the Jew must now live by his wits. And irony is wit's sharpest weapon, with a two-sided blade capable of piercing enemies both without—the Hamans and the czars—and within, our own self-delusion and hubris. Thus, in addition to tales of the Jews' ironic triumphs over Greece, over Rome, over European princes, we also have stories of failure—sexual trespass, intellectual conceit, spiritual arrogance, the foolishness of Chelm.

It is precisely this double-edged vision that has been the secret to our survival. Without the self-aggrandizement made possible through ironic narrative, we could not have held up our heads all these centuries in a world that so often despised us. Without the self-criticism made possible through an irony turned against ourselves, we would not have held on to our faith in something beyond our own wits.

For almost four thousand years, we have been both the teller and the tale, acting all the parts assigned us while at the same time narrating the play. Ours has been one of history's grandest roles but also one of its most exacting. And the final curtain has yet to fall. It cannot, for the last player has yet to strut the boards. When that scene comes, the Story comes to an end.

But until then, we have stories enough to while away the time.

How to Read This Book

This collection contains three hundred stories spanning four thousand years and three continents. To help you find your way through this wealth of material, I have provided a chronological table of contents in the front of the volume as well as several indexes in the back arranged by holiday, by Torah and Haftorah readings, by character types, by symbols, and by topics. In addition, there is a general index of proper names and places and a list of sources.

I hope that these many doors will lead you to all the treasures you seek.

A Note on Methods and Sources

In making my selection of tales, I have been guided by three general principles: how representative the tale is of Jewish tradition, how well it complements the other tales in its particular section, and how well it reads as a story. The choice of stories also reflects my own tastes and biases. I have made no attempt to be comprehensive; rather, my ambition has been to present many of the best tales Jewish tradition has to offer.

In order to offer the most readable narratives, I have occasionally integrated material from several sources. In the biblical stories, I have often incorporated parts of the scriptural account within a larger midrashic framework so that the stories have a discernible unity. I have also omitted several central biblical tales—Noah and the Flood, the story of Ruth, Jonah and the Whale among others— because I feel that the biblical accounts stand on their own as complete narratives without need of or benefit from further midrashic embellishment.

In biblical as well as later stories, I have often woven

together several versions of the same tale, following the ancient model of the Torah itself as well as the more contemporary model of Louis Ginzberg's *Legends of the Jews*. My primary criterion has been literary coherence, not editorial accuracy. For those interested in tracing the separate threads of a particular tale, refer to the list of sources at the end of the book.

Because I have been interested in recovering women's stories and voices within the Jewish tradition, I have restored names for female characters who have remained nameless in most Jewish story collections: Adam's first wife Lilith, Noah's wife Naamah, Lot's wife Edith, Jephthah's daughter Sheilah, and many others. I have also chosen to exclude some stories that are blatantly misogynistic, although my commitment to presenting a *representative* sample of Jewish tales has restrained my hand particularly in the selection of ancient texts.

In arranging the material in chronological order, I have been guided by the *subject matter* of the tales, not by their date of composition. Thus the collection reads more like a folk history than a scholarly compilation. The one exception to the chronological pattern is the final section, "Elijah the Prophet." In his post-biblical incarnation, Elijah has appeared on every stage in our itinerant theater, sometimes as beggar, other times as slave, still other times as supernatural redeemer. To indicate his extraordinary status beyond the constraints of history, I have included stories about him at the end of the collection.

Although the Jewish people now lives on six continents, most of its history has been confined to three: Europe, Asia, and Africa, with the Middle East significantly bridging all three. The first half of this collection focuses on Israel and Babylonia as the crucible of our narrative genius, specifically as embodied in the Bible, Talmud, and *midrash*. The second half tilts unevenly to the side of Europe, especially in that sixty of these tales originate from the hasidic culture of Eastern Europe. Since I have intended this book primarily for an American audience, most of whom trace their origins back to

Europe, I have purposely chosen to bias the collection in that direction.

Finally, I have chosen to end my collection in the nineteenth century with the later Hasidic masters, rather than bring it up to contemporary times. My reason for this is twofold: first, because it is too early to tell which new tales will find a permanent place within the tradition and which will die away; and second, because the folk tradition necessarily implies anonymous authorship, which is exceedingly difficult to achieve in our time and culture characterized as it is by individual achievement and fame. (My own exception to this rule was to include three tales authored by Rabbi Nahman of Bratzlav, although he himself did not write them down. Their stylized characters and plots set them squarely within the folktale tradition.) Perhaps in future years when the dust finally settles over our bones, our own generation's voices will blend with those of past storytellers and add our echoes to our people's timeless tale.

For those who wish to read further within the Jewish tale tradition, I recommend the following works in English:

GENERAL COLLECTIONS

The single most comprehensive collection of Jewish tales is Joseph Bin Gorion's three-volume *Mimekor Yisrael: Classical Jewish Folktales* (Bloomington, IN: Indiana University Press, 1976). This collection contains 1,000 tales spanning the entire tradition, including multiple variants of many tales. The prose is quite readable and unencumbered by scholarly apparatus.

Raphael Patai's *Gates to the Old City* (Northvale, NJ: Jason Aronson, 1988) offers selections from traditional texts, from the Bible to the Hasidic period. Rather than integrate scriptural and later material, Patai keeps all sources separate, so that the narrative material appears more fragmentary than it does within the classical tradition. The English reflects the author's scholarly bias rather than his interest in telling stories. There is an excellent introduction to the collection.

A shorter general collection is Nathan Ausubel's *Treasury of Jewish Folklore*, which has recently been reissued by Crown. This collection, although somewhat dated in its humor, offers a diverse selection of short folktales, including Chelm stories, traditional shtetl *maa' selakh*, and classical tales.

Other good general anthologies of stories include Peninnah Schram's *Jewish Stories One Generation Tells Another* (Northvale, NJ: Jason Aronson, 1987); Howard Schwartz's collections *Elijah's Violin* (New York: Harper and Row, 1983), *Miriam's Tambourine* (New York: Free Press, 1986), and *Lilith's Cave* (New York: Harper and Row, 1988); Zev Vilnay's three-volume *Legends of Eretz Yisrael* (Philadelphia: Jewish Publication Society, 1973, 1975, 1978); and Dov Noy's *Folktales of Israel* (Chicago: University of Chicago, 1963).

BIBLICAL COLLECTIONS

The monumental seven-volume work of Louis Ginzberg, *The Legends of the Jews*, has not been surpassed since its publication earlier in this century (1909–1938). With three volumes of tales, three volumes of notes, and an entire volume devoted to the index, this work contains all the midrashic material based upon biblical narratives. Ginzberg weaves all the tales together into coherent stories, leaving the reader to unravel the strands in the notes. Although this collection is comprehensive, its English is that of the scholar, not the storyteller, so it is more useful as a reference than as a literary text.

Judah Nadich's collection, *Jewish Legends of the Second Commonwealth* (Philadelphia: Jewish Publication Society, 1983), is devoted exclusively to tales covering the period beginning with the return from Babylon exile until the Destruction of the Second Temple. There are extensive notes and introductions.

Regrettably out of print, the poet Hayim Nahman

Bialik's *And It Came to Pass* (New York: Hebrew Publishing House, 1938) is a delightful collection of tales about King David and Solomon. The prose sparkles with wit and charm.

MEDIEVAL COLLECTIONS

Moses Gaster's *The Ma'aseh Book* (Philadelphia: Jewish Publication Society, 1981), is based on an earlier collection by the same name that appeared in Germany in 1602 and enjoyed remarkable popularity among medieval Jews. Its 250 stories include some traditional rabbinic material as well as local folklore and legend.

HASIDIC COLLECTIONS

For many years, Martin Buber's collections of Hasidic tales—the two-volume *Tales of the Hasidim* (New York: Schocken, 1947-1948), *Legends of the Baal Shem Tov* (New York: Schocken, 1955), *Tales of Rabbi Nahman* (New York: Schocken, 1956)—were all that was available in English. These collections still reward the reader, although many scholars now challenge the authenticity of the rather romantic picture Buber paints of these early Hasidic masters.

In addition to Buber, readers can now find many collections of hasidic tales: Meyer Levin's *Classic Hasidic Tales* (New York: Citadel Press, 1966); Louis Newman's *Hasidic Anthology* (Northvale, NJ: Jason Aronson, 1987), which is arranged topically rather than historically; Arnold Band's *Nahman of Bratslav: The Tales* (Mahwah, NJ: Paulist Press, 1978), to name only a few.

In more recent times, Yaffa Eliach has edited *Hasidic Tales of the Holocaust* (New York: Oxford University Press, 1982), a powerful collection of tales arising out of the ashes of World War Two.

MODERN COLLECTIONS

In 1983, Howard Schwartz edited a collection called *Gates to the New City* (Avon), which will be reissued in 1989 by Jason Aronson. This collection brings together 180 stories written during this century, both by noted authors such as Sholom Aleichem, Franz Kafka, and Primo Levi, as well as younger authors from Europe, Israel, and America. These tales are based on traditional materials and attempt to place themselves within the classical midrashic tradition, although most put modern twists on their interpretations.

ILLUSTRATIONS

Page 2—*The Tower of Babel.* Courtesy of the Jewish Theological Seminary, New York, New York.

Page 46—*Abraham in Nimrod's Furnace.* Courtesy of the Chester Beatty Library and Gallery of Oriental Art, Dublin, Ireland.

Page 94—*Pharaoh and the Plague of Frogs.* Courtesy of the Pierpont Morgan Library, New York, New York. M. 638 F. 8.

Page 172—*Yael Kills Sisera.* Courtesy of the Jewish Theological Seminary, New York, New York.

Page 194—*Meeting of Solomon and the Queen of Sheba.* Courtesy of Art Resources, New York, New York.

Page 262—*The Temple at Jerusalem.* Courtesy of the Jewish Theological Seminary, New York, New York.

Page 292—*Rabbinic Discussion at B'nai B'rak.* Courtesy of George Weidenfeld and Nicolson, Limited, London, England.

Page 342—*Purim Costumes and Games.* Courtesy of the Jewish Theological Seminary, New York, New York.

Page 472—*Jewish Holiday Customs.* Courtesy of the Jewish Theological Seminary, New York, New York.

Page 576—*Elijah Ascends in a Chariot of Fire.* Courtesy of the Jewish Theological Seminary, New York, New York.

PART I

IN THE BEGINNING

The Torah teaches that in the beginning God created the heavens and the earth. But legend teaches that the Torah itself preceded creation. The holy words were written in letters of black fire emblazoned upon white fire, the alphabet of creation. All the rest was commentary.

1

The Beginning

Before the heavens and the earth were made, while all still whirled in the chaos of first things, God fashioned the Torah. Eons before the earth cooled and life burst forth upon its fertile soil, the letters of the Torah blazed forth, black fire upon white fire, lighting up the entire universe with its glory.

And then God created a world. But alas! It was not a perfect world, and so God destroyed it. Nine hundred and seventy-four generations sprang forth and perished, and still God labored toward perfection. Until at last God understood that the lower world would always be incomplete and flawed. So God spread over this last created world the Divine Wings of mercy and goodness and shielded it from the harsh glare of heaven's own justice. And so, this world did not perish like the others. It sparkled radiantly in the blackness, a blue-green gem in the diadem of God's love. And God saw that it was a good world.

But Divine Goodness did not end there. For God promised to continue protecting this newborn, imperfect world. Had God not done so, the evil spirits and fierce beasts would soon have put an end to the weaker creatures, including frail beings like ourselves. And so God decreed that each Nisan, at the time of spring, the holy seraphim would swoop down upon the evil spirits and demons and monsters of the night and prevent them from harming humankind. And to this day, the seraphim cover us all with their majestic wings, and there we shelter, unafraid.

And so, too, in Tammuz, at the time of summer, God commanded mighty Behemoth, who dwells in the Thousand Mountains and feasts on the shady jujube tree, to lift up its great horny head and roar but once, but so terrible is this roar that lions and leopards and bears cower in their lairs and lose heart, and so the gentle beasts can nurture their young in peace.

And in Tishrei, at the coming of autumn, the great bird Ziz-Shaddai flaps its monstrous wings and lets out such a fearsome shriek that the falcon and the hawk and the eagle tremble in their nests and fear to prey upon the weaker birds lest the Ziz swoop down upon them and gobble them whole. And so the little birds escape their enemies' sharp talons.

And in winter, in the month of Tevet, the sea boils and fumes, and the mighty Leviathan, whose fins flash with a brilliant flame and whose length exceeds a hundred miles, passes gas in the depths and frightens the bigger fish into their caves, so that the smaller ones can swim unafraid. Even the shark and whale shudder when Leviathan churns the ocean with his great tail and gnashes his ten thousand teeth.

And to watch over all, God appointed the Angels of Mercy surrounding the Heavenly Throne, Michael and Gabriel and Raphael and Uriel, and God banished the Angels of Destruction to the far reaches of heaven, so that above—as below—peace might prevail.

2
The Aleph-Bet

When God was about to create the world, all twenty-two letters of the *Aleph-Bet* leapt off the flaming crown of God and crowded around the Heavenly Throne, pleading, "Create the world through me!"

First the Taf, the last letter of the *aleph-bet*, came forward. "I am the first letter of *Torah*," it said. "Create the world through me, for later on I will give Israel all its laws and stories."

"No," replied God, "for in future days you will serve as a sign—*mayt*—to be placed upon the foreheads of the dead."

So the Taf departed from the Heavenly Throne, its head bowed in shame.

Next the Shin stepped forward. "Lord of the World, create the world through me. Doesn't Your own name, *Shaddai*, begin with me?"

But God again refused. "The words *shav* (lie) and *sheker* (falsehood) begin with you. Depart!"

And so the Shin, like its sister Taf, backed away from God's presence.

And so it was with one letter after another. Resh argued that it began another of God's names, *Rahum* (Merciful), but God reminded Resh that it also began the words *ra* (wicked) and *rasha* (evil). Kof pointed out that it was the first letter in *kadosh* (holy), but God retorted that it also began *k'lalah* (curse). Tzadde's plea for *tzaddik* (righteous) was offset by *tzarot* (troubles); Pey's for *Podeh* (Redeemer) by *pesha* (sin). Ayin, although it began *anavah* (humility), also began *ervah* (immorality). Samekh's hopes rose for a moment when God agreed that it did indeed uphold—*samekh*—the fallen, but it had to submit to God's order that it continue its important task of upholding the fallen rather than creating the world.

Nun boldly marched forward to claim that it began the word *ner* (lamp), which would light the spirits of humankind, but God answered that the same *ner* would also serve as the lamp of the wicked, whose light God would ultimately have to put out. Mem claimed another of God's names, *melekh* (king), but it was soon chastened by being reminded that it also began the word *mehumah* (confusion), a disastrous thing for a new world. Lamed pointed out its revered place at the head of *lukhot* (tablets), the Ten Commandments, but it forgot—until God reminded it—that Moses would shatter the two tablets on seeing the Golden Calf.

Kaf strutted up to the Throne confident of its triumph. "Surely You cannot refuse me," it boasted. "I begin *kissey* (throne) and *kavod* (honor) and *keter* (crown). You *must* begin the world with me!"

But its confidence was short-lived, for God proclaimed that in future years the Ruler of the Universe would clap one palm against another—*kaf*—in despair over the sorrows and misdeeds of Israel.

Then all the other letters were ready to concede victory to little Yud, for did not this letter begin the Awesome Name, the Tetragrammaton? But God gently reminded them all that Yud also started the words *yetzer ha-ra* (the evil inclination), so it would never do to begin the world with Yud.

Then Tet presented itself, arguing that *tov* (good) seemed a fitting note on which to begin a new creation. But God scolded Tet, saying, "Not in the lower world but only in the World to Come will true goodness be found." And so Tet was forced to withdraw its claim.

Khet pleaded for itself, saying, "I too begin one of Your names, *Khanun* (Gracious One)," but it blushed deeply when it remembered that it also began the word *khet* (sin). As for Zayin, it bragged that it began *zakhor* (remember), but God retorted that it also began the word *zayin* (weapon), the origin of human woes. Vav and Heh came forward together to press their case, both being letters of the Sacred Name, but God dismissed them immediately, for they were too exalted to serve the lower world.

Dalet pointed out that it began the word *davar* (the Divine Word), but it was reminded that it also began *din* (judgment), too harsh a note on which to bring a frail world into being. Gimel rushed up with its claim of *gadol* (great), but God rebuked it, pointing out that it also started *gemul* (punishment).

That left only Aleph and Bet. Bet humbly stepped forward and said, "O Source of Blessing, all the inhabitants of this new world will praise You daily through me, saying, *Barukh Attah Adonai*, "Blessed be the Maker of All." And God immediately granted Bet's request, creating the world through it: *"B'reshit*—In the beginning . . . "

Only modest little Aleph had not spoken until now. Because of its humility, God rewarded it by later giving it the place of honor at the head of the Ten Commandments: *"Anokhi*—I am *Adonai* your God."

3
The Sun and the Moon

On the fourth day of creation, the Sun and the Moon began shining in the heavens. At first they were of equal size and power. But this arrangement did not please the Moon. So it began to argue with God.

"Why did You create the world with the letter *bet*?" the Moon asked.

"*Bet* is the second letter of the *aleph-bet* and also the number two," God replied. "By creating the world with *bet*, I have made known to all my creatures that there are two worlds, both created by one God."

"Which is larger," continued the Moon, "this world or the World to Come?"

"The World to Come is larger," said God.

"*Adonai*," said the Moon, its silvery voice rising in irritation, "You have created so many pairs: this world and the next, the next world being greater than this one; heaven and earth, heaven being greater than the earth; fire and water, water being stronger than fire; and two heavenly lights, the Sun and the Moon. But neither light is greater than the other. To keep things in balance, shouldn't one of us outshine the other?"

"And I suppose that it is your wish that I make you the brighter light?" asked God.

"Why, yes," answered the Moon, its bright round form swelling with pride. "I would be pleased to accept . . ."

"Silence!" thundered God, rocking the heavens to their very foundations. "As a punishment for your presumption, I am taking away all but a sixtieth part of your light."

"O Merciful One!" pleaded the shamefaced Moon, "So great a punishment for so small a sin, but a few boasting words?"

And God immediately felt sorry for the Moon and relented. "In the future world, your light will be restored so that you will shine as brightly as at the first."

But the Moon could not leave well enough alone. "And the Sun's light? In the future world, will it be greater than mine or less?"

With that, God's patience gave out. "So you are still competing with the Sun! Very well then, foolish Moon, on that day, the Sun will shine forth with seven times its former brightness."

The Moon was about to protest further, but God silenced it abruptly, saying, "No more from you! It is decided and sealed."

Disconsolate, the Moon departed the Divine Presence. But so downcast was it that it failed to watch its step and so fell, unraveling its silken threads as it tumbled through the heavens. Each silvery thread became a star, shedding its pale light on the diminished Moon as it hung weeping in the sky.

4

Ziz-Shaddai

On the fifth day, God created the birds. The king of the birds is Ziz-Shaddai, whose feet rest upon the earth and whose head brushes the top of the sky. When he flies across the sun, his enormous wings turn day into night.

And what a wonderful taste the flesh of this bird has! So varied is its flavor that it tastes different to each person who eats it, both like this—*zeh*—and like that—*va-zeh*. Hence its name: Ziz. At the End of Days all the righteous will gather at the messianic banquet to feast upon this wondrous dish. And the heavenly waiter will be Moses himself!

Many legends have arisen about this wonderful bird. Once a ship passed by where Ziz was wading, and the passengers saw that the water only lapped at the creature's ankles.

"Surely this is a fine place to bathe," they said, "for the water is not too deep." And they readied themselves to jump in.

Then a heavenly voice thundered out of the sky, saying, "Do you wish to drown yourselves? Once a carpenter dropped his ax just at this spot, and it took seven years for it to reach the bottom."

Then they knew that the bird they had spied was none other than Ziz-Shaddai.

Another time an egg from Ziz-Shaddai's nest accidentally rolled down a mountainside and cracked. The impact felled sixty giant cedars in the forest of Lebanon. The fluid from the cracked egg flooded sixty cities.

But such misfortunes are rare, for God appointed

Ziz-Shaddai to guard the earth from the harsh winds of
storm and winter chill. Its wings spread from one end of
the earth to the other, sheltering us all like God's own
canopy of peace.

5

Leviathan

On the fifth day of creation God also made Leviathan. Just
as Ziz-Shaddai is the King of the Birds, so Leviathan is the
King of the Sea. At first there were two such creatures in
the sea, but so terrible was their power, so insatiable their
thirst, that God destroyed the female, leaving the male to
rule alone. Yet even this single sea monster threatens to
overwhelm the earth, for each day Leviathan gulps down
all the water from the Jordan River as it flows into the sea.
And when he's hungry, his hot breath boils the seas until
they seethe like a stewpot.

How strangely is this creature made! His gigantic fins
blaze with lightning, outshining the sun. His flashing
eyes light up the entire sea. Every day God leaves heaven
to play with Leviathan in the waves.

But oh — the beast's terrible smell! So repulsive is the
odor of his breath that it would kill all living things on
earth were it not for the fact that each morning Leviathan
thrusts his great pointed snout into Paradise to perfume
himself with the heavenly fragrance.

At the End of Days the righteous will feast on
Leviathan along with Ziz-Shaddai and the mighty Behemoth. Leviathan's wife, killed by God at the beginning
of creation, is already prepared for the messianic table,
pickled in brine.

And how will the angels slay this mighty sea dragon?
They will not be able to, for his steely scales will turn back
their swords and spears. No, God will have to send
Behemoth, the King of Land Beasts, to combat him. They

will slash each other to death with their fierce tails. The beasts' flesh will then feed the pious at the final feast of souls. From the shining skin of Leviathan, God will fashion tents to shelter the righteous, and what remains of the skin will be stretched over Jerusalem, its radiant light illuminating the entire world.

6

Leviathan and the Fox

How hard God worked in creating a new world, filled with so many wonderful creatures! When all was finished, it was at last time to rest. But along came the Angel of Death to disturb God's first *Shabbat*. Seeing all the new creatures in God's world, the Angel declared, "Master of the Universe, You fashioned me to be the lord of death. Now give me power over all Your creatures."

"Take a pair of all living things," answered God, "and hurl them into the sea. Then you shall have power over all the rest of their kind."

And that is precisely what the Angel of Death did.

But Fox was too wise for him. When he saw the Angel coming, he began to weep and wail so loudly that the Angel stared at him in amazement.

"Why do you cry so bitterly?" he asked Fox.

"Look in the sea," answered wily Fox. "What do you see?"

The Angel of Death peered down into the water. "Why, I see another Fox!" he cried, for at that moment Fox bent over the water to cast his reflection in the shallows.

"Indeed," wailed Fox, wiping a tear from his long red nose, "two of my friends have fallen into the sea and drowned!" And he lifted up his head and began to cry even more bitterly.

"Then I have no need to drown you," said the Angel

of Death. "Be off with you now, for I have more important things to do than to stand here listening to crying foxes."

And so Fox escaped the Angel's clutches.

Soon after this, when Leviathan gathered to himself all the drowned creatures sent to him by the Angel of Death, he noticed that Fox was not among them.

"Where is he?" he demanded of the smaller fishes.

And they told him of the clever trick Fox had played on the Angel of Death.

"Surely this is the wisest of all creatures," thought Leviathan to himself. "I will not rest until his wisdom is mine!"

So he summoned several fishes and commanded them to bring Fox to him so that he might eat him up and so possess his wisdom.

When they found Fox strolling along the shore, they called out to him, "Is there anyone as wise as you, Fox? Your wisdom exceeds even the great Leviathan's!"

Fox stopped in his tracks and stared out at the sea. When he spotted the silvery heads bobbing up out of the waves, he smiled at them, preening his glossy red fur with one paw. How true were their words! He was indeed the wisest creature on earth. Hadn't he outfoxed even the Angel of Death?

"Leviathan is dying, Fox," called out the fishes, "and he insists that none but you may take his place. He has heard of your wonderful wisdom and would like to meet you before he dies."

"But how will I get to his palace without drowning?" asked Fox, nervously eyeing the tumbling waves.

"Hop on one of our backs and we will see to it that not even the pad of your foot gets wet. Then when we get close to Leviathan's palace, we will show you a way down so that you will be safe from harm. There you will rule over the vast kingdoms of the sea, feeding on such delicacies as you have never tasted before. And your underwater subjects will protect you from all danger so that you will never again be afraid of savage beasts as you are on land."

Fox hesitated for a moment, then decided to accept

their invitation. With one deft leap, he landed on the shiny back of a marlin, and off they swam out to sea. But as they left the shore farther and farther behind, Fox began to have doubts about what he had done. How foolish he had been to trust these fishes with his life. Now he was entirely at their mercy!

Then the marlin confirmed his worst fears. "From this day on, my dear Fox, they will no longer call you wise, but foolish, for as soon as Leviathan sees you, he will rip open your chest and gobble up your heart and then he will be as wise as you." And he began to laugh in his fishy sort of way, spraying bubbles of foam into Fox's face.

But Fox was not about to give up so easily. "My heart, you say? Why didn't you tell me before! For alas, I have left my heart at home."

Instantly the marlin stopped swimming, and Fox felt the fish's strong fins trembling under his paws. "Left it home, you say? But why?"

"Oh, foxes never carry their hearts with them unless they know they will need them. And since you didn't tell me that was what Leviathan wanted, I didn't bring it."

"What shall we do?" the fishes asked each other, churning up the water in their agitation.

Fox smiled, stroking his whiskers, for he was very pleased with himself now. "Calm yourselves, my friends! You only have to carry me back to the shore, and I will run home and bring my heart along with me. But if you don't, beware! Leviathan will surely be angry with you for failing to follow his instructions, and then you will be his supper instead of me. For then I will have no choice but to tell him that it was your fault that I left my heart behind."

"Fox is right," said the tuna.

"Yes, let us bring him back at once," said the swordfish, sawing the air to underline his point.

So they turned around and brought Fox back to the shore. As soon as he felt the solid ground under his feet, Fox scrambled up a cliff and began laughing at the fishes below.

"Come back!" they cried. "You promised!"

"What fools you are!" laughed Fox. "Have you ever heard of an animal who travels without his heart?"

"Then you tricked us!" they cried.

"Yes, indeed I have. I fooled the Angel of Death, and now I have fooled Leviathan. They do not call me wise for nothing!"

When the fishes returned to their King and told him what had happened, he said, "Indeed, he is a crafty fellow and you are all fools."

And right then and there, he ate them all up.

7

The Re'em

On the sixth day of creation God fashioned the beasts of the earth. One of the most wondrous of these beasts was the Re'em.

God made only two of these creatures at the beginning, and no more than two are alive at any one time. For there is not enough food and water on the whole earth to feed more than two of these monstrous beasts. They divide the world between them, the male always dwelling in the east and the female in the west.

Once in seventy years they come together to mate. As soon as the male joins with the female, she turns round her head and bites him so that he dies. Then she remains pregnant for twelve years. For the first eleven years, she moves about and grazes. But in the twelfth year, her belly grows so heavy that she can no longer stand, and she falls down upon her side. There she lies for the next twelve months, spittle drooling from her mouth and watering the grass beside her so that she can feed herself and her growing young.

At the end of the twelfth year, her womb splits open and twin calves emerge, one female and one male. At that instant, the mother dies and the two young depart, one for the east and one for the west. For the next seventy years, they remain apart until, like their parents before them, they meet again to mate and die.

At the time of the Flood, when Noah was commanded to take all the animals into the ark, only the pregnant Re'em was too large to fit inside, so he tied her to the back of the ark and she ran behind, her horned head just reaching above the crest of the floodwaters.

Very few people have encountered this marvelous creature and lived to tell the tale. One such brave soul was King David, when he was still only a shepherd boy tending his father's flocks. One day he chanced upon the Re'em asleep and mistook it for a mountain. Up he climbed until he was perched upon the giant beast's back. Suddenly the Re'em awoke and David found himself high up in the air, caught between the beast's sharp horns. At that moment David vowed that if he were to escape harm this day, he would one day build a temple to God as high as the Re'em's horns, which was very high indeed.

And God heard David's promise and immediately sent a lion to that very spot, which frightened even the mighty Re'em to its knees. As the giant creature bowed its horny head low, David quickly jumped to the ground. And before the lion had a chance to notice the helpless young boy, God sent a deer running by, which the lion chased into the forest.

And so the future king of Israel escaped both monsters without so much as a scratch. And in time, his son Solomon fulfilled his vow.

8

Milham, the Phoenix-Bird

When Adam and Eve ate from the forbidden tree in the Garden of Eden, their minds instantly grasped the terrible truth: One day they would die. Not wishing to be the only living things to meet such a terrible fate, they quickly shared their deadly fruit with all their other companions in the Garden: the lions and the pandas, the unicorns and the dragons, all winged and creeping and scaly beasts, from the tiniest flea to the mighty Behemoth and the Re'em.

Only one creature refused to taste the fruit: the Bird Milham, also known as the Phoenix, who wanted no part of the humans' fatal offering.

"Is it not bad enough that you disobeyed God's command and ate of the Tree of Knowledge of Good and Evil? Do you now wish to kill us all? No, I refuse to eat the fruit!"

No matter how hard the two humans pressed her, Milham stubbornly shook her purple crocodile head and refused to change her mind.

In reward for her loyalty, God granted Milham eternal life. Of all creatures on earth, she alone would never have to die. Never would she feel the sharp blade of the Angel of Death.

"Never is a long time," pointed out the Angel of Death, who was very wise in the ways of earthly creatures. "Surely Milham will follow the bad example set by her neighbors, and thereby forfeit her special privilege. For how can she possibly resist evil forever?"

So God commanded the Angel of Death to build a special city to shelter Milham, a place surrounded by high unbreachable walls. The name of this walled city is Luz. The only way into Luz is through a cave, whose entrance is hidden in an almond tree and kept secret from all other creatures. Luz is the only place on earth forever barred to the Angel of Death. And that is where Milham lives to this very day.

For a thousand years each Phoenix-Bird lives out her life there until her feathers finally drop off and her body shrinks to the size of an egg. Out of this egg a new Milham soon emerges, just like the first, with a lion's feet and tail, a scaly crocodile's head, and twelve shining purple wings. Each day she flies over the earth, her enormous wings catching the rays of the sun as she soars high into the heavens, protecting the tender earth from its scorching flames. She feeds herself on manna from heaven and dew from the earth.

And each night she comes home to roost in the holy city of Luz, there to sleep safe from the reach of sin and the tireless tread of the Angel of Death.

9

The Creation of Souls

Unlike the human body, which was created on the sixth day, the soul was created on the first day before anything else in the world. In that first hour, God created all souls and placed them in the highest heaven where they remain until called to enter the body chosen for them.

When a baby is conceived, Laylah, the Angel of Night, brings the fertilized egg before God who decides its fate: whether it will be a boy or girl, rich or poor, strong or weak, beautiful or ugly, fat or thin, wise or foolish. Only one decision does God leave in the hands of the unborn soul: whether it will be righteous or wicked.

Then God sends the Angel of Souls to the highest heaven to bring back the soul destined for that particular body. Always the soul rebels, for compared to the celestial world, the lower world is but a poor place, full of sorrow and pain.

But God reprimands the rebellious soul, saying, "Hush! For this is why I created you!" And so the soul enters the unborn child and nestles quietly under the mother's breast.

The next morning a second angel carries the soul to Paradise, where it sees all the Righteous enjoying eternal happiness.

"If you follow God's Torah and live a worthy life," explains the angel, "you will one day join these happy creatures here. But if not . . ."

And that night, the angel takes the soul to the gates of Gehinnom, where it sees the Angels of Destruction whipping the wicked souls with burning lashes.

"Such is the fate of those who have devoted their lives to sin and cruelty," the angel says. "It is for you to choose for yourself."

Between morning and night of that day, the angel reveals to the unborn soul its future life: where it will live and where it will die and where it will be buried.

And then at the end of nine months, the angel announces that it is time for the soul to leave the warm refuge of the womb.

"Oh, no!" cries the soul. "For that will be too much to bear!"

But the angel quickly silences it. "So God has decreed. Against your will you were formed, and against your will you will be born. And against your will you will one day die. Such is your fate."

And with that, the angel strikes the newborn baby under the nose, leaving a small cleft there. Then he extinguishes the light shining above its head, and instantly the soul forgets everything it has learned during the previous nine months. And then the baby emerges into the world, crying and afraid.

Each soul spends the rest of its time on earth recovering all that it once knew.

10

The Creation of Adam

When it came time to create the first human being, God turned to the angels to ask their advice.

The Angel of Love urged God to proceed with the task, saying, "For humans will bring affection and caring into the world."

But the Angel of Truth immediately objected with, "On the contrary! They will be full of lies, not love!"

Then the Angel of Justice rushed to humankind's defenses and said, "No, you are wrong! Human beings will practice justice among themselves, clearing away lies to reveal the truth."

But the Angel of Peace objected, saying, "Justice, you say? No, they will do just the opposite! They will fill the world with their quarrels, each claiming to possess a higher truth than the rest. Heed my advice, great King of Kings: Do not ruin Your beautiful new world by creating people!"

What then was God to do? From the beginning it had been part of the Divine Plan to create human beings, but it had also been part of the plan to enlist the angels in this task. That is why God had asked for their advice. And that is also why, to guarantee their consent, the Holy One had even been willing to deceive them, revealing to them the future deeds of only the righteous among humankind, not those of the wicked. Yet even this partial vision of human history was enough to dishearten some of the angels.

And so God had no choice but to force their hand by asking, "Why did I create this world if not for human beings to enjoy? Why did I give the peacock his glorious plumes and the trout his shimmering scales if not to delight the human eye? Of what use is a pantry full of sweets if no guest comes to dine?"

Then the angels, understanding that the matter was already decided, cried out, "How great is Your name in all the earth, *Adonai!*" And God rejoiced in their praise.

God then said to the angel Gabriel, "Bring me dust from the four corners of the earth, and I will fashion a human creature."

But the earth refused to yield up any of its soil to

Gabriel. "One day God will curse me because of these human beings. No, not a single grain of sand will I hand over to you!"

God ignored the earth's objections. Stretching forth one hand, God scooped up some dust and out of it made the first human being. This dust came from all corners of the earth: east and west, north and south. And it was made up of all the earth's colors: red for the blood, black for the bowels, white for the bones, and a rainbow of shades for the skin.

Unlike all future human beings, this first human creature was born fully formed by God's own hands, male and female in one body, appearing like a creature twenty years old. How enormous this creature was, its head reaching all the way to the heavens and its body stretching from the east to the west. So glorious was its form that even its heel outshone the sun.

But this creature was not yet complete, for it lacked a soul. Yet God was uncertain at what point the soul should enter.

"Through the mouth? No, for with their mouths people will come to speak ill of each other. Through the eyes, then? But their eyes will only lead them into sin. Then through the ears? But with their ears they will listen to slander and unholy thoughts. No, only through the nostrils can the soul enter, for the nose can tell the difference between pure and impure things, and keep the righteous away from sin."

So through the creature's nostrils, God breathed in a soul.

How wise this first human being was! When he was barely an hour old, God brought him all the animals in Eden and asked him to give them names.

"You with the hump will be called 'camel' and you with the long neck 'giraffe.' And you with the flat beak and webbed feet, I shall call 'duck-billed platypus.'"

And so it went for hours and hours. As each creature paraded before her, the human named them all: ibis and toad, gazelle and python, ring-necked pheasant and raccoon. Then God asked the namer to choose her own name.

" 'Adam,' " he answered without hesitation, "for it was out of the *adamah*, the humus, that You formed a human being." Adam even gave God a new name: "'*Adonai*,' Lord, for You rule over all the creatures on the earth."

Not only did Adam give names to all living things on earth, but she also invented all seventy languages and alphabets to write them down. And when God showed Adam the whole earth, granting her the ability to see from one end of the globe to the other, Adam pointed out the places where people would live and where they would abandon the land to desolation. And God accepted Adam's design.

Then God divided Adam in two, male and female, and humanity was no longer alone.

11

Adam's Gift to King David

Only one sad note disturbed the wondrous creation of human beings. When God showed Adam all the future generations of the earth—kings and queens, teachers and scholars, judges and evildoers, and all the ordinary people who would make up humankind—he noticed that one radiant soul blazed forth for only a moment, then just as suddenly winked out.

"Whose soul was that?" asked Adam. "How brightly it shone before it vanished!"

"That was the soul of David," answered God.

"But why did it disappear so quickly?"

"It was decreed at the beginning that this soul would live but for a moment on the earth."

"How unfortunate!" cried Adam. "How desperately the earth needs this great soul! What great deeds it might perform for Your people! I will gladly give up some of my own allotted years so that this soul might live out a full measure of days."

And God granted Adam's request. Instead of the hour he was originally given, David lived a full seventy years. And instead of his allotted thousand-year span, Adam's life was diminished by seventy years, so that he died at the age of nine hundred and thirty. And so, because of Adam's sacrifice, the people Israel was later blessed with one of its greatest kings.

12

Lilith

How lonely Adam was that first day as he watched the animals parade by, two by two, each with a companion. And God took pity on him and made him a partner, scooping out another handful of dust from the earth. This creature was named Lilith and she became Adam's wife.

Because this first woman was equal to Adam in every way, having been made by God out of the same earth and on the same day as her husband, she insisted on enjoying equal footing with him in the Garden: sharing the labor and its reward, working side by side to tend the growing things entrusted into their care.

Also in the ways of love between a man and a woman, Lilith wished to share equally, sometimes lying on top of her lover and sometimes below him. For were they not full partners in creation?

But this was too much for Adam to bear, and he complained to God, saying, "Is this why I have been created—to share *everything* with her? When I asked for a companion, I did not mean this!"

When Lilith heard Adam's complaint, she decided to leave the Garden, where she was not welcome, and make a new home for herself far away. Pronouncing the Awesome Name, she flew away to the shores of the Sea of Reeds.

Instantly Adam was sorry that he had driven her away, and he once more cried out to God, "My wife has deserted me! Again, I am all alone!"

So God sent three angels, Senoy, Sansenoy, and Semangelof, to fetch Lilith back to Eden. But she was not willing to return, for she knew that Adam did not desire her the way she was.

"If you do not return with us," threatened the angels, "you will lose one hundred of your children each day until you change your mind."

"So be it," replied Lilith. And she sent them back to Eden empty-handed.

And soon the angels' dire prophecy came to pass.

From that day on, in revenge for her hurt pride and slaughtered children, Lilith has prowled through the night, looking for newborn babies to harm. With her long black hair and great flapping wings, she will sometimes swoop down on day-old baby boys or on baby girls during their first twenty days of life, and suck the breath out of them.

But at heart she is not cruel. For out of compassion for her sister creatures, she has betrayed her own power: "If you inscribe the names of the three angels, Senoy, San-senoy, and Semangelof, in an amulet and tie this charm around your children's neck," she has whispered to the mothers of these innocent babies, "I promise not to harm even one hair on their heads."

And she has never failed to keep her word.

13

The First Wedding

After Lilith deserted the Garden, Adam was again lonely, and again God had compassion on him. A glimmering mist descended upon Adam and he slept upon the ground. Out of his side God drew a rib-bone and fashioned it into a second creature, bone of his bone, like emerging out of like. Next God breathed upon Adam's face with an icy breath so that the two faces, one male and one female, separated, and God gave one of the faces to the new creature now stirring to life. And when Adam opened his eyes after the mist had lifted, he saw his own image staring at him, smiling. And so Eve, the mother of life, came into being.

Seeing how alike they were and how naturally their hearts inclined toward each other, the two human beings fell in love and wished to be married. So God erected a canopy of gold, pearls, and precious stones and personally adorned the couple for their wedding. Never before or since has the earth seen a more splendid wedding. God was the *hazzan*, and the angels the choir, filling the heavens and earth with such sweet melodies that all the birds stopped their singing to listen and marvel.

On that day, God gave the new couple a special wedding gift, a piece of the Divine Name, *yud* for Adam and *heh* for Eve. And so Adam changed his name to *ish* and Eve to *ishah*, adding a holy spark to their union. But God warned them that this gift might not be theirs forever. For if they shut God, *"Yud-Heh,"* out of their hearts and betrayed their love for each other, the divine spark would abandon them and return to God. Then each would lose the added letter from the Divine Name and be left only with the two letters *aleph* and *shin*, which together spell *esh*, fire. And this fire would consume their love and destroy them.

After the couple had pronounced the holy words to each other, the angels rejoiced and drew a curtain of night over them. And Adam and Eve embraced and became one flesh. Thus human love was born upon the earth.

14

The Shamir

On twilight of the sixth day of creation, God created the Miracles: the pit that swallowed Korakh, the mouth of Miriam's well, Balaam's talking ass, the rainbow, the heavenly manna, Moses' rod, the magically suspended letters of the Ten Commandments, the First Tongs that made all other tongs, and the Shamir.

The Shamir was a marvelous creature, no bigger than a single grain of barley, but so strong that it could cut through any substance on earth, even the hardest diamonds. Only lead alone could contain it.

For safekeeping God gave the Shamir to the Hoopoe-bird, who promised to guard it with her life. With the little worm tight in her beak, the Hoopoe flew throughout the earth, dropping the Shamir upon desolate mountaintops so that the mountaintops split open and blossomed forth into life.

For eons, the Hoopoe kept the Shamir safe in Paradise, departing with it only to seed the mountaintops, until one day God borrowed it back for a special task. It was then that the Israelites were wandering on their forty-year journey in the wilderness. Aaron, the high priest, was ready to take on God's holy work in the Tabernacle, but for this sacred work, he needed a special breastplate made of twelve precious stones, one for each tribe. How could the Israelite artisans engrave the tribes' names on these stones without splintering them? For to etch the words required great strength but also the greatest accuracy and craft. Only the miraculous Shamir was capable of such a task.

So Bezalel and his artisans inscribed the names in ink on each of the stones: ruby, topaz, smaragd, garnet, sapphire, emerald, zircon, agate, amethyst, beryl, jasper, onyx. And then God sent the Shamir to perform its work, etching the names into the shimmering surface of the stones, working with such astonishing skill that not one atom of stone was lost.

Then God returned the Shamir to the Hoopoe's charge.

Where did the Hoopoe keep such a powerful creature? What ordinary vessel could possibly hold it? Since lead alone could resist the Hoopoe's bite, the bird sealed up her precious charge inside a box of lead, wrapped in a woolen cloth nestled among a handful of barley grains.

And there she might have kept it forever had not
Solomon needed it to build the Holy Temple in Jerusalem.
But that is another story.

15

The Fall of Satan

After God had created the first two human creatures, all
the angels were summoned to Paradise to pay their
respects. At first they rebelled at the idea. What!—the
inhabitants of heaven bow low before creatures of the
earth! And they would have destroyed Adam and Eve
with fire had not God stretched forth a hand to shield
them. Then God made peace between the angels and the
human beings, and calm reigned in heaven again.

Only Satan refused to bend his will to God's command. For he was too jealous of these earthly creatures to
do them honor. Was he not the greatest of all the angels,
possessing twelve wings while the others had only six?

"You fashioned the angels out of Your own Splendor," he protested to God, "but people out of the lowly
dust!"

"Yet this dust has more wisdom than you!" answered
God.

Now Satan was a wily creature, so he proposed a test
to see who was indeed the wiser of the two.

"Very well," agreed God. "I will bring before you and
before the human beings all the other creatures I have
made, and we will see which of you can guess their true
names by understanding their secret natures. If it is you
who can do this, then Adam and Eve will render you
honor, and you shall sit beside Me near the Throne of
Glory. But," warned God, "if you fail and they succeed,
then you shall be their servant, and they will live peacefully in My garden and tend it."

"Agreed!" cried Satan, and off he sped to Eden.

Certain that he would succeed, Satan insisted that he
try first. But to his great dismay, he failed utterly. The ox

lowed, and Satan named him "Loaf." The cow mooed, and Satan called her "Moon." Then God brought before him the donkey and the camel, and again Satan failed to guess their true names. When the donkey brayed—"hee-haw!"—Satan smugly called out, "Jackdaw!" and the camel's gruff cough fooled Satan into dubbing it "Auk!" Furious at his humiliating defeat, Satan flapped his twelve wings and flew swiftly back to heaven.

Then God brought these same animals before the human beings and helped them guess their names by planting clues at the beginning of each question:

"*Couch* this beast's name in its proper form," God said. And Adam declared, "I shall call this creature 'Cow'!"

"*Don't keep* me waiting too long for this one's name," God said. And Eve called out, "Donkey!"

One after another, the animals presented themselves to their human masters and received their proper names. And God winked at the angels, delighted to see proud Satan humbled at last.

Satan, high on his heavenly perch, shrieked to see himself so shamefully outwitted by these earthly creatures. But he had no choice except to acknowledge their superior wisdom.

Yet still he refused to pay honor to them, and he declared that he would now raise his own throne above God's and rule the heavens together with his own host of angels.

But God spoiled Satan's plans and flung him and his angels out of heaven down to earth. And from that day on, Satan and humankind were forever at odds.

And shortly thereafter Satan took his own revenge.

16

The Fall of Adam and Eve

Of all the creatures in the Garden of Eden, the serpent was the most remarkable. At the beginning he stood upright like a human being and was as tall as a camel. Had envy not wormed its way into his soul, he and his wife would have lived happily with Adam and Eve, providing them with silver, gold, gems, and pearls, and performing all their work in the twinkling of an eye. For the serpent was a wise and skillful creature. But it was precisely his wisdom that led to his undoing.

How the serpent hated to see these human creatures strolling so contentedly in the Garden, calling each beast by its divine name, enjoying God's handiwork!

"Surely I am more clever than they!" thought he. "Yet I am not master here. But perhaps I can change that."

So the serpent approached Eve and asked, "Is it true that you may not eat of *every* tree in the Garden?"

"We may eat of every tree but one," answered Eve, "and that one we may not even touch, or we will surely die."

Now God had not told the man and woman that they might not *touch* the Tree of Knowledge, only that they might not eat of it. But Adam, worried that they might accidentally forget, had forbidden Eve even to touch the tree. And the serpent, knowing this, took advantage of Adam's exaggeration to lead Eve into sin.

Without warning, he pushed Eve against the forbidden tree and said, "See, you have touched it but have not died. So you also may eat its fruit and not die, for God only forbade it to you so that you might not yourselves become creators. For just as God fashions and destroys worlds, so you too, once you have eaten of this wondrous fruit, may bring new worlds into being. And like God, you will be able to destroy life and revive the dead."

Seeing that he now had Eve firmly in the palm of his hand (for at this time serpents did have hands and feet, until they led humanity into sin and so lost them), he went on, saying, "You see, God was afraid that you would eat the fruit and then create new worlds of your own, rivaling this one, for everyone knows that craftsmen in the same trade hate one another. So, quickly now, eat of the tree and claim your power, or God will bring forth new creatures to rule over you."

And stretching forth his two scaly arms, the serpent grabbed hold of the tree and shook it, so that several pieces of fruit fell down at their feet. He picked one up and took a bite, declaring, "See, as I have not died by eating this, neither will you." And he held out the fruit to Eve.

Feeling guilty about breaking God's command, Eve at first only tasted the skin of the fruit, and then emboldened, sank her teeth into its soft flesh. Instantly she saw standing before her the Angel of Death.

"Adam!" she cried, fleeing from the Angel. "Come eat with me!" For she feared that after her death, Adam would marry a new wife and soon forget her. Reluctantly, Adam shared the fruit with his beloved wife, and then they gave all the animals pieces of it to eat, so that they might all face the same fateful end together. Only Milham the Phoenix-Bird refused to eat and so was granted immortal life.

As soon as they had eaten, Adam and Eve became naked, for before this they had horny skin and were covered with a cloud of glory. But with the first taste of the forbidden fruit, the cloud and skin dropped off, and they were ashamed.

Adam then ran to the carob tree and tried to snatch some leaves to wrap themselves in, but the carob tree pulled back in horror, saying, "Here is the thief who has deceived his Creator! Such wicked hands shall take no leaves from me!"

"Nor from me!" shouted the pomegranate and the olive and the almond trees.

Only the fig tree willingly gave up its leaves to the naked couple, for the fig had been the forbidden fruit itself and so shared in their shame.

As soon as they had clothed themselves in leaves, the two human sinners hid from God, taking refuge among the trees of the garden. How they wept cowering there among the thorny briars, for only an hour before they had been like giants, their heads reaching into the clouds, and now they were shrunken to the size of ordinary beasts, easily concealed in the underbrush.

Then God called out to them and they trembled. "Where are you?"

Had they only confessed their crime right then, God would surely have forgiven them at once and taken them back into Paradise, but they were too ashamed, and so they lied.

"I did not want to eat the fruit!" declared Adam. "Eve made me do it! If only You hadn't created her and had left me alone."

"But it was you who asked Me to make you a partner!" answered God. "Do not blame her for your mistakes."

And then Eve tried to wiggle out of her part in the crime. "The serpent made me eat the fruit. He was too clever for me!"

Enraged by their deceit, God ordered them out of the Garden forever.

Then God turned to the serpent, who opened his mouth to argue, but God did not even give him the chance to speak. For clever sinners always have excuses for their sins, and it is best to turn a deaf ear to their crafty words.

"Because of your part in this, you will be punished ten times," God told the serpent. "You will lose the power of speech, and your hands and feet will be cut off, so that you must crawl on your belly in the dust. In the dust you will eat, and human feet shall trample upon your head. The tastiest food and drink shall turn to dust in your mouth, and all will call you cursed. You shall shed your skin in pain, and bear your young only after long waiting. Everywhere people see you, they will try to kill you, and when Israel at last learns to walk wholeheartedly in My ways, you shall be banished forever from the Holy Land."

Adam and Eve also received severe punishments before leaving the Garden. Adam's curse was to till the soil with much hard labor, and Eve's to give birth with much pain. Their children were doomed to wander the earth, and their bodies to be prey to worms after death. Their days were to be few in number and full of sorrow, and at the end of their days, they would be forced to render a truthful account before the Heavenly Court.

Even the Moon suffered because of Adam and Eve's fall. For although the Sun instantly eclipsed its light when the first human beings disobeyed God, the Moon only laughed, and God punished it by making it grow old each month and disappear only to be born again and then age anew.

And the earth, too, suffered when Adam and Eve fell, for it showed no signs of regret when they ate the fruit born of its own soil, and took no notice at all of the first great sin. So the earth was cursed to sprout thorns and thistles out of its breast, and to surrender its sheltering leaves to the cold. And often the golden grain was doomed to wither on the stalk.

Then God drove Adam and Eve from the Garden and shut the gate behind them. At the entrance God stationed the cherubim with swords of fire flashing round and round in their hands. So the Garden was closed forever to humankind.

But God did not send the two humans forth empty-handed to their fate. As a parting gift, God gave Adam and Eve the Torah as a tree of life, since they were now leaving behind the Tree of Eternal Life. "Only hold fast to it," God urged, "and you will one day find yourselves back in Paradise."

Then the angels gave Adam and Eve their parting gifts: sweet spices of cinnamon, saffron, frankincense and myrrh, as well as seeds with which to sow the earth. Comforted by these gifts, Adam and Eve set out on their journey into the world, hearing at their backs as they walked away the fiery crackle of the ever-turning swords.

Only twelve hours had passed since God had first conceived the idea to create human beings. It was on the first day of the month of Tishrei that Adam and Eve were driven from their first home—*Aleph b'Tishrei*, whose letters, rearranged, spell out *B'reshit*, in the beginning. It was a fateful beginning for humankind. But every Rosh Hashanah, on the first of Tishrei, each human being has the chance to reverse the story and re-enter the Garden through the flaming swords of the cherubim. There the Tree of Life awaits, and the serpent is forbidden entrance.

17

Adam and Eve's Repentance

After they were expelled from the Garden, Adam and Eve built themselves a poor hut in the east and sat down there to mourn. For seven days they touched neither food nor drink, but instead raised their voices in sorrow because of what they had done. Then at last, driven out by hunger and thirst, they emerged into the light of day to seek food.

For the next seven days, they could find nothing fit to eat, only food for cattle and wild beasts. Where were the delicacies of Eden now? How could they lower themselves to eat straw and wild thistles after feeding on the sweet fruits of Paradise?

Finally, Eve turned to her husband and said, "Kill me, Adam! Then maybe God will take you back into the Garden, for it is all my fault that we have been driven out."

"Do not speak such foolish words!" cried Adam, tears running down his gaunt cheeks. "We are both at fault, and together we will bear our fate. Perhaps if we look harder, we will find something to quiet our grumbling bellies."

But after nine more days of searching, they still could find no food.

"Our only chance is to ask God to forgive us," reasoned Adam. "Then perhaps God will have pity on us and show us where to find the food we need. Go now to the Tigris River, Eve, and find a large stone there. Set it up in the deepest part of the river and stand upon it so that the water reaches up to your neck. For thirty-seven days, stand there and say nothing, for it is by our lips that we have sinned. Let no food or drink enter your mouth. I will do the same in the Jordan River, fasting and remaining mute for forty days. Then God will surely see our desperate plight and help us."

So Eve departed for the east to stand upon a stone in the Tigris River, and Adam traveled west to the Jordan. Standing amid the swirling water, he called out to all the fish, "Surround me and keep me company in my grief, but do not punish yourselves, for it is only I who have sinned." And all the fish and river creatures surrounded him like a shimmering net, and the waters of the Jordan stood still.

Now when Satan saw what Adam and Eve were doing, he became afraid that God might indeed forgive them and admit them back into the Garden, thus undoing all the crafty mischief he had done with the serpent's help. So he disguised himself as an angel and came to Eve on the eighteenth day that she stood in the Tigris and proclaimed, "Eve! Leave your rock and cease your tears! For God has heard your cries and has forgiven you. Even the angels have pleaded on your behalf. Now God has personally sent me to bring you back to Paradise and feed you from its delights."

So Eve, fainting from her fast and her long days under the scorching sun, stepped out of the river and quickly returned to Adam to tell him the happy news.

But Adam immediately saw through Satan's trick and scolded her, saying, "O Eve, if only you had been more patient! Again you have let this wily serpent seduce you! Where is your repentance now?"

And Eve turned to Satan and cried, "Why then do you torment us, Satan? What have we ever done to you that you hate us so?"

And Satan hung his head in shame and said, "I lost heaven because of my envy for Adam, and I swore to take my revenge. Now we are both robbed of Paradise."

Then Adam lifted his voice up to God and cried, "Take him away from us, *Adonai*, so that we may at least know peace in our exile! Isn't it enough that we have been driven from Your Garden? Must the serpent follow us even here?"

And immediately Satan vanished.

Now the days grew shorter as Adam stood upon that rock in the Jordan River to finish out his forty days as he had sworn to do. Each day the sun sank at an earlier hour, leaving him in the mists of night. How worried the man and woman were each night to see their precious warmth and light disappear behind the mountains, not knowing if it would return, fearful that their terrible sin might eventually extinguish the sun altogether. Each night they wept, praying God to forgive them for the terrible thing that they had done.

And then the days began to grow longer again, and the sun never failed to rise from its bed. Then they understood that all this was according to God's plan. And they wished to give thanks to God for this wonderful order of the natural world, and so Adam sacrificed a unicorn there upon an altar of stones.

Upon that very spot, generations later, another altar was to stand where Abraham would offer up a ram in place of his son. And generations after that, the Holy Temple would also stand in that holy spot. There the people of Israel would offer up their thanks to God and ask forgiveness for their sins.

18

The Cat and the Dog

Why are the Cat and Dog such enemies? It was not always so.

When the Cat and Dog were first created, they decided to become partners and seek their fortunes together. But after three days of searching for food, they could find none, so they agreed to part ways.

"Why should we starve?" reasoned the Dog. "You go

to Adam's house and dwell there, and I shall fend for myself among the wild beasts."

"Very well," said the Cat. "But let us promise each other never to serve the same master."

"Agreed," said the Dog, and so they wished each other well and went their separate ways.

The Cat went to Adam and Eve's house and right away began to gobble up the mice stealing their food. So delighted were Adam and Eve that they warmly welcomed her in and gave her a saucer of warm milk and a fish head for her supper. Then, purring contentedly, she curled up beside their hearth and made herself at home.

The Dog, however, did not meet with such good luck. First he came upon the Wolf's den and made himself a rough bed inside. That night he woke to the sound of footsteps and cried out, "Wolf, Wolf! There are robbers and evildoers at the door!"

"Then go outside and drive them away!" snarled the sleepy Wolf, and the Dog tried to do so, but he was almost torn to shreds by the wild beasts.

So he fled to the cave of the Ape, who would not let him in, and then to the Sheep's pasture, who welcomed him as a friend.

That night the Dog again heard footsteps and he cried out, "Sheep, Sheep! I fear there are robbers and evildoers at the gate!"

"Please help me," cried the Sheep, "for I cannot defend myself against them!"

So the Dog ran outside and began barking at the wolves, but his frantic bark told them that there was a helpless Sheep just behind him, and so one of the wolves snuck past him and gobbled up his friend.

Sick at heart, the Dog left the now empty pasture and went begging for food. He soon came to Adam's house, and the man took him in and fed him.

At midnight that night, the Dog again awoke to the sounds of footsteps and began to bark. Adam rose up and took his bow and arrow and drove the wild beasts away.

"You are a good companion," Adam said to the Dog. "Come live with us, and we will gladly share with you what we have." And Eve made the Dog a warm bed beside theirs, and gratefully he lay down to rest.

But when the Cat heard the Dog's glad bark the next morning, she ran up to him and said, "What is the meaning of this, Dog? You have broken your promise!"

"It is not my fault," insisted the Dog, and he told her all the terrible things that had happened to him since they had parted.

But the Cat insisted that he leave at once.

Then Adam tried to make peace between them, promising the Cat that she would lose nothing by living together with the Dog under one roof.

But the Cat would not change her mind. And the bickering between them became so intense that the Dog was forced to leave the house and seek shelter with Adam and Eve's son Seth. And occasionally he returned to the Cat and tried again to make peace, but the Cat would have no part of it. And thus they continue to this very day.

19

Cain and Abel

Now the serpent lay with Eve, and she became pregnant and gave birth to a son. And she called him Cain, for she said, "I have gotten a son—'kaniti'—through an angel of God." For the serpent had come to her disguised as an angel.

Then she lay with Adam and had a second son and called him Hevel, meaning mist and nothingness, for she said, "Out of mist we have come and into mist this one will soon depart."

And soon after the birth of the two boys Eve had a dream. In the dream the blood of Abel flowed into the mouth of Cain, and Cain lapped it up greedily. And Abel cried out to his brother not to drink it all. When Eve told

Adam her dream he was afraid that it prophesied a tragic end for his younger son, and so he separated the two boys and taught them different trades. Cain became a farmer and Abel a shepherd.

But even that did not help. For Cain was always jealous of his brother. Once Adam told both boys to bring a sacrifice to God from the work of their hands. Abel selected the best sheep in his flock and built an altar where he laid his offering. And God accepted his offering immediately, for it came from his heart.

But Cain was not so generous. He first ate a full meal of the best fruits and vegetables from his garden and then threw what was left over upon the stones of his altar. And God was angry with him and sent down smoke so that his face became dirty with soot. But Cain was not ashamed at God's displeasure.

When Cain saw that God had accepted his brother's sacrifice and not his, he began to mock God before Abel. "What an unjust God this is who rules strictly by whim! See, your sacrifice has been chosen over mine for no good reason! And to think that I used to believe that God ruled the world fairly!"

But Abel answered him, "God *does* reward good deeds. It is only because of my good deeds that my sacrifice was found acceptable to heaven. You did not offer your gift in the proper spirit."

Cain said nothing in reply, but in the dark secret place of his heart, he vowed to take revenge upon his brother.

There was another reason that Cain envied Abel: He desired Abel's beautiful twin sister for his wife. God had arranged that each boy marry the twin sister born with him, so that the generations continue after them. But Cain desired Abel's sister rather than his own, and so began to plot a way to get rid of his brother.

An opportunity soon arose when one of Abel's sheep wandered into Cain's fields and began nibbling at his crops.

Shaking with rage, Cain stormed up to his brother and demanded, "Pay me for the damage!"

Abel calmly replied, "First pay me for the wool that you are now wearing, and for the lamb that you have so willingly eaten!"

When he heard this, Cain's face grew even darker with rage, and he jumped upon his brother and began to struggle with him upon the ground.

Now Abel was stronger than Cain and would have overpowered his brother had Cain not cried out for mercy. Abel immediately let him go, but Cain took advantage of his brother's kindheartedness and began to strike him all over his body with the wooden handle of his plow. Since no one had ever died before, Cain did not know how to kill a man. He kept hitting Abel until at last the wooden handle struck the tender flesh of his brother's neck, and Abel lay still upon the ground.

Then Cain hid himself from God.

"Cain!" called God from the heavens. "Where are you? And where is your brother Abel?"

"How should I know?" answered Cain. "Am I my brother's keeper?"

"Cain, what have you done? Your brother's blood cries out to Me from the ground!"

"Why do You blame me?" Cain snapped back. "It is true that I killed Abel, but it was You who created the evil inclination within me! Why did You let me do it? If You had only accepted my sacrifice as You did Abel's, I would not have raised my hand against him, and he would still live and breathe upon the earth!"

"Silence!" roared God. "Your brother's many wounds cry out to Me! So does the blood of all the righteous souls who might have come from him."

But Cain still refused to accept his guilt. "How was I to know that striking a man would result in his death? No one on earth has ever died before!"

God then lost His patience and declared, "From now on you shall be cursed and the ground you till shall also be cursed. You shall wander the earth and find no rest."

Cain tried to wriggle out of his punishment, and he said to God, "What will people say of You when they see me? That first You banished my parents from the Garden and now You banish their son! You will become known as a God who delights in exile!"

Although Cain's words were mean-spirited and insincere, God now felt sorry for him, and God removed half of Cain's curse so that he would be able to settle in a human city and raise a family there.

Then the wild beasts of the earth rose up to kill Cain and Cain called out to God for help. God put a mark on Cain's forehead, a single horn to warn others not to touch this man who had murdered his brother.

"For although you did kill Abel," said God, "you did not fully understand what you were doing. But from now on, one who sheds blood will pay in blood." And God gave Cain a dog to protect him from wild beasts and sent him on his way.

Cain journeyed eastward and settled in the land of Nod.

In time Cain met the same end that he had brought to his brother Abel. One day his great-grandson Lamech went hunting with his young son Tubal-Cain. Since Lamech was blind, his son would tell him when he saw an animal to shoot at. After a while the boy caught sight of a horned creature in the distance, and Lamech raised his bow and shot an arrow at it. When the boy ran up to see what his father had killed, he found Cain dead upon the ground, a single horn emblazoned upon his forehead. In despair over the deed, Lamech clapped his hands together and crushed the skull of Tubal-Cain, who had invented the very weapons used to kill Cain.

And so Cain's sin came round full circle.

20
Enoch, the Man Who Never Died

Now the generations on the earth grew sinful and began to worship idols. Only one man among them knew what was right in the eyes of God, and his name was Enoch, whose great-great-great-great-grandparents were Adam and Eve. To keep himself from sin, Enoch hid himself in his house and there prayed to God and filled his mind and heart with understanding.

But one day an angel appeared to Enoch and called out to him, "Enoch!"

And Enoch answered, "Here I am!"

And the angel said, "It is time for you to rejoin the world and teach humanity how to walk in God's ways. Leave your house now and go forth among the people of the earth!"

So Enoch left his house and gathered all the people around him, including princes and judges and all the ordinary people who had strayed into sin, and he taught them what God wanted from them. Most of all, he taught them how to live in peace together, and the earth rejoiced that Enoch had come to rule humankind.

Enoch led the people for two hundred and forty-three years, and then Adam died. After his death, Enoch decided to withdraw from the world again, but he was afraid to leave the people too suddenly. So he withdrew himself bit by bit, first going away for three days at a time and then returning for a day to teach, then going away for six days and returning for one. Soon he was appearing before them for only one day a month, then one day a year. And the people missed him greatly and begged him to stay longer, but he would not.

Then one day an angel appeared before Enoch, saying, "God will soon call you up to heaven to rule over the souls there. Finish up your teaching on earth so that your wisdom may remain after you."

And Enoch told the people that soon he would leave them forever, but he did not know when, and he taught them all he knew about living in peace and judging fairly and honoring each other and God's creation.

Then one day a giant horse rode out of heaven on the wings of the wind and stood trembling before Enoch.

"This horse has come to take me away," said Enoch, and he mounted upon its great sleek back and began to ride away. And eight hundred thousand people followed behind him all that day and the next, until Enoch turned to them and said, "Go back to your homes, for all who come with me will surely die."

Then some departed, but many continued on with him until the sixth day, when Enoch said, "Tomorrow I will go up to heaven, never to return. Anyone who is with me on that day will surely die. Leave me now, I beg of you!"

Then most of the people departed, but some still refused, saying, "Wherever you go, we will go with you. Only death will separate us!" And Enoch saw that it was impossible to change their minds.

On the seventh day Enoch rose to heaven in a chariot of fire borne on a whirlwind.

And on the eighth day, messengers came to the place where Enoch had disappeared and found a field covered with great boulders of ice and snow. They split open the great stones of ice crystals and underneath them found the frozen bodies of all those who had been with Enoch on the last day. But of Enoch they could find no trace.

When Enoch reached heaven, God transformed him into a giant angel with thirty-six wings, each as large as the world, and three hundred and sixty-five thousand eyes, each as brilliant as the sun. And God changed his name to Metatron. Then Enoch's body melted into fire, veins and bones and eyeballs and hair and even the heart within his chest. And all around him swirled storms and hurricanes and thunder. Then God taught him the secrets of creation and entrusted him with the treasures of heaven.

21

The Cat and the Mouse

Why are the Cat and the Mouse enemies? It was not always so.

In the beginning the Cat and the Mouse were friends.

But after a time, the Mouse complained to God that there was not enough food to share between them.

Then God grew angry with the Mouse and said, "It is no use trying to fool Me, Mouse, for I know very well why you complain. You would rather eat up your friend Cat for your supper than share your food with her!"

Under God's stern gaze, the Mouse backed off into a corner and lowered his tiny gray head in shame.

Then God said, "Don't you remember what happened to the Moon when she complained to Me about the Sun? As a punishment for her envy, I took away all but a small part of her light. Now you too shall be punished for your complaining. From now on, the Cat shall eat you!"

But the Mouse protested, "Then no mice shall remain in Your world!"

God reassured him. "You will learn to hide in holes, and so some of you shall escape the Cat's keen claws."

Furious at God's judgment, the Mouse ran to the Cat and bit him, and then the Cat turned on the Mouse and bit him. Before long, the Mouse lay dead at the Cat's feet. From that day on, the mice went into hiding in holes whenever they heard the deadly tread of the Cat's silky paws.

When Noah took all the animals into the ark, he made the Cat swear to leave the Mouse in peace, since they all had to live together under one roof for many days. But one day the Cat forgot his promise and leapt at the Mouse to eat him. By a miracle, a hole suddenly appeared in the wall and swallowed up the frightened Mouse. The Cat reached in its long claw to spear the Mouse, but the Mouse opened its jaw wide. In went the sharp claw and ripped open a hole in the Mouse's cheek, but the Cat could not fish the Mouse out of the hole and finally left it there.

Then Noah sewed up the tear in the Mouse's cheek with a needle and thread. To this day, all mice bear two tiny seam-like puckers at each corner of their mouths where that hungry Cat's claws went fishing in vain in that miraculous mousehole in Noah's ark.

22

Nimrod and the Tower of Babel

At the beginning all people spoke one language.

Then Nimrod, son of Cush, grandson of Ham, great-grandson of Noah and Naamah, gathered all the other princes of the earth and declared that he wished to be their king.

"Why should we make you king over us?" they asked.

Then Nimrod reached into a trunk and pulled out the magical garments of skin once owned by Adam and Eve that made the wearer invincible. And when he put these garments on, they made him appear like a giant in their eyes. (He didn't tell them, of course, that his grandfather Ham had stolen these clothes from Noah, for what people would choose a thief as their king? But later, Nimrod got his just desserts, when Esau killed him to steal the garments for himself.)

Then Nimrod chose Shinar as his capital and made a tower there of five thrones—the lowest one of cedar wood, the next of iron, then copper, then silver, then gold. And he sat upon the golden throne with his crown almost touching heaven and declared himself a god.

Then the people said, "Let us make an even greater tower reaching up to heaven. Then we shall make a name for ourselves and not be lost upon the earth."

One group said, "When we reach the sky, we will make war with God." And they shot arrows up into the sky and when the arrows fell back to earth, they were dripping with blood. "See, we have already begun to kill the angels!" they cried. For God wished to fool them into thinking that they could do what they wished. And how easily they were fooled by their high-handed thoughts!

A second group declared, "Let us climb up to heaven and set up our own idols there." And they began dragging the great stone statues up the winding tower.

And the third group said, "Let us take our spears and

lances and pin the angels against the clouds so that they can no longer fly." And they clambered up the endless stairs, brandishing their weapons and whooping like wild cranes.

So high did the tower rise that it took a full year for the workers to travel from the ground to the top. Often bricks would fall before the workers reached the top, and then what a cry would rise up from the people: "A brick! Woe is us, for we have lost a precious brick!"

But if a person slipped and plunged to his death, no one even noticed.

Then God decided to put an end to their foolishness and sent the angels down to mix up their language so that they could no longer understand each other.

Immediately confusion overwhelmed them. When one worker asked for tacks, he was handed an ax, which he angrily threw back at his companion and so split his brain in two. When another asked for water, he was handed mortar, which the thirsty fellow immediately flung at his companion's head so that he became blind, lost his footing, and fell a year long to his death. Soon all work on the tower ceased, for the dead rained to the ground like hail.

Then God punished them further for their sin. Those who had wanted to set up idols in heaven were turned into apes and elephants. Those who had wanted to fling spears at the angels were themselves flung howling into the abyss. And those who had wanted to make war with heaven were scattered over the face of the earth.

From that day on, the place became known as Babel, because there God mixed up their language so that they could do no more than babble on like fools.

Then the earth opened its mouth and swallowed up the bottom third of the tower. Then fire fell from heaven and burned up the top third. All that remains to this day is the middle third, open to the ravages of wind and rain. Yet so tall is even this ruin that it still takes a traveler three days to journey to the end of its shadow. And no king since Nimrod has dared climb again to its broken crown.

PART II

FROM UR TO EGYPT –
THE FIRST FOUR
GENERATIONS

Almost four thousand years ago, an idol worshiper named Abram revolutionized human history by trusting in a Being he could not see. Together with his wife Sarai, he left civilization behind and became a spiritual pioneer. So began Jewish history.

23

The Birth of Abraham

In the land of Ur, far to the east, lived a mighty and powerful king named Nimrod. Even after God had frustrated Nimrod's plan to build a tower reaching to the heavens, he still ruled a vast kingdom with mighty armies and teeming treasure-houses. Throughout the land, Nimrod's word was law. And all the people worshiped him as their god.

One night Nimrod gave a feast in honor of his favorite captain, Terah. How happy Terah was to be so honored by the king! That night Terah vowed that when his wife Amitlai next gave birth to a son, he would name him Abram, meaning "great father," for his father was indeed greatly honored by the king.

On their way home from the feast that night, all the magicians and wise men looked up at the sky and saw an astonishing sight: A bright star suddenly blazed forth from the east and swallowed up four other stars.

In amazement they asked each other, "What can this mean?"

Then the oldest and wisest among them declared, "It can mean only one thing! Soon a child will be born among us who will become so powerful that he and his children will one day swallow up the kings in the land and rule over us all."

His words struck terror in their hearts, and they hurried home, where they prayed fervently to their stone gods.

The next morning they met again. "It is not good to keep this dread news from the king," they agreed, "for when this boy grows up and begins to fulfill the star's prophecy, Nimrod will blame us for having kept this from him."

So they went to the king and told him what they had seen.

"What shall I do?" demanded the king.

"Build a great house," they advised him, "and post guards at the gate. Gather there all the pregnant women in your kingdom. If they give birth to a boy, kill the baby immediately. But if they bear a girl, reward the baby and her mother with much gold and fine cloth. Parade them through the city, proclaiming, 'This is what the king will do to the woman who bears a daughter!'"

Their words pleased the king very much, and he ordered the house built at once. From all over the kingdom pregnant women were brought to the capital and imprisoned there, together with their midwives. In the next few months, seventy thousand baby boys were slaughtered, until the angels cried out to God, "How long will You let this evil Nimrod go on killing! Why should all these innocent babies die?"

God answered them, "Fear not, for you will soon see what I shall do to this wicked king. I shall now set My hand against him and undo his evil ways!"

Then Amitlai, Terah's wife, conceived and carried a son within her. And Terah saw her belly grow round and her face turn green, and he said to her, "I see that you are pregnant! It is the king's order that you go to the house he has prepared and there submit to his will."

But Amitlai did not wish to surrender her son to the king's sword, so she lied to her husband and told him, "I am not pregnant but ill with a stomachache."

Terah did not believe her. "Let me feel your belly."

By a miracle, God moved the child up from her abdomen to a place between her two breasts, so that when Terah pressed on her belly, he felt nothing unusual. And the boy remained there near her heart until the time came for him to be born.

Amitlai was afraid to give birth within the city, so she went out into the wilderness to a cave near a river and gave birth there. And when the baby was born, the whole cave blazed forth with light.

Amitlai lifted up the baby and said to him, "Abram, my son, I am afraid to stay here with you, for if the king finds you, he will kill us both. It is better that I leave you here so that I will not see your death." And she wrapped him in her cloak and laid him gently down in the cave and blessed him. Then she left him there and returned home, heartbroken and afraid.

The baby lay in the cave with no one to nurse him, and he cried out to God. God heard him weeping and sent the angel Gabriel, who nursed him with milk that poured forth from his right index finger.

When Abram was ten days old, he stood up, left the cave, and went walking by the river. There he met the angel Gabriel, who greeted him. "Peace to you, Abram!"

Abram replied, "And to you peace, Gabriel." Then he washed himself in the river and thanked God for keeping him alive.

Twenty days later Amitlai returned to the cave to see what had become of the baby she had abandoned there. She found a grown man walking by the river, and she did not recognize him, for he had grown so large in only twenty days.

"Peace be to you!" he said to her.

And she answered, "And to you peace."

Then Abram asked her, "Why are you wandering here in the wilderness?"

"I am seeking my baby whom I left here twenty days ago."

"What kind of mother abandons her child? Surely wolves and lions and bears have consumed the helpless child!"

Amitlai began to weep, and she said, "Nimrod would surely have killed him had I given birth to him in the city. Already he has murdered seventy thousand baby boys by the sword! I left my baby here in this cave, hoping that perhaps God would have pity on him and save him."

Abram embraced her and declared, "I am your son, Mother!"

She did not believe him. "What! In twenty days you have grown so big that you can walk and speak?"

"Is anything too great for God? Now go to Nimrod and tell him what you have seen here."

So Amitlai hurried home to Terah and told him what had happened in the cave in the wilderness. And Terah hurried to the king and bowed low until the king raised his scepter and gave Terah permission to rise.

"What is it that you wish, Terah?"

"O great and mighty Nimrod! I have come to tell you that the child prophesied by the blazing star has indeed been born and that he is my son Abram! For his sake you slaughtered seventy thousand innocent babies, but his mother lied to me and hid him in a cave and when she went to find him after twenty days, behold! He was walking and talking like a grown man and declaring that there is a God in heaven who sees but cannot be seen and who is even greater than Nimrod!"

When he heard this, the king trembled on his golden throne and called his wise men to him. "What shall be done with this child?"

They answered him. "He is only one child! Send one of your lowest captains to capture him and throw him into prison!"

"No," argued the king, "he is no mere child! Have you ever heard of a child who walks and speaks after only twenty days?"

Then Satan disguised himself as a prince dressed all in black silk and appeared before the king. "Summon all your princes and captains of war and give them weapons and send them out to capture this child. Surely he will not be able to resist such an army!"

The king followed Satan's advice. When Abram saw a great army advancing toward him, their spears and shields flashing in the sun, he became very frightened and cried out to God, "Help me, O God, for surely I am now lost!"

God comforted him and said, "No, Abram, you are not lost, for I am with you. Fear not, for I will deliver you from their hands."

God now sent a mist full of darkness between Abram and Nimrod's army, and they were afraid of it and returned empty-handed to the king.

Then Abram left the wilderness and began teaching God's ways to the people of Ur.

24

Abraham and the Idols

When Abram was about twenty, Terah sent him and his brother Haran to sell idols in the streets of Ur. Haran walked proudly through the city streets, peddling his father's wares, but Abram tied a rope around the necks of his two idols and dragged them face-down through the mud, proclaiming, "Who wishes to buy an idol that is good for nothing? It has a mouth but cannot speak, eyes but cannot see, a nose but cannot smell, ears but cannot hear, and feet but cannot walk. Who wishes to waste his money on dumb things made of stone and wood?"

When the people heard him, they were astonished. Was this any way for an idol-maker's son to behave? How could he say such things about the holy gods?

Then one old woman approached Abram and asked,

"Have you a large idol for me to buy? For the one I recently bought from your brother Haran was stolen last night by thieves."

"If it could not protect itself from thieves," Abram scolded her, "what good was it? Why do you waste your money worshiping an image that is good for nothing?"

"Then whom should I worship?" she asked him.

"Worship the God of heaven and earth, the Creator of all things," Abram told her. "Worship the God of Nimrod and Terah and Abram, the God of north, south, east, and west, the Holy One who made the sun and moon and stars and everything beneath them! Why should you bow down to things of stone and wood or to that beast Nimrod who calls himself a god?"

And the woman listened carefully to everything Abram said. Then she took a stone and with it smashed the idols in her home. That done, she went about the streets, declaring, "Those who wish to save their souls from destruction, let them worship the God of Abram! All else is emptiness and lies!"

When Nimrod heard about the old woman's deeds and how she was attracting many of his people to this new God, he ordered her taken prisoner and brought before him.

"What nonsense are you preaching to the people?" he said to her. "I am your god! I made you, and I keep you alive!"

"No, it is you who are talking nonsense!" she rebuked him. "The only God is the One who made heaven and earth and all that is in it, including the king."

Her words angered Nimrod, and he ordered her head cut off on the spot. But her death did not stop the people of Ur from flocking in ever great numbers to Abram's God.

Not long after this, Abram went to his mother Amitlai and said, "Mother, my father's idols seem especially hungry today. Prepare a fitting banquet for them so that they may eat."

So Amitlai prepared a meal and gave it to her son,

who set the plates before the stone and wood objects and then sat down to watch. When nothing happened, he returned to his mother and declared, "I am afraid that they did not find the food quite to their liking. Perhaps if you prepare an even more sumptuous feast, they will find that more acceptable."

So she selected three choice lambs from their flocks and cooked them with her best skill. Yet the idols did not touch this food either, but sat stone-still upon their shelves.

Then Abram took an ax and smashed all but the largest idol. Then he set the ax in the largest idol's hand.

When Terah heard the noise, he rushed into the room and found all his idols lying in pieces on the floor. In anger, he turned to his son and cried, "What have you done, Abram? Why have you destroyed my idols?"

Calmly Abram replied, "I did not destroy them, Father. When I brought them food to satisfy their hunger, all the smaller idols reached out their hands to take the food first, and the largest idol grew so angry with them that he took an ax and smashed them all to pieces."

Then Terah's face turned red and he shook a clenched fist at his son. "What nonsense you are telling me, Abram! Do these idols have any soul and breath in them that they can move? I myself made them all! And *you* destroyed them and put the ax in that one's hand. How can you tell me such lies and expect me to believe them?"

"And how can you believe that these are your gods, Father? If you made them, how can you worship them? Will they save you from your enemies? Will they protect you from sickness and death? Don't you know that there is one God who made the earth and heavens, who cannot be seen or touched or smashed by an ax? Surely you know better than to worship the work of your own hands, Father!"

Then Abram grabbed the ax from the remaining idol's hand and smashed it, too. Then he departed from his father's home.

25

Abraham in Nimrod's Furnace

Terah was terrified when his youngest son Abram smashed his idols, and he ran to tell King Nimrod. Nimrod had Abram brought before him and asked him to confirm or deny what Terah had said.

"I will tell you the same story I told my father," Abram told the king. "The largest idol became angry at the smaller ones and smashed them all with an ax."

"Surely, Abram," said the king slyly, "you don't expect *me* to believe that story. It's one thing to tell your old father that tall tale, but I am the great King Nimrod who is wise beyond measure."

"Then if you are so wise, King Nimrod," replied Abram, "why do you worship gods made by human hands? And why do you call yourself a god when you will die one day like all men of flesh and blood? No, the only real God is *Adonai* who made heaven and earth! There is none else!"

Nimrod's face twisted into a sinister smile, and he ordered Abram thrown into prison for a year without food or water. "Now we will see what good it does to worship an invisible God!"

God sent the angel Gabriel to care for Abram during the year, and the angel brought him all sorts of delicious foods. And out of the ground within Abram's prison cell arose a sweet spring that provided water for him to drink.

When the year was over, the king sent the prison warden to fetch Abram.

"Surely he is dead!" cried the warden. "What man can live for a year without food or water?"

"So much the better," answered the king. "When you find the body, bury it and the people will forget all about him and his foolish ideas."

But when the prison warden called down to Abram,

"Abram, are you alive or dead?" a strong voice arose out of the pit and answered, "I am alive!"

"How did you stay alive so long?" asked the warden.

"The One who sustains all the living kept me alive and guarded over me. Nothing is too great for the one and only God!"

The prison warden ran to tell the king about the miracle that had happened.

"Impossible!" cried Nimrod.

"Nothing is impossible for the one true God!" answered the warden.

"Not you, too!" said Nimrod. "Are all my people turning against me now?"

"You are a false god, King Nimrod," answered the warden. "Only Abram's God is the true Creator of the World."

Furious, Nimrod called to his guards to chop off the warden's head, but when the metal blade struck the warden's neck, the blade shattered like glass. So the king was forced to let the warden go free.

Then Nimrod ordered that the royal kiln be heated for three days and nights until it burned with a scorching flame. He then ordered Abram thrown inside. So hot was the fire in the kiln that the first prince who approached it was immediately burned up before he could even open the door, and the same thing happened to the next eleven princes who tried to thrust Abram inside.

Then Satan appeared in human form and said to the king, "I will show you how to cast Abram inside the furnace. Fetch me boards and nails and ropes."

And Satan fashioned a *trabuko*, which is a catapult, and they tied Abram's arms and feet and bound him to the device and prepared to fling him into the fire.

Then Satan appeared to Abram and said, "Abram, you still have a last chance to save yourself from Nimrod's furnace. Bow down to him and he will let you live."

But Abram shook his head and cursed Satan so that he left him.

Then Abram's mother came to him with tears in her eyes. "Abram, my son, save yourself from Nimrod's furnace! Bow down before the king!"

"No, Mother," answered Abram. "For Nimrod's fire can be put out with water, but the fire of God lasts forever!"

"May God now save you from Nimrod's fire!" said his mother, and she too left him.

Then they flung Abram into the furnace, and he landed in the midst of the flames. Instantly the flames at the heart of the furnace went out, and the wood burst into flower so that the furnace at that spot seemed like a perfumed garden, although all around the flames leapt with a white-hot rage. And the king and all his servants could see Abram walking unharmed in the midst of the flames.

Then Nimrod ordered that they remove Abram from the furnace. But when the king's servants approached the kiln, flames leapt out and consumed a dozen men, and they could not come near.

Then Nimrod called out to Abram, "Abram, servant of the true God, come forth out of the furnace."

And Abram walked out of the flames, and they saw that the ropes that had bound him were completely consumed, but not a thread of his garments was even singed. And the king and all his people bowed low before him.

But Abram said, "Do not bow before me, for it is God alone who saved me from the flames. God fashioned each of you, and only God deserves your praise."

Then all the people in Ur believed in Abram's God. And Nimrod gave Abram many gifts, including a servant from the royal household named Eliezer. And the king also gave him silver and gold and crystal and many camels.

Then Abram prepared to leave Ur of the Chaldees, the land of his birth, to travel to a new land that God would show him.

26

Nimrod's Dream

Two years after Abram escaped the flames of Nimrod's furnace, Nimrod had a dream.

In his dream, he and his army were camped near the furnace in a valley. Suddenly out of the furnace emerged a man resembling Abram. In his hand was a sword, and he pursued Nimrod, brandishing the sword, and Nimrod fled from him in terror. Then his pursuer flung an egg at him, and the egg cracked open. The liquid from the egg flooded the valley and drowned the entire army, except for Nimrod and three other kings. Then miraculously the fluid streamed back into the shattered eggshell, and the pieces knit together once again into an unbroken egg. Out of the egg hatched a chick that flew to Nimrod's head and pecked out one of his eyes.

Nimrod awoke from his dream shaking with fear. With a trembling voice, he summoned to his bedside all his wise men and asked them to explain what the dream meant.

Anoko, one of his most trusted magicians, said, "Woe to you, mighty Nimrod, for this is a most evil dream! Abram will one day destroy your army and leave only you and three of your allies alive. In time one of Abram's descendants will turn against you and take your life. As long as Abram lives, you will not be safe!"

Then Nimrod ordered Abram captured and put to death. But Eliezer, the royal slave whom Nimrod had given to Abram as a gift, happened to be in the palace on that day and heard the king's fateful decree and ran to warn Abram. Abram fled to Noah's house, where he hid for a month until the king gave up looking for him.

Then Abram gathered together his household and family—his wife Sarai, his nephew Lot, his father Terah, and his mother Amitlai, together with the three hundred people of Ur whom he and Sarai had converted to their new faith, and Eliezer, the faithful servant who had saved his life. Then they departed for Haran.

For three days they traveled in the shadow of the ruined Tower of Babel that Nimrod had erected to defy God, until at last they saw the sun lighting the way westward toward Canaan. All the time they traveled they never once looked back, and the land of their birth slowly faded away to nothing but a distant dream.

27

Abraham and Sarah in Egypt

After Abram and Sarai had left Ur, they traveled west to Haran and then to Canaan, where they settled together with their household and flocks. Soon after they began to dwell in the land, there was a terrible famine, and they were forced to go down to Egypt to find food.

For many days Abram and Sarai journeyed through the desert toward Egypt. As they neared their destination, they forded a stream. In the middle of the crossing, Abram chanced to look down and thus caught a glimpse of his wife's face reflected in the water. Never before had he noticed how radiant she was! Her great beauty filled his eyes with wonder.

"What will the Egyptians say when they see her?" he asked himself. "Surely they will take her from me! It is best that I hide her in a basket so that she will be safe from their grasp!"

So he hid Sarai in a reed basket, loaded the basket onto one of his camels, and came to the gateway of Egypt. There the border guards stopped him and asked, "What are you carrying in that great basket of yours? It is our custom to charge a tax for all goods brought into the land."

"It is nothing but a basketful of barley," answered Abram.

"Perhaps he is lying," they whispered to one another. "Let us charge him a higher tax and see if he will pay."

So they said to him, "Barley, you say? Are you sure it is not wheat you are carrying?"

Their words terrified Abram. What if they were to discover the truth! Surely he would be put to death! So he quickly replied, "Forgive me, I was mistaken. It is wheat that I carry. I will gladly pay the tax on wheat!"

They saw that he was easy prey so they pressed him further. "You seem too eager to pay the higher tax. Maybe it is because you have even more valuable goods inside. Pepper, perhaps?"

Abram's terror increased. From inside the basket he could hear Sarai's quickening breath. "Very well, then— pepper!"

But still they wouldn't let him go. "No, we say it is gold you have in there!"

"Very well, then, gold! I will pay anything you ask, only let me go by! I have come from a land of famine and need to buy food as quickly as possible so that my family back home does not die from hunger!"

But they were still not satisfied to let him pass. "What exactly do you have inside that basket that makes you so willing to pay any price? Obviously we must open it up and see for ourselves."

So they pulled the basket off the camel's back and pried open the lid. Instantly all of Egypt was filled with a blinding radiance, as Sarai's beauty shone forth from within. Each of the guards began to vie with the other to buy this precious treasure from Canaan, but at last word reached Pharaoh himself and he demanded Sarai for his own wife. He had her brought into the palace and showered with gifts—fine cloths, precious pearls and diamonds, servants, herds, and flocks. He even gave her his own daughter Hagar as her handmaid. And he deeded her the land of Goshen for an inheritance.

And then for the first time he noticed Abram standing quietly alongside her. "And who is this man with you?"

"He is my brother," Sarai lied. For she feared that Pharaoh would kill Abram if he found out he was her husband.

And Pharaoh gave him gifts, too, and honored him.

That night when Sarai went to her bridal chamber to await Pharaoh, she cried out to God and God heard her prayers. God sent her an angel, invisible to all but Sarai, who stood by her side with a large stick in one hand.

When Pharaoh came into her bedroom, he stretched forth his hand to touch her shoe, but the angel struck him on the hand until he cried out in pain. He next reached up his hand to stroke her hair, and again the angel rapped him across the knuckles with the stick. All night long Pharaoh tried to touch his new bride, but all his efforts were greeted with blows. Then the whole palace was struck down with a plague of leprosy until Pharaoh fled from the bridal chamber in terror, fearing that he would soon die. All this happened on the fifteenth of Nisan, just as in later years, God would strike down the first-born of Egypt on this same night before liberating the Israelites from their long bondage.

The next morning Pharaoh consulted with his magicians and priests and discovered the reason for his troubles: Sarai was not Abram's sister but his wife! Contrite and bruised, Pharaoh returned Sarai to her husband and gave them all the food they needed and more.

And then, loaded down with the riches of Egypt, Sarai and Abram returned home to the land of Canaan.

28

The Cruel Customs of Sodom

Before the Flood, the earth had been filled with such wickedness that God had had no choice but to wipe the slate clean and start again. And although the people of the earth again returned to sin after the terrible waters receded, still they were not quite so bad as they had once been.

Except in the city of Sodom.

Nowhere on earth was such evil found as in this city and its sister city of Gomorrah. So famous were these cities for their wickedness that travelers would often detour many days out of their way to avoid entering their gates. But it sometimes happened that a stranger would wander in unawares, or perhaps a sudden desert storm might leave a traveler no choice but to seek refuge within their walls for the night. And woe to that traveler if such a thing ever happened!

For as soon as a stranger entered the city gates, three strong men of Sodom would grab the stranger's feet and three would grab his head, and they would carry him to a special bed built by the Sodomites just for this purpose. If the man's body was too short to fit the bed, they would pull at his feet and head like taffy until he stretched to the bedposts. And if his body was too long, they would first chop off his feet and then his legs until he fit just right. Then they would send the bruised and weeping visitor on his way, proclaiming, "This is the way Sodom welcomes strangers into its midst!"

Why were the people of this city so cruel? All because of too much gold. For gold was everywhere in Sodom—in the fields where they plowed, in the rivers where they washed their clothes, on the streets where they peddled their wares. If a farmer pulled up a turnip, he found crumbs of gold clinging to the roots. If a shepherdess lowered a bucket into the well, she would be just as likely to bring up a gold nugget as water.

So much wealth made the people of Sodom greedy. The more they had, the more they wanted. So they continued to devise ways to steal from those poor unsuspecting souls who occasionally stumbled into their midst.

If they saw that a stranger had much silver and gold, they would lure him to the outskirts of town near a teetering stone wall where two Sodomites would skillfully back him up against the wall. Then, while these two distracted him with conversation, a third would dig under the wall on the other side until it collapsed upon the stranger, burying him and his riches. They would then dig out the money, divide it, and strip the stranger of the very clothes on his back, leaving the naked body there for the birds. For that was the only food they ever allowed their birds to have.

Sometimes they would invite a rich traveler into their homes and shower him with even more gold. But the gold they gave him was smeared with strongly scented oil. That night, while the unsuspecting guest slept, they would sniff out his treasure and rob him of everything, driving him out the next morning with only the shirt on his back.

So heartless were they that they refused to feed strangers anything but gold and silver, so that those who ate a meal in Sodom always left hungry.

Once a beggar came to Sodom. To everyone's amazement, the man stayed on for days, inexplicably remaining alive even though no one gave him a penny or a crumb of bread. Then they discovered that Lot's daughter Paltit had been sneaking the beggar food in her water jug, and as a punishment, they burnt her alive.

One of Paltit's friends also tried to feed a stranger on the sly, but she too was discovered. Her punishment was even worse. The people of the city smeared her from head to foot with sweet honey and left her to be stung to death by the bees.

It was after this last cruel deed that God decided to put an end to Sodom's wickedness forever.

29

Lot's Wife

God sent two angels to Sodom to rescue Lot and his family before the city was destroyed. When the two strangers knocked on the door, Lot's wife Edith trembled from head to toe. Had not her daughter Paltit recently been killed by the people of the city for showing even a small kindness to a stranger? How could she admit these strangers into her home, feed them, and shelter them, and still escape her neighbors' wrath?

So she refused to open the door.

But Lot waited until cover of night and then quietly snuck the strangers in, hoping in that way to escape detection.

When his wife found the guests already inside the house, she let out a frightened cry. "Out they go, Lot! We shall never remain alive as long as they stay under our roof!"

The angels tried to reassure her. "We have come to spare you from the destruction that God will soon bring down upon this wicked city. Fear not, for we will protect your family from harm."

But Edith was too upset to listen to them. "You don't know the people of this city as I do! They will stop at nothing to punish us all!" And turning to Lot, she declared, "If you insist on keeping these strangers here with us, let us divide the house in two. They will stay under *your* roof tonight. Let the consequences be on your head!"

To calm his wife, Lot agreed to the arrangement. Then he asked her to prepare a meal for their guests. But when his wife went to the pantry to get salt, she saw that she did not have enough to prepare dinner. So she went next door to borrow some.

"Salt—at this hour of the night?" complained her sleepy neighbor when Lot's wife knocked on her door. "Why not wait until morning?"

"Because our guests are hungry now and need to eat," answered Lot's wife. Then she bit her tongue, for she had let the cat out of the bag. But it was too late. Grabbing the pot of salt from her suspicious neighbor's hand, she hurried home, finished preparing the meal, and awaited the morning with growing dread.

Like wildfire the news spread throughout Sodom that Lot and his family were entertaining guests in their home. The next morning an angry crowd gathered at the door to demand that they hand over the strangers to the people of the city. But Lot refused to surrender them, for he knew only too well what they would do to these strangers if they got their hands on them. He even offered to turn his own daughters over to his neighbors—to work their evil will upon them—but his wife stood firm and would not let them out of the house.

Then the angels came to Lot's aid, blinding the murmuring Sodomites outside so that they could not even find their way to Lot's door to force their way in. Then the angels said to Lot, "The time has come to turn your backs on this evil place and flee for your lives. For God will now destroy this city and everyone in it. Only you will escape alive."

Lot's sons-in-law only laughed at the angels' warning, refusing to leave the city. So Lot and his wife took their two daughters and fled out the door, while all around them the people still groped blindly and cried out for revenge.

As Lot's family ran toward the hills, the angels shouted after them, "Whatever happens, don't look back!"

And then the rain that had been falling upon Sodom and Gomorrah that morning turned yellow and hot and began scorching everything it fell down upon.

Without pausing for breath, Lot and his family kept running, hearing the hiss of the poison rain falling heavily upon the plains, feeling the ground shaking under their feet as the walls of Sodom and Gomorrah crumbled. They had almost reached a safe place when Edith felt an uncontrollable urge to turn around to see what had become of her home.

When she looked back, she beheld the awesome *Shekhinah* of God sweeping over the burning cities of the plain, transforming all beneath its wings into darkness and ruin. Instantly she turned into a pillar of salt, for it was through salt that she had betrayed her angelic guests. To this very day she stands at the edge of the desolate plain, licked by the cattle until by nightfall only her feet remain. But every morning she grows anew, until the cows lick her down again to the ground.

30
Abraham's Impatience with the Old Man

Who was more hospitable than Abraham! No traveler ever left his tent without a meal and a pleasant rest in the cool shade. No stranger ever forgot Sarah's generous hand or her kind words.

One day an old man wandered into their camp, tired and dusty from his long trek through the wilderness. Eagerly Abraham invited him inside the tent, but the old man refused, saying he preferred to sleep outside. But Abraham pleaded with him until he changed his mind. Then Sarah hurried to bring their guest cool water and cakes of meal, which he gobbled up with great gusto.

When they had finished their meal, Abraham offered up a simple prayer of thanksgiving to God. The old man watched him curiously.

"What is this *Adonai* you speak of?" he asked Abraham. "I have not heard of this god in my travels."

"Not heard of *Adonai!*" exclaimed Abraham. "Why, this is the one true God, Creator of heaven and earth, unseen but seeing all."

The old man shook his grizzled head. "I know only the gods of my youth. I am too old to believe in such things as invisible gods."

"When the sun goes down at night," said Abraham, "who watches over the earth? And when the wind blows, who sends it forth? There is only one Power behind all things and that is the everliving God. God made everything—you, me, the stars, the sands. How can you not see that, old man?"

But the old man simply shook his head and repeated, "I am too old for such strange ideas. I know only the gods of my youth."

Abraham now became angry and pointed a shaking finger at his guest. "Then out with you, old man! I will not have such a stubborn fool under my tent."

Slowly the old man gathered up his few belongings and headed out into the desert night.

As soon as he was out of sight, God spoke to Abraham. "Where is the old man who came to shelter under your tent?"

"I have chased him away, for he denied You!"

Then God's voice grew angry and blasted Abraham like a hot wind. "Abraham, you do not understand anything at all! All these years I have been patient with this old man. I have fed him and clothed him and taken care of his simple needs. I have not minded that he does not worship Me. But you—you lost patience after only one night!"

Abraham felt overcome by a terrible sadness, for he had disappointed God. "Forgive me for my impatience."

"It is not I who deserve your apology, Abraham, but the old man," answered God. "Go find him and beg his forgiveness."

So Abraham wrapped his cloak around his shoulders and hurried out into the desert night, calling for the old man. And he found him not far off, shivering from the cold.

"Forgive me," begged Abraham. "I was wrong to send you away. Please return to the shelter of my tent."

The old man forgave Abraham and followed him back to the tent, where he spent a peaceful night.

The next morning, after the old man had departed, God again spoke to Abraham. "Now you understand Me better, Abraham. In future times, when your children sin against Me, they too will understand that I will never lose

My patience with them altogether. No matter how much I chastise them, I will not forsake My covenant with them. You and your children will always be welcome under the shelter of My tent."

And so it has come to pass.

31

The Birth of Isaac

Sarah grew older and older, and still she was barren. Her hair turned white, and her skin puckered into a thousand wrinkles. But still no child entered her belly as God had promised her and Abraham.

Then three messengers came one day to their tent and told the old couple that they would soon bear a son. When Sarah heard the news, laughter creased her old face.

"Shall I, whose bent spine can barely carry me from sunrise to sunset, now cradle a fat baby in my arms? Surely I am too old for such fairy tales!"

And God heard her laughter and scolded her. "Is anything too difficult for Me, Sarah? Did I not rescue Abraham from Nimrod's flames and you from Pharaoh's lust? Have a little more faith than that!"

And Sarah felt ashamed of herself for laughing.

And thus, a year later, on the first day of Passover, Sarah did give birth to a healthy baby boy, and they called him Isaac, which means "laughing boy," for his mother had laughed at the thought of bearing him in her old age. Sarah was ninety years old and Abraham one hundred when Isaac was born to them.

That day the whole world rejoiced with the old couple. All the barren women in the world gave birth at the same time. The blind all regained their sight, the lame their sure step, the mute their voices, the mad their reason. And Abraham's white hair turned black as pitch, and Sarah's wrinkles became smooth as ivory.

Now there were those who doubted that such a miracle as this could have happened. And they accused Abraham and Sarah of finding an orphan child by the road and claiming him as their own. But God had foreseen such doubts and had commanded the angel who has charge over embryos to fashion a child exactly in the likeness of his father. And indeed, anyone looking at Isaac could have no doubt of his lineage.

Abraham and Sarah gave a great feast to celebrate Isaac's circumcision on the eighth day after his birth. And another miracle happened then, for Sarah's breasts so overflowed with milk on that day that she nursed the one hundred babies who came to the feast. Those whose mothers were thinking only pious thoughts as their babies suckled at Sarah's breast became converts to Sarah's faith when they grew up. And in future years, all righteous Gentiles and pious converts descended from these same suckling babes.

But as for those mothers who were only using their babies to test Sarah, suspicious of miracles such as these, their children grew up to be powerful rulers in the world. And when God revealed the Torah at Sinai, they all lost their kingdoms, for they did not accept the Torah.

And on that day the sun shone forth with such brilliance as had not been seen since Adam and Eve had departed the Garden. And it will not shine as brightly again until the End of Days.

32

The Akedah

After Abraham had celebrated the birth of his son Isaac, Satan appeared before God and said, "Why do You honor Abraham above all Your children on earth? He is not worthy of such praise!"

"And why do you speak ill of him, Satan?" God asked.

"Long have I wandered the earth," said Satan, "observing Your creatures, and I have seen that they are all alike, even the great Abraham. When they want something, they pray to You and burn sacrifices on their altars. But as soon as You have granted their requests, they forget all about You. Look at Abraham! Now that he and Sarah have a son in their old age, they spend all their time feasting and playing with the child, but they do not honor You at all."

"Abraham is an upright man," God replied, "honoring guests within his tents, living humbly and peacefully among his neighbors. Surely if I were to ask him to do anything, even to sacrifice his own son Isaac on an altar, he would not hold back."

Now these words were precisely what Satan had been waiting for. "Agreed!" he cried, clapping his twelve wings together with undisguised delight. "I accept Your wager! Let us see if Your servant will indeed hold nothing back from You!"

And he flew off, confident of his certain victory over God.

God now spoke to Abraham, "Abraham!"

And Abraham answered, "Here I am!"

"Take your son . . ."

"But I have two sons," protested Abraham, "Ishmael and Isaac."

"Your only son . . ."

"But each one is the only son of his mother."

"Whom you love . . ."

"But I love them both!"

"I mean Isaac."

Then Abraham's heart froze within his breast. "And where shall I take him?"

"To the land of Moriah and there offer him to Me as a sacrifice."

"And what shall I tell his mother Sarah?" asked Abraham, his heart breaking.

But God said nothing more.

So Abraham approached Sarah in her tent and said,

"Our son Isaac is already thirty-seven years old, but he knows little of God's ways. It is time for me to take him to a teacher so that he can learn how to serve God."

"And where can you find such a place out here in the wilderness?" asked Sarah, fear gripping her heart.

"I will take him to Noah's son Shem and his son Ever."

"Very well, Abraham, but do not keep him there long, for he is all that I have. I am old and have not much longer to live."

That night Sarah stayed up with Isaac, advising him from the wisdom of her many years. The next morning she gave Isaac a turban set with a splendid jewel and placed it on his head. Then she embraced her only son and wished him well on his journey.

Accompanying Abraham and Isaac to Mount Moriah were two others, Abraham's older son Ishmael and his servant Eliezer, whom Nimrod had given Abraham long ago when he had escaped the fiery furnace. Seeing Abraham's solemn face and noting that he had brought no animal along to sacrifice, the two guessed Abraham's plans and began rejoicing in their good fortune.

"When Isaac is dead," said Ishmael, "I will inherit all of Abraham's riches, for I am the first-born!"

"What a fool you are!" Eliezer rebuked him. "Abraham has already cast you out together with your mother and sworn not to give you anything. No, it is I who will inherit everything, for have I not been a faithful servant all these years?"

Then a voice issued forth from heaven and silenced them both. "Neither of you will inherit, for I have other plans for this child of Abraham and Sarah!"

When Satan saw the small caravan approaching Mount Moriah, he suddenly grew worried that God might win the wager after all. So he disguised himself as an old man and appeared before Abraham in the road.

"Where are you going, foolish old man? Do you think God really wants you to sacrifice your only son? What has

Isaac done to deserve such an end? Surely this idea does not come from God!"

But Abraham knew it was Satan speaking, and he chased him away.

Then Satan disguised himself as a young man and appeared before Isaac.

"Do you understand what your father is doing, Isaac? He is going to sacrifice you to his God! Do not let this foolish old man do such a thing, for why should you die when you are still in the prime of your youth?"

Isaac told his father what the stranger had said, and Abraham warned him that it was Satan speaking, and together they sent him packing.

Then Satan changed himself into a swift brook in their way. When they came to the bank, they began to wade across, but soon found themselves up to their necks in the raging waters. Abraham again recognized the hand of Satan, for there had never been water in this place before.

"Leave us, Satan, and no more of your tricks! For we are doing God's will, and you are powerless to stop us!"

Satan fled in terror at the sound of Abraham's voice, and the stream suddenly became as dry as bone.

On the third day of his journey, Abraham looked up and saw Mount Moriah in the distance. At the top of the mountain, a pillar of fire reached from earth to heaven and a cloud of glory swirled around it.

Abraham turned to Isaac and pointed toward the place. "What do you see there, Isaac?"

"I see a pillar of fire upon the mountain," replied Isaac, "and the glory of God in the cloud."

Then Abraham knew that Isaac was acceptable as a sacrifice to God. He then asked the two others with him, "What do you see there in the distance?"

And they answered him, "We see nothing more than a mountain like other mountains."

Then Abraham said to them, "Stay here with the donkey then, for you are just like him. Isaac and I will go to Mount Moriah and worship God there. We will return to you this evening."

Abraham then strapped the wood upon Isaac's back, and he himself took the fire and the knife. And as they proceeded up the mountain, Isaac asked, "Father, I see the wood, the fire, and the knife, but where is the lamb for the sacrifice?"

And Abraham gazed sadly upon his son and replied, "God has chosen you for the sacrifice, Isaac."

And Isaac said, "I am ready to do God's will."

Abraham was pleased with Isaac's words, although he was also heartbroken because of them. And when they reached the mountaintop, they built the altar together. Then Abraham piled wood upon the altar and tied Isaac upon it with strong ropes.

"Hurry with the task, Father," urged Isaac as he lay there upon the rough wood, "for you are an old man and I am young, still thirsty for life. Move quickly or I might struggle and deflect your knife and make myself unfit for sacrifice."

And as Abraham raised up his knife to kill his son, Isaac said, "When I have been burnt by the fire, take my ashes back to my mother Sarah and ask her to keep the casket in her chamber so that she can remember me at all times."

Abraham now turned away to hide his tears. "We will survive you but a few days, Isaac, before we follow you down to the grave."

Then Abraham mounted the altar and laid his knees upon Isaac's chest and raised his knife high. And his tears fell upon Isaac's face, and Isaac's fell down upon the wood, and from heaven the tears of the Angels of Mercy rained down upon the knife so that it lost is sharpness. But so terrified was Isaac by the falling blade that life escaped him and he died.

Then God declared, "Now you see, angels, why I have created humankind! Had I listened to you at the beginning when you cried, 'What is the human soul that You are mindful of it?' I would not have known my friend

Abraham, who this day proclaims my unity throughout the world!"

God now called out to the angel Michael, "Quick! Stretch out your hand and stop Abraham!"

And Michael called out, "Abraham, do not lay your hand upon your son!"

Then Abraham suspended his hand in mid-air and looked heavenward. "First God commands me to do this thing, and now a voice forbids me. Which voice should I obey, teacher or disciple?"

Then a mighty voice filled the heavens and declared, "Abraham, do not harm the boy! Because you did not withhold your precious son from me, I shall bless you and make your children as many as the stars in the sky and the sands in the sea, and through you all the nations of the world shall be blessed."

When Isaac heard the heavenly voice, he came back to life and declared, "Blessed is God who revives the dead!"

Then Abraham said, "Can I leave here without offering a sacrifice of thanksgiving?"

God replied, "Look behind you, Abraham, and you will find your sacrifice."

Abraham turned around and saw a ram caught in a thornbush. This was Satan's doing, for when the ram had run toward Abraham to offer itself for the altar, Satan had tangled its horns in the bush. Now Abraham freed it and offered it up to God in place of his son Isaac, and God accepted his sacrifice.

This was no ordinary ram that Abraham sacrificed that day on Mount Moriah. For it had been created at twilight on the sixth day of creation for just this purpose, and every part of it was destined for a holy task. The skin became Elijah's garment, the sinews the ten strings of David's harp, and the ashes part of the altar in Jerusalem. But most special of all were the two horns. One was destined to sound at Sinai when God revealed the Ten Commandments, and the other will announce the End of Days.

God revealed to Abraham on that day that the spot on which he had bound his son Isaac was the holiest spot on earth. Here Adam had performed his first sacrifice, and Cain and Abel theirs, and Noah his. And on this spot the Holy Temple would one day rise where the children of Israel would offer up their sacrifices of atonement and thanksgiving to God.

Full of joy and gratitude, Abraham and Isaac now hurried back down the mountain to return to Sarah waiting for them at their camp.

But Sarah was not there. For after Abraham and Isaac had left for Mount Moriah, Satan disguised himself as an old man and came to Sarah and said to her, "Where have your husband and son gone?"

"To a distant place to study Torah," she replied.

"Poor woman!" Satan cried. "They have lied to you, for Abraham has taken your only son Isaac to Mount Moriah to sacrifice him to God."

Then Sarah's whole body trembled and she felt the breath leaving it. But she forced herself to be strong and to answer Satan, "All that God has commanded Abraham, may he do with a full heart."

Then Satan departed, disappointed in all his designs. As soon as he was gone, Sarah packed some food in a sack and left the camp to inquire what had happened to her husband and only son.

When she came to Hebron, she asked for them, but no one there had seen them. Then she sent her servants to Shem's house, but no one had seen them there, either. In anguish she cried out, "All my life did I wait for a son, and now he is no more. O Isaac, my son, my son, if only I had died in place of you!" Then she forced herself to be as still as stone, and declared, "God is just. My heart rejoices that my son has done what he has been commanded to do."

Then Satan appeared to her again as an old man and said, "Stop your tears, Sarah, for I lied to you before when I told you that your son was dead. Abraham did not sacrifice him on Moriah. God has spared your only son."

At Satan's words Sarah's heart filled up with such joy that it burst, and she died at once.

When Abraham and Isaac returned home, they learned that Sarah had gone to Hebron to seek them. So they journeyed to Hebron and there discovered that Sarah had died. Then they lifted up their voices in a great cry and wept. On that day Abraham lost his youth, which he had regained at the birth of Isaac, and became an old man, bent and gray. And Isaac refused to be comforted for his mother.

Then Abraham buried his beloved wife in a cave in Machpelah, beside Adam and Eve. When Adam and Eve learned that Sarah was to lie next to them, they wished to leave the cave, "on account of our sins and her good deeds," but Abraham promised to pray for them so that they would lose their shame and would merit a grave near Sarah. When they heard Abraham's words, they lay back down in peace.

And the whole land mourned Sarah for many days. days.

33

Eliezer's Mission to Seek Rebecca

After the death of Sarah, Abraham and Isaac were lonely. No longer did their tents glow with the special Sabbath light she kindled from week to week. No longer did their bread taste of the blessing of her hands, nor did the needy come to their camp to seek comfort from her soft words.

Abraham now called his servant Eliezer and said to him, "It is time for my son Isaac to marry. But he shall not marry a woman from this land. You shall travel to the land of Haran where my brother's family lives and take a wife from there. God has already chosen the proper bride for him."

"But what if she refuses to return with me?" said Eliezer. "Perhaps Isaac can go there . . ."

"No!" cried Abraham. "When God called me forth
from my father's house and brought me to this land, God
promised to give it to my children after me. If the woman
does not wish to return with you, then you are no longer
bound by your oath to me."

Eliezer now prepared for his long journey, taking
with him ten camels and ten servants to carry the many
gifts he brought. And God sent two angels to travel with
him, one to guard him and one to guard Isaac's bride.

As they set out on their way, the earth rushed
forward to meet them with such eagerness that the
journey lasted only a few hours instead of the many days
it normally required.

When he reached Haran, Eliezer stopped at the well
and prayed to God for guidance. "The maidens of Haran
will soon come to this well to water their flocks. Please
show me by a sign that one of them is the bride destined
for my master's son. If one maiden offers to give me drink
and also to water my camels, then I shall know she is the
one You have intended for Isaac. And let all the others
refuse to give me drink."

Then as he waited there, the young maidens of Haran
came to the well to water their flocks. All of them refused
to give Eliezer water, except for one young woman who
eagerly brought him water and also watered his thirsty
camels, although he had not asked her to. This was the
daughter of Bethuel, son of Abraham's brother Nahor—
Rebecca, who had been conceived on the very day
Abraham had brought Isaac to Moriah to be sacrificed to
God. Eliezer could see that she was as kind as she was
beautiful, and he gave her a gold nose-ring and two gold
bracelets and asked to meet her family.

When Rebecca's brother Laban saw Eliezer coming,
bearing so many gifts, he wished to kill him and steal all
that he had, for Laban was a sly and greedy man. But then
Eliezer, who was a giant, lifted up two of his camels, one
in each hand, to cross a nearby stream, and Laban
thought better of it.

When they sat down to eat, Laban renewed his scheming and told his father Bethuel about all the gold and silver and jewels Eliezer had brought with him. So they cooked up a dish of poisoned food and set it before Eliezer. But Eliezer did not wish to touch a morsel of food until he had accomplished what he had set out to do, so he pushed aside the dish and told them why he had come.

"Your kinsman Abraham wishes to marry his only son Isaac to your daughter Rebecca," Eliezer told Bethuel. "Together they will inherit all that he has, a great fortune in lands, herds, tents, and servants. They will be among the most powerful in the land of Canaan, and their children will inherit after them."

His words pleased Rebecca's family, and they agreed to the match.

As they were listening to Eliezer, God sent an angel to move the dish of poisoned food from Eliezer's place to Bethuel's, and he ate from it without thinking what he was doing, and he died.

Then Eliezer wished to depart at once with Rebecca to return home to Abraham's camp, but her family wanted her to remain for a week to mourn her father Bethuel. Spurred on by the impatient angel waiting outside, Eliezer said, "Let Rebecca herself decide."

When they asked Rebecca, she said, "I am ready to leave with Eliezer."

So they gave her their blessing and she departed. But their blessing did not come from their hearts, and so it became a curse, and Rebecca remained barren for many years.

Again, as on Eliezer's previous journey to Haran, the earth rolled forward so eagerly to meet them that their return journey lasted only a few hours. They left at noon and were at Abraham's camp by three o'clock.

When they approached Abraham's camp, Rebecca looked up and saw a young man in the fields, praying the *minhah* prayer that he had written. She was instantly struck by his extraordinary beauty and the sweet fragrance floating in the air around him, for the place where he prayed was near the gates of Paradise.

At that moment a voice addressed her from heaven and told her that she was destined to be this man's wife and the mother of Jacob and Esau. But when she heard Esau's name, her heart was filled with such dread that she fell off her camel and injured herself.

Then Isaac took her to Sarah's tent, which had remained empty for three years, and became her husband. And all the miracles that had vanished at the death of Sarah returned to the camp. The cloud of glory once more hovered over Sarah's tent. And each Sabbath eve, when Rebecca kindled the Sabbath candles, light filled the tent and did not depart during the rest of the week. The blessing returned to the dough Rebecca kneaded, and the needy once more gathered at the tent gates, which stretched wide to accommodate them all.

In every way Rebecca was like Sarah, and Isaac was at last comforted for the death of his mother.

To reward his servant Eliezer for completing his mission so successfully, Abraham granted him his freedom. And God added to Abraham's gift by granting Eliezer a privilege given to few mortals: to enter the gates of Paradise alive.

34

The Birth of Jacob and Esau

For twenty years Rebecca and Isaac remained childless. At last they went to Mount Moriah and prayed to God to give them a child. And God heard their prayers and answered them.

But when Rebecca had been pregnant for seven months, she began to wish that she had never prayed for children. For the twins she carried inside her struggled fiercely and caused her endless pain. Even in the womb, they never stopped fighting. When she passed by a heathen temple, Esau pounded against her body, struggling to get out, and if she passed by a synagogue or a house of study, Jacob butted his head up against her belly.

The two brothers argued with each other from sunup to sundown. Esau would say, "There is only the world of earthly pleasure awaiting us once we are born," and Jacob would argue back, "No, there are two worlds, this one and the next, and I will gladly give up this one to possess the World to Come."

They each enlisted an angel on their side, Esau calling upon the evil Samael, who was none other than Satan, and Jacob calling upon the archangel Michael. And the two angels fought so furiously that the Heavenly Court had to intervene to stop their warfare, or Rebecca would surely have died. She might have died anyway, for Esau threatened to kill her if his brother emerged first from the womb. So Jacob had no choice but to let Esau be born first.

Rebecca asked other women she knew if they too suffered so greatly in carrying their children, and when they told her they did not, she went to Shem to ask why she must suffer so.

"My daughter," he whispered to her, "let me tell you a secret. Two nations struggle in your womb, and how should your body hold them, if the whole world itself will prove too small to contain their strife? Each one owns a world, one the Torah, the other sin. One will give birth to Solomon, who will build the Temple; the other to Vespasian, who will destroy it. One will be Rome and the other Israel, and they will be at each other's throats until the end of time."

And when at last it came time for Rebecca to give birth, more extraordinary events took place. For when Esau emerged, he already had all his hair, a full beard, and all his teeth, and his skin was blood-red, a sign of his bloodthirsty nature. Jacob, on the other hand, was sweet and smooth-skinned, and he came forth from the womb already circumcised.

Because of Esau's ruddy color, Isaac was afraid to have the baby circumcised at eight days, fearing that poor circulation might endanger the baby's life, but when the boy reached the age of thirteen he refused to be circumcised, unlike his uncle Ishmael, who had willingly undergone a *brit* at that age. So he remained uncircumcised for the rest of his life.

Instead of the sign of the covenant, Esau was born with the figure of a serpent emblazoned in his skin, the symbol of all that is hateful to God.

Esau's name described his condition at birth: *asui*, fully formed, for he sprang forth full-grown from Rebecca's womb.

Jacob's name, *Yaakov*, revealed even more about his life: *ekev*, heel, since he emerged from the womb holding on to his brother's heel, as he would grasp after his brother's birthright in later years; and *akav*, deceitful, for he would cheat his brother of his inheritance and in turn be cheated by Laban. The numerical values of the four letters of his name also carried great significance: *yod*, ten, standing for the Ten Commandments; *ayin*, seventy, standing for the seventy elders, leaders of Israel; *kof*, one hundred, for the hundred ells of the Temple; and *bet*, two, for the two tablets of stone.

Later on he would receive a new name, Israel, one who struggles with God. For even before his birth, he knew struggle, and struggle would dog his heels all the days of his life.

35

Jacob's Flight from Esau

After Jacob stole the birthright from his brother Esau, he was forced to flee, for Esau vowed to kill him. With only the clothes on his back and the barest sustenance for his journey, he fled eastward, with Esau hot on his heels.

Two days later he neared Mount Moriah, where his father Isaac had once been bound on the altar, and he paused to rest, for it was noon and the desert sun blazed overhead.

Then a voice rang out from the heavens, "You shall camp here tonight on this mountain!"

Jacob looked up at the sky. He had many more hours of daylight left, and in the distance the dust clouds of Esau's men swirled ever closer.

And then a miracle happened, one of five miracles that accompanied Jacob on his flight from Esau. God wanted Jacob to spend a night at the site of the future Temple, so God caused the sun suddenly to sink below the horizon so that it was the dead of night. And Esau was thus forced to halt in his pursuit, and Jacob lay down safely to rest on Mount Moriah.

Jacob gathered twelve stones from the altar his grandfather Abraham had made many years before, and he prayed to God, "If I am indeed destined to become the father of twelve tribes, let these stones knit themselves together as one."

And the second miracle happened: The twelve stones fused together into one stone and became as soft as down. Jacob laid his tired head upon the pillow and slept.

That night he dreamed a dream: A ladder stretched from the earth to the heavens, and angels descended and ascended its golden rungs. On it he saw the two angels who had gone to Sodom to warn Lot and his family, and the angels of the Four Kingdoms–Babylon, Media, Greece, and Rome. God also showed him that night the Revelation at Sinai, Elijah's ascent to heaven in a fiery chariot, the Temple in its glory and its destruction, Nebuchadnezzar's futile attempt to burn Mishach, Shadrach, and Abedneggo in the fiery furnace, and Daniel's encounter with the dragon Bel.

Then God spoke to Jacob in the dream and said, "I now make you a promise, Jacob, as I have made promises to Abraham and Isaac before you. The land you are now lying on will be an inheritance for you and your children after you" (for God had rolled up the whole of Canaan and placed it under Jacob's pillow). "And just as the land survives all things," God continued, "so your children will survive all the nations of the earth. And just as the land is trampled upon, so too your children, if they depart from My ways, will be trampled upon by all nations of the earth."

Then Jacob awoke from his dream and cried out, "How awesome is this place! This is none other than the House of God, the very gateway to heaven!"

And Jacob picked up the pillow he had lain upon and poured oil upon it that had rained out of heaven, and God engraved the Holy Name on it and sank the stone into the center of the earth, where it became the *Even Shetiyah*, the Foundation Stone. In later years this stone became the center of the Sanctuary. Those who learn the secret of the Name engraved on it gain mastery over nature, and over life and death.

Then the third miracle happened as Jacob went on his way. As with Eliezer and Rebecca before him, the earth raced forward to meet him as he journeyed eastward, and he arrived in Haran in the twinkling of an eye.

At the well in Haran, he saw a great crowd of people milling around, waiting to water their flocks and herds.

"Why do you not water your animals?" he asked them. "They seem very thirsty in the hot sun."

"There are not yet enough of us to roll away the stone," they told him. "For it takes all the men of the village to move it."

Then Jacob lifted up his eyes and saw a young maiden approaching with her flock. It was Rachel, daughter of his uncle Laban. When he saw her, Jacob leapt up and rolled off the great stone from the mouth of the well as easily as if it had been a cork in a bottle. This was the fourth miracle.

And the final miracle that occurred was that the water then rose up out of the depths of the well to the very rim so that no one had to draw it forth. And there it remained for the twenty years Jacob dwelled in Haran, working for Laban.

And Jacob married Rachel and her sister Leah in Haran, and brought prosperity to Laban's house.

36
Jacob Wrestles with Samael

After twenty years of working for Laban, Jacob gathered his wives, his eleven sons and one daughter, his many servants and vast flocks, and headed home to Canaan. Yet even after all this time, he still feared his brother Esau's anger, for could Esau ever forgive him for stealing his birthright and blessing?

Jacob journeyed westward until he came to the banks of the River Yabbok, and there he camped with his vast household and possessions. And that night they all forded the river and camped on the other side.

Then Jacob returned to the opposite bank of the river, for he had forgotten to bring along some pots and pans. And when he reached the shore, he met a shepherd there with many sheep and camels.

The shepherd said to him, "I am tired, for I have worked hard all day. Please carry my sheep across, and I will carry your pots."

And Jacob agreed to do as the man wished.

In the twinkling of an eye, all the pots and pans flew through the air to the opposite bank. But when Jacob began to carry the man's sheep across the Yabbok, he always found the same number of sheep awaiting him on the bank. All night he ferried the sheep across on his back, but after many hours, the shepherd's flock was no smaller than before, although many sheep now grazed on the other bank as well.

"You are a wizard!" cried out Jacob in frustration. "Stop your witchcraft at once!"

Then the shepherd touched the ground with his staff and it shook. Fire burst forth and lapped at Jacob's heels.

But Jacob was not frightened by the wizard's tricks. "What is fire to one who is made of fire? For God said of me, 'Jacob's house shall be a fire and a flame!' Now go away and let me cross!"

But the shepherd then changed his appearance into a terrible angel, and he was none other than Samael, Esau's guardian angel, who had come to struggle with him. And they began to wrestle there on the banks of the Yabbok, and they struggled together until the dawn began to break.

In the end Jacob proved too strong for Samael, and the angel could not prevail against him. "Perhaps he is not a man at all, but a celestial being," thought Samael, and he reached up to touch Jacob on the thigh, for angels have no joints, but men do. And he found the joint there and pinched it, so that Jacob cried out in pain, but he still would not let Samael go.

"Let me go," begged Samael, "for I am needed to sing in the heavenly choir this morning."

But Jacob said, "I will not let you go unless you bless me first."

"Very well," said Samael when he saw he had no choice. "What is your name?"

"Jacob."

"No more will you be called Jacob, but you will receive a new name: Israel, God-wrestler, for you have struggled with heaven and triumphed."

Then Jacob asked him, "And what is your name?"

And Samael said, "How can you ask me my name?" and he vanished.

And when Jacob left that place to rejoin his camp, he limped because the angel had pinched him in the hollow of his thigh. And he called the place Peniel, for he said, "I have seen angels here face to face—*panim el panim*—and have still lived to tell the tale."

Thus filled with the spirit of God, Jacob went forth to meet his brother Esau, and they embraced each other and made peace.

37

Asnat

Shechem, the son of Hamor the Hivite, raped Dinah, Jacob's daughter, and she became pregnant and gave birth to a daughter whom they called Asnat. Her brothers found it hateful to look upon her, for she was the sign of their sister's shame, and so they drove her out from their midst.

But Jacob felt sorry for her, for she was his own granddaughter and the daughter of an Israelite, and he would not send her off without a gift. He took a tablet of gold and engraved upon it the story of her birth and hung it around her neck. Then he laid her under a thornbush to protect her from the sun.

A caravan of merchants passed by and found her and took pity on her and carried her down to Egypt. There Potiphar saw her and was struck by her beauty. And he took her into his house and adopted her as his own daughter, for he and his wife were childless.

Potiphar tried to read the strange writing on Asnat's tablet but could make no sense of it at all. And he showed it to the wise men of Egypt, but they too were completely mystified. And shortly after this, a new slave came into Potiphar's household whose name was Joseph, but no one showed the tablet to him since he was only a poor slave.

One day Zuleika, Potiphar's wife, tried to seduce Joseph, for he was extraordinarily beautiful, but he resisted and she accused him before Potiphar of trying to rape her. And little Asnat, then only eleven months old, witnessed the scene, and spoke up in Joseph's defense, and so he was only thrown into prison instead of hanged. And because of her noble deed, she was destined to become Joseph's wife.

When Asnat grew up, she was astonishingly beautiful. She was slender like Sarah, graceful like Rebecca, and radiant like Rachel. Many Egyptian nobles wished to

marry her, even Pharaoh's first-born son. But she refused
to marry any man and shut herself up in a palace next to
Potiphar's house with her seven maids.

In the first of the seven years of plenty, after Joseph
had been redeemed from prison and elevated to viceroy of
Egypt, he came to Potiphar's house. Potiphar now
schemed to marry his daughter Asnat to Joseph, for was
he not the most honored man in Egypt next to Pharaoh?
But when he told Asnat of his plan, she rejected it
immediately.

"What! I, marry your former slave, son of a Canaanite
shepherd, whose only merit is that he can interpret
dreams? Never!" And she stormed out and locked herself
up in her palace.

But curiosity soon got the better of her. When Joseph
arrived a few minutes later, she stole a glance at him from
the window of her palace. So overwhelmed was she by
his beauty that she felt instantly contrite for her rash
words and prayed to God that she might be his wife.

When Joseph caught her staring at him, he asked her
father to order her away, for he knew that his beauty
bewitched women, and he wished to remain free of the
Gentile women around him. But Potiphar urged him to
meet Asnat, since Joseph was the first man in whom she
had ever shown any interest.

When Asnat entered the room, Joseph saw the gold
tablet around her neck and asked to read it. When he
realized that she was his kinswoman, daughter of his
sister Dinah, he was overjoyed. But when Asnat reached
out to embrace him, he rebuffed her. "You are an idol-
worshiper, who bows down to dead gods and eats the
bread of vanity. I cannot kiss you."

Then he called upon God to pour the Divine Spirit
into Asnat and open up her eyes.

When Asnat returned to her apartment, she was overcome with shame at Joseph's words, and she took off her
stately robes and put on sackcloth and ashes. Then for
seven days she mourned and repented of her heathen
ways.

On the eighth day an angel appeared to her and announced that she had been born anew. And he showed her a honeycomb more wonderful than any she had ever seen or smelled.

The angel broke off a piece from the honeycomb and gave it to Asnat. "This honey was produced by the bees of Paradise as food for the angels and the righteous. Take a bite."

When Asnat bit into the honeycomb, her mouth was filled with the most remarkable sweetness.

"From now on," said the angel, "your body shall bloom like the eternal flowers of Paradise. You shall have inexhaustible strength and youth, and your beauty shall never fade. And may God bless you and make you like your name: a fortress—*hasna*—surrounded by a wall."

Then the angel flew up to heaven in a chariot of fire drawn by four fiery horses. And Asnat knew she had been in the presence of no ordinary being.

Before going to see Joseph, she washed herself and saw reflected in the water a face of exquisite beauty, like an angel. Joseph did not recognize her when he saw her.

"Who are you?" he asked.

"I am Asnat, your kinswoman. I have cast away my idols and am now prepared to be your wife as the angel has promised me." And she told him about her recent visitor and the honeycomb he had given her to eat.

Then they embraced each other and became betrothed. And all of Egypt celebrated their marriage. Pharaoh himself set gold crowns on both their heads and forbade all work during the seven days of their wedding feast.

And in time, Asnat and Joseph had two sons, Ephraim and Menasheh, whose descendants became two of the twelve tribes, and so Asnat conveyed a double blessing upon Joseph's house.

38

Kimtas the Physician

When Joseph was flung into prison after the incident with Potiphar's wife, he met Pharaoh's chief butler and baker who had been jailed for displeasing their master. Pharaoh had found a fly in his winecup and a pebble in his bread, and had sentenced to death the two perpetrators of these crimes.

One morning when Joseph brought them their water for washing, he found both men unusually depressed.

"What is the matter?" he asked them.

"We have both dreamed dreams," the baker told him, "and we do not know what they mean. And there is no one here in this prison who can help us."

"Tell me your dreams," replied Joseph eagerly, "and God will put wisdom in my heart to understand them."

The butler and baker laughed at him. "You? You are only a slave! Can a donkey tell fortunes in the stars? You cannot be serious!"

Joseph smiled calmly at their mockery and asked them, "Have you ever heard of Kimtas, the famous physician?"

"Indeed we have," the two men replied. "But what has he to do with our dreams?"

"Let me tell you a story about him," said Joseph, and this is what he told them:

"Kimtas was one of the greatest physicians in Egypt, but he was not satisfied with his knowledge. He always wanted to increase it. One day he decided to travel throughout the world to learn even more about the art of healing. So he packed up his medicines in a knapsack and set off. He visited many foreign lands, never charging for his services, seeking only more knowledge and greater art, never fame and fortune for himself.

"After many months, he came to the outskirts of a

city and lay down to rest, for he was tired from all his traveling. As he slept, a vagabond came by and saw his rich clothes. Taking off his own rags, the vagabond stripped Kimtas of his clothing and left his pile of rags beside the sleeping man. He did not touch the battered knapsack of medicines lying beside Kimtas.

"When the physician awoke, he found himself naked. Seeing only the rags nearby, he quickly dressed himself and went on his way.

"As he passed through the streets of the city, he heard a great wail coming from a house, and he entered to see what was the matter. Inside he found three physicians huddled anxiously around the sickbed of a young boy, while the boy's parents wrung their hands and wept.

"Forgetting he was wearing only rags, Kimtas stepped boldly up to the boy's bed. 'Let me have a closer look. Ah, yes, I see what the problem is. Fortunately I can help. If you'll permit me to treat your son . . .'

" 'You—treat my son!' shouted the boy's father. 'How dare you mock me in the hour of my distress? You are only a dirty vagabond looking for a handout! How can you claim to be a doctor? These three men here are the best doctors in the city, and they have had no success thus far. Out with you!'

And grabbing Kimtas by the scruff of his neck, the father roughly booted him out of the house. Shortly after this, the three doctors shrugged their shoulders and left as well, declaring that the boy was beyond help.

"As soon as they were all gone, the boy's mother turned to her husband and said, 'Perhaps we were too hasty with that poor man. What harm could it have done to let him try?'

" 'Your head has been turned by your sorrow,' her husband said to her. 'Did you not see how poorly the man was dressed? And I would bet that all he had in that knapsack of his was a dry crust and a pair of old shoes. No, he was a madman who somehow got the crazy notion into his head that he was a physician.'

"And as they were talking, the boy on the bed let out a sharp cry and died. And the parents lifted up their voices in grief until they had no strength left to cry.

"Kimtas came to the marketplace of the city and announced, 'I am Kimtas the great physician. Let all who are afflicted with disease come to me and I will heal them.'

"All the people gathered around him and laughed, for the man was clearly mad. He spread his medicines out upon the ground, and they were astonished to see such a colorful array of bottles in every color and shape.

" 'If you are really the famous Kimtas,' one bystander called out, 'then why are you dressed in rags?'

"And he told them how he had been robbed and stripped naked.

"Finally one man covered all over with sores approached the ragged stranger and asked to be healed. Kimtas carefully poured a small amount of oil from a small purple vial and rubbed it on the man's sores, and they instantly disappeared. When the people saw what had happened, they crowded around Kimtas and showed him all their ailments, and Kimtas healed them all.

"Then the father of the boy who had died the day before heard what Kimtas was doing in the marketplace, and he came to the physician and said, 'I alone am guilty of my son's death, for had I not scorned you because of your rags, my son might still be alive today. I now see that a person must be judged by his manner, his deeds, his intelligence, and his merits, not by his clothes.'

"And so," finished Joseph, "I too may look like a slave who has no wisdom to interpret dreams, but like Kimtas, I was robbed of my possessions and sold into slavery. In truth I am the son of a great, noble, and pious man, and have been cast into prison for no crime that I committed."

And the butler and the baker took Joseph's words to heart and told him their dreams. And Joseph told the butler that his dream meant that he would regain his freedom in three days, and he told the baker that in three days he would lose his head. And so it came to pass.

And in time Joseph regained his freedom, too, and like Kimtas, exchanged his prison rags for the golden robes of Egypt.

39
Joseph and Benjamin

When Joseph's brothers returned to Egypt with their youngest brother Benjamin, Joseph looked at his brother and felt the tears welling up in his eyes. But the time had not yet come for him to reveal himself to his brothers, so he hid his tears.

Then Joseph called for his silver goblet and announced, "I will now seat you all according to your proper place in your family."

And he pretended to consult the goblet as if he were a wizard, and he astonished them all by seating Reuben as the first-born, then placing Simeon, Levi, Judah, Issachar, and Zevulun with Reuben as sons of the same mother. Then he studied the goblet again, turning it this way and that, and seated Dan and Naftali together at a second table. And then he stared deeply into the bowl of the cup and pronounced Gad and Asher sons of the same mother.

Then he turned to Benjamin and said, "You are the only son of your mother and so am I, so you will sit beside me at my table."

Joseph then gave all the brothers delicacies from his own table, but to Benjamin he gave even more than the others. And when Asnat saw how much Joseph favored Benjamin, she asked him why he did so, and he whispered to her that here was his own brother, son of the same mother, and she too gave Benjamin sweet things from her own plate. So did Joseph's sons Ephraim and Menasheh when they saw how much their parents honored this Canaanite stranger. So Benjamin received five times the favor of his brothers.

Then Joseph asked Benjamin, "Do you have any children?"

"I have ten sons," answered Benjamin.

"And what are their names?" asked Joseph.

"All their names tell the story of my poor brother Joseph's misfortune," explained Benjamin, and he told him their names: " 'Swallowed Up' (Bela), and 'First Born' (Bekher), and 'In Captivity' (Ashbel), and 'Stranger' (Gera), and 'Pleasantness' (Naaman), and 'Big Brother' (Ekhi), and 'Crown of My Head' (Roshi), and 'Wisdom from My Father's Mouth' (Muppim), and 'Wedding Canopy That I Did See' (Huppim), and 'Went Down to Slavery' (Ard)."

And when Joseph heard all this, he was so overcome with feeling that he had to leave the room to hide his tears. Then he washed his face and returned to the table.

Then Joseph called for his astrologers to bring the star charts to him, and he asked Benjamin if he knew how to read them.

"Like all Hebrews, I am wise in the stars and seasons," said Benjamin.

"Then if your brother Joseph did indeed go down to Egypt and if he still lives," said Joseph, "these charts and instruments should tell you where he can be found."

And Benjamin gazed into the stargazing instruments of Egypt and found to his astonishment that his brother Joseph was seated right beside him. But before he could cry out to the others, Joseph silenced him with his finger.

"I am indeed your brother Joseph," he whispered to Benjamin, "but the time has not yet come to reveal myself to the others. I am going to send them away now and then call them back. If they are willing to trade their lives for yours, then I will know they have repented of the evil they did to me long ago. And only then will I make myself known to them."

Then Joseph tested his brothers, and this time they did not fail him.

PART III

FROM SLAVERY TO
FREEDOM

*After four hundred years of slavery in Egypt,
one man arose to redeem the Jews and return
them to their destined course. That man was
Moses.*

40

The Birth of Moses

Sixty years after Joseph died, Pharaoh dreamed a dream: An old man stood before him holding a pair of scales in one hand. On one side stood all the inhabitants of Egypt, men, women, and children, and on the other, one small lamb. But the lamb outweighed all of Egypt.

Pharaoh awoke frightened from his dream and summoned all his wise men to interpret the dream. Only Balaam, son of Beor, could make sense of the dream.

"Alas!" proclaimed Balaam. "This is an evil dream for the House of Pharaoh! A baby boy will soon be born to the Children of Israel who will spell the doom of Egypt."

"How can I avert this evil, Balaam?" cried Pharaoh.

Balaam smiled cunningly and said, "There is only one way to save Egypt. Command that every male child born to the Hebrew slaves be killed!"

Balaam's suggestion pleased Pharaoh, and he ordered it done immediately. But Shifrah and Puah, the two midwives of the Hebrew women, did not obey Pharaoh's orders. Furious, Pharaoh had them brought to his palace.

"Why have you disobeyed my orders?" he demanded of them.

"But we did not disobey you," they said, falling on their faces before him. "These Hebrew babies thrust themselves out of their mothers' bellies so fast that we always arrive too late to do our duty!"

"Perhaps a little reward might help," said Pharaoh. "An honored place in my harem, for instance . . ."

But they refused.

Then Pharaoh threatened to burn them alive, and again they held firm. Angrily Pharaoh sent them away, warning them to obey his orders from now on or to forfeit their lives.

Now when the Hebrew slaves heard Pharaoh's evil decree, they raised their voices to heaven and despaired. Then Amram, one of the leaders of the slaves, declared, "Why should we bear children only to feed them to the crocodiles? Let us divorce our wives so that we will not have any more sons to give up to Pharaoh." So many of the Hebrew men separated themselves from their wives.

But not all did. Those who continued to conceive and bear children took their newborn sons to the fields and left them there. And God sent an angel to watch over and protect these babies. And the angel gave each infant two pebbles to suck on, one that yielded milk and the other, honey. And God caused the babies' hair to grow long and to swaddle them as a garment. The earth yawned wide and swallowed up the infants until they grew older, and then they sprouted out of the ground like new grass. And although the Egyptians tried to plow them under like weeds, still they thrived and grew.

But most of the Hebrew slaves refrained from conceiving children, for they feared Pharaoh's decree.

Then the spirit of God rested upon Miriam, Amram's daughter, and she chastised her father. "You are worse than Pharaoh, Father! For he wishes to murder only our sons, but you would kill all our children. He robs them only of this world, but you take from them also the World to Come!"

And Amram hung his head in shame.

"Behold," continued Miriam, for God had endowed her with the gift of prophecy, "a son will be born to you and my mother Yokheved who will redeem our people from bondage."

Then Amram and all the other Hebrew men remarried the wives whom they had divorced.

And although Yokheved was already old, she now regained her youth. Her wrinkles vanished and her skin softened to the silky flesh of a young maid, and she conceived. Six months later, on the seventh of Adar, Yokheved gave birth to a son. And when this baby was born, the whole house filled up with light as brilliant as the sun and moon shining together. And the baby was miraculous to behold, for before he was one day old, he began walking about and speaking as though he were full-grown.

And Yokheved hid the child for the first three months, so that Pharaoh's murderers could not find him.

Then he was too big to hide any longer, and she decided to surrender him to the Nile—into God's hands, not Pharaoh's.

41

Moses in the Bulrushes

When she realized that she could no longer hide her infant son, Yokheved fashioned an ark of bulrushes, smeared it with pitch on the outside, and laid the baby inside. Then she set the ark adrift on the Nile.

Amram then summoned his daughter Miriam and said to her, "Now what has become of your proud prophecy concerning this child? When you first prophesied that we would bear a son to redeem our people, I kissed the head that beheld such vision. But here is what I think of that vision now!" And he cuffed her rudely on her head and sent her off.

Miriam waded in the reeds along the bank to watch over the baby and learn his fate.

That day was a day of scorching heat. Leprosy and boils afflicted all the inhabitants of Egypt. Thermutis, daughter of Pharaoh, summoned her servants and went down to the Nile to bathe, for she too suffered from the plague tormenting the land. But there was a second plague tormenting Thermutis: the idolatry of her fathers. And so she wished to immerse herself in the cleansing waters of the Nile to rid herself of sin.

And as she came down to the bank, she saw the tiny ark floating among the reeds, and she asked her maids to bring it to her. But her servants were afraid that it was one of the Hebrew children, and they refused to touch it. They urged her to leave it alone, for such was Pharaoh's decree. But the angel Gabriel appeared just then and seized all the maids but one and thrust them into the bowels of the earth.

Then Thermutis herself reached forth her hand to take the ark, and although the basket floated sixty feet from the shore, her arm stretched out over the waters and grasped it. And at that moment, her leprosy vanished and her skin became as pure as snow.

When she looked inside, she saw that it was indeed one of the Hebrew children, for he was circumcised, a boy of exquisite beauty with the *Shekhinah* of God's Glory shining around his head. And she became afraid because of her father's decree and decided to abandon the child to his fate. But Gabriel came at that moment and rapped the child on the head so that he began to cry. And Thermutis took pity on him and determined to save him, for she was childless and had longed for a son.

She gave him the name 'Moses,' one who draws out, for she said, "I drew him out of the water, and he will draw his people out of bondage in days to come."

Then God said to her, "I will bless you, for you have a good heart. Although Moses is not your child, you treat him as such. And although you are not My daughter, I will call you My daughter." And God changed her name to Bitiah, which means 'daughter of God.'

Bitiah then sent for an Egyptian nursemaid for the baby, but the child refused to suck at her breast. For God had decided that Moses should not draw nourishment from Egypt.

Then Miriam stepped forward and said to Princess Bitiah, "I know of a Hebrew nursemaid for the child." And she ran home and brought back Yokheved to nurse her own son.

Then Bitiah said to Yokheved, unaware of the hidden truth of her words, "Here is what is yours. Take him and nurse him, and I will pay you two pieces of silver for your wages."

On that day the astrologers of Egypt told Pharaoh the happy news: "Once Egypt was threatened by an Israelite boy whose doom lay in water, and now that threat is past." And Pharaoh reversed his evil decree, and they stopped drowning Hebrew children in the Nile.

But the astrologers did not understand their own divining, for what they had seen—the watery doom awaiting Moses—was not death in the Nile but the curse of the waters of Meribah, where Moses would later strike the rock and thus seal his fate. But the Egyptian magicians were fooled into thinking that they had saved Egypt by casting Hebrew boys into the Nile, and so Moses was saved. And later Egypt would meet its own watery doom at the shores of the Sea of Reeds.

Because of the merits of Moses, the six hundred thousand Israelite boys conceived on the same night as Moses were not thrown into the Nile and drowned. And they accompanied him out of Egypt into the wilderness.

And because she saved Moses' life, Bitiah was rewarded by being permitted to enter Paradise alive.

42

The Coal and the Crown

Moses grew up in Pharaoh's palace and became a prince in Egypt. And he was a wise and beautiful child.

When he was three years old, he dined at a feast given by his grandfather Pharaoh and his grandmother, Queen Alfar'anit. At the table were also his mother Princess Bitiah, the evil magician Balaam ben Beor, and all the nobles of Egypt.

Suddenly Moses grabbed the crown from Pharaoh's head and put it on his own head. When Pharaoh and the other princes saw this, they were terrified, for surely this was an astonishing thing!

"What can this mean?" cried out Pharaoh.

Balaam declared, "Listen to me, Pharaoh, and I will interpret this sign, as I once unraveled your dream and so saved Egypt from destruction. Think not that this baby is without wisdom, for he is a Hebrew child and he has learned cunning from his people. Just as Abraham lied to a Pharaoh before you when he said that his wife Sarah was his sister, just as Isaac did the same to Avimelech, and Jacob deceived his brother to steal his birthright, so this child is bent on deceit and rebellion. When he grows up, he will snatch the kingdom from you as he has just snatched the crown from your head. I advise you to kill him at once and thus avert certain disaster."

Balaam's words seemed wise to Pharaoh, and he would have carried them out immediately had not the angel Gabriel appeared then, disguised as one of Pharaoh's wise men.

"Let us not act too hastily, my lord," said Gabriel, "for it is also possible that the child acted innocently, his eyes beguiled by the glitter of gold. Let us make a test: Place before the child a sparkling jewel and a hot coal. If he reaches for the jewel, we shall know that he acts with understanding and we shall kill him. But if he reaches out his hand and grabs the coal, then he acts without understanding and shall live."

And Pharaoh found Gabriel's words pleasing and ordered it done.

When they placed the jewel and the coal before Moses, he reached out to touch the jewel, but Gabriel stretched out an invisible hand and guided his hand toward the coal. When the child felt the burning coal in his hand, he instantly thrust it into his mouth to quench the fire and so burned his tongue. And from that day on, Moses was slow and clumsy in his speech.

When the nobles and wise men saw what had happened, they agreed that the child had acted without malice, and they spared his life. And so Moses grew to manhood in Pharaoh's palace.

43

Moses, King of Ethiopia

When Moses reached manhood, he learned that Pharaoh's enchanter, Balaam ben Beor, had sought to kill him when he was still a child, and his anger blazed against Balaam, and he wished to punish him. But Balaam learned of Moses' plan and, together with his two sons, Jannes and Jambres, fled to Ethiopia where he sought refuge with King Nikanos.

Shortly after this, Moses' eyes were opened to his people's sad plight in Egypt, and he tried to ease their burdens by going among them and offering words of encouragement. He even bent his own back to their labors so that the Egyptians were amazed. But Pharaoh concluded that Moses was only trying to set an example for the slaves, so he did not become alarmed by Moses' actions.

Then one day Moses went walking among the Hebrew slaves and he saw an Egyptian taskmaster beating one of the Hebrews. And Moses became enraged and pronounced the Awesome Name, and the Egyptian instantly fell down dead.

Moses buried the corpse in the soft sand and retreated back to the palace. But two Israelite brothers, Datan and Aviram, began to spread the report among the Hebrews that Moses had killed an Egyptian, and then they appeared before Pharaoh and told him of it.

Pharaoh ordered Moses thrown into prison and executed. They led Moses up to the scaffold, and tried ten
times to cut off his head, but the sword merely glanced off
his neck, which was as hard as ivory. Then God sent
down the angel Michael disguised as the executioner, and
the executioner He transformed into the likeness of
Moses. And Michael cut off the executioner's head with
his own sword, and Moses escaped to Ethiopia.

At that time a war broke out between Ethiopia and
the nations of the East, which had been under Ethiopia's
rule. Nikanos, King of Ethiopia, took a great army and
went to fight his enemies in the East. And he left his
capital in charge of Balaam and his two sons.

While Nikanos was away fighting, Balaam had himself declared king, and he set his two sons over the
remaining army as generals. And he had the people build
high walls around the city. On two sides they made the
walls too high to scale; on the third side, they dug canals
and diverted the river into them; and on the fourth side,
Balaam and his sons summoned by their magic arts
poisonous scorpions and snakes, so that it was impossible
to pass that way.

When Nikanos returned victorious from the war in
the east, he was surprised to see the walls of his city built
up so high. "It must be that my people, fearing my death,
have walled themselves in against their enemies."

But when he approached the gates and called for the
guards to let him in, he was met with a hail of arrows.

The next day the king sent a party of soldiers to ford
the canals, but they drowned in the fierce currents. Then
they built rafts, but again the currents capsized them and
they drowned. On the third day, soldiers tried to advance
past the scorpions and snakes, but the deadly reptiles
killed one hundred and seventy men.

Then Moses appeared in Nikanos's camp. The soldiers were amazed at his appearance, for he was tall like
a palm, radiant as the sun, and strong as a lion. That day
King Nikanos appointed him general of the army.

Then Nikanos sickened and died, and the soldiers
chose Moses to be their king. And they piled their cloaks

in a great heap and set Moses on top of it and declared, "Long live the king!" Each man brought a gift—gold nose-rings, coins, onyx stones, pearls, and silver—and they gave them to Moses.

Moses was twenty-seven when he became king of Ethiopia, and he reigned there for forty years.

On the seventh day of his reign, the soldiers came to Moses for advice. "For nine years we have been besieging the city. We have not seen our wives and children all this time. How can we prevail against Balaam and his sons?"

Moses said, "Go to the forest, each of you, and find a stork chick and bring it here." And they did so.

Then Moses said, "Raise these chicks until they are grown, and teach them to hunt like hawks."

When the storks were grown, Moses ordered them starved for three days. Then he said, "Put on your armor and take your swords." And they did.

Then he said, "Mount your horses and each of you take your stork and follow me."

They came to the side of the city where the snakes and scorpions were, and they loosed the storks upon them. The storks devoured all the serpents. Then the soldiers attacked the city and conquered it.

When Balaam saw that all was lost, he pronounced a magic spell and flew through the air with his sons, and they returned to Egypt.

And the people loved Moses and made him king over the whole land, and they gave him Nikanos's widow Adoniah as a wife. But Moses remembered Abraham's words to his servant Eliezer: "You shall not take a wife from the daughters of Canaan." And he did not lie with Adoniah as a husband.

After forty years, Adoniah's son Monarchos became king over Ethiopia, for Adoniah said to the people, "It is better for you to serve the son of your former king than a stranger, a slave of the king of Egypt."

And the people sent Moses away with gifts, for they loved him very much. Moses was afraid to return to Egypt because of what he had done there, so he journeyed on to Midian.

44

Moses Marries Zipporah

In Midian lived a man named Jethro who had seven daughters. Jethro was a priest who spent his life serving idols. But after a time, Jethro came to lose faith in these statues of stone and clay, and he began to turn his heart to God. And the people of Midian despised Jethro and his daughters, and made life hard for them.

Jethro's daughters were shepherds, and each day when they came to the well to water their flocks, the other shepherds taunted them and would not let them approach the well until all the other sheep had been watered.

Moses journeyed from Ethiopia to Midian, and stopped at the well there to refresh himself. This was the same well at which Jacob had long ago met his beloved Rachel. At that moment, the other shepherds were bullying Jethro's daughters, and as Moses looked on, several of the men picked the young women up and threw them into the well. Moses ran forward and fished them out. Then he gave their flocks water to drink, and even watered the other shepherds' herds, although clearly they did not deserve such favors.

Out of gratitude, the daughters invited Moses home to meet their father. One of the daughters, Zipporah, found special favor in Moses' eyes because she was so modest, and Moses asked her to marry him.

But Zipporah said, "You should not ask such a thing!"

"Why not?" asked Moses.

"Because first you must pass a test. My father has a tree in his garden, and only the man who can uproot that tree may marry any of us. So far, every man who has tried has been devoured by the tree as soon as he touches it."

"Where does this tree come from?"

"It is the rod created at twilight on the Sixth Day of

Creation," Zipporah explained. "God gave it to Adam, who gave it to Enoch, who gave it to Shem. Then it passed on to Abraham, Isaac, and Jacob, and Joseph inherited it when Jacob went down to Egypt. When Joseph died, the Egyptians stole it and brought it to Pharaoh. My father, who was a magician in Pharaoh's court, saw it and understood its power, for on it was engraved the Awful Name and the Ten Plagues that will one day ruin Egypt. So he stole it and brought it to Midian. One day he stuck it into the ground, and it instantly sprouted and sent forth flowers. Only the man who can pull this rod out of the ground may ask my hand in marriage."

Then they brought Moses to Jethro's tent. When Jethro saw Moses with his daughters, he asked them who this stranger was and they told him, "He is an Egyptian who saved us from the other shepherds."

And Moses stood nearby and said nothing.

But his silence at that moment cost him dearly. For had he corrected them and introduced himself as a Hebrew, not an Egyptian, he would have been permitted to enter the Promised Land forty years later. But he allowed them to call him an Egyptian and was thereby doomed to die in the wilderness.

Moses then stepped up to the tree and grabbed hold of it, and with one tug, pulled it out by the roots. When he brought the tree to Jethro, Jethro thought to himself, "Surely this is the Israelite prophet of whom Pharaoh dreamed and the wise men foretold, who will one day spell the doom of Egypt."

And he seized Moses and threw him into a pit, expecting him to die there.

But Zipporah schemed to save him, and she told her father that she wished to stay home from then on while her six sisters tended their flocks, so that she could take care of Jethro and their household. And while she was home, she smuggled food into the cistern where Moses lay, and so kept him alive for seven years.

At the end of seven years, she said to her father, "Do

you remember that man you cast into the pit seven years ago after he uprooted the rod in the garden? Uncover the pit and see if he still lives. If he has died, we should bury him, for the smell of death will fill the house. But if he is still alive, we shall know he is one of the truly righteous in the world."

"Do you remember his name?" asked Jethro.

"Moses, son of Amram and Yokheved."

So Jethro went to the pit and uncovered it and called down, "Moses! Moses!"

And Moses replied, "Here I am!"

And Jethro said, "Now I know that you are a holy man who will redeem his people and bring ruin to Egypt."

Then Jethro raised Moses from the pit and gave him Zipporah as his wife. But he made Moses promise that the children of this marriage would be divided equally between the Israelites and the Egyptians. The first child they called 'Gershom,' which means 'a stranger there,' for God had not failed to aid him even there, in a strange land. And Moses circumcised the boy on the eighth day.

When their second son was born, Moses and Zipporah decided to return to Egypt to be among the Israelites there, for they knew that Jethro would not let them raise this second child as a son of God's covenant.

On the way to Egypt Satan appeared as a serpent and swallowed Moses whole down to his feet. And Zipporah realized that this was because they had not yet circumcised their second son. So she took a knife and circumcised the child's flesh and sprinkled the blood on her husband's feet, which dangled out of the serpent's mouth.

And at once a voice spoke forth from heaven and proclaimed, "Spit him out, Satan!"

And Satan spat Moses out, and he stood unharmed before his wife and child.

When they reached Egypt, Datan and Aviram, leaders of the Hebrews, met Moses and said to him, "Have you come to kill us as you killed the Egyptian?"

And Moses became afraid and returned to Midian for two more years, until God was revealed to him in the Burning Bush and told him, "Go down to Egypt and tell Pharaoh to let My people go!"

45

The Thornbush

One day Moses was out tending his flock when he noticed that one lamb had strayed off. He went in search of it, and as he drew near the slopes of Mount Horeb, his eyes were struck by a strange sight: A thornbush burned with an unearthly black fire but the branches remained unsinged. He drew nearer and the mountain began to shake and rumble, but it became still again as soon as his sandals touched the mountainside. For several moments he stood there and stared at the fire, and then he noticed that bright-colored flowers bloomed within the flames. Then he discerned within the fire the spirit of the angel Michael, dancing among the tongues of flame.

Suddenly a voice came out of the bush and said, "Moses! Moses!"

And Moses was amazed to hear the voice of his father Amram, for he did not know that his father still lived. With his own voice full of joy, he replied, "Here I am!"

And the voice said, "Take off your shoes, for you are standing on holy ground!"

It was then that Moses looked up and noticed that no birds flew overhead nor nested anywhere on the mountain. And he knew that this must indeed be a holy place. Quickly he removed his shoes.

"What is it you want, Father?" Moses asked.

Now it was not really Amram who had spoken to Moses out of the Burning Bush but God. But it would have so terrified Moses to hear God's voice that God had used Amram's voice at first. Now, however, the voice changed, swelling with greater power and thundering out of the flaming thornbush. "It is not your father who speaks to you, Moses, but the God of your father, the God of Abraham, the God of Isaac, and the God of Jacob."

And Moses hid his face, for he was afraid.

And God commanded Moses to go down to Egypt to demand of Pharaoh that he let the Israelites go. God showed Moses that the rod he had plucked out of Jethro's garden was to be a sign before Pharaoh and his magicians. And God also told Moses a new name by which to call God before the Hebrew slaves: "I AM THAT I AM!" God then gave Moses a promise for the people, that they would be redeemed and brought to a good land flowing with milk and honey. And then God ceased speaking, and the bush became what it had been before, a lowly bramble of thorns.

Moses stood wondering at what he had just seen. Why had God chosen to speak to him out of the lowly thornbush? Why not the stately palm or the graceful acacia or the venerable olive tree? Then the angel Michael revealed to him all the reasons why the thornbush had been selected for this holy task.

"First, because pagans cannot make idols from the thornbush, for the wood is too brittle and slight.

"Second, because nothing in nature is too insignificant to merit God's attention. Sometimes, in fact, the humble things deserve more honor than the grand, for they are not corrupted by pride or ambition.

"Also, because Israel itself is like the thornbush, for in its exile, Israel is the lowliest of the nations. and just as the thornbush bears flowers and thorns alike, so Israel carries within its midst the righteous and the wicked. And just as the thornbush needs much water, so too Israel can only prosper by drawing deeply from the Source of Life, the Torah.

"And the numerical value of the word 'thornbush'— 'ha's'neh'—equals one hundred and twenty, to teach you that you will live for that many years and that for that many days, the *Shekhinah* will rest on Mount Horeb, which is also called Sinai, when God reveals the Law.

"But most important of all," finished Michael, "God chose the thornbush to teach us that holiness resides not in lofty mountains nor in towering cedars but in the modest spirit."

And Moses took Michael's words to heart and lived his life by their wisdom. Thus he was known as Moses, the humble servant of God.

46

The Ten Plagues

Moses and Aaron appeared before Pharaoh and demanded, "Let My people go!"

But Pharaoh refused, for he needed the Hebrew slaves to build his pyramids and treasure-cities.

Then God sent ten plagues to punish Egypt. Three plagues, those of water and earth, God sent through Aaron and not through Moses, for Moses had been aided by the Nile when he was a baby and by the ground when he had buried the Egyptian taskmaster, so it was not right that he should bring harm to these things. Three plagues, those of fire and air, God sent through Moses, and one plague the brothers brought together. The last three plagues God brought without human intervention, so that Pharaoh could feel the full power of heaven.

Each plague paid the Egyptians back in kind for what they had done to the Children of Israel:

They had made the slaves draw water for them and had forbidden them their ritual baths, so the waters of Egypt turned to blood.

They had made the slaves fish for them, so frogs came out of the rivers and into their homes.

They had made the slaves sweep their houses and streets, so the dust itself turned to lice.

They had made the slaves catch wolves, lions, and bears for their circuses, and had sent them far from their families to hunt these wild beasts, so wild beasts swarmed into their houses and devoured them, even the infants in their cradles.

They had made the slaves tend their flocks far from home, so disease came and struck down their cattle.

They had made the slaves prepare their baths, so they were stricken with itchy boils that could not be relieved by bathing.

They had made the slaves plow and sow their fields, so hail rained down and destroyed their crops.

They had made the slaves plant trees and guard the fruit, so locusts came and ate what the hail had missed.

They had thrown the slaves into dungeons, so the darkness of hell descended and imprisoned them in their houses.

They had thrown the male children of the Israelites into the Nile, and so their first-born were slain.

Many wondrous things happened during this plague year in Egypt. And although Pharaoh's magicians could duplicate the plagues at the beginning, in the end they were forced to acknowledge the hand of God in what happened. Not before this time nor since has the world seen the like.

The first plague was blood. All the waters of Egypt turned to blood, except where the Hebrew slaves lived. In wells and in vessels of wood and stone, the water turned to blood. The very spit from the Egyptians' mouths came out as blood upon the ground. Even the juice within fruits turned to blood when the Egyptians bit into them. And if an Egyptian drank from the same cup as an Israelite, the water turned to blood in the Egyptian's mouth, while in the Israelite's mouth it remained pure and sweet.

Only a single frog appeared at the beginning of the second plague, but then he began to croak, calling all his companions out of the rivers and marshes and ponds. And they swarmed all over the land. They were able to break through even marble and metal and make their way into all the houses of Egypt.

"Make way!" the frogs declared to the walls, and the walls split in two.

So eager were the frogs to do God's will that they leapt even into the red-hot bake-ovens and devoured the bread baking there. God rewarded these zealous frogs by saving them from the flames. And when all the other frogs died after the plague, these frogs in the bake-ovens survived. And their descendants are the crocodiles, which today rule over the Nile.

But in Goshen where the Israelites lived, no frogs came.

Next came the plague of lice. Although Pharaoh's magicians were able to imitate the first two plagues, they were powerless to duplicate this plague, for their art only allowed them to produce things larger than a barley-grain, and lice are smaller than that. In addition, magicians lose their power when their feet cannot touch the ground, and the lice covered the earth like a carpet, stinging the Egyptians' feet wherever they stood.

But in Goshen where the Israelites lived, no lice came.

The fourth plague brought wild beasts into the cities of Egypt—lions, bears, wolves, panthers, and so many birds of prey that the sun and moon were darkened in the sky. And they devoured many of the Egyptians. And when the plague was over, even those animals killed by the Egyptians came back to life and fled the land so that the Egyptians could not profit from their skins and flesh.

But in Goshen where the Israelites lived, no wild beasts came.

Then came the plagues of cattle disease and boils, and these afflicted the Egyptians greatly. The magicians tried to imitate all these plagues, and they did, but they were unable to reverse the effects afterward, and so suffered from their own plagues for the rest of their days.

But in Goshen where the Israelites lived, no cattle disease or boils came.

Next came hail. Now as a rule, fire and water are bitter enemies, but in this plague they were reconciled.

Fire burned within the hailstones as a wick survives surrounded by flame. Hailstones mounted up to the sky in great walls and prevented the people from carrying off the carcasses of the animals smitten by the hail. And if they succeeded in salvaging the meat, eagles and hawks swooped down and snatched the meat from their hands. And the hail pelted the fields and broke down even the tallest trees.

But in Goshen where the Israelites lived, no hail fell.

Then Pharaoh begged Moses to take away this plague, so Moses prayed to God, and the hail froze in midair and the thunder ceased.

Then Pharaoh hardened his heart again and would not let the people go.

Then God brought locusts that ate every growing thing in the land. The Egyptians caught many of the locusts and preserved them in brine as a delicacy, since all their food was being consumed in the fields. But when this plague ended with yet another of Pharaoh's false promises, God sent a strong west wind to blow all the locusts into the Sea of Reeds, and even the pickled locusts flew out of their pots and departed, so that the Egyptians did not benefit from the plague.

But in Goshen where the Israelites lived, no locusts came.

Then God sent the plague of darkness. For the first three days, the darkness was not too thick, and the Egyptians could move about. But for the following three days, the blackness thickened, for it emerged out of the depths of hell, and the Egyptians were not able to move so much as an inch. Those who were standing on the third day remained standing until the sixth day; those who were lying down could not get up. So thick was the darkness that it could be felt like a dense vapor.

But in Goshen a celestial light shone, and the Children of Israel could see by it even into the dwellings of the Egyptians. They saw the Egyptians hiding their valuables under cover of the darkness, and when the time came to leave Egypt, the slaves pointed out these hiding places to their former masters, and so stripped Egypt of its riches.

There was another reason for this plague of darkness. Among the Children of Israel themselves there were many wicked people, those who were idolaters, or who did not wish for freedom from their masters, and God put an end to them under cover of darkness. And the Israelites buried them without the Egyptians knowing. For the vast multitude that eventually left Egypt was but a small fraction of the Israelite people. The rest perished at God's hand during the plague of darkness.

Then Pharaoh hardened his heart one last time, and God brought the last, the most terrible plague of all: the slaying of the first-born.

When Pharaoh decided to let God bring this last plague upon his people, he made a grave error, for he thought that only the first-born sons of Egypt would die, and he was willing to sacrifice these to his own greed and ambition. But God decreed that the first-born daughters would also die, as would the oldest member of each household, whether first-born or not, and the first-born of other nations who served the Egyptians. Even the first-born who had already died were dragged from their graves by dogs, and the monuments erected to their memories crumbled into dust that then swirled out of sight.

And on that night all the idols of Egypt were destroyed. Those made of stone crumbled into dust, those of wood rotted, and those of metal melted away. Thus the Egyptians were not able to blame their tragedy upon the wrath of their own gods.

And all of Egypt raised its voice in sorrow, for the Angel of Death had spared no house, from the dungeon to Pharaoh's palace. Only Pharaoh himself, a first-born son, escaped the Angel's terrible sword, for God was not through with him yet.

But in Goshen where the Israelites lived, the Angel of Death passed over their homes. And together they shared the Paschal Lamb and prepared to go forth from Egypt, out of the house of bondage.

47

The Crossing of the Sea of Reeds

The Children of Israel marched forth from Egypt into the wilderness, and after three days, they arrived at the shores of the Sea of Reeds. Then they looked back and saw the army of the Egyptians pursuing after them, and their hearts melted within their breasts.

"What have you done to us?" they cried out to Moses. "Now the Egyptians will punish us for all the plagues God has brought upon them, and for all the treasures we took from them when we left Egypt!"

And, indeed, the situation they found themselves in was desperate. Before them was the sea, behind them the Egyptian chariots, and on either side of them the wild beasts of the wilderness.

Then Moses prayed to God. "I am like a shepherd who has brought his flock to the edge of a cliff and cannot get them down. You alone have the power to rescue this people, for You alone created heaven and earth, the seas, and all that is in them. We turn to You in our hour of . . ."

"Moses!" interrupted God. "My children are in trouble. The sea blocks their way, the enemy is almost upon them, and you stand there praying! Sometimes long prayer is good, but at other times it's best to be brief. For the sake of Adam for whom I gathered the waters together, for the sake of Abraham who was ready to sacrifice Isaac to Me, I now promise to divide the sea and let My children go through to safety."

"But what about Samael?" asked Moses. "He will use all his power to thwart us! Even now he holds up our sins to heaven to accuse us!"

"Then I shall do what the wise shepherd did when his flock was threatened by a wolf. He threw a strong ram to the wolf, and while the two of them struggled, he carried the rest of the flock across the stream. Then he ran back and snatched the ram out of the wolf's jaws."

And that is just what God did. He surrendered Job to Samael and said, "While Samael busies himself tormenting Job, I will lead Israel safely through the sea, and then I shall come back and rescue Job from the hands of the Accuser."

Then God said to Moses, "Stretch out your rod over the sea and divide it. Tell the sea, 'I am the messenger sent by the Creator of the world. Uncover your paths so that My children can pass through on dry land.' "

But when Moses did as God commanded, the sea refused to part, saying, "Why should I do what you say? You are only a human being, and besides, I am three days older than you since I was created on the third day and you were not created until the sixth."

Moses reported to God what the sea had said.

Then God asked Moses, "What does a master do to a stubborn servant?"

"Beats him with a rod," replied Moses.

"Then do so!" ordered God. "Lift up your rod and divide the sea!"

But still the sea refused to divide. Moses pleaded with God to command it to obey.

"If I were to command it," said God, "it might never return to its former state, but instead remain dry forever. No, you must command it again, but this time I will send with you a likeness of my strength, and then it will surely obey you."

So God sent the Spirit of Divine Strength to be at Moses' right hand. When the sea saw this, it cried out to the earth, "Make hollow places for me to hide in, for I am afraid of God!"

Then God caused a strong east wind to blow, the same wind with which God chastises the nations. This same east wind brought the Flood, toppled the Tower of Babel, destroyed Jerusalem, and will one day bury Rome, and it is this wind that punishes the sinners in Gehinnom.

And the waters of the Sea of Reeds divided, and not only these waters but all the waters on the earth—in cisterns, in wells, in caves, in bathtubs, in pitchers, in bottles, in drinking cups, in glasses. And they all remained divided until the Children of Israel had passed through the dry land in safety.

Even before the waters had piled up into walls and the land had dried out, Nakhshon, Prince of Judah, leapt into the sea. Close at his heels was the entire tribe of Benjamin. And the rest of Judah then pelted the Benjamites with stones for stealing their honor of being the first to cross the sea. But God did not become angry with them, for their rivalry was motivated by holiness, not malice, and God rewarded them both for their zeal: The *Shekhinah* came to dwell in Benjamin's share of the land, and the tribe of Judah gave rise to the royal house of Israel.

Ten miracles accompanied Israel's crossing of the Sea of Reeds: The sea divided; the waters united in a canopy over their heads; twelve paths spread before them, one for each tribe; the waters became transparent so that each tribe could see all the others; the soil under their feet was dry but turned to mud when the Egyptians tried to pass through; the walls of water were soft when the Israelites passed by them but turned to jagged rock when the Egyptians passed through, and dashed them to bits; the waters reached sixteen hundred miles into the sky, and every nation on earth could see the waters.

In addition, the waters nourished the Israelites as they passed through. Whatever their hearts desired, the sea yielded up. If a child asked for an apple or a barleycake, all his mother had to do was reach her hand into the water and pluck one out. And through the salty water flowed a sweet stream that quenched the Israelites' thirst as they crossed through.

But the greatest of the miracles were the witnesses who came out of their graves to watch the Children of Israel cross the sea—the three Fathers and the six Mothers, for God carried them to the shore of the Sea of Reeds to see these miracles unfold.

Then Uzza, the Angel of the Egyptians, came forward to plead the Egyptians' case before God. "They call you

Just, but You are about to drown Your children in the sea. What wrong have they done? If You condemn them for making Your other children slaves, then consider that these slaves have been paid their wages, for did they not take much silver and gold with them when they left Egypt?"

And God answered Uzza before the Heavenly Court. "My friend Joseph once helped the Egyptians survive a great famine. To repay this favor, what did they do? They enslaved Joseph's children! When I sent Moses and Aaron to Pharaoh, he said to them, 'Who is this God that I should listen to you and let Israel go?' Because he denied Me, I sent ten plagues upon him, yet still he pursues My people and wishes to return them to bondage. Does he not deserve to drown in the sea?"

Then Uzza said, "Even if my people deserve punishment, are You not the God of Mercy? Take pity on the works of Your hands!"

God was about to yield to Uzza's pleas, but then the angel Michael sent Gabriel to Egypt, and he returned immediately with a brick that he held up before the Heavenly Court.

"The Egyptians used a Hebrew child as mortar for this brick! Will You have compassion on a nation that has done this?"

Then God resolved to put an end to Egypt.

First God cast Uzza himself into the sea. And after him God tossed in Rahab, the Angel of the Sea, for Rahab, too, had spoken up on Egypt's behalf, saying, "Is it not enough that Israel has escaped from bondage? Egypt should suffer no more for their sakes." So Rahab and his army perished in the depths of the sea.

As soon as the last of the Israelites reached the opposite shore of the sea, the Egyptians plunged in after them. And God met them in battle. The Egyptians shot arrows, and God hurled back fiery hail. They advanced with gleaming swords, and God sent down lightning. Pharaoh flung missiles, and God answered with coals of fire. They sounded trumpets and horns, and God thundered in the heavens. To lure them into the water, God caused fiery mares to swim in the sea, and the horses of the Egyptians dashed in after them.

God also fought with a pillar of cloud and a pillar of fire. The cloud turned the soil into mud, and the fire boiled the mud, so that the horses became mired and could not move.

Then God blew with a hot breath, and the sea covered them. And God shook the sea and pitched them into the abyss. Like lentils tossed in a stewpot, they flew about in the boiling water and then sank to the bottom of the sea.

Thus, all the Egyptians were drowned, except for Pharaoh himself. When he heard the Children of Israel singing their victory song on the other shore, he lifted up his hands to heaven and declared, "I believe in You, O God! You are righteous and I am wicked. There is no God but You."

Then Gabriel descended and placed an iron chain around Pharaoh's neck and said to him, "Villain! Yesterday you said, 'Who is this God that I should listen and let Israel go?' And now you say, 'God is righteous!' "

Gabriel then dropped Pharaoh into the depths of the sea, where he stayed for fifty days. Then the angel flew him to Nineveh and made him king there. And many centuries later, when Jonah came and prophesied the destruction of the city because of the evil the people did there, Pharaoh covered himself with sackcloth and ashes and proclaimed for all to hear, "Let all fast within our gates, for there is no God besides the One God, whose judgments are true and faithful."

Pharaoh never died, and never will die. He sits at the gateway to hell, and when the kings of the nations enter, he says to them, "You fools! I denied God, and God sent plagues down upon me and sent me to the bottom of the sea. Now see what has become of me!"

Then, before he lets them into hell, he makes them all acknowledge God's sovereignty, which, of course, they do.

48

Manna from Heaven

The unleavened bread that the Children of Israel brought with them when they left Egypt lasted thirty-one days. And when it was gone, many of the people complained to Moses, "Have you brought us out of slavery only to have us starve in the wilderness? It would have been better for us to stay in Egypt, for at least there we were well fed!" Already they had forgotten the bitterness of slavery.

But Moses did not lose his temper with them, for he knew the ways of the multitude, how easy it is to be swayed by others in distress. And God, too, forgave them for their grumbling, for they still carried their slavery within them.

Then God said, "Tomorrow morning manna will rain down from heaven and feed you."

This manna was created on the second day of creation and was ground by the angels. (Even now the angels work the celestial mills in the third heaven, making manna for the righteous who dine on this wondrous bread in Paradise.) So miraculous is manna that all who eat it become like the angels in strength. In addition, they no longer have to empty their bladders or bowels, for manna dissolves entirely in the body. But if a person sins, the manna no longer dissolves, and that person becomes like an ordinary mortal with ordinary needs.

The taste of manna is like nothing else on earth. It does not need to be cooked or prepared in any way, yet it possesses the flavor of any food imaginable. One only has to wish for a particular dish, and that is the taste of the manna in his mouth. To children it tastes like mother's milk; to youths, bread; to the old, honey; and to the sick, barley soaked in oil and honey.

Before the manna rained down from heaven each morning, a north wind came to sweep the floor of the desert. Then came a rain to wash the sands clean, then dew that froze into a tabletop, sparkling like the finest gold. The dew also floated above the manna like a cover to keep off insects.

The manna fell like shining pearls and gave sustenance to the entire people.

For the pious, it fell within the doorways to their tents. For the mass of the people, it fell in the fields around the camp and could be gathered without much difficulty. But for the wicked, it could only be collected after much searching. And no matter how long or hard each person harvested, no matter how full or empty each one's basket, everyone's portion was always the same: one *omer* per Israelite.

Six days of the week the manna fell, and on the sixth day, a double portion fell, so that the people could gather enough for the Sabbath. For none fell on the day of rest. And Moses warned the people not to save any overnight on the other days, for it would spoil. God sent them manna daily to teach them to have faith each day.

But Datan and Aviram, who never ceased to make trouble for Moses, paid no attention to Moses' command and hoarded the manna in their tents overnight. The next day great swarms of worms arose from the manna hidden in their tents and slithered in long trains throughout the camp so that all knew what they had done.

Even lawsuits were decided by the manna. If a husband and wife came before Moses and accused each other of unfaithfulness, Moses would say to them, "Let the manna decide." And the next day, if the manna fell before the husband's tent, then he was in the right. But if it fell before the tent of the wife's parents, then she was vindicated.

The manna continued to fall for the forty years the Children of Israel wandered through the desert. It ceased the day they entered the Promised Land. Only one measure of it remained after that, kept in an earthen vessel set before the Holy Ark. King Josiah hid it together with the Ark and the jug of sacred oil before the Temple was destroyed. And in messianic times Elijah will bring it out of hiding and restore it to its rightful place.

49

Miriam's Well

After receiving the miraculous manna, the Children of
Israel were content for a time and devoted themselves to
studying God's Torah and living righteously. But they
soon grew tired of being so good and returned to their old
ways.

Then water disappeared from their camp and they
cried out in their thirst, "What have you done, Moses?
Have you brought us out of Egypt only to kill us with
thirst?"

Moses grew impatient with them and scolded them.
"Have you already forgotten all that God did for you?
What an ungrateful people you are!"

But God urged Moses to forgive them. "Try to act like
Me, Moses. I return good for evil, and forgive them their
sins. Go before them and lead them as a shepherd leads
his flock. Now take some of the elders of the people to
Mount Horeb and bring water out of a stone. Hit one of
the rocks there with your rod, and water will come forth."

For God wished to show them that the rod Moses
carried could bring blessing as well as destruction. It had
brought the plagues and had split the Sea of Reeds, and
now it would bring life-giving water.

So Moses did as God commanded.

When they came to Horeb, Moses said to the elders,
"Choose a rock, and I will make water flow from it."

So they pointed to a rock, and Moses struck it with
the rod in his hand. Instantly water gushed out of it in a
powerful stream. God called that spot 'Massah' (Trial) and
'Meribah' (Tribulation) because the people murmured
against God there and tried God's patience.

This rock became Miriam's well, which accompanied
the people for the next forty years. It was created on the
second day of Creation along with the manna and was
given to the Children of Israel as a reward for the merits

of Miriam the prophet. It was a sieve made of stone, and water gushed out of it at all times.

When the people camped, the well would settle itself opposite the Tabernacle. Then the leaders of the twelve tribes would bring their staffs before it and declare, "Spring up, O Well!" And the water would shoot up as high as pillars, then flow into great rivers. And the people would sail in ships down these rivers to the oceans, and haul up the world's treasures from the deeps.

These rivers separated the camp into different parts so that the people needed to sail on ships to visit each other. And the waters emptied into plains that surrounded the camp and sustained all kinds of fruit trees that grew there. Because of the miraculous powers of the water, these trees always bore fruit. And all sorts of fragrant herbs grew on these plains, and the people used these herbs for perfumes. Also mosses and grasses grew there and provided soft beds for the poor who had no pillows or mattresses of their own.

When Miriam died, the well disappeared temporarily, but it was restored due to the merits of Aaron and Moses. And when the people entered the Promised Land, Miriam's well disappeared forever and was hidden in the Sea of Tiberias.

But in the End of Days, it will be restored to us and will provide healing water for all the world.

50

We Will Obey and We Will Hear

Before the Torah was given to the Children of Israel, God offered it to all the other nations of the earth so that they could not complain later, "If only You had offered it to us first, we would have certainly accepted it!"

The first nation to whom God offered the Torah asked, "What is in this Torah?"

God said, "You shall not murder."

They quickly rejected it, for they said, "We live by the sword."

The next nation asked, "What is in it?"

And God replied, "You shall not commit adultery."

And they also refused it, for they said, "We are all the children of unchastity. How could we accept this Torah?"

The third nation asked, "What is in it?"

And God said, "You shall not steal."

They laughed and shook their heads, for they said, "We make our living by robbing each other blind. This Torah of Yours is not for us!"

The next nation asked, "What is in it?"

And God answered, "You shall not lie."

They rejected it rudely, for they said, "We cannot give up the law of our fathers, for they have taught us to shun the truth and profit by deceit."

And so it went with all seventy nations of the earth. Each one rejected the Torah, since to accept it would mean changing their ways completely, which they were unwilling to do.

Then God came to Israel, and said, "Will you accept My Torah?"

"What is in it?" they asked.

"Six hundred and thirteen commandments."

And they said, "All that God has spoken we will obey and we will hear."

God was pleased with their words and gave Israel the Torah for an inheritance throughout their generations.

51

The Contest of the Mountains

While the nations were rejecting the Torah, the mountains were fighting with each other for the honor of being chosen as the site of Revelation.

Mount Tabor boasted to Mount Hermon, "The *Shek-*

hinah should rest upon me, for in the days of the Flood, I alone kept my head above the waters. I am the highest mountain and am therefore the only one worthy to receive the *Shekhinah*."

Mount Hermon replied, "No, upon me shall the *Shekhinah* rest, for when the Children of Israel wished to pass through the Sea of Reeds, I placed myself between the two shores and held back the waters so that they could pass through safely."

Then Mount Carmel spoke up and said, "My feet touch both dry land and sea, so the *Shekhinah* can choose either place to rest her spirit. Indeed she could do no better than to choose me."

Then a voice thundered out of the heavens. "Hush! The *Shekhinah* will not rest on any mountains that are so proud and quarrel among themselves! I prefer the low mountains, and Sinai foremost among these, because it is the smallest and most insignificant of all."

The other mountains took offense and complained, "Are You going to play favorites, and not even reward us for our good intentions?"

God replied, "Because you were quarreling over My honor, I will reward you. You, Tabor, will help Deborah in her fight against Sisera, and Carmel, you will aid Elijah against the priests of Baal. And in times to come, Hermon, the heavenly Jerusalem will descend upon your crown."

Then God addressed Sinai. "I have chosen you for the honor of receiving My law, not only because you are so humble, but also because no one has ever worshiped idols upon your slopes, for your crown is too far below the clouds to interest the heathens. And you also share a noble past, for once you were joined with Mount Moriah, where Abraham went to sacrifice his son Isaac. Then you separated yourself and came to the desert. And I will bring you back to Moriah at the End of Days and build My new Temple upon you."

So God gave the Torah to Israel upon little Mount Sinai.

It was fitting that it was in the desert that the Revelation took place, for although Israel received the Torah first, it does not belong to Israel alone but to the whole world.

52

Our Children Shall Be Our Guarantors

Even though the people of Israel were eager to accept the Torah, still God hesitated to give it to them.

"Bring Me guarantors who will assure Me that you will observe it, and then I will give you My Torah."

And the people said, "Our ancestors will be our guarantors."

But God rejected their claim. "Your ancestors are in My debt. Abraham, Isaac, and Jacob all sinned in some way and lost faith in Me. No, they will not do as guarantors."

So the people said, "Our prophets will be our guarantors."

But God rejected these as well. "No, your prophets will fail Me, too. 'Like foxes in the desert' they will become. Have you no one else to be your guarantors?"

And the people said, "We will give You our children as our guarantors."

Then God smiled and said, "These are good guarantors!"

Then the mothers brought their babies nursing at their breasts and the pregnant women came, too. And God made the bellies of the pregnant women as transparent as glass and spoke to the children in the womb. "Behold, I am giving your parents My Torah. Will you guarantee that they will keep it?"

And the babies answered, "Yes!"

Then God said, "I am your God."

And they answered, "Yes!"

"You shall have no other gods but Me."

"No other!"

And they answered each commandment with a re-sounding 'Yes!' and each prohibition with a firm 'No!'

Then God gave the Torah to their parents.

53

Divine Blackmail at Sinai

Did Israel accept the Torah entirely of its own free will? Not exactly . . .

When the people approached Sinai, God lifted up the mountain and held it over their heads, and said, "If you accept My Torah, well and good. But if you don't, you will find your graves under this mountain!"

Then all the people burst into tears and poured out their hearts to God. "All that God has said we will obey and we will hear!"

Then God sent down one hundred and twenty thousand angels with a crown and a sash of glory for every Israelite. And the people kept these divine gifts until they sinned with the Golden Calf, and then the angels came and took these gifts back. God also bestowed on them that day a heavenly radiance that shone from their faces, but that too they lost because of their sins.

Only Moses retained his radiance, even in the grave. And if today a crack were to appear in his tomb, the light shining from his corpse would be so powerful that it would destroy the whole world.

54

The Revelation at Sinai

All of Israel stood at the foot of Mount Sinai, and a heavy cloud rested on the mountain, swallowing up its crown in darkness.

And on the sixth day of Sivan, fifty days after Israel came forth from Egypt out of the house of bondage, the people heard loud thunder upon the mountain and saw terrible lightning. The sound of a thousand shofar blasts shook the ground under their feet, and the people trembled in great fear. God churned up the clouds and rattled the earth to its foundations, and even the heavens were afraid.

The rulers of the earth quaked on their thrones and came to the great enchanter Balaam. "Help us!" they cried. "God is bringing another Flood upon our heads!"

"Fools!" answered Balaam. "God promised never to destroy the earth again through water."

"Then fire!" they said. "God will rain down hot flames upon us, and we will all perish!"

Balaam only laughed at them in their distress. "Neither fire nor water is coming to destroy the earth. All the commotion you hear comes from Mount Sinai, where God is about to give the Torah to Israel."

And the rulers heaved a great sigh of relief and declared, "God will bless the people of Israel with peace!"

The earth, too, trembled on this day, for she believed that the end of time had come, when she would have to account for all the blood she had absorbed into her soil, all the murdered souls she had swallowed up, beginning with Abel. It was only when she heard the first words of the Ten Commandments that she became calm again.

Then Mount Sinai rose into the air until its summit reached the Divine Throne, and a cloud shrouded its sides. And a vast array of angels gathered upon the mountain on all four sides, and God appeared from all directions at once and filled the heavens with the Divine Glory. And although the mountain was small, there was room to spare for all the angels upon it.

The first word God spoke was, *'Anokhi'*: "I am." This was not a Hebrew but an Egyptian word. Why did God address the people in Egyptian? To welcome them back after their stay in a foreign land, for when people travel far from home, it is natural for them to become accustomed to a foreign tongue and to forget their own.

But when the people heard the words issuing from God's mouth, borne by lightning and thunder, and when they saw the fiery torches lighting up the darkened sky, they flew back in terror twelve miles from the mountain and died of fright.

When the Torah saw this, it turned to God and said, "Master of the world! Have You given me to the living or to the dead?"

God answered, "For your sake, I will bring them back to life." And God rained down the dew of resurrection, and the people returned to life.

But still the people were so terrified that they could hardly stand, so God sent two angels for each of the Israelites, one to lay a hand upon each of their hearts so that the soul might not leave the body, and the other to lift each head to behold the Divine Splendor.

Then the invisible Word thundered forth from the heavens and rolled into their ears and asked each one of them, "Will you accept the two hundred and forty-eight positive commandments, one for each bone of your body?"

And the people answered as one, "Yes!"

Then the Word rolled out of their ears, kissed their mouths, then rolled back into their ears and called, "Will you accept the three hundred and sixty-five prohibitions in the Torah, one for each day of the year?"

And again the people shouted, "Yes!"

Then the Divine Word rolled out of their ears and kissed them on the mouths again.

Then God opened the seven heavens and the seven earths and said to them, "You are My witnesses this day! I have delivered this people out of slavery and given them My Torah. If they obey My commandments, I will be merciful, gracious, and eternally patient with them, full of goodness and truth, but if they rebel, I will be a stern judge. Had they not accepted My Torah, I would not punish them for sinning. But since they have accepted it, they must now obey."

God wished to show Israel the Unity of the Divine Presence, so God ordered all of nature to stand still. No feathers flapped, no beasts bellowed, no worms wiggled, no tempests tossed, no seraphim serenaded the heavens with their 'Holy, Holy, Holy!' All was unnaturally still until an echoless voice announced, "I am the Lord Your God!"

These words were heard by all the inhabitants of the earth in all seventy languages. Even the dead awoke to the sound and flew to Sinai to see God revealed, and the souls of the not-yet-born also gathered at the foot of Sinai. All prophets and teachers flocked to hear their special share of revelation, which they would later reveal to humankind. All who heard God's voice that day heard the same words, but to each the voice sounded different, as if God were addressing that person alone.

And after they had heard the first two commandments—"I am the Lord Your God" and "You shall have no other gods before Me"—the people could stand no more. They pleaded with Moses to come between them and the Awful Voice, for they feared that they would die if they heard all that God had to say to them.

So Moses alone received the other eight commandments and reported them to the people. But as a result, the people did not take the other commandments to heart as they had the first two. They forgot some of Moses's teachings, and they sinned. If only they had had the courage to listen to God directly! For when they heard God declare, "You shall have no other gods before Me," the evil impulse was banished from their hearts. But when they demanded that Moses be their go-between, the evil impulse snuck back into their hearts and took root there forever.

Moses stayed up on the mountain for forty days and forty nights. God spoke to Moses face to face and revealed the Law to him, and even more.

55

Moses and the Angels Wrestle over the Torah

On the day that God gave Israel the Torah, the sun did not set but remained in the sky for an extra twenty-four hours. Then Moses ascended the mountain and prepared to meet God.

A cloud floated down and hovered before Moses. Before he could decide whether to jump on top of it or grab hold of its rim, the mouth of the cloud sprang open. With trepidation, Moses stepped into the cloud, and off it flew.

Inside he met Kemuel, the Porter Angel, who demanded, "What are you doing here, son of Amram, in this place that belongs to the angels of fire?"

"I come not of my own will," answered Moses, "but to fulfill a mission for the Holy One, to bring the Torah down to Israel."

Kemuel held out his hand to bar Moses' way, and Moses struck him, and he dissolved into the cloud.

Then Moses met Hadarniel, who roared at him with fiery lightning flashes. "What are you doing here, son of Amram, in the place of the Holy and Most High?"

Moses trembled down to his soles and began to weep, until God thundered at Hadarniel out of the heavens, "You angels have given Me trouble from the very beginning! I have summoned Moses here to give the Torah to Israel. Leave him alone!"

Hadarniel shrank back and said, "I did not know that, O Lord of the World! I will be glad to be his messenger and disciple."

Then Hadarniel took him to Sandalfon, also called "The Wheel," who fashions crowns for God. But the fire blazing forth from this giant angel proved too much for

Hadarniel, so he was forced to leave Moses in Sandalfon's charge.

Now Sandalfon is terrible to look at and so tall that it would take a human being five hundred years to climb to the crown of his head. When Moses saw him, he began to cry and almost fell off the cloud. But God reached down a hand and shielded him from the flames of Sandalfon. Then Moses came to the Angels of Terror who surround the Throne of Glory, the mightiest and most terrifying of all the angels. They wished to scorch Moses with their fiery breath, but God told Moses, "Grab hold of My throne, and no harm shall come to you."

Then the angels demanded, "What is this human being doing here?"

And God said, "He has come to receive the Torah."

"Let us have the Torah!" cried the angels. "Why do You wish to give it to those who live in the dust?"

Moses now plucked up his courage and said to them, "In the Torah it is written: 'I am the Lord Your God who brought you out of the land of Egypt, out of the house of bondage.' Have you been slaves in Egypt? Did God redeem you? Why do you need the Torah? And it is also written: 'You shall have no other gods.' Are there idol-worshipers here, that you need the Torah to remind you not to bow down to idols? And it is also written: 'You shall not swear false oaths.' Do you do business here in heaven? And the Torah says: 'Remember to keep the Sabbath.' Do you have jobs that you must rest? Or parents whom you must honor? Or wives and husbands whom you must remain faithful to? And is there money in heaven that you fear you might steal? Or a murderer among the angels? And are there donkeys and oxen up here that you covet for your own? No, you do not need the Torah! But we human beings do."

And the angels had to admit that Moses was right. They raised up their voices in praise to God. "O God, how excellent is Your name in all the earth!"

Moses stayed in heaven for forty days and nights

learning the Torah from God. But when he started to go back down to earth, he encountered the Angels of Horror and the Angels of Terror and the Angels of Trembling and the Angels of Quaking, and in his fear he forgot everything he had learned. So God called Yefefiah, the Prince of the Torah, and this angel gave Moses the Law written out on a scroll, so that it would be there for all to read.

As farewell gifts the other angels gave Moses secrets of the Torah and holy remedies. Even the Angel of Death gave him a remedy against death. And Moses went down to the people to share with them all that God had commanded.

56
Moses Visits Akiva's Classroom

When Moses reached heaven, where he was to receive the Torah, he found God busy decorating the letters of the Torah with elaborate crowns. He stood watching without saying a word.

Then God said to him, "Don't you know how to say *Shalom*?"

Moses replied, "Should a servant greet his master first?"

"You might at least have wished Me success in my work!"

Moses replied, "May You succeed in all Your works!"

Then Moses stared at the ornaments God had made on the letters of the Torah, and he asked what they meant.

God told him, "In later years there shall live a man named Akiva, son of Joseph, who will fashion a mountain of laws based on every dot crowning these letters."

Moses said, "Show me this man!"

So God transported Moses to Rabbi Akiva's classroom, and Moses took a seat on one of the back benches.

He listened to the master and his students discussing the law but could not follow a word they said. And Moses was ashamed of his own ignorance.

Then he heard one of the students asking Akiva, "Master, how do you know that this is so?"

Akiva answered, "This is a *halakhah* given to Moses on Mount Sinai."

It pleased Moses to hear such wisdom credited to him, even though he himself did not understand it.

"Surely this is a great teacher!" he thought to himself.

When he returned to heaven, Moses said to God, "Why do You give the Torah to Israel through me when You have such a teacher as this in Your world?"

God thundered at him, "Be silent! This is My decree!"

Then Moses asked God, "Now that I have seen this man's great learning, may I also see his reward?"

And God said, "Turn around and look!"

So Moses turned around, and he saw a vast amphitheater filled with people, and there in the center stood the aged Rabbi Akiva, surrounded by Roman soldiers, and they raked his flesh with sharp iron combs until he died.

Moses cried out, "Is this the reward for such great learning?"

God replied, "Be silent! This is My decree!"

And Moses held his peace.

57

The Golden Calf

When Israel agreed to accept the Ten Commandments, God decided to reward the people with a second gift: immortal life. But then came the incident of the Golden Calf, and as a result of that terrible sin, this second precious gift was never bestowed. All of Israel's suffering from that moment on, including the dark centuries of

Exile, stem from this single episode when Israel betrayed its God.

For when Moses went up to Mount Sinai to receive the Law from God, he promised the people that he would return in forty days. But at noon on the fortieth day, Satan used his wizardry to conjure up the image of the lifeless Moses, floating in his coffin midway between heaven and earth. And when the people saw it, they cried out, "Look what has become of Moses who brought us out of the land of Egypt!"

Panic-stricken, they ran to Aaron and pleaded with him to make them a god that they could carry with them, such as the Egyptians had.

When Miriam's son Hur heard their request, he became incensed and rebuked them. "O you fickle people! Have you already forgotten the miracles God did for you?"

In their anger, the people killed him on the spot, and then, pointing to his corpse, they said to Aaron, "If you will make us a god, it will be well with you, but if not, we will do the same to you as we did to him!"

Aaron did not fear for his own life, but he feared for the very soul of his people, for he thought that God might not forgive them if they killed him, who was God's high priest and prophet. So he decided to take their sin upon himself rather than let them doom themselves.

But he still hoped that he could delay them long enough for Moses to return and so prevent their sin altogether. So he said to the men, "Bring me your wives' jewelry and the jewelry of your sons and daughters," thinking that these others would refuse to give them up. And he was right about the women, for they did refuse to donate their ornaments to make an idol. And not only did they refrain from sin at this moment, but they later refused to listen to the evil counsel of the ten spies whose courage failed in the face of the Canaanite giants, and they also never begged Moses to take them back to Egypt. God rewarded the women for their faithfulness by letting them all live to enter the Promised Land, with the exception of Miriam. Even Yokheved, the mother of Moses, lived to cross the Jordan at the age of two hundred and fifty. And God also gave the women the New Moons as their special holidays.

But although the women refused to give up their jewelry, the men would not be denied, so they pulled off their own earrings and brought them to Aaron so that he could fashion for them an idol of silver and gold. And when Aaron threw the ornaments in, a golden bull emerged out of the flames and began to bleat before the people.

Now both Moses and Aaron were indirectly responsible for this Golden Calf that emerged out of the fire. For when the Children of Israel were about to leave Egypt, Moses went to the shores of the Nile to retrieve Joseph's coffin and carry it out of Egypt as the Children of Israel had promised Joseph long ago. In order to summon up the coffin from the riverbed, Moses took four leaves of gold and engraved on each an image from the four corners of the Divine Throne: the lion, the human being, the eagle, and the bull. First he threw in the leaf with the image of the lion, and the river grew turbulent and roared. Then he threw in the second leaf with the human image on it, and the scattered bones of Joseph drew together and knit themselves into a complete body. Then he threw in the third leaf with the image of the eagle, and the coffin flew to the river's surface.

But he did not need the fourth leaf since he could retrieve the coffin without it, so he gave the leaf with the image of the bull to an Israelite for safekeeping and then forgot about it. This was one of the ornaments the people now brought to Aaron, and it was this gold leaf that gave rise to the Golden Calf. Satan hid himself within the body of the calf and began to bleat. So the people were fooled into thinking that this was a living creature that now stood before them.

But the people were not content with a single god, so

they made twelve more, one for each tribe, and they gathered the heavenly manna to offer as a sacrifice. So great was God's love for the people that, even in their apostasy, God did not withdraw the manna from them, but continued to nourish this wayward people in the wilderness.

Then Aaron tried to delay the people again, offering to build an altar with his own hands for this new god. But by the next morning, Moses had still not appeared, and the altar now stood complete before the people. And they began to worship their false gods and to act sinfully.

God now wished to destroy this rebellious people and to begin all over again with Moses, but Moses pleaded on their behalf, until God softened and forgave them. For Moses said to God, "To judge fairly, a judge must also be held accountable to the law, and so You must accept Your own law to allow another to absolve You of Your vows. For though You have vowed to destroy anyone who worships other gods besides You, You can now repent of Your vow before me and be absolved."

And God said, "I repent of the evil I swore to bring to My people."

And Moses replied, "I absolve You of Your oath!"

But when Moses himself descended from the mountain with the two tablets of the Law, his own anger blazed forth, and he wished to punish the people for their faithlessness. When he looked now at the tablets, he saw that the writing, black fire upon white, had suddenly vanished, leaving only blank stone. And the two stones now weighed him down, whereas before the letters had buoyed up the tablets so that they were as light as air.

In his great anger, Moses flung the tablets to the ground and they shattered.

Then the oceans wished to leave their beds and flood the world, but Moses pleaded with them to remain where they were. And when they would not be appeased, he took the Golden Calf, burnt it, ground it into powder, and scattered it upon the waters. But still the oceans were not appeased. Then Moses made the people drink the bitter water. And the oceans were calmed.

This bitter water was one of three judgments God brought down upon those who had worshiped the Golden Calf. The Israelites who had been seen by witnesses worshiping the calf drank the bitter water and died. Those who had sinned without witnesses died soon after from the plague that God sent into the camp. And those who had been warned ahead of time not to worship the calf but did anyway were killed that day by the Levites. In all, three thousand Israelites died because they had sinned before God.

And the people repented of the evil they had done, and God forgave them, as did Moses. Then Moses went back up the mountain to receive the second set of commandments, and the mountain remained shrouded in a dark cloud for the next forty days.

58

The Pouch of Gold

After the incident with the Golden Calf, Moses ascended Mount Sinai a second time. And he was still bewildered by all that he had seen the last time, particularly the bitter fate of Rabbi Akiva, and so he again pressed God about Divine Justice.

"Why do the good suffer and the evil prosper?" asked Moses. "Is there no justice in the world?"

And God said to Moses, "Behold!"

Moses looked down from Mount Sinai and saw far below a man on a river bank, stooping down to drink. And as the man bent over the water, his purse fell out of his pocket, but he failed to notice. Then the man stood up and went on his way.

A short time after this, another man came along and

found the purse. When he opened it, he discovered that it was filled with gold coins. Quickly he pocketed the purse and ran off.

Soon an old man came along who stopped at the river to drink. Then he lay down on the bank and fell asleep.

When the first man realized what had happened, he ran back to the river and found the old man sleeping on the bank.

"Give me back my money!" he shouted.

The old man woke up and looked around, bewildered by the other man's excited shouts. "What money? What are you talking about?"

"You are the only one who could have taken my pouch!" shouted the first man, and he drew his sword and pierced the old man through the chest.

Moses watched this scene in horror. "Show me Your ways, O God, so that I can understand what I have just seen! Why has this innocent man been murdered while the true thief has escaped punishment?"

Then God explained to Moses. "The man who found the money was once robbed of this purse by the man who lost it, and the old man, whom the first man killed, long ago killed the father of his own murderer. Thus justice has been done."

And Moses was appeased.

But God added, "Do not think that you understand all My ways because of what you have seen here today. You cannot possibly grasp all the workings of My hands, for that is beyond the understanding of the human mind. Be content that you have seen even the shadow of My justice, which is more than most people come to know."

Then God placed Moses in a cleft in the rock and passed before him so that Moses could see God's back. And so radiant was even the back of the Divine Presence, that its reflection on the rock illumined Moses' face so that it shone from that day on.

Then on the tenth of Tishrei, the Day of Atonement, Moses descended from the mountain to bring the second tablets of the Law to his penitent people.

59

The Spies

When the Children of Israel approached the borders of Canaan, they came to Moses and said, "Before we enter this land, let us send spies into it to see how strong the people are and how fortified are their cities." So eager were they to force Moses' hand in this matter that the younger men pushed their elders rudely out of the way and spoke insolently to Moses.

Then God said to Moses, "How little faith this stiff-necked people has! For in Egypt they ridiculed My promise to free them, and now again they doubt that I will give the Canaanites into their hands. Send spies if you wish, Moses, but do not pretend that I have ordered it."

Moses chose one man from each tribe except Levi, and each was the most worthy in his tribe, so that even God approved of Moses' choices. But even though these men were originally pious, they now turned wicked. They decided among themselves to bring back an evil report from the land, so that the people would be forced to remain in the wilderness and not settle in Canaan. For these men feared that they would lose their own positions as heads of their tribes if Israel settled in the land.

Only Caleb of the tribe of Judah and Hoshea of the tribe of Ephraim refused to go along with their wicked plan. It was at this moment that Moses changed Hoshea's name to Yehoshua—Joshua—saying, "May God be your salvation (*Yeshua*), and protect you from the evil influence of the others."

As soon as Moses changed Hoshea's name to Joshua, Yud, the smallest letter of the *aleph-bet*, rejoiced. For ever since God had changed our mother Sarai's name to Sarah, substituting a *heh* for the *yud* at the end of her name, little Yud had been inconsolable. "Why have You taken me away from pious Sarah?" it forever complained to God.

But now it had been chosen to head Joshua's new name. So Yud wiped away its tears and was content.

Moses gave the spies many instructions about their mission. "Travel in secret between the cities. But show yourselves openly once inside, saying to the inhabitants: 'We come only to buy pomegranates and grapes.' Do not destroy the idols or the high places but simply look carefully at the people and the land, noting their virtues and flaws. If you find the people living in the open, know that they are a brave people who do not fear their enemies. But if they live behind high walls, know that they are cowards whom we need not fear. Most important, find out if Job still lives, for he is the only pious man in the land of Canaan, and his merits might shield the inhabitants from our swords."

Even though the spies discovered that Job had recently died, still their hearts failed them when they traveled in the land, and thus they sealed Israel's fate for the next forty years.

Moses sent them first to the south of Canaan, the poorest section of the land, for like a clever merchant, he wished them to see the poorer goods before the better, and thus be favorably impressed. And, indeed, when they reached Hebron farther north, they were immediately struck by its beauty and richness. And as they traveled the land, God helped them by sending a plague to each city they spied out, so that the inhabitants were too busy burying their dead to trouble with strangers.

They might have mustered their courage and brought back a favorable report had they not encountered the giants who lived in the land. Some were so tall that the sun only reached to their ankles, and when they walked, huge plots of land shot up from under their feet.

When the spies came to the city of Kiryat Arba, the "City of Four," where the giant Anak and his three sons lived, they hid in a cave to escape the giants. But they discovered to their horror that the cave was actually the rind of a pomegranate that the giant's daughter had thrown away. Before they had a chance to flee, the giant girl bent down and picked up the rind with all twelve spies in it and threw it into the garden. Luckily, she never noticed that there were men inside, and so they managed to escape.

They might not have escaped from the other giants, however, had Moses not given them two secret weapons: his sapphire rod and the secret of the Divine Name. Whenever they found themselves in danger, they had only to pronounce the Name or lift up the rod, and they were saved from harm.

By this time, they were so terrified of the Canaanites that they wished to return to the Israelite camp without taking any of the bountiful fruits back with them, but Caleb held up his sword and threatened to fight them all unless they brought fruit back to the Israelite camp. So they cut down a grape vine that yielded enough wine to last the Israelites for the forty years in the wilderness. So heavy was this vine that it took eight of them to carry it. The ninth spy carried a single pomegranate, and the tenth a fig. Neither Joshua nor Caleb carried anything, for it would not have been fitting for these princes of Israel to carry burdens like common workmen.

When they returned to the Israelite camp, the ten spies began their report favorably, so as to fool the people into listening to them. "The land we have seen does indeed flow with milk and honey," they began, and then they began to strike fear in the people's hearts, "but the people are very strong and live in walled cities, and we even saw giants there. It is impossible for us to overcome them."

Then Joshua rose to refute them, but they shouted him down. "How dare you speak to us about conquering this land! You have no children, and so stand to lose nothing if you die in battle! But we have our sons and daughters to think of!" And so they silenced him.

Then Caleb rose to speak. The others did not try to silence him, because he had pretended to agree with them while they were in Canaan, and so they did not suspect he would now speak against them.

"Moses took us out of Egypt," he declared, "and split the sea for us, and gave us manna. If now he told us to climb to heaven on ladders, we should obey him!" And his voice was so mighty that he could be heard twelve miles away. But even his loud voice did not impress the people, and they preferred to follow the evil counsel of the other ten spies.

"The land is a wicked land," they said, "that eats up its inhabitants with disease. And when we saw the giants, we were as grasshoppers in our own sight, and in theirs."

Now God spoke, annoyed at the faithless spies. "It does not offend Me that you say, 'We were like grasshoppers in our own sight,' but how do you know how you appeared to the Canaanites? You might have appeared as angels to them!"

Yet nothing Moses or Caleb or even God could say could change the people's minds. They were convinced that the land was beyond their reach and that they would surely perish if they tried to conquer it. They even tried to convince Moses that God hated the Israelites. "If a human king has two children and two fields, one field watered by a river and one only by rain, does he not give the field watered by the river to his favored child, for the other field is dependent upon the whim of heaven? God led us out of Egypt, which is watered by the life-giving Nile, and is now trying to force upon us Canaan, which depends on the fickle rains for food. Is this the act of a loving God?"

Then the people tore their clothes and began to mourn their fate, and soon a loud wailing filled the entire camp of Israel. It was on the ninth day of Av that the people raised their voices in lament, and God grew angry with them and said, "Today you weep without cause, but in the future I shall give you reason to weep on this day." So God decreed that in the future, the Temple in Jerusalem would be destroyed on this very day, and the Children of Israel would forever know the Ninth of Av as a night of tears.

Then the people rose in rebellion against Moses and Aaron, and they tried to set up Datan and Aviram as their new leaders, and to raise their hands against Moses and Aaron. But God sent the Cloud of Glory to protect them. When the people saw that Moses and Aaron had vanished, they hurled stones into the cloud to try to kill Moses and Aaron inside.

At last God lost patience with the spies and with the people who listened to their wicked counsel, and He determined to destroy them all. But Moses pleaded with God for mercy, and the sentence was softened.

"For your sake, Moses, I will spare this people, but I will nonetheless collect the debt owed Me for their faithlessness. For the next forty years they will pay Me back, one year for each day the spies spent in the land. All males who were twenty years or older when I redeemed them from Egypt will die in the wilderness, and the sands will swallow them up."

So each year for the next forty, on the eighth day of Av, the people dug their own graves and spent the night in them, and the next morning, on the Ninth of Av, a herald went forth through the camp and declared, "Let the living separate themselves from the dead," and about fifteen thousand Israelites remained lifeless in their graves. For forty years, no Israelite died on any day but this, which was the day that the people had greeted the spies' report with tears and ashes. Only in the fortieth year did the Ninth of Av pass without death.

As for the ten spies themselves, since it was through their tongues that they had sinned and brought disaster down upon the whole people, God punished them by making their tongues stretch out of their mouths until they reached down to their navels, and then out of their tongues grew worms that pierced their navels, and thus they died.

When the people heard God's stern judgment upon them, they cried out bitterly and declared their readiness to enter the Promised Land. But it was too late.

And so began the Israelites' long exile in the wilderness.

60

The Rebellion of Korakh

After the people had been condemned to wander forty years in the wilderness, one man arose to stir them to more rebellion. This was Korakh, son of Izhar, nephew of Amram, who was Moses's father. Korakh was a jealous man, for he envied his older cousins Moses and Aaron for their great power and popularity, and he envied his younger cousin Elizaphan for his position as a prince of the Levites.

Korakh went among the people and tried to stir them to rebellion. And his prophet's eye misled him, for he looked into the future and saw that one of his descendants would be the great prophet Samuel and that twenty-four other descendants would be levitical singers and psalmists in the Temple. And he assumed that it was his own merits that would protect him from God's wrath now. But alas, poor Korakh failed to see that it was his three sons who would merit these distinguished descendants, for they would repent of their father's rebellion and so save themselves and their children after them. As for Korakh, his sins would lead him straight to hell.

Korakh had once been Pharaoh's treasurer. While serving in the palace, he had discovered one of the three treasure-houses built by Joseph during the seven years of plenty and had claimed it for himself. So vast was this fortune that it took three hundred white mules to carry just the keys to the treasure. And it was because of this great wealth that Korakh became so proud, and it was because of his pride that he sinned.

Korakh's co-conspirators in his rebellion were Datan and Aviram, who never ceased plotting against Moses. It was they who had revealed to Pharaoh Moses' killing of the Egyptian taskmaster, they who had urged the Israelites to return to Egypt at the Sea of Reeds, and they who had led the people in revolt after the spies returned from

Canaan. Now they joined Korakh in challenging Moses and Aaron's authority.

Korakh came before the people and began to mock the Torah. "What foolish laws we have received through Moses! Not to yoke together an ox and an ass! To put blue fringes on our garments! To nail *mezuzahs* to our doorposts even if our houses are filled with holy books! Why do you wish to follow this man and his unreasonable Torah?"

And the people took his words to heart and accused Moses of lording it over them. They even accused him of leading an immoral life and lusting after their wives.

Finally Moses could stand no more and said to God, "I do not mind if they insult me or my brother, but when they insult Your Torah, they must be punished. If these men die a common death, I will declare that the Torah was not given by You. But if the earth opens up its mouth and swallows them up, then all will know that You are Truth and that Your Torah is truth."

Then Moses said to Korakh and his two hundred and fifty followers, "Tomorrow, come before the Tent of Meeting with your fire-pans and burn incense to God, and we will then see whom God accepts."

The next day the mouth of hell approached the spot where Datan and Aviram stood with their families, and the ground opened up and swallowed them. This was the pit created at twilight of the Sixth Day of Creation. Not only did it swallow the people but their possessions also. Even the sheets at the launderers and the rolling pins at the bake-ovens rolled toward the pit and fell in. And even their names disappeared from any documents upon which they were written.

The rebels did not plummet to their deaths all at once, but the ground digested them slowly, opening up only enough to swallow their legs, then wider to engulf their abdomens, then narrowing over their heads. And just before they vanished into the ground, they cried out, "Moses is truth, and his Torah is truth, and the Torah has been given by God!"

As for the two hundred and fifty rebels who offered

incense in their fire-pans, they were consumed by fire that rained down out of the heavens.

But the worst punishment of all was Korakh's, for he died both ways, by fire and by the pit, so that neither Datan and Aviram nor the others could complain to God of unfairness. First, he was transformed into a ball of fire, and then the fireball rolled toward the pit and disappeared into the bowels of the earth

To this day, Korakh and his followers suffer in hell, rising to the surface of the earth every thirty days, to the exact spot where they were swallowed by the mouth of hell. And anyone who puts his ear to the ground at that spot can hear them call on those days, "Moses is truth, and his Torah is truth, but we are liars!"

In later times, when the Temple was destroyed, God sank the Temple gates deep in the earth until they reached the very edge of hell. Korakh and his followers grabbed hold of the gates, saying, "If these gates return to earth, we shall then be lifted up also." So God appointed them keepers of the Temple gates, and thus they await the coming of the Messiah, when they will rejoin their people once again.

61

The Waters of Meribah

After almost forty years had passed in the wilderness, Miriam the prophet, sister of Moses and Aaron, died on the first day of Nisan. Then the well that had accompanied the Children of Israel throughout their wanderings vanished, for it was only because of Miriam's merits that it had provided water to the people.

The people came to Moses and Aaron to complain about the lack of water. When Aaron saw the mob approaching, he said to his brother, "Look, Moses, the people have come to express their sympathy about Miriam."

But Moses knew the people better than that and he said, "No, my brother, see how disorderly they are! They come without leaders and without ranks. They have come to demand something from us!"

And sure enough, the people crowded around the two sons of Amram and said to them, "Wasn't it bad enough that so many of us died by a plague at the time of the Golden Calf and that so many of us were swallowed up by the mouth of hell and that so many of us were consumed by fire when Korakh incited us to rebellion? Now are we all to die of thirst?"

Before Moses and Aaron could reply, they said, "Why don't you ask God to have pity on us since Miriam's well has disappeared with her death?"

Moses and Aaron did not fault the people for their complaints, for they knew that distress turns people's heads and tries their faith, and God too understood their plight and forgave them.

God now said to Moses and Aaron, "Stop grieving over the death of an old woman and help My children who are dying of thirst! Go to the rock the people shall choose and speak to it, that water may come forth from it. Make sure not to strike it but only to speak to it, for the merits of Abraham and Sarah, Isaac and Rebecca, Jacob, Rachel, and Leah will suffice to draw water out of the stone by your command alone."

Then Moses took the rod on which was written the Holy Name of God and went to draw water out of the rock. All the people followed him, many stopping at different rocks along the way, hoping that they might perform the miracle themselves.

Some grumbled, "Moses was once a shepherd, so he knows how to divine water in the desert. He will try to trick us into thinking that his word has brought water out of the rock, but in truth the water will spring from a hidden source. The only way we can be sure that he has brought forth water from stone is for us to choose the rock!"

Now for forty years, Moses had tried to keep his

anger in check, although the people continued to try his
patience. And for all that time, he had succeeded. But on
this one occasion, he failed, and now he shouted at the
people in unbridled rage, "You stiff-necked people who
insist on teaching your own teacher! Do you think I can
bring water only out of the rock you choose? I tell you that
I will bring water only out of the rock that *I* have chosen!"

Every single Israelite heard his angry words, for God
had hollowed out the space in front of the rock so that it
could hold the entire people. And Moses' anger blazed
even hotter, and he lifted the rod in his hand and struck
the rock that God had commanded him only to speak to.

At first only a few drops oozed out of the stone, and
the people mocked Moses, saying, "Are we then only
babies still nursing at our mother's breast?"

Moses became angrier still, and he struck the rock a
second time. This time great streams of water gushed out
and drowned many of the people and flooded the whole
desert.

Then God said to Moses, "I told you not to strike the
stone but to speak to it only! Because you dishonored Me
in front of the people and because Aaron did not stay your
hand or tongue, neither of you will enter the land but will
die here in the desert. Only in messianic times will you
lead Israel into the Holy Land."

Then Moses cried out to God, "If it is Your judgment
that I die in the desert like the rest of the people, at least
write in Your Torah that my sin was different from theirs!
Let future generations know that I failed to sanctify Your
Name at the rock in Kadesh, not that my heart failed in
courage before the inhabitants of Canaan."

And so it was written.

Thus Moses' doom was sealed because of the waters
of Meribah, which means "strife," because he strove there
with the people instead of comforting them, and strove
with the rock instead of trusting in God. And because
Moses' death was brought about by water, God did not
declare the Second Day of Creation "good" when he first

brought forth water upon the earth. For although water once had saved Moses, it now defeated him.

62

The Death of Aaron

Not long after Miriam's death, it was Aaron's turn to die. God said to Moses, "I have an important matter to discuss with you, but it saddens Me greatly."

Moses asked, "What is it?"

And God said, "It is time for Aaron to die. He is not to enter the land because he stood by silently at the waters of Meribah."

Moses cried out to God, "Master of the Universe, You rule heaven and earth, and everything is in Your hands! The whole world depends upon Your will. Yet I cannot tell my brother he is about to die, since I am unworthy, for he is older than I."

Then God said, "You need not tell him of his death beforehand. Only take him and his son Eleazar up to Mount Hor, and speak gently to him there, and strip him of his priestly robes and put them upon Eleazar. Then I will take his soul. But I myself cannot prepare him for his death, for I am too ashamed."

When Moses heard God's words, his heart filled with sorrow and he wept bitterly. So deep was his grief that his soul almost left his body. But God had commanded him to perform this task, so he set out for the Tent of Meeting to find Aaron.

For forty years, it had been Moses' custom to walk each morning from his tent to the Tabernacle with the elders, priests, and all the people behind him. Always he would walk at the head of the procession in the center, with Aaron at his right side and Eleazar at his left. This morning, however, Moses changed the customary order, putting Aaron in the center and himself on Aaron's right.

Aaron was surprised at the change and asked Moses, "Why have you done this thing?"

"Wait," replied Moses, "I will tell you when we get to the Tabernacle."

When the people saw Aaron in Moses' place, they rejoiced greatly, for they loved Aaron even more than Moses. Ever since the incident with the Golden Calf, Aaron had been trying to atone for his part in Israel's sin. He would go from household to household, teaching the *Sh'ma* to those who did not know how to recite it, teaching Torah to those who did not understand it, and teaching the people how to pray. Even dearer to his heart was his wish to make peace in every dwelling, between the learned and the unlettered, among scholars, and between husbands and wives. So many marriages were saved by Aaron's peacemaking that eighty thousand boys bore his name and later mourned his death. So when the people saw him now marching in the center of the morning procession, they imagined that Aaron had supplanted Moses in rank, and they were overjoyed.

When they came to the Tabernacle, Aaron said, "Now tell me what God has commanded you this day."

But Moses put him off. "Wait until we reach Mount Hor."

When they reached the foothills of the mountain, Moses said to the people, "Stay here until we return to you. Aaron, Eleazar, and I will go to the top of the mountain and hear what God has to say to us. Then we will return to you here."

When they got to the top of the mountain, a cave suddenly appeared. Moses said to Aaron, "Come inside with me."

This was a difficult moment for Moses, for God had commanded him to strip Aaron of his priestly robes and put them on Eleazar. So he said to Aaron, "Perhaps inside this cave there are graves that will make your priestly garments impure. It is best that you take them off and put them on your son."

As soon as Aaron took off the first of the eight priestly robes, a celestial garment miraculously appeared to array his body, and soon he was wearing eight celestial robes to replace the eight earthly garments he gave up to his son.

Then Moses turned to Eleazar and said, "Wait here for us until we come out of the cave."

When they went inside, they found a couch, a prepared table, and a lighted candle, and all around the couch angels stood awaiting them.

Yet still Aaron remained ignorant of God's design, and he said to his brother, "When will you reveal to me why you brought me here? Even if it involves my own death, I would gladly accept it since it comes from God."

Then Moses said, "Since you yourself have mentioned your death, know that this is the reason I have brought you here. I was afraid to tell you before now. But take heart: Your death will be a remarkable one. The angels themselves have come to wait upon you."

But Aaron cried, "Why didn't you tell me before, Moses, so that I could bid farewell to my mother, my wife, and my children?"

Moses tried to comfort him. "You almost died forty years ago when you allowed the people to worship the Golden Calf, but I pleaded for your life then, and God granted you these additional forty years. Now I envy you your death, Aaron, for when you die, I will bury you, but I will have no brother to bury me. And when you die, your sons will inherit your priesthood, but strangers will inherit my place."

And Aaron was comforted by his brother's words.

Aaron now lay down upon the couch. Then the *Shekhinah* descended and kissed him, and his soul departed. When Moses left the cave, it vanished at once so that no one would know the place where Aaron had died.

When Eleazar saw Moses descending alone, he cried out, "O my teacher, where is my father?"

And Moses replied, "He has entered Paradise."

When they came down the mountain and the people saw that Aaron was not with them, they cried, "Where is Aaron?"

And Moses told them that he was dead.

But they did not believe him. Some thought that Moses had killed him because he envied Aaron's greater popularity with the people. Others thought that Eleazar had killed his father to inherit the priesthood. And others thought he had been taken alive to heaven. Then Satan stirred up the evil urge within the people's hearts so that they wished to stone Moses and Eleazar.

Moses appealed to God for help. "Show them Aaron's coffin so that they will know that he is indeed dead, or they may even make a god of him."

So God commanded the angels, "Lift up Aaron's coffin!"

And the people saw Aaron's coffin floating midway between heaven and earth, and God and the angels sang lamentations over it.

All Israel mourned for Aaron for thirty days, for the people had loved him dearly.

63

The Giant Og

The giant Og was the son of Shemhazael, one of the fallen angels. When the great Flood covered the earth, he persuaded Noah to let him ride on the roof of the ark and to feed him each day through a hole in the roof. In return for this favor, Og promised to serve Noah and his descendants forever. And later Noah's descendant Nimrod gave Og, whose other name was Eliezer, to Abraham as a present when Abraham escaped the fiery furnace.

Never in his life did Og use a wooden chair or bed,

for he would have broken them with his huge body. Only iron chairs and beds could hold him. Daily the giant devoured a thousand oxen or other animals and drank a thousand measures of water or wine. Once when Abraham scolded him harshly, Og became so frightened that one of his teeth fell out, and Abraham made the tooth into an ivory bed for himself.

When Og was eight hundred years old, Moses and the Children of Israel met him in battle at Edrei. Moses was afraid to fight Og, for he said, "I am only one hundred and twenty years old, and Og is eight hundred. How could he have attained such an old age if not for his good deeds? How can I possibly defeat him?"

But God reassured Moses. "He will be like a green leaf in your hand. I have already decreed his downfall, for he once lusted after Sarah, to make her his wife, and he later cast an evil eye upon Jacob and his family when they arrived in Egypt. It is time for him to meet his end."

When Og discovered the Israelite camp outside the city of Edrei, he said to himself, "I shall tear up a mountain and throw it at them and crush them." And he pulled up a mountain three miles wide and put it upon his head and came marching toward the Israelite camp.

When Moses saw the sun grow dark—for the mountain blotted out the sun—he feared that the people of Edrei had built high stone walls overnight around their city. But then he saw Og approaching with a huge mountain balanced atop his head.

Then God sent an army of ants to drill a hole into the mountain so that it slipped down around the giant's neck and was caught fast by the huge tusks protruding from his mouth. And while Og struggled and bellowed with blind rage, Moses took an ax and leapt twenty feet into the air and struck Og in the ankle so that he fell down and died.

All of Og's lands fell to the Children of Israel without another blow.

Years later, a hunter chased a stag three miles

through a cave until the animal fell to his arrows. When he emerged from the cave, he discovered that it was not a cave at all but rather the thighbone of Og, King of Bashan, the last giant on earth.

64

Balak and Balaam

After the Children of Israel had defeated the giant Og, they came to Moab and camped there. When Balak, King of Moab, saw their vast numbers and heard what they had done to Og and his brother Sihon, he was terrified for his own kingdom.

Now Balak was a great magician. Whenever he wanted to perform magic, he consulted a special bird he had made. Its feet, body, and head were made of gold, its mouth of silver, and its tongue came from the ancient Yadua bird. For seven days Balak would offer sacrifices to this magical bird, and then its tongue would begin to move. Then he would prick it with a golden needle, and it would utter terrible secrets and mysteries. But now as Israel approached Moab, a flame suddenly leapt up and burned the golden wings of the bird. Thus Balak knew that disaster was in store for his kingdom.

So he sent messengers to Midian, where Moses had once dwelled, and asked them, "What is the secret of this man's strength?"

And the Midianites replied, "His mouth."

So they decided to seek out a man whose strength was also in his mouth, and set him against Moses. That man was Balaam, the greatest and last of the heathen prophets, grandson of Laban, who had long been an enemy of Israel. Balaam's name meant "devourer of nations," and he did indeed use his sorcery to curse and defeat kings and princes.

Balak first sent several elders to Moab and Midian to Balaam to request that he come to Moab to curse Israel.

But Balaam said to them, "Stay with me overnight, and I will consult God to see what I am to do."

God appeared to Balaam that night and asked him, "Who are these men with you?"

In asking this question, God was testing Balaam as Cain had once been tested. For when Cain killed his brother, God had asked him, "Where is your brother Abel?" And instead of answering, "O God, all is known to You. Why then do You ask me?" Cain had replied, "I do not know. Am I my brother's keeper?"

Balaam also failed the test, for instead of answering God's question, "All is known to You. Why then do You ask me?" he boasted, "Even though You have not made me famous in the world, still kings come to ask my help. See, Balak, King of Moab, has sent for me to curse Israel!"

Balaam's arrogant reply angered God. "Those whom you wish to curse will instead be blessed by you. Israel is the apple of my eye, and you wish to curse it! Now your own eye shall be blinded!" and Balaam immediately lost sight in one eye.

The next morning Balaam sent Balak's messengers away, saying, "You are not distinguished enough to be ambassadors to someone like me." For he hoped that his answer would insult Balak so that he would send no more messengers, because Balaam now understood that he could not curse Israel, and he knew that he might be humiliated if he tried.

But Balak did not take offense at Balaam's answer, and instead sent back even more noble messengers. And again Balaam asked them to stay overnight while he sought God's counsel, saying, "Even if Balak were to give me a house full of silver and gold, I can only do what God commands me."

This time God told Balaam, "Go with these men, but you will speak only words that I put in your mouth."

So Balaam rose the next day, thinking that he now had God's permission to curse Israel and reap a great reward from Balak. He saddled his ass and started on his way.

This was no ordinary ass that Balaam rode, for it had been created at twilight on the sixth day of Creation, along with the other miracles. Jacob gave the ass to Balaam as a bribe so that he would not give wicked advice to Pharaoh in whose court he served as a magician. But Balaam did give evil counsel to Pharaoh, urging him to make the Israelite slaves make bricks for his treasure-cities, and he later urged Amalek to attack the Israelites from the rear. So wicked was Balaam that even the Angel of Mercy turned against him, and now, as Balaam rode to meet Balak, it was this angel who appeared to his ass and blocked her way with a drawn sword. But to Balaam, the angel remained invisible.

Three times the ass refused to advance against the angel, and three times Balaam beat her, for he did not see the angel or his sword. Finally the ass lay down in the road and refused to move another step, and Balaam continued to beat her until God opened the ass's mouth, and she said to her master, "What have I done to you that you have beaten me three times?"

Balaam replied, "You have mocked me! If only I had a sword in my hand, I would kill you!"

"If you cannot even kill one ass without a sword," answered the ass, "how do you expect to defeat an entire people with only your mouth?"

And Balaam could not answer her.

Then the ass said to him, "Am I not your beloved ass whom you have known as intimately as a man knows his wife?"

Then God opened Balaam's eyes and he saw the Angel of Mercy standing before him, and he fell down on his face in fear.

"Why have you beaten your ass three times, Balaam, for if she hadn't turned aside when she saw my sword, I would surely have killed you! You are now free to go on your way, but you will only speak the words that I put in your mouth."

When the ass had finished speaking, she died, for God did not wish the heathens to worship her as a god. And God also wished to spare Balaam the disgrace of having people point to his ass and say, "This creature got the better of the prophet Balaam!"

When Balaam at last arrived in Moab, Balak greeted him and said, "Here is this people Israel that covers the face of the land. Curse them now, that my armies might defeat them!"

First the king sacrificed many oxen and sheep on the altars he erected. Then Balaam and Balak went up to the mountain and looked out over the multitude of Israel.

Balaam drew upon all his magical arts to curse Israel. He was the only magician on earth who could pinpoint the precise moment in time, lasting only for a fraction of a second, when God grows angry each day, during the third hour of the morning when the pagan kings worship the sun. And he alone knew how to read the sign of its occurrence, when the red rooster's comb turns white.

But so great is God's love for Israel that on this one day, God did not become angry for even this brief moment, so that Balaam was not able to saddle his curse to God's wrath.

Then Balaam tried to gain God's consent for his curse by offering sacrifices on the many altars Balak had erected, but God rejected his offerings, saying, "Better is a dry crust and peacefulness than a house full of fatted lambs and discord." But Balaam was not easily put off, and he offered still more sacrifices.

Then God rebuked him. "Balaam, enough! Don't you understand that I prefer a dinner of grass where love is found to all your oxen where hatred reigns? Sweeter to Me were the *matzah* and bitter herbs of the freed slaves than all these sacrifices you offer to Me with gall in your heart!"

Then God caused an angel to lodge in Balaam's throat so that only blessings could come out of his mouth. Three more times Balaam tried to curse the Children of Israel, but each time the angel put only words of praise on his tongue. "How good are your tents, O Jacob! Your dwelling places, O Israel! Blessed be everyone who blesses you, and cursed be everyone who curses you!"

And God endowed Balaam's voice with extraordinary

power on that day so that every inhabitant of the earth heard his praise for Israel. Not only did he bless Israel, but he also foretold the future kingdom of David and the End of Days. And when he finished speaking, the spirit of prophecy deserted Balaam, and he fell from the rank of prophet to lowly sorcerer.

When Balaam saw that he could not prevail against Israel by his words, he devised a different strategy to defeat them. He advised Balak to erect tents near the Israelite camp, and to seat old women in their doorways to sell linen garments to the Israelites. And the old women lured the men inside the tents, where the young women of Moab awaited them, adorned and perfumed. The Israelites became drunk and slept with these women and worshiped their gods. Then God sent a plague, and twenty-four thousand Israelites died.

Thus Balaam at last succeeded in cursing Israel.

But Balaam met his end soon after, for when Israel met the Midianites in battle, Balaam tried to escape by flying up into the air behind a cloud, but Zaliah the Danite, himself a master of sorcery, flew up after him and killed him with a sword engraved with a serpent on both sides and bearing the words, "Kill him with that to which he belongs." So Balaam died by the sword.

His corpse was not buried but rotted on the ground where it fell, and out of the worm-eaten bones emerged poisonous snakes, which magicians used for enchantments. Only Solomon knew how to reverse these enchantments, and he later imparted these secrets to the Queen of Sheba. But with their deaths the secrets disappeared.

65

Moses Resists His Fate

When Israel was ready to enter the Promised Land, Moses thought to himself, "Now God will reverse my fate, for how many times have the people sinned and been forgiven! Surely, God will allow me to enter the land with my people and will not have me die on this side of the Jordan!"

God was not pleased by Moses' presumption and at that moment sealed his doom. But when Moses heard that his death was imminent, he tore his clothes, sat down in the ashes, and prayed fifteen hundred prayers for mercy. Then he drew a circle around himself and announced, "I will not budge from this spot until God suspends the judgment upon me."

Then heaven and earth trembled, for they feared that the world was about to be destroyed because of Moses' threat. But a heavenly voice declared, "I hold the souls of all living things in my hand, even that of Moses. And his time has come to die."

God commanded the herald angel Akraziel to lock all the heavenly gates so that not one of Moses' prayers could get through, and all the angels were forbidden to carry his prayers heavenward. Moses' prayer rose up on its own, slashing and tearing like a sword, borne by the power of the Holy Name, but even it could not penetrate the heavens, since God's command had shut them up.

Then Moses pleaded with God to annul the decree of his death. "Where is Your sense of fairness? You owe me wages for forty years of labor. Did I not do Your bidding in Egypt and then in the wilderness?"

But God did not answer him.

Then Moses said, "Where is Your mercy? When the people sinned with the Golden Calf, You wanted to destroy them, but I pleaded with You to spare them, and You did. Spare me now!"

But God did not answer him.

Then Moses said, "It was through me that You performed Your miracles, splitting the Sea of Reeds, giving the Torah to Israel, raining down manna from heaven. If You let me live, I will proclaim Your greatness to the next generation and keep the people from sin."

And finally God spoke. "If you live, the people will make a god of you and worship you."

But Moses protested, "Once before You tested me

with the Golden Calf, and at that time I prevented the people from worshiping idols. I would do so again if they worshiped me. Why then must I die?"

Then God said, "Whose son are you, Moses?"

"Amram's son."

"Whose son was he?"

"Izhar's son."

"And whose son was he?"

"Kehat's son."

"And whose son was he?"

"Levi's son."

"And from whom did they all descend?"

"From Adam and Eve."

"And what happened to all of them?"

"They died."

Then God asked Moses, "Why, then, do you wish to have a different fate from theirs?"

Moses replied, "Adam and Eve stole the forbidden fruit and ate it. But what did I ever steal from You?"

God said, "Did I tell you to kill the Egyptian?"

"You killed all the first-born of Egypt! Shall I die for killing a single Egyptian?"

God grew angry and said to Moses, "Are you My equal? I kill and restore to life, but can you revive the dead?"

Then God took pity on Moses and tried to comfort him about his approaching death. "Think of all the honors I have bestowed upon you, Moses! I reversed the order of nature for your sake, raining down bread from the sky and causing water to sprout from the earth. I spared Israel by your word. I named the Torah after you, calling it 'the Five Books of Moses.' I hid you in the cleft of the rock and showed you my Glory. Through you I gave Israel the Ten Commandments and the Sabbath and the law of circumcision. Through you I brought Israel out of slavery. I made you unique in the world."

And Moses was comforted by God's words. But still he begged to be allowed to cross the Jordan.

Then God grew impatient with him. "Speak no more

to Me about this! It is better that you die here, Moses, for if you were to enter the land, you would be buried by human hands in a coffin and tomb fashioned by human hands. But if you die here, My hands will fashion the coffin and tomb, and My hands will bury ou."

Seeing that God could not be swayed, Moses turned to the Earth to intercede on his behalf. But the Earth refused. "No, your fate is like mine, for 'you are dust, and to dust you shall return.' "

Moses then went to the Heavens, but the Heavens also refused. "I cannot help you, for 'the heavens shall vanish away like smoke.' "

So it was with the Sun and the Moon, the Stars and the Planets, the Hills and the Mountains, the Rivers and the Deserts. They were all powerless to prevail against God's will, for they were all subject to the heavenly decree.

Then Moses appealed to human intercessors: Joshua and Eleazar and Caleb. But Samael interfered with their prayers and snatched them away before they could ascend to heaven. And they came weeping to Moses, "We cannot pray for you, for Samael has closed up our mouths."

Then Moses appealed to the Children of Israel to pray for him. "Over and over, I have saved you from God's wrath. Return the favor now, I beg of you, and save me from death."

But when the people began to pray, God sent one hundred and eighty-four thousand angels, led by Zakun and Lahash, to seize their words so they could not reach the Divine Throne. But Lahash was filled with compassion for Moses and tried to release the people's words so that they could fly up to God. Then Samael bound the angel with chains of fire and brought him to the Divine Throne, and God expelled him from the inner heaven for disobedience.

Brokenhearted, the people came to Moses and said, "The angels will not let us pray for you."

Then Moses began to weep, and God grew very

angry with him because he would not accept his fate. Then Moses prayed, "*Adonai, Adonai,* a God full of compassion and grace, slow to anger, and full of mercy and truth, forgiving wickedness and error and sin."

And God's anger melted, and with a voice full of kindness, God said to Moses, "I have made two vows, Moses, that you are to die and that Israel is to be destroyed. I can only cancel one of these vows. If you are to live, Israel must die."

Moses cried out, "What a crafty God You are! Of course, I must choose my own death over that of the whole house of Israel!"

God now asked Moses, "Why are you so afraid to die?"

"I fear the sword of the Angel of Death."

God said to him, "I will not deliver you into his hand."

Then Moses at last accepted his fate and argued no more with God.

66

Only a Glimpse of the Promised Land

On the seventh day of Adar, a voice declared out of the heavens, "Moses, you have only one more day to live!"

Moses set to work writing thirteen Torah scrolls, one for each tribe and one for the Holy Ark, for he thought that he could escape death that way, since the Torah is a tree of life to all who hold fast to it. Surely, he thought, the sun will set before I finish my task, and thus my fate will be averted.

But the sun declared, "I will not set as long as Moses lives!"

And indeed, by the time Moses finished writing the thirteenth scroll, not even half the day had passed.

Moses then gathered all the people together and gave them the Torahs and urged them to follow God's laws faithfully. Then he summoned Joshua and clothed him in a purple robe, set a crown of pearls upon his head, and seated him on a golden throne. And Joshua addressed the people and sang praises to God.

When Joshua finished speaking, a voice rang out of heaven, "Moses, you have only five more hours to live!"

Then Moses read out of the Torah he had written, and Joshua explained it to the people. And Joshua's face shone like the moon, but Moses' shone like the sun.

When they were finished speaking, a voice rang out of heaven a second time, "Moses, you have only four more hours to live!"

Then Moses became alarmed and began to plead with God, "Turn me into a bird that I might fly across the Jordan, or make me a fish, changing my two arms into fins and my hair into scales, so that I might leap across the Jordan and see the land of Israel."

But God answered, "If I were to do that, I would be breaking My vow."

"Then let me hang from a cloud and see the land below me."

"That would still be breaking My vow."

"Then cut me limb from limb and throw me piecemeal across the river and revive me on the other side so that I might see the land."

"That too would mean breaking My vow."

"Then at least let me *see* the land before I die."

And God said, "You may have your wish."

So God led Moses to the top of Mount Nebo, which is also called Mount Avarim and Mount Hor and Mount Pisgah, and showed him the land. God gave Moses extraordinary powers of vision so that he could see from one end of the country to the other, and from the beginning of time to the end. And that day Moses saw the whole history of Israel unfold before him: the conquest of the land under Joshua, and defeat of the Philistines at the hand of Samson, the reign of David, Solomon's Temple built and destroyed, the Exile and the Return. And God took Moses up to heaven to show him the heavenly Jerusalem. And there he met the Messiah.

Moses asked him, "When will this heavenly city descend to earth?"

The Messiah answered him, "God has made this known to no one."

"Can I not at least see a sign?"

God answered him, "First I shall scatter Israel over all the earth as a shovel scatters the dust, and then I will gather them in. And that is when the heavenly Temple will descend to earth."

Then Moses was overjoyed and went back down to the mountain to meet his fate. And the Angel of Death followed after him, but Moses refused to give up his soul to anyone but God, since that was the bargain they had struck. And he waited patiently upon the mountaintop for God to come for him.

67
The Kiss of the Shekhinah

When God saw that Moses was prepared to die, God sent the angel Gabriel to bring his soul to heaven. But Gabriel refused and said, "How can I presume to take a soul that outweighs six hundred thousand mortals?"

Then God ordered Moses' guardian angel Michael to bring him Moses' soul, but he also refused. And Zagzagel, Moses' heavenly teacher, likewise refused.

Then Samael came to God and said, "Is Moses greater than Adam, who was created in Your image? Or than Abraham, who let himself be cast into a fiery furnace for Your name's sake? Or than Isaac, who laid himself upon the altar as a sacrifice? Or than Jacob and his twelve sons? Not one of them escaped my sword. Give me permission to fetch Moses' soul!"

And God replied, "From which part of him will you extract his soul? From the face who saw My face? From the hands that received the Torah? From the feet that touched My Cloud of Glory?"

But Samael would not be denied. "I will do it whichever way I will do it. Only let me try!"

And God said, "You have My permission to try."

So Samael flew off to take Moses' soul. In his hand he wielded his flashing sword, and his body was robed in cruelty and wrath. With a face terrible to behold, he now approached Moses, who was at that moment at work writing the Holy Name. Darts of flame shot from Moses' mouth, and his face shone like the sun. When Samael saw him, he was seized with fear, and his eyes grew dim because of the radiance lighting up Moses's face. His body was suddenly wracked with pain like a woman in labor.

Moses said to him, "Samael! God says that there is no peace for the wicked. Leave me at once, or I will chop off your head!"

"Why are you angry with me, Moses? Give me your soul, for your time has come."

"Who sent you?"

"The One who created all souls."

"I will not give it to you!"

And Samael said, "Since the creation of the world, all souls have been given into my hands."

Moses said, "I am greater than all souls who came before!"

"How is that possible?"

And Moses said, "I came forth circumcised from my mother's womb. At the age of three days I walked and talked. When I was three months old I prophesied that I would receive the Torah from God's own hand. At the age of six months I snatched the crown from Pharaoh's head. When I was eighty I brought ten plagues upon Egypt and led Israel out of bondage and split the Sea of Reeds. I spent one hundred and twenty days upon Mount Sinai like an angel, neither eating nor drinking, and there received the tablets of the Law. I killed the giants Sihon and Og. How dare you presume to claim my pure soul? Go away, for I will not give it to you!"

And Samael fled in terror and reported to God what Moses had said.

Then God bellowed at him, "Go back and fetch Me Moses' soul or I will give your job to someone else!"

And Samael said, "I cannot!"

"Why not?"

"Lightning and fiery darts shoot from his mouth. I cannot stand before him!"

"Go back and bring Me his soul! How happy you were at first to take on this task, but now that you see how great this man is, you are afraid. Do not come back to Me without his soul!"

So Samael drew his sword and in a fierce rage flew again to Moses, saying, "Either I will kill him or he will kill me."

When Moses saw him coming, he lifted up his rod with the Holy Name engraved on it and drove Samael away. And as Samael fled, Moses pursued him and struck him with the rod and blinded him with the radiance of his face. And he would have killed him, but a voice now thundered out of the heavens, "Let him live, Moses, for the world needs him." So Moses let him go.

Then the same voice declared, "Moses, your last second is at hand!"

Moses cried, "My God, in love You created the world and in love You guide it. Treat me also with love and deliver me not into the hands of the Angel of Death!"

God replied, "Do not fear. I Myself will bury you."

Then God descended with three angels, Michael, Gabriel, and Zagzagel. Gabriel arranged Moses' couch, Michael spread a purple cloth upon it, and Zagzagel laid down a pillow for his head.

Then God said to Moses, "Cross your feet, fold your hands across your breast, and close your eyes."

And Moses did as God commanded.

Then God spoke to Moses' soul. "My daughter, for

one hundred and twenty years, you have dwelled in this righteous man's body. Now it is time to leave it and come to Me."

But the soul replied, "Is there a body so pure in all the world? In all this time not even a fly has rested upon it! I love this body and have no wish to leave it."

"Do not regret leaving it, my daughter, for I will take you to My Heavenly Throne, and you will sit beside Me."

"No, *Adonai*, I wish to remain with this righteous man. Ever since You revealed yourself to Moses at the Burning Bush, he has lived apart from his wife so that he could devote himself entirely to Your service."

And when Moses saw that his soul was reluctant to leave him, he himself gave her permission to depart and she did. Then the *Shekhinah* kissed Moses upon the mouth, and he died.

To this day no one knows where Moses is buried. God laid his body to rest atop Mount Nebo, where Aaron and Miriam died before him. An underground passage leads from his grave to the Cave of Machpelah, where the bodies of the Patriarchs and Matriarchs lie. And to this day, Moses' body has shown no signs of decay, so that it is as pure and whole as on the day he died.

68
The Death of Moses — An Ethiopian Tale

When Moses first led the Children of Israel into the wilderness, he asked God to tell him when he would die.

God said, "On a Friday."

So every Friday Moses put on his funeral shroud and waited for the Angel of Death. But many years passed, and the Angel of Death never came. So Moses forgot all about God's warning, and in time reached the age of one hundred and twenty years.

One Friday when he went to pray on Mount Sinai, a young man greeted him in a strange voice. "Peace unto you, Moses!"

Moses was frightened by the youth's eerie voice and he asked, "Who are you?"

"I am Suriel, the Angel of Death. I have come to take your soul."

Moses pleaded with him, "Give me only a few more hours to say farewell to my family."

And Suriel said, "As you wish."

So Moses hurried down the mountain and came into the Israelite camp. For a moment he hesitated, unable to decide whether to go first to his mother or to his wife. Then a heavenly voice said, "Go first to your mother Yokheved."

So Moses went to the aged Yokheved's tent and embraced her and kissed her goodbye. Then he went to his wife Zipporah's tent, and he told her and his two sons that he was about to die. And they wept so bitterly that Moses too began to cry.

God asked him, "Are you crying because you do not want to die or because you fear death?"

Moses replied, "My father Amram is dead and so are my father-in-law Jethro and my brother Aaron. Who then will take care of my widow and orphans?"

God said, "Have you forgotten how I took care of you when your mother cast you adrift on the Nile? I will also watch over your children."

Then God said, "Stretch out your rod over the Sea of Reeds and divide it."

Moses did as God had commanded him, and a huge stone rolled out of the sea. He then split the stone with his rod, and two worms crawled out, one small and one large. The small worm said, "Praised be God, who has not forgotten me at the bottom of the sea!"

Then God said to Moses, "Behold! If I have not forgotten this little worm at the bottom of the sea, neither will I forget your children!"

Moses then left his tent and went walking, and he

came upon three angels, disguised as young men, digging a grave.

"For whom are you digging this grave?" asked Moses.

"For the beloved of God."

"Then I will help you," said Moses, and he picked up a shovel and began to dig.

Then the angels said, "We don't know whether the grave is big enough. Would you go down into it? The person who will be buried here is about your size."

So Moses jumped down into the grave, where he met Suriel, the Angel of Death.

"Peace to you, Moses, son of Amram and Yokheved!"

And Moses answered, "Peace to you!" And then he died.

And the angels buried him in the grave, whose whereabouts remain a secret to this very day.

PART IV

IN THE DAYS OF THE JUDGES

When the Israelites entered Canaan, they faced
hostile enemies without and moral frailties
within. Without a central leader to unite them,
they often strayed after foreign gods or fell prey
to foreign swords. But occasionally leaders arose
to deliver them. These were the judges, who
guided the people until Saul was crowned king.

69

The Birth of Joshua

Once a saintly couple dwelled in Jerusalem, and they had no children. They prayed for a child, and God heard their prayers. But after the woman conceived, her husband continued to weep and to fast day and night.

His wife said to him, "Why do you weep and fast when we are about to have a child? You should rejoice and give thanks to God who has answered our prayers!"

Then her husband confessed to her that God had spoken to him in a dream and told him that this son who was about to be born to them would one day cut off his father's head.

The woman gave birth to a son, and she called him Joshua. She took the baby and put him in a little ark smeared with pitch and set him adrift on the sea. And God sent a great fish to swallow up the ark with the baby inside.

Not long after this, the Pharaoh made a great feast and invited all his ministers and servants. A fisherman caught the fish that had swallowed the little ark and gave the fish to Pharaoh as a gift. When they cut it open, they were surprised to find inside a little boy, crying. Then Pharaoh summoned a wet nurse to suckle the child, and he was raised in the court of Egypt. When he was grown, Pharaoh appointed him chief executioner.

Now it came to pass that Joshua's father broke one of the Pharaoh's laws and was condemned to death. They brought him before the chief executioner, who cut off his head. Then they gave the executioner the dead man's wife as a bride, as was the custom in those times.

But when Joshua came into his mother's bedroom, the strangest thing happened: Milk flowed from the woman's nipples and filled up the whole bed. Joshua reached for his lance to kill her, for he was convinced that she was a witch. But she remembered her husband's prophecy from long ago and cried out to him, "I am not a witch, but your own mother who suckled you with these very breasts!" And she told him of his father's prophecy and of the ark she had placed him in as an infant.

Then Joshua remembered the tale he had heard of how he was rescued from the belly of a great fish, and he threw down his lance in grief and begged her forgiveness. And he atoned for the killing of his father and abandoned his old ways.

That is why he is called Joshua *"bin Nun,"* which means "son of the fish" in Aramaic. But the spies with whom he later entered Canaan called him "the beheaded one," both because of his former name, Hoshea, which lacked the *yud* at its head and was thus cut off, and also because he cut off his own father's head while he was Pharaoh's executioner in Egypt.

70
The Battle of Jericho

When the Children of Israel were ready to enter the Promised Land, Joshua sent two spies to scout out the land. To make sure that these spies did not fail him as the ten spies had failed Moses forty years earlier, he sent his trusted friend Caleb and the priest Pinkhas, grandson of Aaron. Accompanying them were two demons who had offered their services to Joshua but had been refused. Not to be put off, they had secretly entered the bodies of Caleb and Pinkhas and had transformed the two men into monsters so frightful that they terrified all the inhabitants of Jericho.

In Jericho, Caleb and Pinkhas found shelter at the inn of Rahab, a woman who had formerly been one of the greatest sinners in that city. But when she heard that the Israelites were at the borders of Canaan, she had converted to the Israelite faith and had begun to worship God and repent of her former ways. In reward for her piety, she later became the wife of Joshua and the ancestor of Jeremiah, Ezekiel, Huldah, and six other prophets.

When the king's soldiers came to search Rahab's house, looking for the spies, Pinkhas said to her, "Do not fear. I am a priest, and God's priests are like angels, visible when they wish to be seen, invisible when they do not." So Rahab hid Caleb, but Pinkhas remained in plain view. And although the soldiers several times came face to face with Pinkhas, they never saw him.

In gratitude for her help, the spies promised to spare Rahab and her family when the Israelites captured Jericho. They told her to tie a red cord in her window to identify her dwelling. Then she lowered them down by a rope, and they brought their report back to Joshua.

Joshua then gathered the people and led them to the banks of the Jordan River. As soon as the Levites bearing the Ark of the Covenant set foot in the water, the waters piled up on either side of them in walls three hundred miles high, and the Children of Israel passed through on dry land. The ark remained in the riverbed until all the people had crossed over. Then a miracle occurred, and the ark moved on its own to the other side, dragging the Levites after it.

When they reached the city of Jericho, Joshua commanded the people to march around the walls once each day for six days, while the Levites blew their *shofarot*. On the seventh day they were to march around Jericho seven times, with the Levites blowing their *shofarot*. And on the last circuit, the people were to shout a great shout.

They did just as Joshua commanded. And when they shouted after the seventh circuit on the seventh day, the walls of the city trembled and groaned and came tumbling down with a great thundering sound, and then they plunged into the earth all the way down to farthest Sheol.

And thus began the conquest of the land under the leadership of Joshua bin Nun.

71

Joshua's Last War

When Joshua and the people of Israel had conquered all of the land of Canaan, Shobakh, King of Armenia, united the forty-five kings of Persia and Media and prepared to wage war against Israel.

Shobakh sent a messenger to Joshua with a letter that said: "Greetings from the kings of Armenia, Persia, and Media to Joshua! You are a ravaging wolf who has destroyed our land, killed the thirty-one kings of Canaan, and turned our cities into a wasteland! We have vowed to seek revenge! In thirty days we will come to meet you in battle, each of us bringing an army of sixty thousand warriors armed with arrows and swords, and we will utterly destroy you!"

Joshua sent back the following reply: "Fools! In the name of the Lord of Hosts, who destroys the wicked and upholds the righteous, who performed miracles in Egypt and split the waters of the Sea of Reeds, I declare that we will meet you in battle and annihilate you from the face of the earth. God knows that you carry evil within your hearts and that you bow down to idols that are full of emptiness and vanity. God will surely deliver you into our hands!"

The messenger took Joshua's letter back to Shobakh and his allies, and they were terrified by his words.

Then Shobakh summoned all his wise men and magicians, including his mother, who was a powerful witch, and said to them, "Is this a foolish thing we are about to do? Will we be utterly destroyed?"

Shobakh's mother told her son, "Have no fear of this people Israel! Come see what your mother will do to them!"

Meanwhile, Joshua gathered twelve thousand men, and they marched out to meet Shobakh's armies at the Oak of Dread in Kimon. And Shobakh's mother cast a spell upon the Israelite army so that they all became bound to the oak and could not move. Then she conjured up seven iron walls around them to hem them in.

Joshua prayed to God, "O God! Remember the merits of Abraham and Jacob and Moses, and save us now!"

Then a dove fluttered down and landed next to Joshua. Joshua wrote a letter to his cousin Nobah, king of the two-and-half tribes of Israel who had settled on the east bank of the Jordan, and he asked Nobah to come to his aid. He put the letter in the dove's mouth, and she flew off with it toward the east.

When Nobah received Joshua's letter, he called all the men of Reuben, Gad, and half the tribe of Manasheh and told them of Joshua's plight. He also summoned the priest Pinkhas, grandson of Aaron, to come with his trumpets. And they marched swiftly against Shobakh's forces.

Then Shobakh's mother declared that she saw a star rise out of the east that would defeat all her magic arts. And when she told this to her son, Shobakh threw his mother off the wall and went out to meet Nobah's army.

When Nobah's army neared the Oak of Dread, Pinkhas blew a mighty blast upon his trumpet, and the seven iron walls came crashing to the ground. Then the two Israelite armies came together and went out to meet their enemies and prevailed against them that day. Nobah killed Shobakh, King of Armenia. And soon all forty-five kings fell into Israel's hands.

72

Yael and Sisera

The Children of Israel settled in the land of Canaan. And in time they forgot what Moses had taught them in the wilderness, and they began to stray after false gods and evil ways. So God sent an enemy against them.

This enemy was Jabin, King of Hazor, who oppressed them terribly. But even worse than Jabin was his general Sisera, a mighty giant who had conquered the whole world by the time he was thirty. So powerful was his voice that one shout would topple stone walls and root wild beasts to the ground in terror. When he took a bath in the river, enough fish became tangled in his beard to feed an army, and it took nine hundred horses to pull his chariot.

But even though God sent Sisera to chastise Israel, God also had compassion on them and sent a redeemer for Israel. This was Deborah, judge and prophet. Before God chose her for her special task, Deborah used to make candles for the divine service in the sanctuary. It was her custom to make the wicks as thick as possible so that the light would last as long as possible.

God said to her, "Because you have wished to bring light to My house, I will spread your light throughout the land."

So Deborah became a judge in Israel, and people came from far and wide to hear her wisdom.

Deborah summoned her husband Barak and said to him, "God has commanded you to take ten thousand men from the tribes of Naftali and Zevulun and to march to Mount Tabor, where you will meet Sisera in battle. God will deliver Sisera's army into your hands."

"If you will go with me," said Barak, "I will go. If not, I will not go."

So on the first night of Passover, Deborah girded herself for battle and went out with Barak's troops to meet the enemy by the River Kishon. And Sisera brought his nine hundred iron chariots to the river and prepared to do battle.

Deborah said to Barak, "The Lord is marching before you! Go down the mountain and destroy Sisera!"

So Barak and his ten thousand men charged down Mount Tabor and routed Sisera's army. The enemy troops were seized with panic and fled on foot. And Barak's soldiers pursued them and killed every one of them, except Sisera, who escaped on horseback.

Sisera came to the tent of Yael, whose husband was Hever the Kenite, a friend of King Jabin. And he asked for asylum there.

Now Yael was extraordinarily beautiful, and her voice was the most seductive voice ever possessed by a woman. And she had adorned herself in beguiling robes and precious jewels to bewitch Sisera.

She welcomed Sisera. "Come in and eat, and then sleep until evening, to refresh yourself after battle. And this evening I will satisfy your hunger even more."

Then Sisera decided that he would take this woman home as his wife as soon as all danger was past.

He said to her, "I thirst for milk."

So she went out to milk her goat. And while she was milking, she prayed to God, "Show me a sign that You will now help me. If Sisera wakes up and asks for water when I go back into the tent, I will know that You are with me."

When she went back into the tent, Sisera awoke and begged for water. And Yael gave him water mixed with wine, and he fell back into a heavy sleep.

Then she took a tent spike in her hand and again prayed to God, "Show me a second sign. If Sisera does not wake up when I drag him out of bed, then I will know that You will deliver him into my hand."

She dragged his huge body onto the floor, but he did not wake up. Then she prayed to God a third time, "Strengthen my arm, O God, for the sake of Your people!"

Then she took a hammer and drove the tent spike into Sisera's temple. As he died, he cried, "O that I should die by the hand of a woman!"

Then Barak came to Yael's tent, and she showed him the corpse of Sisera. Barak sent it to Sisera's mother Temakh, whose name means "may she be destroyed." And he sent this message with the body: "Here is your son, whom you expected to return laden down with spoils!"

Now Temakh was a sorceress. Before Sisera had set out for battle, Temakh had consulted her oracles and had seen a vision of her son lying in a Jewish woman's bed. But she had misinterpreted the vision, thinking that Sisera and his soldiers would take many women captives. Instead, a woman had taken him captive and blotted out his life.

Deborah ruled Israel for forty years, and all this time there was peace in the land.

73

Gideon

After Deborah died, the Israelites slipped back into idolatry. The person most responsible for their sin was a Midianite sorceror named Aud who made the sun shine at midnight and thus convinced the Israelites that Midian's gods were more powerful than their own. So they turned to Baal and other idols, and even worshiped their own images reflected in water.

Then God punished them by sending Midian to oppress them. The people took refuge in mountain caves to escape from their enemy. But while they were hiding there, the Midianites, the Amalekites, and the Kedemites swooped down upon the land and destroyed the Israelites' crops and herds, so that the people were left with nothing.

On the first night of Passover, Gideon of the tribe of Manasheh cried out to God, "Where are all the miracles that You performed in Egypt, redeeming our ancestors from slavery?"

And God answered Gideon, "I have chosen you to redeem Israel now!"

Why did God choose Gideon? All because Gideon was a good son. While the Midianites ravaged the land, his father was afraid to thresh the barley in his field, so Gideon used to do it for him. And because of this kindness to his father, God now chose Gideon to redeem Israel. Because Gideon had risked his life to save his father's barley, God later strengthened Gideon's heart through a barley loaf.

Soon after, an angel appeared to Gideon, and Gideon asked him for a sign to confirm that he was in truth going to redeem his people from Midian's hand. And the angel asked Gideon to pour water over a rock, and asked him to choose what the water would change into.

"Half fire and half blood," said Gideon.

When Gideon poured the water over the rock, half of the water turned into blood and half into fire, but the fire did not dry out the blood, nor did the blood put out the fire.

Then Gideon asked for another sign. He laid a fleece upon the ground, and said, "By morning, let the fleece be wet with dew, but the ground remain dry." And so it happened.

Then Gideon said to the angel, "Do not be angry with me if I ask for yet one more sign. Didn't Moses himself ask for several signs before going down to Egypt? I will lay the fleece down again, and this time let the ground be wet, but the fleece remain dry. If this comes to pass, then I will know that I am meant to lead my people to victory over Midian."

And everything happened exactly as Gideon had said.

Then Gideon broke down the altar to Baal and built a new altar on top of the rubble, and there he sacrificed a bull to God. Then he gathered thirty-two thousand men from the tribes of Asher, Zevulun, Naftali, and Manasheh to fight the Midianites.

But God said to him, "You have too many soldiers! The people might think that it was they themselves and not I who won this victory over the enemy. Send home all those who are afraid to fight."

And twenty-two thousand men left.

Then God said, "You still have too many troops. Tell them to go to the river to drink, and those who lap the water like dogs shall remain in your army. Those who kneel down to drink shall return to their homes." For God knew that the men who kneeled down at the riverside were still worshiping their own images reflected there and were not wholehearted in their faith.

All but three hundred knelt down to drink.

Then God said, "With these three hundred I will deliver Midian into your hands."

But Gideon was afraid to attack the enemy with so few soldiers. Then God said, "Sneak into the Midianite camp tonight and listen to what they say. It will give you the courage you need."

So Gideon stole into the enemy camp, which stretched out over the plain like the sands of a limitless shore, and eavesdropped at one of the tents. And he heard a man telling another man a dream he had had that night: "A loaf of barley was spinning through our camp like a whirlwind, and it struck one of the tents and flipped it upside down so that it collapsed."

And the other man said, "That can only mean that Gideon will soon defeat us in battle." For God had remembered Gideon's kindness to his old father.

Then Gideon's heart swelled with courage, and he returned to his camp and summoned his soldiers.

"God has given us victory!" he declared. "Every man

now take an empty jug and put a lit torch inside it. Then take a *shofar* and follow me. Do as I do, and Midian will fall into our hands."

Then they divided themselves into three columns of one hundred men and silently crept into the enemy camp. Then Gideon blew his *shofar* and broke his jug, and the rest did the same. And they shouted, "A sword for *Adonai* and for Gideon!"

The Midianites were so startled to see their camp suddenly lit up and to hear the noise of so many trumpets that they began attacking each other with their own swords and soon fled in panic. And Gideon and his men pursued the enemy and defeated them that day, and peace ruled the land for the next forty years.

74

Jephthah's Daughter

The next judge after Gideon was Jephthah.

Now the Ammonites waged war against Israel, and Jephthah led the people against the enemy. Before the battle, Jephthah vowed a vow to God. "If I am successful in this war, I promise to sacrifice the first thing that meets me on my safe return."

God was angry with Jephthah for making such a thoughtless vow. "The first thing that meets him! And what if that turns out to be a dog? Will he sacrifice a dog to Me? I shall punish him for his foolish vow by turning it against his first-born!"

That day Jephthah did win the battle against the Ammonites, and he returned home victorious.

Now Jephthah had a daughter, his only child. And when he returned home, she ran out to greet him, dancing and playing her harp.

When Jephthah saw her running out toward him, he cried out, "O my poor daughter! How fitting is the name

I gave you at your birth—'Sheilah,' the one who is demanded! But I have vowed a vow to God, and I cannot go back on my word."

Sheilah said to her father, "Why do you mourn my death, Father? Remember Abraham, who gladly went to sacrifice his only son Isaac on Mount Moriah, and Isaac, who consented with a joyous heart? Do what you have sworn to do. Only one favor do I ask of you before you fulfill your vow: Give me two months to go with my friends to the mountains to cry over my lost youth. And do not think that I mourn my own death, Father, but know that it is your careless vow I regret most of all. For when you made it, you were not thinking of me, your only daughter, but of some dumb beast. Therefore, I fear that God will not consider me an acceptable sacrifice and that my death will be in vain."

Then Sheilah called her companions and prepared for her death. But before she left home, she decided to ask the sages of her people if what she was doing was according to the Torah, for she suspected that it was not. Did not the Torah allow only animal sacrifices? Hadn't God stayed Abraham's knife? But the sages all agreed that Jephthah must do as he had sworn. For they had all forgotten the Law.

Only one man could have proven Jephthah wrong, and that was Pinkhas the high priest. But Pinkhas refused to lower himself to go to an ignoramus like Jephthah, and the princely Jephthah refused to bow to the authority of Pinkhas. Their petty rivalry cost Sheilah her life. But God punished them for their pride. Jephthah died a horrible death, being dismembered limb by limb. And from that moment on, the Divine Spirit abandoned Pinkhas, and his priestly dignity departed.

When Sheilah saw that it was useless to change her father's mind, she went up to the Mountain of Snow, Mount Hermon, and stayed there with her women friends, mourning her lost youth, and the husband and children she would never know. Then she returned to Gilead and submitted herself to her father's will.

Every year in the month of Tevet, the young women of Israel return to the mountains and mourn for Jephthah's daughter.

75

Samson

Again the Israelites sinned and whored after false gods, and God sent the Philistines to oppress them for forty years.

At that time, there lived a man named Manoah of the tribe of Dan and his wife Hezlalponit of the tribe of Judah, and they were childless. One day an angel appeared to Hezlalponit and said to her, "You will soon give birth to a son. Be careful not to drink any wine or eat any forbidden foods when you are pregnant with this child. And when the child is born, do not cut his hair, for he shall be a Nazirite to God even in the womb. And he shall one day save Israel from the Philistines."

When she heard this, Hezlalponit ran to Manoah and said to him, "A man of God came to me, so terrible to look at that he seemed not of this earth. I was afraid to ask him his name. And he told me, 'You are going to have a son. Do not drink wine or eat forbidden food, and do not cut the boy's hair, for his life will be devoted to God.' "

Manoah cried out to God, "Please send Your messenger again and let him tell us what we are to do with this child who will be born to us."

So God again sent the angel to Hezlalponit as she was sitting alone in the field. And she ran to fetch Manoah and brought him to the field.

"Are you the man who spoke to my wife?" asked Manoah.

"Yes," answered the angel.

"May your words come true! What shall we do with this child who will soon be born?"

The angel answered, "Your wife is to drink no wine nor eat any forbidden foods. She must do exactly as I commanded her."

"Stay awhile," Manoah said, "and we shall prepare a kid for you to eat."

"No," said the angel, "I will not eat your food. Offer it to God."

"Then at least tell us your name, so we can honor you when the baby is born."

"Do not ask me my name! It is unknowable!"

Then Manoah and Hezlalponit offered a sacrifice to God upon a rock, as the angel had commanded. And as the flames soared heavenward, the angel mounted them and flew up to heaven. Manoah and Hezlalponit fell upon their faces in fear. And the angel never appeared to them again.

A year later Hezlalponit gave birth to a son, and they called him Samson, for like the sun, shemesh, they hoped that Samson would spread light over his generation.

Samson grew up and became a man. His strength was superhuman. He was a giant of a man, measuring seventy-five yards between his shoulders. His only defect was that he was lame in both feet. And whenever the spirit of God filled him, his hair began to rustle and flutter and ring like a loud bell. Then strength flowed into his arms and legs, and he was as powerful as an army of men.

But Samson lusted after a daughter of the Philistines, and he went down to Timnah to visit her. On the way, he met a lion and tore it apart with his bare hands. But he told no one.

A year later he went with his parents to Timnah to marry the Philistine woman. On the way, he took a detour to look at the carcass of the lion he had killed the year before, and he found that bees had made a hive there, and the skeleton was full of honey. And he scooped out some of the honey and ate it, and gave it to his parents when he rejoined them on the road.

When they came to the wedding feast, he presented

a riddle to the thirty guests gathered there: "Out of the eater came something to eat, and out of the strong came something sweet."

He said to them, "If you can solve this riddle within seven days, I will give each of you linen robes, but if you cannot, each of you owes me a linen robe."

After three days, the guests could still make no sense of Samson's riddle. So on the fourth day they came to Samson's wife and said to her, "Wheedle the answer out of your husband, or we will burn down your house!"

So the woman cried and pleaded with her husband until he could take it no more, and he told her the answer to the riddle. And at sunset of the seventh day, they came to Samson and said, "What is sweeter than honey or stronger than a lion?"

Samson was enraged, and he went to Ashkelon and killed thirty men there, and gave their clothing to the wedding guests. Then he returned to his parents' house in a fury. And his wife's father married her to one of the wedding guests.

When Samson returned to his wife at the season of the wheat harvest and discovered that she was married to someone else, he was furious. His father-in-law offered Samson his younger daughter instead, but Samson refused.

Then Samson took three hundred foxes, tied their tails together, two by two, and lashed lit torches between each pair of tails. Then he turned the foxes loose in the wheat fields of the Philistines and burned them to the ground.

The Philistines came to Judah to take Samson captive, and the Israelites there bound Samson with ropes to turn him over to them. But Samson snapped the ropes as if they were thread. Then he grabbed the jawbone of an ass, which was the same ass that Abraham had ridden to Mount Moriah, and mowed down a thousand Philistines that day. And from then on, they called that place Ramat Lekni, Jawbone Heights.

Afterwards, he was overcome by a great thirst and he cried out to God, "You have granted me a great victory today, but am I now to die of thirst?"

God performed a miracle, and a spring of water flowed out of Samson's own mouth.

Samson then slept with a whore in Gaza, and the Gazites planned to ambush him at dawn. But at midnight Samson left the whore's bed and went to the town gates and pulled both gates out of the ground. And he carried them on his shoulders and set them up on a hill near Hebron.

Then he fell in love with a pagan whore named Delilah, whose name means "she who makes poor," and indeed she eventually robbed Samson of his eyes, his wisdom, and his piety. And the lords of the Philistines offered Delilah eleven hundred shekels of silver to betray her lover. She tried to coax the secret of his great strength out of Samson, but he misled her three times.

"Only tie me up with fresh tendons that are used for bowstrings, and I will be completely helpless," he told her.

But when the Philistines came to take him, he burst his bonds as easily as fire eats straw.

Next she tied him up with new ropes that had never been used, but he snapped those, too. And when she braided his hair into her loom, he pulled out the thick peg binding him there as if it were a hair.

But at last he became weary of her nagging, and he confided his secret to her. "No razor has ever touched my head, for I have been devoted to God's service from the womb. If anyone were to cut my hair, I would be as weak as any ordinary man."

Delilah knew that she had finally won, and she told the Philistines. When Samson was asleep that night, she cut off the seven locks of his hair, and his great strength abandoned him.

She called out to him, "Samson, the Philistines are upon you!"

This time Samson could not break his bonds, and the Philistines took him captive and gouged out both his eyes.

And thus he who had gone astray after his eyes lost his eyes.

They brought him down to Gaza and chained him in bronze chains and made him a mill slave. And the Philistines brought their women to Samson, hoping to breed a race of giants, and Samson fell prey to his own lust and slept with them.

Meanwhile, his hair began to grow back.

Then the Philistines made a great feast to their fish-god Dagon, and they brought the blind Samson into the temple, where three thousand Philistines were gathered. And Samson asked the boy leading him to place him between the two pillars holding up the temple. Then he prayed to God, "*Adonai*, give me strength just one more time to take revenge on the Philistines."

And he pulled on both pillars, and they began to sway. And Samson cried out, "Let me die with the Philistines!"

He pulled with all his might, and the temple came crashing down upon Samson and all the lords of the Philistines. All three thousand people inside died, and all the people crowded around outside as well, so that forty thousand Philistines died that day.

As he died, Samson whispered, "Go forth, my soul, and do not grieve. Die, my body, and weep not for yourself."

Even after his death, Samson was a shield to his people. For the Philistines feared him so much after what happened in the temple of Dagon that they dared not attack Israel for the next twenty years.

76

The Birth of Samuel

The last of the judges and the first of the prophets was Samuel, son of Elkanah and Hannah.

For a long time Hannah was barren, and she went to

her husband Elkanah and persuaded him to take a second
wife. So he married Peninah, and she bore him ten sons.
But Elkanah continued to love Hannah even more than
Peninah.

Elkanah was the only righteous man of his generation, and it was for his sake that God did not destroy the
world, which had grown so sinful. In fact, Elkanah turned
many hearts back to God, for each year he took his entire
household on pilgrimages to Shiloh to offer sacrifices
there, and people would see him and be inspired by his
example. The first year five other families joined him on
his pilgrimage. The next year ten came, and soon the
entire town accompanied him. And each year Elkanah
chose a different route to Shiloh, so that he could turn
many souls back to God.

Hannah came to Shiloh with Elkanah and prayed to
God in the sanctuary there. "*Adonai*, do You create things
for no reason? You have given us ears to hear with and
eyes to see with and a nose to smell with. Why then did
You give me these breasts if not to nurse a baby? Angels
don't eat, drink, give birth, or die, but live forever.
Mortals, on the other hand, do all these things. If I am an
angel, then let me live forever. But if I am mortal, let me
do my part in transmitting life."

The priest Eli saw Hannah's lips moving but heard no
sound and assumed that she was drunk. And he chastised her for her improper behavior in a holy place.

But she said to him, "You are mistaken. I have only
been speaking out of my great pain."

Then Eli said, "Go in peace. May God hear your
prayers and answer them."

And shortly after her return from Shiloh, Hannah
became pregnant.

Then a voice came out of heaven and declared to all
the people that a great man was about to be born, and his
name would be Samuel, meaning "his name is given by *El
Elyon*, the Most High God." And every woman who gave
birth to a son that year named him Samuel. The mothers
would gather each day to boast about their sons, each

trying to prove that *her* Samuel was the one foretold in the prophecy.

Then in her one hundred and thirtieth year, Hannah gave birth to a son, and she too called him Samuel. Like all the prophets, the baby was born after only seven months of pregnancy. And his parents, too, were prophets.

As the boy grew, Hannah told stories about him to the other mothers, and they all agreed that his deeds surpassed those of their sons. And Hannah knew that he was destined to be a great leader of the people.

The Israelites now cast lots to see who would be their judge, and the lot fell to no one. And they cast lots again, and the same thing happened. But when they cast lots a third time, the lot fell on the city of Ramah. And they cast again, and the lot leaped out at Elkanah's name. So they came to Elkanah and said, "Come rule over us."

But Elkanah refused.

So they prayed to God, and God answered them, "Not Elkanah but his son shall be your prince and prophet."

"Which of Peninah's ten sons shall be this prince and prophet?" they asked.

God said, "None of Peninah's children, but the child born to the woman Hannah who was barren. And I shall love him as I loved Isaac."

When Samuel was two years old, Hannah brought him to Shiloh to serve God under Eli's care. And each year Hannah returned to Shiloh on the annual pilgrimage and brought Samuel the new coat that she had made for him. God repaid Hannah for the loan of her son, and gave her three more sons and two daughters.

And Samuel grew up in the sanctuary at Shiloh and became the first prophet of Israel.

PART V

DAVID AND SOLOMON

Saul was the first king of Israel, but he forfeited the throne when he defied God's command. Then Samuel anointed the shepherd boy David, and he wrested the crown from Saul. David the warrior conquered Jerusalem, and his son Solomon built God's Holy Temple in its midst. David conquered the hearts of Israel, but Solomon earned their wonder.

77
The Selection of David

Saul was Israel's first king. But when he disobeyed the King of Kings, his kingdom was torn from him and another man was chosen in his place. This was David, whose house ruled Israel for a thousand years and whose descendant will one day sit again upon the throne of Israel.

After Saul had forfeited the kingdom, God spoke to the prophet Samuel. "How long will you continue to feel sorry for Saul? I have rejected him and have chosen another in his stead. Now fill your horn with oil and go to Bethlehem to the house of Jesse, for I have chosen one of his sons to rule after Saul."

So Samuel went to Bethlehem and came to Jesse's house. And the first son he saw was Eliav, the eldest, and Samuel was impressed by Eliav's stature and bearing. "Surely this is the one destined to rule Israel!" he thought.

But when he tried to pour the holy oil on Eliav's head, it refused to flow from the horn. The same thing happened with the next six sons.

Then Samuel asked Jesse, "Have you any more sons?"

"My youngest, who is a shepherd in the fields," replied Jesse, and the other sons scoffed when he mentioned this last son, for this boy was only their half-brother, the son of one of Jesse's slaves.

"Bring him here," said Samuel.

So he sent for David, the youngest son. And when Samuel saw the young man, he was terrified, for David's hair was bright red and his skin ruddy.

"A second Esau!" cried Samuel. "A man of blood!"

But God told Samuel, "Yes, this one will indeed shed much blood, but those he shall strike down will deserve their deaths because of their sins."

And as David now walked over the threshold of Jesse's house, the horn of oil leaped out of Samuel's hand and flew to David's head, where it poured itself out. As soon as the oil touched his hair, the drops crystallized into pearls and diamonds that adorned him like a prince. And when Samuel reached up to retrieve the horn, it was as full of oil as before.

When David's brothers saw this miracle, they cried out, "How is this possible? David is the son of a slave! How can he become king over Israel?"

Then Nazbat, Jesse's wife, stepped forward and spoke. "You are mistaken, my sons. David is not the son of a slave, but my very own son. Years ago, when I saw how your father was tempted by one of his slaves, I disguised myself as that slave and so deceived him and conceived his son. And when my child was born, I pretended that it was the slave's child and so kept my deception a secret from your father. But I knew that this child was destined for great things, for he was born with the sign of the covenant already upon him."

And so at the age of twenty-eight, David became the next king of Israel. But his anointing was not made known to Saul. And when the evil spirit came to Saul, he sent for David to play his lyre for him. So David came to live in the king's house. And his music soothed Saul's troubled spirit, and for a time he found peace.

78

Goliath

David and Goliath were cousins. David's great-grand-mother was Ruth the Moabite, and Goliath's was Orpah, Ruth's sister and sister-in law. Both women were daughters of Eglon, King of Moab.

Because Orpah shed four tears when she parted from her mother-in-law Naomi, she was granted the privilege of giving birth to four giants. Goliath was the strongest and the greatest of these. And because she walked forty steps with Naomi before turning back to Moab, Goliath was permitted to show off his great strength and skill to the Israelites for forty days before being killed by David.

David's three older brothers joined Saul's army to fight the Philistines. One day Jesse gave David some parched corn and bread and said to him, "Bring this food to your brothers in the valley of Elah and see how they are doing. When you are there, try to summon up the courage to fight this giant Goliath, for it is your duty as a member of Judah to protect the Benjamite Saul, just as the first Judah once watched out for his youngest brother."

So David came to Elah and brought food to his brothers. When he saw the nine-foot champion of the Philistines standing in the valley below, he decided to fight him.

It was evening when David arrived at Saul's camp. And he heard Goliath fling his challenge at the Israelite soldiers as he had done every night and morning for forty days: "Send a man out to fight me. If he kills me, the Philistines shall become your slaves. But if I kill him, you shall be our slaves." And as always, Goliath timed his challenge to coincide with the Israelites' reciting of the *Sh'ma,* for he took special pleasure in frustrating their devotion to God.

When Saul heard that David wished to fight Goliath, he gave the young shepherd his royal armor, which was twice David's size, but astonishingly it fit David perfectly.

Then Saul knew that this young Bethlehemite had been anointed to be his successor, for holy oil has the power to transform a person's stature.

To allay Saul's jealousy, David returned the king's armor and went forth to meet Goliath dressed as a simple shepherd, armed only with a slingshot and his staff. Five smooth pebbles flew into David's hand of their own will and fused there into one stone. Just so, Abraham, Isaac, Jacob, Aaron, and God fuse their wills together to safe-guard Israel.

Then David marched out to meet Goliath. As he neared him, David cast his evil eye upon the giant, and Goliath became rooted to the ground and stricken with leprosy.

Then Goliath cursed David, "Am I a dog that you come to fight me with a stick? I will feed your carcass to the sheep!"

Then David knew that Goliath was doomed, for his mind was so confused that he thought that sheep could eat meat. And he shouted back at the giant, "And I will feed your carcass to the birds!"

When he heard that, Goliath looked up to see if there were any birds flying overhead. As he did so, the visor on his helmet lifted just a crack. At that moment, David shot his stone through the space in the armor and hit Goliath right between the eyes. The giant began to fall backward, but an angel descended and pushed him forward so that he landed on the mouth that had so long cursed God.

Goliath was wearing several layers of armor, and David did not know how to remove it to cut off the giant's head. Then Uriah the Hittite stepped forward and told David that he knew how to take off the armor, but he would only tell him if David promised to find him an Israelite wife. David accepted, and Uriah showed him that the suits of armor were all fastened at Goliath's heels. Then David removed the armor and cut off Goliath's head. And soon after, Bathsheba became Uriah's wife.

When the Philistines saw that their champion was dead, they fled in panic. The Israelites pursued them and looted their camp. Then David brought Goliath's head to

Saul, and the king took David into his service. And the people loved David even more than Saul.

79

The Spider

One day David was in his garden, and he noticed a spider's web glistening with morning dew.

"How wise You are, O God, and how wonderful is the world You have created. But of what use is the spider who weaves garments that no one wears?"

God answered David, "The time will come when you will need this creature, and then you will understand why it was created."

Not long afterward Saul's evil spirit again visited him, and he pursued David in order to kill him. David fled to the wilderness and hid in a cave. Saul's men pursued him there and began to search the caves looking for him.

As David cowered at the back of his cave, he heard the footsteps of the soldiers nearing the mouth of the cave. And he gave himself up for lost.

But just then he noticed a spider overhead, and as he watched, it began spinning a web in front of him, stretching from the roof of the cave down to the floor.

Moments later, when Saul's men entered the cave, they saw the web and said, "Look, here is an unbroken spider's web. Surely no one has come in here for days!" And they left without searching the cave.

So David was saved from certain death. And never again did he question God's wisdom in creating the spider.

80

The Hornet

It was not only the spider whose purpose David questioned. The hornet, too, provoked his scorn.

"Why did You make a creature," he challenged God, "who does nothing but sting?"

Then God proved to him just how valuable the hornet was.

Once when David was fleeing Saul's soldiers, he came upon the king's troops asleep in their camp.

"Here is my chance," he thought, "to prove to Saul beyond a doubt that I bear him no ill will, even though his heart has been set against me."

In the dead of night he stole into Saul's camp and crept into the tent of Saul's general, Avner, who was a giant. Between Avner's spread-eagled legs lay a jug of water. David's plan was to steal the jug but spare Avner's life, proving thereby that he harbored no enmity toward Saul. But when David stepped between the giant's legs and grasped the jug, Avner groaned in his sleep and drew his powerful legs together, pinning David between them like a nut in a nutcracker.

David was certain that the giant would soon awake and kill him. But at that moment a hornet flew into the tent and stung Avner on one knee. In his sleep the giant grunted and parted his legs. David ran out of the tent and fled to safety in the hills.

And David never complained about hornets again.

81

The Jars of Honey

During the reign of King Saul there lived a very rich old man who had a beautiful wife. When the old man died, the wicked lord of the city wished to take the widow by force and sleep with her. Not wishing such an evil fate, the woman determined to leave the city. Before she left, she took all her gold and put it at the bottom of two large clay jars. Then she filled the jars with honey and entrusted the jars to a neighbor who had been a friend of her husband's. But she did not tell him about the gold at the bottom of the jars. Then she fled to a faraway city.

One day the widow's neighbor gave a wedding feast in honor of his son. When the cooks were preparing for the feast, they ran out of honey. The master of the house thought to himself, "Surely my friend will not mind if I borrow a little honey from the jars she left in my keeping."

But when he dipped his ladle into the jar, he saw the gold coins shimmering at the bottom. Quickly he emptied all the gold from the two jars and refilled them with honey.

After some time, the lord of the city died, and the woman returned home. She came to her neighbor, and he returned the two jars to her in the presence of witnesses.

But when the woman went to remove the gold from the jars, she found only honey.

"The thief!" she cried. "He has betrayed my trust and made me a pauper!"

She ran to the judge of the city and told him what had happened.

"Do you have any witnesses who saw you hand over the gold to him?" asked the judge.

The woman had to admit that she had none.

"Then I cannot help you," the judge said.

So she went to King Saul, who sent her to the Sanhedrin. But they, too, required witnesses to uphold her case.

On her way back from the court, she passed some young boys playing in the street. Among them was David, who was then still only a young shepherd.

"Listen to my sad tale!" she called out to them. And she told them what had happened.

"Go to the king," said David, "and ask him to grant me permission to judge your case."

So she went back to Saul and told him what the shepherd boy had said.

"Bring the boy to me."

She brought David before Saul, and Saul asked him, "Is it true that you can solve this case?"

David replied, "I have faith that God will aid me."

"Then you have my permission to judge," said Saul.

David ordered the woman to bring him the two jars and the neighbor to whom she had entrusted them.

When the man stood before him, David asked him, "Are these the jars this woman gave you for safekeeping?"

"Yes, the very ones," answered the man.

David ordered the honey from the jars poured into other vessels. That done, he took a hammer and smashed the empty jars. Then he fell to his knees and felt around the broken shards until he found a piece of the jar that had two gold coins stuck to it. This piece he now held up before the woman's neighbor. "Here is your pledge! Return what you stole from this woman!"

And the man paid back all the gold he had stolen.

Then all of Israel knew that the spirit of God dwelled within David.

82

The Witch of Endor

When the prophet Samuel died, all the people mourned his death. None mourned his passing more than King Saul.

Then the Philistines marched against Israel and camped near Mount Gilboa. When Saul saw their mighty army, his heart melted, and he asked God if Israel would triumph over their enemy in the coming battle. But God did not answer Saul, not in dreams, nor through prophets, nor through the oracle of the Urim.

So Saul decided to consult Zephaniah, the Witch of Endor, whose name means "the hidden one."

However, Saul himself had outlawed sorcery in the land, so that he would be breaking his own law by consulting a witch. Therefore he disguised himself and went to see her at night.

"Whom do you wish me to summon?" asked the witch.

"The prophet Samuel," said the king.

But when Zephaniah conjured up Samuel's spirit, she shrieked, for the prophet stood before her upright instead of head downward and feet in the air, as spirits usually appear.

"What do you see?" asked Saul. For in witchcraft only the conjurer sees the spirit but cannot hear its voice, and the seeker sees nothing but can hear the spirit speak.

"You are King Saul," cried the witch, "for spirits only stand upright before a king! Do not kill me, my lord, for I only act on your command!"

"Do not fear," Saul reassured her. "No harm will come to you."

Then Zephaniah shrieked again. "He is not alone! I see Moses with him and the souls of the righteous. They must think that the Judgment Day has come."

"What does Samuel look like?" asked Saul.

"He is an old man dressed in a robe that is torn in one corner."

Then Saul knew that it was indeed Samuel who had risen from the grave.

"Who disturbs my rest?" demanded the spirit of Samuel.

"I am in great trouble," said Saul. "The Philistines are attacking, and God has turned away from me. I receive no answer either from dreams or prophets. You are my only hope."

"Why do you ask me if God has indeed become your enemy? God is doing what has been foretold: 'The kingdom has been torn from you and given to David, because you disobeyed My command to bring vengeance down upon Amalek.' Tomorrow God will deliver Israel into the hands of the Philistines. And when the sun next sets, you and your sons will be with me."

"Can I escape death?" asked Saul.

"Yes, if you flee from battle. But if you accept God's judgment, you will join me tomorrow in Paradise."

Then Saul fell on his face, terrified by Samuel's words.

But that night he told his generals, "We will go into battle tomorrow and emerge victorious. And my three sons will distinguish themselves in battle."

For Saul's heroic spirit accepted God's judgment, and he hoped by his death to atone for his sins. The next day the Philistines attacked Israel and defeated Saul's army on Mount Gilboa. And Saul's sons Avinadav, Jonathan, and Malkhi-shua died that day, and Saul himself was mortally wounded by the Philistine archers and died by the hand of his armor-bearer Edad the Amalekite, as God had ordained.

83
Bathsheba

David was one of the pious few over whom the evil inclination had no power. Why then did he lust after Bathsheba, a married woman? Why did he give way to sin? Because God wished sinners to take an example from David: "See how even the great David has done wrong and repented. Go learn from him!"

David's sin with Bathsheba, however, was not as great as it might appear. For from the first, Bathsheba was destined to be David's wife. But God decided to punish David for his lighthearted vow to Uriah the Hittite after the death of Goliath. In return for Uriah's help in removing Goliath's armor, David promised to find Uriah an Israelite wife. And this was the very woman David later would come to desire.

Vanity also contributed to David's undoing, for once he complained to God, "Why do people say 'God of Abraham, God of Isaac, and God of Jacob,' but not 'God of David'?"

And God replied, "I tested Abraham, Isaac, and Jacob, but I have never tested you."

"Then test me now!" cried David.

God said to him, "I will test you, and I will give you a privilege I never granted your forefathers: I will tell you ahead of time that you will fail the test and that a woman will be your downfall."

One day Satan appeared to David disguised as a bird. David threw a dart at him, but the dart missed and broke through a wicker screen where Bathsheba was combing her hair. At the sight of her extraordinary beauty, David's lust was aroused, and at that moment he contrived to send her husband Uriah to the battlefront, where he would face certain death.

For twenty-two years after he married Bathsheba, David repented of his sin. Every day he cried for a whole hour. And for a short time, he even suffered from leprosy on account of his sin and lost the blessed company of the *Shekhinah*. But the worst punishment of all was the rebellion of his beloved son Absalom, which utterly broke David's heart.

84

Absalom's Rebellion

David's son Absalom was a giant. He was so big, in fact, that someone standing in the eye-socket of his skull would sink down to his nose. But the most extraordinary thing about him was his hair, which weighed as much as two hundred silver shekels. Since he had taken the vow of a Nazirite, he only cut it once a year, so that it covered his head like a tangled bush.

David loved Absalom more than any of his sons. And Absalom took advantage of his father's special love to rebel against him and to sow the seeds of discord among the people. When David heard that Absalom had set himself up as king in his father's place, he was devastated. He decided to start worshiping idols, so that his people would think that he deserved to be deposed from his throne and to be replaced by his son. But his friends prevented him from committing idolatry.

Then David sent his army against Absalom's men, and they defeated them in the forests of Ephraim.

As Absalom was fleeing David's men on his mule, he passed under a great oak tree, and his thick hair became tangled in its branches. The mule bolted from under him and left him hanging in the tree. But when Absalom reached for his sword to cut himself loose, he saw yawning below him the black mouth of hell. So he stayed in the tree, preferring to hang there rather than to drop down into hell.

Then Yoav, David's general, came upon Absalom hanging in the tree, and he thrust three darts into his chest. Then ten of Yoav's armor-bearers finished Absalom off with their swords. And they cut off his head and threw his body into a great pit and covered it over with stones.

When they told King David that his son Absalom was dead, David cried out, "O Absalom! O my son, my son, Absalom! If only I had died instead of you! O Absalom, my son, my son!"

And David's soldiers were humiliated because the king had turned their victory celebration into a day of mourning.

Absalom descended into hell and was put in charge of ten heathen nations. And whenever the Avenging Angels sit in judgment of the nations, they wish to punish Absalom anew for his great sin. But a heavenly voice always calls out, "Do not burn or chastise him! He is the son of My servant David!" And so he is left undisturbed on his throne.

What really saved Absalom from the fiery scourges of hell was the eight repetitions of his name by his father David. When the Angel of Death heard David's lament, he even re-attached Absalom's head to his body before carrying him to hell. But even though Absalom is spared extreme torments, he is barred forever from the World to Come.

David paid dearly for his excessive love of his rebellious son. Each time he cried out "My son!" in his lament, he lost a son: Absalom, Amnon, Adoniyah, Bathsheba's first child, and four others. And eight of Israel's kings died a violent death like Absalom.

As a further punishment, Absalom died childless. Before his death he had set up a pillar in the Valley of the King to keep his name alive, since he had no sons. And it is called Absalom's Monument until this day.

85
The Brave Avishai

David was a mighty warrior. Not only did he kill the giant Goliath with a single stone, but he could kill eight hundred men with a single arrow. But David became too proud of his skill in battle and boasted, "There is none to compare with me in this world nor will there be any like me afterward!"

So God decided to punish David for his pride.

God sent Satan disguised as a deer to lure David into the land of the Philistines. And there David saw a tower. He went inside and saw an old woman spinning at a wheel. This was Orpah, the mother of Goliath, but David did not recognize her. She recognized him, however, and determined now to avenge her son's death.

She broke off her thread and said to David, "Please bring me my spindle."

And David did. But as he bent over, the spindle caught him by its point. Then Orpah seized him and pinned him under the legs of the bed on which she sat in order to break every bone in his body.

David prayed to God, and God created a hollow space under the bed so that David was not crushed.

Then Ishbi, Goliath's brother, came to the tower. His mother said to him, "Guess what I caught today, my son!"

"What did you catch, Mother?"

"David, who killed your brother!"

"Give him to me," cried Ishbi, "so that I can kill him!"

"There is no need," said Orpah, "for I have broken every bone in his body. Look under the bed."

But when Ishbi peered under the bed, he saw David sitting in the hollow space, unharmed. "He is alive!"

Then Ishbi thrust his lance into the ground with its point facing the sky, and he seized David and threw him up in the air so that he would land on the point of the lance. But God suspended David in midair.

Just at that moment, Avishai, nephew of David and one of his most trusted generals, was washing for the Sabbath, and he saw the water turn to blood. A moment later a dove landed nearby and began plucking out her feathers, crying and wailing.

"The dove is the symbol of the people Israel," thought Avishai. "Surely the king is in trouble!"

And he mounted the king's horse and was in the land of the Philistines in the twinkling of an eye, for the ground shrank miraculously as he rode. He first met Orpah, and he killed her with one blow. Then he saw David suspended in midair over Ishbi's lance.

"Give me your lance," demanded Avishai, "so that I might kill him!"

And Ishbi gave him the lance, and he immediately ran Ishbi through with it.

Then Avishai spoke the Name of God, and David floated back to earth.

When he returned to his palace, David declared, "Where now is my strength and where is my bravery!"

And never again did David boast of his might.

86
The Egg and the Boiled Beans

Once King David gave a great feast and invited all his servants. One servant was so hungry that he ate his entire appetizer before the meal began. Embarrassed, he asked his neighbor if he could borrow one of his eggs.

"Certainly," replied the man, "if you promise to pay me back all the profit a single egg can produce when I ask for it."

And the other servant agreed.

Many years later, the lender of the egg appeared before the borrower and demanded repayment. Gladly the borrower gave him an egg, but the other man insisted that he owed him much more. So the two men went to King David to settle their dispute.

On the way into the city, they passed young Solomon sitting by the gates.

"Where are you going?" Solomon asked them.

"To King David," said the lender, "to find out which of us is right."

"And what do you disagree about?" asked the king's son.

"I borrowed an egg from this man and now he wants repayment," said the borrower. "He claims that I owe him more than a single egg, and I say that that's all I owe him."

"Go then to King David and present your case to him," said Solomon. "Then return here and tell me what he said."

So the two men went on their way.

When they told their story to King David, he said to the servant who had borrowed the egg, "You must pay what you owe."

"And how much is that?" asked the nervous borrower.

Then the royal treasurer spoke. "If one egg hatches one chick in the first year, and the second year that chicken produces eighteen more chicks, and each of them produces eighteen more chicks during the third year . . ." and he calculated a vast sum.

"You must pay what you owe," repeated the king.

Distressed, the borrower left the palace and came to Solomon. Almost in tears, he told him what had happened.

"I will help you," said Solomon, "but you must do exactly as I tell you. Take a handful of beans and boil them. Then go to a field alongside the road on which the king's men normally ride and sow the boiled beans in that field. When they ask you what you are doing, tell them that you are sowing boiled beans."

The man did exactly as Solomon said. When the king's men saw him, they asked him what he was planting.

"Boiled beans," he answered.

"Madman!" they cried, and they reported the strange matter to the king. David had the man brought before him.

"Whoever heard of sowing boiled beans?" exclaimed King David.

"And whoever heard of a boiled egg hatching out a chick?" answered the man.

"Aha!" cried David. "I see Solomon's hand in this!"

And the man admitted that it had indeed been Solomon who had told him to sow the boiled beans.

Then David summoned Solomon and the two servants to the palace. "It was my mistake," admitted the king, "not to find out whether the egg in question was hard-boiled or fresh. Because it was an appetizer, it almost certainly was hard-boiled." Then he turned to the borrower and said, "Pay this man the single egg you owe him."

Then all the people marveled at the wisdom of one so young as Solomon.

87

The Sack of Flour
and the Wind

While David still sat upon the throne, there lived in Jerusalem a poor widow who was known for her great charity. Every day she used to bake three loaves of bread.

Two she gave to those poorer than herself, and the third she kept for her own needs.

One day a man dressed in rags appeared at her front door. "Three days ago the ship I was traveling on sank in a storm," he told her. "By some miracle, I was washed ashore. But all my possessions now lie at the bottom of the sea. And for three days I have had nothing to eat. Please help me!"

Moved by the man's sad tale, the widow gave him a loaf of bread and sent him on his way.

Soon after, a second man knocked at the door, looking even more ragged than the first, and cried, "Take pity on me, kind lady! Three days ago, I escaped from slave traders who captured me and carried me far from my home. All this time I have had nothing to eat, and I am ready to die!"

So the widow gave this man, too, a loaf of bread and sent him on his way.

As soon as he was gone, a third poor man appeared, hardly able to stand up on his two legs, and said to her, "If you have a heart, my friend, help me! I was walking on the road and robbers attacked me and stole all I had. For three days I have wandered in the forest, eating nothing but grass. If you have even a crust of bread, please give it to me."

And the widow gladly gave him her last loaf of bread.

Then she went to King David to beg for flour so that she might satisfy her own hunger. The king gladly gave it to her, and she put the sack of flour on her head and started on her way home. But suddenly a wind rushed out of the sea and snatched the sack from her head.

Desolate, the woman returned to David's palace to complain about her bad fortune.

"What sin have I committed that I deserve to be robbed like this?" she moaned. "Is this the reward for charity?"

David was about to give her another sack of flour when his young son Solomon spoke up and said, "You should not let the wind get away with this, Father!"

"What nonsense are you speaking, Solomon?" said the king. "Am I God that I can summon the wind here to give an accounting of its deeds?"

Then Solomon said, "Then give me your crown and scepter, Father, and let me sit upon your throne this once. I will command the wind to appear."

So David seated his young son upon his throne. Then Solomon ordered the winds to appear before him, and they blew into the palace with a great blast of hot breath. Solomon first asked the east wind, "Why did you rob this poor widow of her flour?"

The east wind replied, "It was not I who robbed her, my lord! I did not leave my realm today."

The south and west winds gave the same answers.

But the north wind confessed to the crime. "Yes, it was I who took this woman's sack of flour, but I had a good reason. I saw a rich merchant ship sinking into the sea with a great hole in its side, so I stole this woman's sack of flour to plug up the hole and save the ship."

At that moment, three merchants burst into the room, followed by three servants carrying heavy sacks of gold. "Take these gold coins," they cried, "and give them to the poor of the city, for we wish to give thanks for the great miracle that happened today."

"What miracle is that?" asked Solomon.

"We were at sea and a great storm arose. For hours we were tossed about like a withered leaf, and then the ship began to sink. We gave ourselves up for lost. Then suddenly the ship righted itself, and we sailed safely into harbor. The gold coins in these sacks represent a third of the wealth we carried on board."

"Let us go down to the harbor and investigate this miracle," said Solomon.

And when they examined the ship, they discovered a sack of flour wedged into a large hole in the keel.

In gratitude, the merchants gave the widow the sacks of gold, and she became wealthy beyond her dreams. But she did not change her ways and continued to open her hand generously to the poor.

And Solomon gave his father back his crown and throne. But David knew that Solomon was destined to sit there again one day and rule the people with a wisdom exceeding his.

88

The Death of David

When David grew old, he asked God to tell him when he was going to die.

But God said, "No one may know the day of his death."

Then David said, "At least tell me on which day I am going to die."

"On the Sabbath," answered God.

"Why not on a Friday?"

"I delight in your study of the Torah on the Sabbath and do not wish to sacrifice even one of these days."

"On a Sunday, then!"

"No, for I have ordained that your son Solomon will begin his reign on a Sunday, and one reign may not overlap another by even a second."

So David spent every Sabbath from then on studying Torah from sunset to sunset, because the Angel of Death may not take a soul when it is engaged in study.

Then one Sabbath, which also happened to be the Festival of Shavuot, while David was studying Torah as usual, he heard a rustling sound in his garden, as if someone were climbing in his fruit trees. He threw down his book and ran outside to see who it was. But it was only the Angel of Death who had tricked David into abandoning his study so that he could seize his soul.

As soon as David set foot on the stairs leading into his garden, they collapsed under him and he died.

Since it was the Sabbath, the king's body could not be moved. So Solomon summoned several eagles, and they spread their broad wings over David's body to shield it from the sun.

And the next day Solomon ascended to the throne of Israel.

89
Solomon's Gift of Wisdom

When Solomon was still a young boy but already sat upon the throne of Israel, God came to him in Gibeon in a dream and said to him, "Solomon, My son, ask Me for anything you wish and I will grant your request."

Solomon said, "O God, You were kind to my father David, because he was faithful to You and ruled Israel justly and with a generous heart. And now You have set me on my father's throne, although I am still only a boy. My people are so many, and my experiences so few. Please grant me an understanding heart so that I may rule my people wisely."

And God was pleased by Solomon's request and said, "You could have asked for a long life or great wealth or victory over your enemies. But instead you asked for wisdom, and you shall have your wish. You shall be able to understand the language of all the birds and beasts. No one has ever been wiser than you, Solomon, not even the great Moses himself! Nor will anyone ever surpass your wisdom! And although you did not ask for great wealth, long life, or triumph over your foes, you shall have these, too. All these gifts shall be yours – if you walk in My ways and follow My commandments as your father did before you."

Then Solomon woke up from his dream. And he wondered if God had really spoken to him or whether it had been a spirit beguiling him in his dreams.

Then he heard the birds squawking and twittering to each other in his garden below. And he heard one suddenly cry out, "Silly birds – stop all this noise! Don't you know that God has just given Solomon the ability to understand what we say and to make us do as he wishes!"

Then Solomon knew that the dream had indeed been sent by God.

"Nonsense!" chirped another bird. "How can a human being rule over us? Human beings are stuck on the ground while we can fly up into the heavens. Only the eagle, who lives high in the mountains, can be our king."

"We'll see about that," whispered Solomon. Then he thrust his head out of his window and thundered, "Birds, be quiet! King Solomon commands you!"

Instantly all was quiet in the garden.

"Where is the bird who a moment ago talked so boldly? Come here at once!"

The poor little bird came fluttering to Solomon's finger, shaking as if her little heart would break.

"So," grumbled the young king, "you think that the eagle is stronger than I. We shall soon see about that. I command you to fly to the desert and summon the great White Eagle, mightiest of the birds, to Jerusalem. Then we shall see who is king over the birds!"

"He will kill me if I speak so boldly to him!" stammered the little bird.

Then Solomon attached a letter to the bird's foot with a gold ring and placed the royal seal upon it. And the little bird flew off, shaking with fear.

The next day, as the sun rose, Solomon's guards felt a great blast of wind howling down upon their heads. Then came a second blast, then a third. And their hearts melted within them.

Then a fourth blow shook the palace to its foundation. In flew the great White Eagle, sparks of fire blazing from his gold eyes, his white beak flashing like a sharp sword. As soon as his broad wings stopped beating, a little bird peered out from one of them and then darted behind the king's golden throne.

"Why have you summoned me here?" demanded the Eagle.

"To show you my power," answered the king.

Then Solomon ordered his guards to sound the *shofar*. Within moments, the vast throne-room filled with birds—parrots and peacocks, hawks and hummingbirds, cranes and cuckoos. The noise in the room was deafening.

Then the king cried, "Silence!"

And instantly they all hushed.

Then Solomon turned to the White Eagle, who towered above all the other birds like a mighty tree. "I command you, King of the Birds, to come back here once each month. Upon your wings, I shall keep watch over my great kingdom."

And so each month, the White Eagle returned to Jerusalem. And King Solomon mounted his broad wings and shepherded the skies over Israel.

90

Solomon and the White Lion

One day, as King Solomon was riding through his kingdom on his splendid black Arabian stallion, he overheard two donkeys arguing in a field.

"Fool!" said one. "Here comes the great Solomon, King of Israel, and you stand there eating grass and braying like an ass! On your knees, if you value your life!" And the first donkey fell to his knees in the tall grass.

"Hee-haw!" brayed the second donkey. "Solomon may be king over Israel, but he certainly does not rule over me! Whoever heard of a king ruling over subjects he cannot even understand?" And with that he stamped his hooves and brayed even louder.

The other donkey trembled and buried his gray muzzle ever deeper into the mud.

"Besides," continued the second donkey, "how can the weak rule over the strong? Surely the lion, king of the beasts, would make this Solomon cower on his throne. If they were to meet, the lion and the man, we would see who was the true king."

Solomon listened in silence to this debate between the two donkeys. Then he called to them from his black horse, "Silence! Do you not know before whom you stand? I am Solomon, King of Israel! God has given me dominion over all the beasts of the field and the seas and the air. All living things are my subjects!"

When the second donkey heard the king's angry words, his legs collapsed under him and he fell upon his belly.

"Foolish fellow," laughed the king. "They do not call you an ass for nothing. But your words are not completely without sense. A king must be able to master all his subjects. You are right. If I cannot subdue the lion, I am not his king. Go at once to the Desert of Palmyra and summon the great White Lion to see me."

The poor donkey cried out bitterly, "Do not send me, O king, to be killed by the lion! I will die of fright just hearing his awful roar!"

But the king would not listen to the donkey's pleas. He tied a small leather pouch around the donkey's neck. "Carry this letter from me, and no harm will come to you. Now be off!"

A month later, as Solomon sat in judgment upon his throne, a great thundering shook the palace. Soon there came a second terrible roar, more powerful than the first. Then a third, which made Solomon's servants and all his subjects fall trembling upon their faces. Only Solomon sat unafraid upon his great golden throne.

Suddenly a fierce lion rushed into the room, roaring thunderously and gnashing his sharp teeth. His white fur shone like the sun, and his mane billowed like the sea. In his eyes flashed gold fire.

Behind him crawled the poor donkey, his teeth chattering and his bones knocking against each other so loudly that it seemed as if any moment he would shatter into a thousand pieces. The leather pouch still dangled, dusty and worn, from his scrawny neck.

"Be still!" commanded Solomon.

Still growling, the lion crouched down upon his great haunches and glared at Solomon.

"Bring water and meat for my guest!" ordered the king.

With one bite, the lion devoured all the food the king's servants brought to him.

"You are indeed a great king," said Solomon to the lion. "But I am even greater. In the forest you rule unchallenged, but here I am your master."

Reluctantly, the lion bowed his stately head before Solomon. The king's subjects looked on in astonishment — and kept their distance.

"From this day on," commanded the king, "you will leave the Desert of Palmyra once each month and come here. Upon your back, you will carry me to the desert, where I will build a magnificent palace of glass. You will then be free to do as you wish until I summon you to take me home."

And so it came to pass. Each month, two weeks after the White Eagle swooped into Jerusalem, the White Lion roared into the palace and bore the king away to his great glass palace in the wilderness of Palmyra.

And the donkey returned to his field to graze and bray to his heart's content — as long as the king was not nearby.

91
The Two-Headed Cainite

Asmodeus, King of the Demons, wished to test Solomon's wisdom, so he came to him and said, "Is it true that you are wiser than all men?"

And Solomon replied, "So God has promised me."

Then Asmodeus said, "I will now show you something that even you have never seen."

Asmodeus stuck one of his long, hairy fingers into the ground and up sprang a two-headed man.

Solomon asked him, "Who are you?"

"I am a descendant of Cain," answered the creature.

"And where do you come from?"

"From Tevel, the highest of the seven underground worlds under the earth."

"Do you have a sun and moon there?" asked the king.

"Indeed we do, and we also plant fields and herd flocks."

"Where does the sun rise in your world?"

"It rises in the west and sets in the east," answered the Cainite.

"Do you wish to remain in this world or return to your own?" asked Solomon.

"I wish to return to Tevel," he answered.

But Asmodeus was not able to return him underground. So the man married a wife of the earth, and they had seven children. Six were like their mother, but the seventh was born with two heads like his father. In time the Cainite acquired many fields and livestock, and after many years he died a wealthy man.

But when it came time to divide up the inheritance, the two-headed son demanded a double portion. The other sons claimed that he was only entitled to a single share.

Unable to decide the matter, they brought their case to King Solomon, who for once was completely baffled. So he asked the Sanhedrin to rule on the case, but they, too, were at a loss. Then he prayed to God. *"Adonai,* when I was only a boy, You promised to grant me wisdom. Give me now the wisdom to decide this case justly."

The next day, when the seven sons of the Cainite appeared before Solomon again, he ordered both heads of the two-headed man covered with a cloth.

"If one head can tell what I am doing to the other," he declared, "then they belong to one being. But if not, they are two."

Then he poured boiling water over one of the heads.

Immediately both heads cried out, "We are dying, we are dying! We are not two, but one!"

So Solomon ruled that the two-headed son was entitled only to a single share, like his brothers.

92
The Maid, the Youth,
and the Thief

Once three merchants went on a journey. As the sun began to set on Friday evening, they decided to bury their money in a safe place, since it is forbidden to carry money on the Sabbath. But when they went to retrieve the money at the conclusion of the Sabbath, it was gone! Each accused the two others of having stolen it, but no one confessed to the theft.

So they presented their case to King Solomon.

"Before I decide your case," said Solomon, "let me ask your help on another matter. I know you are all wise men who have traveled the world and seen many things. I would like to ask your advice on a problem presented to me by the King of Rome. Perhaps you can help me solve it."

The three men were, of course, flattered to be consulted by the wise Solomon. "Tell us the problem," they said, "and we will try to help you."

Then the king told them this tale: "Once a girl and a boy became betrothed to each other when they were very young. They made a promise at that time that they would not marry anyone else without the other's permission. Soon after, the boy moved to a different city. When they grew up, the girl became engaged to another man but refused to marry him until she had obtained the consent of her childhood friend. So the girl and her fiancé filled several sacks with silver and gold and traveled to the city where the friend of her youth now lived.

"When the girl told her friend that she wished to marry a different man, he gladly gave his blessing to the couple, refusing to accept any money to release the girl from her childhood oath.

"Then the happy couple began their journey home, but were surprised along the way by an old thief who wished to steal both the girl and the money.

" 'You are welcome to the money,' the girl said to the

thief, 'but please spare me.' Then she told him about the mission they had just completed and added, 'If a young man like my friend can control his passion, how much easier it should be for an old man like you! Shouldn't you be filled with the fear of God at your age?'

"And the old thief took her words to heart and stole neither the girl nor the money, but let her and her fiancé go in peace.

"Now," said Solomon to his three listeners, "I have been asked to decide which of these three acted most nobly: the maid, the youth, or the thief?"

The first merchant said, "The maid, for she kept her oath."

The second merchant said, "The youth, for he controlled his passion and did not stand in the way of his friend's happiness."

The third merchant said, "The thief, of course! He could have kept the money and still let the girl go!"

Then Solomon pointed at the third merchant and declared, "There is your culprit! By his admiration of the thief, he has displayed his own greed and given himself away."

The man confessed his crime and showed the others where he had hidden the money.

93

The Three Brothers Who Went to King Solomon to Learn Wisdom

There were once three brothers who went to Jerusalem to learn wisdom from King Solomon. Solomon appointed them officers of his court, and they served him for thirteen years. At the end of that time, the oldest brother said to the others, "For thirteen years we have served the king, but we have learned nothing. All this time we have not seen our wives or our possessions. Let us now go to the king and ask his permission to return home."

When he heard their request, Solomon summoned his treasurer and had him set before each brother one hundred gold coins.

Then the king said to them, "Choose one of these things: either three words of wisdom or one hundred gold coins."

The brothers talked it over, and all three decided to take the money.

But when they reached the outskirts of Jerusalem, the youngest brother changed his mind. He tried in vain to convince his brothers to return with him, saying, "Did we come to Jerusalem and serve the king for thirteen years only to make money?" But they refused to exchange their gold for wisdom.

So the youngest brother returned to the palace alone and said to the king, "Take back your gold, my lord, and teach me wisdom, for that is what I came here to learn."

Solomon was pleased by the young man's words, and he said to him, "Here are the three words of wisdom I have to teach: First, when you are on a journey, always prepare your camp while it is still light. Second, never cross a river when the water is high, but wait until it subsides. And third, never reveal a secret, not even to your own wife."

The youngest brother thanked the king and went on his way.

He caught up with his brothers and they asked him, "And what did you learn from the king?"

"What I learned, I learned," he answered. And his two brothers laughed at him.

When the sun began to set, the youngest brother, recalling the king's advice, dismounted from his horse and began to make camp in a clearing where there was ample grass, water, and shelter. But his brothers refused to stay with him.

"We can still cover more miles before it is night," they said.

"You may not find grass and water for your horses or shelter for yourselves," he cautioned them.

"What a fool you are!" they said. "You threw away money for nothing!"

"Do as you wish," said the youngest brother, "but I will camp here tonight."

And the brothers rode on.

The youngest brother then cut branches for a shelter, built a warm fire, and fed his horse. Then he lay down in peace.

The brothers, however, kept riding, and by nightfall found themselves on a barren mountaintop. There they could find neither water nor grass for their horses nor wood for a fire. And after they fell asleep on the rocky ground, a sudden snowstorm arose, burying both brothers in an icy grave.

The next morning the youngest brother got on his horse and rode on until he reached the spot where his brothers lay dead. He wept over them and buried them. Then he took their gold coins and continued on his way.

Soon he came to a river swollen by the melting snow. Remembering the king's words, he sat down on the bank to wait for the water to subside. As he sat there, two of the king's servants came along, leading two donkeys carrying sacks of gold.

"Why aren't you crossing?" they asked him.

"Because the water is too strong and swift," he answered.

"Coward!" they jeered at him, and began crossing with their donkeys. But the powerful current swept them away and drowned them.

The youngest brother waited until the waters went down and then retrieved the sacks of gold and went on his way.

When he reached his home, his brothers' wives asked where their husbands were.

"Still serving the king and learning wisdom," he replied.

With the money he had, the youngest brother bought land and vineyards and houses and herds. His wife asked him where he had acquired so much wealth, but he refused to tell her.

"Don't you love me?" she cried.

But he remembered what Solomon had told him and kept his secret to himself.

Still his wife continued to pry and nag and complain until at last he gave in and told her everything that had happened to him since he had left Solomon's palace.

Soon after, the two of them had an argument, and the youngest brother struck his wife in anger.

"Are you going to murder me like you murdered your two brothers and the king's servants?" she yelled at him.

When the other brothers' wives heard this, they went straight to Solomon and demanded justice. Solomon sentenced the youngest brother to death.

As they were leading him to the place of execution, he asked to speak to the king.

"O great and wise Solomon!" he cried as he stood before the king's throne. "I am one of the three brothers who served you for thirteen years in order to learn from you. I was the only one who exchanged gold for wisdom. And the wisdom you taught me twice saved my life. But I failed to follow your third piece of advice and so have forfeited my life."

And he told him all that had happened since he had left the king's service.

Then Solomon recognized him and said, "Do not fear. The money you took from your brothers and my servants is yours to keep. And so is your life."

The king ordered him released and he returned in peace to his wife.

That is why Solomon wrote in his book of proverbs: "It is better to acquire wisdom than much fine gold."

94

Buried Treasure

Once a merchant went on a journey. On the eve of the Sabbath, he found himself outside an unfamiliar town.

"To whom can I entrust my money?" he wondered. "I know no one in this town."

Looking around to see that no one was watching, he buried his money under a stump in a field and went into town to spend the Sabbath. But the man who owned the field saw him bury the money, and as soon as the merchant was gone, dug it up. Two days later, when the man returned for the money, it was no longer there.

The merchant went to King Solomon and complained about the theft.

"Find out who owns the field and tell him that you buried only part of your money in a secret place. Explain to him that you wish to hide the rest of your money and ask his advice: Should you bury it in the same secret place or in a different place, or should you leave it with a trustworthy person? He will no doubt advise you to bury it in the same place so that he can get his hands on it. But he will soon realize that if you go to the stump and find the first money missing, you will not want to leave any more there. So he will return the money he stole to the hole under the stump."

The merchant followed Solomon's advice. And as Solomon had predicted, the owner of the field quickly returned the stolen money to its hiding place under the stump, expecting to double his profits this way.

But the merchant outfoxed him. That night he removed all the money and went on his way. And the next morning, the thief found only an empty hole under his stump.

95

The Game of Chess

In his wisdom Solomon invented the game of chess, and no one in the world could play it better than he.

One day he was playing chess with his chief minister, Benaiah ben Yehoyada, and the minister soon found himself in danger of checkmate. Suddenly there was a commotion in the street below, and Solomon ran to the window to see what was going on. While the king was distracted, Benaiah removed one of Solomon's knights from the chessboard. When Solomon returned to the game, he failed to notice that his knight was missing and continued to play as before. Not only did Benaiah escape checkmate, but he went on to win the game.

The king was greatly distressed by this, for he had never before lost a game of chess to anyone. So he replayed the game in his memory, and saw in his mind's eye that his knight had mysteriously disappeared at some point in the game.

"It must have happened when I was at the window," he concluded.

Now the king did not like to suspect Benaiah, who was his favorite minister, but he did want to get to the bottom of the mystery, so he devised a way to flush out the thief. But meanwhile he acted as if nothing had happened and treated Benaiah as favorably as before.

One evening at the hour of dusk, Solomon noticed two men slinking by in the street below, carrying two empty sacks over their shoulders.

"Surely these are thieves!" thought the king.

Quickly he changed out of his royal robes and dressed as one of his own servants. Then he ran down to the thieves and said to them, "My friends, I am schooled in the same trade as you. Here are the keys to the king's treasury," and he dangled a ring of keys before their noses. "For a long time I have been planning to steal from the king, but I have been afraid to act alone. If you now join me, we will all be rich men."

"Tell us what we should do," replied the thieves, "for we must not fail in this. To steal from the king means death if we are caught."

"Wait until night when the palace is asleep. Then we can go about our business without being discovered."

In the dead of the night Solomon took them to a chamber in his treasury where brass objects were kept.

The thieves wished to fill their sacks with these, but Solomon said, "Keep your hands off! I will show you far more precious treasures!"

Then he took them to a second chamber where silver objects were kept. But again he would not let them put anything in their sacks.

The third chamber contained gold and all kinds of precious jewels. "Take these," said Solomon, "and while you are filling your sacks, I will stand guard outside to make sure that nobody comes."

Solomon left the room and locked the thieves inside. Then he changed back into his royal clothes and summoned his servants.

"I have discovered thieves trying to steal my treasures!" he said. "I have trapped them inside with their spoils. Make sure that neither of them escapes!"

The next day Solomon gathered together the members of the Sanhedrin, including his minister Benaiah, and said to them, "What should be done to a thief who has stolen from the king?"

Now when Benaiah heard the king's words, he was sure that the king was talking about his crime of stealing the knight from the chessboard. And he thought to himself, "If I say nothing, the king will leave judgment to the Sanhedrin, and they will no doubt punish me severely for my deed. But if I confess now before the king and ask his forgiveness, perhaps I will be spared."

So Benaiah fell to his knees before Solomon and said, "My lord king! I am the thief! During our last chess game, I stole your knight and thereby won the game. Please forgive my sin and spare me severe punishment!"

When the king heard Benaiah's words, he laughed and said, "Relax, my dear Benaiah! I was not thinking of you when I asked the Sanhedrin for judgment. I have already forgiven you and forgotten your deed. No, the reason I have called the Sanhedrin together was to punish two thieves I caught stealing my treasures."

And the Sanhedrin tried the thieves and sentenced them to death.

And Solomon was happy, for he had succeeded in flushing out Benaiah's crime without the minister's suspecting a ruse.

And no one ever beat Solomon at chess again.

96

The Jug of Milk and the Serpent

Once a man was walking along with a jug of milk on his shoulder, and he came upon a serpent crying out in pain.

"Why are you crying?" asked the man.

"Because I am dying of thirst," answered the serpent. "Tell me what you have in your jug."

"Milk," answered the man.

"If you give me some of your milk to drink, I will show you a hidden treasure that will make you wealthy beyond your dreams."

So the man gave the serpent milk to drink. Then he said to the serpent, "Now show me the treasure."

The serpent took the man to a large stone, and when the man rolled it aside, he found a fabulous treasure underneath. But when he bent down to gather up the treasure, the snake coiled around his neck and began to strangle him.

"What are you doing?" cried the man.

"I am killing you," answered the serpent, "because you are robbing me."

"Let us go to Solomon's court for judgment," said the man, and off they went, the snake still coiled tightly around the man's neck.

"What do you wish?" King Solomon asked the serpent when the two appeared before him.

"I wish to kill this man," answered the serpent.

"First come down from his neck," ordered the king, "for it is not fair that you should have an advantage over him in court."

So the serpent slithered down to the floor.

"Now finish what you have to say," ordered Solomon.

"I wish to kill this man," said the serpent, "because it is written in the Torah: 'And you shall strike at their heel.' "

"But isn't it also written," said Solomon, " 'They shall strike at your head'?" Then he turned to the man and said, "Now do so!"

And the man crushed the serpent's head with his heel.

97

Life and Death in the Power of the Tongue

Once the king of Moab was deathly ill. His physicians announced that the only hope for him was to drink the milk of a lioness. But not even the king's most courageous soldiers, the Lion-men of Moab—whose hair and beards were like lions' manes and who wore lions' skins and iron shoes shaped like paws on their feet—not even they would volunteer to milk the wild lioness in her lair.

So the King of Moab sent a messenger to his neighbor King Solomon, asking him for help. And Solomon called his chief minister Benaiah ben Yehoyada and said to him, "Are you willing to go to the mountains and milk the lioness in her lair?"

Benaiah said, "For your glory and for the glory of the God of Israel, I will go!"

Benaiah took ten goats with him and went to Mount Hermon where the lions dwelled. There he found the lair of the lioness where she was nursing her cubs. On the first day he threw a goat to her, but he himself stayed far away from her den. On the second day, he threw her another goat, but this time he moved a little closer to her.

By the tenth day, she was so used to him that she let him play with her cubs and milk her teats.

Benaiah filled a skin with her milk and hurried back with it to King Solomon. Solomon gave the milk to the King of Moab's messenger and said to him, "Tell your king that my minister Benaiah risked his life for this milk. May the king be healed by it. Now go in peace and may God watch over your tongue."

The messenger traveled back toward Moab and stopped along the way to rest. That night he had a dream: All the parts of his body were quarreling with one another.

The legs said, "We are most important, for if we hadn't walked to the lioness's lair, Benaiah could not have brought back milk to the king."

And the hands said, "But if we hadn't milked the lioness, there would certainly be no milk."

The eyes argued, "If we had not shown Benaiah the way, he would never have found the lair."

And the mind said, "If I had not shown him how to befriend the lioness, he could never have milked her."

Then the tongue piped up, "No, you are all wrong! I am more important than all of you put together, for without speech, nothing is possible!"

Then the others all jeered at the tongue and said, "Who do you think you are, you boneless flap of skin who lives in a dark, gloomy hole!"

And the tongue replied, "Wait and see! You will soon admit that I am the master of you all."

When the messenger awoke the next morning, he remembered his dream and was troubled. At last he arrived at the king's palace, and he presented Solomon's gift to the king.

But when he started to speak, it was as if a demon had taken possession of his tongue: "Here is the bitch's milk you asked for, your majesty," he said to the king.

The King of Moab flew into a rage. "What! I ask for the milk of a lioness and you bring me the milk of a dog! You shall lose your head for this insult!"

And the messenger was taken to prison to await execution.

That night the messenger had another dream. This time all the limbs of his body were trembling uncontrollably, and the tongue said to them, "See, what did I tell you? Will you now admit that I am your master?"

"Yes!"shouted all the organs and limbs at once. "We admit it, only please save us from death!"

When the man awoke from his dream, his tongue said to the executioner, "Take me to the king!"

When he stood before the royal throne, he said, "Your majesty, why did you order me hanged? Haven't I brought you a cure for your illness?"

"Then why did you tell me you had brought me milk from a *bitch*?" asked the king.

"What does it matter what it's called as long as it cures you, your majesty? But I apologize for my tongue's carelessness. You see, a lioness is sometimes called a bitch by hunters, but I should not have used that word in the presence of a king."

And the messenger's words appeased the king, and he forgave him. Then he drank the milk and was cured.

Then all the limbs and organs said to the tongue, "We acknowledge that you are master over us!"

And when word of this matter reached Solomon's ears, he wrote in his book of proverbs: "Life and death are in the power of the tongue."

98
The Circle of Death

Once an otter came to King Solomon and complained, "Your majesty, didn't you decree that wild creatures must live in peace together?"

"And who has violated my decree?" demanded the king.

"The weasel," answered the otter. "When I went

down to the river to hunt for food, I gave my babies to the weasel to watch over and it devoured them all. He deserves to die!"

So Solomon summoned the weasel and asked him, "Did you kill the otter's children?"

The weasel replied, "Yes, your majesty, but I didn't do it on purpose. You see, I heard the woodpecker pounding on the war drums, calling me to battle, and as I rushed to fight, I accidentally trampled the otter's children."

So Solomon called the woodpecker and asked him, "Did you summon the weasel to war by thundering on your drum?"

And the woodpecker replied, "I did, my lord, but only because I saw the scorpion sharpening its dagger."

So the king had the scorpion brought before him and said, "Why were you sharpening your dagger?"

The scorpion answered, "Because I saw the tortoise polishing his armor."

The tortoise told the king, "I was only polishing my armor because I saw the crab honing its sword."

And the crab explained, "I was honing my sword because I saw the lobster swinging its javelin."

And when the lobster stood before the king, it said, "I was swinging my javelin because I saw the otter coming down to the water to devour my children."

Then the king turned to the otter and said, "The weasel is not guilty. He who sows death shall reap it."

99
Ziz-Shaddai and the Queen of Sheba

Solomon was king over all the beasts and birds and creatures of the sea as well as over all human rulers in the east, west, north, and south. One day he gave a great feast and invited all the neighboring kings. And when he was emboldened by wine, Solomon called for all living creatures to sing and dance before him.

What bedlam then broke out! Elephants pranced, monkeys swung from the rafters, and leopards kicked up their heels. Fleas hopped, bees pirouetted, and dragon-flies did loop-de-loops. And the birds filled the air with riotous song.

Then Solomon noticed that one bird was missing: the great Ziz-Shaddai.

So Solomon commanded that Ziz-Shaddai be brought before him.

"Do not be angry," said Ziz-Shaddai when he stood before the king. "For the past three months I have been flying over the whole world, not even stopping to eat or drink, in order to see whether there exists anywhere on earth a kingdom that does not accept you as their king."

"And what have you found?" asked Solomon.

"There is one such kingdom," said the bird, "far to the east, whose capital city is Kitor. Its soil is like precious gold, and silver lies in the streets like dust. And its trees are watered by the rivers of Eden. The people there do not know how to wage war, nor has anyone ever told a lie. The ruler of this kingdom is Bilkis, the wise and beautiful Queen of Sheba. If you wish, O great king, I will fly there and bring her back to you in chains."

Ziz-Shaddai's words pleased Solomon, and he wrote a message to Bilkis and bound it to the bird's foot. Then the king sent him off to Kitor to bring back the Queen of Sheba to Jerusalem. So Ziz-Shaddai flew off to the east, and all the other birds followed after him.

The next morning at dawn, when the Queen of Sheba went out to worship the sun, the skies suddenly darkened. Looking up in terror, she saw a cloud of birds filling the air above her. She fell to her knees and tore her clothes.

Then Ziz-Shaddai swooped down and alit next to the queen. Bilkis removed Solomon's message from the bird's foot and read it to her ministers: "Greetings from the great Solomon, King of Israel! God has made me king over all the living creatures as well as the spirits and demons. If you will come to my kingdom and acknowledge my power, I will show you greater honor than I have shown any other sovereign. But if you refuse, I will send my armies to defeat you. Who are these warriors of mine? The beasts, birds, and demons whom I will command to destroy you utterly."

When Bilkis's ministers heard Solomon's message, they advised their queen to ignore his threats. "Who is this Solomon who speaks so boldly? We've never even heard of him!"

But Sheba ignored their advice. She gathered many ships and filled them with precious jewels. Then she ordered six thousand young men and women to board the ships, all of them born in the same year, on the same hour, at the same moment, and all identical in size and bearing, and dressed in purple robes. The captain of the fleet carried a letter to Solomon from the queen: "Greetings to Solomon, King of Israel, from Bilkis, Queen of Sheba! We would be most honored to visit your kingdom. And although it should take a full seven years to reach Israel from Kitor, we shall complete our journey in only three, to please you, O great Solomon."

Then the Queen of Sheba boarded one of the ships, and they set sail for Solomon's kingdom.

Solomon received Bilkis in his glass palace in Palmyra. When the queen saw the glass floor, she thought that the king was floating in water and so raised her skirts to wade to him. Then Solomon saw her hairy legs and concluded that she was a demon, for demons are covered everywhere with hair. But Bilkis soon proved herself a woman of flesh and blood, and delighted Solomon with her wisdom.

100
Sheba's Riddles

In order to test Solomon's wisdom, the Queen of Sheba asked him many riddles.

And here was the first: "When it is alive, it does not move, but when it has its head cut off, it does move."

And Solomon answered, "The timbers of a ship."

Next she asked him, "What is this? A wooden well with iron buckets that bring forth stones and pour out water."

And Solomon answered, "A jar of eye makeup, for kohl is crushed from stone and makes the eyes water when rubbed on."

Then she asked, "A woman says to her son: 'Your father is my father, your grandfather is my husband, you are my son, and I am your sister.' "

And Solomon answered, "One of Lot's two daughters who slept with their father."

"What is this?" asked the Queen of Sheba. "The dead lived, the grave moved, and the dead prayed."

And Solomon answered, "The dead one who lived and prayed was Jonah, and the grave that moved was the whale."

Then the Queen of Sheba ordered a cedar tree cut down and the two ends sawed off so that they looked identical. She then had the trunk brought before Solomon and asked him, "Which end was the root and which the top?"

Solomon ordered his servants to throw the trunk into the river. One end sank down so that the trunk was floating upright in the water. He then said to Bilkis, "The end that sank was once the root and the other end the top."

And she exclaimed, "How wise you are, Solomon! You truly deserve your reputation! But I have a few more riddles for you. Perhaps you will be stumped yet."

Next she asked him, "There is a room with ten doors. When one is open, nine are shut; when nine are open, one is shut. What is it?"

And Solomon answered, "The womb. The ten doors are the ten openings in the human body: eyes, ears, nostrils, mouth, the two holes for eliminating waste, and the navel. When the child is in the womb, its navel is open and all other passages are closed. When the child is born, the navel is closed and all the other passages are opened."

Then she asked, "Seven leave and nine enter, two pour and one drinks. What is this?"

And Solomon answered, "The seven days of menstruation end when the nine months of pregnancy begin. The mother's two breasts pour out milk, and the baby drinks."

And Bilkis said, "The next one will surely defeat you, Solomon! It is a many-headed beast! And here it is: A tempest goes before it, and it cries and moans. It bows its head like a reed. It is the glory of the rich and the shame of the poor, the glory of the dead and the shame of the living, the delight of the birds and the sorrow of the fish. What is it?"

And Solomon answered, "Flax, for it makes sails for ships that moan in the storm. It provides fine linen for the rich and rags for the poor, a burial shroud for the dead, and a rope for hanging the living. As seed it nourishes the birds, and as a net it traps the fish."

Then she asked, "What was never born but was given life?"

And Solomon replied, "The Golden Calf."

Then the Queen of Sheba said, "This is my last riddle, Solomon. Answer this and I will declare you the wisest man on earth: What land has only seen the sun once?"

And Solomon answered, "The bed of the Sea of Reeds when God divided it."

And Bilkis, the Queen of Sheba, declared, "I did not believe my ears when they told me you were the wisest king who ever lived, but now I have seen that it is true. Happy are your servants who daily drink in your words of wisdom!"

101

The Bee and the Queen
of Sheba

One day as King Solomon lay beneath a fig tree napping, a bee landed on his nose and stung him there. The king awoke with a startled cry and behold! His nose was swollen like a plum.

"Who has dared to sting the king?" he roared. But the bee had already fled for her life.

Then Solomon commanded all the bees and wasps and hornets and gnats and mosquitoes and flies to appear before him. Soon the garden was filled with such buzzing that it sounded like a forest being felled by a thousand saws.

King Solomon pointed to his nose, which had by now swollen to the size of a tomato.

"Who has done this?" he asked. "Who has dared attack the king?"

Now an even louder buzzing filled the garden as the insects asked one another, "Who has s-s-stung S-S-Solomon? What a craz-z-zy thing to do!"

"Silence!" roared the king. Immediately the buzzing ceased. Then a small bee flew toward Solomon and hovered trembling before his great, throbbing nose.

"A thousand pardons, your majesty!" she said. "I am only a young bee, still unable to tell the difference between a flower and a sweet, lovely nose such as the king's."

The corners of Solomon's eyes and mouth began to curl up in amusement. But his smile quickly vanished when a new needle of pain pricked his nose, which had swelled to the size of a melon.

"Why should I not punish you for your foolish error?" he asked sternly, although there was again a twinkle in his eye. "I have ordered mighty warriors punished for less!"

"I am but a small, insignificant creature," answered the clever bee. "But if you spare my life, I will one day repay you for your kindness."

The king laughed. "You—pay back the king? What nonsense!" Then he smiled. "But since you have spoken so cleverly, I will let you go. Now go quickly before I change . . ."

The bee was out of sight before he could finish his sentence.

In a few days the king's nose had shrunk back to its former size, and the king soon forgot all about the bee's promise.

Then one day the Queen of Sheba came to Jerusalem to visit Solomon and test his wisdom. To her astonishment Solomon easily solved all the difficult riddles she put to him.

Then she laid before him the most difficult test of all. She summoned fifty young men and fifty young women, each carrying a bouquet of flowers. They lined up in a straight row at the other end of the vast throne room, far from Solomon.

"Only one of these bouquets is real," she told Solomon. "The rest are made by human hands. In your great wisdom, O King of Israel, tell me which of these hundred bouquets was made by God alone."

How distressed Solomon was by Sheba's words! At last the clever queen had outsmarted him. How could he tell the flowers apart? At this great distance, they all looked exactly alike! Suddenly he heard a fierce buzzing outside the window.

In flew a bee, the very one Solomon had long ago forgiven for stinging his nose. Only Solomon heard her buzz into his ear, "Fear not, your majesty! I shall unlock this riddle for you."

Quickly the bee flew across the room and began threading her way through the hundred bouquets. In a matter of seconds she had found the one real bouquet. Triumphantly she sped back to the king and whispered the answer in his ear.

"This is truly a difficult nut to crack, my dear queen," announced Solomon, stepping down from his throne, "but with God's help I will succeed."

And he strode confidently across the room and plucked the real bouquet from the hands of a startled young man.

When the Queen of Sheba saw that Solomon had guessed correctly, her dark eyes grew round with wonder.

"Surely Solomon is the wisest man on earth!" she declared.

No one but Solomon heard a small voice echo hers, "The wis-s-sest indeed!"

102
How the Hoopoe Got Its Crest

Once each month Solomon rode upon his White Eagle to the secret pleasure palace he had built for himself in the wilderness of Palmyra. One day as he rode upon the wings of the giant bird, the sun beat down upon him so intensely that he thought he would die. Suddenly a flock of Hoopoes flew by, and seeing the king's distress, gathered themselves together, wingtip to wingtip, so that they formed a sheltering canopy over the king.

In gratitude for their kindness, Solomon summoned the King of the Hoopoes and said to him, "Ask me whatever you wish, and I shall grant it to you."

For a day and a night the Hoopoes considered Solomon's offer. The next day, their king appeared before Solomon and said, "Here is our wish, my lord: May we be given golden crowns to wear upon our heads?"

Solomon laughed. "Your wish is granted! But know, my friend, that it is a foolish thing you have asked for. It will lead you straight into the hunter's snare. But when such evil overtakes you, return to me and I will remember your kindness and help you again."

The King of the Hoopoes left Solomon's palace with a golden crown upon his head. Soon all of the Hoopoes sported golden crowns, as Solomon had promised. And their pride swelled and so did their vanity, so that they hardly deigned to speak any more to the other birds. At every stream and river and at the shore of the sea, the Hoopoes gazed for hours into the water to admire their beautiful new crowns.

Then one day a hunter saw a Hoopoe with its golden crown and wished to catch it. So he set a trap and placed a mirror inside it. And the Hoopoe flew into the trap to admire itself in the mirror and was caught. Then the hunter wrung the bird's neck and brought the crown to a brass smelter.

The cunning smelter saw that the crown was made not of brass but of gold, but he lied to the hunter and said it was only made of brass. And he gave the hunter a few small coins and told him that he would buy any more crowns the hunter brought him.

But the next time the hunter trapped a Hoopoe, he met a goldsmith on his way into town. When the goldsmith saw the crown in the hunter's hand, he told him that it was made of gold. And he paid the hunter handsomely for the crown and asked for more.

When word of this began to spread, people abandoned their shops and fields and began hunting Hoopoes for their golden crowns. Soon the sounds of whizzing arrows and clanging traps rang throughout the forests and hills, and the Hoopoes became fewer and fewer in number until only a handful remained.

Then the King of the Hoopoes came to King Solomon with a heavy heart and said, "How right you were, my lord king, to call our wish for golden crowns foolish! Now our own vanity has brought evil down upon our heads. Please help us before we are all dead!"

Solomon replied, "Indeed you have brought this trouble upon yourselves, but because you were once so kind to me, I will help you again. No longer shall gold crowns adorn your heads, but instead you shall wear a simple crest of feathers. Thus your beauty shall no longer entrap you."

From then on all the Hoopoes wore crests of feathers upon their heads. And without their gold crowns, hunters no longer pursued them, and they increased in number. Throughout the land they lived in peace and none made them afraid.

103

How the Temple Site Was Chosen

On Mount Moriah in Jerusalem there once lived two brothers. One had a wife and children; the other was unmarried. They all lived together in one house in perfect harmony. Each day the two brothers would rise early and together work their fields.

When it was harvest time, they reaped their grain and brought the sheaves to the threshing floor. There they divided the sheaves into two equal piles and went home.

That night the brother who had no family said to himself, "I am alone, but my brother has a wife and children to feed. Why should my portion be equal to his?"

So he rose from his bed and went to the threshing floor. He took some sheaves from his own pile and added them to his brother's.

That same night, the other brother said to his wife, "It is not right that my brother has the same number of sheaves as I. For I have a greater share of happiness since I have a wife and children, but he is all alone."

So the brother and his wife went secretly to the threshing floor and put some of their own sheaves on the single brother's pile.

The next morning the two brothers rose early and

went to thresh their sheaves. Both were astonished to find the piles still equal. That night they both went again to the threshing floor and met each other there. When they realized why they were both there, they embraced and kissed each other.

That is why God chose their field as the site of the Holy Temple, for it was there that two brothers showed their great love for each other.

104

Asmodeus and the Shamir

After Solomon had been king for many years, God commanded him to build a Temple in Jerusalem.

"My House must be built without tools of iron," said God, "for out of iron, nations make swords, shields, and spears to wage war. It was because of his own bloody hands that I did not permit your father David to build Me a Temple."

"But how can I cut stone without iron tools?" asked Solomon.

"With the Shamir!" answered God.

"And where can I find the Shamir?" asked Solomon.

But the heavenly voice was silent.

So Solomon summoned his chief minister Benaiah ben Yehoyada and said to him, "At twilight on the Sixth Day of Creation God created the Shamir, a miraculous little creature that can cut through any substance on earth but lead. I need the Shamir to build God's Temple, but I do not know where it is. The only one who knows is Asmodeus, King of the Demons."

"But surely he won't tell you!" said Benaiah.

"Then I must capture him and make him tell!" said Solomon.

"And how do you propose to do that?"

"Asmodeus lives on a very high mountain," answered the king. "Each morning before he leaves to do his day's mischief, he places a giant stone over his drinking well so that no one else can drink from it while he is gone. Each night when he comes back, he checks to see that no one has drunk from his well, then drinks his fill and falls asleep."

Then Solomon lowered his voice so that no demon might overhear and warn Asmodeus about the king's plans.

"I want you to go to Asmodeus's mountaintop and bring with you a strong chain, a drill, a bundle of wool, a skin of wine, and my magic gold ring with the Secret Name of God engraved upon it.

"After Asmodeus leaves in the morning, drill a hole at the bottom of the well and drain out all the water. Then plug up the hole with half of the wool. Drill a second hole near the top of the well, below the stone lid, and fill the well with wine. Then plug up that hole, too, and wait for Asmodeus to return home."

Benaiah did exactly as the king had commanded. Taking with him a chain, drill, wool, wine, and the king's magic ring, he traveled for many days until he reached Asmodeus's mountaintop on the other side of the wilderness of Palmyra. Then he crouched behind a boulder waiting for the Demon King to depart. As soon as he was gone, Benaiah drained the water from the well and refilled it with wine. Then he crouched behind the boulder to await Asmodeus's return.

Just as the sun was setting, Benaiah heard the giant's horny chicken-feet scrambling up the mountain. Just as Solomon had said, the first thing Asmodeus did was to check the great stone on top of his well. Satisfied that no one had tampered with it, the giant removed the stone. Then he reached down one hairy hand and scooped up a lakeful of water. How surprised he was to taste wine! Laughing, he reached down for more. Within moments, he had drained the entire well. Suddenly he fell to the ground like a stone, shaking the mountaintop so that Benaiah had to hang on to the boulder to keep from falling off.

When Benaiah was sure that Asmodeus was fast asleep, he crept out from his hiding place and tied the heavy chain around Asmodeus's thick, hairy neck. When the demon awoke hours later, he tried to escape, bellowing like a mad bear. Then Benaiah showed him Solomon's magic ring.

"It is no use trying to escape, Asmodeus," he told the giant demon. "God is mightier than you."

Benaiah brought Asmodeus to Solomon's palace, where the king sat upon his throne, waiting for him.

"Tell me, Asmodeus," commanded Solomon. "Where is the Shamir?"

Asmodeus grumbled, "I know, but I will never tell you!"

Then Solomon held up his magic ring and glared at the demon. "In the name of God, I command you to tell me!"

Asmodeus lowered his hairy head and snorted, "God gave the Shamir to the Hoopoe. She has hidden it in a secret place."

"And where is the Hoopoe's nest?"

"Far, far away, on a mountain on the other side of the sea. But she will never part with it!" Asmodeus warned Solomon. "She has promised God to guard it with her life." And he laughed so loudly that the cedar rafters of the ceiling rattled like dry bones.

Then Solomon imprisoned Asmodeus in his deepest dungeon and sent Benaiah to bring back the Shamir. This time he gave his minister a piece of glass, a lead box, and enough food for a long journey.

Benaiah traveled for many days, across the sea, through forests and deserts, until he came to the Hoopoe's nest. He hid himself and waited until the Hoopoe flew away to find food for her babies. Then he put the piece of glass over her nest.

When the mother bird came back with a worm in her

mouth, she discovered a strange, invisible wall separating her from her babies. She could see them but not touch them.

Off she flew and soon came back with a small creature in her beak. She dropped it on the glass, which shattered instantly. At that moment, Benaiah jumped out from behind the rock, shouting and wildly waving his arms. The Hoopoe was so surprised that she flew away. Benaiah quickly scooped up the Shamir in the lead box and raced down the mountain. He hardly stopped to eat or sleep until he reached Jerusalem.

When the Hoopoe realized what had happened, she was so desolate that she jumped off the mountain and drowned herself in the sea.

Solomon immediately set to work building a beautiful Temple for God in Jerusalem. The tiny Shamir cut all the stones to make the floors and walls.

At last it was done. The great Temple, covered with gold inside and out, shone like the sun itself. But when Solomon commanded Benaiah to bring him the Shamir, it had disappeared! All the king's servants searched high and low but it was nowhere to be found.

To this day no one has ever seen the Shamir again.

105

The Craftsman's Wife and the Glass Vial

When King Solomon was building the Temple in Jerusalem, he sent messages to all the neighboring kings requesting that they send him their best craftsmen to help build the Temple. And soon the most able carpenters and stonemasons and weavers and metalworkers flocked to Jerusalem. And Solomon paid them many times their usual wages for their work.

In one faraway city lived a craftsman who was known throughout his country as a man of exceptional talent. The king of that city had this man brought to his palace, and the king ordered him to go to Jerusalem to answer the Israelite king's summons.

But the man refused, for he had a wife of extraordinary beauty, and he feared that she would be seduced by another man if he left her for such a long time.

"I shall give you a choice," said the king. "Either go to Jerusalem—or die!"

When the man came home that night, his wife immediately saw that something was wrong. Her husband's usually cheerful face was downcast, and he spoke few words to her.

"What is wrong?" she asked him.

And he told her what the king had said.

To his surprise, his wife laughed merrily. "Is that all? By all means, go to Jerusalem! You need not worry about me. I promise you that I will guard my virtue with my life and that no man but you shall have me, not even if he should be a king"

But her husband would not be persuaded. "There is none so fair as you in all the world," he told her. "Even if your heart wishes to remain true, perhaps some man will take you by force or by deceit."

Then his wife took a glass vial, put in it a cotton wick and a burning coal, and sealed up the vial.

"Take this," she said to her husband, "and wear it around your neck at all times. If the coal does not burn the wick, know that I have not been burned by a sinful passion either, but have remained pure. However, if the wick begins to burn, know that I too have been inflamed by an unholy desire and that all is lost."

Reassured by his wife's words, the man rejoiced with her that night, and the next morning he set out for Jerusalem.

One day as Solomon was overseeing the Temple workers, he noticed a strange glass vial hanging around the neck of one of his new foreign craftsmen.

"What can this possibly mean?" he asked himself, and he had the craftsman brought to him.

The craftsman told the king why he was wearing the unusual necklace.

"Impossible!" thought Solomon to himself. "No woman can resist temptation forever!" And he determined to test the craftsman's wife to see if the vial would indeed reveal her unfaithfulness.

The next day he sent two exceptionally handsome young men to the woman's house with much gold and gifts, and instructed them not to return until they had seduced her.

When the two young men arrived at the woman's house, she offered them good food and wine, and then showed them to their room. But as soon as they were inside, she locked the door. For the next month, she had her servants bring them ample food and drink every day, but would not let them out of their room. For she understood that they had come to seduce her, and she suspected King Solomon's hand in it.

All this time Solomon had been daily observing the craftsman's vial, confident that the wick inside would soon burst into flames. When it did not after an entire month, he determined to investigate the matter himself.

Disguising himself as a merchant and taking with him two trusted attendants, he set out for the city where the craftsman's wife lived. She fed Solomon and his attendants royally, then showed them to their rooms. The next day she did the same.

On the third day she brought Solomon a basket of hard-boiled eggs, each painted a different color. Then she took an egg of each color and said to her guest, "Tell me, my lord king, which of these eggs tastes the best?"

Solomon drew back, astonished. "Which of us are you calling king?"

The woman smiled. "It is no secret that you are a king, my lord, for royalty shines out of your eyes. And I suspect that you are Solomon, since your words disclose great wisdom. If so, tell me, O wise Solomon: Which of these eggs has the best flavor?"

And Solomon said, "What a foolish question, woman! Even though these eggs look different on the outside, they all taste the same inside!"

The craftsman's wife smiled again and said, "So it is with women, your majesty. Although some are beautiful on the outside and some ugly, yet they are all the same inside. And just as a person throws away the eggshell, no matter how finely colored, and eats what is inside, so too it is the inside of a woman that one values, not what is on the outside.

"Now, since that is the case, why did your majesty go to so much trouble to sleep with me simply because of my colorful shell? I knew immediately that the two young men were sent to seduce me, and I expected that you would come yourself when they didn't return after a month.

"But of what use is it, my lord, to try to ruin my virtue? You are the king of kings, and I am but a poor woman of little means. You have the power to do whatever you desire with me. But I know that you are a wise man, and that you know how vain are the pleasures of this world."

Her wise words pleased the king, and he said to her, "Blessed are you and blessed is the husband who has you for his wife! When I saw the vial hanging around your husband's neck and learned its purpose, I wished to test you to see if it was indeed possible to stay entirely free from sin. Now I know that you are a woman of valor. From now on, you shall be as a sister to me, and I shall honor you for the rest of my life."

Then the woman released the two young men from their room, and they feasted and rejoiced all evening. And the king returned to Jerusalem and told the craftsman all that had happened. Then he paid him many times his wages and sent him home to his wife.

Husband and wife rejoiced together and loved each other ten times more than before. And for the rest of his life, King Solomon honored the craftsman and his wife, and held them dear to his heart.

106

Solomon and Naamah

For many years after the Temple was completed, Solomon kept the demon Asmodeus prisoner in his dungeon. One day Solomon said to him, "How can you call yourself King of the Demons if I, a mere man of flesh and blood, can hold you captive?"

"Release me from my chains and give me your magic ring," answered Asmodeus. "Then we shall see who is king."

Confident of his own power, Solomon granted Asmodeus's wish. Instantly the demon seized the king's crown, and with a single flick of his powerful wing, hurled Solomon four hundred miles from Jerusalem.

Asmodeus then flung Solomon's magic ring into the sea, where it was swallowed by a fish. For Asmodeus thought, "If anyone should gain possession of the ring, he will know what I have done."

Then the Demon King disguised himself as Solomon and sat down upon his golden throne.

When Solomon fell to earth, he found himself in an abandoned field. Bewildered, he looked down into a pool of rainwater and behold! His royal robes had turned to rags, his face was now covered with a dirty beard, and the thin furrow that had once ringed his brow—the mark of Israel's kings—was gone.

Sadly, Solomon cut a wooden staff for himself and began to wander the countryside as a beggar, crying, "I am Solomon! Once I was King of Israel! Now I rule only the dust!"

People thought him mad. Children ran after him, laughing and throwing stones.

Back in Jerusalem, Asmodeus managed to convince the entire court that he was the real king. He made sure never to show the royal servants his feet, lest they discover that they were like a rooster's. And he refused to see Benaiah or Solomon's wives, for they knew the real king too well.

For three years Asmodeus reigned in Solomon's place, while the poor beggar-king wandered in foreign lands. Solomon in his wisdom soon realized that God was making him atone one year for each of his three sins: taking too many wives, too many horses, and too much silver and gold.

At the end of three years, Solomon came to the foreign capital of Ammon. A servant of the Ammonite king came to the market where Solomon was begging and hired him as a cook.

One day Solomon asked the master cook if he might prepare a meal for the king. Recalling the dishes from his own royal table, Solomon prepared a feast unlike any ever seen before in the land of the Ammonites. The king immediately elevated Solomon to chief cook.

The king of the Ammonites had an only daughter, Naamah, a beautiful and kindhearted girl. Naamah fell in love with her father's cook, for he was a handsome man despite his coarse clothes. When her father learned of her wish to marry his poor cook, he became furious.

"Are there no worthy princes in my kingdom that you must settle for one of my servants?"

But Naamah would not change her mind. At first the king desired to kill them both. But then he took pity on Naamah, his only daughter, and sent them off together to die in the wilderness.

"Let me not see their love or their death," he said.

Solomon tried to persuade Naamah to return to her father's palace, but she would not leave him, for she loved him dearly. After many days they came to the seashore and there bought a fish to satisfy their great hunger. When Naamah cut open the fish, she found in its belly Solomon's magic ring with God's Holy Name engraved upon it.

Solomon placed the gold ring upon his finger. Instantly his rags turned into purple velvet cloth, his face began to shine, and a thin line creased his smooth brow. Then Solomon told the astonished princess who he was and all that had happened to him. He vowed to make her his queen and her firstborn son king after him.

Then they made their way to Jerusalem. At first the king's ministers only laughed at Solomon's claim that he was the true king. But when he showed them his magic ring and the furrow of a crown on his forehead, they all believed him. Then they realized that for three years no one in the palace had ever seen the king's feet.

Then Solomon strode fearlessly into the palace where Asmodeus sat upon his golden throne.

"Remove your shoes, impostor!" demanded Solomon.

As soon as he saw the real king, Asmodeus let out a fierce howl and jumped out of his shoes, revealing the horny yellow claws of a chicken. Then he unfurled his great black wings, which had been hidden so long under his robe, and spread them wide so that one touched heaven and the other hell. And then, still shrieking, he flew away to his dark and lonely mountain, never to be seen again.

Then Solomon ordered a great wedding feast and invited all the kings and queens from near and far. How great was the joy of the King of Ammon when he recognized his daughter and his cook whom he had given up for dead!

As he had promised, Solomon made his new wife Queen of Israel. And a year later she gave birth to a son, whom they named Rehoboam. And in time Rehoboam became king after Solomon.

107

The Mysterious Palace

Even more wondrous than the White Eagle and the White Lion was Solomon's Flying Cloak. It was sixty miles long and sixty miles wide, made of green silk cloth woven with threads of fine gold. On it were pictures of every living thing in God's creation: birds and beasts, flowers and trees, crawling things and the monsters of the deep. On this magic cloak Solomon would fly throughout the world, rising so high that the earth seemed no bigger than a ripe gourd. So swift did it fly that he could eat his breakfast in Jerusalem and his dinner in Timbuktu.

One day as he was flying upon his magic cloak with a company of demons and spirits, Solomon glanced down and saw the most splendid palace he had ever seen. It was built all of gold and shone like the sun.

But when he stood before its golden walls he could find no way inside. No gates or windows broke the smooth gold surface of the walls.

Solomon sent one of the demons to the roof. The demon soon returned accompanied by a magnificent black eagle.

"Is there any way to enter this palace?" Solomon asked the eagle.

"I do not know, your majesty," answered the eagle, "for I am but seven hundred years old. But I have a brother who is two hundred years older than I. Perhaps he may know."

"Summon him!" commanded the king.

Soon a white eagle stood before Solomon, even more majestic than his younger brother. But he, too, did not know the answer to Solomon's question.

"But I have a brother who is four hundred years older than I," the white eagle said to Solomon. "Perhaps he will know."

The third brother was a great golden eagle, so ancient that he needed to be held up on either side by his two younger brothers.

"I have not seen it with my own eyes," he croaked, "but I once heard my grandfather speak of a gate in the western wall. If you dig there, perhaps you will find it."

Then Solomon commanded the four winds to blow away the centuries of dust piled before the western wall. There he found an old iron gate and beside it, in a cavity in the wall, a glass box containing four keys, one of iron, one of brass, one of silver, and one of gold. Above the gate was an inscription:

Know that we who lived in this palace were once happy, enjoying all that our hearts desired. But famine came upon us and we ground our pearls into flour but still had no bread to eat. So we left this palace to the eagles and died.

Let no one enter here but a king.

With the iron key Solomon unlocked the door and found behind it a brass gate, then a silver one, then one of gold. Inside the gold door he found many rooms filled with precious things. There were pillars of crystal, floors of gold, domes of rubies, emeralds, and pearls. In the walls glittered sapphires, shining like stars.

On the floor of the farthest room, Solomon found a silver scorpion. When he picked it up, the floor in front of him yawned open, revealing an underground cavern more beautiful than anything he had seen so far. Sweet perfume and music drifted through the air like a dream. In this room, seated upon an ivory throne, was a lifelike statue, around whose neck hung a silver tablet on a golden chain. But when Solomon drew near the statue, it breathed out fire and smoke from its nostrils.

Then Solomon pronounced the Secret Name of God, and the statue instantly fell to the ground, shattering into a thousand pieces. The king picked up the tablet but discovered to his dismay that the words were written in a language he did not know. Despite all his wisdom he could make no sense of it.

Suddenly a beautiful maiden entered the room. She walked soundlessly toward the king and took the silver tablet from his hand. In a sweet, infinitely sad voice she read the words:

I am Shadad, son of Ad.
King of kings was I once.
Lions and bears trembled at my name!
The world proclaimed my glory and might.
I ruled over thousands of princes;
On thousands of horses I rode;
Thousands of warriors I struck down.
But before the Angel of Death I was powerless.

The maiden paused. Then with silver tears flowing down her pale cheeks, she read the last words: "You who read this, remember: Nothing remains in a man's possession but a good name."

Then she withdrew as silently as she had come.

Solomon then mounted his Flying Cloak and returned home, a sadder but wiser man. And he wrote in his book of wisdom: "Vanity of vanities, all is vanity!"

108
The Ruby Serpent

Solomon knew that he was the wisest king in the world, but he wished to prove it. So he decided to make a test to demonstrate his extraordinary wisdom.

He gave a great banquet to which he invited all the neighboring kings and queens. After they had eaten and drunk their fill, Solomon announced, "I say that there is nothing in the world more powerful than love! Human hands cannot built walls high enough to keep true love out."

His guests laughed gaily at his bold words.

Solomon smiled. "We shall see who has the last laugh." Then he said, "To prove my claim about love, I will command a tower to be built on a faraway island. There I will lock up my beautiful young daughter Keziah. Then we will wait to see what happens."

The guests all looked at each other and shook their heads. Surely Solomon had gone mad!

Over the next few months Solomon's Flying Cloak flew hundreds of workers to a secret island where they built a tall stone tower. Its walls were so smooth that no human hand or foot could ever hope to scale them. Beside the tower grew a great oak tree, whose lowest branches were one hundred feet above the ground and whose massive trunk was as thick as fifty men standing together.

At the top of the tower was a room with a single window. There the princess would live—alone. From this window she could see the green forest below and the wide ocean all around.

When the work was completed, the Cloak flew Solomon and Keziah to the room at the top of the tower.

Solomon took his daughter's hand in his and said to her, "Do not fear, my little dove. No harm will come to you here. Each day, my White Eagle will bring you the tastiest foods from the royal table. And a beautiful bird will perch in this oak tree to talk to you and keep you company."

But at his words the princess began to cry.

"Do not be sad," said the king. "I promise you that soon someone will come to rescue you. Then you will leave this tower forever."

Then he flew off upon the Flying Cloak, leaving Keziah all alone.

Far to the north lived a Hebrew merchant who had an only son named Natanyah, a wise and handsome boy. The merchant loved Natanyah and gave him everything he wanted, except for one thing: He would not let his son go to sea. Many years before, the merchant's beautiful young wife had drowned at sea. The merchant was afraid that the same thing would happen to his only son.

But Natanyah wanted to sail in a ship more than anything in the world. Every day he asked his father, "When will you let me go to sea, Father? Please, if you love me, let me go!"

Finally his father gave in. When the day came for Natanyah to sail, the old merchant gave him a small box. Inside the boy found the largest ruby he had ever seen, so bright he had to shield his eyes with one hand.

"I captured this jewel from a powerful serpent," said the merchant, "and gave it to your mother on her wedding day. May its magic powers protect you in your travels."

Happily, Natanyah grasped the ruby, leapt aboard the ship, and waved good-bye to his father. But the merchant's heart was seized by a terrible fear as he watched the ship sail away.

After a few days a great storm arose at sea. When the ship was about to sink, the merchant's old servant tied Natanyah between two wine sacks and tied a waterskin around his neck. Then Natanyah tied the leather pouch containing the ruby around his waist. A moment later a huge wave swept him overboard into the boiling sea.

For days Natanyah drifted, drinking from the waterskin to quench his terrible thirst. Suddenly he saw above him a great White Eagle, which swooped down and plucked him out of the sea with its powerful claws. The bird carried him to a deserted island and dropped him in the middle of a beautiful forest.

After wandering for many hours, Natanyah saw, on top of the island's only mountain, a tall stone tower standing alone.

"Surely this belongs to pirates or a sorcerer," he thought.

But when he came near the tower, Natanyah saw at the top a young girl talking to a gaily colored bird perched upon her finger. How beautiful she was! She had long, black hair like silk, golden skin, and tiny hands like a kitten's paws. Natanyah instantly fell in love with her.

"But how can I reach her?" he wondered.

Then he remembered the ruby. Hadn't his father said that it had magical powers? Maybe it had brought him here to rescue the princess in the tower. He took it out of its leather pouch and rubbed it between his fingers.

Suddenly a giant speckled serpent slithered out of the bushes and seized the gleaming ruby in its mouth. Before Natanyah could stop it, the snake sped to the tall oak tree beside the tower and coiled around it like a giant screw.

Then magically, the tail slithered down and wrapped itself around Natanyah's hands, pulling him up. He scrambled up the serpent's twisted body as though scaling a ladder. When he reached the top of the tree, he saw that the snake's neck had stretched itself out to the window of the tower like a stiff beam. Eagerly Natanyah bounded across it and leapt down.

There on the stone floor lay his ruby, and looking up at him with startled black eyes was the princess in the tower.

"You have come at last!" she cried. "Now we are two!"

The two embraced and told each other all that had happened to them.

The next day Solomon noticed that the White Eagle took two portions from the royal table to bring to the tower. Immediately he ordered his Flying Cloak to fly him and his ministers to the island to see what had become of the lonely princess.

Imagine their amazement to find Princess Keziah sitting together with a handsome young man!

The Cloak then flew them all back to the palace, where Natanyah's old father awaited them, flown there upon the wings of the White Eagle. Soon afterward, the young couple was married amid great festivity.

"And now," said the king to the wedding guests, "do you acknowledge how wise I am? Has not love conquered all?"

All eyes turned toward the young bride and bridegroom who blushed beneath their gaze. Love shone in their eyes as brightly as the brilliant red ruby now sparkling upon Princess Keziah's smooth, honeyed brow.

109
This Too Shall Pass

Benaiah ben Yehoyada was King Solomon's most trusted minister. He used to boast that he had never failed to do what the king asked of him.

One day Solomon decided to humble Benaiah to put an end to his boasting. So he summoned his minister and said to him, "Benaiah, there is a certain ring I want you to find and bring to me. I wish to wear it for Sukkot. That gives you six months to find it."

"If it exists anywhere on earth, your majesty," replied Benaiah, "I will find it and bring it to you! But what makes this ring so special?"

"It has magic powers," answered the king. "If a happy man looks at it, he becomes sad, and if a sad man looks at it, he becomes happy."

Now Solomon knew that no such ring existed in the world, but he wished to give his minister a little taste of humility.

"You shall have it in time for Sukkot!" promised Benaiah, and eagerly he left the palace to begin his search.

But as hard as he looked, he could not find the ring. He searched all the jewelry shops in Jerusalem, but no jeweler had ever heard of such a ring. He asked caravan drivers who traveled to far-off markets in Egypt and Babylon and the Spice Lands of the East, but they had never run across it. He asked ship captains who sailed the seven seas, but they too were ignorant of such a ring.

Spring passed and then summer, and still Benaiah had no idea where he could find the ring. As Sukkot neared, he became so sad that he avoided seeing people, especially the king.

On the night before Sukkot, he decided to take a walk in one of the poorest quarters of Jerusalem.

"Perhaps," he thought, "a miracle will happen and I will find the ring tucked away in some forgotten corner of a poor jeweler's shop."

But as dawn began to light up the eastern sky, he still had had no luck.

Then he passed by a young merchant who had just begun to set out his day's wares on a shabby carpet in front of his shop.

"Have you by any chance heard of a magic ring that makes the happy wearer forget his joy and the broken-hearted wearer forget his sorrows?" asked Benaiah. "If you have such a ring, you may ask any price, and I will pay it."

The young merchant shook his head. But nearby, his grandfather overheard Benaiah's question, and he now beckoned to his grandson with one gnarled finger. He whispered something into his grandson's ear, which made the young man smile broadly.

"Wait!" he called out to Benaiah, who had begun to walk away. "I think I can help you."

Benaiah's heart almost stopped beating, and he ran back to the young merchant. Baffled, he watched the man take a plain gold band from his carpet and engrave something on it. But when Benaiah read the words engraved on the ring, his face broke out in a wide smile.

"This is it!" he cried, and he emptied his purse of gold coins into the merchant's hands. Then he ran swiftly through the dark streets to the king's palace, grasping the gold ring tightly in his hand.

That night the entire city welcomed in the holiday of Sukkot with great festivity. In the palace, Solomon presided over a magnificent feast for all his court. Benaiah sat down near the king, concealing the ring in his pocket until the king should ask for it.

"Well, my friend," said Solomon, "have you found what I sent you after?"

All the ministers laughed, and Solomon himself smiled. Poor Benaiah! He had finally failed his king and would feel the sting of shame. But Solomon was prepared to redeem his minister's honor by now revealing to him that he had been sent on a wild goose chase.

But to everyone's surprise, Benaiah held up a small gold ring and declared, "Here it is, your majesty!"

As soon as Solomon read the inscription, the smile vanished from his face. For the jeweler had written three Hebrew letters on the gold band: *gimel, zayin, yud,* which begin the words *"Gam zeh ya'avor"*—"This too shall pass."

At that moment Solomon realized that all his wisdom and fabulous wealth and tremendous power were but fleeting things, for one day he would be nothing but dust. And the amusement he had felt just a moment before now gave way to sorrow.

Solomon beckoned to his minister and said, "I have always known you were faithful, Benaiah, but now I know that you are truly wise."

Then Solomon slipped the ruby signet ring off his finger and replaced it with the gold band that Benaiah had brought him.

"I shall always wear this ring, my friend," he said, "and keep its wisdom close to my heart. And you shall have this ruby ring as my thanks to you."

And until the day he died, Benaiah never once failed to do whatever the king asked of him.

PART VI

TALES OF THE SECOND COMMONWEALTH

In 586 B.C.E. Jerusalem fell to Babylon. Fifty years later the Persian Cyrus allowed the captives to return home to rebuild the ruins. Most chose to stay in their adopted home; a brave remnant made the long trek back to Jerusalem. For the next five centuries, foreign powers challenged Jewish life both in Israel and in the Diaspora. Then, in 70 C.E., Rome reduced Jerusalem to ashes and exiled the Jewish people from their holy land.

110
The Tale of Tobit

After the reign of Solomon, the twelve tribes divided into two kingdoms, Israel in the north and Judah in the south. Then Assyria came and conquered the northern kingdom and scattered its ten tribes to the winds.

Among those carried off into exile were Tobit, his wife Hannah, and their only son Tobias. They came to the city of Nineveh and settled there among their exiled countrymen. Although he was now living among strangers with foreign ways, Tobit did not forsake the God of Israel or the Torah, but continued to live righteously. He gave generously to the poor, acted justly, and did not bow down to foreign gods. And whenever he saw the abandoned corpse of a Jew lying in the street, he himself would bury it.

Once Tobit traveled to the city of Ragae in Persia, now called Teheran, where he met a poor merchant. He lent the man a considerable sum of money, and the man promised to repay him some day.

Then the king of Assyria died and his son, Sennacherib, came to the throne. Sennacherib hated the Jews, for they had shamefully defeated him in Jerusalem, and he ordered many Jews executed. Against the king's orders, Tobit buried the bodies. Then Sennacherib ordered Tobit killed and his property confiscated. Tobit fled from the king's wrath and hid himself among his kinsmen.

Then Sennacherib died at the hands of his own son, and a new king ascended the throne. This king did not hate the Jews, and he ordered Tobit's house restored to him.

But a new misfortune soon struck Tobit. One day as he gazed into the sky, a bird's droppings fell into his eyes, and he became blind. Always a faithful man, he did not curse God, but instead prayed for his own death.

At the same time in the distant city of Ecbatana in Persia, a young kinswoman of Tobit's named Sarah was also praying for death. For she had married seven husbands, one after the other, and all seven had died on their wedding night at the hands of Asmodeus, King of the Demons. So she too longed to die to escape her shame.

Now that he could no longer support himself because he was blind, Tobit decided to send his son Tobias to Ragae to reclaim the loan he had made long ago. He instructed Tobias to find a trustworthy guide to accompany him. Tobias went to the marketplace and hired a man named Azariah, who was really the angel Raphael in disguise.

When the two reached the Tigris River, Tobias stopped to wash. As he knelt on the bank, a great fish suddenly leapt out of the water and frightened him. Raphael told Tobias to seize the fish by the fins, kill it, and take out its heart, liver, and gallbladder. He revealed to Tobias that burning the heart and liver would drive away evil spirits and that the gallbladder could cure blindness. So Tobias salted the organs and wrapped them safely for the journey.

Next they journeyed to Ecbatana, where Tobias's kinsmen lived. Along the way, Raphael urged Tobias to marry Sarah, since he was her only eligible kinsman.

Tobias, however, feared that he would meet the same fate as all her other husbands. But his companion assured him that the fish's heart and liver would protect him. So reluctantly he agreed to do what his companion suggested.

That night, after the wedding ceremony, Sarah's father dug a new grave beside the seven other graves behind their house, certain that he would be laying the body of his daughter's latest bridegroom there the next morning. Then he and his wife went to bed with heavy hearts.

When the newly married couple went into their bedroom that night, Tobias unwrapped the fish's heart and liver and laid them upon the hot coals in the fireplace. Then Asmodeus appeared, his great wings stirring up a whirlwind in the room and his hairy body reeking of the grave. But when Tobias fanned the bitter smoke toward him, he fled shrieking from the room.

The next morning the couple emerged whole and smiling from their room. When Sarah's parents saw them, they rejoiced and feasted with them for the next fourteen days. During this time, Raphael traveled to Ragae and returned with the sum of money owed to Tobit. Then Sarah's father gave the newlyweds half of his property and promised them the other half upon his death. Then they started home for Nineveh.

As they approached Tobit's house, Tobias saw his blind old father stumbling toward them in the road. Tobias ran forward and anointed his father's eyes with the fish's gall. Instantly the white scales clouding them dropped off, and Tobit regained his sight. He embraced his son and his new bride and welcomed them joyously into his home.

When Tobias told his father how Azariah had helped him on his journey and had cured Tobit's blindness, Tobit sent for the guide to reward him. But when he stood before him, Raphael revealed to them who he really was and then suddenly vanished from sight.

Tobit lived to a very old age, performing many deeds

of charity and goodness. Before he died, he warned Tobias and Sarah that Nineveh would one day be destroyed, as Jonah had prophesied. And when Tobit died, they moved to Ecbatana with their children and inherited Sarah's parents' estate.

In their old age, Sarah and Tobias received word that mighty Nineveh had fallen. And they were very pleased indeed.

111

Shadrach, Mishach, and Abednego

A few generations after the conquest of the northern kingdom of Israel, Nebuchadnezzar swooped down upon Judah with his mighty army and conquered it. His forces destroyed Jerusalem and burned God's Holy Temple to the ground. Those who escaped the enemy's sword were exiled to Babylon.

Among the exiles were four princes of Judah—Daniel, Hananiah, Mishael, and Azariah. The conquerors gave them new names—Belteshazzar, Shadrach, Mishach, and Abednego—and taught them a new language and new customs. In time they entered the king's service and gave him wise counsel. Daniel remained in the king's court and the other three became officers in the province of Babylon.

But they did not forsake the ways of their people or their God.

Then Nebuchadnezzar had a great golden statue made and set it up in the plain outside his capital. And he commanded all his princes and officials to attend the dedication of the statue and to bow before it. Anyone who failed to appear would face death in a fiery furnace.

From near and far they came, speaking all languages, and wearing all manner of costume. And they all bowed before the king's statue.

But Shadrach, Mishach, and Abednego failed to appear, and several men came to the king to report them. "Who do they think they are?" raged the king when he heard their report. "No one disobeys the king and lives to boast of it!"

So the three Israelites were seized and bound with strong cord. Then Nebuchadnezzar's servants brought them to the mouth of the fiery furnace.

Before they were thrown into the fire, the king said to them, "Why do you insist on adhering so steadfastly to your God when all your fellow Israelites have bowed before my idol?"

And they answered him, "You are king when it comes to taxes and tribute and other earthly affairs, but in this matter you are only Nebuchadnezzar. We will not obey your command."

When the king heard their words, he was so enraged that he ordered the furnace made seven times hotter, so his servants fed pitch and oil to the flames. And the flames leapt seventy-five feet out of the furnace and consumed the servants.

Released from their hands, Shadrach, Mishach, and Abednego fell into the furnace. As the flames danced around them, they cried out to heaven, "*Adonai*, save us!"

Then Gabriel, the Angel of Fire, descended into the furnace and cooled the flames surrounding the three men while he fanned the flames outside. The fire grew so hot that Nebuchadnezzar himself was half burned when he tried to peer inside. What he saw astonished him: Four men were strolling peacefully among the flames, their clothing unscorched, their hair unsinged. Three of them he recognized as his ministers, but the fourth seemed not a creature of this earth.

Then he ordered the three Israelites to come out of the furnace. They emerged from the flames with the songs of *Hallel* upon their lips, and the king gaped in awe.

As soon as they left the furnace, it rose high in the air and broke apart, the pieces raining down upon the heads of the onlookers like great hailstones. Then the enormous golden statue that Nebuchadnezzar had erected crashed to the ground and shattered.

And on that day Nebuchadnezzar issued a decree: "Whoever slanders the God of Shadrach, Mishach, and Abednego shall be torn limb from limb and his house confiscated, for there is no other God who is able to perform wonders like theirs!"

And the king promoted the three princes of Judah, and their names became known throughout the land of Babylon.

112
Susannah and the Elders

In Babylon there lived an Israelite woman named Susannah who was pious and good-hearted and also very beautiful. Her husband Yehoyakin was also a righteous man, more honored than any other Israelite in Babylon. Behind their house was a private garden where Susannah walked with her handmaids and bathed each evening.

Every day two elders would come to Yehoyakin and Susannah's house to judge the people. When they saw Susannah's beauty, their hearts were inflamed with desire, and they wished to lie with her. Day after day they schemed and awaited their chance.

One afternoon, after all the people had gone home, the two men climbed to the roof and hid themselves there. Soon Susannah came into the garden below with her servants. She sent them away to bring her anointing oils, and then she undressed herself.

When the two elders saw her naked body, they jumped down from the roof and shouted to her, "Lie with us now, Susannah, or we shall tell everyone that you were making love here with a young man!"

Fearful for her life and honor, she cried out, "God of Israel, save me from these wicked men!"

But when her servants and family came running, the

elders accused her of lying with a young man, as they had threatened. They brought her before the people and said, "We saw this woman entering her garden with her servants, but she sent them away and a young man appeared and lay with her. We tried to catch him but he ran away."

All the people were astonished, for Susannah had always been such a pious and modest woman. But how could they doubt the words of elders who were the judges of the people? So they grabbed hold of Susannah and dragged her off to stone her.

Susannah prayed to God for deliverance, and God heard her prayers and answered them.

The spirit of God entered Daniel, who was then only a young man in the king's court, and he called out to the people, "Wait! Is this what the Torah teaches—to kill a person without a proper investigation? Bring the elders to me, and I shall get to the bottom of this matter."

So they brought the elders to Daniel, and he separated them. He said to the first, "Tell me the truth—and remember that an angel is standing by to split you in two! Under what tree were they sinning?"

"An oak tree," answered the first elder with confidence.

"There is no oak tree in Susannah's garden!" said Daniel. And the people went to investigate and confirmed Daniel's words.

Then he questioned the second elder and asked, "Under what tree were Susannah and the young man lying—and remember that an angel is waiting nearby to slice off that lustful head of yours!"

"A mulberry tree . . . I think," said the second elder, less confident than his friend.

"There is no mulberry tree in Susannah's garden!" said Daniel, and the people confirmed that this was so.

Then the people seized the lying elders and stoned them instead of Susannah. Susannah and her family thanked Daniel and praised God for sending him. And all of Israel acknowledged Daniel's wisdom.

113

Bel and the Dragon

Once when Darius the Persian, King of Babylon, was celebrating the feast of the god Bel, he said to his trusted counselor Daniel, "If only you would believe in the power of Bel, who consumes all this food set out before him!"

He pointed to the bull, the ten rams, the hundred doves, and the seventy loaves of bread arrayed before them on the long table.

"How can his majesty believe in something that is only vanity and death?" replied Daniel. "Bel is no more than the work of human hands. How can he eat? How can he drink? No, it is the priests who eat this food in secret and fool the people into believing it is Bel. If you will give me permission, I will prove it to you."

And Darius said, "So be it."

So Daniel ordered all the gates and doors of Bel's temple locked except the main entrance. Then he had the king's servants bring him ashes, and he scattered them around the table set for Bel. But the priests were not told of this.

When he had finished, Daniel and the king left through the main entrance, locked the door behind them, and set the royal seal upon it. The next morning they inspected the seal and found that it had not been disturbed during the night.

"See, Daniel!" said the king, delighted. "No one has been here!"

Inside they found only bones and crumbs on the table. Overjoyed, the king cried, "Now you must acknowledge Bel's power! Only he could have eaten the food we left for him."

But Daniel shook his head and pointed to the ashes on the floor. "Then whose footprints are these, your majesty?"

Darius bent down and saw in the ashes many foot-prints of men, women, and children. "So, my priests have lied!" he said. "Bring them to me at once!"

When the priests were brought before the king, they confessed that they had entered the temple through secret tunnels and had eaten all the food themselves. Then the king ordered the temple of Bel destroyed so that not one stone remained standing.

But still the nobles of Babylon were not convinced that their gods were things of vanity and death, as Daniel claimed.

"Let Daniel meet the Sacred Dragon and prevail over him, and then we shall believe in his invisible god!" they declared to the king.

This Sacred Dragon lived in a cave outside the city. Every day people would bring offerings there and throw them down before the mouth of the cave. Then the Dragon would emerge, rear up on its great hind legs, and quickly gobble up the animals they had brought for a sacrifice.

"If Daniel can defeat this *living* god," said the nobles, "then we will believe what he says about our gods." Secretly, they were convinced that Daniel would meet his end in the Dragon's cave.

So the king asked Daniel if he could defeat the Dragon as he had defeated Bel.

"Not only will I destroy him," answered Daniel, "but I will do it without using sword or spear. This Dragon is only a crawling thing like a worm, and God gave us dominion over such detestable things. It is the nobles I fear, not the Dragon."

"You have my word that I will protect you from them," promised the king.

So Daniel took two iron combs used for combing flax and glued them back to back so that their sharp tines faced outward like a porcupine. Then he covered the iron tines with fats and honey so that they were completely hidden from view.

He then went to the Dragon's cave and tossed his offering into the Dragon's gaping mouth. And the Dragon swallowed it whole. But when it entered his belly, the fats melted and the tines thrust into the Dragon's soft organs so that he died.

The next day when the nobles came to bring their sacrifices to the Dragon, they saw no movement at the mouth of the cave. Instead, a dreadful stink filled the air. When they entered the cave, they found the Dragon's lifeless body swarming with maggots and snakes.

The nobles were enraged. "What has this Jew Daniel done to us, killing both our gods and making us a laughingstock before the king! Let us kill him before he destroys us all!"

But the king uncovered their plot and had them all executed before they could harm Daniel. And that was the end of Bel and the Dragon.

114

The Strongest Thing in the World

Darius, King of Persia, had three bodyguards—a Persian prince, a Hindu prince, and Zerubbavel, prince of Judah, grandson of King Yehoyakin. One night when King Darius was asleep, the three men decided to hold a contest among themselves.

"Let us each declare what is the strongest thing in the world," they agreed. "When the king awakes, he will choose which of our answers is best."

So they each took a slip of paper and wrote down their answers.

The Persian wrote, "Wine is the strongest thing in the world, for it banishes sorrow and gives birth to joy."

The Hindu wrote, "The word of the king is the strongest thing in the world, for all must bow to his will—or die."

And Zerubbavel wrote, "The power of woman is the strongest thing in the world, for she can humble even kings. But stronger than all these things is Truth, for the earth requires it, the heavens acknowledge it, all of creation kneels before it. It is perfect. To it belong power and glory. Blessed be the God of Truth!"

They placed their slips of paper under the king's pillow and quietly left the room.

When the king awoke, he summoned all his advisors and ministers to hear the words of his three bodyguards. When the first two defended their answers, the ministers and advisors praised their wisdom. But when they heard Zerubbavel's answer, they cried in one voice, "Mighty is Truth! Nothing can compare to it!"

The king then turned to Zerubbavel and said, "You have won the contest, young prince of Judah. Now you may name your prize. What is your wish?"

"Only one thing do I desire, your majesty," answered Zerubbavel, "to lead my people out of captivity back to their home and to rebuild God's Temple in Jerusalem. Give us permission to leave and to bring back with us the holy vessels taken by Nebuchadnezzar."

"Granted!" declared the king.

Before he died, Darius instructed his successor Cyrus to give Zerubbavel all that he had promised him. And Zerubbavel led the captives home to Jerusalem. There they rebuilt the ruined Temple. It was Zerubbavel who found the celestial fire hidden by Jeremiah at the destruction of the Temple, and with it they rekindled the Eternal Flame.

It was at this time that Zerubbavel, whose name means "planted in Babylon," received his Hebrew name, Nehemiah, which means "comforted by God." And God decreed that he would join Elijah at the End of Days to herald the Messiah and summon all the scattered exiles back home.

115

The Capture and Release of the Evil Inclination

Soon after the return from Babylonian exile, the Jewish people again returned to sin. Fearful of another national catastrophe, Ezra and the other leaders prayed to God to erase the evil inclination from every heart in Israel.

"Although it is good for us to triumph over our evil inclination," they said, "it is better to have no evil inclination at all, so that we receive neither punishment nor reward."

In response to their prayers, a note fluttered down from heaven with a single word written upon it: "Truth." And they knew that their prayers had been answered.

For three days and nights they fasted. Then the Evil Inclination came charging out of the Holy of Holies like a fiery lion.

"This is the Evil!" cried the prophet Zechariah.

They tried to seize the beast but only managed to grasp a single hair and pull it out. The creature bellowed so loudly that its cry was heard a thousand miles away.

"How shall we capture this monster?" asked the frightened people.

"Place it in a lead pot," said Zechariah. "But take care not to destroy it, or the entire world will perish."

For three days they held it captive in the lead pot. But during this time, the chickens stopped laying eggs, for sexual desire had vanished from the world. Not one egg could be found for the sick in all of Palestine.

"What shall we do?" the people cried. "If we kill this evil creature, disaster will befall us, but if we keep it captive, we shall no longer have eggs. And we cannot ask God to rob it of half its power, for God does not do things by halves."

So they lifted the lid of the pot and blinded the

creature and set it free. And it once again roamed the world, but its power was greatly diminished. No longer did hearts incline to such evil deeds as in earlier times.

116
Alexander Enters Jerusalem

Alexander led a great army out of Macedonia and conquered every land in his way. Mighty Egypt fell before him. So did Edom and Gaza and Tyre. Then he prepared to take Jerusalem.

The night before he marched on the city, he had a dream: An angel dressed in white linen appeared before him brandishing a fiery sword. The angel lifted the sword above the king's head and prepared to strike him.

"Wait, my lord!" Alexander cried. "Why do you wish to kill me? I am your slave!" And he bowed low to the ground.

The angel replied, "It is I who have brought you all your victories. God has sent me to subdue all the peoples in your path. But now you have set your heart on doing evil to God's people and God's holy city. So you must die!"

"I will turn around then, and return home."

"No!" said the angel. "You will enter Jerusalem as you have planned. But when you meet a man who bears my image and dress, bow before him and do whatever he asks of you. If you do not, that day will be your last."

When the king awoke from his dream, he was furious. Was he not Alexander the Great, conqueror of the world? He would bow before no man!

But when he approached the gates of Jerusalem and saw the high priest Hananiah walking toward him, dressed all in white and wearing a flashing diadem upon his head, Alexander leapt off his charger and prostrated himself on the ground before him.

His generals were astounded. "What are you doing, Alexander?" they cried. "This behavior is not befitting the ruler of the world!"

Then he told them his dream, and they fell silent.

Alexander then said to Hananiah, "Blessed be the God of Israel who has such love for you and your people! To acknowledge your God's great power, I shall give much gold to your craftsmen to erect a statue of me so that you may set it in your Holy of Holies as a memorial."

"We cannot accept your gift, your majesty," said the priest.

Alexander's face darkened. "And why not?"

"God forbids us to bow to any graven image. But let me suggest another memorial that will be far better than the one you propose."

"And what is that?"

"Give your gold to the priests to sustain them and the poor among our people. In return, every male child born to our priests this year in the whole of Judah shall be given the name Alexander. In this way your memory shall never depart from our midst."

Hananiah's words pleased Alexander, and he did as the high priest requested. Alexander then made a covenant of peace with the people of Judah and gave them many gifts.

And then he departed to conquer the remainder of the world.

117
The Fair Judgment

Once Alexander crossed the Mountains of Darkness and came to a land ruled entirely by women. He wished to make war with them but they said to him, "If you defeat us, what honor will you gain? And if we defeat you, imagine your shame!" So he made peace with them instead.

Then he said to them, "Bring me bread."

And they brought him a loaf made of gold.

"Do human beings eat gold?" he asked.

"Was there no bread in your own country that you have come to take ours?"

"It was not your wealth that brought me here," said Alexander, "but your laws."

Then they led him to a room where one of their judges sat. Two men came before the judge.

"I bought a piece of land from this man," said his companion, "and I found a great treasure buried in the ground. So I said to the seller, 'Take back this treasure, for I did not buy this when I bought your land.' "

The second man said, "When I sold my land to this man, I sold everything in it from the sky above to the netherworld below. I have no wish to rob the buyer of that which is rightfully his."

The judge said to the first man, "Have you a daughter?"

"Yes," said the man.

"Have you a son?" she asked the second man.

"Yes," he replied.

"Then marry them to each other and let them share the treasure."

So they did.

Alexander laughed when he heard the judgment.

"Why do you laugh?" they asked him.

"In my country, the king would have judged differently. I would have ordered both men killed and then would have taken the treasure for myself."

"Does the sun shine in your kingdom?" they asked Alexander.

"Yes."

"Do you have cows and sheep and goats there?" they asked him.

"Yes," said Alexander.

"Then it is for their sake that the sun shines and the land gives forth food," said the women, "for the people do not deserve it."

When Alexander left this land, he wrote on the gates, "I was a fool until I came here and learned wisdom from the women."

118
Alexander and the Eyeball

Once Alexander decided to travel until he came to the end of the earth. So he mounted his horse and rode until he came to the mountains. For six months he and his army rode along the mountain road until they came to a great plain. In the middle of this plain stood a tall and beautiful gateway with words engraved upon it in a strange language.

Alexander called Menahem the Scribe and had him translate the words. And this is what they said: "This is the gateway of *Adonai*—only the righteous shall enter here."

"Surely this is the Garden of Eden," said Alexander. "And surely I am among the righteous!"

But when he stepped toward the gate, a voice thundered from within, pronouncing, "No uncircumcised man may enter!"

So that night Alexander circumcised himself, and his physicians healed him with herbs. But he kept it a secret from his soldiers.

The next day Alexander again approached the gate and said to the gatekeepers, "Pay me tribute and I shall leave here in peace."

They handed him a little box. Inside Alexander found an eyeball. Alexander tried to lift the eyeball out of the box, but it was too heavy. Then he placed it on a scale and weighed it against all his silver and gold, and it outweighed all his treasures.

"Why do I need this?" he asked the gatekeepers.

"It is to remind you," they answered, "that the eye is

never satisfied, no matter how much gold and silver a person acquires."

"How can I lift it?" asked Alexander.

"Take a pinch of dust and sprinkle it over the eye."

So Alexander sprinkled a little dust upon the eye. Instantly it grew as light as mist.

"Let this remind you," said the gatekeepers, "that your eye will not be satisfied until you return to the dust from which you came."

Alexander carried the eye back to Macedonia, where he placed it among his most precious treasures.

119
Alexander Has Horns

On the top of his head Alexander had two horns that he hid under his hair. Each week he hired a barber to cut his hair, but he was so ashamed to reveal his secret to the barber that he had the man killed as soon as he had finished cutting his hair. Soon only one barber, an old Jew, remained in the city.

"I cannot kill him, for then who will cut my hair?" said Alexander.

So he made the barber swear an oath not to reveal the king's secret to anyone. If word of the secret reached the king's ears, Alexander warned him, the barber would lose his head.

For weeks the barber kept the secret to himself. Finally he could keep it in no longer. He went to a cave and shouted at the top of his lungs, "Alexander has horns! Alexander has horns!" Relieved at last of his terrible burden, he returned home to his family, certain that the secret was still safe.

Through this cave ran a stream, beside which reeds grew. One day a shepherd entered the cave and cut a reed to make himself a flute. But when he began to play the flute, it sang out, "Alexander has horns! Alexander has horns!"

Others overheard the flute's song, and word of it soon reached the king's ears. Enraged, Alexander sent for the barber to order his execution. But when the barber told the king the truth, the king forgave him and let him go.

For just as kings may have horns, caves may have ears.

120

Judith and Holofernes

Once Holofernes, king of the Greeks, marched against Jerusalem with a mighty army and laid siege to the city. The Jews trapped within the city walls suffered greatly from hunger and thirst, and they cried out in their misery. One woman in particular, a beautiful young widow named Judith, lifted up her voice and prayed that she might help her people out of their distress.

God heard her prayers and answered them.

One day Judith went with her maidservant to the city gates and asked the gatekeepers to let her through.

"What?" they said to her. "So that you can betray us to the enemy! Have you fallen in love with one of the soldiers outside? Or perhaps you have your eye on Holofernes himself!"

Then she said to them, "Heaven forbid! I have faith that God will help me triumph over our enemy."

And they let her pass.

She came before the king's guards and said to them, "I have a secret to tell the king."

So they brought her to Holofernes. She said to him, "My lord, I am the daughter and sister of prophets. Yesterday I overheard them saying that the Jews will soon fall into your hands. So I fled the city to save myself before you destroyed my people."

Judith's words pleased the king, as did her extraordinary beauty. He wished to marry her, but she said to him, "First I must immerse myself in the spring outside your camp, for I have just finished menstruating and must purify myself. Please tell your soldiers not to stop me or my maidservant when we go to the spring tonight. When I return, I shall gladly become the king's wife."

That night Holofernes invited all his generals and princes to a sumptuous banquet in her honor. When they had all become drunk, they stumbled back to their tents, leaving the snoring king alone with Judith and her maid. The two women lifted the king's heavy sword and cut off his head. Then they wrapped Holofernes's head in a cloak and hurried down to the spring.

When the Greek soldiers saw them, they said to themselves, "These must be the two Jewish women the king told us not to disturb."

So they let them pass.

When the two women reached the gates of Jerusalem, the gatekeepers refused to let them in, for they feared that they had betrayed the city.

"Open up, for a miracle has happened!" cried Judith. "I have killed Holofernes!"

Still they did not believe her. "Isn't it bad enough that you went whoring with the enemy? We will not let you destroy us as well!"

Then Judith pulled Holofernes's bloody head out of the cloak.

"Hear O Israel!" they cried. "*Adonai* is our God! *Adonai* is one!"

That night the people of Jerusalem celebrated Judith's great victory over the Greek king. The next morning they armed themselves and went out to meet the enemy. When the Greeks ran in to Holofernes's tent to tell him of the Jews' attack, they found him lying headless in his bed. Then they panicked, fleeing their camp with the Jews hot on their heels. The Jews chased them as far as Antioch. Then they returned to the Greek camp and despoiled it.

121
The Legend of the Septuagint

One day Ptolemy Philadelphus, King of Egypt, summoned his royal librarian and said to him, "I would like to build a library greater than any the world has ever seen. In this library I want a copy of every book in the world."

So the royal librarian gathered many camels and slaves and set forth. Three years later he returned to Alexandria.

"Have you gathered every book ever written?" Ptolemy asked him.

"No, your majesty, only about half of them. My camels could carry no more than that."

"Then set out again," ordered the king. "Do not return until you have collected a copy of every single book in the world."

Three years later, the librarian returned.

"Well," said the king, "have you succeeded this time?"

"Your majesty," boasted the librarian, "I have brought you books from the Spice Lands of the east, from deepest Africa, from across the ocean, and from the Mountains of Darkness. From . . ."

"Enough!" roared the king. "Only answer my question!"

The librarian lowered his head and muttered, "Not quite, your majesty. One book has eluded my grasp. It is the holy book of the Jews, containing all their laws and wisdom."

"Why have you not procured a copy of this book?" thundered Ptolemy. "I will pay the price!"

"It is not a question of money, my lord, but . . ."

"Go on!" cried the king.

"One of your scribes tried to copy this book, but he became mad and had to abandon the effort. Another lost his sight and only regained it when he vowed never to try again."

"Then we shall get a copy written by a Jew!" said the king. "But I must have this book!"

"It's not so easy, your majesty," said the librarian. "For these books are written in a language called Hebrew, which is difficult to understand. Even the Jews in Israel do not speak it anymore."

"Is there nothing we can do, then?" sighed Ptolemy, sinking back into his throne.

"Perhaps if we ask their high priest Eleazar to send us translators. . . ."

"Excellent!" shouted the king. "Do it at once! And spare no expense!"

So the king wrote a letter and sent his officer Aristeas to Jerusalem to deliver it to Eleazar. And he also sent many precious gifts.

The high priest was delighted by the king's interest in the Torah. He chose seventy-two sages who knew both Hebrew and Greek, each seventy-two years old and seventy-two inches high, and each weighing seventy-two kilos. Then, they set off for Egypt, each carrying a copy of the Bible.

For ten days Alexandria celebrated their arrival. Then Ptolemy sent them to the island of Pharos, where each one was given a separate house so he could work undis-turbed—and isolated from the others.

At the end of the seventy-two days, Ptolemy had the seventy-two Jewish elders brought back to Alexandria, and he had his own scribes examine their translations. To their great surprise, the Egyptian scribes discovered that the translations were absolutely identical—to the letter! All seventy-two versions had even changed the name of the unkosher animal "hare" to "slender-footed" when translating it into Greek, because the name of Ptolemy's wife meant "hare" in Greek and they did not wish to offend the queen.

Then the king ordered a great banquet in honor of the

completion of his library and invited all the scholars in Egypt. At the banquet, he had his librarian read portions of every holy book contained in the library. All the scholars agreed that the wisdom of the Jews surpassed them all.

Then Ptolemy issued a decree that all Jewish slaves in his kingdom be freed at once, for he said, "Any people who have given the world such a book should never be slaves to anyone."

The next day the seventy-two sages started home for Jerusalem, laden down with gifts from Ptolemy Philadelphus, whose name means "brotherly love."

122
The Death of Nicanor

Angered by the Jews' refusal to abandon their God and embrace the way of the Greeks, the wicked Antiochus, King of Syria, sent his viceroy Nicanor to Jerusalem to subdue this rebellious people. Along with Nicanor, Antiochus sent a decree: From this day on, no Jew could observe the Sabbath, or circumcise his son, or observe the New Moon Festival. Anyone caught doing so would be put to death.

Mattathias, son of Yohanan the high priest, had a daughter named Hannah who was engaged to be married to a prince of Israel. But just before her wedding, one of Nicanor's soldiers seized her by the hair, spread open a Torah scroll, and lay with her upon it. Afterward, the Greek soldiers sprinkled pig's blood around the holy altar.

Hannah's brother John vowed to take revenge upon the Greeks for his sister's disgrace. He made himself a small dagger and hid it in his robe. Then he appeared before Nicanor.

"Why are you people so stubborn?" Nicanor asked him. "Don't you understand that I could burn all of you like dry straw blown before the wind? No god in any other country has ever triumphed over my armies. Why should your God fare any differently?"

To Nicanor's great surprise, John replied, "You are right, my lord. That is why I have come to you today—to submit to your will. I am ready to do whatever you say."

Nicanor smiled broadly. "So at least one of you has come to his senses! Good! From now on, you will sacrifice your offerings with swine's blood. And you shall wear a Greek crown upon your head when you do it."

John leaned forward and whispered, "I fear my people's anger, your majesty. If they see me doing these things, they will surely stone me!"

Then he lowered his voice still further. "Yet I think I know a way to carry out your orders without being thwarted by my own people. But first you must send everyone out of the room. For I fear Jewish informers."

So Nicanor sent away his advisors and guards. As soon as they were alone, John took out his dagger and stabbed Nicanor in the heart. Then John fled the palace and hid in the hills.

Soon John and his brothers—Judah, Simon, Jonathan, and Eliezer—gathered together a small band of Jewish fighters and led them in revolt against the Greek army. And with God's help, the Maccabees triumphed over the greater enemy forces and won back Jerusalem and the Holy Temple.

Then the Jews took Nicanor's body and cut off his hands, feet, and head, saying, "Thus justice is done to the mouth that spoke with arrogance, to the hands that were raised against Jerusalem, and to the feet that hurried to do evil against Judea." And they hung the pieces upon the city gates.

From that day on these were known as "Nicanor's Gates," and the thirteenth of Adar, the day on which Nicanor was slain, was celebrated each year as "Nicanor's Day."

123
Shame Destroys Jerusalem

In Jerusalem there once lived a man who had a friend named Kamza and an enemy named Bar Kamza. One day the man held a banquet, and he sent his servant to invite his friend Kamza. But the servant became confused and brought Bar Kamza instead.

"Get out of my house!" shouted the host when he saw his enemy seated among his guests.

Bar Kamza's face turned bright red. "If you will only let me stay," he said, "I will gladly pay for all the food and drink I consume."

"No!" said the host.

"Then I will pay for half of the banquet," offered Bar Kamza.

"No!" answered the host.

"I will pay for the entire banquet!"

Without another word, the host stormed over to his uninvited guest, picked him up by the scruff of neck, and tossed him into the street.

Bar Kamza thought to himself, "Not even the rabbis who were there tried to prevent my humiliation! I will teach them all a lesson!"

So he went to the Romans to inform on his countrymen. "The Jews are rebelling against Rome," he said.

"Prove it," said the Roman governor.

"Send them a sacrifice," said Bar Kamza, "and see if they will offer it on the Temple altar."

So the Roman governor selected a calf without blemish and sent it with Bar Kamza. But on the way, Bar Kamza made a small mark on the white of its eye, which made it unfit for Jewish sacrifice although still acceptable to the Romans.

The rabbis wanted to offer it anyway, so as not to offend Rome, but Zechariah ben Avkulus objected and said, "People will say that it is now fine to offer animals with blemishes. It sets a bad precedent!"

So they decided not to sacrifice it.

But then they began to worry about Bar Kamza. When he reported their actions to the Roman governor, would not the governor's wrath come down upon their heads?

"Let us kill Bar Kamza so that he doesn't inform on us," they said.

But Zechariah ben Avkulus again objected and asked, "Do we now kill people simply because they blemish a sacrifice?"

Again they bent to his will.

And the wrath of Rome did indeed come down upon their heads. Jerusalem was destroyed, the Temple burned, and the Jews exiled from their land.

"Do you see how serious it is to embarrass a person?" taught Rabbi Eleazar. "For to defend Bar Kamza's honor, God was willing to destroy even the Holy Temple!"

124
Beyond the River Sambatyon

When the Jews were exiled to Babylonia after the Destruction of the First Temple, among them were the Levites, whose task it had been to sing in the Holy Temple. Nebuchadnezzar commanded them to appear before him with their harps and sing to him.

"How can we sing before Israel's enemy?" they said. "If only we had sung more of God's praises when the Temple still stood, it might not have been destroyed!"

With tears in their eyes, they hung their harps in the willow boughs along the Euphrates River and then slashed their fingers with sharp knives so that they could no longer play. Then they came before Nebuchadnezzar and held up their bloody hands. Enraged at their impudence, the Babylonian king ordered them all executed in the morning.

That night the Levites and their families prayed to

God and prepared themselves to die in order to sanctify the Holy Name. But when the morning mist lifted, they found to their surprise that they were no longer in Babylon, but in a strange and beautiful land they had never seen before. Everywhere fruit trees were in blossom, and the air was filled with a sweet fragrance. On three sides, the land was bordered by the sea, and on the fourth side flowed a wide river in the midst of which boulders rolled and crashed with a ceaseless thunder.

This was the River Sambatyon. For six days of the week, the rocks in the river's midst continued their tireless churning. But on the Sabbath they rested, and the river was as still and smooth as glass. To keep out enemies, a curtain of fire arose on the opposite bank and remained there until the following sunset, when the rocks resumed their weekday commotion.

The Levites soon discovered that their new land was a paradise. The trees and flowers bloomed twice each year, and the seeds sown in the fields produced a hundredfold. Grandparents never saw a grandchild die before them, and the old left the earth in perfect health. There were no soldiers, judges, or guards among them, for all was peaceful and just.

Only once did someone not of the tribe of Levi cross the Sambatyon. It happened soon after the Destruction of the Second Temple, when an evil pagan priest, a warlock, ruled Jerusalem and tormented the Jews left behind after the Roman siege. He was a giant of a man, and like Goliath, he challenged the Jews to send a champion to defeat him in wisdom, or he would destroy them all.

The sages in Jerusalem drew lots to choose one of their number to cross the Sambatyon and summon a champion from among the inhabitants there. The lot fell upon one of the youngest among them. Before he left, they made him divorce his wife, for he would have to desecrate the Sabbath to cross the river on the one day that it was still. But they gave him no permission to desecrate the Sabbath to come back.

He traveled for many days and finally arrived at the

banks of the Sambatyon. Swiftly he passed through the fiery wall into the lands of *B'nai Moshe*, the descendants of the Levites, and he told them of his mission. They, too, drew lots, and the lot fell upon a dwarf, hunchbacked and lame. He, too, divorced his wife, crossed the Sambatyon, and made his way to Jerusalem.

When the giant warlock saw the hunchbacked dwarf, he laughed. "So this is whom you have sent to challenge me! Then prepare to lose your lives."

The people of Jerusalem erected a wide platform in the middle of the city for this contest of wits, and the two men climbed up and stood upon it. First it was the warlock's turn. Chanting magic incantations, he made wheat grow right out of the wooden boards of the platform. But the dwarf conjured up roosters that quickly devoured the wheat.

Then it was the dwarf's turn. He made two giant trees sprout up out of the platform. Within seconds their leafy tops pierced the clouds.

"Now show your power," challenged the dwarf. "Bring the treetops down to the ground."

So the warlock summoned all his power and made the treetops bow low to the ground. But as soon as the warlock grabbed hold of the uppermost branches, one in each hand, the dwarf caused the treetops to spring back into the sky, splitting the warlock right down the middle. Then the dwarf conjured up two great millstones that floated in midair and ground the two halves of the warlock's body until nothing remained but dust, which the dwarf scattered to the winds.

And then suddenly he, too, vanished into the air.

PART VII

THE SAGES OF THE TALMUD

With the Destruction of the Second Temple, followed by the disastrous Bar Kochba Rebellion sixty-five years later, darkness threatened to swallow up the Jewish people. In order to preserve the vast teachings of the oral tradition, the rabbis agreed to write it down, and these commentaries and elaborations on the written biblical text became the Mishnah and Talmud. Many of these teachings had to do with the halakhah, the laws guiding Jewish life. But many others belonged to the aggadah, the imaginative tradition of fable, legend, moral teaching, mysticism, and folk wisdom. The rabbis figured as both heroes and spinners of their own yarns.

125

Honi the Circle-Maker

Once there was a terrible drought in the land of Israel. It was already the month of Adar, which usually marks the end of the rainy season and the beginning of spring, but no rains had fallen all winter long.

So the people sent for Honi the Circle-Maker.

He prayed, but still no rains came. Then he drew a circle in the dust and stood in the middle of it. Raising his hands to heaven, he vowed, "God, I will not move from this circle until You send rain!"

Immediately a few drops fell, hissing as they struck the hot white stones.

But the people complained to Honi, "This is but a poor excuse for rain, only enough to release you from your vow."

So Honi turned back to heaven and cried, "Not for this trifling drizzle did I ask, but for enough rain to fill wells, cisterns, and ditches!"

Then the heavens opened up and poured down rain in buckets, each drop big enough to fill a soup ladle. The wells and the cisterns overflowed, and the wadis flooded the desert. The people of Jerusalem ran for safety to the Temple Mount.

"Honi!" they cried. "Save us! Or we will all be destroyed like the generation of the Flood! Stop the rains!"

Honi said to them, "I was glad to ask God to end your misery, but how can I ask for an end to your blessing?"

The people pleaded with him, and he finally agreed to pray for the rain to stop. "Bring me an offering of thanksgiving," he told them, and they did.

Then Honi said to God, "This people that You brought out of Egypt can take neither too much evil nor too much good. Please give them what they ask so that they may be happy."

So God sent a strong wind that blew away the fierce rains, and the people gathered mushrooms and truffles on the Temple Mount.

Then Shimon ben Shetakh, head of the Sanhedrin in Jerusalem, said to Honi, "I should excommunicate you for your audacity, but how can I, since you're Honi! God coddles you as a father does his young child. The child says: 'Hold me, Daddy, and bathe me, and give me poppyseeds and peaches and pomegranates,' and his father gives him whatever he wants."

So it was with Honi the Circle-Maker.

126
Honi and the Carob Tree

Once when Honi was out walking, he came upon a man planting a carob tree.

"How long will it be before this tree bears fruit?" Honi asked.

"Seventy years," the man replied.

"How do you know you'll be alive in seventy years?"

"Just as I found carob trees when I came into the world," answered the man, "so I am now planting carob trees for my grandchildren to enjoy."

Then Honi lay down and fell asleep. While he slept, a rock enveloped him so that he slept undetected for seventy years. When he awoke, he saw a man gathering carobs under a nearby tree.

"Did you plant this tree?" Honi asked him.

"No, my grandfather did," answered the man.

"Then I have been sleeping for seventy years!" cried Honi.

Then he went to his house. "Does Honi the Circle-Maker still live here?" he asked.

"No," they told him, "he died long ago, but his grandson lives here."

"I am Honi," he said. But they didn't believe him.

He went to the House of Study and sat in the back of the room. The rabbis were discussing the Law, and they said, "This teaching is as clear to us as it was in the days of Honi the Circle-Maker. They say he used to come here and answer all the rabbis' questions."

Honi stood up and declared, "I am Honi!"

But they didn't believe him, either. He prayed for mercy, and he soon died.

Later Rava taught, "That is why people say—'Either give me fellowship, or give me death ' "

127
The Hidden Jewel of Shimon ben Shetakh

Once Shimon ben Shetakh bought a donkey from an Arab. When his disciples went to claim it, they found a precious jewel hanging around its neck.

They came to Shimon ben Shetakh and said, "Master, now you no longer need to work, for the Lord's blessing brings wealth."

"How is this so?" he asked them.

"We found this precious jewel on the donkey you just bought."

"Did the Arab know about this?"

"No," they answered.

"Then return it to him at once. I bought a donkey, not a jewel."

When they returned the jewel to the Arab, he exclaimed, "Blessed is the God of Shimon ben Shetakh!"

128
The Witches of Ashkelon

In Ashkelon lived two good friends, both pious students. One died and appeared to his friend in a dream, strolling among the orchards and springs of Paradise. Then the dreamer saw Miriam, the daughter of Mr. Onion-Leaves, with the hinge of the door of Hell stuck in her ear.

"Why is she being punished like that?" the dreamer asked his departed friend.

"Because she fasted and bragged about it."

"How long will she have to stay like this?" asked the dreamer.

"Until Shimon ben Shetakh dies. Then we shall lift the door out of her ear and stick it in his."

"Shimon ben Shetakh, the head of the Sanhedrin!" cried the dreamer. "But what has he ever done to deserve such punishment?"

The spirit of his friend replied, "When he became the Nasi, he vowed to destroy all the witches in the land, but there are still eighty witches living in a cave right here in Ashkelon, causing ruin in the world. It is your job to tell him so."

"I am afraid to go before such a great man and rebuke

him," protested the dreamer. "He is the Nasi and will not believe a poor student like me."

"Don't be so sure," the spirit assured his friend, "for he is a modest man. But if he doesn't believe you, show him this sign—take out your eyeball and then put it back into its socket, and it will be as it was before."

The next day the student went before Shimon ben Shetakh and told him about the witches. He was about to show him the sign, but the Nasi stopped him, saying, "I know that you are a pious man and can perform wonders. But you must understand that I took that oath in my heart, not with my lips."

Even so, the next day Shimon ben Shetakh took with him eighty young men and led them to a sheltered place near the witches' cave. Then he gave them each a cloak and a new pot to keep out the rain that was falling.

Shimon said to them, "When I whistle once, put on your cloaks and pots. When I whistle a second time, come and take hold of a witch and lift her up from the ground, for witches are powerless when their feet lose contact with the earth."

Then Shimon ben Shetakh stood at the mouth of the cave and shouted, "Ho! Open up for me, for I am one of you!"

They opened the great wooden door sealing the entrance and asked him, "How did you get here without getting wet?"

He answered, "I walked between the raindrops, since I am a warlock."

"Why did you come here?"

"To learn and to teach," he said. "Let each of us show our skill."

Then one witch recited a spell and conjured up a loaf of bread. A second witch conjured up meat; a third, cooked vegetables; a fourth, wine.

Then they turned to him and said, "What can you do?"

He said, "I can whistle twice and bring you eighty young men to gladden your hearts."

They cried, "Yes, we want that!"

So he whistled once, and the eighty young men put on their cloaks and pots. He whistled a second time, and they came into the cave, lifted up the witches, and hanged them all.

And that was the end of witchcraft in Ashkelon.

129
Hillel the Snow Scholar

When Hillel was a young man, he used to earn only half a *zuz*. Half of that he spent on food and shelter, and the other half he paid to the doorkeeper at the House of Study, so that he could hear the teachings of the rabbis.

One winter's day, he did not have enough money to gain entrance to the House of Study, so he went up to the roof and eavesdropped through the skylight. All that day heavy snow fell, and by evening he was completely covered. Yet Hillel hardly noticed, for his mind was totally absorbed by the words of Torah being spoken in the room below.

But when night fell, he discovered that he could not move, because his limbs were frozen with cold, so he lay there all night long. The next day, when Shemaiah and Avtalyon came into the House of Study to teach, they saw that it was unusually dark in the room. They glanced up and saw that the skylight admitted no light. When they went up to the roof, they found young Hillel, lying almost lifeless in the snow. They gave him dry clothes and warmed him by the fire until the redness returned to his cheeks.

From that day on they gave Hillel permission to enter the House of Study without paying. And they dismissed the doorkeeper.

In later times when anyone would say, "I cannot study because I am too poor and can spare no time from my need," the sages would say to that person, "Are you poorer than Hillel was?"

And that question would always silence all complaints.

130
Hillel and Shammai

Once a Gentile came to Shammai and said to him, "I will convert to Judaism if you teach me the whole of the Torah while I stand on one foot."

Shammai hit him with his builder's T-square.

Then the man came to Hillel and proposed the same thing.

Hillel immediately accepted him as a convert and told him, "Do not do to your neighbor that which is hateful to you. All the rest is commentary. Go and study it!"

131
The Patience of Hillel

Once a man made a bet with another man for four hundred *zuzim* that he could make Hillel lose his temper.

The first man went to Hillel's house on a Friday afternoon, when Hillel was preparing for the Sabbath. When Hillel heard the knock on his door, he wrapped his wet head in a towel and went to let the man in.

"What can I do for you, young man?" asked Hillel.

"I have a question to ask you."

"Ask, my son, ask," said Hillel.

"You are a Babylonian, are you not? Then can you tell me why the heads of the Babylonians are so round?"

"That is because their midwives are not very clever," answered Hillel.

"Ah!" said the man, and went away.

A short while later, he returned and knocked on Hillel's door. Again Hillel wrapped himself up in a towel and came to meet him.

"I have another question," said the young man.

"Ask, my son, ask," said Hillel.

"Why do the people of Palmyra have teary eyes?"

"It is because the wind blows the desert sands into their eyes," answered Hillel.

Satisfied, the man went away, and Hillel returned to his bath.

But a short time later, the man returned a third time.

"What can I do for you, young man?" asked Hillel when he came to the door.

"I have another question to ask you," said the man.

"Ask, my son, ask," said Hillel.

"Why do Africans have such wide feet?"

"It is because they live near marshes and swamps, where the ground is soft."

Without even thanking him, the man went away. And all this time, Hillel's temper remained calm.

When the man knocked a fourth time, Hillel again wrapped himself up and came to the door.

"What is your wish, young man?" he asked.

"I have many more questions to ask, but I am afraid you will get angry with me," said the young man.

"Ask all the questions you wish, my son," said Hillel.

"Are you the man they call 'Hillel, Prince of Israel'?"

"I am," replied Hillel.

"How happy I am that there are not more of you!" cried the young man.

"Why is that?" asked Hillel.

"Because on account of you, I lost four hundred *zuzim*!"

"You may yet lose another four hundred before Hillel loses his temper," laughed Hillel. "Better that you should lose four hundred times four hundred *zuzim* than that I should get angry in the presence of God, whose patience is without end."

And before Hillel could say another word, the young man stormed off to pay off his bet.

132
Yohanan and Vespasian

When the Romans besieged Jerusalem, there was a terrible famine within the city, but the Jewish zealots inside would not let anyone out to negotiate with the enemy.

Yohanan ben Zakkai called his nephew Abba Sikra, leader of the zealots, and said to him, "How long will you allow Jerusalem to starve?"

"What can I do?" complained Abba Sikra. "If the others find out that I spoke to the enemy, they will surely kill me!"

"Then I will go to the Romans," said Yohanan. "Find some way for me to leave the city."

"If that is your wish," said his nephew, "here is how you can succeed. Pretend that you are dying, and then your students can smuggle you out of the city in a coffin."

So Yohanan ben Zakkai feigned death, and his students, Rabbi Eliezer and Rabbi Yehoshua, carried him to the city gates in a coffin.

But when they reached the gates, the guards grew suspicious and wished to pierce Yohanan's body with their lances.

"What would the Romans say," Yehoshua argued, "if they saw his body like that? They would say that we ourselves killed him!"

So they let them pass.

When Yohanan reached General Vespasian's tent, he said to him, "Peace unto you, O King!"

Vespasian replied, "With your own words, you have just brought down two sentences of death upon your head. The first, because you called me a king when I'm not. And the second, because you waited too long to come and pay homage to your king—if that is truly what I am."

Yohanan said, "I do not deserve the first penalty, because you are soon to become a king, for who but a king is worthy of capturing Jerusalem? Neither do I deserve the second, because my own people prevented me from coming to you to pay you honor."

At that moment, a messenger arrived from Rome to tell Vespasian that Caesar had died and that Vespasian was the new Caesar.

Vespasian said to Yohanan, "I am now going away. My son Titus will take my place. But I wish to reward you for the truth of your prophecy. Ask and it shall be given to you."

Yohanan said, "Give me the Academy of Yavneh and its sages, the dynasty of Rabban Gamliel, and a doctor to heal Rabbi Zadok, who has been fasting for forty years to save Jerusalem."

And Vespasian granted his wishes.

Thus the Torah was saved from destruction.

133
Titus and the Gnat

Vespasian left Judea to become the new Caesar, and his son Titus captured Jerusalem. After his victory, Titus brought a whore into the Holy Temple and lay with her upon an open Torah scroll. Then he thrust his sword through the Veil of the Holy of Holies, and the Veil began to bleed.

Titus cried, "Behold, I have killed God!"

Then he ripped off the Veil and filled it with the silver and gold Temple vessels. These he loaded into his ship, and he set sail for Rome. Then a storm arose at sea and threatened to drown him.

"What kind of God is this who only has power in the water?" sneered Titus. "You drowned Pharaoh in the Sea of Reeds and overcame Sisera with a flood. Now You try to triumph over me in water. If You are so mighty, I dare You to make war against me on dry land!"

And a voice called out of heaven "Wicked son of a wicked father! I have a small creature in My world called a gnat. Go onto the dry land and make war against it!"

When Titus reached Rome, a gnat entered his nose and gnawed at his brain for seven years. One day Titus passed a blacksmith's shop, where a smith was pounding on an anvil. The gnat heard the pounding and stopped his gnawing.

"Here is a remedy for my pain!" cried Titus.

So each day he had a smith brought to him who pounded on an anvil. The Gentile smiths received four *zuzim* for their work, but the Jewish smiths received nothing, for Titus said, "Isn't it enough that you see your enemy reduced to this shameful state?"

But after thirty days the gnat got used to the pounding and resumed his gnawing.

When Titus died, they opened up his brain and found there a creature as big as a swallow, weighing two pounds. Some even claimed that its beak was made of copper and its claws of iron.

Before he died, Titus instructed them to burn his body and scatter the ashes over the seven seas so that the God of the Jews could not summon him to heavenly judgment. But each day the angels gather his ashes together and bring him before the Heavenly Throne, where God judges him according to his wicked deeds. Then they burn him again and scatter his ashes over the seven seas.

134
Hanina ben Dosa's Heel

Once a poisonous lizard was biting people and killing them. They told Hanina ben Dosa about it, and he said, "Show me its hole."

They showed him the hole and he placed his heel upon it. The lizard bit his heel and then died.

Hanina ben Dosa carried the lizard's body to the academy and said to the rabbis, "It is not the lizard that kills but sin."

The rabbis declared, "Woe to the sinner who meets a poisonous lizard and woe to the lizard who meets Hanina ben Dosa's heel!"

135
Bread from Twigs

Hanina ben Dosa and his wife were very poor. Every Friday, his wife would burn twigs in her oven to make smoke so that her neighbors would not know she had no bread to bake.

One Friday afternoon, one of her neighbors, a meddlesome, mean-spirited woman, decided to embarrass Hanina's wife. "I know that the oven is empty," she said to herself. "I will go and see for myself."

When she knocked on the door, Hanina's wife ran into her bedroom. The neighbor came into the house and peered into the oven. How surprised she was to find it full of baking bread!

"Hurry, woman!" she cried. "Bring your breadshovel or the loaves will be burned to cinders!"

But Hanina's wife was already on her way with the long, wide paddles in her hands, for being Hanina ben Dosa's wife, she was quite used to miracles.

136

The Missing Table Leg

Once Rabbi Hanina ben Dosa's wife said to him, "How long must we be so desperately poor?"

Hanina said, "What can we do?"

"Pray to God to give you something."

So Hanina prayed, and a hand reached down from heaven grasping a golden table leg and gave it to him.

That night Hanina had a dream: All the righteous were seated in Paradise, eating at three-legged golden tables, while he and his wife were eating at a golden table with only two legs.

When he awoke, he said to his wife, "How would you like to eat at a golden table with only two legs in Paradise when all the other righteous souls have tables with three?"

So she said to him, "Ask God to take the leg back."

Hanina prayed, and the hand again came down and took the leg back.

This was an even greater miracle than the first, for what heaven gives, it never takes back.

Except this once.

137

The Law Is Not in

Heaven

Rabbi Eliezer ben Hyrcanus used every argument in the world to support his opinion that a certain oven was ritually clean, but the other rabbis opposed him.

He said, "If the *halakhah* is with me, let this carob tree be uprooted from the earth!"

And the carob tree rose into the air and flew five hundred feet before it crashed to the ground.

But the rabbis said, "You cannot prove anything with a carob tree."

Then he said, "If I'm right, let this stream of water flow backwards!"

And instantly the stream reversed its course and flowed the other way.

But the rabbis said, "A stream can't prove anything."

Then Eliezer ben Hyrcanus shouted, "If the law is with me, let the walls of this study house prove it!"

And the walls immediately began to teeter, but Rabbi Yehoshua reproached them and said, "Is it any of your business, walls, if scholars disagree about the Law?"

And out of respect for Rabbi Yehoshua, the walls stopped falling. But out of respect for Rabbi Eliezer, they did not right themselves either. Thus they remain tilted at an angle to this day.

Then Eliezer raised his voice and called out, "If the *halakhah* is with me, let heaven itself prove it!"

And a heavenly voice rang out, "Why are you opposing Rabbi Eliezer? Don't you know that the Law is always as he says?"

Rabbi Yehoshua now jumped to his feet and cried, "The Torah is not in heaven!"

What did he mean by that?

Rabbi Jeremiah explained, "The Torah was given to Israel on Mount Sinai. Therefore, we need not listen to heavenly voices, for the Torah itself teaches us that the majority rules in matters of Law."

Later, when Rabbi Nathan met the prophet Elijah, he asked him, "What was God's reaction to Rabbi Yehoshua's outburst?"

Elijah replied, "God smiled and said, 'My children have gotten the better of Me! My children have bested Me!' "

138
The Conversion of Onkelos

Onkelos, the nephew of Titus, converted to Judaism and became a great scholar, translating the Torah into Aramaic so that the common people could understand it.

When Caesar heard that Onkelos had embraced Judaism, he sent messengers to bring him back to Rome. But Onkelos taught Torah to the messengers, and they joined him in his new faith.

Caesar again sent messengers, this time instructing them not to enter into debate with Onkelos lest he convert them, too. When the new messengers arrived, Onkelos said to them, "Let me ask you only one question."

"What is it?" they asked.

"When the master of the house walks in a dark street, who lights his way?"

"His slave," they replied.

"Not so with the God of Israel," said Onkelos. "When the slaves left Egypt and wandered through the desert, God lit *their* way with a pillar of cloud by day and a pillar of fire by night."

As soon as the messengers heard this, they embraced Judaism.

When Caesar heard about the fate of his second delegation, he became furious and dispatched one more set of messengers, this time warning them not to speak or to listen to Onkelos.

When they arrived, Onkelos placed his hand upon the *mezuzah* in his doorway.

"What is that?" they asked him.

"Let me first ask you a question," he said. "When a king enters his house, who guards the door?"

"His ministers and servants," they replied.

Onkelos said, "The opposite is true of the God of the Jewish people. The King of Kings guards our doors while we, God's servants, remain safely inside. How much God must love us!"

And they, too, embraced Judaism.

When Caesar heard this, he decided to send no more messengers to Onkelos.

139
A Box of Dust

There once was a man named Nahum of Gam Zu. Why was he called that? Because no matter what happened to him, he would always say, *"Gam zu le'tovah* — this too is for the best."

Once the rabbis wished to send a gift to Rome. They chose Nahum of Gam Zu as their ambassador, for he was experienced in miracles. They filled a small box with precious jewels, gave it to Nahum, and sent him on his way.

He came to an inn and stayed there for the night. While he slept, his hosts broke into his room, stole the jewels, and refilled the box with dust.

When Nahum arrived in Rome, he presented the gift to Caesar. But when Caesar opened the box, he found only dust.

"The Jews are making fun of me!" he cried. And he ordered Nahum executed.

When Nahum heard Caesar's words, he said, "This too is for the best."

Then Elijah appeared as one of Caesar's officers and said, "I have heard that the Jews have a certain magic dust that once belonged to their ancestor Abraham. When Abraham would throw the dust at his enemies, it would turn into swords and destroy them."

At that time, there was one country that Caesar had been unable to conquer with his army. So he took

Nahum's dust and used it against this enemy and quickly defeated them. In gratitude, Caesar ordered Nahum's box refilled with precious jewels and sent him home with great honor.

On the way back, Nahum stopped at the same inn. His hosts were surprised to see him still alive, and they were even more surprised to hear about his great triumph in Rome.

"What did you give to Caesar?" they asked him.

"What was in this box," he told them, and he showed them the box filled with jewels.

The next day he departed for Israel. Thinking that their soil must indeed have magical properties, the innkeepers demolished their inn and put some of the dust in a box. This they presented to Caesar, claiming it had the same miraculous powers as Nahum's dust.

But when the Roman legions tried to use the dust against their enemies, it proved to be nothing more than dust, so Caesar had the innkeepers executed.

140

Ugly Vessels

Once the daughter of Caesar said to Rabbi Yehoshua ben Hananya, "Why is such glorious wisdom contained in such an ugly vessel as you?"

He said to her, "In what kind of vessels does your father keep his wine?"

"Clay vessels," she replied.

"People who are as important as you should keep their wine in vessels of silver and gold!" Yehoshua said.

So she told her father to put all his wine in gold and silver vessels, and he did. But the wine soon soured.

Her father asked her, "Who told you to do this?"

"Yehoshua ben Hananya."

So Yehoshua was brought before Caesar. Caesar asked him, "Why did you tell my daughter to put wine in silver and gold vessels?"

"I was only following her own wisdom," he said. "She told me that precious things belong in precious vessels."

"But surely there are beautiful people who are scholars!" said Caesar.

"Were they ugly," Yehoshua replied, "they would be even greater scholars!"

141

God Is Everywhere

Caesar said to Rabban Gamliel, "Is it true that God is everywhere that ten Jews can be found?"

"Yes," replied Rabban Gamliel.

"How many gods you must have in order for God to exist everywhere that there are ten!"

"Yes, God is everywhere that there are ten," said Gamliel, "but there is still only one God. And I will prove it! "

He called for one of Caesar's servants. As soon as the man entered the room, Gamliel struck him on the head.

"Why did you do that?" cried the servant.

"Why did you let the hot sun shine upon your master's house?" asked Gamliel.

"But the sun shines all over the world!" said the servant. "How can anyone keep it out?"

"If the sun, which is only one of God's countless servants, shows itself at the same time all over the world, how much more so must God, the Creator of heaven and earth!"

And Caesar acknowledged Gamliel's wisdom.

142
The Pious Cow

Once a pious Jew fell on hard times and was forced to sell his cow to a Gentile. The cow worked for her new owner for six days but refused to work on the Sabbath. The Gentile beat her, but she still refused to stand up and pull the plow. Indignant, he brought the cow to the Jew and demanded his money back.

The Jew whispered in the cow's ear, "Dear cow, you must do as the man says! Because of my sins, I was reduced to poverty and had to sell you. Now you are working for a non-Jew and can no longer observe the Sabbath as you once did. Now please get up and plow!"

And the cow immediately rose to her feet and began to plow.

"You are a wizard!" cried the Gentile. "Even when I beat her, I could not get her to move, but you whispered a spell into her ear and she obeyed at once! Take her back and give me my money, for I cannot run to you for help every time she decides to stop working."

"No, I am not a wizard," the Jew said. "It is only that this cow had become accustomed to having one day of rest in the week, as God commanded on Mount Sinai."

"Wonder of wonders!" cried the Gentile. "Here a dumb beast who can neither reason nor speak recognizes her Creator, yet I, made in the image of God, do not."

The Gentile went and became a Jew and studied much Torah until his fame spread throughout the land. And he became known as Yohanan ben Torta, "son of the cow," for it was a cow who first led him to God.

143

How Rabbi Akiva Became a
Scholar

One of the three wealthiest men in Jerusalem was Kalba
Savua. So hospitable was he that even dogs came away
from his door completely satisfied, hence his name:
"Sated Dog." Kalba Savua had a daughter named Rachel,
as kindhearted as she was beautiful. Although Rachel
could have married any of the wealthy young men in the
city, she chose for her husband a poor ignorant shepherd
named Akiva. When her father discovered her secret
betrothal, he disinherited her, leaving her penniless.

"Because of me, you have lost everything," lamented
Akiva. "But I promise you that when I shall have money,
I shall buy you a Jerusalem of gold to wear upon your
head!"

Although they were quite poor, Rachel and Akiva
were nonetheless very happy together. Having no money
for a bed, they slept on straw, and every day Rachel
combed the straw out of Akiva's hair, and he combed it
out of her long black tresses. One day Elijah appeared to
them disguised as a poor man and asked for some straw
for his wife who was about to give birth.

"See how fortunate we are!" cried Akiva. "This man
doesn't even have straw!"

After they had been married for a short time, Rachel
urged her husband to go to Lydda to study Torah in the
academy there.

"But I am too old to begin!" protested Akiva. "I am
already forty with gray hairs!"

"Nevertheless you should try," she said.

Akiva went to Lydda and stopped at the well there
for a drink. He noticed that the stone rim of the well was
notched and grooved.

"Who did this?" he asked.

They told him, "The rope that rubs against the stone every day when we draw water."

"Well," said Akiva, "if something as soft as rope can cut something as hard as stone, then how much more so can the keen-edged words of Torah etch themselves in my soft head."

So he went to the kindergarten where the little children sat, and he soon learned the *aleph-bet*. After that, they taught him Torah and that, too, he took in quickly.

Then he went to the academy in Lydda and studied with the rabbis there until he had learned all that they had to teach him.

While he was away studying, Rachel suffered dire poverty in order to support him. She even cut off her beautiful black hair and sold it to buy food. Her former friends and neighbors became her masters, and her rich clothing turned to rags.

After twelve years, Akiva returned home with twelve thousand of his students. As he stood outside his house, he overheard a neighbor mocking his wife Rachel: "Some husband you have! He went off to study twelve years ago and has left you a widow!"

"I would have him study another twelve years," replied Rachel, "as long as he doesn't come back to me as ignorant as when he left."

Then Akiva turned around and went off for another twelve years of study.

In the twenty-fourth year, he returned home with a following of twenty-four thousand students. Rachel came out to meet him, her hair white and her clothing in tatters. Akiva's students tried to chase her away, but Akiva saw her and held them back.

"Leave her alone!" he cried. "All the Torah we have we owe to her!"

When Kalba Savua heard that a famous scholar was in town, he went to see him, but he did not recognize his former shepherd. He said to Akiva, "I have a problem to put before you, Rabbi. I once made a vow to withhold all my wealth from my daughter because she married a man unworthy of her, an ignorant shepherd. But they tell me she lives in extreme poverty and lacks many things. Please absolve me of my vow, so that I might help her now."

"Would you have disinherited her if she had married a sage like me?" asked Akiva.

"If he had known even a single blessing, I would have given him half my wealth."

"I am your daughter's husband!" declared Akiva.

Then Kalba Savua embraced him and gave him half his wealth.

Akiva made Rachel a gold crown with the image of Jerusalem engraved upon it, as he had long ago promised. And when his students complained that he was lavishing too much attention on his wife, he replied, "I have not shown her half the honor she showed me! How greatly she suffered on my account!"

144
Everything God Does
Is for the Best

Akiva used to teach, "It is always good to say: 'Everything God does is for the best.'"

Once Akiva went out walking and he came to a town. He wanted to stay there for the night, but they wouldn't give him lodgings.

He said, "Everything God does is for the best."

He went out to the field and slept there overnight. He had with him a candle, a rooster, and a donkey. During the night, the wind blew the candle out, a cat came and ate the rooster, and a lion came and ate the donkey. But Akiva said, "Everything God does is for the best."

That same night an army passed by where Akiva was sleeping and captured the town, killing most of the inhabitants.

"How right I was to say that everything God does is for the best!" exclaimed Akiva, "for had they let me stay in the town, I would surely have been killed! And had my candle been lit or had the rooster crowed or the donkey brayed when the army passed this way, that too would have brought about my end!"

145
Charity Saves from Death

The fortunetellers told Rabbi Akiva that on her wedding day his daughter would be bitten by a snake and would die. As the day of the wedding approached, Akiva became more and more worried.

On the day of the wedding, his daughter took off her brooch and stuck it into the fence, and it pierced the eye of a poisonous snake that happened to be coiled there. The next morning she pulled out the brooch and found the snake impaled upon it.

Akiva asked her, "What good deed did you do to merit such a reward?"

She said, "Last night a beggar came to the door, but everyone was too busy preparing for the wedding banquet to attend to him. So I gave him my own portion."

"You have performed a great *mitzvah*" said her father. "As the Book of Proverbs teaches: Charity saves from death."

146
The Debt Paid by the Sea

Once the Jews in Israel needed money, so they sent Rabbi Akiva to a rich Roman matrona to borrow it.

"Who will guarantee your loan?" she asked him.

"Whoever you name," he replied.

"Very well," she said. "I will take the sea and God as your guarantors."

When the time came to repay the debt, Akiva was too ill to travel to her house and thus failed to appear with the money.

So the Roman matrona went down to the seashore and prayed to God, "Creator of the Universe! It is known that Akiva is ill, so I appeal to You as his guarantor to repay his debt."

God caused the daughter of Caesar to become mad, and she filled up a chest with jewels and gold and tossed it into the sea. The wind carried the chest from Rome to Israel, where it washed up near the matrona's house. When she opened the chest, she found her loan more than repaid.

When Akiva recovered from his illness, he hurried to the matrona's house to repay the debt. "A thousand apologies for failing to repay you sooner," he said.

Then the matrona explained to him that his guarantors had already repaid the debt, and she told him to keep the money for himself. And so more was added to the wealth Akiva had already inherited from his father-in-law Kalba Savua.

147

The Doctor and the Farmer

Once when Rabbi Ishmael and Rabbi Akiva went walking in the streets of Jerusalem, they met a sick man who said to them, "My masters, tell me what I can do to become well."

They told him what remedies to take.

Then he asked them, "Who made me ill?"

"The Holy One, Blessed be He," they replied.

"If so, why do you interfere with God's handiwork? If

God made me ill, why do you presume to make me well? Are you not sinning against God's will?"

They asked him, "What is your work?"

"I am a farmer," he replied. "See, here is my scythe in my hand."

"Who created your vineyard?" they asked him.

"The Holy One, Blessed be He," he said.

"If so, why do you interfere with God's handiwork? God created it, and now you cut off its fruits."

"But if I do not go out with my scythe and till it and manure it and weed it, it will yield nothing!" protested the farmer.

"You fool!" said the rabbis. "Just as your vineyard cannot grow without the care of a human hand, so too your body cannot remain healthy without care. Medicine is the manure and the physician is the farmer who tills the soil."

And he took their medicines and was cured.

148
The Four Who Entered Paradise

Four entered Paradise to study the heavenly mysteries: Ben Azzai, Ben Zoma, Aher the Other One, and Rabbi Akiva.

Ben Azzai gazed upon the *Shekhinah* and died. Ben Zoma gazed and went mad. The Other One betrayed his faith and went astray. But Akiva entered in peace and departed in peace.

149
The Death of Rabbi Akiva

When the Romans issued a decree forbidding the study of Torah, Akiva gathered people around him in public places and taught them Torah.

Pappus ben Yehudah asked him, "Master, aren't you afraid of the Romans?"

Akiva answered, "Let me tell you a story: Once a fox was walking along the shore when he saw fish darting back and forth in the water. 'What are you fleeing?' he asked them. 'The fishermen's nets,' they replied. 'Why not come out onto the shore?' suggested the sly fox. 'Once your ancestors and mine lived side by side upon the land.' But the fish replied: 'If we are in danger in the sea where we live, how much greater will the danger be in a place that spells our death!' "

"So it is with us," Akiva told Pappus. "If we are in danger when we study Torah, which is our Tree of Life, imagine our danger if we no longer cling to it!"

In a few days Akiva was arrested and imprisoned. They led him out for execution just at the time for reciting the morning *Sh'ma*. As the Roman executioners were tearing his flesh from his body with iron combs, he continued to recite his prayers.

His disciples cried, "Master, even now? This far?"

Akiva answered, "All my life I wondered how I could fulfill the commandment to love God with all my soul. Would I ever be able to give up my soul to serve God? Now that I have the opportunity, should I not seize it?"

He reached the end of the *Sh'ma* and held the word 'One' to his last breath. And then he died.

The angels cried, "Is this the Torah and is this her reward?"

A voice burst forth from heaven, "Happy are you, Akiva, for you have inherited the joy of eternity!"

150

The Martyrdom of Hanina ben Teradyon

Like Rabbi Akiva, Hanina ben Teradyon also defied the Roman ban and taught Torah in public places. And like

Akiva, he too was arrested and condemned to death. The Romans ordered him wrapped in a Torah scroll and burned. The executioner wrapped him in the scroll, lit a fire beneath him, and then placed wet wool sponges over his heart so that he would not die quickly.

Hanina's daughter cried, "Woe to me, Father, that I should see you like this!"

Hanina answered, "How good for me, my daughter, that you should see me like this!"

His disciples asked him, "Our master, what do you see?"

He said, "I see the scrolls being consumed by fire and the letters flying up."

Then he began to cry.

His disciples asked him, "Master, why are you crying?"

He replied, "If I alone were being burned, it would not be difficult for me, but the Torah scrolls are burning, too!"

The executioner said to him, "Rabbi, if I remove the wool sponges from your heart so that you die quickly, will you bring me life in the World to Come?"

"Yes," replied Hanina.

"Swear to me," said the executioner.

So Hanina swore.

Then he added wood to the fire and took away the sponges so that Hanina's soul departed. Then the executioner himself leapt into the fire and died.

A voice came forth from heaven and said, "Rabbi Hanina ben Teradyon and the executioner are welcome to enter the World to Come!"

151
Spitting in the Rabbi's Eye

Once there was a woman who went to synagogue every Sabbath evening to hear Rabbi Meir teach, for his words uplifted her soul. Her husband once came home from his prayers to find the house empty. When his wife at last returned, he swore an oath that he would not let her into his house again until she spit in Meir's eye.

"That I should do such a shameful thing to such a great rabbi—never!" said his wife, and she returned to her parents' house.

When Meir heard of the incident, he found out where the woman lived and traveled there. He stood in the doorway of the women's section of the synagogue and said, "I am Rabbi Meir. Does anyone here know how to whisper a spell to heal eyes? For mine have failed me."

The other women said to the one who had been banished from her home, "Whisper a spell over his eyes and spit in them so that your husband will release you from his oath."

Then they said to Meir, "Rabbi, there is only one of us here who can perform such a charm," and they left the woman there by herself.

She started to run after them, but Meir seized her hand and said, "Whisper the charm over my eyes, and heal me!"

"Rabbi," she said, "I do not know any charms!"

"Then spit seven times in my eyes, and God will do the rest."

"I cannot!" she protested.

But he would not let her go until she spat seven times in his face. Then he led her to her husband and said, "Tell him that you have spat in my eye not once but seven times!"

Then Meir returned to the synagogue, and the woman to her home.

152

Rabbi Meir and His Sister-in-Law

Hanina ben Teradyon had two daughters. One of them was Beruriah, the wife of Rabbi Meir. After Hanina was executed by the Romans, they took his other daughter and placed her in a Roman brothel.

When Beruriah heard of this, she said to her husband, "With God's help, deliver my sister from that evil place!"

Taking four hundred *zuzim* with him, Meir disguised himself as a Roman nobleman and went to the brothel where his sister-in-law was being held captive.

He said to her, "Take this money and lie with me."

But she refused, saying, "There are so many others more beautiful than I!"

Then he knew that she had not surrendered herself to sin.

He went to the brothel-keeper and offered him the money to release her. "If Caesar should demand her, give him half of this money," said Meir. "But if he should order you killed for releasing her, pray to the God of Meir and you will not be harmed."

"How do I know you are telling the truth?" asked the keeper. "Give me a sign."

Meir took him to the place where the Caesar's royal dogs were kept chained. These dogs were so savage that they bit everyone who came near. But when they leapt at Meir, he cried, "My God, deliver me!" and they shrank back in terror.

So the brothel-keeper took the money and released Meir's sister-in-law from captivity.

When Caesar heard of this, he ordered the keeper executed. But when they tried to cut his head off, the keeper cried, "O God of Rabbi Meir, save me!" and the blade glanced off his neck without leaving so much as a scratch. Then the keeper told Caesar what had happened, and Caesar ordered Meir's image engraved upon the gates of Rome so that he could be captured.

A guard spotted Meir and pursued him. But just then Elijah appeared disguised as a prostitute and embraced Meir in the middle of the street.

"Surely this could not be the holy Rabbi Meir!" declared the guard, and passed him by. And so Meir escaped.

Then Rabbi Meir, Beruriah, and her sister left Rome
and went to Babylon, far from Caesar's reach.

153
The Two Jewels

One Sabbath Rabbi Meir went to the House of Study to
deliver his afternoon sermon. While he was gone, his two
sons died suddenly. When he returned home, he asked
his wife Beruriah, "Where are the boys?"

Not wishing to disturb his Sabbath peace, Beruriah
replied, "They have gone somewhere and will soon
return."

She handed him the wine goblet and he performed
the *havdalah* ceremony separating the Sabbath from the
weekdays. As he ate his supper, he again asked for his
sons.

"Do not worry," Beruriah assured him. "I am certain
that they are safe."

After he had concluded the blessing after meals, she
said to him, "Meir, I have a question for you."

"Ask," he said.

"A while ago, a man came to the house and left two
jewels with me for safekeeping. Now he has returned and
asked for his jewels back. Should I give them to him?"

"Of course!" cried Meir. "Anyone who keeps a
pledge must return it to its rightful owner when he calls
for it."

Then she took him by the hand and led him to their
sons' room, where the boys' lifeless bodies lay upon their
beds. "Did you not tell me," she said to him, "that we
must return the jewels when their owner asks for them
back? '*Adonai* gives and *Adonai* takes away. Blessed be the
name of *Adonai*.' "

154
Beruriah

Great was the wisdom of Beruriah! She of all women gained the rabbis' respect, and her words are recorded alongside those of the great sages. When her husband Meir prayed for the death of sinners, she counseled him to pray rather that they repent of their sins. Her husband followed her advice, and the sinners soon abandoned their evil ways. How often did she rebuke the rabbis for their low opinion of women! How often did she prove them wrong by her own sharp wit!

But to some of the rabbis, a woman such as Beruriah inspired envy and uneasiness, so they decided to put her to the test. Even her husband Meir went along with this scheme, and it was he who finally persuaded one of his students to try to seduce her. After many attempts, the man at last succeeded, and Beruriah fell into his trap.

So ashamed was she at her own weakness that she hanged herself. And so guilty was Meir for his part in her undoing that he left Palestine and went into exile after her death.

Once Beruriah's voice was silenced, no woman ever taught again from the pages of the holy Talmud.

155
The Punishment of Rabbi Meir

When Rabbi Meir came to Jerusalem for each of the three Pilgrimage Festivals, he would stay in the home of Yehuda the Cook. Yehuda's wife was a gracious hostess who always treated Meir with the greatest respect.

In time Yehuda's wife died and he remarried. The

next time Meir came to Yehuda's house, he was greeted by a strange woman.

"Where is the wife of Yehuda the Cook?" he asked her.

"I am his wife. His first wife has died, and I am now the mistress of his house. My husband has commanded me to serve you food and drink with my own hands and to make up your bed. I promise that I will be even more careful about your honor than Yehuda's first wife."

Now Rabbi Meir was an exceptionally handsome man, and as the hostess served him his meal, she felt desire welling up within her. So she gave him much wine until he was drunk. She made up his bed, laid him in it, and took off his clothes. Then she lay down beside him and slept with him all night.

The next morning she rose before he awoke. Rabbi Meir dressed and went off to the House of Study to pray. When he returned, Yehuda's wife served him lunch, but this time she acted boldly before him, laughing and flirting with him. Meir turned his eyes toward the floor in order to avoid looking at her.

"Have you no shame?" he rebuked her.

"Shame?" she replied. "How dare you act so high and mighty with me! You felt no shame last night when you lay with me!"

"That is a lie!" cried Meir.

"How else could I have learned about the birthmark on your back?" she asked him.

Then Meir knew that she was speaking the truth, and he felt ashamed. "I have lost the Torah that I have studied for so long!" he cried bitterly. "What shall I do now? How can I atone for my sin? I shall go to the head of the yeshivah in Babylonia and put myself at his mercy!"

So Meir went home, put ashes on his head and tore his clothes, and prepared himself for the long journey.

"What are you planning to do?" his family asked him.

"I shall go to the rosh yeshivah in Babylonia and ask him to sentence me for my sin."

"No, don't go!" they told him. "Your sin was unintentional, so God will surely forgive you. If you go, you risk ruining your reputation and shaming your children."

"God will surely *not* forgive me if I cover up my sin," replied Meir. "No, I must go and accept my punishment."

So he went to the *rosh yeshivah* in Babylonia and confessed his sin. "Master," he said, "whatever you decide, even if it be feeding me to wild animals, I shall accept your judgment."

The next day, they brought him before the *rosh yeshivah* and he said, "We have studied your case and have decided that you should be fed to the lions in the forest."

The *rosh yeshivah* then called two strong men and said to them, "Tie Rabbi Meir's hands and legs and bring him to the place in the forest where the lions dwell. Climb a tall tree and watch what happens. If they devour him, bring me his bones, and I shall mourn him with all my heart, for he willingly accepted the punishment of heaven. If not, bring him back to me."

So they bound Meir's hands and feet and brought him to the place in the forest where the lions had their lair. At midnight a roaring lion came and sniffed at him but did not harm him. The next morning they brought him back to the *yeshivah*.

"Take him back tonight and watch again," the *rosh yeshivah* instructed them.

The next night at midnight a lion came roaring out of the forest, sniffed Rabbi Meir, and turned him over, but the lion did not harm him. The next morning they brought him back again to the *rosh yeshivah*.

"Take him to the forest one last time," the *rosh yeshivah* told them, "and tell me what happens. If the lion does not harm him this third time, we shall know that heaven has forgiven him."

So they took him back and left him to the lion. At midnight a roaring lion came, sniffed him, and then took an olive-sized bite out of him. Then it went away.

They brought the wounded Meir back to the *rosh yeshivah*.

"Since the lion took no more than a small bite, we know that he has been spared the punishment of heaven," declared the *rosh yeshivah*. And he called for the doctors to heal him.

When Rabbi Meir returned home, a heavenly voice spoke to him and said, "Rabbi Meir is destined for the World to Come!"

156
Shimon bar Yohai and the Cave

Once Rabbi Yehuda, Rabbi Yose, and Rabbi Shimon bar Yohai were sitting together, and Yehuda ben Gerim, a proselyte, came and sat down with them.

Yehuda said, "How great are the works of the Romans! They have built marketplaces, bathhouses, and bridges."

Yose said nothing.

Shimon bar Yohai said, "How selfish are the works of the Romans! They have built marketplaces to show off their whores, bathhouses to pamper themselves, and bridges to tax travelers."

Yehuda ben Gerim spread their words until they reached the ears of the Romans.

The Romans said, "Yehuda who praised us shall be praised. Yose who said nothing shall be exiled. Shimon who condemned us shall be condemned to death."

So Shimon bar Yohai and his son Elazar went into hiding in the House of Study. Every day Shimon's wife brought them bread and water. When the Romans increased their persecution, Shimon said, "Perhaps they will torture her and she will be forced to betray us."

So they went and hid in a cave. A miracle occurred, and a carob tree grew up near their cave and a spring of water bubbled up from the rock. In order to preserve their clothing, they stripped themselves naked and sat in sand up to their necks. Thus they studied each day. Only when they prayed did they dress themselves. This way their clothes lasted for the twelve years they lived in the cave.

At the end of twelve years, Elijah came to tell them that Caesar was dead and his edicts repealed. So they emerged from the cave. Everywhere they saw people plowing and planting.

Shimon cried, "For shame! They are giving up eternal life to busy themselves with the vanities of this world!"

With blistering scorn, Shimon and Elazar gazed upon the world they had abandoned for so long. And whatever they looked upon burned up with fire.

A heavenly voice declared, "Did you come out only to destroy My world? Go back to your cave!"

They went back for another twelve months. Then a heavenly voice announced, "Even the worst sinners are forgiven in twelve months. Leave your cave!"

This time whatever Elazar's gaze consumed, Shimon's healed. Shimon said to his son, "Our learning alone can sustain the world!"

One Sabbath eve, they came upon an old man carrying two bunches of myrtle.

"What are these for?" they asked him.

"To honor the Sabbath," he answered.

"But why do you have *two* bunches?" they asked him.

"One to *remember* the Sabbath day and one to *keep* it," he replied.

Shimon declared, "How dear are God's commandments to Israel!"

And thus they were reconciled to the world.

157
The Most Precious Thing in the World

In Sidon there once lived a couple who had been married ten years but were still childless. The husband wished to divorce his wife, and he went to Rabbi Shimon bar Yohai for advice.

"Do you still love each other?" Shimon asked him.

"Yes," answered the man.

"Then remain together as husband and wife," advised Shimon.

"No," replied the man, "for without children the marriage is not a marriage."

Then Shimon said to him, "You made a great feast when you married your wife. Now that you are about to part from her, make another feast."

So he did. At the feast his wife gave him wine until he was drunk. Then he said to her, "Before you leave this house, take out the most precious things to keep for yourself."

After he was asleep, she had the servants pick him up and carry him to her father's house. When he awoke, he did not know where he was.

"Why am I here?" he asked his wife.

"You told me to take the most precious things with me," she replied. "I have followed your directions. I took the most precious thing."

Her husband was deeply moved by her love for him. They returned to Shimon bar Yohai and told him of their decision to stay together. He blessed them and prayed for their happiness.

A year later they had a son.

158
The Exchange of Sons

Hadrian, the wicked Emperor of Rome, decreed that Jews could no longer circumcise their sons. But when a son was born to Rabban Shimon ben Gamliel, Shimon circumcised him so as not to disobey a power higher than Rome. This son was Judah the Prince.

A Roman officer in the city heard of this and ordered

the baby brought to him. When he saw that the child had indeed been circumcised against the will of Rome, he commanded that the baby and his mother appear before Hadrian for judgment.

On the way to Rome, Judah's mother stopped at an inn run by a Roman named Severus. Shortly before their arrival a son named Antoninus had been born to Severus. When Judah's mother told her hostess why she was traveling to Rome, the Roman woman said, "Take my child who is not circumcised and give me yours. Take him with you to Rome and thus save your life and the life of your son."

When she arrived in Rome, she was brought before Caesar. The officer who had accused her was also there. He said, "Your majesty, this woman violated your law and circumcised her son. Do with her as you see fit."

But when they inspected the boy, they discovered that he was uncircumcised. Enraged, Hadrian said to the officer, "My decree forbade circumcision! Why then have you brought me an uncircumcised child?"

The great men of Rome explained, "So powerful is the God of Israel and so beloved his people that a child who was once circumcised has been made whole again!"

Hadrian ordered the officer executed and his own decree repealed, and he sent Antoninus and Judah's mother home in peace. When they reached the home of Severus, the mothers took back their own sons.

Antoninus's mother said, "Since the Holy One performed a miracle through me and my son, let my son and yours be friends forever."

When Antoninus grew up, he studied Torah with Judah the Prince and became wise in the ways of Israel. And when he became Caesar, he remained friends with the man who had once suckled at his mother's breast, and in time inherited the World to Come.

159
Miriam bat Tanhum and Her
Seven Sons

In time Rome supplanted Greece as the master of Palestine, and then even harsher times fell upon the Jewish people. The wicked Emperor Hadrian ruled them with an iron fist so that it became dangerous to live by the Torah's teachings. Idolatry and sin defiled the land.

Once Hadrian captured a Jewish widow and her seven sons. He had the seven brothers imprisoned separately, and then he had the oldest brought before him while his widowed mother looked on.

"Bow down to this idol!" Hadrian commanded him. "Your brothers have already done so."

"God forbid that they have!" answered the oldest son. "But even if they had, I still would not bow down before a false god made by human hands."

So they took a sword and cut off his head.

Then the second son was brought before Hadrian.

"Bow down to this idol!" ordered Hadrian. "Your brothers already have."

"God forbid that they have!" replied the second son. "But even if they had, I still would not bow before an image of emptiness!"

And they cut off his head, too.

So it went for the next four sons until only the youngest, a boy of three, remained.

They brought the little boy before Hadrian. The emperor said to him, "Bow down before this idol! Your brothers have already done so."

The youngest son ran to his mother and asked, "What should I do, Mother?"

With tears in her eyes, she said, "Your brothers await you in Paradise."

So the boy came back to the emperor and said, "I refuse to deny my God."

Then Hadrian beckoned to him and whispered, "You don't have to bow to the idol, little one. I will only throw down my ring, and you can bend down to pick it up. That way the people will think you are bowing before the idol."

"Woe to you, mighty Caesar!" said the boy. "If you are ashamed before your own people who are only flesh and blood, should not I be even more ashamed to fool my God who is the Creator of heaven and earth?"

"If your God is so great," Hadrian taunted him, "why doesn't He save you from my hands?"

"You are not worthy to have miracles performed through you," retorted the boy.

Then Hadrian ordered him killed, too.

Just before the executioner cut off his head, Miriam begged the king and said, "Please let the blade sever both our heads at once!"

But Hadrian refused. They cut off the boy's head while his mother looked on. And all the nations of the world wept and tore out their hair.

Then Miriam kissed the heads of her dead sons and said to them, "Tell Abraham that he should not boast of the one son that he was ready to offer to God on Mount Moriah. For I have given seven!"

Then she climbed up to the roof of Hadrian's palace and threw herself off.

At that moment a voice from heaven was heard weeping, "Happy is the mother of sons!"

160

The Inheritance of a Fool

There once was a man who made a will stating that his son should inherit nothing until he became a fool. Rabbi Yose ben Judah and Rabbi Judah the Prince went to Rabbi Joshua ben Karkha to ask him to explain this. When they arrived at Rabbi Joshua's house, they saw him crawling on his hands and knees with a reed in his mouth, following behind his young son. Not wishing to embarrass him, they hid themselves and only went to talk with him after he had gone inside the house.

When they asked him to explain the matter of the strange will, he laughed and said to them, "Can't you see that such a thing has already happened to me? For when a man lives long enough to have children, he starts to act like a fool."

161
Joseph the Sabbath-Lover

Once there lived a poor man whom everyone called Joseph the Sabbath-Lover, for he would spend his last penny to buy food and wine to honor the Sabbath.

Near Joseph lived a rich man who owned much property. One day a fortuneteller told him, "Joseph the Sabbath-Lover will consume all your wealth."

So he sold all he had and with the money bought a large jewel that he sewed into his turban. One day when he was crossing the river in a ferry, the wind blew the turban off and flung it into the river, where it sank and was swallowed by a fish.

That Friday a fisherman caught the fish and brought it to the marketplace.

"Who will buy this fish?" he cried.

Everyone said to him, "Take it to Joseph the Sabbath-Lover for he always buys fish for the Sabbath."

So he did, and Joseph bought it. When he cut open the fish, Joseph found the jewel that he sold for thirteen piles of gold coins.

A wise old man said to him, "He who lends to the Sabbath is amply repaid by the Sabbath."

162
The Suffering of Animals

Judah the Prince suffered a toothache for six years and had trouble urinating for seven. Why?

Once he was walking through the butchers' quarter, and he saw a calf run away from a butcher. The animal ran up to him and pressed against his side as if to say, "Save me from the butcher's knife!"

But Judah seized it and handed it back over to the butcher. He said to the butcher, "Slaughter it, for that is why it was created."

Because of his heartless words he suffered pain for thirteen years.

At the end of these thirteen years, he saw his maidservant sweeping the floor one day when a weasel scurried out of a hole. The servant raised her broom to kill it, but Judah cried, "Do not kill it! For did not King David declare: 'God's mercies are over all His works?' "

Since he took pity on the weasel, God took pity on him and ended his suffering.

163
Rabbi Hiyya and the Pomegranate

Rabbi Hiyya feared that his evil inclination was too strong, so he did not sleep with his wife for several years. Frustrated, his wife donned courtesan's clothing, painted her face, and came to Hiyya while he was studying in the garden. He did not recognize her and asked who she was.

"A courtesan," she replied.

Hiyya felt himself suddenly aroused. "What is your fee?" he asked her.

"That pomegranate at the top of the tree," she replied.

With one leap he jumped to the top of the tree and seized the fruit. He gave it to her, and they lay together. Then Hiyya rose and went off by himself to weep, overcome with remorse.

When he returned home, he found his wife, modestly dressed as always, kindling the fire to make dinner. He jumped into the oven and was consumed by the flames kindled by his own wife.

164
How Resh Lakish Became a Sage

Rabbi Yohanan was the most handsome man in the world. One day Resh Lakish the Robber was walking along the Jordan when he saw Rabbi Yohanan bathing. Thinking he was a woman, Resh Lakish jumped in.

Rabbi Yohanan said to him, "How great is your power to study Torah!"

Resh Lakish said, "How beautiful you would be if you were a woman!"

Rabbi Yohanan said, "If you will study Torah, you may marry my sister, who is even more beautiful than I."

Resh Lakish agreed. He repented of his sins, married Rabbi Yohanan's sister, and began to study Torah. In time he became a great scholar.

One day Rabbi Yohanan and Resh Lakish had an argument about how to purify a sword, a knife, a spear, and a sickle. Rabbi Yohanan lost his temper and said to Resh Lakish, "You robber! You know all about such things because they are part of your trade."

Resh Lakish replied, "What is the use of studying Torah if I am treated now no differently than I was before?

Just as I am called 'master' now, so was I called that when
I was still chief of the thieves!"

Rabbi Yohanan replied, "It is better to study Torah
because in so doing you gain a share in the World to
Come."

So angry was Rabbi Yohanan with Resh Lakish that
he gazed upon him sternly and made him ill.

The wife of Resh Lakish went to her brother and
begged him to allow her husband to live. "What will
become of me and my children if he should die?" she
cried.

"I shall care for you and your children," answered
Rabbi Yohanan.

Shortly after this Resh Lakish died.

Rabbi Yohanan grieved greatly over his death. The
sages sent Rabbi Eleazar ben Pedat to comfort him. The
two studied Torah together. To everything that Rabbi
Yohanan said, Eleazar replied, "Yes, I have been taught
the same thing."

Rabbi Yohanan became angry. "When I would state
my view of the law to Resh Lakish, he would always raise
twenty-four objections and then answer them himself. He
sharpened my mind, while you agree with everything I
say. Don't I already know that I am correct?"

Then Rabbi Yohanan tore his clothes and cried,
"Where are you, son of Lakish?"

So long and deeply did he mourn Resh Lakish that he
lost his mind. The rabbis prayed for compassion upon
him, and he died, and they buried him.

165
Abbaye's Suspicions

Once Abbaye overheard a man ask a woman to walk with
him several miles to a nearby town. Fearing that the man
planned to seduce the woman, Abbaye decided to follow

them and keep them from sin. But when the couple came to a forest at the edge of a marsh, the man said to his companion, "How pleasant it has been to walk together," and then they parted company.

Abbaye said to himself, "Had I been with the woman, I might have desired to seduce her! Not their evil inclination, but *my own*, compelled me to follow them!"

Then Abbaye stepped out on the bridge over the swamp and prepared to throw himself in. Just then an old man appeared and said to him, "The greater the man, the more powerful the evil inclination."

And Abbaye returned home in peace.

166
The Tithe

Once there was a pious farmer who owned a large field. Every year the field yielded a thousand measures of grain, of which the farmer set aside one hundred measures as a tithe for the poor.

When he was about to die, the man called his son and said to him, "My son, I am leaving this field to you. Be careful to tithe each year, for that is why the field has rewarded me so well."

The year after the father's death, the field produced a thousand measures, as it had always done, and the son set aside one hundred measures for the poor. But the next year he set aside only ninety measures, and the field produced less at the next harvest. Each year he decreased the measures he set aside, and each year the harvest was poorer. Finally the field yielded only one hundred measures of grain.

His relatives came to see him wearing their finest holiday clothes.

"Why do you rejoice when I have suffered this misfortune?" he cried. "You should have compassion for me!"

"Why should we not rejoice?" they replied. "Before, you were the householder and God was the priest, since to the priest belongs the tithe. But now God is the householder and you are the priest, for your field only produces a tenth of what it once did."

Chastened by their words, the son tithed fully that year. The following year, the field once more produced a thousand measures of grain, as it had in the days of his father.

167
The Weasel and the Well

Once a young girl went walking and lost her way. She came to a well and climbed down the rope to get something to drink. But when she tried to climb out, she found that she could not pull herself up. So she began to weep and wail.

A young man came along and heard her cries.

"Are you a human being or an imp?" he shouted down.

"I am a human being," she said.

"Perhaps you are deceiving me!"

She swore that she was not.

Then he pulled her out by the rope and wished to lie with her. But she said, "Is this the way a man of Israel behaves? Let us pledge ourselves to each other, and promise not to marry anyone else."

So they made a covenant to marry each other when they came of age.

"Who shall be our witnesses?" asked the young woman.

At that moment a weasel was scampering by the well. "Let this weasel and this well be our witnesses!" declared the young man. "By them we swear not to be false to each other."

Then they parted and went their separate ways.

The young woman kept her promise. No matter how

many suitors her parents proposed for her, she refused to marry any of them, and finally she lost her mind, tearing her own clothes and the clothes of her suitors if they approached her. So they left her alone.

The young man, however, soon forgot his oath and married another woman. They had a child, but one day he was strangled by a weasel. They had a second child, but she too died when she fell into a well and drowned.

"How strange this is!" said the young man's wife. "If our children had died ordinary deaths, I would have accepted heaven's judgment. But these were no ordinary deaths! Tell me what you have done to deserve such punishment!"

And her husband told her about the vow he had taken in his youth.

"You must honor your vow or more evil will befall us," said his wife.

So he divorced his wife and went to the city where the young madwoman lived.

"I shall marry her with all her faults," he declared to her parents. And they accepted him, though they had little hope that he would fare any better than all the others.

When he approached his betrothed, she came at him with her long nails outstretched, ready to tear his clothes, but he cried, "Weasel and well!" and she instantly regained her reason.

They married and had many children, and prospered in all that they did.

168
The Birthday of the Messiah

On the day the Temple was destroyed, the Messiah was born.

Soon after, a man was plowing when suddenly his

cow began to moo. A passerby heard the sound and stopped to talk to the farmer.

"Who are you?" he asked him.

The farmer replied, "I am a Jew."

"Jew, Jew!" cried the passerby. "Unharness your cow and unhitch your plow!"

"Why?"

"Because the Temple of the Jews has been destroyed."

"How do you know?" asked the farmer.

"Your cow has told us."

Then the cow mooed again.

"Jew, Jew!" cried the passerby. "Harness your cow and hitch your plow, for the Messiah has been born."

"What is his name?" asked the farmer.

"Menahem son of Hezekiah," replied the stranger.

"Where does he live?"

"In Birat Araba near Bethlehem in Judah."

The farmer sold his cow and became a merchant of children's clothing. He went from place to place until he came to Birat Araba. But when he came to the house of Hezekiah, the mistress of the house did not buy any garments.

"Mother of Menahem!" he said. "Come buy linen garments for your son."

"Alas for my son!" she cried. "May the enemies of Israel choke!" she cried.

"Why do you say this?" asked the merchant.

"Because on the day that my son was born, the Temple was destroyed."

The merchant said, "Just as the Temple's destruction is tied to your son's birth, so too is its rebuilding."

She said, "I cannot buy clothes for him for I have no money."

"Do not trouble yourself about that," said the merchant. "Take the garments and pay me in several days when I return."

Several days later he returned to her house and asked, "What deeds has your son done since I left?"

"Soon after you departed," wailed the mother, "stormy winds came, snatched him out of my hands, and carried him away!"

The merchant said, "Be comforted, for God has hidden him in Paradise until the world is ready to be redeemed."

PART VIII

IN THE LANDS OF THE DIASPORA

For over a thousand years after the decline of the talmudic academies in Babylonia and Palestine, Jews wandered on foreign soil, carrying other people's tales upon their backs along with their wares. They carried tales from India, Persia, and Arabia to Europe, where the tales took on a life of their own. In the process of transmission, these stories entered the Jewish narrative tradition and were in turn transformed and made ours.

1. FAITH

169
Ariel, or the Pious Man
and the Lion

A pious Jew in Hebron once had to make a perilous twelve-day journey over the desert to a distant city. Before leaving, the Jew offered the caravan leader several extra gold pieces if he would agree not to travel on the Sabbath. The man promised to do what the Jew asked.

But on Friday afternoon, the leader refused to halt his camels. So the Jew found himself faced with a terrible dilemma: If he remained alone in the desert, he risked death from wild beasts, but if he desecrated the Sabbath, he would surely forfeit his share in the World to Come. He chose to remain behind.

When the sun set, the Jew received the Sabbath Queen with joyful singing, then prayed the evening prayers and ate his simple meal. Just as he was about to lie down to sleep, a fierce roar shattered the desert silence, making every bone in his body tremble.

Across the sands strode a magnificent lion, its golden skin gleaming in the bright moonlight. As the lion came nearer, the Jew began reciting the words of the *Sh'ma*, certain that the next moment would be his last.

But when the lion reached him, it lay down peacefully at his feet, looking up at him with great kindness. Then the Jew understood that God had sent the king of the desert to safeguard him through the night.

The next morning when he awoke, the lion still lay quietly nearby. The Jew rose, prayed the Sabbath morning prayers, ate his second meal, and studied. And during it all, the lion looked on, silent, with that same look of great tenderness in his golden eyes.

At sunset the Jew made *havdalah*. As soon as the candle flame had been extinguished, the lion walked over to him and lay down at his feet. The Jew mounted upon the great beast's back, and off they rode, the man riding the lion. Swift as the wind ran the lion until the man spied a line of camels on the horizon. As they drew nearer the Jew recognized his caravan.

As soon as he saw them, the caravan leader dismounted from his camel and fell to his knees.

"Forgive me!" he cried. "Now I understand that you are a man of God!"

The moment the Jew dismounted from the lion's back, the great beast bounded swiftly away toward the mountains until he was out of sight. Then the Jew climbed upon a camel, and the caravan continued on its way.

From that day on the Jew was known as Ariel, Lion of God. And his descendants, who still live in Hebron, are known by that name to this very day.

170
The Wooden Sword

Shah Abbas was a wise and just ruler who would often disguise himself as a dervish and slip out among his people to see how they lived. One evening he saw a light in a poor hut and went in. A Jew sat in front of a dish of simple food, singing praises and songs of thanksgiving to God.

"Is a guest welcome?" the Shah asked.

"A guest is a gift of God," replied the Jew. "I do not have much, but you are welcome to share it with me."

After they had finished eating, the Shah said to him, "What is your work?"

"I am a cobbler," he answered. "All day long I walk about the streets of the city and mend shoes. With the few pennies I earn, I buy food for myself."

"And what will you do tomorrow?" asked the Shah.

"Blessed is God day after day," answered the Jew.

The next day the Shah issued a decree that cobblers could no longer mend shoes without a permit. When the Jew heard of the new law, he went to the well and drew water for people in exchange for a few pennies.

When the disguised Shah returned that evening to the poor hut, he found the Jew sitting as usual, singing and praising God.

"What did you do today?" he asked him.

"When I left my house this morning, I learned that I could no longer mend shoes, so I drew water and thus earned enough to buy bread."

"And what if the Shah should forbid the drawing of water tomorrow?"

"Blessed is God day after day," answered the Jew.

The next day the Shah issued a decree banning the drawing of water. When the Jew learned of it, he went and cut wood for several people in exchange for a few pennies. That night when the Shah returned, he found the Jew eating and singing as usual.

"What did you do today?" he asked the Jew.

"I found that I could no longer draw water, so I cut wood."

"And what if the Shah should forbid the cutting of wood tomorrow?" asked the Shah.

"Blessed is God day after day," said the Jew.

The next day the Shah sent messengers throughout

the city proclaiming that all woodcutters must report for guard duty at the palace. The Jew went and was given a sword and told where to stand guard. Since he could not earn money that day, he went in the evening to the storekeeper and exchanged the steel blade of his sword for food. Then he went home and fashioned a wooden blade and attached it to the hilt of the sword. He was still working on the blade when the disguised Shah arrived.

"What are you doing?" the Shah asked him.

"I had to guard the palace today, so I could not earn money to buy food," the Jew told him. "I gave my sword blade as a pledge to the storekeeper, and now I am making a wooden one to replace it."

"And what if they should check swords tomorrow?" asked the Shah.

"Blessed is God day after day," answered the Jew.

The next day the captain of the guard summoned the Jew and placed a prisoner in his charge. "This prisoner has been condemned to death," he told the Jew. "You must cut off his head."

"I cannot," answered the Jew. "I have never killed a man in my life."

"It is the Shah's order!" said the captain. "You must obey!"

The Jew grasped the hilt of his sword and cried aloud to the crowd gathered to witness the execution, "God of the Universe! You know that I am no murderer! If the man who stands before me deserves to die, let my sword be a sword of steel. But if he is innocent, I pray that You turn this steel blade into a blade of wood!"

And when he drew forth the blade—behold! It was made of wood. The people gasped in astonishment. Then they let the prisoner go free.

After this, Shah Abbas summoned the Jew to the palace, embraced him, and revealed his true identity. He made the Jew one of his chief counselors and cherished him as a friend all the days of his life.

171
The Sabbath Loaves

Once there was a *Marrano* who left Portugal and came to Israel. He and his wife settled in the holy city of Safed, where they both joyously embraced the faith of their ancestors.

One Sabbath the man went to the synagogue and heard the rabbi deliver a sermon about the special Sabbath loaves the priests used to prepare in the Temple when it still stood in Jerusalem.

"But because of our sins," concluded the rabbi, "we have stopped bringing God these special loaves as we did in times past."

When the service was over, the *Marrano* hurried home and said to his wife, "Dear wife, please make two Sabbath loaves that I can bring as an offering to God. Be sure to use only the finest flour, and make sure your hands are pure when you knead the dough."

And his wife did as he asked.

That Friday afternoon, he brought the two loaves to the synagogue and set them down before the Holy Ark.

"Almighty God!" he cried. "Please accept our offerings, for we offer them with all our heart. My wife and I hope that You find these loaves tasty and that the sweet smell pleases You. We pray that You will not be disappointed in us."

As soon as he had left the synagogue, the *shammash* came in to prepare the room for the evening prayers. He found the *Marrano's* loaves in front of the ark.

"Praise be to God who has provided for all our needs!" cried the *shammash*. "Some generous soul has put these loaves here so that I and my family can celebrate the Sabbath in joy and gladness." And he ran home to give the loaves to his wife.

Just before sundown the *Marrano* hurried back to the

synagogue and discovered that the loaves were gone. How great was his joy to discover that God had accepted his offering!

And so it went each week: The *Marrano* and his wife would offer the loaves, and the *shammash* and his family would consume them. Both rejoiced in their good fortune.

One Friday the rabbi came to the synagogue early to prepare his sermon for the next day. While he was concealed behind the lectern, the *Marrano* came in and laid his two loaves before the ark. As always, he pleaded with God to accept his offering, and then he turned to go, his heart and step lifted by joy.

But before he reached the door, the rabbi stepped out from behind the lectern and called to him, "You fool! Do you really think that God needs your bread? Do you really think that God has a body and an appetite? It is a great sin to think so! It must be the *shammash* who has been eating your loaves!"

He called in the *shammash* and questioned him.

"Yes, rabbi, it was I who took the loaves," admitted the *shammash*. "All this time I thought that some kind soul had taken pity on me and my family and left the loaves there for us."

"You see!" cried the rabbi to the shamefaced *Marrano*. "It is just as I said. Imagine thinking that God was eating your loaves!"

The *Marrano* now burst into tears. "Oh, rabbi, what a sinner I have been! When I heard you talk about the special Temple loaves in your sermon, I misunderstood your words and so committed a terrible transgression. Will God ever forgive me?" And he began to cry again.

At that moment, a messenger arrived from Rabbi Isaac Luria, the holy Ari.

"My master says that you are to go home and set your house in order," declared the messenger, "for tomorrow you will die. It is the will of heaven."

Upset by these grave words, the rabbi hurried to the Ari and asked him to explain his message.

"Not since the Holy Temple was destroyed has God

derived such pleasure as from the two loaves offered by this simple *Marrano* and his wife," said the holy Ari. "Each Sabbath the Holy One looks forward to the words of thanksgiving and praise that this simple Jew pours forth from the depths of his heart. But in shaming this pious man, you have robbed God of one of His supreme pleasures. And because of this, you have been sentenced to death. It is useless to pray for forgiveness, for your fate has been sealed."

So the rabbi went home and made out his will. And the next day at the conclusion of the Sabbath, the words of the Ari came true, and he died.

172
The Man Who Kept the Sabbath
and the Bear Who Kept Him

Once three men went on a journey. On Friday afternoon they found themselves in the middle of a forest. As darkness began to descend, two of the men became afraid and said, "We cannot stay here, for the woods are filled with robbers and dangerous beasts. Let us keep traveling until we find shelter for the night. For it is better to desecrate the Sabbath than to die!"

But their companion refused to accompany them, and he bade them farewell. When they were gone, he set up his tent and began to recite the Sabbath evening prayers. Then he sat down upon the bare ground and began his simple Sabbath meal.

Suddenly a bear appeared before him, a beast so huge that it towered over his tent. But instead of devouring him, it came over to him and gently took bread from his hand. Then the man finished his meal, recited the grace, and lay down to sleep. All night the bear stood watch over him.

The next day he said his prayers, ate his meals, and

studied, while the bear stood quietly by, watching and guarding him. At the conclusion of the Sabbath, the two set off through the forest.

That same night robbers came upon the other two travelers and stole all that they had. Moments later, the bear and his companion reached them. Instantly the great beast rushed at the two hapless travelers and tore them to pieces. But the pious man he left unharmed.

When the robbers saw this, they asked the pious man, "Who are you?"

"I am a Jew," he replied.

"How do you come to have this bear with you?" they asked him.

"The king gave him to me as a companion so that no one should harm me."

Then the robbers grew afraid, for they thought: "Surely this man is beloved of the king!"

"Let us give him all our money," they said to each other, "or he may betray us to the king and cause us to be hanged. Perhaps we can purchase his silence."

So they gave him all the money they had stolen, and then they departed. The pious man proceeded on his way to the edge of the forest accompanied by the bear. As soon as he was safely out of the woods, the bear disappeared back into the trees and was never seen again.

173
Only the Dead Lose Hope

Once there was a rich man who believed in giving charity only to those who have lost all hope, for only they depend totally on another's kindness.

One day when he was walking along, he saw a poor man in rags lying on a rubbish heap. He thought to himself, "Here certainly is a man who has lost all hope," and he offered him a coin, saying, "I see that you need this, for your hope is cut off in this world."

"No," answered the poor man, "it is your hope that is cut off, not mine."

Shocked by his reply, the rich man said, "Why do you curse me when I wish to do you good?"

"Don't you know that God casts down the high and proud and raises up the humble? Just because I lie here in the ashes doesn't mean that my hope is cut off. I believe what the Psalmist says: 'God raises up the poor from the dust and the needy from the rubbish heap.' "

"Then tell me," asked the rich man, "who are those whose hope is cut off in this world and need my charity?"

"The dead," replied the other, "for they have no more hope."

So the rich man went to the cemetery and buried one hundred coins in a grave.

"This is for you, dead man," he said to the grave. "Keep these coins, for you have lost all hope and need my charity."

Then he went home.

In time, the wheel of fortune turned, and the poor man became rich, and the rich man, poor. So poor did the rich man become that he had not even a crust of bread to eat. Then he remembered the coins he had buried in the cemetery and went there to dig them up. People saw him digging there and thought that he was trying to steal the shrouds from the dead. So he was arrested and brought to the mayor of the town, who was none other than the poor man who had now become the richest man in town.

When the people accused the formerly rich man of trying to steal the shrouds of the dead, he said to the mayor, "God forbid that I should commit such a sin!" And he told him the whole story of the poor man's curse and how he had buried money in the cemetery.

When he finished his tale, the mayor said to him, "Don't you recognize me?"

"No," answered the formerly rich man.

"I am that poor man who lay on the rubbish heap! I am he whose hope you thought was cut off! God remembered me and raised me up so that now I am the mayor of this town."

And he embraced the accused man and said to him, "You see, my friend, you should never rely on your money. But since you did want to give charity when you once had the means, I shall now take you into my house and take care of you all the days of your life."

And so he did.

174
The King's Loaves

Once there were two beggars who went daily to the palace to beg at the king's gate. Every day the king gave each of them a loaf of bread. One of the beggars would always thank the king for his generosity. But the other thanked God for giving the king sufficient wealth to give charity.

The second beggar's words always hurt the king. So the king decided to teach him a lesson. The king ordered his baker to bake two identical loaves, but in one he had him conceal precious jewels. Then he instructed the baker to give the loaf with the hidden jewels to the beggar who always thanked the king for his charity.

The next day the baker went to the king's gate and handed the two loaves to the beggars. He took great care not to confuse the two, for he feared the king's wrath if he should make a mistake.

When the beggar with the special loaf felt how heavy and hard it was, he concluded that it was poorly made and asked the other beggar to exchange loaves with him. The second beggar, always eager to help a friend, agreed. Then they went their separate ways.

When the second man bit into the loaf, he discovered that it was filled with jewels. He thanked God for his good fortune, grateful that he would no longer have to beg for his bread.

The next morning the king was surprised to find only the first beggar at the palace gate. He had the baker brought before him and asked him, "Did you mix up the two loaves I had you bake?"

"No, your majesty," answered the baker. "I did exactly as you commanded."

Then the king turned to the beggar and asked, "What did you do with the loaf you received yesterday?"

The man replied, "It was hard and poorly baked so I gave it to my friend in exchange for his."

Then the king understood that all his riches had indeed come from God and that only the Holy One can make a poor man rich and a rich man poor. Not even a king can change the will of heaven.

2. LOVE

175

Sincere Friendship

A father who was about to die called his son to his bedside and asked him, "My son, how many friends do you have?"

The son replied, "About one hundred, Father."

The father said, "How fortunate you are! I have only one half of a friend." Then he said to his son, "Perhaps if you test your friends, you will discover you have fewer friends than you think."

The son agreed to put his friends to the test.

"Take a calf," instructed the dying man, "kill it and cut it into pieces. Put the pieces in a bag, take it to your friends, and ask them to bury it without asking any questions."

So the son killed a calf and brought the bloodstained

bag to his closest friend. But when the man saw the blood, he feared that his friend had committed a murder and so refused to do what he asked. So it went with all his friends. Chastened, the son returned to his father's bed and reported what had happened.

"Now go to my half of a friend," instructed the father, "and ask him to bury the bag."

The son did so, and the man buried the bag in his garden without asking a single question. Only then did the son reveal to him that it had only been a test.

When the son again stood before his dying father, he said to him,"I now understand, Father, how rare true friends are. But tell me," he continued, "if the friend you have now is only half a friend, have you ever had a whole friend?"

"Unfortunately not," answered the father, "but I have heard of one," and he told his son this story:

"Once there were two merchants, an Egyptian and a Babylonian. One day the Babylonian came to visit the Egyptian in his home. The host gave a seven-day feast to honor his friend, but on the eighth day his friend fell mysteriously ill. Wise men were called in to examine him, and they declared that he was suffering from a secret love. The host brought before him all the women of the household, but he turned away from them all.

"Then the friend disclosed his secret love: She was the young woman whom his host had raised since childhood and was intending to marry now that she had come of age.

"Hearing of this, the host said, 'You may have her for your wife, for I do not wish you to die.' So he gave his betrothed to his friend, and the couple returned to Babylonia.

"Soon the wheel of fortune turned, and the Egyptian lost all that he had. He traveled to Babylonia to ask his friend for help. Near the city where his friend lived, he suddenly felt overcome with despair.

" 'Why should I go on living?' he asked himself. 'I have lost the woman I love and my entire fortune. What is there left for me?'

"Just then soldiers came upon him. 'Have you seen a man fleeing this way?' they asked him. 'For a murderer has just escaped from the prison.'

" 'I am that murderer,' said the Egyptian, for he had no wish to live and was glad to submit himself to the executioner's rope.

"They brought him into the city and led him to the place of execution to be hanged. But among the crowd gathered to witness the execution was his old friend, who recognized him and ran toward the gallows, crying, 'Stop! I am the true murderer! This man is innocent! Hang me in his stead!'

"So they put the noose around the second man's neck over the protests of his friend.

"Witnessing this scene was the real murderer, who had come that day to see an innocent man die in his place. So moved was he by the friendship of these two friends that he now came forward and confessed his crime and was immediately hanged.

"The Babylonian merchant, learning of the recent bad fortune of his friend, took him into his household and made him heir to everything he had.

"My son," concluded the dying father, "these two were whole friends."

176

The Bail

Once there were two friends who loved each other so dearly that they were seldom ever apart. But circumstances finally forced them to separate, and one left his home and settled in a faraway land.

It happened that while one friend was visiting the other in his new home, war broke out between the two countries. The foreign visitor was arrested as a spy and sentenced to execution. He asked the king's permission to return home first to settle his affairs.

"Your majesty, my business has always operated totally on trust," he explained. "I have kept no records of the debts owed me. If I were to die now, my wife and children would not know who owed me money and would be left penniless."

The king laughed. "How do I know you'll return if I let you go? What man comes back for his own funeral?"

Then his friend came forward and said, "I will go to prison in his place. If he does not return on the date set for his execution, I shall die in his stead."

And the king agreed to the plan.

So the foreigner left for his own country, and his friend went to prison in his place. On the morning of the execution date, the condemned man had still not returned. So they led his friend to the gallows and prepared to take his life.

Just then, the other man appeared and demanded to be hanged as originally decreed. But his friend refused to let them remove the noose from his neck. Back and forth they quarreled, each insisting that he should die in the other's stead.

Finally the king called for silence.

"What an extraordinary friendship this is!" he cried. "Never in my life have I seen the like! I hereby pardon you both. Only one thing do I ask in return: that you both consent to be my friends, for friends such as you are as precious as the finest gold."

And the three became fast friends for the rest of their lives.

177

The Bird That Sang to a
Bridegroom

The young experience a strange kind of happiness. Their soul imagines itself immortal, as Adam and Eve once were, for it is still innocent of passion or evil thoughts. But it is only a dream . . .

Once a young man in the East became engaged to be married. As the day of his wedding approached, he felt overcome by deep sadness, for he knew that he was about to forfeit his immortality in exchange for the pleasures of this world.

On the eve of his wedding he went into the forest and prayed, "O Holy One of Blessing, before I leave Paradise and take my wife to heart, grant me but one glimpse or sound from eternity, even if it costs me some of my heavenly portion."

Suddenly a bird began to sing in a nearby tree. So sweetly did it sing that the boy felt his heart fill with an inexpressible joy.

"Thank you, God!" he cried as he bent his ear to the wonderful sound.

Then the bird flew off. Eagerly he ran home to tell his bride-to-be what he had just experienced in the forest.

But when he reached his home it was dark. From inside came no sound of merriment, no bustle of hurrying servants preparing for the wedding feast, no strains from the musicians, no happy voices.

He ran to his bride's bedrooom window and knocked, but a stranger thrust his head out and rudely asked, "What do you want?"

"Where is my beloved, my bride?"

"There is no bride here!" snapped the man, and he slammed the shutter in the boy's face.

Bewildered, the boy wandered through the streets of his town, but he recognized no one. He went to the synagogue and found only strangers within. Desperately, he called out the names of his family.

Suddenly an old man's voice interrupted him. "Who calls the names of the friends of my youth?"

"It is I," said the boy, "the bridegroom to be married tonight."

The old man asked him, "Are you the bridegroom who disappeared mysteriously forty years ago?"

"That is impossible!" cried the boy.

"Come with me," said the old man. And he led him to the cemetery and showed him the graves of his mother and father. The boy began to weep. Then the old man led him to another grave.

"Read what is written on the stone," he told the boy.

Through tear-filled eyes, the boy read, "Here lies she whose beloved vanished without a trace and who later died of a broken heart."

Then the boy fell to the ground and wept until he could weep no more. When he looked up, he saw standing before him the Angel of Death.

"You asked for more than humankind has been granted," the Angel told him. "Beneath your noble aspirations lay pride and vain curiosity. You wished to separate holiness from love, which is impossible. But God has taken pity on you and will make your suffering short. I have been sent to lead you back to Paradise."

And the Angel took the boy's soul, and he died.

178
The Clever Wife

Once there was a king who declared that he would only marry a woman who was willing to break off all relations with her parents after the wedding and never see them again. Despite this harsh condition, many women wished to be queen, and so the king held a contest to choose one of them to sit beside him on the throne. After the wedding, the king spent most days away from the palace attending to matters of state, and so his new wife was almost always alone. After several months she died of loneliness.

The king mourned her, and then declared another contest to choose a new queen. But this queen, too, he neglected, and she too died of loneliness. So it went for many years, queen succeeding queen, and the king burying them all.

Once an only daughter wished to become the new queen. Her parents tried to discourage her, but she insisted on trying her luck in the king's contest.

"Do not worry, my dear Mother and Father," she told her parents before she left them. "I promise that I will see you again."

Since she was both beautiful and graceful, the king chose her for his new bride. After the wedding, he left her alone as he had all the others.

In a few days the new queen became bored. So she took a goatskin, blew it up, dressed it in men's clothing, and painted a face on it. Then she proceeded to pour out her sorrows to it.

Whenever the king was with her, she responded happily to his attentions, but when he was gone, she held long conversations with her doll. After several months, the king was surprised to find her so well and happy. None of his previous queens had adjusted so well to their solitary lives in the palace.

"Perhaps she is betraying me," he thought to himself.

So he drilled a hole in the wall of her bedroom and spied on her. And soon he saw her conversing with a strange man.

"Aha!" he said to himself. "So I am being deceived!"

Then he ordered his guards to watch if anyone was stealing in and out of her room. They watched carefully but discovered no one coming in or going out.

A few nights later, he concealed a dagger in his robe and invited his wife to come into his room. When she stood before him, he drew forth the dagger and demanded, "Where is your lover?"

"Come with me and I will show you," she said.

She led him to a cupboard in her room. The king flung open the door and plunged his dagger deep into the goatskin doll. Blood flowed from the doll onto the floor.

"What is this?" he cried.

She said to him, "This is my sorrow and my grief. If

I had not told this doll all that was in my heart, I would
have burst from all my suffering."

And at last the king understood that he had been the
cause of his wives' deaths, and he repented of his hard-
heartedness. He revoked his cruel decree and invited his
wife's parents to come visit her in the palace.

And so she kept her promise that she would see them
once again.

179
The Revival of the Dead

In Jerusalem there once lived a poor scholar and his wife
who were childless. At that time there was a terrible
famine in Israel, and the scholars of the city drew lots to
choose one among them to go abroad to seek help from
their fellow Jews in the Diaspora. The lot fell upon the
poor childless scholar.

When his wife heard of it, she wept bitterly, "How
can you leave me alone in my old age? For I have no child
to comfort me, and who knows when you shall return!"

"Let us pray to God," said her husband. "Perhaps we
will have a child in our old age."

So it happened. The old woman conceived, but the
husband could not delay his departure any longer and so
set sail before the child was born.

A few months later, the wife gave birth to a handsome boy whom she named Solomon. So wise was the
child that he soon learned the whole Torah, and after that
the Mishnah and Talmud. Every day he would study with
his companions upon the roof of his house, where it was
cool. Twice a day his mother would bring him his meals
there and visit with him.

One afternoon as he strolled upon the roof awaiting
his mother's visit, an eagle suddenly swooped down
upon him, seized him in its strong talons, and carried him
off, leaving only his shoes behind. Swiftly it bore him

over the sea until they reached Spain. Then it dropped him into the king's garden and flew away.

When the king's guards found a strange youth lying on the ground, still as death, they summoned physicians who attended to him until he recovered.

When at last he opened his eyes, he asked, "Where am I?"

"You are in Spain," they told him, "in the king's palace." And they brought him meat and wine to revive his spirits.

But the boy refused to eat or drink. "I am a Jew," he told them. "The Torah has forbidden these foods to me."

"What then can we bring you?" they asked.

"Honey, nuts, and fruits," he told them.

So they brought them to him.

When the boy had regained much of his strength, he spent his days wandering in the garden, reciting all the Torah and holy words that he remembered. But he often wept, wishing that he had his books with him. The king learned of his unhappiness and sent messengers throughout his kingdom to buy him the books he wanted. And he built for the boy a beautiful house in the garden in which to study.

Meanwhile, the boy's mother, having discovered her son's empty shoes on the rooftop and presuming him dead, mourned him day after day, bitterly lamenting her lonely fate.

One night the king's daughter found herself unable to sleep and went into the garden to walk among the trees and flowers there. She knew nothing of the strange boy in the garden, for her father wished to protect her since she was but a young girl. She saw a light in the window of the little house where Solomon lived and drew closer to investigate.

Hearing her footsteps, Solomon looked up and saw in the window the most beautiful face he had ever seen. Instantly fear seized his heart, for he imagined that this was a demon come to distract him from his studies. So he bent over his holy books and tried to banish the beautiful face from his mind.

Then the king's daughter spoke to him, but he pretended to hear nothing. She returned to the palace, bewildered by what she had seen.

A short time later she returned with an interpreter, thinking that the boy had not understood her words. But this time he answered her questions in her own language. So she sent the interpreter away and began to converse with the stranger herself.

"What are you studying?" she asked him.

"I am a Jew," he told her. "These are the books of my faith."

"Tell me what is in them," she said.

So he told her about the Torah and the ways of his people. And they conversed until it was almost dawn. Then she returned to the palace, her heart filled with a strange new happiness.

The next night she returned to Solomon's house, and he taught her more words of Torah. Night after night, the two young people studied and conversed together until the princess came to love this stranger and his teachings.

One night she said to him, "I wish to become a Jew."

"It will be too difficult for you," said Solomon.

But the more he tried to dissuade her, the more she insisted, until he had to yield. "If that is your wish," he told her, "then you must keep it a secret."

"I will," she promised.

"Tomorrow night when you come here," Solomon instructed her, "bring with you clean garments. Take off the clothing you are wearing and immerse yourself completely in the garden pool. Then put on the new garments."

The next night the princess did as Solomon had instructed her. When she emerged from the water, she said the blessing he had taught her and put on the new garments.

Then Solomon said to her, "You are now a new person and you need a new name. No longer will you be called Mary but Sarah. You must be careful not to eat impure foods or to transgress God's holy laws."

After that she asked him to teach her the *aleph-bet*, and then the prayers and blessings, and he did. With each meeting their love grew stronger until they vowed to marry. They exchanged signet rings as a sign of their everlasting love.

But the next night, as Solomon awaited his beloved by the garden pool, the eagle came and bore him off again in its talons, carrying him over the sea and dropping him back upon his rooftop. A servant found him there the next morning and summoned his mother, who rejoiced to find her lost son returned to her. In time the physicians healed him and he returned to his friends in the House of Study. But not for one moment could he banish the memory of his beloved Sarah from his thoughts, and he would frequently break off his studies to sigh, "Oh, Sarah!" His friends and family worried greatly about him, thinking that his terrible experiences must have confused his mind.

Meanwhile, Sarah returned to the garden only to find her beloved Solomon gone without a trace. Night after night she wandered along the garden paths, seeking him, until at last she gave up hope and took to her bed. The worried king and queen called in the court physicians, but they were unable to cure her.

Soon after this the poor scholar returned home from his travels. How great was his joy to find a son so handsome and wise within his house. But he soon saw that Solomon was greatly troubled, and he questioned the boy until he finally learned the secret of his distress.

"I will go to Spain and find this Sarah of yours," he told his son. "And with God's help I will bring her back to you."

Solomon gave his father the ring Sarah had given him so that she would believe his father's words. The next day the old man set sail for Spain.

Disguising himself as a physician, he came to the king's palace and announced that he could cure the ailing princess. When they brought him in to her, he asked them all to leave so that he could consider her case with no distractions. So they left him alone.

He approached her bed and whispered to her, "Sarah, my daughter, I am the father of your beloved Solomon."

At first she did not hear him, so great was the sleep brought on by her illness. But at last she opened her eyes and saw the old man by her side.

Again he whispered, "Sarah, my daughter, I am the father of your beloved Solomon. He has sent me here to find you."

Suddenly her cheeks flushed with life, and she sat up in her bed, her eyes wide with astonishment. "Is it possible? Is Solomon still alive?"

"Yes, my daughter," he said, "and here is his ring." And he showed her the signet ring she had once given to Solomon to seal their love. Then she knew that he spoke the truth.

The father then went out of the room and announced to the king and queen that he had cured the princess. They gave her food and drink, and in a few weeks she was restored to health, looking even more beautiful than before.

Then he appeared before the king and queen and said, "Your daughter needs a change of climate to complete her cure. Let me take her on a sea voyage, and then she will fully regain her health."

"She is in your hands," they answered.

So the princess gathered all her jewels and gold and kissed her parents good-bye. Then they set sail for Israel.

As they neared the end of their voyage, Solomon became gravely ill, for he feared that his father's efforts would fail and that he would never see his beloved Sarah again. Just as Sarah and his father reached the gates of Jerusalem, Solomon breathed his last breath and died.

When they arrived at the poor scholar's house, they found everyone weeping. Sarah ran to Solomon's room and found his lifeless body on the bed.

"Leave me, all of you!" she cried. "Leave me alone with my love!"

So they left her and she lifted up her voice to heaven

and prayed, "Dear God, Master of Life! I have abandoned my father and mother and the land of my birth to come here and seek shelter under Your wings. It was this youth who first opened my eyes to the joys of Your Torah and commandments. Have pity upon him and restore him to life so that all the world may know that You are a God who restores the dead to life. If not, then take my life, too, for I have no wish to live without my beloved. Blessed be the Lord who listens to our prayers!"

Then she stretched out her body over the dead youth's lifeless form and placed her mouth upon his mouth and her eyes upon his eyes.

"Solomon!" she cried. "Solomon, do not abandon me! I shall not move until my spirit joins with yours!"

Suddenly the form beneath her shuddered. She rose up and looked upon Solomon's ashen face. Then his eyes opened and he looked around.

"I am Sarah," she told him. "I have come to you, my love." And she kissed him.

But he was still unable to speak, so she gave him water to drink and food to revive his strength, and at last he sat up. She called in his parents, who rejoiced greatly to find him restored to life.

"Blessed be God who revives the dead!" they cried.

Then they set up the marriage canopy, and the couple was married with great joy and singing.

180
The Will of Heaven

Once the king and his minister went traveling in the countryside in disguise and met an old holy man with a long white beard. The man was writing notes on slips of paper, then tossing them into the air.

"What are you doing?" they asked him.

"I am writing questions and tossing them up to

receive the answers," he told them. "From the first note I have learned that you are the king and his minister, and from the second note, I have learned that the queen has just given birth to a daughter."

The king and his minister were astonished by the holy man's words, and they asked him what was in the third note.

"The third note tells me," replied the old man, "that a woman who lives nearby has just had a son who is destined to be your daughter's bridegroom."

"Tell us this woman's name and where she lives," commanded the king, and he did.

They rode until they came to a poor hut where they found the woman and her newborn son.

"Surely this cannot be my daughter's husband!" cried the king.

He offered the woman a large sum of gold for the baby but she refused.

"How can I give you my own child?" she said.

"If you do not, you will both die of hunger," said the king. "But if you accept this money, you can have more children and feed them well. I promise that your son will have a good and happy life."

So the woman agreed to give her son to the king in exchange for a large sum of gold.

The king commanded the minister to take the child to a nearby mill and fling him upon the millwheel. But the child's garment caught upon a nail and stopped him from falling into the turning wheel. Before long the miller came out and found the child hanging upon the nail.

"Blessed be God!" cried the miller. "Here is a child to help me in my old age."

So the miller adopted the boy as his son, and the boy grew and began to help him in the mill.

One day the king said to his minister, "Do you remember the prophecy of the holy man? What do you think of it now?" And he laughed triumphantly.

"Maybe he is not dead, your majesty," replied the

minister. "With God's will, all is possible. One cannot escape fate."

"But you threw the child upon the millwheel with your own hands!" cried the king.

They decided to visit the mill. They found the miller grinding flour with the aid of a young boy.

"Who is this boy?" they asked him.

"He is my son," he told them.

"Tell us about his birth," they said. And the miller told them how he had found the boy hanging on a nail beside the millwheel and had adopted him as his son.

They offered the old man a large sum of money for the boy, and at last the miller agreed to hand over the boy.

"This time I will kill him with my own hands!" declared the king after they left the miller. They came to a deserted crossroads, and the king began to beat the boy with his sword until he lay bloody and lifeless in the dust.

"Enough!" cried the minister. "You have broken every bone in his body!"

So they left him there.

Soon after, a physician came by on his way to visit a sick woman. When he came to the crossroads, his horse refused to follow the path to the woman's house. The physician beat him, but still the beast would not budge.

"Then I shall let him go his own way," said the man.

The horse walked a few steps until he came to the lifeless body of the boy. The physician found one beating nerve in the boy's heart and managed to revive him. When the boy was well again, the physician adopted him as his son and made him his assistant.

Years passed. One day, the king said to his minister, "Remember the prophecy of the old holy man? Do you still think that the boy is alive?"

"Perhaps, your majesty," replied the minister. "With God's will, all is possible. One cannot escape fate."

They returned to the crossroads and proceeded to the nearest town. There they found a large crowd gathered, and they asked one of the bystanders what was happening.

"An excellent physician has come here," he told them, "and people have come from near and far to ask his advice."

Among the crowd walked a youth handing out slips of paper with numbers of them. The king asked the bystander about him.

"Several years ago, the physician found him lying almost dead in the road. He healed his wounds and then adopted him as his son."

The king could not believe his ears. He went to the doctor and offered him a large sum of money for the youth. Reluctantly, the doctor agreed. Then the king sent the young man to one of his ministers with a sealed letter that read, "Put the bearer of this letter to death at once."

The youth set off to see the minister. But by the time he reached the city, the gates were closed. Weary and hungry, he lay down on the ground, placing the king's letter under his head.

Meanwhile in the palace, the princess awoke from a troubled sleep and glanced out of her window. By the light of the moon, she saw a young man lying just outside the city walls.

"How handsome he is!" she thought.

Then she noticed something under his head. Lowering a rope out of her window, she sent her servant out to bring it to her. When she read her father's letter, she was enraged that he wished to kill this handsome youth. She wrote a new letter, instructing the minister to send the young man to her so that they could be married. Then she sealed it with the royal seal and sent her servant back outside to place it under the youth's head.

The next morning the young man came to see the minister and handed him the letter. The minister sent him to the princess and then instructed the servants to make preparations for a royal wedding.

That day the king was called off to war, and he remained away from the palace for three years. Meanwhile, the princess married her young man and they had three children. When the king returned from the wars, he was greeted by three young children at the city gates.

"Who are these children?" he asked the minister who accompanied them.

"They are your grandchildren, your majesty," replied the minister.

"My grandchildren!" exclaimed the king. "But who gave my daughter permission to marry?"

"Why, you did, sire," said the surprised minister. "It was written in the letter you sent me."

The king then called his daughter and demanded an explanation. She told him how she had switched the letters so that the youth who was now her husband should be spared from death.

"Now I understand," said the king, "that everything I did was to no avail. I could not change the holy man's prophecy or my daughter's fate. With God's will, all is possible. One cannot escape fate."

Then he embraced his son-in-law and made him heir to his kingdom.

3. REWARD AND PUNISHMENT

181
The Kamzan (The Tongs)

Once there was a *mohel* who was so greedy that he was known as the *kamzan*—"the tongs"—because he never parted with his gold. Each day he would spend hours in front of his coffer, admiring his wealth. Yet he believed himself a righteous man, for he never charged the poor for his services.

One day a stranger came to him to ask him to perform a circumcision. Seeing the man's wealthy carriage, the *kamzan* was eager to go with him. For hours they drove until they reached the wilderness. Alarmed, the *mohel* asked the stranger where they were going, but the man did not answer him.

At last they reached a magnificent mansion, and the carriage came to a halt. The stranger got out and went inside. When the *kamzan* entered the house, he was greeted by the baby's mother who whispered to him, "Be warned, my friend. My husband is not like you and me, but is a spirit. Do not drink or eat anything while you are here, and refuse any gifts offered you. Otherwise your life is in peril."

They came to a large room where there was a table set with a great feast. The host invited the *mohel* to eat and drink, but the *mohel* remembered the woman's warning and refused.

"Only let me go home," pleaded the *mohel*, but the host did not seem to hear him.

Then they came to a room filled with silver objects. The host asked the *mohel* to choose whatever his heart desired. Reluctantly, the *mohel* refused.

They came to a room filled with gold objects and another with precious jewels, but each time the *mohel* shook his head, although it pained him to turn down such costly gifts. But he remembered the woman's warning and stood firm.

Then the host brought him to an empty room where many keys hung upon the wall. As the *mohel* looked at the keys, he recognized one as the key to his own coffer.

As if reading his mind, the host said, "Yes, *mohel*, it is your own key."

When he heard these words, the *mohel* became as pale as death.

"When a man orders a coffer," his host told him, "two keys are made. One belongs to him and the other to

God. If God's key is not used, we keep it here. You see, a person is not the master of his own money. If he keeps putting money in but never takes it out to give to those less fortunate, then his soul is locked inside that coffer."

Every bone in the *mohel's* body trembled as he listened to the spirit's words. For at last he realized that the spirit was none other than the Angel of Death.

The spirit continued, "Remember all that you have seen here today, *mohel*. You will not have a second chance. Now take God's key home and use it, so you can be master of your own money."

From that day on the *mohel's* hand was always open to the poor and needy, and no one ever called him *kamzan* again.

182
The Three Sons in the Orchard

Once a king had three sons. He announced that he would bestow riches and honor only to him who performed good deeds. He said to them, "Go out into the world, be strong, and perhaps you will be transformed. Travel far and remain there until I send for you. Then tell me of your deeds and I shall reward you."

The sons were sad to leave their father and the land of their birth, but they bade farewell and traveled beyond the rivers of Cush. They came to an orchard guarded by three gatekeepers—one very old, one lame and covered with boils, and one awesome in splendor.

The first gatekeeper said, "Enter the orchard, but know that you must leave it."

The second one said, "Eat as much as you wish, but you may not carry anything out."

The third one said, "When you eat of the fruit of the orchard, beware the beautiful and choose only the good."

The three sons entered the orchard. Inside they found beautiful trees, flowers, and birds, sweet water flowing in clear streams, and gold, crystal, and precious jewels lying everywhere upon the ground.

The first son filled his belly with all the wonderful fruits in the orchard, and he kept eating until he felt as though he might burst.

The second son filled his pockets with jewels and gold, but he still wanted more, so he made his coat into a bag and filled that, too. Even that did not satisfy him, and he continued to gather more and more precious things until his body became stooped and his flesh began to waste away, since he did not take the trouble to feed it.

The third son sought only to understand the ways of the garden. He listened to the animals, studied the streams and pools, and examined all the growing things in the soil. And everywhere he went, he searched for the gardener of this magnificent orchard, but he was nowhere to be found. He ate only enough to sustain him and took for himself only a few jewels.

One day a servant of the king arrived with a message that said, "Come to me right away!"

As soon as the first son stepped outside the orchard gates, his belly became swollen and he died. When the second son stepped outside, the gatekeepers took away all his jewels. With a broken body and spirit, he came to the palace gates and called out, "I am the son of the king!" But his body was so broken from the weight of all those jewels and gold, and his bearing so diminished, that they did not believe him but threw him into the dungeon.

The third son left the garden still handsome and full of youthful strength. Remembering the words of the second gatekeeper, he placed his jewels in his mouth so they could not take them from him.

As he ran toward the palace, he thought to himself, "At last I will meet the gardener!" and his heart thrilled within his breast.

The people received him with great love. So did his

father the king, who embraced him and asked him what had happened to him during his travels. The son described the wonderful orchard and gave his father the jewels that he had taken.

"But I still wish to meet the gardener," the son told his father. "Do you know who he is?"

Then the king took his son to a room and spoke words of wisdom to him. No secrets were hidden from him, no questions left unanswered. And the son's heart was filled with an inexpressible joy.

Then his father bestowed great honor upon him and placed his seat next to his own throne, and there he sat forever.

183
The Jar of Tears

Once there was a great drought, and the rabbi called all the people of the city to the synagogue. They prayed day and night, but still no rain fell. Then the rabbi declared a fast and asked God to answer their prayers.

A voice came forth from heaven, saying, "God will send rain only if Rahamim, who always sits in the corner of the synagogue, prays for it."

The Rabbi called the *shammash* and told him to bring Rahamim to the synagogue.

"What do you want with him?" asked the astonished *shammash*.

"He must come up on the *bimah* and pray for rain," answered the rabbi.

"But he's an ignoramus!" protested the *shammash*.

"Call him," ordered the rabbi.

When the *shammash* brought Rahamim back to the synagogue, Rahamim asked the rabbi, "What do you want of me?"

"Go up to the *bimah* and pray for rain," said the rabbi.

"But I do not know how to pray!" said Rahamim. "There are so many others who know more than I."

"Nevertheless," said the rabbi, "it is you who must pray."

The next day the rabbi called all the people together to pray. The synagogue was filled to bursting. All eyes were on the *bimah*, where everyone expected to see the rabbi leading them in prayer. How great was their amazement to see poor Rahamim standing up there before the Holy Ark!

Before he began the service, Rahamim said, "Please wait a few minutes. There is something I must get."

He ran out of the synagogue and returned a few moments later, carrying a clay jar with two spouts.

"Now I ask that you pray with all your hearts," he told the congregation.

So they opened the ark, and the people poured out their hearts to heaven, wailing bitterly and beating their breasts. Then Rahamim lifted up his jar, first placing one spout to his eye, then the other to his ear.

Instantly there was a rumble of thunder, and then the skies opened up, drenching the earth with rain.

The rabbi asked Rahamim, "Why did you bring that jar here, and what did you do with it?"

"Rabbi, I am only a poor man," Rahamim replied. "What I earn as a cobbler barely feeds my many children. Every day they cry for bread, and I have none to give them. When I hear their cries, my heart breaks and I too cry. I collect my tears in this jar. I have asked my wife to bury the jar with me when I die. When you asked me to come here to pray, I looked into the jar and said: 'Master of the Universe, if You do not send rain, I will break this jar in front of all these people.' Then I listened in the other spout and heard a voice that said, 'Do not break it!' And then it began to rain."

The rabbi said, "How true are the words of our sages: 'The gates of tears are never closed.'"

184
The Rich Beggar and the Wonderful Purse

Once there was a poor man who wished for a fortune. Suddenly he noticed a small purse lying on the floor of his house. When he picked it up, a heavenly voice declared, "Inside this purse you will find one coin. When you remove it, another will appear in its place. You may take from it as many coins as you wish, but you may not spend even one of them until you throw the purse into the river, where it will turn into a fish."

The poor man opened the purse and found a single coin inside. When he took it out, he found another coin where the first had been. All that day and all that night he drew coins from the wonderful purse, until he had filled a large sack with gold coins.

The next morning he discovered that he was hungry, but there was no food in the house. Yet he was unwilling to spend any of his gold coins for food, so he went out to the streets to beg. He spent the few coins that he received to buy bread, then returned home and filled up another sack of gold from the purse.

The next day he was hungry again, so he took the purse down to the river to throw it in. But he could not bring himself to throw away the source of his good fortune. So again he went to beg on the streets.

So it went day after day. Often he went down to the river to throw the purse in, but he could never bring himself to do it. When he died many years later, they found his house full of gold, but not a crust of bread anywhere.

185

Have Mercy on Animals,
Not Men

Once an old man on his deathbed told his son, "Have mercy on animals, but not on men." Then he died.

One day the son went walking and came upon a dove with a broken wing. He brought her home and paid the doctor to heal her. Another time he went walking and came upon a snake lying almost dead in the dust. He wrapped the snake in his handkerchief, brought it home, and paid the doctor to heal it as well. Each day he fed the two animals, and they soon recovered their health.

Another time he went walking and came upon a man who had been stoned for some crime but had not died. It was the law that a man who survived stoning was allowed to go free. The man lay moaning on the ground, his body covered with blood.

"Please help me," he cried, "for I am near death!"

The son thought, "My father was surely wrong when he warned me not to have mercy on men." He carried the man home, bound up his wounds, and nursed him until he recovered. In gratitude the man gave his rescuer one of his six chests of gold.

Not long after this a thief stole a chest of gold from the king. When the man who had been stoned and rescued heard of it, he went to the king and said, "Your majesty, I know who stole your chest of gold."

"Aren't you the man who was stoned not long ago?" asked the king.

"Yes," he replied. "I was rescued by camel drivers and in time regained my health."

"How do you know who stole my chest of gold?" asked the king.

"Does it matter?" answered the man. "What matters is that you can catch the thief and gain back your gold."

So the king sent messengers to the son's house, and they found his chest of gold. They did not examine the chest carefully to see whether it was indeed the king's chest but instead threw the son in prison and brought the chest back to the king's treasury. The king rewarded the man who had told him of the thief, making him vizier and paying him handsomely.

Then the king's soldiers took the son outside the city and stoned him. He did not die but lay groaning in the dust, covered with blood. The dove and the snake became alarmed when their master did not return home to feed them, so the dove flew off to look for him. She found him lying almost lifeless in the dust and brought water to him in her beak until his thirst was slaked. Then she flew home and told the snake what she had found.

"Wrap me in this handkerchief and take me to the palace," said the snake.

So the dove wrapped the snake in the handkerchief and flew him to the palace. The snake entered the princess's bedroom and coiled himself around her so that she could not eat. No one could remove the snake from her, for they feared his terrible fangs, and soon the princess sickened from hunger and fright until she was near death. The king promised a handsome reward to anyone who could save her.

At this time several men happened by where the son was lying wounded in the dust.

"Are you alive?" they asked.

"Yes," he said. "Tell me what is happening in the city."

So they told him about the snake who was strangling the princess to death.

"I can cure her," said the man.

So they brought him to the palace and led him to the princess's room. The snake hissed angrily when he first entered the room, but when the man laid his handkerchief on the floor, the snake slithered off the body of the princess and coiled up inside the handkerchief. The king was amazed at this and asked him how it was done.

"It is nothing, your majesty," he said. "I once showed mercy toward this snake, and now it is returning the favor."

Then the king asked him, "Did you steal my chest of gold?"

"No," answered the man. "Examine the chest you took from my house, and you will see that it is not yours."

The king's treasurer examined the chest and saw that it was as the son said.

"My father was right to tell me not to show mercy to men," the son told the king, "for it was a man, not an animal, who betrayed me."

Then the king ordered his vizier to come before him. The frightened vizier confessed that he had lied when he had accused his rescuer of stealing the king's chest.

"How dare you bite the hand that saved you?" said the king.

He commanded his soldiers to take the vizier outside the city walls and stone him. And this time he died.

186
The Hunter and the Bird

Once a hunter caught a bird in his net. The bird pleaded with the hunter to let her go. In return, she promised to give him three pieces of wisdom. After he swore to release her, she said to him, "Do not seek what you cannot obtain. Do not regret what you have lost. Do not believe what cannot be." Then the hunter let her go as he had sworn to do.

She flew to the top of a tree and called down to him, "Foolish hunter! If only you had held on to me, you would have discovered that I had a pearl the size of an ostrich egg inside me!"

The hunter started to climb the tree to recapture the bird, but he fell and bruised himself all over.

The bird called down a second time, "How quickly you have forgotten what I just taught you! Here you already have sought after that which you cannot obtain, you have regretted the loss of the pearl, and you have believed the impossible, that a giant pearl could fit inside my tiny belly. How many men are like you!"

And with that, she flew away.

187
The Three Friends

Once a man had three friends, one dearest to his heart upon whom he lavished much affection and gifts; a second, less dear but still the recipient of much affection; and a third, less dear and often neglected.

The wheel of fortune turned, and the man lost all he owned. The king commanded him to appear before him, but the man feared to go, for what tribute could he give the king? So he went to his first friend and asked for help. But the man spurned him, giving him only a ragged piece of clothing. He went to the second friend, but he too turned him away, offering only to accompany him to the palace and then turn back.

But the third friend received him gladly and offered to share with him all that he had, despite the disregard the man had shown him earlier.

The first friend is a person's wealth that cannot accompany him even to his grave; all he takes with him is his shroud. The second friend is a man's family and friends, who must abandon him at the grave. The last friend is his charity and good deeds, which precede him to the next world and stand by him forever.

188

Abraham the Carpenter and the
Money Hidden in the Tree

In a village near Jerusalem there lived a rich Jew and his wife. Once a Gentile came to their home to borrow money. The woman went upstairs and opened the chest where they kept their gold. But when she reached in to take some coins, a voice called out, "Do not touch it! It is not yours!"

Frightened, the woman went downstairs and told her husband what had happened. He went up and opened the chest. The voice again called out, "Do not touch it! It is not yours!"

The man asked, "To whom does it belong?"

"To Abraham the Carpenter," answered the voice.

Saddened by this discovery, the man took the money from the chest, cut a hole in a tree in his garden, and hid the money there. Then he and his wife went out into the streets to beg.

Soon after this, there was a great flood that carried away many houses and trees, including the tree with the money hidden inside it. A fisherman found the tree floating in the river and said, "What a good piece of timber this is! I am sure that my friend Abraham the Carpenter would be happy to have it." So he brought the tree to Jerusalem where Abraham lived.

When Abraham began hewing the tree to make a table, he found the treasure inside it. He was overjoyed at his sudden good fortune and thanked God with all his heart.

Not long after this, the couple to whom the treasure had once belonged decided to travel to Jerusalem to see whether the money had found its way to its true owner. They came to Abraham's house and knocked on the door.

It was Friday afternoon, and Abraham's wife was preparing for the Sabbath. When she saw the poor old couple at the door, dressed in tatters and begging for bread, she invited them in to spend the Sabbath.

But when the two beggars saw their own silver cups on the table, they began to weep.

"Why are you weeping?" asked Abraham's wife.

At first they refused to tell her. But she pressed them until they told her the story of the mysterious voice that had made them surrender their treasure to its true owner. Then Abraham's wife told them how her husband had found their treasure in the uprooted tree.

"Please take back what is yours," she told them. "We have enough without taking your things."

"No, they are yours," replied the poor couple. "We must have sinned, and so have lost everything."

When Abraham's wife told him about the poor couple's misfortune, he instructed his cook to bake a cake and hide 100 silver coins inside. This cake he gave to the old couple on Sunday morning, although they were reluctant to take anything from him.

On their way home they came to a place where they had to pay a toll. Since they had no money, they gave the tollkeeper the cake that Abraham the Carpenter had given them.

"How fortunate!" thought the tollkeeper. "Now I have a beautiful gift to give Abraham the Carpenter in honor of his son's wedding."

So he gave the cake to Abraham. And thus the treasure returned to its rightful owner.

The old couple died in poverty, for they had never given charity and God punished them by taking away their wealth. As for Abraham and his wife, whose hands were always open to the poor, they lived happily to a ripe old age and they never lacked for bread.

189
Slander Slays Three

Once there was a man who had three daughters, one a thief, one a lazy good-for-nothing, and the third a slanderer. A man came and wished to marry the three daughters to his three sons.

"No," said their father, "for they are unworthy."

But the other man persisted, and the three couples were married.

The father of the three sons put the thieving daughter in charge of all his money and the lazy daughter in charge of all his servants. And each morning he came to the daughter who was a slanderer to inquire about her health.

After some time, the girls' father came to visit them.

"Thank you, Father, for sending me to this house," said the daughter who had once been a thief. "For I have repented of my evil ways."

The second daughter likewise praised her father, for she too had changed her wicked ways.

But the third daughter said, "May you be cursed, Father, for sending me here! For you have married me to two husbands, not to one. As soon as the son goes to work each morning, the father comes to force himself upon me. If you do not believe me, hide under the bed and see for yourself."

So the next morning, the father hid under his daughter's bed as soon as her husband left for work. A few moments later, the father-in-law came into the room and kissed his daughter-in-law on the forehead as he did every day.

"Leave me alone!" she cried. "My father is here!"

At that her father came out from under the bed and killed him. When the sons heard of this, they came and killed their father-in-law. Then they killed the slanderer herself.

So it is that slander slays three: the one who spreads the slander, the one who listens to it, and the one who is slandered.

190
The Man Who Never Took an Oath

Once there was a pious man who never took an oath. When he was about to die, he told his son, "All the riches I have acquired are mine because I never took an oath. Promise me that you will not take an oath, either."

So the son promised, and then his father died.

As soon as it became known that the old man was dead, a scoundrel showed up on the son's doorstep.

"Your father owed me a large sum of money," he said, "that he never paid me back. Now that he's dead, I demand that you pay me!"

The son insisted that this was not true, so they went before the judge.

"Will you swear before God that your father never borrowed money from this man?" the judge asked the son.

Remembering his promise to his dying father, the son refused to swear. The scoundrel, on the other hand, did not hesitate to swear that his lie was the truth, so the judge ruled in his favor. And the son had no choice but to pay him the money he claimed was his.

So it went every day. One after another, rascals and rogues showed up at the son's house, making more and more preposterous claims, yet still the son refused to swear that they were liars. So he lost all that he had, and the judge threw him into prison since he could no longer pay his debts.

To free him, his wife went to work, doing laundry down by the river. One day a ship captain saw her and was struck by her beauty. He asked her to wash his shirt and gave her a coin for her wages. Immediately she ran to the prison and bought her husband's freedom. But when she went to the captain to bring him his shirt, he kidnaped her and sailed away.

When the husband discovered that his wife was gone, he took his children and went in search of her. They came to the sea, and he took a job as a shepherd. One day when he went to tend his flock, the same ship captain who had stolen his wife saw the children playing on the shore and kidnaped them, too.

Bereft of his wife and children, the heartbroken man went down to the water to end his life. "Once I had riches, a wife, and children, but now I have nothing," he lamented. "Better that I should die from a serpent's bite or from drowning than live another day in such misery!"

Just then a voice spoke to him from heaven, saying, "Dig under the tree behind you and you shall find a great treasure, because you kept your promise to your father never to take an oath."

So the man dug and found a treasure beyond his wildest dreams. He thanked God for the gift and prayed that he be allowed to see his wife and children again. Then he went to the king and asked permission to build a house by the sea so that he could charge a tax for the king's treasury to all ships that passed by. The king gladly granted his request.

Every time a ship passed by, he went aboard to search for his lost wife and children. But every search proved futile.

One day a ship came by and anchored at his dock. When he went aboard, he immediately recognized his wife and children, but they did not recognize him, for he had become noble and prosperous.

He went up to the captain and asked, "Where did you get this woman and her children?"

"From a faraway country," answered the captain.

When the woman heard this, she began to weep, for she now recalled her former life, when she had been so happily married and had lacked for nothing.

When her husband saw her tears, he burst out, "I am your husband!"

Overjoyed, the family embraced and wept many happy tears. Then the husband turned to the captain and said, "I shall send you before the king to decide your fate."

"But he will surely kill me!" cried the captain. "Take everything I have, only let me go!"

So they took all the treasures that were on the ship and let the captain sail off. Now they were even richer than they had been before. All this happened because the son kept his promise to his father never to take an oath.

191
Cast Your Bread upon the Waters

Once there lived a man who performed many deeds of charity. Before he died, he made his son swear that he would follow his father's example and always stretch out his hand to the poor.

"The Bible tells us," said the dying man, " 'Cast your bread upon the waters, for you shall find it after many days.' Heed this teaching, my son, and you shall never suffer want."

The son promised to do what his father asked.

After his father died, the son went down to the shore each day and cast a loaf of bread into the sea. And each day a certain fish ate it. In time the fish grew so large that the other fish went to complain to King Leviathan.

"So large has this greedy creature grown that he swallows twenty of us in one bite!" they cried. "We can no longer live together with him!"

Leviathan summoned the fish and asked him, "Your brothers and sisters who live in the teeming depths of the sea are not half as large as you who live by the ocean's edge. How do you account for this?"

"There is a man who feeds me every day," explained the fish. "Each morning he casts a loaf into the sea, and I gobble it up."

"Bring me that man!" commanded Leviathan.

The next day the fish dug a tunnel in the sand where the man always stood to cast his loaf and placed his gaping mouth at the bottom of the tunnel. When the man stepped there, he fell down into the hole and was swallowed up by the fish, who brought him before Leviathan.

"Spit him out!" ordered the King of the Fishes.

So he spat him out, and Leviathan swallowed him.

"Why have you cast bread into the waters each day?" asked Leviathan.

"Because my father taught me to do so," replied the man.

Then Leviathan spit him out and kissed him and offered him a gift: either half the treasures of the deep or the knowledge of all the languages of human beings and beasts. He chose the latter, so Leviathan instructed him until he understood all the tongues on earth.

Then Leviathan brought him to a far shore and flung him up on the sands. Lying there, he looked up and saw two ravens flying overhead.

One raven said, "Father, I see a man lying there. Is he alive or dead?"

"I don't know, my son," replied the other.

"I shall go down and pluck out his eyes, which are my favorite dainties," said the younger bird.

"Do not go!" warned the father, "for if he is alive, he will capture you and kill you!"

But the son did not heed his father's words and flew down to the man lying motionless on the shore.

The man had understood everything the ravens said,

and when the bird landed on his head, he grabbed it by its feet.

"Father, Father!" cawed the captive bird. "I am lost!"

"Alas, my son!" the father cried, "if you had only listened to me!" Then he flew lower and said to the man, "May God grant you the wisdom to understand my words! Let my son go, and I will show you a treasure beyond your wildest imaginings!"

Immediately the man released the bird. The grateful father said, "Dig under your feet and you will find the treasures of King Solomon."

He dug in the sand and found chests filled with jewels and pearls and much fine gold. From that day on, he and his family never suffered want. And he continued to stretch out his hand generously to the poor, just as he had promised his father.

192

Had Gadya

Once a father bought a little kid for his child for two *zuzim*.

Then along came a cat that ate the kid that a father bought for two *zuzim*.

Along came a dog that bit the cat that ate the kid that a father bought for two *zuzim*.

Along came a stick that beat the dog that bit the cat that ate the kid that a father bought for two *zuzim*.

Along came a fire that burned the stick that beat the dog that bit the cat that ate the kid that a father bought for two *zuzim*.

Along came water that quenched the fire that burned the stick that beat the dog that bit the cat that ate the kid that a father bought for two *zuzim*.

Along came an ox that drank the water that quenched the fire that burned the stick that beat the dog that bit the cat that ate the kid that a father bought for two *zuzim*.

Along came a slaughterer who killed the ox that drank the water that quenched the fire that burned the stick that beat the dog that bit the cat that ate the kid that a father bought for two *zuzim*.

Along came the Angel of Death who killed the slaughterer who killed the ox that drank the water that quenched the fire that burned the stick that beat the dog that bit the cat that ate the kid that a father bought for two *zuzim*.

Along came the Holy One who killed the Angel of Death who killed the slaughterer who killed the ox that drank the water that quenched the fire that burned the stick that beat the dog that bit the cat that ate the kid that a father bought for two *zuzim*.

Had Gadya — all because of one little kid!

4. FIGURES IN HISTORY

193
Rashi's Companion

Solomon ben Isaac, known as Rashi, was the greatest Jewish scholar of his generation. When he reached his sixtieth birthday, he wished to know who would be his companion in Paradise, for all the righteous share a table there with one other soul.

"Surely my companion will be a righteous and learned man!" thought Rashi.

That night God revealed to him in a dream that his future companion would be Don Abraham Gerson the Tzaddik, who lived in Barcelona.

"Surely this Don Abraham is an old man with white hair and a long, white beard," thought Rashi when he awoke the next morning, "a pious man whose wrinkled face is pale from years of study but whose eyes are still clear and filled with wisdom."

Eagerly he prepared himself for a long journey and then set off for Spain.

When he reached Barcelona, he went straight to the synagogue. There he was received with great honor, for the name of Rashi had already spread far and wide. His hosts insisted that he share a meal with them, lead them in prayer, and teach them words of Torah.

Finally Rashi was unable to contain himself any longer. "Where might I find Abraham the Tzaddik?" he asked them.

They all shook their heads. No one by that name lived in Barcelona. Disappointed, Rashi turned to go. Then he had an idea.

"Have you by any chance heard of Abraham Gerson?"

"Abraham Gerson!" they cried. "But he is an apostate! He eats food prepared by Gentiles, violates the Sabbath, and never sets foot in the synagogue. What do you want with him?"

Rashi was very surprised to hear these things about his future companion in Paradise, but he thought, "Perhaps I have been sent to bring him back to the right path."

So he went to Abraham Gerson's house. How surprised he was to find himself standing before a magnificent mansion! A servant ushered him inside, where he saw broad marble staircases, beautiful gardens, and servants scurrying to and fro in gold livery.

"There must be some mistake," thought Rashi. "What sins have I committed to merit such an unholy companion in the World to Come?"

Just then Don Abraham Gerson appeared. He was a young man of about thirty, very handsome and proud.

"I am Rabbi Solomon ben Isaac," declared Rashi. "I come in the name of God!"

"I am sure that you do," answered Don Abraham, smiling. "So you are the famous Rashi! Your name has reached us even here in Spain. Let us be friends. I invite you to come to my wedding tomorrow."

"Is it a Gentile woman you are marrying?" asked Rashi.

"No."

"Surely a wealthy woman then?" said Rashi.

"No," answered Don Abraham.

Just then a servant interrupted their conversation. "There is a poor woman outside who wishes to be admitted."

"Let her wait," replied Don Abraham.

"How can you be so heartless?" protested Rashi. "Perhaps she is in dire need."

So they went to the woman and asked her what she wanted.

"I do not come to beg for bread," she told them, "for Don Abraham has already distributed alms to the poor in honor of his wedding tomorrow."

"What then do you want of me?" asked Don Abraham, growing impatient.

"I have come to you for advice," she said. "I am a poor woman, a widow with four children. Three of my children are too young to work for wages, so my oldest son must support us all. Now he is dangerously ill, and I fear we will be left without anyone to support us."

"I will be glad to send my own physician to tend your son," offered Don Abraham.

"No, it is not disease that has stricken my son but disappointed love. He had hoped to marry a poor girl whom he loves dearly, but the girl's parents are forcing her to marry a rich man against her will."

"Why are you telling me all this?" asked Don Abraham.

"Because you are that rich man!" cried the mother, pointing an accusing finger at the startled man.

"What is your son's name?" asked Don Abraham.

"Don Abraham ben Manuel," she replied.

"You and your family are invited to my wedding

tomorrow," said Don Abraham. Then without another word, he turned and walked away.

Rashi ran after him. "Don Abraham!" he cried. "Do not be overly distressed by this woman's words. People cannot die of love. The young man will soon recover."

"No," answered Don Abraham. "I fear he will not."

"In time he will find another woman, and this one will become only a fond memory."

"No," said Don Abraham again. "There is only one sun in heaven. Take it away and all is dark. Life without love is nothing."

"Nonsense!" said Rashi. "Time heals all wounds. But you are right to be concerned about the family. Until the son recovers, they are in need of help."

"Indeed they are, Rabbi," said Don Abraham, and his voice carried an infinite sadness. Then his face brightened and he said, "Remember to come to my wedding tomorrow!"

Bidding him goodbye, Rashi departed and returned the next day.

When he entered Don Abraham's house, he found the marble pavement strewn with flowers, the courtyard filled with many guests wearing rich, brightly colored clothes, and a beautiful wedding canopy set up in the center. In one corner huddled the poor widow and her four children, her eldest son leaning weakly upon her arm. A hush suddenly fell over the crowd as the veiled bride was led to the canopy to stand beside Don Abraham. Then the marriage contract was read.

"There has been a terrible mistake!" announced Don Abraham at the conclusion of the reading. "The bridegroom's name is not Abraham Gerson but Abraham ben Manuel. I have only been the matchmaker in this marriage. Tomorrow I am going abroad to conduct some business. I leave Don Abraham ben Manuel in charge of my affairs while I am gone." He paused, and Rashi saw that his eyes were filled with tears. Then he smiled through the tears. "Come here, young man," he beckoned to the pale young man in the corner. "I want to wish you and your new bride a long life and much happiness!"

As soon as the young man stood under the canopy, the rabbi concluded the ceremony, and then the musicians began to play. The newly married couple seemed not to hear a sound, so lost were they in each other's gaze.

Rashi now turned to Don Abraham and said, "You are indeed worthy to share my table in Paradise!" And he told Don Abraham about the dream sent to him by God.

Don Abraham smiled and said, "I am delighted to have such an excellent companion in the next world. For as you can see, I shall be coming alone."

194
Maimonides and the Limekiln

The wisdom of the great Maimonides, the Rambam, was famous throughout the world. Even the Caliph in Cordoba was impressed by his excellent philosophy and character and befriended him. But there were others, particularly a certain spiteful courtier, who were jealous of Maimonides's intimacy with the Caliph and vowed to destroy him. This courtier was forever accusing Maimonides of treason, but the Caliph refused to listen to his malicious slander.

One day the courtier came to the Caliph and said, "Your majesty, the Jew has been slandering you! He has been saying that your mouth gives forth an evil-smelling odor."

So the Caliph sent for Maimonides.

Meanwhile the courtier went to Maimonides and said, "The Caliph has confided in me that he finds your breath offensive, but he says nothing to you for fear of offending you."

So Maimonides went to the Caliph, his mouth covered with a handkerchief so as not to offend him.

When the Caliph saw Maimonides enter with the handkerchief over his face, he was furious. So at last the courtier had told him the truth! Why else would Maimonides be covering his face if not to protect himself from the Caliph's breath?

The next day the Caliph went to the section of the city where the lime-burners worked and ordered them to throw into the kiln the first person who said, "Have the Caliph's orders been carried out?" Then he called Maimonides and sent him to the limekiln to ask that very question.

On his way there, Maimonides was stopped by a mother worried about her sick daughter.

"Noble sir, please help her!" she cried. "I know that you are a great physician. Please go to my daughter and heal her!"

So Maimonides went with the mother, sent for the appropriate medicines, and healed the daughter. When he finally reached the limekiln, he found the lime-burners laughing.

"Have the Caliph's orders been carried out?" asked Maimonides.

"Yes," they answered him.

Then he returned to the palace to report their answer to the Caliph. The Caliph was astonished to see him.

"Did you follow my orders?" he stammered.

"Yes, your majesty," answered the Rambam. "I only delayed for a moment in order to attend a sick girl. Then I went to the limekiln and did as you commanded."

Puzzled, the Caliph sent for the lime-burners.

"Why did you not follow my orders?" the Caliph demanded.

"But we did, your majesty!" they protested. "A man came and asked the question, so we threw him into the limekiln as you commanded. Here is his ring."

The Caliph instantly recognized the ring of his courtier, and his mouth dropped open.

"What is it, your majesty?" asked Maimonides.

"This death was meant for you," said the Caliph, "to punish you for your insult about my breath."

"*Your* breath!" cried Maimonides. "But he told me that it was *my* breath that offended you!"

"God is indeed just," declared the Caliph. "You escaped death because you gave comfort to a sick girl, but he met his end because he was so eager to see you destroyed."

And the Caliph never again doubted Maimonides's loyalty.

195
Ibn Ezra's Bad Luck

A man's fate is irreversible. Rabbi Abraham Ibn Ezra and Maimonides, the Rambam, were born on the same day at the same hour, but the Rambam was born when the Wheel of Fortune was at the top and Ibn Ezra when it was at the bottom.

Ibn Ezra's mother was a widow, and they were always poor. Whenever Ibn Ezra would decide to sell something, the price for that item would go down the next day. Whatever he tried to do always ended in failure.

Once Maimonides decided to help his friend by giving him money, but he knew that Ibn Ezra was too proud to accept charity. So he left a purse filled with gold coins near his friend's house. Surely he could not fail to find it on his way to the House of Study the next day!

That morning, Ibn Ezra awoke and said to himself, "How can I complain about my own troubles? What if I were blind and could not even walk without stumbling? Far better is it to be poor and sighted than rich and blind."

He went outside his house and said to himself, "Today I will walk to the House of Study with my eyes closed so that I shall know what it would be like to be blind."

So he set off with his eyes tightly shut and walked right past the purse of gold coins.

When he reached the House of Study, Maimonides asked him, "Did you discover anything this morning?"

"Yes," replied Ibn Ezra. "I discovered how fortunate I am to have the use of both my eyes. I walked all the way here with my eyes closed, and now I see how difficult is the lot of the blind!"

Then Maimonides realized that it was impossible to change the fate of someone who is born when the Wheel of Fortune is upside down.

Ibn Ezra himself agreed, for he once wrote about himself:

An unlucky planet
Cursed this life of mine.
If I sold candles for my trade,
The sun would always shine.

No matter what I do,
I fail at what I try.
Were selling shrouds my trade,
No one would ever die!

196

Pope Elhanan

Once a son was born to Rabbi Simeon the Great of Mayence, whom they named Elhanan. One Sabbath a Gentile woman came in to tend the stove, and she saw little Elhanan playing with his nurse, for his parents were away at synagogue. She picked up the boy and took him out of the house. The nurse said nothing, for she thought that the woman wished only to play with the child for a while. But when she did not return, the nurse became alarmed and went in search of the child. But she could find no trace anywhere of the woman or the child.

When the parents returned from synagogue, she told them what had happened, and they too searched the city but to no avail. The child was gone. So they tore their clothes and wept.

The Gentile woman took the child that she had stolen to a monastery, where he was raised as a Christian. Because of his sharp and inquisitive mind, he became a great scholar and eventually rose to the position of cardinal in Rome. When the old Pope died, Elhanan was named the new Pope.

But all this time, he knew that he had been born a Jew. Yet, because of the honors and riches he had acquired in his new faith, he could not bring himself to return to the faith of his ancestors.

Now the desire grew in him to see his father, Rabbi Simeon. So he thought of a scheme to force his father to come to him in Rome. He issued a papal decree forbidding the Jews of Mayence to circumcise their sons, to keep the Sabbath, or to immerse themselves in the ritual bath. He thought, "They will send their greatest leaders to ask me to annul my decree. Surely Rabbi Simeon will be at their head."

And so it came to pass. The Jews of Mayence were devastated by the Pope's decree, so they appealed to the bishop of the city to have it repealed. But the bishop said to them, "This order comes from the Pope himself. I am powerless to undo it."

So they sent a delegation to Rome. At its head, as Elhanan had predicted, was Rabbi Simeon. They came to the Jewish community of Rome and told them what had happened.

"How odd," said the Roman Jews when they heard of it, "for this Pope has always been such a good friend to the Jews. Daily he converses with Jewish scholars, plays chess with Jews, seeks their wisdom. What have you done to bring God's wrath down upon your heads through this Gentile?"

They declared a fast and gave much charity to avert the evil decree.

Then they went to the cardinal and asked him to speak to the Pope on behalf of the Jews of Mayence.

"I cannot," said the cardinal, "for it was his idea alone to issue this decree. You must go to him yourself."

So the delegation went to St. Peter's and asked for an audience with the Pope.

"I wish to see only the leader of the delegation!" declared the Pope.

Rabbi Simeon came in and saw the Pope playing chess. The son recognized the father, but the father did not recognize the son. Then the Pope began to converse with Rabbi Simeon on all manner of topics. Rabbi Simeon was amazed at the range of his knowledge. He knew as much about Jewish books and philosophy as any Jewish scholar. Then they sat down to play chess. Although Rabbi Simeon was the best chess player in Mayence, the Pope easily beat him. In every way the Pope's mind surpassed his own.

Then the Pope sent everyone away so that they could be alone.

"Father, do you not recognize me?" he cried, and he began to weep.

"How would I recognize your holiness?" asked Rabbi Simeon. "I have never before been to Rome."

"Did you not lose your young son when a Gentile woman carried him off on a Sabbath?" said the Pope. "I am that son!"

Rabbi Simeon was astonished to hear his words and did not believe them.

"It is true, Father," continued the Pope. "I am your son who was lost to you all these years. I have never forgotten who I am and have longed to return to the faith of my birth."

"Return then, my son," said Rabbi Simeon. "Blessed is God who redeems the captive!"

The Pope's face darkened. "Long have I known that I was a Jew, but I could not bring myself to give up the comforts of this life. Will God forgive me?"

"Repentance awaits all those who turn back," answered Rabbi Simeon. "God will show mercy to anyone who opens up his heart."

"Go home in peace, Father," said the Pope, "and show the letters I will give you to the bishop. He will annul my decree. Tell no one what you have heard today. I must first do something here, and then I will come to you in Mayence."

So Rabbi Simeon returned to Mayence and gave the Pope's letters to the bishop. The Jews of the city rejoiced greatly to have the Pope's harsh decree annulled.

As he had promised, Rabbi Simeon told no one about his son except his wife, who rejoiced greatly to learn that he was still alive. In Rome, the Pope wrote a letter against his adopted faith and left it with instructions that it was to be read by all his successors. Then he fled Rome in disguise, came to Mayence, and resumed the faith of his parents. He became an even greater scholar than before, and his fame spread throughout the Jewish world.

In gratitude for his son's return, Rabbi Simeon wrote a hymn of praise for the Second Day of the New Year. In it he included the phrase: "God has shown grace"— *Elhanan.*

197
Rabbi Amnon of Mayence

Rabbi Amnon, the leader of the Jews of Mayence, was a wealthy and handsome man of good family. The bishop of the city wished to convert him, so he sent messengers to him day after to day. One day, when Amnon had grown tired of their endless arguments, he said to them, "Give me three days to consider what you have said."

As soon as they had gone, Amnon was stricken with shame. How could he have had any doubts about his faith?

In three days the bishop sent for Amnon, but he refused to come. So the bishop had him brought against his will:

"What is your answer?" asked the bishop.

"I will sentence myself," declared Amnon. "Let the tongue that expressed doubt be cut out!"

"No," said the bishop, "your tongue shall not be cut out, for it spoke the truth. Rather your legs and hands, which refused to obey me, shall be cut off."

So they cut off his hands and feet and poured salt in his wounds. As they cut off each joint, the bishop asked him if he was ready to convert. "No!" he said each time, so they sent him home with his severed members beside him.

Then the people knew that he was truly worthy of his name, Amnon, "a man of faith."

On Rosh Hashanah, he asked to be taken to the synagogue. There he composed the *Unetanneh Tokef* prayer, which he recited to all assembled: "We acclaim this day's pure holiness, its awesome power. . . . The great *shofar* is sounded. A still, small voice is heard. . . . 'The day of judgment is here!'"

Then he died. Three days later he appeared to Rabbi Kalonymus ben Meshullam in a dream and taught him the entire hymn, ordering him to teach it to Jews throughout the Diaspora.

But others say he died in Cologne. Just before he died, he instructed his students to take him back to Mayence and bury him beside his ancestors there.

"It is too dangerous!" they told him.

"Then prepare my body for burial, lay my coffin in a ship, and set it afloat on the Rhine."

When he died, they did as he had instructed them.

Without pilot or crew, the ship traveled upstream against the current and arrived in Mayence. When the Christians tried to seize hold of the ship, it leapt backward out of their hands.

But when the Jews of the city gathered on the shore, the ship neared them and did not leap away. They boarded the ship and found a letter: "My brothers and sisters in the holy community of Mayence, I have departed this world and ask that you bury me by the graves of my ancestors. Peace be with you!"

But when the Jews tried to remove the coffin and bring it to the Jewish cemetery, the townspeople attacked them and tried to steal the coffin. But it stayed where it was and could not be lifted. So the townspeople built a church above it. No matter how much money the Jews offered for the coffin, the leaders of the city would not turn it over.

Then one night several young Jews went outside the city and took a hanged man down from the gallows, dressed him in a white shroud, and exchanged his body for that of Rabbi Amnon's. Then they buried Amnon beside the graves of his family, and there he rests in peace to this day.

5. ISRAEL AMONG THE NATIONS

198
The Pound of Flesh

In Rome many years ago there lived a Jew named Shylock. In time the Wheel of Fortune turned upon Shylock, and he found himself in debt to a certain Gentile named Antonio Zavello. When the time came to repay the debt, Shylock found that he did not have sufficient funds. So Antonio demanded that on the following day, Shylock either pay him with a pound of his own flesh or else hand over to him his beautiful young daughter Jessica.

The Pope at this time, Sixtus IV, would often disguise himself as a beggar and go out among the people of Rome to see how they lived. On this particular evening when he slipped out of the Vatican, he chanced upon two beggars wolfing down a huge meal of meat and wine, licking their fingers with loud smacks of delight.

"Whose hand has been so generous today?" Sixtus asked them.

"Antonio Zavello," they told him.

"Surely he must have something wonderful to celebrate!" exclaimed the Pope.

"Indeed he has," answered one of the beggars. "The Jew Shylock owes him one thousand zecchini, which he claims he cannot pay. So tomorrow Antonio is taking it out of his hide!"

"The last debt he'll ever owe!" laughed the other beggar.

Disturbed by the beggars' words, the Pope hurried to the Jewish ghetto. It was twilight, the hour just before the gates were closed for the night, locking the Jews of Rome in and their enemies out. As Sixtus watched, a richly dressed nobleman and his maidservant came out, stopping by the gate to converse. Sixtus concealed himself in the shadows and listened to their words.

"That was his last chance, Portia," said the nobleman. "Now he has no choice but to pay his pound of flesh tomorrow."

"He may yet change his mind, Antonio," said Portia.

"Ah!" thought Sixtus to himself. "The beggars had indeed been telling the truth!"

"So I would prefer it," replied Antonio. "But if I can't have Jessica's sweet young flesh, I'll settle for his tough gristle. As long as the Jew pays me."

Laughing, the two strolled off toward the wealthier neighborhoods of Rome.

Moments later, a young girl hurried toward the ghetto gates just as they were closing. Her wild hair and faltering steps betrayed her distress.

"Can I be of help?" asked Sixtus, stepping out of the shadows.

"How can a beggar help repay a debt of one thousand zecchini?" she declared. "My father is about to lose his life unless I save him!"

"Return in peace to your home, Jessica," said the Pope.

"But how did you know my name?" cried the startled girl.

"Trust me," he said, smiling. "Your father's debt will be repaid."

And before she could ask more, the beggar disappeared mysteriously into the night. Puzzled but now full of hope, Jessica returned to her father's house.

The next morning, a huge crowd gathered around the wooden platform that Antonio had ordered erected for the public flaying. In the middle of the platform stood old Shylock, trembling with fright, his hands bound with rough cords. Next to him stood the executioner, dressed in a black hood and bare-chested, a cruel cat-o'-nine tails dangling from one black-gloved hand. On the other side stood Antonio, already looking triumphant.

The executioner raised his whip, but before the cat-o'-nine tails bit into Shylock's flesh, a magnificent coach came racing up to the platform. The coat of arms on the coach door identified it as the property of the Holy See. Quickly the executioner lowered his hand.

"What is the meaning of this?" demanded Antonio.

The papal messenger stepped down from the coach and held out a small leather pouch. "His Holiness the Pope wishes to repay this man's debt," he announced.

"I refuse to accept!" cried Antonio. "This man will pay me the pound of flesh he owes!"

He nodded to the executioner, who once again raised his whip high in the air.

But now out of the coach stepped an imposing figure dressed in purple robes. The crowd gasped when it recognized Pope Sixtus himself.

Even Antonio abandoned his bluster and fell to his knees.

"I stand as a witness against you, Antonio!" declared the Pope. "It is against our law to extort virtue from young maidens, and you have done so. You have thereby forfeited your life. You have only one hour to live."

Without waiting for Antonio's reply, the Pope climbed back into the coach and left the scene in a swirl of dust. Within the hour, the executioner had released the old Jew and taken Antonio's life on the very platform he had ordered built for Shylock's pound of flesh.

199
The Pasha's Lance

Once when the Pasha of Jerusalem visited the Tomb of David, his lance slipped out of his hand and fell through a grate into the tomb. Immediately the Pasha ordered one of his servants lowered into the tomb to retrieve it. For this was no ordinary lance, but one encrusted with precious jewels and crowned with gold.

Minutes later, they pulled the lifeless body of the servant out of the tomb. Then the Pasha ordered another servant lowered into the tomb, but the same thing happened. So it was with the third and fourth servants.

"Your majesty!" cried one of his chief ministers. "If you do not stop, we shall all soon be dead!"

"I will not leave this spot until I have my lance back!" declared the Pasha.

"Then send a messenger to the *Hakham* of the Jews," advised the minister. "Tell him that he must send a Jew to retrieve the lance or all the Jews of the city will die. Surely one of them will succeed in retrieving your lance, for this people has a special place in David's heart."

When the *Hakham* received the Pasha's message, he

burst into tears and tore his clothes. How could he ask one of his own people to set foot in such a holy place? He would surely be condemning that man to death. He pleaded with the Pasha's messenger to give him three more days to reply, then summoned all the Jews of the city to the synagogue. For three days, the Jews of Jerusalem prayed and fasted. Many went to the Tomb of Rachel to beg that she intercede for them in heaven.

On the morning of the fourth day, the *Hakham* said to the people, "Who among you will go down to the tombs of the kings?"

No one came forward.

"Then we must draw lots," said the *Hakham*.

The lot fell upon the *shammash*, a poor, simple man.

"I am the servant of the God of Israel!" he declared, and he prepared his soul for death. Saying farewell to his family and friends, he climbed Mount Zion where the Pasha and his men eagerly awaited him. In the synagogue, the Jews continued to pray, hoping that a miracle might save the synagogue attendant from heaven's wrath.

Carefully the Pasha's men lowered the *shammash* into the tomb and waited. Moments passed, but no sound came from below. Just as the Pasha was about to order the rope raised up, a thin voice cried out from the tomb, "Pull me out!"

Quickly they pulled on the rope. The first thing that emerged was the gold point of the Pasha's lance, then the shaft, sparkling with precious jewels in the bright sun. Finally the pale face of the *shammash* rose out of the tomb. He held the lance out to the Pasha, whose face betrayed the greatest astonishment and awe.

All of the Pasha's men fell on their faces and cried, "Blessed be the God of Israel!"

From that day on the Pasha held the Jews in his domain in the greatest esteem.

As for the Jews themselves, they rejoiced greatly in their good fortune and heaven's grace. But the joy was greatest in the house of the simple *shammash*, who received many gifts from the community and from the

Pasha himself for his brave deed. Many wished to know what had happened to him in the tomb, but his lips remained sealed.

Only the *Hakham* ever heard his story: As he had stood trembling in the gloom, an old man, dressed in gleaming white robes, had appeared before him and silently handed him the lance.

200

The Bullet in the Mirror

Once there was a king who was a great astrologer and diviner. One day he wished to discover whether anyone else had been born under the same star as he. So he consulted the stars and discovered that in a certain city, on a certain street, in a certain courtyard lived just such a man by the name of Rabbi Hayyim ben Moses ben Attar.

The king was astonished to learn that it was a Jew who shared his birthstar, and he very much desired to meet this Rabbi Hayyim. So he summoned all his ministers and princes and said to them, "I am now going on a long journey to faraway lands to learn how other kingdoms are governed. While I am gone, I appoint the viceroy to rule in my stead."

Then he took one of his slaves, exchanged his royal robes for simple clothing, and rode from land to land until he reached the city where Rabbi Hayyim lived. But when he came to Hayyim's house, he was dismayed to find that the man whose star he shared lived in a poor hovel made of mud and straw.

The king stooped under the low doorway and blinked his eyes in the gloom. From across the room a voice cried out, "Enter, my lord king!"

The king was startled. How did the man know he was a king? Was he not in disguise?

"I am not a king," he protested.

"Why do you try to hide it, my lord?" laughed Rabbi Hayyim. "It is obvious to me that you are a king!"

The king saw that it was no use pretending any longer. "But how did you know my true identity?" he asked.

"Every man has a guardian angel who accompanies him wherever he goes. Behind you stands an angel clearly befitting a king. But tell me," Rabbi Hayyim went on, "why did you come all this way to see me?"

"I will not conceal the truth from you," replied the king. "I have consulted the heavens and have learned that you and I were both born under the same star. But I am surprised to discover that you are such a poor man."

"Ah!" answered Rabbi Hayyim, smiling. "But I am greater than you!"

"How can you say such a ridiculous thing?" protested the king. "You are but a poor man, while I am a great king!"

"I will show you," answered Rabbi Hayyim, and he took a mirror and held it up to the king. "Can you see your kingdom within this glass?"

The king looked in the mirror and saw a host of kingdoms before him. "Give me a moment to find mine among so many lands."

"Turn around, your majesty," said Rabbi Hayyim, "and then look again."

The king did as Rabbi Hayyim asked, and when he gazed in the mirror once more, he saw the familiar fields and mountains of his own kingdom.

"Can you find your royal capital?" asked Rabbi Hayyim.

"It is a large kingdom I rule over," said the king, "with many great and small towns. Give me a moment to find the capital among them."

"Turn around, your majesty, and then look again."

This time when the king turned around and peered into the glass, he saw his royal city with his palace gleaming brightly upon a hill.

"Now can you see your bedchamber?" asked Rabbi Hayyim.

"My palace has hundreds of rooms," protested the king. "Give me a minute to puzzle out which is my bedchamber."

"Turn around, your majesty," said Rabbi Hayyim, "and then look again."

The king turned around, and when he gazed again into the mirror, he saw his own bedchamber where his queen was preparing herself for bed. His heart instantly began to ache, and he felt a powerful longing to return home. As he looked on, the door to the chamber opened, and the viceroy walked in. The queen seemed startled.

"What are you doing here?" she cried.

"Let me into your bed, my beautiful queen," said the viceroy. "Am I not the king now?"

But the queen drew back from him and held out both her hands as a shield.

"If you do what I ask," said the viceroy, "we will rule this great kingdom together. When the king returns, we will poison him and so ensure the throne for ourselves. But if you do not," and his voice now became menacing, "you will pay dearly for your refusal."

As he listened to the viceroy's words, the king felt rage well up in him. But at the same time, he was beset by doubt.

"How do I know that what I am seeing is real?" he asked Rabbi Hayyim. "Perhaps it is all an illusion conjured up by your magic arts."

"Then take the gun in your hand," said Rabbi Hayyim, "and shoot the viceroy in the mirror!"

The king aimed his gun at the viceroy and shot a bullet straight into his heart. Instantly the man fell down dead at the queen's feet.

Startled by the noise and by the viceroy's inexplicable death, the queen looked around in alarm. Where had the shot come from? Had someone concealed himself in her chamber? In her distress, she summoned the palace priest and told him what had happened. They searched the room but found nothing.

"What a fortunate coincidence," said the priest. "Here at last is our chance to destroy those hateful Jews in our kingdom. We shall bury the body, and then summon witnesses to testify that the viceroy was last seen in the Jewish quarter of the city."

The king heard all these things and was very disturbed by them. He took his notebook and wrote down the exact date and time that the viceroy had died. Then he said to Rabbi Hayyim, "Have no fear, my friend. Your people will not be blamed for something they did not do. If these matters be true, then I shall surely know that you are indeed greater than I."

When the king returned home, his ministers told him that the Jews of his kingdom had killed the viceroy, and they urged him to order the Jews killed or expelled.

"It is no simple thing you ask of me," answered the king. "We must be certain that justice is done. Therefore, I will hold a trial to which I shall invite the greatest judges from near and far to render judgment. In their number I will also include a Jew. Let no one call me an unjust king."

So the king invited judges from all the nations near and far, and he also sent an invitation to Rabbi Hayyim ben Moses ben Attar. When the Jews of the kingdom heard of the coming trial, they put on sackcloth and ashes and declared a fast, for they feared the worst.

Then the king went to the queen's bedchamber and asked her what she knew about the viceroy's fate. She swore that she knew nothing. He asked her a second time, promising that no harm would befall her if she told him the truth. Still she insisted that she knew nothing. Then he became angry and threatened her with death unless she told him all that she knew. So she told him what had happened in her bedchamber, naming even the hour and minute that the bullet had stopped the viceroy's heart. When the king took out his notebook and compared what he had written down in Rabbi Hayyim's house, the times matched exactly!

"Great is the God of Israel!" declared the king.

On the day of the trial, the king held a great banquet. The judges and princes dined and drank to their heart's content until they were quite merry. Then Rabbi Hayyim declared, "Let us now have wine that has been aged well and not decanted."

To which the king answered, "My cellars are open to you!"

So the king and all his guests went down into the cellar to look for wine. The priest urged them to go down a certain passageway, but Rabbi Hayyim led them down another. As soon as they entered the room where the barrels of wine were kept, they smelled a strong stench, like rotting meat.

"What is this stench?" they asked.

"Only the dankness of the underground air," hastily answered the priest.

But Rabbi Hayyim searched the ground until he found one spot that was of a different color than the rest of the earthen floor. The king ordered them to dig in that spot. They soon uncovered the body of the dead viceroy, still dressed in his royal garments.

"Who did this?" demanded the king. "I will have you all killed!"

So frightened did they all become that they said, "It was not we ourselves who did this, but the priest who saw in the viceroy's mysterious death a chance to destroy the Jews."

Then the king ordered the priest and the false witnesses executed, and the charges against the Jews dismissed. It was a day of thanksgiving and great rejoicing for the Jews of the kingdom. As for Rabbi Hayyim ben Moses ben Attar, the king invited him to come live in the palace, where he served as his chief counselor for the rest of his days.

201
In Pursuit of the White Gazelle

In Germany there once lived a prince, so just and honest that he was much beloved of his people. This prince had many advisors, but none was closer to his heart than the Jew Meyer Rothfels. When the time came for the prince to die, he called his young son Erhard to his bedside and said to him, "My son, a prince whose judgments are fair and whose heart is generous commands the respect of his people. Do as I have done, and your reign shall be long and prosperous."

"I shall," promised the young prince.

"But even the wisest ruler," continued the father, "sometimes finds himself beset by doubts and trials. If that should happen to you, Erhard, call upon the Jew Meyer Rothfels, who has been my most trusted advisor. He will never fail you."

Prince Erhard promised to do all that his father asked, but in his heart he thought, "Let me never sink so low that I have to go to a Jew for help!"

Shortly after this, the old prince died and Prince Erhard became the new ruler. True to his word, the young prince ruled his kingdom with a just and generous heart, so that his people loved him even more than they had loved his father. But in time, Erhard forgot his father's words and began to rule his people harshly. The Jews especially suffered under his heavy hand. One day he decided to banish them from his kingdom.

Meyer Rothfels, who had long since become a stranger to the palace, hurried to Prince Erhard to plead for a reprieve. But his pleas fell upon deaf ears.

"By this time tomorrow," declared the prince, "I do not want to find a single Jew within my borders. Any Jew who remains behind will face certain death!"

Brokenhearted, Meyer Rothfels left the palace and

returned home, where he prepared himself to leave the land of his birth.

As soon as Rothfels was gone, Prince Erhard entered his bedchamber to eat his breakfast. As he gazed out of the window, he saw a beautiful white gazelle limping in the garden below. Seizing his bow and arrow, he ran outside. The gazelle bounded off into the woods, and the prince chased after her.

Hour after hour he pursued her, but she continued to elude him. Finally he had her within range of his arrows. But when he drew back his bow to shoot, she gazed up at him with such mournful eyes that he did not have the heart to kill her.

"I shall take her alive and keep her for a pet," he declared, lowering his bow.

But no matter how fast he ran after her, the little gazelle ran still faster, and he never seemed to get any closer to her. After hours of pursuit, he noticed that the shadows had lengthened on the forest floor and that the sky was rapidly growing darker.

"I shall have to sleep in the forest tonight," said Erhard. "Perhaps the little deer will make her bed nearby, and I shall catch her in the morning."

He gathered leaves and moss to make a bed for himself and lay down for the night. When he awoke the next day, he realized that he was lost. As for the gazelle, she was nowhere in sight. For the next sixty days he wandered, ragged and hungry, in the forest. He ate what he could scavenge—roots and berries and wild game. When his arrows were gone, he was often forced to hide from wild beasts. Then winter came, and snow began to fall, so that life became even more miserable.

At the end of sixty days he met a charcoal-burner in a clearing.

"I am Prince Erhard," he announced to the roughly dressed man. "If you give me food and drink and a bed for the night, I will see that you are richly rewarded."

The man stared at Erhard as though he were a

madman. Enraged, Erhard raised his hand to strike the man, but then he looked down at himself. On his feet were strips of skin from a wild animal he had killed, and his clothes were ragged and threadbare. He knew that his face was covered with a wild beard and that his hair fell long and dirty around his neck. Why shouldn't the man consider him mad?

Erhard bowed his head and mumbled, "I am a poor wanderer, lost in the forest. Could you spare a few scraps of bread and provide me a pallet of straw for the night?"

The charcoal-burner felt sorry for this ragged stranger and took him into his hut, where his wife gave him food, a sturdy set of clothes, and a warm bed. The next day the charcoal-burner took Erhard into the forest and gave him an ax with which to chop wood. For the next sixty days, Erhard worked hard for his new master. To his surprise, he discovered that his troubles seemed to leave him while he was working. He also realized that he was more thankful for the simple food, the warm bed, and the cheerful human companionship of the charcoal-burner and his wife than he had been for the rich pleasures of court life.

At the end of sixty days he bade farewell to the charcoal-burner and his wife, collected his meager wages, and set out to find his way home. When he came to a town, he took lodgings at an inn and went to bed. But during the night, robbers came and stole the few pieces of silver he had wrapped up in his handkerchief. So he was forced to beg for his next meal. Then he found work as a cobbler's apprentice and earned enough money to buy his dinner.

So it went. He wandered from town to town, taking whatever jobs he could find and earning only enough to buy food and a simple roof over his head each night. The journey stretched on from weeks to months, until at last he reached the capital city.

This time he knew better than to reveal his true identity to the palace guards. Surely they would not believe that this ragged and dirty wanderer was their prince! So he nosed about the city to find out who had taken his place in the half-year he had been gone. To his astonishment there was no word of any change in the palace. So—an impostor had stolen his throne!

Erhard went to the palace gates and peered in. There was his beautiful garden where he had first seen the little white gazelle months before. If he could only get inside and see who had stolen his throne!

As he stood gazing through the iron bars, an old Jew dressed in a long black coat and black hat came hurrying through the gates. He recognized Meyer Rothfels. Erhard suddenly remembered his father's dying words: "If you ever find yourself in trouble, go to Meyer Rothfels." How fortunate that this was the very man now coming toward him!

"Kind sir," Erhard said to the old man, "will you help me now as you once helped my father?"

Openmouthed, Meyer stared at the wretched young man standing before him. Then he recognized Prince Erhard under the torn clothes and wild beard.

"Come with me, sire," he said, leading Erhard by the arm. "It is best that we talk in private."

Once inside his house, Meyer gave Erhard a new suit of clothing, cut his hair and beard, and set a meal before him. When Erhard had eaten his fill, Meyer said to him, "Now tell me, my friend, what evil fortune has befallen you?"

"Have you heard nothing then of my disappearance?" cried Erhard. And he told Meyer all of his adventures since he had first left the palace in pursuit of the white gazelle. As Meyer listened, his eyes grew round, but he said nothing.

"And now," said Erhard when he had completed his story, "tell me who has taken my place in the palace!"

Meyer took Erhard by the hand and brought him to a little door in the palace wall that Erhard had never seen before. They made their way through a maze of dark corridors until they found themselves outside Erhard's bedroom.

"Where is he?" cried the young prince, bursting into the room. "Where is the impostor?"

But the room was empty. Meyer walked over to the dressing table and picked up a mirror and handed it to Erhard. "Look in there," he said. "There is your impostor! You have been gone from the palace only one hour."

Amazed, the prince stared at his own image in the glass.

"It is a miracle from God!" exclaimed Meyer Rothfels. "One hour ago I saw you dash out into your garden and run after a wounded white gazelle." He poured the prince a cup of tea from the pot sitting by his bed. "Taste this tea, my lord," he said. "It is still warm."

Just then a servant entered the room. "Is my lord finished with his breakfast?" he asked.

"How long ago did you bring it to me?" asked Erhard.

"About an hour ago, sire," answered the servant.

"So it is true!" cried Erhard. "But in this one hour I have learned enough to last me a lifetime!"

His eyes now fell upon the edict he had signed that morning banishing the Jews from his kingdom. He seized it and threw it into the fire. "Now I know what it is like to be homeless and without friends," he said.

From that day on, Meyer Rothfels was once more a frequent visitor at the palace, and Erhard was beloved of his people once again.

6. FOOLS

202

A Box of Bones

A rich merchant and his wife once had a dim-witted son.

When the boy grew up, his mother said to him, "It is time that you learned a trade. Go to the fair and buy there something of value that you can sell at a profit when you return home."

The merchant gave his son a bag of coins and sent him off. The first thing the boy saw at the fair was a man selling pipes. He bought a box of pipes, thinking, "Surely I will make a handsome profit from these!"

But when he returned to his house and opened the box to show his parents, he discovered that every pipe had broken on the journey home. His father boxed his ears, and his mother scolded him soundly.

"Go back again," she told him, "and buy something that will not break on the journey home!"

So the boy took a second bag of coins and set off.

Not far from the fair lived a poor Jewish farmer who was at that moment in a most unfortunate predicament: He was unable to pay back the large debt he owed to his Gentile landlord. To punish him, the landlord locked the Jew in the barn until he starved to death. Then the landlord took the dead Jew's bones, put them in a box, and ordered his servant to sell them at the fair.

When the merchant's son arrived at the fair, he came upon the servant selling the box of bones.

"A box of Jewish bones for sale!" cried the servant.

Without a moment's hesitation the boy bought the box, brought it to the holy burial society, and then buried the bones in a Jewish cemetery.

When he returned home, he proudly announced to his parents, "What a good deed I did today! I bought a Jew's bones and buried them in the Jewish cemetery."

That night the merchant had a dream: "If you want your son to succeed in life," said the voice in the dream, "go out tomorrow morning and take as your son's partner the first Jew you meet."

The merchant woke up and thought to himself, "Only a fool listens to dreams!"

But the dream returned two more times that night, so the merchant knew that he must do what it said.

The next morning he went out early and came upon a poor Jew bearing a sack over his shoulder.

"Where are you going?" asked the merchant.

"To the fair," the man replied.

"You need not walk there," said the merchant. "You can ride on my wagon. For from this moment on, you and my son shall be partners."

So the merchant's son and his new partner set out for the fair. They came to a dense forest and camped beside a stream. Then the partner said to the merchant's son, "Wait here until I return."

In a short while he came to a small house in a clearing. Peering through a chink in the wall, he saw a band of thieves dividing up their spoils. In one corner he saw severed hands, legs, and heads; in the other, jewels and mounds of gold coins.

He knocked on the door and said. "I too am a thief. Let us be partners. I will take you to where the merchants are camped on their way to the fair. But only one of you must come with me at a time."

Eagerly the thieves agreed to his plan. One by one they followed the partner to a certain place in the forest, and one by one he cut off their heads. Then he returned to the merchant's son, and together they rode to the thieves' house. After filling several sacks with jewels and gold, they continued on their way.

As the Sabbath approached, they came to an inn.

"We wish to spend the Sabbath here," they told the innkeeper.

"But I have no food!" he protested.

"Take these gold coins and buy whatever you need," they told him.

So the man and his wife prepared a Sabbath meal, and they all sat down to eat. But during the meal they noticed that every so often a hand mysteriously appeared through a doorway, into which the innkeeper slipped food. Not wishing to disturb their hosts' Sabbath, the two travelers asked no questions about the hand until after the *havdalah* ceremony.

"To whom does that hand belong?" asked the merchant's son. "And why doesn't its owner let himself be seen?"

"If you were to give me all the gold in creation," said the innkeeper, "still I would not tell you!"

But they would not let him rest until he told them.

"That hand belongs to our daughter," he said. "Three times has she been wed, and three times her husband has died on the wedding night."

"I have a new husband for her," declared the partner.

"No!" cried the innkeeper. "He too will surely die!"

But the partner insisted until at last the innkeeper agreed to marry his daughter to the merchant's son.

Then the innkeeper said to his wife, "Buy candles, for tomorrow we shall be in mourning." And they both began to weep bitterly.

After the wedding ceremony, the partner said to the merchant's son, "Let us divide up our fortune, for tomorrow we must part ways."

So they divided up the jewels and gold that they had taken from the thieves' house.

Then the partner said, "Now let us divide up the bride."

"How can we do that?" cried the merchant's son. "You cannot divide a woman in half. Either I will pay you for your share or you will pay me for mine."

But the other man insisted on dividing her with a sword. He tied the trembling girl to a tree and raised up his sword to split her in two.

But before the blade descended, the girl's mouth popped open, and a huge snake slithered out. With one swift blow, the partner chopped the snake in two.

The next morning the bride's parents were overjoyed to see the groom still alive. So was the bride.

As for the partner, he packed up all his possessions and prepared to leave. Before setting off, he said to the merchant's son, "Go home with your new wife, and live a long and happy life. Tell your father that I am the man who appeared to him three times in his dreams. And tell him also that I am the Jew whose bones you bought and buried. Thus have I paid you back for your kindness." And then he vanished.

203
The Two Husbands

In the east there once lived a woman named Shafika who had a simpleton for a husband. Shafika ran the household, cared for the children, and earned the money to keep them all fed and clothed. All her husband managed to earn was shame and ridicule, for he was a very stupid man.

One day Shafika's friend Rahama came to visit her.

"Woe is me!" cried Shafika. "No wife has ever had a more foolish husband than I!"

"That's what you think!" answered Rahama. "You could search far and wide, and still not find a man as stupid as my Shimon."

The two wives decided to have a contest to see which of their husbands was the more foolish. First Shafika called her husband Hangal in to her.

"Hangal," she said, "go up to the roof and bring down a loaf of bread for your lunch."

When Hangal was halfway up the ladder, he shouted down, "Shafika! You must help me! I am on the middle step of the ladder, and I do not know whether I am climbing up or coming down."

"Stupid husband!" shouted Shafika. "Tell me what is in your hands."

Hangal looked at his hands and saw that they were empty. "I have nothing in my hands!" he cried.

"Then you are still on your way up to the roof," said Shafika. "For if you had already been there, you would have a loaf in your hands."

"What a wise wife I have!" exclaimed Hangal.

He climbed up to the roof, took a loaf of bread, and began to climb down. But halfway down, he called again to Shafika, "O wise wife of mine, help me again! Am I coming up or down?"

"Look at your hands!" cried Shafika.

Hangal looked at his hands and saw that he was carrying a loaf of bread. "I have a loaf in my hands," he shouted.

"Then you are coming down, stupid, for how else could you have gotten the bread!" Then Shafika turned to Rahama and said, "Have you ever seen a more foolish man in all your days?"

"Come to my house and judge for yourself," answered Rahama, and so the two women went to Rahama's house.

Rahama filled up a jug of water and handed it to her husband Shimon. "Take this grain to the miller," she said to him, "and have him grind it into flour. Hurry, for our guest is hungry."

Shimon did as he was told. When the miller saw the water in the jug and heard Shimon's foolish words, he decided to have some fun with him.

On that day a Hindu was sleeping just outside the mill. The miller said to Shimon, "Go take a nap beside the Hindu. I will wake you when I have finished grinding the wheat."

So Shimon lay down beside the Hindu and fell asleep.

While he was sleeping, the miller cut off Shimon's beard and replaced his hat with the Hindu's turban. Then he woke Shimon and said to him, "Here is your grain. Go home in peace."

When Shimon arrived home, he looked so different that he shocked the two women waiting for him. "Who are you?" asked Rahama. "Where do you come from?"

"I am married to one of you, but I don't remember which one," answered Shimon.

Rahama handed him a mirror.

"Curse that miller!" cried Shimon when he saw his

own shaven face in the glass. "He woke the Hindu by mistake and gave him *my* grain! *Me* he left sleeping in the sun. I had better run back there immediately and ask him to wake me up before I get sunstroke!" And off he ran.

Shafika now turned to Rahama and said, "You win, my friend. I am fortunate compared to you. May God help you!"

204
The Voice from the Tree

Once a trickster and a simpleton became partners. On their way to the city, they found a purse full of gold.

"Let us divide it in half," said the simpleton, "and each take his share."

But the trickster wished to keep all of the money for himself, so he said, "Let us take now only what we need and conceal the rest. Then we can return later and take more whenever we need it."

So they took a few coins for themselves and buried the rest under a great tree beside the road. Then they went on their way to the city. That night the trickster returned and took the rest of the money.

A short time later the two returned to the tree. When they discovered that the purse was gone, the trickster cried, "Ho, thief! How could you have stolen from your own good friend?"

"I stole nothing!" insisted the simpleton. "Let us go to the judge and let him decide."

So they went to the judge. "Where are your witnesses?" the judge asked the trickster. "For if it were not for witnesses, thieves would rule us all."

"The tree is my witness," declared the trickster.

"Then we shall go tomorrow to the tree and let it prove your words."

That night the trickster went to his old father and said

to him, "I have sworn that the tree will bear witness to the simpleton's guilt. Go now to the tree and conceal yourself there. When the judge asks who took the money, say, 'The simpleton.' For if you do not do this, they will surely discover that it was I who took the money, and I will be forced to return it."

"My son," said the old man, "there are some tricks that ensnare the trapper. Have you not heard of the bird that the Arabs call the Algon?"

"No," answered the trickster.

"The Algon always made her nest near the adder's den, and the adder always ate the chicks. Each time this happened the Algon cried and moaned over her evil fortune. Once a crab heard her and told her, 'The young kite is an enemy of the adder. Go and catch many fish and with them lay a trail from the kite's nest to the adder's den.'

"The Algon followed the crab's advice. The young kite snapped up the fish one by one until he came to the adder's den, and then he ate the adder as well. But he was still hungry, so he retraced his steps until he came to the Algon's nest. Then he gobbled up the Algon and her chicks."

"Such a fate will not befall us," said the trickster to his father. "We need not fear such a simpleton as this one!" And he pleaded with his father so long and so pitifully that the old man agreed to do what his son asked. So that night the father hid himself in the hollow trunk of the tree.

The next morning the judge, the simpleton, the trickster, and a group of townspeople came to the tree. "Who stole the money?" the judge asked the tree. "I call upon you as a witness."

"The simpleton took it!" came a voice from inside the tree.

So astonished was the judge to hear a human voice that he ordered them to pile wood around the base of the tree and light a fire to burn the spirit inside it. When the smoke reached the old man, he leapt out of the tree, crying in pain. The judge ordered him and his son beaten for their knavery. Then he forced the trickster to repay the simpleton every coin that he stole.

205
The Story of Kunz and the Shepherd

There is a proverb that says: "You will be left behind as Kunz was left behind to tend the sheep." And here is why it says this:

The king had many counselors, the least of whom was Kunz. Yet despite his lack of wisdom, Kunz succeeded in winning the king's heart. For whenever the counselors came together to advise the king, it was Kunz who told the king of their advice, claiming that it was he who had first thought of it.

Of course, the other counselors resented Kunz, and one day they came to the king to complain of his deceitfulness.

"But isn't Kunz the wisest among you?" asked the king, surprised by their words. "He has told me so himself!"

"All lies!" they declared. "It is our wisdom he has stolen. Test him alone and you will see how foolish he really is."

So the king called Kunz and said to him, "My dear Kunz, you know that you are dearer to me than all my counselors. That is why I now turn to you for to help. For a long time I have been troubled by three questions that I cannot answer."

Kunz's chest puffed out with pride when he heard the king's words. "Ask, your majesty, and I will be glad to answer these questions for you."

"Where does the sun rise? How far is the sky from the earth? What am I thinking?"

"These are difficult questions, your majesty," said Kunz nervously. "I will need three days to answer them."

"Very well," answered the king. "You may have three days. When you return with the correct answers, I will reward you handsomely for your great wisdom."

When Kunz left the palace, he said to himself, "Surely I cannot think clearly in the city, for it is too full of noise and distraction. I shall go into the country to think."

He came to his own meadow, where he found a shepherd tending his flock. Kunz walked back and forth at the edge of the meadow, muttering loudly to himself, "Where does the sun rise? How far is the earth from the sun? Who can tell me these things? And who can tell me what the king is thinking?"

The shepherd overheard him and said to him, "You seem to be troubled by something, master. Why not share your troubles with me, for perhaps I can help?"

Kunz thought to himself, "Maybe my shepherd is a scholar and can answer the questions." So he said to the shepherd, "The king has asked me three questions that I cannot answer: 'Where does the sun rise? How far is the sky from the earth? What am I thinking?' No matter how hard I think, I cannot discover the answers to these questions."

"Give me your fine court clothes and take my rough ones," said the shepherd."While you stay here to tend the sheep, I will go to the palace and pretend to be you. When I answer the questions, the king will think that I am you, and he will reward you handsomely for your great wisdom."

The plan delighted Kunz, and he lost no time exchanging clothes with his shepherd. While he stayed behind tending the sheep, the other made his way to the palace.

As the shepherd had predicted, the king mistook him for Kunz and said to him, "Well, have you the answers to my three questions?"

"Indeed I have, your majesty," answered the shepherd.

"Where does the sun rise?" asked the king.
"The sun rises in the east and sets in the west," answered the shepherd.
"And how far is the sky from the earth?"
"The sky is as far from the earth as the earth is from the sky," answered the shepherd.
"And what am I thinking?" asked the king, convinced that he would stump his counselor at last.
"You are thinking that I am your counselor Kunz, but I am not. I am his shepherd. Yesterday my master came to where I was tending the sheep muttering to himself, 'Where does the sun rise? How far is the sky from the earth? What is the king thinking?' I told him that if he changed clothes with me, I would come to you and answer the questions in his stead. So here I am in his fine clothes, and he is in my rough ones, tending the sheep."
"You are indeed a wise fellow!" exclaimed the king. "Remain here with me and be my counselor. We shall let Kunz remain where he is, tending the sheep."
And that is why they say: "You will be left behind as Kunz was left behind to tend the sheep." May it never happen to us!

7. THE FANTASTIC

206
Joseph de la Reina

In Safed there once lived a holy man named Rabbi Joseph de la Reina, who spent his days and nights studying the mystical writings of the *Kabbalah*. So much did he immerse himself in pure waters and fast and pray that in time he lost almost all attachment to this earth and drew near to the angels.

Then Elijah appeared to him and taught him all

manner of secret knowledge, including the Blessed Names of God. Then Joseph's soul became filled with the desire to bring the *Shekhinah* down to humankind and to end the reign of Samael on the earth.

But when he told Elijah of his wish, the prophet disappeared. For many days and nights Joseph wept and prayed, crying out, "Elijah, Elijah, return to me! Where have you gone?"

At the end of forty days, Elijah returned and said to him, "You rubbish heap of dust and ashes, why have you been disturbing the heavens with your prayers? Don't you know that greater souls than yours have tried to bring about the Redemption and have failed? These are hidden secrets that no one may know!"

But Joseph would not be put off. He pronounced the Awesome Names and said to Elijah, "I will not let you go until you tell me what I wish to know."

"Very well," answered Elijah. "Go with your disciples to the Mountains of Darkness. There you will find a large dog whose color is blacker than black. This is none other than Satan himself. When you find this black dog, you must bind it at once with this iron chain upon which is engraved the Holy Name of God. Then you must slaughter the beast without delay. Be careful not to let him deceive you in any way, for he is the wiliest of creatures. You must show no mercy whatsoever. If you do, all shall be lost. Here also is some pure incense that the priests once prepared for the Temple, so that you may withstand the dreadful stink of Satan. If you succeed in all this, you shall indeed bring the Messiah to redeem humankind. This is all I am permitted to tell you."

And with that, Elijah vanished.

With great joy Rabbi Joseph ran to tell his disciples all that Elijah had revealed to him. For three days they prepared themselves for the journey, fasting, praying, and immersing themselves in holy waters.

At the end of three days, Elijah reappeared and guided them to the Mountains of Darkness. Then, without a word of farewell, he left them. They soon came upon a great black dog whose stench was so powerful that they almost turned back. But Joseph bravely ran up to the beast and threw the chain around its neck. When it saw that it was bound, it began to cry and howl, begging them to release it. But they recited the Secret Names and refused to show any mercy.

Then the dog realized that it would have to use deceit to save itself, so it said to Joseph, "You may do with me as you wish, for I see that I am powerless to subdue you. Only one thing do I ask of you: Permit me to sniff a little incense to revive my spirit."

Joseph thought to himself, "What harm can incense do?" So he held up a few grains of the incense to the beast's nostrils. Instantly fire flared out of the nostrils and consumed the incense, then swirled up around them until they were completely ringed by flame. Several of Joseph's disciples died instantly, and the rest fell to the ground in terror.

"Lord of the Universe!" cried Samael in triumph. "Did You not write in Your Torah, 'You shall not bow down to idols!'? See, these men have served me by offering me pure incense from Your Temple!" And with a wicked laugh, he flung Joseph and his disciples from the mountaintop.

Some died from the fall, some went mad, and the rest returned shaken and bruised to their homes in Safed, never breathing a word to anyone about what had happened.

As for Joseph himself—he was flung all the way to France and landed near the palace of the king. Although his mind was deranged by the fall, he nevertheless retained the mystical teachings, and the Jews of the city gave him a house and treated him with the respect befitting a holy man.

The Queen of France at that time, Dolphina, was an exceptionally beautiful woman, and Joseph began to lust after her. So he used his magic arts to summon angels who conveyed her to his bed at night. When she awoke in the morning back in her own bed, it seemed to her as if she had lain with a strange man in her dreams, and she was very frightened. After several months of these dreams, she told her husband.

"Describe this man to me," said the king.

So she described Joseph to him. He sent messengers all over the country, and they reported back that the man who had been inhabiting the queen's dreams was none other than Joseph de la Reina, for his strange ways and wild looks had made him known throughout the land.

The king sent the messengers to Joseph's house, but they could not find him anywhere.

Then a voice spoke out of the air, startling them: "Whom do you seek? I am here! Tell the king that I do not wish to come to him!"

Frantically they searched for the voice but could find no sign of Joseph. So they returned to the king and told him that the man he sought had the power to render himself invisible.

"Then I shall order the Jews to bring him to me!" declared the king.

When the Jews heard the king's decree, they became very frightened, for they knew that great harm would befall them if they failed to bring Joseph to the king. So they sent a message to Joseph, saying, "If you refuse to go to the king, we shall blow the *shofar* against you and ban you from our synagogues and study houses, so that the Holy Names will serve you no longer."

When Joseph heard this, he knew that he was lost, for he had no power against his own people. So he climbed to the top of a nearby mountain and threw himself off. Such was the end of the man who tried to force the hand of God.

207
The Grateful Dead

In Jerusalem there once lived a wealthy man to whom an only son was born in his old age. The old man doted on the child and gave him anything his heart desired. But when the boy reached the age of six, his father began to fear that he might be corrupted by the vanities of this world. So the father equipped a special room to serve all the boy's needs and arranged to have him tutored by a private teacher. For the next ten years the boy learned Torah and Talmud until he was wise in God's ways. And all this time he did not venture out into the world.

Then the father became gravely ill, and he knew that he would soon die. He called his son to his bedside and said to him, "My son, my life is at an end. It is time for you to inherit all that I possess. But you have no knowledge of the world's ways, for I have shielded you all these years. Yet without such knowledge, all my wealth will be lost, and you will be forced to beg for your bread!"

So the father showed his son all the treasures of his house and taught him the ways of trade and the marketplace. And because the young man was so clever, he soon became as skilled in commerce as he was in study, and his father's heart swelled with pride.

Then the father felt his end drawing near, and he said to his son, "Let not the Torah depart from your lips, for worldly knowledge is of little worth if the heart is not wise in God's ways." And then he died.

The son took a purse full of money and set out to see the world. He came to Constantinople, where he saw a large iron casket hanging on a chain in the marketplace. The casket was guarded by a soldier.

"What is this?" he asked the soldier.

"It does not concern you," answered the soldier.

But the young man begged the soldier to tell him and even gave him some gold coins, until the soldier finally told him the story of the iron casket.

"The Sultan had a Jewish treasurer whom he honored greatly," the soldier explained. "But the other ministers envied him and accused him of stealing from the Sultan's treasury. When the Sultan examined his treasury, he discovered that a large sum was indeed missing! So he summoned the Jew and said to him, 'Show me where every penny has gone over the last twenty years

since you have been my treasurer.' The Sultan's words
terrified the Jew, for who can account for every penny
over twenty years? He pleaded for mercy, but the Sultan
would not listen. He ordered the man executed and his
body hung in this casket until the Jews of the city pay him
all the money missing from the treasury."

"And how much is that?" asked the young man.

"A vast sum," answered the soldier, and he named
the amount.

The young man went to the palace and asked for a
private audience with the Sultan, saying that he had a
secret to tell him. When he was alone with the Sultan, he
spoke so wisely that the Sultan said to him, "Ask for any
favor and it shall be granted."

"I wish to repay the money missing from the Sultan's
treasury, and in return I ask that you release the treasurer's body to me for burial."

The Sultan agreed. The young man gave him all the
money he had inherited from his father. Then he said,
"Announce throughout the city of Constantinople that
every man, woman, and child must attend this man's
funeral." And so it happened that not a person remained
home that day, not the newborn babies in their cradles
nor the old people in their beds. Indeed, the Sultan's
treasurer was more honored in death than he had ever
been in life.

A few days later, the Sultan summoned the young
man and said to him, "I have one thing to ask of you."

"Your will is my command, my lord," answered the
young man.

"I wish to inherit the reward for this commandment
that you have done."

"Ask anything else, my lord," answered the young
man, "but this is beyond my power to give. All my life I
have desired to perform such a commandment as this,
which will honor me even more in the next world. How
can I give up its reward? Perhaps I shall never have
another opportunity to perform such a commandment,
even if I were to acquire great wealth and power."

The Sultan found the youth's words very wise and sent him on his way in peace.

So the young man continued his journey throughout the cities of the world, and finally boarded a ship to return home. But a few days out to sea, a mighty storm arose and wrecked the ship, so that the young man found himself cast adrift in the sea. He looked up and saw a great stone pillar rise up out of the sea. He swam toward it, and it led him to a deserted island. Finding himself all alone without hope of rescue, he began to weep, when suddenly a great white eagle swooped out of the sky and bore him off upon its wings. In a few moments, he was back in his own courtyard in Jerusalem.

When he looked around for the eagle, he discovered that it had vanished, but before him stood a man dressed in white. The young man began to tremble, for this man did not look like a being of this earth.

"Do not fear," said the man, touching him lightly on the arm. "I am the Sultan's treasurer for whom you performed the final act of kindness. In gratitude I saved you from death, for I was the stone pillar and the eagle. Happy are you in this world, and great will be your reward in the next." Then he too disappeared into the night.

For the rest of his life, the son was wealthy and honored by all, and he lived to a ripe old age, studying Torah and performing many deeds of charity.

208
Soothsaying Dogs

Once an old Jew went walking and met old Father Abraham along the way.

"Peace unto you," said Abraham.

"Unto you peace," replied the old man.

"Ask any favor and it shall be granted to you," said Abraham.

Surprised by his unexpected good fortune, the old man blurted out, "I wish to understand the language of birds and beasts!"

"So be it," said Abraham, and then he vanished.

The old man hurried home to his poor hut, where he found his two dogs barking to each other. To his amazement, he found that he could indeed understand their speech.

"We shall eat well tomorrow," said one dog, "for in a few hours the old couple's cow will die."

As soon as he heard that, the old man took the cow to market and sold her.

The next day he again heard the dogs barking to each other.

"We shall eat well tomorrow," they said to each other, "for in the morning a fire will break out in the cellar, and while the old man and his wife try to put it out, we will be able to snatch all their food."

When he heard that, the old man removed all his possessions and sold his house.

On the third day he heard the dogs barking to each other, and this time he craned his ear in dread. "Woe unto our master, for tomorrow a great disaster will befall him! When the sun sets, his wife will breathe her last."

In great distress the old man ran to the rabbi for advice, for he could think of nothing to save his wife from the Angel of Death. He told the rabbi everything: how he had met old Father Abraham and been granted his wish, how he had sold his cow and house after he had heard his dogs prophesying their destruction, and how he was now helpless to save his wife from death.

When he had finished his tale, the rabbi said to him, "You old fool! Don't you see that Abraham was doing you a favor by granting your request? Your cow and house were meant to be sacrificed in place of your wife, but you misunderstood the dogs' words and sold them instead. Now your wife must die, for that is God's will."

And when the sun set the next day, the old man closed his wife's eyes and sat down to weep.

209
The Demon Wife and the
Broken Oath

In Israel there once lived a merchant named Shalom who had an only son named Dihon. Dihon was a wise and pious boy, and his father loved him with all his heart. When Shalom was about to die, he called Dihon to him and made him swear an oath that he would never go to sea, for he said to him, "My son, all that I have will soon be yours. You and your children will want for nothing as long as you live. I acquired this wealth in my travels, but the way was fraught with dangers, and many times I feared that I would never again see the land of my birth. That is why I wish to bind you to this oath, for I wish to spare you from a terrible death. If you break your oath, all my wealth will be in heaven's hands, and you will be left penniless."

The son swore to do what his father asked, and then the old man died.

Some time later sailors appeared at the son's door.

"Are you Shalom the merchant?" they asked him.

"I am his son," replied Dihon. "My father is dead."

"To whom did he will his treasures overseas?" they asked.

"He told me nothing of such treasures," confessed Dihon.

"Then he must have been out of his wits!" they cried. "For we have brought here a ship filled with gold and silver and precious jewels, and this is only a small portion of what remains to him in distant lands. Since you are his son, all this wealth now belongs to you."

Before Dihon could reply, they brought the ship's cargo to him — sacks filled with gold coins and silver bracelets and priceless treasures beyond measure. And while Dihon stood in the threshold, his mouth agape and his eyes nearly popping out of his head, the captain of the ship said to him, "Come with us now and we will show you the rest of your father's fortune."

Sadly Dihon shook his head. "I swore an oath to my father never to go to sea."

"But your father must not have been in his right mind when he made you swear that oath," they said to him, "for did he not conceal from you the vast fortune that should be yours, waiting for you in distant lands?"

Still Dihon refused to go with them. "My father was thinking of my own welfare when he made me promise not to go to sea. For the sea is filled with perils."

"But did he not endanger his own life when he sailed the seas in search of fortune? Is it fair that you remain at home when he himself did not?"

And they continued to plead with him until at last he gave in and sailed off with them. Soon a mighty storm arose and the ship sank, drowning all aboard except Dihon. He drifted to a deserted island, where he saw a giant owl perched in a tree. Suddenly the owl swooped down and bore him away. As they flew over another part of the island, Dihon thought he heard words of Torah being chanted below.

"Surely this is a place where Jews live!" he said to himself.

So he threw himself off the owl's back and landed amidst a crowd of men. But these were not ordinary men but rather demons who fell upon him and would have torn him to pieces had not Asmodeus, their king, intervened on his behalf.

"Let us kill this man," the demons cried, "for he has broken his oath to his father and so deserves to die!"

"Let me test him and see if he deserves such a death," said Asmodeus. Then he asked Dihon questions about Torah and Mishnah and all the laws, and Dihon answered each question brilliantly. "How wise he is!" exclaimed Asmodeus. "Surely he only broke his oath to his father because the sailors bewitched him with talk of treasure. A sin committed unintentionally does not merit death."

Then Asmodeus brought Dihon to his palace and studied Torah with him for three years. At the end of that time Asmodeus went off to war to fight his enemies, and he left Dihon in charge of his entire household.

"Here are the keys to every room in my palace," said the Demon King, "all except one. While I am gone, my servants have orders to obey you and grant your every request. Only one thing do I forbid you: to enter that room for which you have no key."

After Asmodeus left, Dihon began to explore his vast palace, and in time came upon the forbidden room. As he stood outside the locked door, he heard a woman's voice singing, a voice so enchanting that he found himself rooted to the ground. Softly he knocked on the door, and the voice abruptly stopped. He heard footsteps approaching, and then he found himself face to face with the most beautiful woman he had ever seen.

"Who are you?" she demanded angrily.

"I am Dihon," he said. "Asmodeus has entrusted his palace to me until he returns home. Who are you?"

"I am Asmodeus's daughter," she said. "And my father is already on his way home to punish you for disobeying his orders. He will cut off your head as soon as he sees you."

When he heard this, Dihon fell to his knees and begged for mercy. "I had no evil intentions when I knocked on your door," he said. "Please spare my life!"

Impressed by his soft words and pleasant appearance, the heart of the demon princess softened, and she said, "Very well, I shall spare your life. But only on one condition: You must ask my father to let us marry when he returns."

And Dihon agreed.

When Asmodeus returned from his wars, he stormed into the palace, brandishing his sword. Seeing Dihon, he roared, "Why have you disobeyed me? For this you shall die!"

Dihon fell to his knees and said, "My lord king, I only entered the forbidden room because I loved your daughter and wished to marry her. Now, I beg you, give your permission for us to marry."

Dihon's words pleased Asmodeus, for in truth, he had been planning to marry his daughter to Dihon, since the man was so wise in the words of Torah. So they married, and in time the demon princess bore a son. They named the boy Solomon.

But as the years passed, Dihon found himself missing his own human wife and children, and one day he sighed so deeply that his demon wife heard it and asked him about it.

"How I miss my home and family!" cried Dihon.

"Am I not beautiful?" cried the demon princess. "Have you not fabulous treasures at your command? What do you lack here?"

"My wife and children," answered Dihon, and he sighed again.

"Then you may return to them for a brief time," she said, "but then you may see them no more. Name the time you need."

"Grant me one year," said Dihon, and his demon wife agreed.

Then Dihon swore an oath that he would return in one year, and his wife sent him off on the back of a one-eyed hunchback who brought him to his home in one day. When Dihon saw his wife and children again, he embraced them and shed many happy tears. Then he turned to the hunchback and said, "Tell your mistress that I am not her husband and she is not my wife, for I am human and she is a demon. And tell her that I shall not return to her in one year!"

The hunchback reported Dihon's words to the demon princess, but she did not believe him. "Surely one so versed in Torah would not swear falsely!"

So at the end of one year, she sent the hunchback back to the city where her husband lived. But Dihon again refused to return to her, and he sent the hunchback away with unkind words.

"Perhaps he is ashamed to be borne by a hunchback,"

thought the princess, so she sent more honorable messengers dressed in splendid robes and jewels. But Dihon sent them away also, repeating his pledge never to return to the demon king and his demon wife.

So the princess decided to go herself, bringing with her young Solomon. But no matter how much she pleaded with Dihon, he would not be persuaded to abandon his human family for his unearthly one. Even his young son's tears failed to move him.

So the princess put her case before the congregation of the city and declared, "This man broke the oath he made to his father and so was cast adrift in the land of the demons. My father saved his life, and I in turn saved him from my father's wrath. We married according to the laws of the Torah, and he swore an oath before God that he would return to me after one year. He has returned evil for kindness and broken his oath. If he does not wish to return to me, let him fulfill the terms of the marriage contract and pay me what he owes."

The leaders of the congregation agreed that her words were just, so they read the words of the *ketubah* and discovered that Dihon had promised a vast sum of money to his demon bride. When they demanded that he pay the sum in order to divorce his wife, Dihon refused, and he declared that he would never return with her to Asmodeus's kingdom.

"I only swore these oaths to her in order to save my life," he said, "and the law states that an oath taken under duress is not a valid oath."

Realizing that she could not change Dihon's mind, the demon princess declared, "So be it. Since my husband has made a mockery of God's name and of me, I shall leave him to his shame. But I ask one favor before I go: I should like to part from him with a kiss."

Finding her request reasonable, the leaders of the congregation demanded that Dihon comply. So she kissed him on the lips and drew the lifebreath from him so that he died.

Then she pointed to her young son and proclaimed,

"If you do not wish me to slay all of you, you will marry Solomon to the daughter of one of your most worthy leaders and set him above you to rule over you. For now that my husband is dead, I do not wish to keep his son with me to remind me of my shame. Give him the lion's share of his father's property so that he shall never lack for anything."

And they did what she asked, and the demon princess returned to her father's palace alone.

210
The Scorpion in the Goblet

There once lived a pious man who had an only son named Rabbi Yohanan. When the old man was about to die, he called his son to his side and said to him, "Swear to me that after I die, you will go to the market and buy the first thing someone tries to sell you. Bring it home and it will safeguard you."

Rabbi Yohanan promised to do what his father asked. Then the old man shut his eyes and died.

When the period of mourning was over, Rabbi Yohanan went to the marketplace and saw a merchant selling a beautiful goblet.

"How much do you want for that goblet?" asked Rabbi Yohanan.

"One hundred gold coins," replied the merchant.

"I will give you sixty," said Rabbi Yohanan.

"I will not sell it for sixty," said the man and walked away.

Remembering his promise to his dying father, Rabbi Yohanan ran after him and said, "Very well. I will give you one hundred gold coins."

"The price is now two hundred," said the merchant.

"Two hundred!" cried Rabbi Yohanan. "Before, you asked only one hundred, and that is all I shall pay."

"Then I shall keep the goblet," answered the man and walked away.

Rabbi Yohanan said to himself, "I dare not break my oath to my father. I must give the man what he asks."

So he ran after the merchant and offered him two hundred gold coins.

"Now the price is one thousand," said the merchant.

"One thousand!" cried Rabbi Yohanan. "But it is not worth even half that much! Who would pay one thousand gold coins for a single goblet?"

"Be that as it may, if you want the goblet you must pay what I ask, or I shall sell it to someone else."

"I have no choice," sighed Rabbi Yohanan, "for I promised my father on his deathbed." So he gave the man one thousand gold coins and brought the goblet home.

All this occurred just before Passover. When it came time for the *seder*, Rabbi Yohanan's wife took the beautiful goblet and set it in the middle of the table. But when Rabbi Yohanan removed the lid to pour wine into the goblet, he found a smaller goblet inside. And when he lifted the lid on the smaller goblet, he was astonished to find inside a little scorpion. Rabbi Yohanan gave it some food, which it gobbled up. Then it leapt out of the goblet, scrambled up Rabbi Yohanan's chest, and kissed him on the cheek. After eating a few more morsels from the table, the little scorpion leapt back inside the smaller goblet, which Rabbi Yohanan then placed in the large one and covered over with the lid.

"Surely my father meant for us to care for this creature," said Rabbi Yohanan to his wife. "Let us feed it and see what good fortune it brings us."

But the more they fed the scorpion, the bigger it grew, until it outgrew the small and large goblets and had to be housed in its own little pen that Rabbi Yohanan built for it in the yard. But in a short time it outgrew that as well, and its body swelled to fill the entire yard. Soon Rabbi Yohanan and his family had nothing left to eat themselves, so Rabbi Yohanan sold his own *tallit* to buy the creature more food.

But soon that too was gone, and the family was left destitute. Then Rabbi Yohanan and his wife fell to their knees and prayed to God, saying, "Lord of the Universe, please help us! We have cared for this creature in order to honor our father's memory. But now we fear that our children will starve, for we have given it all that we have, and nothing remains to us. Have mercy on us, O Holy One of Blessing, and show us who this creature is and what its fate will be."

Then the scorpion opened its mouth and said, "God has heard your prayers and has given me permission to speak to you. You have indeed given me all that you have and I wish to return your kindness. Ask for anything and it shall be granted you."

"Teach me the language of the birds and beasts," said Rabbi Yohanan. And the scorpion did so.

Then he turned to Rabbi Yohanan's wife and said to her, "You have opened your heart to me and treated me as one of your own children. Ask for any favor and it shall be yours."

"Kind sir," she said, "grant me sufficient wealth so that I can sustain my family and keep them from want."

"Both of you follow me to the forest," said the scorpion, "and bring with you wagons and horses."

So they followed him to a clearing deep in the forest. Then the scorpion opened its mouth wide and cried out in hisses, squawks, hoots, and wails until every wild creature in the forest appeared in the clearing, each one bearing a precious jewel in its mouth. All these treasures Rabbi Yohanan and his wife loaded onto the wagons until they groaned under the heavy weight.

Then Rabbi Yohanan turned to the scorpion and said, "Praise be to God! Such wealth exceeds even our wildest dreams! As long as we live, we shall want for nothing. But tell us, Scorpion, who are you and how did you come to have such awesome powers?"

"I am a son of Adam," replied the scorpion. "Before Eve was formed, Adam had intercourse with all the wild beasts in the Garden, including my mother. I am the son of that union. For one thousand years I dwindle away until I am no bigger than a grain of sand, and for the next thousand years I grow until I tower above the hills. So it has been from the beginning, so it will be until the end. For although I am a son of Adam, I do not share his mortality."

"If you are indeed Adam's son," said Rabbi Yohanan, "then bless me!"

"May God save you from the evil fortune that will befall you!" said the scorpion.

"What evil fortune?" cried Rabbi Yohanan, but the scorpion was already gone.

Word of Rabbi Yohanan's fabulous wealth and astonishing wisdom soon spread throughout the kingdom, until it reached the ears of the king. Wishing to see for himself, the king invited Rabbi Yohanan to the palace and was so impressed by what he saw and heard that he made Rabbi Yohanan one of his most trusted advisors. But the other advisors were very envious and longed to see Yohanan's downfall.

Now the king was unmarried, and his advisors urged him to marry so that he would have an heir.

"Give me three days," said the king, "and then I will tell you my answer."

On the second day, the king went into the garden to meditate on this matter of choosing a queen. As he sat lost in thought, a raven flew overhead and dropped a single strand of golden hair that landed at the king's feet.

The next day the king came to his advisors and declared, "I shall marry the woman whose hair matches this golden strand. If you fail to find her, you shall all lose your heads."

The advisors consulted together and agreed that only Rabbi Yohanan had the wisdom to do what the king asked. So they sent him to the king.

As Rabbi Yohanan approached the palace, a large raven flew overhead and cawed, "May God save you from the evil fortune that will befall you!" How astonished Rabbi Yohanan was to hear from the raven's mouth the very words once spoken to him by the scorpion! How his heart hammered with dread!

The king said to him, "You are the wisest of my counselors, Rabbi Yohanan.Therefore I charge you with the task of finding the woman whose hair matches this golden strand. She is the only one who shall be my queen."

"This is a most difficult thing you ask of me," protested Rabbi Yohanan. "Who ever heard of finding a woman by a single hair?"

"Nevertheless," said the king, "this is your task. If you fail, you and all your people shall perish."

"Very well," said Rabbi Yohanan, "I will do what you ask. But I shall need three years to find her." And the king agreed.

Rabbi Yohanan packed three loaves of bread and ten gold coins and set out for the forest, where he had last seen the scorpion. First he came upon a huge dog who was howling in great distress.

"What ails you, my friend?" asked Rabbi Yohanan.

"For many days have I wandered here with nothing to fill my belly," complained the dog. "I shall die if I do not eat soon!"

So Rabbi Yohanan gave him one of his loaves of bread.

In one bite, the dog gobbled down the whole loaf. "May God redeem you from the many troubles you will soon encounter!" he cried. "And may I find a way to repay you for your kindness." Then he ran off into the forest.

A short while later, Rabbi Yohanan met a giant raven whimpering in pain.

"What ails you, my friend?" asked Rabbi Yohanan.

"I have not eaten in many days," cawed the raven. "I am near death."

So Rabbi Yohanan gave him the second loaf of bread. The raven wolfed it down greedily, then said, "You will not regret this, kind sir. Someday I will do you a favor in return." And flapping his great black wings, he flew off.

Soon Rabbi Yohanan came to a river, where he saw a fisherman casting for fish. Fearing that he would lose his last loaf of bread, Rabbi Yohanan quickly ate it and then drank some water from the river.

The fisherman cried out to him, "Will you buy the first fish that swims into my net?"

"How much will you charge me?" asked Rabbi Yohanan.

"Those ten gold coins in your pocket," answered the fisherman.

Rabbi Yohanan thought to himself, "How did he know what was in my pocket? This must be a sign from God!" So he agreed to pay the fisherman the ten gold coins for the first fish snared in his net.

Moments later, when the fisherman hauled in his net and cast the flapping fish within it upon the bank, he gasped in astonishment. Never in all his years of fishing had he caught a fish even half this big!

The fish now spoke to Rabbi Yohanan, saying, "Kind sir, you can see that I am too big to eat or carry. Please throw me back into the river. I promise to return the favor someday. And may God save you from the evil fortune that will soon befall you!"

Rabbi Yohanan did what the fish asked. When the fisherman saw this, he cried out in anger, "That fish was worth one hundred gold coins, yet you threw it back!"

"God has mercy over all creatures," answered Rabbi Yohanan, and he continued on his way.

Soon he saw a magnificent city rising on the opposite bank of the river. At the river's edge he saw a young woman standing. By her royal bearing and gleaming golden hair, Rabbi Yohanan knew that she was the woman he sought.

When she saw Rabbi Yohanan looking at her, the young queen with the golden hair called the ferryman nearby and said to him, "There stands a holy man who wishes to take me to marry a wicked king. A raven stole a strand of my hair and carried it to this king, and now he has sent this holy man to bring me back. If he can pass three tests, I will go with him. Now bring him to me."

So the ferryman brought Rabbi Yohanan to her and she said to him, "Why have you come here?"

"To find the woman whose hair matches this strand," answered Rabbi Yohanan. "The king of my country wishes to marry her."

"I am she whom you seek," answered the queen. "Stay here one month, and I will give you my answer."

So Rabbi Yohanan stayed in her kingdom for one month. During his time he was treated like a prince, receiving dainties from the royal table and being attended by the queen's own servants.

At the end of the month, the queen summoned him to her and said, "I will now go with you if you can perform three tasks for me. Here are two empty barrels. Fill one with water from the Garden of Eden and the other with water from Gehenna. Then bring them back to me."

"What human being can do such a thing?" cried Rabbi Yohanan.

"If you do not do what I ask," said the queen, "I will not go with you."

"Very well," sighed Rabbi Yohanan. "I will try, for if I do not, my people will surely perish."

The ferryman took Rabbi Yohanan back across the river. He sat down upon a fallen tree and began to weep.

"God of the Universe!" he cried. "Send me the raven who once promised to help me!"

Instantly the raven flew down to him and said, "The Lord has heard your cries and answered them. Command what you will and I will perform the deed."

"Here are two barrels," said Rabbi Yohanan. "Take one to Gehenna and fill it with water from the river there. Then take the other to Eden and fill it with water from the river there. Then bring them back to me."

With the barrels dangling around its neck, the raven flew off. First it came to Gehenna. As it swooped low to scoop up water from the river, it narrowly missed being burned to death from the stinking fumes rising from the boiling foam.

Then it flew to Eden, where it bathed in the perfumed waters of the river before filling the other barrel. This water instantly healed its feathers and skin, which had been blistered and singed by the vapors rising from Gehenna's river.

Both barrels filled, the raven flew back to the forest where Rabbi Yohanan anxiously awaited its return.

He presented the barrels to the queen and said to her, "See for yourself whether I have accomplished that which you asked of me."

The queen smelled the evil stench of the waters of Gehenna and the sweet fragrance of Eden and knew that Rabbi Yohanan had indeed succeeded in his task.

"There is yet one more task I ask of you," she now said to him. "Twenty-five years ago my father gave me a ring set with the most beautiful stone. But one day when I was walking by the river, it fell from my hand and was lost. Bring me that ring, or I will not accompany you to your king."

"Twenty-five years is a long time!" cried Rabbi Yohanan. "Who could ever hope to find such a small thing in such a vast place after so many years?"

"Nevertheless, if you do not bring it to me, I will not go with you."

So Rabbi Yohanan went to the place on the riverbank where he had thrown back the huge fish and sat down to pray, "God of all Creation! Once I did a good deed for a fellow creature and it promised to help me someday. Send me that fish!"

Instantly the great fish thrust its head out of the water and said, "I myself do not have the queen's ring, but I know who does. I shall summon this fish before Leviathan for judgment."

So the great fish went to the fish who had swallowed the queen's ring and brought him before the King of Fishes. He told Leviathan all about Rabbi Yohanan's trials, and Leviathan ordered the other fish to surrender the ring. Then the great fish swam back to Rabbi Yohanan and spat the ring out upon the bank.

But before Rabbi Yohanan could pick it up, a wild pig came charging out of the forest and swallowed the ring. At that moment the huge dog to whom Rabbi Yohanan had given his first loaf of bread sprang out from behind a tree and tore the pig to pieces. Then he seized the ring in his teeth and dropped it at Rabbi Yohanan's feet.

Rabbi Yohanan brought it to the queen, and together they set out for the palace of the wicked king.

When Rabbi Yohanan reached his home, he discovered that in the three years he had been gone, his wife had died and his children had been robbed of all they had and had been sold into slavery by the envious ministers. So he found the children and ransomed them and clothed them and gave them food. Then he brought the golden-haired queen to the king.

"Let us marry at once!" cried the king when he saw her.

"In my country we do not marry so hastily," said the queen. "Give me a year to prepare myself with incense and oils. Then we shall be wed."

And the king agreed.

The king wished to reward Rabbi Yohanan for bringing his bride to him, so he elevated him above all the other ministers and gave him his signet ring. The other ministers envied him more than ever and plotted his downfall. One day when he was out walking, they fell upon him and cut him to pieces. When the queen heard of this, she was very distressed, for Rabbi Yohanan had become dear to her heart. She found his mutilated body, reassembled the pieces, and then touched them with the stone in her ring. Instantly the pieces knit themselves together into a whole, even more handsome and youthful than before. Then she poured upon his head some water from Eden, and immediately his skin flushed with life, and he began to breathe again.

When the king and his ministers heard of this they

said, "Let us now make war on all our enemies, for if we die, the queen can bring us back to life."

So they marched off to war and all but one servant were killed in battle. This servant came to the queen and said, "My lords are all dead! Come restore them to life!"

So the queen reassembled the pieces and touched them with her ring, and they all became whole. But instead of pouring water from Eden upon them, she sprinkled them with the waters of Gehenna, and they were all instantly burnt to ashes.

Then she said to the people of the kingdom, "It is not I who restore the dead to life but God. It is not right that the wicked should receive the same reward as the righteous."

Then the people made Rabbi Yohanan their king, and the golden-haired queen became his wife. And they lived a long and happy life together, ruling their kingdom with justice and wisdom.

211
The Serpent Prince

Once a poor, pious orphan had a dream:

An old man appeared and gave him a diamond and said to him, "You will sell this diamond and become rich. Then you will marry and have a beautiful daughter whom you must cherish, for you will one day have to give her up in exchange for this jewel." Then the old man vanished, and the boy awoke from his dream.

Everything happened as the dream foretold. The boy found a diamond in his hand when he awoke. He sold it and became a merchant, wandering from town to town selling his wares. In time he married and had a daughter.

One day when he was walking through the forest, a serpent suddenly appeared in his path. Although he was terrified, the merchant found that his feet were rooted to the spot. A voice now addressed him from somewhere above his head, saying, "Promise to marry me to your daughter, or this serpent in your path will kill you."

Trembling with fear, the merchant agreed. Suddenly the serpent vanished, and the merchant's feet were freed from their mysterious paralysis. Without a backward glance, he rushed home to tell his wife and daughter what had happened.

As he neared the edge of the forest, the voice rang out again and said, "If you fail to keep your oath, you will surely die!"

When he returned home, he found to his dismay that his beautiful house and garden were gone, replaced by a miserable hovel. His wife and daughter stood in rags to greet him, and he noticed that his own rich clothes were likewise reduced to tatters. Then the merchant remembered the dream of his youth: The old man's prophecy had come true.

Many months later, there was a knock at the door of the poor cottage, and when the merchant opened it, he found a giant serpent standing before him. His shining scales and fiery eyes were terrible to look upon, and he stood as tall as a man upon the threshold.

"I am the one to whom you promised your daughter," the serpent declared.

"I would rather die than hand her over to a monster!" cried the merchant.

But the daughter gladly offered herself to the serpent in order to save her father's life, and the father reluctantly agreed. Then the serpent and his beautiful young bride went into the other room in the house and locked the door. As soon as the door was shut, the serpent shook himself and shed his serpent's skin. How astonished the daughter was to find a handsome young man standing before her!

"If you wish to be my wife, you must not tell anyone, not even your parents, what you have seen here," he warned her. "I will leave you each morning, but will return to you each night."

The next morning, the parents approached the locked room with dread. Surely their daughter had not survived the night! To their surprise, she emerged from the room, radiant and singing. But when they plied her with questions, she refused to disclose to them what had happened on her wedding night nor where her bridegroom had gone.

Day after day, they pleaded with her to tell them the secret of her serpent husband, until finally she relented and told them of his strange metamorphosis each night. That night her husband appeared to her as he had first come: in a serpent's skin.

"You have broken your word, and therefore I must leave you," he said to her in a voice filled with great sadness. "Do not try to look for me, for you will not find me." And with that, he vanished.

Heartbroken, the daughter locked herself in her room and refused to be comforted. She began to pine away, and her parents feared for her life.

One day a young neighbor girl was playing with her doll when a dog came along and snatched it from her hand. She chased after the dog but could not catch up with it. Suddenly a fox leapt out from behind a rock, and the dog dropped the doll to pursue the fox. But when the child ran up to find the doll, she found only the yawning mouth of some animal's burrow.

Thinking that the doll must have fallen into the burrow, she climbed down into it and soon came upon a huge underground cavern in the midst of which stood a magnificent palace. She went inside the palace and found a table richly set with food and drink, but there was no one there.

Just as she was about to eat something from the table, she heard a sound. She hid under the bed nearby and saw a huge, glittering serpent slither into the room. She was about to scream when the serpent shook himself and shed his skin. How amazed she was to see standing before her a handsome youth dressed in velvet clothes befitting a prince!

The young man ate his dinner and then knelt down to pray. Never in her life had she heard such a strange prayer: "I pray that a young woman will come here soon, burn my skin, and release me from my curse."

Then the young man picked up his skin, tossed it out the window, and lay down upon the bed. When she was certain that he was asleep, the girl came out of hiding and crept nearer for a closer look. There in the young prince's hand was a handkerchief that she recognized as belonging to the young woman who lived next door. Without making a sound, she hurried out of the burrow and ran to her neighbor to tell her what she had discovered.

The next day the two of them went back to the burrow and hid under the bed until the prince had eaten his dinner and fallen asleep. Then the merchant's daughter seized the serpent's skin, ran outside the palace, and burned it until only ashes remained.

The next morning when the young prince awoke, he was astonished to find himself still a man. He turned around and saw his bride standing beside him. Joyously he embraced her and said, "Once I was the son of a king, but my mother died and my father married a wicked woman who turned me into a serpent so that her own son could be king after my father's death. Now that you have burned my skin, the spell has been broken, and the evil witch has herself been reduced to ashes."

The couple returned home and rejoiced with the girl's parents. That night the merchant had a dream: The old man who had first given him the diamond returned and now absolved him of his earlier vow.

In time the king of the country died, and the young couple became the new king and queen. Together they ruled wisely and well, performing many acts of charity and bringing honor to their parents' name.

212
The Werewolf and the Ring

There once was a pious rabbi who performed many deeds of charity. He gave generously to the poor and also supported a *yeshivah*, where he raised up many children to a life of Torah. But his wife was as mean-spirited as he was kind.

In time the rabbi gave away all of his money. So poor did he become that he could no longer give charity nor support the students in the *yeshivah*.

"Surely I am being punished for some sin I have committed," he thought. "It is best that I leave this town, for I can no longer do any good here."

So he gathered together fifty of his students and told them of his plan to leave. They insisted on going with him, offering to share their few pennies with him so that they could buy food along the way. That night they slipped out of town secretly, so that nobody knew where they had gone.

Wherever they went they were received with great honor, for the people could see that the rabbi was a holy man and that his students were devoted to him. But after a year of wandering, their clothes became ragged and their faces gaunt. Finally their money ran out, and they were forced to beg for their meals. People began turning them away, fearing they were vagabonds.

One day the fifty students said to the rabbi, "Master, for a year we have followed you from town to town, learning from you and sharing with you all that we had. But we can no longer continue this way. We wish to return home to our parents' houses and marry."

"Stay with me only until after the Sabbath," said the rabbi. "Then you are free to return home." And the students agreed to do what the rabbi asked.

On Friday morning they came to a small wood, where they stopped to study Torah together. The rabbi walked into the wood to find a stream in which to wash. As he was bending over the water, he saw a small weasel run by with a gold ring in its mouth. He chased after the weasel until it dropped the ring. When he picked it up, he saw an inscription engraved on the gold band: "Although I seem unworthy, my value is priceless."

The rabbi knew at once that this was a magic ring. So he said, "I wish that I had a purse filled with gold coins." Instantly a purse appeared before him.

He ran back to his students and said to them, "In the town nearby I have a rich friend who will surely lend me the money to buy you new clothes and send you on your way with full stomachs."

So they went to the nearest town, and the rabbi bought them all fine clothes and enough food for a magnificent feast. Then he bought a coach fit for a prince and said to them, "Let us now return home, for my rich friend has lent me enough money so that I can once again support my *yeshivah* and give charity to the poor."

As they made their way home, they were received with much honor by the very people who had closed their doors to them when they had been destitute. Finally they reached their own town and were welcomed with joy and celebration.

The rabbi's wife was astonished to see her husband's rich clothes and stately coach. "How did you become so rich?" she asked. "When you left, you were but a poor man."

The rabbi refused to tell her the secret of the ring, for he knew that she would try to use it for evil gain. But she begged and cried so bitterly that at last he showed it to her. As soon as she slipped it on her finger, she said, "I wish my husband were a werewolf, running through the forest with the wild beasts."

Instantly the rabbi disappeared from the house and found himself in the forest, covered with fur and snarling with rage. From that day on he ran wild among the trees, devouring beasts and terrorizing the charcoal-burners who came to the forest to gather fuel. Soon no one ventured into the forest, except one charcoal-burner who befriended the werewolf and shared his poor hut with him.

Then the king of the country offered a reward to anyone who could kill or capture the werewolf: the hand of the princess and the throne after his death. The next day a young knight stepped forward and declared that he would try his hand at the task.

Deep in the heart of the forest, the knight came upon the hut of the charcoal-burner who had befriended the werewolf and asked him where the beast was.

"Do not try to fight him," warned the man, "for he will surely kill you!"

But the knight refused to heed the charcoal-burner's warning. When the werewolf returned to the hut that evening, the knight raised his sword to pierce him through. Enraged, the beast sprang into the air to tear his throat, but the charcoal-burner drove him back. Once again the knight raised his sword and again the werewolf rushed forward to tear him to pieces, but as before the charcoal-burner drove him back.

Now the werewolf was trembling with rage, and he rushed forward and sank his teeth into the knight's leg. As he prepared to meet his death, the knight turned his eyes toward heaven, asking God to save him from the wolf's jaws and promising not to harm him. Instantly the werewolf released the knight and began wagging his tail, as friendly as any house dog. The two started off through the forest, the werewolf trotting on ahead, acting as the knight's guide through the treacherous woods. When wild beasts threatened to attack them, the werewolf tore them to pieces. When a hare or fox crossed their path, the werewolf caught it and brought it to the knight for his supper.

When they reached the palace, everyone was amazed to see the ferocious beast so tame and so devoted to the knight. They wished to kill it, but the knight said, "This beast has saved my life many times and has provided me with food. If you do not try to harm him, he will not harm you."

True to his word, the old king gave the knight his daughter's hand in marriage, and when the old king died, the knight became the king in his place. All this time he kept the wolf with him as a pet, and they often went hunting together in the forest.

One winter's day they set off to hunt for game. The werewolf ran on ahead and disappeared from sight. When the king found him, he was digging in the snow with one paw, forming words in some strange language that the king did not recognize. But one of the king's advisors recognized the writing as Hebrew and translated the message to be, "O King, remember all the kindnesses I have shown you, sparing your life when you tried to take mine and protecting you from wild beasts. I have a wife who has put a curse on me by means of a magic ring. I beg you to go to my town and get the ring back so that I can become a human being again. Do it for the sake of our friendship," and the werewolf then showed him a sign by which to recognize the ring.

The king now disguised himself as a merchant and came to the town mentioned in the werewolf's message. He asked where he might buy some gold rings.

"The rabbi's wife is the only one wealthy enough to have such things," they told him. And they showed him where she lived.

All this time, the rabbi's wife had used the ring to make herself fabulously wealthy, but she had shared none of her wealth with the people of the town. Whenever they asked her where her husband was, she told them, "He has gone away for four years. He will return as he did the last time."

The king came to her house and asked to see her rings. When she brought them out, his eyes almost leapt out of his head. Never in his life had he seen such exquisite stones! Diamonds, rubies, emeralds, and sapphires beyond compare! Then he recognized the ring he was seeking. He asked to buy it, but the woman refused to sell. So he bought two other rings, and when the wife was not looking, he slipped the magic ring onto his finger. Then he paid her and left. Only after he was gone did she realize what had happened, and she tore her hair and wept bitterly over her loss.

The king brought the ring back to the werewolf and slipped it on one of his claws. Suddenly before him stood a naked man, whom the king immediately covered with his cloak. All the courtiers and nobles were amazed at the transformation, and they shrank back from fear. But the rabbi assured them that he was only a man who had been changed into a wild beast by magic. He did not tell them the real secret of the ring, for then the king would have surely kept it for himself.

Then the rabbi bade farewell to his benefactor and returned home. As he approached the town, he grabbed hold of the ring and said, "I wish that my wife were a donkey, standing in the stable and eating from a trough."

When his students saw him, they rushed up to him and asked him where he had been all this time. But he said, "If you wish to be kind to me, do not ask me."

Then he asked them, "Where is my wife?" although he knew very well that she was in the stable.

They said to him, "When we heard you had returned, we ran to tell her the news, but she was nowhere to be found."

"She will return," said the rabbi, "in due time."

From that day on, the rabbi resumed his former life, giving generously to the poor, supporting the *yeshivah*, and teaching his students. After a time he held a banquet for all the people of the town. The tables groaned under the weight of so much food. At the conclusion of the meal the rabbi announced, "Since God has been so good to me, I am taking a vow to build a new synagogue here. My donkey shall carry all the stones to build it."

How hard the donkey labored to carry the stones for the new synagogue! She lost her sleekness and her belly and became as scrawny as a plucked chicken. Her thin legs barely supported her own weight. But she could not complain to anyone, because donkeys are but dumb beasts.

When the synagogue was complete, the rabbi held another banquet to which he invited all of his wife's relatives. At the end of this meal, he announced that he had put a curse upon his wife and turned her into a donkey for the rest of her life. His wife's relatives begged him to undo the curse, but he refused. In time the rabbi died and his wealth passed on to his children. But the magic ring disappeared, and the rabbi's wife remained a donkey all her life.

As they say, many a person digs a pit for others and falls into it herself.

213
The Golem of Prague

In the city of Worms lived a righteous and holy man named Rabbi Bezalel. At that time the Christians of the city made life very bitter for the Jews, for every year at Passover time, they falsely accused them of killing Christian boys and using their blood to make *matzah*. So enraged did the Christian population become at their own slander that no Jew was safe at this season, and the Jews of the city felt as oppressed as their ancestors had in the days of Pharaoh.

On the first night of Passover in the Jewish year 5273 (1513 C.E.), Rabbi Bezalel's wife felt labor pains come upon her in the middle of the *seder*. The guests ran out into the street of the Jewish Quarter to fetch a midwife and suddenly came upon several people carrying a dead Christian child in a sack with the intention of leaving his body on a Jewish doorstep. Realizing that their evil plot was now uncovered, the troublemakers ran off in panic, taking the body with them. Thus miraculously a blood libel was averted.

That night a son was born to Rabbi Bezalel and his wife, and they called him Yehudah Lavi, which means Judah the Young Lion. For his father said, "Like the first Judah he will feed on prey and save us from our enemies."

Judah grew up and became a saintly and learned rabbi known as the Maharal. Eventually he moved to Prague, where he continued his studies in the Torah and the Talmud as well as the Holy Mysteries. During this time, too, the Jews of Prague like the Jews of Worms, suffered from constant threats of blood libel, and Judah finally decided to ask God for help.

That night he conjured up a dream. In it a verse was revealed to him containing ten Hebrew words in alphabetical order: "Create a Golem of Clay, Destroy Those Tearing Israel's Heart."

After seven days of fasting and prayer, on the twentieth of Adar 5340 (1580 C.E.), Rabbi Judah took with him his son-in-law Yitzhak Katz and his disciple Yaakov Sasson and went at night to the banks of the Moldau. Out of the river clay he fashioned a man lying on his back, and on the creature's tongue he placed a slip of paper on which was written the Unutterable Name of God. On his forehead he wrote the Hebrew word *Emet*, meaning Truth.

Then Yitzhak walked around the clay figure counterclockwise seven times, reciting mystical combinations of letters, and the body began to glow like burning coals. Then Yaakov walked around seven times, reciting other combinations of letters, and the fire died down and mists rose from the clay, and hair and nails sprouted on the body. Then Rabbi Judah himself walked around seven times, and they all recited, "And God breathed into him the breath of life," and the creature began to breathe and opened its eyes. But it could not speak.

Then the Maharal commanded him, saying, "Stand up," and he did. They dressed him in servant's clothes and took him home. As three they had come; as four they returned.

The creature became the Maharal's servant. People

called him "golem," meaning simpleton, but the Maharal called him Joseph, after the half-demon, half-man in the Talmud who had so often come to the aid of the rabbis. Joseph's powers were extraordinary: He was as strong as ten men, invulnerable to fire or flood, and could become invisible.

Time after time Thaddeus, the evil priest of Prague, tried to destroy the Jews, but the Maharal always sent his golem to save them. Invisible and indestructible, Joseph thwarted all plots of blood libel and personally brought the offenders to justice. He also discovered Thaddeus's ruse to kidnap and convert a young Jewess and stole her back before Thaddeus could carry out his plan.

But always the Maharal worried that someone would discover the golem's secret or misuse his powers. He repeatedly warned his wife not to call upon Joseph to do household tasks. But once she sent him to the river to fetch water for the Sabbath. How pleased she was when he returned moments later with two brimming buckets. But she did not know how to stop him, and Joseph continued to fetch water until they were all in danger of perishing in a flood. Only the Maharal's timely return saved them from drowning.

Another time she sent Joseph to catch fish, and again he took her literally at her word. Soon the entire household was slithering in fins and scales, and only the Maharal's intervention saved them from suffocation.

And then, at last, the golem's mission was at an end. After many years of persecution, King Rudolph took pity on the Jews of Prague and issued a decree forbidding any more blood libels against them. That year Passover was celebrated without incident, and the Jews began to breathe easier.

A few weeks later the Maharal commanded Joseph to go up to the attic of the synagogue and lie down there among the old prayerbooks and *tallesim*. Two hours later the Maharal, accompanied by his disciples Yitzhak and Yaakov, went up to the attic and found Joseph lying there asleep.

Now they performed a ceremony to take back from

the golem the life they had once give him. Each of them walked seven times clockwise around Joseph's sleeping body, reciting the mystical combinations of letters in reverse. Then the Maharal removed the slip of paper from Joseph's mouth and erased the first letter on his forehead, changing *emet* to *met*, meaning "dead."

And then the golem was no more. Instead, at their feet lay a lifeless lump of clay in the figure of a man. They removed the golem's clothes and burned them, then covered up the body with two old prayer shawls. The next day the Maharal announced that his servant Joseph had run away in a fit of rage. He also issued a decree that no one must ever again go into the synagogue attic for fear of starting a fire among the old prayerbooks.

Some say that the *shammash* of the synagogue, Abraham Hayim, overhearing what happened that night, later snuck into the attic and brought the lifeless body of the golem to the home of his son-in-law Ascher, a cabalist, asking him to use his mystical powers to revive the creature. But immediately after this, a plague broke out in Prague that killed two of Ascher's children. So they placed both children in one coffin and the body of the still lifeless golem in the other and buried this second coffin on Gallows Hill near the Neistaedter Gate, where it rests to this day.

Others say the golem will come to life again only when the Messiah comes, not as the Joseph of the Maharal or the Joseph of the ancient rabbis, but as yet a third miraculous creature, to do God's will on earth.

8. FOX FABLES

Berechiah ben Natronai HaNakdan, also known as Benedictus le Puncteur or Blessed the Punctuator, was a Jewish scribe who lived in France at the end of the twelfth and beginning of the thirteenth centuries. Drawing from the fables of Marie de France and the Latin Romulus *collection, both based upon the tales of Aesop, as well as from the Persian* Kalila and Dimna *fables, he wrote his own Jewish version called "Fox Fables" (Mishle Shualim), recounting his tales in biblical Hebrew and drawing traditional moral lessons for the reader's instruction.*

214
The Dog, the Cheese, and the Water

What does not supply a need gives no pleasure; the eye is not satisfied with merely looking.

Once a dog seized a piece of cheese in the house and ran with it until he came to a bridge. Looking down into the water, he saw the reflection of the cheese in his own mouth and thought, "If only I had that cheese, too! Two pieces are better than one."

But when he opened his mouth to seize the second piece, the first fell out and sank to the bottom of the stream. He tumbled in after it, but when he emerged, he had nothing in his mouth but mud and weeds.

So taught the wise Solomon: Be happy with what you have in your hand and your possession, and do not envy what is another's.

215
The Wolf and the Crane

If one serves a sinner, it is reward enough simply to escape in one piece.

A wolf once got a large bone stuck in his throat. He pleaded with the lion to gather together all the creatures of the forest to help him. So the lion summoned all the birds and beasts, but none would help the wolf.

"It is a trick," they said. "He seeks only an excuse to swallow us alive like the pit. It is better that we keep our distance."

But the wolf cried out to them in his distress, "Help me, please! For I fear that I will soon die!"

His pitiful cries melted their hearts.

"The crane has a long neck and a beak that is strong, sharp, and narrow," they said. "He is the one to help you."

So the wolf turned to the crane and said, "Have mercy on me, Crane! In return for this favor, I promise to give you all that I possess."

"Open your mouth *wide*," said the crane.

So the wolf opened his jaws wide. The crane thrust his long beak down the wolf's throat and plucked out the bone. Then he said to the wolf, "Where now is my reward?"

The wolf threw back his head and howled in laughter. "Whoever heard of such a thing? Was my mouth not made to destroy? What creature has ever come out of my jaws alive? Be thankful that you have escaped with your life. Now flee before I have a change of heart!"

And the crane flew away in terror.

216
The City Mouse and the Country Mouse

One who seeks great things will be tossed about and will finally cry out in bitterness.

Once a city mouse went to visit his cousin in another city. On the way he passed through a forest where some country mice were playing. For a short while he lodged with one of them, and when he was ready to return home, he invited his host to stay with him in the city.

"Better is one day in my courtyard," he said, "than a thousand here in the blast of the storm wind! In winter how will you find food when the grass withers? Come with me to the grain bins, where wheat and barley are plentiful."

So they went to Bethlehem, the "House of Bread," and entered the granaries. While they were eating, a man came and the mice ran to hide. When he was gone, the city mouse came out and resumed his eating, but the country mouse cowered in fear under a pile of straw.

"Why did you speak ill of the country?" he cried. "Better is a dry crust eaten in peace than a rich table in a house of terror. You flee in panic before every man who comes. In my place I find joy and singing, the beauty of Carmel and Sharon. In yours, only the chatter of fear."

And that day the country mouse returned home.

217
The Crow and the Fox

Great is the power of pride, even surpassing greed.

Once a crow sat in a fig tree with a piece of cheese in its mouth. A fox came under the tree and said, "Noble, handsome, and sweet bird, good, agreeable, and lovely bird, happy indeed is your mate! For you are surely the most beautiful bird in the forest! And if you were to sing, your songs would probably surpass those of all the other birds! Let us see whether your voice matches your fine bearing and plumage."

Hearing this, the crow thought to himself, "I will let him hear my voice, and he will praise me even more!"

So the crow opened his mouth to sing and the cheese fell to the ground. The fox gobbled it up and continued on his way.

218
The Lion, the Mouse, and the Snare

Better to be good and kind to all, for there are a time and occasion when every creature can return the favor.

Once a lion was sleeping in the desert when a mouse stepped on his paw and woke him.

With one slap of his mighty paw, the lion pinned the mouse by the tail and roared, "Your time has come, sinful creature! Why did you wake me?"

"I am innocent," squeaked the mouse. "I know I behaved foolishly, but I did not do it on purpose. Let your anger give way to loving-kindness. Why should a mighty king bother to crush a vile mouse?"

The mouse's wise words softened the lion's heart, and he let him go.

"You will not be sorry," said the mouse as it ran off. "One day I will repay you for your kindness."

The lion laughed at the mouse's bold boast and went back to sleep.

It came to pass at midnight at the season when the lions roar that the lion fell into a hunter's snare. The more he tried to escape, the more entangled he became.

The mouse heard him roaring and rushed to his aid.

"Here I am, Mouse!" cried the lion when he saw the tiny creature standing outside the net. "Help me!"

"The time has come to repay your kindness," said the mouse. "I shall call my brothers and sisters to sever your bonds."

The mice came flocking in great numbers and gnawed the strands of the net with their sharp teeth. As soon as the lion was free, he bounded back to his lair, unharmed.

As the sages teach: At times a giant may be strangled by a fly.

219
The Cicada and the Ant

Rid yourself of laziness, and you shall not suffer want.

A cicada once came to an ant to ask for food for the winter.

The ant refused, saying, "All summer long you slept and did not prepare for the hard times to come. What a fool I would be to give you the food I worked so hard to gather!"

The cicada answered, "All summer long I learned to sing songs to chase the sorrows from my heart. All the creatures who listened told me my songs were sweet! But now the winds of winter chill my heart."

"Then go to the house of the rich man," said the ant, "and sing to him when you are hungry! For to me your songs are but vain gusts of wind. Leave me in peace! Because I have no sweet voice nor any strength, I have filled my tent with good things. But you foolishly basked in your vanity. And now when the north wind blows, you will find no sustenance in your songs. For slumber will always awake to find itself in tatters and laziness in the rags of death."

220
The Mouse Seeks a Wife

If you run after honor and power, they will quickly flee from you.

A mouse wished to marry, but he desired a wife of rare virtue—whose beauty was without equal, whose body required no food, and whose heart would not pursue him when he went wandering.

First he went to the sun and said, "With everlasting love have I loved you. I will betroth you unto me."

The sun replied, "Just hours ago my face was darkened by the night. For the sun forever rises and sets. It is far better that you take a wife from your mother's kin and birthplace."

"No," said the mouse, "it is you I wish to wed."

"Always does the cloud conceal me," said the sun. "Go to her. She will not turn her face from you."

So the mouse went to the cloud. "This day have I labored and found my beloved, my beautiful one, my perfect one," declared the mouse. "By the sun's counsel I take you and will never forsake you."

"The One who watches upon the height of heights placed me in the power of the wind," replied the cloud, "and the wind shifts me east, west, north, and south. If you wed me, you will forever be a wanderer upon the earth. Forsake the handmaiden and take the mistress: Go to the wind."

So the mouse went to the wind in the desert. "Be not ashamed to marry a lowly creature like me," he said. "For you will be mine and I yours."

"Only a fool would marry me," said the wind, "for my breath is powerless against the wall. Go to her, for she will be your fortress in time of distress."

So the mouse went to the wall. "I come to you by the counsel of the Sun and the Cloud and the Wind," said the mouse, "and I will betroth myself to you in loving-kindness and mercy."

"Not out of loving-kindness do you come but out of scorn—to mock me!" lamented the wall. "For although I am a wall and my breasts are like towers, the mice have made a hundred holes in my side! I can no more hold them back than a sieve can hold back water. If you wish to marry a worthy bride, go to the mice and wed one of them!"

So the mouse returned to his mother's birthplace and married one of his own kin. And his heart filled with joy at his good fortune.

221
The Sun, the Wind, and the Man

The wise achieve more by their wisdom than the strong by their strength.

Once the Sun and the Wind had an argument about who was stronger.

The Sun claimed, "Because of my innocence and beauty, I have been made ruler of the day. Mine is the glory and the splendor, and I am like heaven itself in purity."

The Wind replied, "At night you are no lónger seen, but I rule both day and night. My deeds are known throughout the land. I split mountains and shatter rocks. Surely I am stronger than you!"

Just then a man came by.

"Let the man decide," said the Sun. "Whoever can make him remove his coat will be lord over the other."

First the Wind blew, but the man only wrapped his coat more tightly around himself. And when the Wind blew harder, the man tied the loops of his garment together and covered his head with his shirt. Soon the Wind grew weary and abandoned his efforts.

Then the Sun cast off his robe of darkness and gazed down upon the man with a steady eye. In a short time the man flung off his garments and fled naked from his sight.

222
Two Apes and a Lion

When the deceitful are full of envy, each arouses hatred in the other.

Two apes once came before their king, the lion, each seeking a gift. Knowing how envious they were of each other, the lion said to them, "I will give you what you ask on one condition: One of you must first whisper his request in my ear, and the other must remain silent. I will grant the first one's request, and then double it for the second, to reward him for his restraint."

The first ape said to himself, "I will remain silent, for that way I will gain twice as much as my fellow." And he stood before the king with sealed lips.

Then the second ape said in his heart, "I am even more clever than he. For I will turn his desire for gain into evil."

So he leaned toward the lion and whispered in his ear, "Your majesty, honor now your vow. I wish to have one of my eyes put out."

The lion replied, "So be it according to your will."

And he pierced the first ape's eye with his claw, then put out both of the other ape's eyes.

And so they both received just rewards for their guile.

223
The Lion, the Man, the Pit, and the Snake

The time is short, the work much, and the master of the house is pressing.

Along a path, a lion lay in wait for passersby. A man saw the lion, heard its roar, and fled to an empty pit. There he found spikes lining the walls of the pit, and he clung to them, feeling himself safe. But then he noticed a poisonous serpent at the bottom of the pit.

"I shall climb out as soon as the lion departs," he thought.

Then two rats, one white and the other black, emerged from a hole in the wall of the pit and began gnawing at the spikes under the man's feet.

"Alas for the lion! Alas for the serpent! Alas for the rats! Alas for hunger and thirst!" cried the man. "There is but one step between me and death!"

Then God brought forth honey from the rock walls of the pit, and the man ate it and forgot what was above and below him.

Suddenly the rats bit through the spikes, and the man plunged to the serpent below. Never again did he see his family and friends, and his home knew him no more.

The lion that lies in wait is death, and the pit is the world. We are all strangers here in this world, but each of us feels at home. The evil inclination in our hearts is the serpent. The white rat is the day, the black rat the night: Together they combine to consume us utterly.

But we do not perceive our end. The honey that is the pleasure in this world beguiles us. The wise say, "The pleasure of this world is poison smeared over with honey. Therefore, I give thanks and praise to my Creator for all that I have. Those who do not do as I do know only trouble and confusion."

224
The Stag and the Dogs

He who boasts of great might will fall, and no one will help him.

Once a stag went to drink at a stream, and he saw his antlers reflected in the water.

"Who can compare with me on account of my great horns?" he thought. "They are perfect in grace and beauty, like stairs ascending to the heavens. If anyone quarrels with me, I can gore him and prevail!"

Just then a pack of hunting dogs sprang upon him. The stag fled in terror, choosing to run through the dense forest instead of the high ground. As he ran, his antlers became entangled in the branches and the dogs caught him and slaughtered him.

Thus pride goes before a fall.

225
The Ape and the Leopard

Love your children equally, for if you love one more and put your hope in him, a sudden turn of fortune's wheel may tear him away.

There was once an ape who lived with two younger apes upon a rock. He loved the little one and hated the big one. One day a hungry leopard came forth to destroy them.

"While he eats one of us, the other two can escape," thought the ape. "I will surrender to him the one I hate."

So he put the little one under him and the larger one on his back, thinking to shake him off as he ran. But the one on his back held on tightly and would not let go. All this time the leopard continued to gain on them, until he was almost upon them. So he was forced to abandon the one he loved and flee with the other. And the leopard devoured the little one, and the other two escaped.

Then the older ape's heart turned to the one he had hated, and his hatred gave way to love. And he took pity on him, as a parent takes pity on the child who cares for him.

226
The Starling and the Princess

One filled with wisdom has an observant eye and an attentive ear.

Once a princess raised a starling and taught him to speak. She locked him in a golden cage and brought him to her room. But because he was not free to come and go, his heart was filled with sadness.

One day a knight came to the king and queen and asked them to guard his house and lands while he went traveling. On his way out of the palace, he passed the princess's room. From his gilded cage, the starling addressed him.

"My soul is weary from my barred prison," said the starling. "Although I have done no wrong, I was stolen from my family and shut up here among humankind. I ask that you remember me in your travels, kind sir, and if ever you see a bird like me, tell him of my plight and bring me back his reply."

The knight promised to do as the starling asked.

Near the sea, the knight saw a starling and told him of his fellow's plight. Suddenly the bird fell down and lay lifeless upon the ground. The knight threw water upon him, wrapped him in his cloak, and tried to revive him, but it was no use. The bird was dead.

The knight then went on his journey, and when he returned he told the princess's starling what had happened. The bird thanked him, and the knight returned to his home.

The next morning the princess found her bird lying dead at the bottom of his golden cage. She threw water upon him, held him in her hands, and tried all she could to revive him, but all life seemed gone from him. She wept and cast him aside upon the ground. As soon as she left the room, the starling spread his wings and flew away.

PART IX

THE HASIDIC PERIOD

In 1740 a simple peasant in Eastern Europe named Israel ben Eliezer revealed himself as a baal shem, *a wonder-worker and holy man. Within one generation, this man's religious teachings had ignited the hearts and minds of millions of Jews, resulting in one of the most remarkable mass movements in Jewish history: Hasidism. After the Baal Shem Tov's death, his disciples and their disciples spread his message of spiritual ecstasy and service of the heart throughout the communities of Eastern Europe. The primary vehicle of inspiration and instruction for these God-intoxicated Hasidim was the tale.*

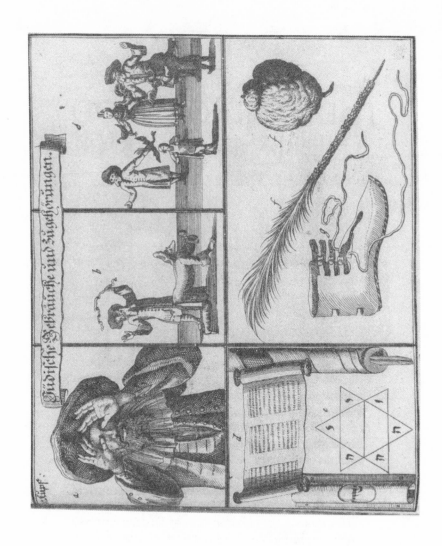

1. THE BAAL SHEM TOV

227
The Werewolf

When Rabbi Eliezer was about to die, he called his son Israel, later known as the holy *Baal Shem Tov* (Besht), to his bedside and said to him, "My son, there will come times when the Evil One will try to overpower you. He will fill the world with his terrible presence until all seems lost. But do not be afraid, for God will be with you, and you will prevail."

Then he closed his eyes and died.

After Rabbi Eliezer's death, the people of the town had compassion on the orphan Israel and tried to send him to school like all the other boys. But Israel preferred the forest and fields to the stifling schoolroom and kept running away from the stern schoolmaster, until they gave up on him and let him roam free in the wild places outside the town.

When he was twelve, he came to all the parents of the town and offered to guide their children to school each day through the woods and fields that he knew so well. And so each day Israel gathered the schoolchildren and led them back and forth to *heder*. In a short time the parents were astonished to see their pale, stoop-shouldered children running and laughing through the streets with garlands of flowers woven through their hair. Joy and song filled the town as never before.

The angels themselves took pleasure in the children's newfound joy. Their own songs of praise took on a new sweetness, and even the Divine Radiance burned brighter in the heavens.

Only one soul grew darker amidst all this light: Satan, the Evil One, who feared that his dominion on earth might suffer as a result of young Israel's influence. So he searched for a way to overpower his human adversary. He finally found it in the troubled heart of a charcoal-burner who lived in the forest near Israel's home. This charcoal-burner from time to time was overcome by fits of rage so terrible that he was transformed into a savage beast, a werewolf, who struck terror into the townspeople, although he never harmed a soul. One night when the charcoal-burner was asleep, Satan thrust his hand into the man's chest, plucked out his heart, and buried it underground. Then he enthroned his own black heart between the charcoal-burner's ribs.

When the charcoal-burner awoke, he felt overcome by such terrible despair that he tore out of his hut and raced into the forest, howling and snarling, white foam dripping from his mouth. Soon he came upon Israel and the children on their way to school, and he terrified them so utterly that many of the children that night came down with raging fevers. Fortunately Israel managed to escape with all the children unharmed, but the next day the parents refused to surrender their children to him for fear that the beast would attack again.

Then Israel remembered his dying father's words: "Do not be afraid of the Evil One, for God will be with you and you will prevail."

So he went back to the parents and pleaded with them, until at last they yielded to him. And he talked to the children, too, and convinced them that no harm would befall them in the forest.

The next morning Israel led the frightened children along the path until they reached the place in the forest where the charcoal-burner had attacked them. Suddenly out of a tangle of thorns burst the werewolf, snarling and baring his sharp white teeth. Remembering his father's words, Israel calmly approached him and reached out his hand.

Then the beast seemed to grow before his eyes, swelling into a huge black shape that blotted out the morning sun and filled the earth with darkness. Israel bravely entered the darkness and walked until he saw something glowing red, fluttering like a great wing. It was the beast's heart, and when he drew closer, Israel saw that it was filled with immeasurable sadness and pain. He reached out his hand and encircled the heart and instantly felt its fury ebb until it lay still within his hand. Then he laid it down upon the ground, which swallowed it up so that not even a trace remained. And instantly the sun returned, and the birds began to sing again.

Israel and the children continued on their way. In a clearing near the edge of the forest, they came upon the body of the charcoal-burner. How peaceful he looked in death, as if an unseen hand had smoothed the lines of his once troubled face, and a vision of heaven had filled his gaze. Israel closed his eyes, and then led the children, singing, out of the forest.

228
The Yom Kippur Flute

There once was a villager who, during the Days of Awe, used to pray in the Baal Shem Tov's synagogue. This man had a son who was such a simpleton that he could not even recognize the shapes of the letters nor recite a single prayer. Each year the man left his son home when he went to the synagogue, for he told himself, "What good will it do to bring such a fool to pray?"

But when the boy became thirteen, the age of *bar mitzvah*, his father decided to take him to synagogue on Yom Kippur, for he feared that the boy would eat out of ignorance during the fast day.

Now the boy always carried a flute with him, because he spent his days tending sheep on the mountain. This day, too, as he and his father traveled to Medzibozh, he carried the little flute in his pocket. That evening during *Kol Nidre*, he resisted many times the urge to take out the flute and play it. And all the next morning, during the long morning service, he tried to put the flute out of mind and instead concentrate on the strange black letters swimming before his eyes in the prayerbook. But when it finally came time for the *musaf* prayer, he tugged on his father's sleeve and asked if he might play a tune on his flute.

"Heaven forbid!" cried his father in alarm. "Not now!"

So the boy restrained himself. But when the time for *minhah* came, he again asked his father if he might play the flute. Again his father forbade him.

"If only I could take it away from you," said his father, "and so remove from you the temptation to sin, but I am forbidden even to touch such things today."

Still, as a precaution, he held onto the boy's pocket so that the boy could not take out the flute and play.

As the service drew to a close, the boy could no longer restrain himself. Just before the start of the concluding *Neilah* prayers, he threw off his father's hand, grabbed the flute, and blew a single powerful note upon it.

In horror the father looked toward the Baal Shem Tov, expecting to see fierce anger blazing in his eyes. But to his great surprise, the Baal Shem Tov's face was calm, and his voice betrayed no agitation as he swiftly chanted the *Neilah* prayers. Listening more closely, the father heard in the rabbi's voice a marvelous sweetness he had never heard before.

At last the service was over. As soon as the final *shofar* blast was blown, the father rushed forward to apologize for his son's improper behavior. But before he had a chance to say a word, the Baal Shem Tov smiled at him and said, "Do not be angry with your son, for the voice of his flute eased my burden. In his heart burned such purity of purpose that his prayer lifted up all the others, carrying them straight up to the gates of heaven."

229
The Baal Shem Tov and the Professor of Pozna

Once the Baal Shem Tov stayed in Brod at the house of a rich man. One day he asked the son-in-law of his host if he wished to spend the Sabbath with him in Pozna, where the son-in-law had been born and raised. The youth was delighted at the chance to visit his parents after an absence of over three years, and he obtained permission from his father-in-law to leave that Thursday.

As soon as they departed, the Gentile wagoner fell asleep at the reins, and the horse went his own way. They traveled all that day and through the night, and the next morning came to a desolate path winding through a field. The Baal Shem Tov woke the driver and asked him to draw some water from a well hidden in the tall grass.

"But it's only a few more hours until *Shabbes* begins!" cried the young man. "If we don't hurry, we will be forced to spend the holy Sabbath in a field instead of at my parents' house!"

"We will be in Pozna by *Shabbes*," calmly answered the Baal Shem Tov. Then he recited the blessing and they drank.

In a short while they were on their way again. Once more the wagoner fell asleep, and the horse proceeded on its own.

Soon they came to a ruin at the edge of a wood, and the Baal Shem Tov called to the horse to halt. Unable to restrain himself, the young man seized the rabbi by the arm.

"But the sun is almost at the treetops, Holy Master! We will never reach Pozna in time!"

Instead of answering him, the Baal Shem Tov climbed out of the wagon and knocked at the door of the ruin. Moments later an old leper came out. Although his body was covered all over with sores and bandages, his face shone with an inexpressible joy. He embraced the Baal Shem Tov and invited them all inside. Then he and the Baal Shem Tov secluded themselves in a room. A half hour later they emerged and embraced like brothers who would not see each other again for many years. Then the three travelers climbed back into the wagon, and the Baal Shem Tov ordered the driver to continue the journey.

By this time the young man had completely despaired of reaching Pozna in time for the Sabbath. When the wagoner fell asleep for the third time, he stared out over the wild countryside and resigned himself to spending the next twenty-four hours in misery. But just as the last rays of the sun were lengthening on the ground, he looked up and saw rising before him the familiar walls and buildings of Pozna.

They entered the city, and soon he saw, not a hundred feet away, his very own house and garden. As they drew nearer, he could already picture his father's joy at this unexpected visit and the shining radiance of his mother's face as she gazed upon him after such a long separation. How brightly the *Shabbes* candles would burn tonight!

But just then the wagon turned away from his street and began to take them toward the students' quarter of the city, where Jews never dared set foot. For several years ago a Jew had accidentally wandered into that part of the city and had been stoned to death. The young man's heart now filled with dread, but when he glanced over at the Baal Shem Tov, the rabbi's face showed nothing but its usual calm. In fact, it was beginning to glow with the added soul of *Shabbes*.

When they reached the students' quarter, they stopped at the only Jewish house on the street, inhabited by a tailor who made clothes for the students. The tailor was frightened to see them, but he could not turn them away on the Sabbath. Quickly he drew them inside and locked the door. In the street outside, the students, who had heard the clatter of the wagon and the horse's hooves, had already begun to gather stones and murmur against the uninvited guests.

"Have you ten for a *minyan* among your workers?" the Baal Shem Tov now asked the tailor.

"Only eight," answered the tailor.

"Then we make ten!" the Baal Shem Tov said, and he began to prepare himself for the evening prayers.

Outside, the murmuring rose to a fierce clamor. The young man glanced out of the window and saw a crowd of students gathered in the street, grasping stones and gesturing angrily toward the tailor's house.

"We are surely lost!" he thought.

But the Baal Shem Tov did not seem to notice the rising storm outside. Calmly he led the ten men in prayer. When the service was over, he opened the door and gazed steadily upon the students. Instantly they dropped their stones in terror and fled. They ran to the home of their professor and cried, "Either this man is a powerful wizard or he is a holy man of God!"

Now this professor to whom they turned in their distress was very learned in the teachings of the Jews. He spoke the Holy Tongue and knew well the Bible and the Talmud. When he heard the students' words, he went himself to the tailor's house and stood outside the door, listening to the songs and prayers of the Baal Shem Tov, but saying nothing. The next morning he returned and this time entered the house, but still he said nothing to the

Baal Shem Tov nor did the latter speak to him. All through the morning and afternoon prayers, he stood and listened, never uttering a single word, his eyes never leaving the Baal Shem Tov's face. And all who saw this marveled and were amazed, none so much as the youth from Brod.

At the Third Meal the Baal Shem Tov gave a *d'rash* on the Torah that was full of great wisdom and light and holiness. And the professor listened with special intentness but still said nothing. Then the Baal Shem Tov recited the grace after meals, prayed the evening prayer, and made *havdalah*.

As soon as the *havdalah* ceremony was over, the professor left the tailor's house without a word and returned home. The Baal Shem Tov, too, bade farewell to his host and called for the youth and wagoner to climb back into the wagon. Within the twinkling of an eye, they were back in Brod.

As soon as their journey was at an end, the young man could no longer restrain himself and demanded an explanation of all the strange events he had just witnessed.

"For I am heartsick," he said, "that I traveled all that way, even to my own threshold, yet still did not see my parents nor the house of my youth! Surely there was some purpose to our journey, some holy reason that we stopped at the well in the deserted field, visited the old leper, and spent the Sabbath with the tailor in the students' quarter."

"I shall reveal two of the secrets to you now," answered the Baal Shem Tov, "but the third will become known to you only after many days. The field where we stopped for water was the burial place of two Jews who long ago became lost and were murdered by robbers. Their souls could not ascend to heaven until another Jew passed by there and cleansed the air with a blessing.

"As for the old leper," continued the Baal Shem Tov, "know that in every generation there is a Messiah born to redeem the world. If the world proves worthy of redemption, he will reveal himself. But if not, he departs on a certain Sabbath at the Third Meal. It was made known to me that this leper was the Messiah of our generation and that he would depart at the end of this very Sabbath. I knew that he desired my company, but I did not wish to bring sighing to my Sabbath by parting from him on that day, so I met him before the Sabbath began."

"But why then did we spend *Shabbes* at the tailor's house?" cried the young man. "Surely that brought sadness and sighing to us all!"

The Baal Shem Tov only shook his head. The next day he departed the city.

In time the young man became a great scholar. After some time he said to his father-in-law, "I wish to engage in commerce, for it is good to combine study with worldly things."

So his father-in-law gave him some money, and he traveled to Germany to buy merchandise. He came to a certain city on the eve of the Sabbath and asked if there was a holy rabbi in that city.

"Indeed there is," they told him, "Abraham the True Proselyte, a saintly and learned man famous throughout this region."

So the young man went to the home of this saintly rabbi and spent the Sabbath with him. He was amazed at the extent of the man's wisdom and the depth of his understanding.

At the Third Meal, the rabbi began to deliver a *d'rash* on the Torah, and the youth recognized it as the same one he had heard in Pozna many years before.

"Where did you learn that *d'rash*?" he asked the rabbi.

"Have you heard it before?" replied the rabbi.

"Yes," answered the young man. "I heard it from the lips of the Baal Shem Tov himself!"

Suddenly the rabbi's hands began to tremble, and his face became very pale. "Are you the young man who accompanied the Holy Master to Pozna on that Sabbath in the students' quarter?"

"I am he," replied the youth.

"Then I shall reveal to you that I am the professor who stood silently listening to the Baal Shem Tov during that Sabbath. So holy were his prayers, so inspiring his songs, that I was unable to tear myself away from his presence for even a moment. And when I heard his *d'rash* at the Third Meal, I was moved to repent of all the evil in my heart and forsake my former ways. His journey to Pozna was all for my sake, to redeem the sparks of my soul and bring me under the wings of the *Shekhinah*. For after his visit, I fled my home and became a proselyte here. Whenever I have honored guests, I share this *d'rash* with them, for it was this teaching that redeemed me."

And thus the youth discovered the third secret of his journey to Pozna with the holy Baal Shem Tov.

230
Two Socks on One Foot

Once there was a man who used to sin without remorse. On Rosh Hashanah every year, at the time of *Tashlikh*, he would take his sins to the lake in a sack and cast them away. Then he would go back to his sinning.

Now this man and his wife, who was a saintly woman, had no children. So they came to the Baal Shem Tov and asked him to intercede for a child. Because of his wife's good deeds, the Baal Shem Tov agreed to do so. A year later the woman bore a healthy baby boy.

With a heart full of joy, the man returned to the Baal Shem Tov to thank him for his help. But the Baal Shem Tov only shook his head sadly when the man stood before him.

"Your son's life is in mortal danger because of your sins," he warned him. "When your son reaches the age of *bar mitzvah*, he will go to the lake and drown, for the lake is angry with you, since you have blackened its waters with so much sin."

"Is there no way to save him?" cried the anguished father.

"If you keep him away from the water on his thirteenth birthday, the curse will be annulled."

"This we will surely do!" cried the man.

"It is not as easy as that," cautioned the Baal Shem Tov. "Thirteen years is a long time. By the time your son reaches the age of *bar mitzvah*, you will have forgotten all that I have told you. But God will send you a reminder: On the day your son puts two socks on the same foot, that day your son must not go near the water or he will surely die!"

The man thanked the rabbi for his advice and hurried home to tell his wife.

The years passed and the son grew to be a handsome, learned, and pious boy, the apple of his parents' eye. In time the parents forgot all about the Baal Shem Tov's dire prediction, for the boy was strong and healthy and seemed safe from all harm.

But on the day of his thirteenth birthday, he rose early and began to dress, and by accident put two socks on the same foot. He came to his mother and asked her for the missing sock. Suddenly terror seized her heart, for she remembered what the Baal Shem Tov had told them thirteen years before.

She ran to tell her husband, and together they locked the boy in his room. No matter how loudly he protested, they refused to let him out. That day was an especially hot summer's day, and the boy cried out bitterly for a glass of water. But even that they would not give him. Finally, he fell asleep on his bed, exhausted and forlorn.

As the sun began to set, a ghostly hand rose out of the lake, followed by a second hand, and then a head. The last of the bathers looked on in horror as the head slowly gazed along the shore, apparently looking for something.

Then an angry voice burst forth, "One is missing!"

Moments later the head slowly sank back into the swirling black waters from which it had emerged.

And so the boy was saved from a terrible death, and the father from the path of sin.

231
The Vengeful Widow

Once the Baal Shem Tov and several of his disciples went on a journey and stopped to rest at an inn. The innkeeper asked them where they were going. They told him that the Baal Shem Tov was to officiate at a wedding that *Shabbat* in Berlin.

"Berlin!" cried the inkeeper. "That's ten days' ride from here. Even if you rode day and night, you could never arrive by this coming *Shabbat*."

"Our master will arrive in time," they assured him.

Eager to prove them wrong, the innkeeper announced that he, too, had business in Berlin and would like to join them on their journey. At sunset they set out and drove all night. To the sleepy innkeeper, it almost seemed as though the horses flew through the air, and when he opened his eyes the next morning, he was astonished to find himself within view of the great city of Berlin.

At the outskirts of the city, the innkeeper parted company with his companions and made his way into the heart of Berlin. There he heard the shocking news that a young bride had just died on the eve of her wedding to a rich man. Thinking of his miraculous journey of the night before, the innkeeper ran to the house of the grief-stricken groom and told him that the Baal Shem Tov had just arrived and might be able to help him. So the groom hurried to the outskirts of the city and asked the Besht to intercede with heaven on his behalf.

"Wrap the bride in her shroud and carry her to the cemetery," ordered the Baal Shem Tov. "Bring, too, her veil and wedding garments. Then lay her in the grave, but do not cover her."

The groom did as the Besht requested.

Then the Baal Shem Tov stood above the open grave and peered down at the lifeless bride, his own face drained of all color and his body stiff, as though bereft of life. Suddenly the young woman's cheeks flushed and she sat up.

"Put on her veil and bring her to the canopy at once!" commanded the Besht.

Quickly they bedecked the young woman in her wedding garments and brought her under the *huppah*. As the Besht pronounced the wedding blessings, the bride suddenly cried out, "He is the one who absolved me!"

"Be silent!" ordered the Besht, and she said no more.

As soon as the ceremony was over, the Besht departed.

Then the bride told her story, and she said, "Once my husband was married to my aunt. When she realized she was about to die, she became jealous of me, certain that my uncle would marry me once she was in her grave. So she made us both swear never to marry each other. But after she died, we were gradually drawn together until we could no longer deny our love and decided to marry. Last night the widow returned to exact vengeance upon me for the broken vow, but the Besht interceded in the Heavenly Court, demanding that the dead woman relinquish her claim on the living. And the Court ruled in his favor.

"When I heard the rabbi pronounce the wedding blessings just now, I immediately recognized the voice of the man who had defended me in heaven."

And then the couple and all their guests rejoiced at the wedding feast with thankful hearts.

232
The Forgotten Story

When the Baal Shem Tov was about to die, he called his disciples and instructed each one as to how he was to conduct his life after the master's death. Rabbi Simon was the last one called.

"You will become a storyteller," the Besht told him, "traveling from place to place, speaking of my life and teachings."

"But what kind of life is that?" protested Rabbi Simon. "To wander without a home, begging for my meals, to be forever a pilgrim."

"Nevertheless," answered the Besht, "this is the work you will do. I promise that you will come to a good end."

And then the Baal Shem Tov died.

So Rabbi Simon sold all his possessions and became an itinerant storyteller, as his master had commanded. He wandered from town to town, telling stories of the miracles performed by the holy Baal Shem Tov, teaching the Besht's wisdom through tales. In exchange for his words, people fed and sheltered him, but it was a hard and lonely existence, and often he wished his master had chosen another life for him.

After many years, word reached Rabbi Simon that there was a Jew in Italy who especially sought out tales of the Baal Shem Tov and would pay the teller handsomely for the privilege of hearing them. So he traveled to Italy and arranged to spend *Shabbat* with this man.

At the end of the Sabbath evening meal, the host eagerly called upon Rabbi Simon to tell the guests a favorite story about his master, but when he tried to recall a story, he discovered to his dismay that he had forgotten them all. Try as he might, he could not retrieve a single memory of his beloved master. With a troubled heart, he apologized to his host.

"Do not be concerned," replied the host with a smile. "Perhaps the excitement of a new place and unfamiliar faces made you temporarily forget. You shall tell us a tale at lunch tomorrow."

But the next day the same thing happened. When Rabbi Simon opened his mouth to tell a story at the end of *Shabbat* lunch, not a single word escaped his lips. His memory was completely blank!

Again his host told him not to trouble himself too

much about it. "Maybe you are exhausted after the long journey," he reassured Rabbi Simon. "Rest yourself during the afternoon, and we shall hear your tale this evening."

But at the Third Meal, Rabbi Simon was still unable to recall even a single incident from the Baal Shem Tov's life. At the conclusion of the Sabbath, his host kindly bade him farewell, inviting him to return to Italy if he should ever regain his memory. Then, over Rabbi Simon's protests, he handed the storyteller a bag of gold coins and sent him on his way in his own handsome coach.

As Rabbi Simon approached the border of the country, a memory suddenly flashed through his mind. Overjoyed, he shouted to the coachman to return to his master's house at once.

"I remember a story!" he cried as he dashed through the front door. "It came to me suddenly as I reached the border."

"Rest first," urged his host. "You must be tired from your journey."

"No, I must tell it immediately, or else it might vanish," said Rabbi Simon. And this is the story he told:

"Once just before the season of Passover, the Baal Shem Tov was troubled about something, and he called for his coach to take him on a journey. He asked me to accompany him. In the twinkling of an eye, we were on a narrow street in a strange city. All the houses on this street were locked up tight. I knocked on one door and they let us in, but it was clear that they were not pleased by our arrival. The people inside the house seemed very frightened about something. They warned us that the Christians of the city were about to take revenge upon the Jews, for it was almost Easter, a dangerous time for our people.

"The Baal Shem Tov seemed untroubled by all this. Without asking permission of his hosts, he opened one of the shuttered windows and looked out upon the square in front of the church. The others thought he had lost his mind and yelled at him to close the window, but he seemed not to hear them. Calmly he ordered me to go out to the square and ask the Bishop, who had just risen to speak to the crowd gathered there, to come into the house to speak with him.

" 'Say to him in Hebrew,' he instructed me, 'Come at once, for Israel, the son of Eliezer, wishes to speak with you.'

"With a heart quivering with fear, I did as my master instructed me. The Bishop bent down and whispered in my ear that he would come to my master as soon as he finished delivering his sermon. But when I gave this message to the Besht, my master sent me back immediately to demand that the Bishop waste no time in obeying the summons. How frightened was I to walk back again through that angry mob to deliver my master's stern demand. But to my great surprise, the Bishop immediately left with me this time, not saying a word to his followers about where he was going.

"For several hours the two men remained secluded together in a room. Outside, the crowd grew more and more restless. Those of us inside held our breath, not knowing what these strange events meant. Finally the door opened and the Baal Shem Tov came out alone, his face shining with joy. Without speaking, he left the house and got into his coach. I followed him, and within the space of one breath, we were back in our own village.

"I never learned what happened that day between my master and the Bishop," concluded Rabbi Simon. "After we returned from our journey, he never spoke of that day again."

When he had finished speaking, Rabbi Simon looked at his host and was surprised by how agitated the man seemed. His body trembled all over, and his face was as pale as death.

"I can tell you what happened," he whispered in a low voice, "for I was that Bishop. I was born a Jew, but in my youth I forsook the faith of my ancestors and eventually rose to the rank of Bishop in my adopted faith. My hatred for what I once was slowly ate away at my spirit until my heart knew only a desire for vengeance. It was then that the Baal Shem Tov resolved to struggle with my afflicted soul and win it back from the Evil One. As I felt his own spirit triumphing over my own, I tried to cast him off by delivering a sermon designed to stir up hatred against the Jews, but I was unable to resist his second summons and so escaped the grasp of the Evil One.

"After my secret meeting with the Baal Shem Tov, I confessed to my superiors that I could no longer serve the church with a whole heart, so I surrendered my position, left the church, and came to Italy to live as a Jew again."

"What else did my master say to you that day?" asked Rabbi Simon.

The host smiled at him. "He told me that one day someone would come here and tell me this story, and that would be a sign that my former sins had been fully forgiven. All this *Shabbat* my soul has been struggling to rid itself of its burden of sin, but only at the last minute did it truly repent. That's when the story finally returned to you."

Then the host invited Rabbi Simon to remain with him for the rest of his days, and he cared for him as one of his own family.

233
The Disturbed Sabbath

After the close of *Shabbat*, the Baal Shem Tov would often call for his carriage and go traveling. On one particular Saturday night, three of his disciples accompanied him as he set out. As so often happened on these midnight journeys, the horses paid no attention to the driver's bidding, but chose their own course, carrying the four travelers into the wilderness, where they wandered for three days. Then they entered a dark forest, where they remained for another three days until it was the eve of *Shabbat*.

Suddenly they saw a light ahead of them. It came from a poor dwelling standing alone in a clearing. When they knocked at the door, a poor peasant came out.

"May we stay with you over the Sabbath?" asked the Baal Shem Tov.

The peasant eyed them suspiciously. "You are *Hasidim*, are you not?"

"We are," said the Besht.

"Then you may not enter!" bellowed the man. "I despise your false piety and your strange ways. I will not have you in my house!"

"But the Sabbath is about to begin, and we have no other place to stay!" protested the four travelers.

"Very well," the peasant grumbled. "You may stay, but only if you do exactly as I say. No special privileges because you are holy men."

Reluctantly the Besht and his companions agreed to their host's inhospitable conditions.

It was the most unpleasant *Shabbat* any of them had ever spent. Their host did not even bother to change out of his rough working clothes, but instead began the Sabbath prayers as soon as they entered the house, mumbling the words rapidly and without feeling. At the meal, he performed the Sabbath rituals with equal indifference, rushing through the blessings as if they were unpleasant chores. The food on the rough wooden table was meager and poorly cooked, and the host wolfed it down without a word of Torah or song. Remembering their promise not to ask for special privileges, the guests bore it all in silence. That night they slept on the bare floor, kept awake most of the night by the peasant's loud snores.

The next day was no better. Although the four visitors longed to go off by themselves to pray and study in peace, they were forced to remain with their host, for the only other room in the house remained locked. From sunup to sundown they had no choice but to endure the peasant's impious behavior in silence.

As soon as the Sabbath was over, the Baal Shem Tov

instructed his followers to lie down to sleep so that they might get an early start the next morning.

"For," he said to them, "we must leave this dreadful place before we lose our very souls."

But when they arose the next morning, they were astonished to see the door to the locked room now ajar and an elegantly dressed woman standing in the threshold.

"Don't you recognize me, Rabbi?" she asked the Baal Shem Tov.

"No," he said, "but you obviously recognize me."

The woman nodded.

"Then if you know who I am," he continued, his voice rising in anger, "why did you allow your husband to treat us so unkindly on the holy *Shabbat*?"

"Once I was a poor orphan girl," said the woman, "and you took pity on me and took me into your household as a servant. For several years I served meals at your table. But because of my youth and unsteady hands, I often dropped things and was then severely scolded by your wife. On one particular *Shabbat*, I tried to carry a brimming tureen of hot soup to the table, but I dropped it and spilled soup everywhere. Your wife slapped me in front of everyone, and you sat at your place and said nothing.

"Because of your silence, it was decreed in heaven that you lose your portion in the World to Come. Then I married my husband, who is a hidden *tzaddik*, and he revealed your fate to me. Together we prayed for a reprieve, and at last it was revealed to us that your heavenly portion would be restored to you if you suffered one disturbed Sabbath in this life, for the Sabbath is a foretaste of the World to Come. And now that you have done so, your rightful place awaits you in Paradise."

Instead of returning home that morning, the Besht and his disciples remained with the holy couple until the following *Shabbat* and celebrated it with great joy and thanksgiving.

234
The Second Chance

Once a rich man came to the Baal Shem Tov because he wanted to impress him with his own learning. But the Besht paid no special attention to him. When the man was about to leave, he handed the rabbi a pouch of gold coins.

The Besht smiled at him. "Tell me, good sir, what do you lack and how would you like me to intercede on your behalf?"

"I lack nothing, holy master!" said the rich man. "I only came here because your fame has spread far and wide, and I wished to meet you. I had hoped you would find my learning worthy of notice."

"You are sure that there is nothing you lack?" asked the Besht. "All others who come to see me want something—a child, a cure, a change in their fortunes."

"I am quite sure," answered the rich man. "I have a good wife, fine children, and enough money to satisfy my every need."

"Then let me give you a story to carry home with you:

"Once there lived two wealthy families in a certain town, each of whom had a son. The two boys became close friends and loved each other dearly, but when they came of age, their parents married them off, and each moved to a different city. Although they continued to write to each other, they gradually became absorbed in their new lives and grew apart.

"In time the wheel of fortune turned, and one of the two men lost all that he had. He came to his friend and told him his sad tale. The rich man ordered an accounting of all that he owned and then divided up his possessions, giving half to his childhood friend. In a short while, the second man doubled and redoubled his wealth so that he became even richer than he had been before his loss.

"In time the wheel of fortune turned again, and the once rich friend now lost everything. He came to his friend and asked for help. But the man had become greedy and stingy and refused even to admit him into his house. And so the destitute man died in the street.

"Soon after this the rich man died.

"They each went to their eternal rest, the poor man to Paradise, and the rich miser to Gehinnom. But the poor man pleaded with heaven to give his friend a second chance. So it was granted to both of them to return to earth in the same station they had left it.

"The poor friend was reborn a beggar and the rich friend an even wealthier man than before. And neither recalled the life he had lived previously. The beggar's wanderings eventually brought him to the rich man's door, but when he knocked, the owner of the house scoffed at him and refused him alms.

" 'Do not turn me away!' pleaded the beggar, 'for you hold my life in your hands!'

" 'I have never given before,' laughed the miser, 'and I don't intend to start giving now!' And he struck the beggar so hard that the man fell down dead."

The Baal Shem Tov now said to the rich man who stood before him, "Do you still maintain that there is nothing you lack?"

At once the rich man fell to his knees. "Rabbi, I am that cruel man! Tell me what I can do to save my soul."

"Go home and begin giving to all the poor in your town. And see in each needy face the beggar whom you struck down in your heartlessness."

So the rich man returned home and did as the Besht instructed him.

235
The Gold Buttons

The Baal Shem Tov was once sitting at the Friday night table with his disciples when all of a sudden he burst out laughing. Surprised, the disciples looked at each other, but none dared ask him the reason for his strange behavior.

After the *havdalah* ceremony, however, they plucked up their courage and came to him. "Holy master," they said, "why did you laugh last night?"

"Come with me," the Besht said to them, "and I will show you."

So they climbed into his carriage and set out. As usual the horses followed their own lead and sped into the darkness as if borne by the wind. Near dawn they reached a village and stopped at a poor hut.

When they knocked at the door, they were greeted by an old man.

"Are you Shabtai the bookbinder?" the Baal Shem Tov asked him.

The old man nodded.

"Tell us what you did this past *Shabbat*," the Besht ordered, "and leave nothing out. You need not be ashamed to tell us everything."

"Holy Rabbi," said the old man, "I am but a poor, unlearned man. All my life I have made a good living binding books, but now that I am old, I have little work and am reduced to poverty, for I have no children to support me. This past Friday I discovered I had not even one penny to give my wife to prepare for the Sabbath, but I did not wish to ask for charity. When I left for synagogue, I instructed my wife not to accept or ask for alms, although I knew that sadness was weighing upon her heart at the thought of a Sabbath without candles, wine, or bread.

"Then I went to the synagogue. With all my heart I prayed that God would remember us on this day and deliver us from our need. When I returned home, I saw lights burning in the window, and I feared that my wife had given in to her sadness and begged for a few coins. And when I went inside, I found the table laid with a magnificent feast.

" 'Dearest wife,' I said to her, 'I cannot blame you for disobeying me, for what is a *Shabbat* without joy?'

"But she only laughed at me and said, 'Since I had no Sabbath meal to prepare, I spent the afternoon cleaning the house. I even cleaned out the old trunk and found my wedding dress at the bottom. On the sleeves were several gold buttons that I sold to the goldsmith for so much money that tonight we will have the best Sabbath meal of our lives!'

"And then, holy Rabbi," said Shabtai, his cheeks flushing with shame, "I laughed aloud and whirled my wife gaily around the room, dancing with her as if I were a youth of twenty. If I have sinned, tell me what penance I can do to atone."

The Baal Shem Tov laughed. "How can happiness be a sin? The angels themselves surely smiled upon your rejoicing that night. May God bless you both with a son in your old age. Call him Israel after my name."

And a year later the old couple had a son whom they named Israel, and the boy grew up to be the holy Maggid of Kozenitz.

236
The Bird's Nest

Once a beautiful bird came to the king's garden and nested high in a tree. The king wished to catch the bird, so he commanded his servants to form a human ladder to reach the top of the tree. Just as the highest man reached the nest, the man at the bottom weakened, and the human ladder collapsed.

"So it is with us," taught the Baal Shem Tov. "We all depend on those lesser and greater than us to bring down God's love. But when one of us weakens, everything collapses and we all must begin anew."

237
Slacken the Reins

Rabbi Jacob Joseph of Szarygrod was one of the Baal Shem Tov's fiercest opponents. Three things in particular bothered him about the practices of the Besht and his disciples: the unrestrained joy of their celebrations, the eccentricity of their services, and the unorthodoxy of the Besht's *Shabbat* afternoon sermons, which were embroidered with mysteries and folktales. To him such practices presented a dangerous threat to the tradition.

One day the Besht came to Szarygrod and began telling a story in the marketplace. First one man stopped, then a second. Then came the women, their baskets and ladles in hand, and they, too, stopped to listen to the holy rabbi weaving his magical tale. Last came the *shammash*, who stood riveted to the spot, his mouth and eyes gaping like open stewpots.

When Rabbi Jacob Joseph arrived at the synagogue for the morning prayers, he was annoyed to find the doors still locked. At just that moment the Besht finished his tale and released the *shammash* from his spell. Frantically the man ran to the synagogue to unlock the doors. But before he could fit the key into the lock, the rabbi began to scold him so roundly that he thought his head would burst.

Suddenly the Baal Shem Tov came up to them.

"*Shalom aleikhem*," he said to Rabbi Jacob Joseph.

"What do you think you are doing," the rabbi shouted at him, "keeping people from prayer?"

"Let me tell you a story," answered the Besht calmly. The rabbi was so surprised by the Besht's words that he caught his breath and listened. "I once drove with a team of three horses. Not one of them could neigh. A peasant approached and told me to slacken the reins, and then they all neighed. Do you understand?"

At that Jacob Joseph burst into tears.

"You need to be uplifted," said the Baal Shem Tov.

From that moment on, Jacob Joseph began to afflict himself, fasting one week of each month. The Baal Shem Tov returned to Szarygrod and said to Jacob Joseph, "God wants joy, not gloom. Eat!"

And the rabbi began to eat. In time, he moved to Polnoye and became a devoted disciple of the Baal Shem Tov.

238
Paying God's Wages

Once when Rabbi Jacob Joseph of Polnoye was studying, a man approached him and asked him, "What is your name and where are you from?"

"Why are you bothering me?" complained the rabbi. "I am Rabbi Jacob Joseph, originally from Szarygrod."

"Do you make a good living?" continued the man.

Jacob Joseph now flew into a rage. "Can't you see that I'm learning Torah? You are keeping me from my studies!"

"But you are keeping God from his living," said the man, "for the Holy One makes a living from human praises. When I asked you how you were doing, you should have replied, 'Praise be to God, I am doing well.' But you are too busy studying to pay God's wages. You never talk to anybody."

Then the man vanished.

Jacob Joseph tried to return to his books, but he could no longer concentrate. So he went to the Baal Shem Tov and asked him for an explanation.

"Well," said the Besht, "Elijah got the better of you, didn't he?"

239
The Happy Drunkard

Once the Baal Shem Tov took his disciples to a particular gravesite, sat down beside the grave, and poured a bottle of whiskey upon it. When his astonished disciples asked him what he was doing, he told them the following story:

When Ivan the Terrible ruled Russia, there lived two wealthy Jewish families in a certain town. The fathers agreed to marry off their only son and daughter to each other and set them up in business. And so it came to pass.

After the wedding, the groom Shimon spent all his days in the House of Study, while his wife Masha managed the business. Daily Masha tried to persuade Shimon to take an interest in the business but Shimon always said, "We have enough money," and kept studying.

Once a wealthy merchant wanted to sell Masha a shipment of unusual merchandise that was sure to fetch a handsome profit. But he would only accept Shimon's signature to seal the agreement. After much coaxing, Masha managed to pry Shimon loose from his books so that he could sign the document. And then the most extraordinary thing happened: When Shimon saw the lovely merchandise, his eyes opened as if for the first time, and he became suddenly interested in his store. Each day he spent more and more time in the store and less time with his books, until he abandoned the House of Study altogether.

Then Masha persuaded Shimon to go himself to St. Petersburg to buy goods, so that they would not have to pay a middleman. At that time Jews were not allowed to enter the city, so she made Shimon tuck in his *tzitzit*, put on a fur hat, and pose as a Gentile. He arrived in St. Petersburg and booked rooms at one of the most elegant inns in the city. The merchants he contacted were impressed by the size of his orders, and the wealthiest of them gave a banquet at his home in Shimon's honor.

And what a banquet it was! The gowns of the ladies dazzled Shimon's eyes, the crystal chandeliers and gilded mirrors made his mouth drop open, and the delicate painted china made his fingers tremble. But what made him tremble even more was all the unkosher food the waiters set before him. But Shimon had no choice but to eat it all, for if he refused, would that not betray him as a Jew?

After the dinner, his host asked him to dance with his beautiful young daughter. Shimon's heart stopped within his breast. He, a married man, dancing with an unmarried woman, a Gentile no less! But would his host not be gravely insulted if he refused? And had it not been Masha's idea in the first place, this risky charade among Christians? So Shimon led the trembling young girl out onto the dance floor.

A few moments later, there was a loud shriek.

"Papa," cried the host's daughter, "this man is a Jew!"

For while he was dancing, Shimon's *tzitzit* had worked free and were now dangling over his belt.

As the horrified guests looked on, the host marched over to Shimon and pointed a gun at his head. "How dare you come to my house, Jew? But since you are my best customer, I will give you a choice: either convert or I will kill you!"

"Give me three days to think about it," said the frightened Shimon.

"Very well," said the host. "Return in three days with your answer."

When Shimon returned to the inn, he thought about what he should do. He could try to sneak out of St. Petersburg, but the truth was that he had become fascinated by life in the big city and had no wish to return home. So he decided to convert, convincing himself that God had more use for him alive than dead.

The wealthy merchant was delighted with Shimon's decision and gave him his only daughter Catherine in marriage. Shimon became a partner in his father-in-law's factory. For ten years Shimon and Catherine lived happily together, raising five children.

Then one day Shimon glanced at his calendar and noticed that the day was marked off as a Jewish holiday — Yom Kippur, the Day of Atonement. Despite his ten years of living as a Gentile, Shimon's Jewish heart broke when he thought now of his former life and the sins he had committed against his own people.

Desolate, he went into the garden to find the gardener, known to all as "the happy drunkard," since he was always so carefree. But today Shimon found him sitting on a bench, crying.

"Why are you crying?" asked Shimon. "You are always so happy!"

"If you promise to keep my secret, I will tell you," answered the gardener.

So Shimon swore to tell no one what he heard that day.

"I am a Jew," confessed the gardener, "and today is Yom Kippur. On this day every Jew appears before God as a holy angel. How do you think I appear today to God?" And he began to cry even louder.

"Promise to tell no one my secret," said Shimon, and the gardener swore. "I too was once a Jew, but I abandoned my wife and learning to come here ten years ago. I have had a good life here with my new wife."

"Since today is Yom Kippur," said the gardener, "promise to do whatever I tell you."

And Shimon promised.

"Tell your father-in-law and wife that you have a fine business opportunity in Amsterdam. Take your money and go home to your wife. Tell her that you were kidnapped ten years ago and were just released. Then return to your studies and do not set foot in your store again. The people here will think you have been captured en route to Amsterdam. Now go in peace."

Shimon did exactly as the gardener instructed him.

After Shimon disappeared, Catherine mourned for him for a whole year, for she loved him very dearly. On the anniversary of his departure, she went into the garden to seek solace from the happy drunkard. Instead, she found him crying.

"Why are you crying?" she asked him. "You are always so happy!"

He told her the same story he had told Shimon, making her first swear to tell no one.

"I too am overcome with sorrow today," she told him, "for I grieve for my lost husband whom I love with all my heart."

"Would you like to know what happened to him?" asked the gardener.

"Do you know?" cried Catherine. "Tell me!"

"Only if you agree to do whatever I ask of you," said the gardener.

And Catherine agreed.

"First swear to me that you and your children will convert to Judaism."

And Catherine swore.

The gardener went on. "Tell your father that you cannot live without Shimon and that you now have a clue where he might be. Then take your children and go to that town. God will show you the rest of the way."

So Catherine took her five children and traveled to the town where Shimon lived. She took rooms in a local inn and asked the innkeeper if he knew a Jew named Shimon.

"Shimon!" exclaimed the innkeeper. "He's the richest Jew in town!"

"I would like to meet him," said Catherine.

"Impossible!" said the innkeeper. "He stays in the House of Study all week long and only returns home for *Shabbat*."

Catherine handed him a few rubles.

"The only way you might meet him," said the innkeeper, "is to wait outside the ritual bath on Friday afternoon when his coach stops there on the way home."

So on Friday afternoon Catherine took her five children and stood outside the ritual bath waiting for her husband. Shimon soon emerged, his face shining with the joy of the coming Sabbath, but when he recognized Catherine and his children, all the color drained from his cheeks.

In a few moments he regained his calm. "Catherine, it is almost time for the Sabbath. Go to my house and tell my wife Masha that you are business acquaintances and will be my guests. Do not tell her who you really are. After the Sabbath, I will take care of everything."

So Catherine and her children spent the Sabbath at Shimon's home. As soon as the holy day was over, Shimon took them and Masha to the rabbi and told him the whole story, not omitting one detail. Then he explained that he did not love his wife Masha, for she lived only for business and gain, whereas he sought more from life than material things.

Then Shimon went over to Catherine and stood by her. "Rabbi," he said, "this woman has loved me all these years, and it was she who gave me the strength to return to my people. Tell me, which of these two women was destined for me in heaven?"

The rabbi was silent for a long time and then said, "Your true soul mate is Catherine from St. Petersburg."

So Shimon divorced Masha. The rabbi instructed Catherine and her children in the Torah, and they became Jews. Then Shimon married Catherine in a Jewish ceremony.

On the anniversary of Catherine's departure from St. Petersburg, her father, who missed her and his grandchildren very much, went into the garden to be cheered up by the happy drunkard. But instead he found him in tears.

"I came here to have my spirits lifted," said the father, "but I see that you too are in trouble. Tell me what is the matter."

"Swear to me that you will tell no one my secret," said the gardener.

And the father swore.

And the gardener told him the same story he had told Shimon and Catherine.

"Now let me tell you my story," said the father. "I have an only daughter and five grandchildren whom I miss very much."

"I will tell you where they are if you promise to follow my instructions exactly," said the gardener.

And the father promised.

"Sell everything you own and convert to Judaism. Go to the town whose name I shall give you, and there you will find your daughter reunited with her husband. She will welcome you gladly."

"Thank you!" cried the happy father.

"But what will happen to me if you leave me here?" said the gardener in a mournful voice. "Take me with you when you go."

So they left together. As they approached the outskirts of the town, the gardener died, and the father buried him in a clearing in the forest.

The Baal Shem Tov concluded his story and shouted, "*L'chayim,* holy drunkard!"

2. EARLY MASTERS

240
The Rabbi Who Thought Friday
Was Shabbat

Once the Yanover Rebbe traveled to a relative's wedding in a distant city. Along the way he stopped to *daven minhah*. When he went looking for a stream to wash his hands, he became lost and wandered in the forest for many days. After a while, he lost track of time and became confused, thinking that a certain day was Friday, when in fact it was the day before. A few days later, he at last made his way out of the forest and came to a city, where he hired a carriage to take him back to Yanov. But when people tried to correct him about the date, he insisted that his reckoning was correct, even though he was actually wrong by one day. For weeks, he continued to observe Thursday night and Friday as the Sabbath, despite the fact that his own followers observed the next day.

Frustrated and in despair, his disciples traveled to Nikolsburg and appealed to Rabbi Shmelke, the Yanover's childhood friend, for help.

"Do nothing to embarrass him," advised Shmelke. "I shall travel to Yanov and see what I can do."

So Shmelke came to Yanov and agreed to spend the Sabbath with his boyhood friend. That Thursday night the two men sat down together to a Sabbath meal. While the Yanover was not looking, Shmelke slipped a sleeping potion into his wine. In a short while the Yanover fell asleep at the table and slept until Saturday. When he awoke and went to the House of Study, he was surprised to find his followers there dressed in their Sabbath finery and reciting the Sabbath prayers. From that day on, the Yanover celebrated *Shabbat* on the same day as everyone else.

But to his dying day, he believed that everyone else had finally come to his senses and started to follow his own example. And no one ever told him otherwise.

241

The Return of the Rich Man's Soul

When Rabbi Aaron of Karlin died, Shlomo, his younger friend and a fellow disciple of the Maggid of Mezritch, refused to take his place as Rabbi of Karlin. Then Rabbi

Aaron appeared to Shlomo in a dream and promised him that if he should take the rabbinic post, he would be granted the power of perceiving the reincarnation of souls. So Shlomo became the next Rabbi of Karlin.

Soon after this, a rich man sent Shlomo a large sum of money, asking him to pray on behalf of his departing soul. At the same time, word reached Shlomo that a poor woman was about to give birth but was struggling in the throes of a difficult labor. With his new clairvoyance, Shlomo was able to see that this baby could not be born until the rich man died, for the rich man's soul was destined to pass into this child. And indeed, the woman gave birth at precisely the moment the rich man breathed his last.

Shlomo sent the rich man's money to the poor mother and her newborn son, for he thought, "This money really belongs to the child." And it sustained them for several years.

After some time the rich man's youngest son reached the age of *bar mitzvah* and, as was the custom, the family invited all the poor to share in the feast. The poor woman brought her young son with her and took a seat at the paupers' table. But the boy was not content to sit there and demanded a place of honor at the guests' table so that he could eat the choicest foods and wine.

"Who does he think he is?" cried the rich man's family.

But Rabbi Shlomo insisted that they give in to the boy's demands, for was he not the father of the *bar mitzvah*?

At the end of the feast the hosts distributed copper pennies to the poor. But when they tried to hand a few pennies to the poor woman's son, he threw them back, demanding gold.

"Is your son always like this?" they asked his mother.

The embarrassed woman protested that he had never in his life behaved this way before.

Rabbi Shlomo demanded that they give the boy what he asked, for he thought to himself, "After all, it is really his."

But this time the rich man's sons refused, and they picked up the boy by the scruff of his neck and threw him out of the house.

When Rabbi Shlomo saw how unkindly they treated their own father, he prayed to heaven to revoke his extraordinary gift, and his request was granted.

242
Let Them Eat Stones

A rich *Hasid* once came to Dov Baer, the Maggid of Mezritch, and asked for his blessing.

"How do you eat each day?" asked the Maggid.

"With great simplicity," answered the rich man. "I eat only dry bread with a little salt."

"Dry bread and salt!" exclaimed the Maggid. "Why don't you treat yourself to meat and wine since you are so wealthy?"

The Maggid continued to chastise the man until he promised to start eating a more expensive diet.

After he had left, the Maggid's disciples asked him, "What difference does it make whether he eats dry bread or meat?"

"It matters a great deal," answered the Maggid. "If he is used to rich foods, then he will understand that a poor man must at least have a dry crust with a little salt. But if he is only used to dry bread and salt, he will imagine that the poor can content themselves with stones."

243
Reb Haim and the Three
Lawsuits

One of the Berdichever Rebbe's followers was Reb Haim, a ragpicker who eventually became a rich man. When Reb Haim died, the Berdichever himself attended his funeral.

Since Reb Haim had not been a particularly pious Jew, the Berdichever's followers were surprised by the rebbe's decision.

The Berdichever said to them, "Reb Haim had three lawsuits in my court and won all three. The first involved a soldier in the czar's army who was taken away for forty years and managed to accumulate ten thousand rubles during that time. When it was time to return home, he tied the money in a red handkerchief and carried it to Berdichev, ready to marry and start a business. But a pickpocket stole the handkerchief from him near the river. The next day Reb Haim took a walk and noticed the soldier pacing back and forth by the river. He asked him what he was doing.

" 'I have lost my life savings and have no choice now but to end my life,' replied the despondent soldier.

" 'Describe the handkerchief and the money,' said Reb Haim.

"And the soldier did.

" 'You are in luck!' cried Reb Haim. 'Yesterday I was walking here by the river, and I found your handkerchief with the money. I took it home with me, hoping that the owner would make himself known to me.'

"Reb Haim took the soldier home, gave him ten thousand rubles from his own money—for, of course, he hadn't really found the soldier's handkerchief—and sent the man happily on his way.

"Soon the real thief heard about Reb Haim's generous deed and came to him with the stolen money.

" 'Take it,' he said to Reb Haim, 'for I no longer want it.'

" 'Return it yourself to the man you robbed,' insisted Reb Haim, and the thief did.

"Then the soldier came to my court," said the Berdichever, "and tried to return the money to Reb Haim, but he refused to take it, claiming it wasn't his. And the court ruled in favor of Reb Haim.

"The second case involved a poor teacher who wished to travel to another city to make more money to support his wife, but she didn't want him to go, for she feared she would not have enough to live on while he was gone.

" 'Go to Reb Haim,' her husband said. 'I will ask him to lend you five kopeks every Friday for the Sabbath.'

"He went away, and his wife went every Friday to get her five kopeks. When her husband returned later with his earnings, he asked her how she had managed while he was gone.

" 'The five kopeks I received from Reb Haim permitted me to make ends meet,' she told him.

" 'But I forgot to arrange for the loan before I left!' cried the husband. 'We must go and pay him back immediately.'

"They went to Reb Haim and offered to pay back every kopek he had given the woman. But Reb Haim refused to take a single coin.

" 'If you had arranged this with me ahead of time,' argued Reb Haim, 'I would gladly accept repayment now. But it so happens that giving the five kopeks was my own idea, and you cannot repay me for my own charity.'

"And again my court upheld Reb Haim's opinion.

"The third case involved a rich man who fell on hard times and came to Reb Haim for a loan of five thousand rubles. As he left, he said to his benefactor, 'May God bless you twofold for this kindness.'

"Shortly after this, someone came to Reb Haim and told him that a local noble had just lost heavily at cards and was selling a yoke of oxen to pay his debts.

" 'You must buy them, Reb Haim,' insisted his informant.

" 'But what do I know about oxen?' said Reb Haim.

" 'Nevertheless, buy the oxen!'

"So Reb Haim bought the oxen for five thousand rubles and sold them for fifteen.

"When the rich man returned to repay his debt, Reb Haim refused to accept the money.

" 'You didn't say that you would repay me but that God would. And God has repaid me twofold. You don't owe me a kopek.'

"And for the third time, my court sided with Reb Haim.

"So," concluded the Berdichever, "when a person wins three such lawsuits in my court, I should go to his funeral and pay my respects."

244
The Shofar Blower

One Rosh Hashanah the Berdichever Rebbe searched for someone to blow the *shofar*. He asked each one who came forward, "What are your mystic thoughts when you blow the *shofar*?"

None of the answers he heard pleased him.

Finally one man came to him who confessed that he was unlearned and had no mystic thoughts.

"Then what do you think about when you blow the *shofar*?" the Berdichever asked him.

"I think of my four unmarried daughters who need husbands," the man replied. "I say to God, 'I am doing my duty to You by blowing the *shofar*. Now You do Yours for me.' "

And the Berdichever chose him to blow the *shofar* that year.

245
The Missing Ruble

Rabbi Pinkhas of Koretz used to support ten young men with a weekly stipend so that they could study Torah. Every Friday Yaakov would go to the rabbi's house and collect the ten rubles, which he and his fellow students needed to buy food for the Sabbath.

But one week Rabbi Pinkhas gave Yaakov only nine rubles. Not wishing to embarrass the rabbi, Yaakov said nothing about the missing ruble, but instead pawned his own fur hat to provide for his family's Sabbath needs. That evening he appeared at *shul* wearing only his weekday hat, but Rabbi Pinkhas appeared not to notice. So Yaakov was unable to point out to him his error in counting.

The next Friday the same thing happened. When Yaakov came to collect the students' weekly stipend, Rabbi Pinkhas handed him only nine rubles. This time Yaakov pawned his Sabbath clothes and came to *shul* wearing only his threadbare weekday garments. But again Rabbi Pinkhas noticed nothing. And again Yaakov had no choice but to remain silent.

When the same thing happened the third week, Yaakov was desperate. He had nothing of value left to pawn. How was he to feed his family? Then a friend, hearing of his distress, offered to lend him some wheat to sell at the market. Reluctantly, Yaakov accepted his offer. He understood that this choice meant the end of his days as a student, but what choice did he have? Without the rabbi's ruble, he could not support himself or his family.

So on the next market day, Yaakov went to market and sold his wheat for a good profit. With a portion of the money, he bought food for his family. The rest he invested in more wheat. In a short time, he became a prosperous merchant. To wheat he added other wares — cloth, spices, tea. His customers knew that his scales were honest and his merchandise good, so they flocked to him in larger and larger numbers. Business flourished, and his children's cheeks grew fat.

In time Yaakov's reputation as a smart and honest businessman even reached the ears of the duke, and one day he summoned Yaakov to his estate.

"Look around you," the duke said to the Jewish merchant. "Is there anything that I lack?"

Yaakov looked at the duke's stately mansion with its

costly furnishings, its many servants, and its vast lands. Indeed, here were riches befitting a king!

"But alas," sighed the duke, "there is one thing I do not have—children. Of what use is all my wealth with no one to inherit it? When I die, who will remember me and honor my memory? Without children, I will quickly be forgotten. Therefore, I wish to preserve my memory in stone. For this purpose, I have hired a sculptor to fashion my likeness on a tombstone, but I wish two precious jewels for the statue's eyes. Jewels of such rare quality can only be purchased in Amsterdam."

As Yaakov listened to the duke's words, he thought to himself: "Why is he telling all this to *me*? What have I to do with this statue?"

As if reading his mind, the duke now said, "I have heard of your reputation as an honest and clever businessman. That is why I wish to send you to Amsterdam to buy these two jewels for me. You will be rewarded handsomely for your efforts. I will give you three days to think it over."

Yaakov went home and thought over the duke's offer. On the one hand, the journey was dangerous, for the north seas were treacherous for ships. But if he was successful, he would then have enough money to quit his business and return to the study of Torah without having to worry about his family's welfare. Torn over his decision, he decided to seek Rabbi Pinkhas's advice.

But Rabbi Pinkhas refused to see anyone during the three days that Yaakov came to call upon him. So Yaakov made the decision himself: He would accept the duke's offer.

The next day they set sail. Fortunately the seas were calm, and Yaakov began to dream of the new life of study he would begin as soon as he returned home.

But the captain of the ship had other plans for him. His curiosity aroused by Yaakov's bulging luggage, he ordered one of his sailors to search Yaakov's cabin secretly, and thus discovered that the Jewish merchant was

carrying a great sum of money. So he devised a scheme to
steal the money and dispose of its owner.

In a short while the ship stopped at an island so that
the passengers could rest. The captain told Yaakov that he
would blow four whistles when it was time to return to
the ship, but he told the other passengers to return on the
third whistle.

Carrying only his bag of holy books, Yaakov left the
ship and went off to find a quiet place to study. When he
heard the third whistle, he began to pack up his books to
return, but as he looked up, he saw the ship sailing away,
leaving him behind. He ran to the shore and screamed for
them to return for him, but it was too late. He was
stranded on the island, and the duke's money was gone!

Rather than despair, Yaakov looked around and soon
found a stream, some fruit trees, and a cave for shelter.
Immediately he set to work building a lookout tower of
stones so that he could survey the entire island. When he
climbed the tower, he spotted a campfire burning some
distance away.

Eager for companionship, Yaakov made his way to
the spot where he came upon a man tending the fire. With
a broken heart, Yaakov poured out his sad tale to the
stranger, but the man said nothing.

"Why do you remain silent?" asked Yaakov.

Without looking up from the fire, the man replied, "I
will only tell you that my name is Hershel." And then he
again fell silent.

That night Yaakov returned to his cave, determined
to find out more about his strange companion on the
island. The next day he sought out Hershel and told him
more about his life in Koretz, his family, and his teacher,
Rabbi Pinkhas. Hershel listened intently but still said
nothing.

And so it continued: Each day Yaakov sought out
Hershel and talked to him, sometimes speaking of his
former life in Koretz, sometimes studying his holy books.
Gradually Hershel came to trust Yaakov and to teach him

how to find the best fruit on the island. Each day Yaakov invited Hershel to study with him, and finally Hershel accepted.

One day Hershel said to Yaakov, "My good friend, I have something to confess to you. I too am from Koretz. The reason that I am on this island is that I deserted my family there."

Yaakov was shocked, but he said nothing.

The next day Yaakov climbed his lookout tower and began scanning the horizon for ships. A few days later, he spotted one, and began waving his shirt to attract attention. His efforts were successful, and the ship's captain sent a boat to pick him up.

As Yaakov stepped into the boat to leave, Hershel suddenly felt a great longing for the family he had abandoned and cried out, "Do not leave me here alone! Take me with you!"

So the two left the island and came to the nearest port. For many months they wandered as beggars from town to town until at last they reached Koretz. As they entered the town, they met a man who told them that a fire had just that day destroyed the duke's entire estate and taken the duke's life. And Yaakov felt a great burden lifted from his heart.

When they approached the center of town, they were struck by the air of excitement filling the streets. It was late Friday afternoon, and the Jews of Koretz seemed to be preparing for a special *Shabbat*. Penniless and in rags, neither man wished to return to his family just yet, so they went to the *shul* to pray and then followed the huge crowd back to the rabbi's house.

Surrounded by all his followers, Rabbi Pinkhas raised his cup for *kiddush*, but then set it down without saying a word. Slowly his eyes searched the crowd until they fell upon Yaakov and Hershel huddling in a back corner. A broad smile spread across his face.

"Friends," said the rabbi, "tonight we have two special guests with us. Let us welcome back Yaakov, who has been away a long time. Let me explain why he was gone so long. I sent him on a mission to bring back Hershel to his family, and I see that he has succeeded, for there is Hershel standing beside him. Welcome back, Hershel! And *yasher koakh*, Yaakov! It is now time for you to reclaim your rightful place in the study hall."

And then Rabbi Pinkhas recited the *kiddush*.

246
Two Kinds of Gifts

In Rabbi Zusya's town there lived a wealthy merchant who saw how poor Zusya was and left twenty pennies in his *tefillin* bag so that the rabbi might provide for himself and his family. The merchant soon discovered to his surprise that the more he gave to Zusya, the wealthier he himself became.

Now this merchant knew that Zusya was a disciple of the great Maggid of Mezritch, so he thought to himself, "If I have done so well giving to Zusya, how much better will it be for me if I give to his master!"

So he traveled to Mezritch and gave a handsome gift to the Maggid. But contrary to his expectations, his fortunes soon took a turn for the worse, and he began to lose money in his business. Within a short time, he lost everything he had.

Distraught, he came to Zusya and demanded an explanation.

"When you gave to me," explained Zusya, "not caring if it was Zusya or some other in need, God gave to you and did not care who you were. But when you sought out an especially worthy recipient for your gift, God did the same."

247
Blows

Once when Zusya and his brother Elimelekh were on a journey, they stopped at an inn where a Gentile wedding was being celebrated. Tired from their travels, the two brothers immediately went to sleep in a corner.

The merrymakers, quite drunk by this time and eager for mischief, grabbed Zusya and beat him up. Then they returned to their merrymaking with renewed gusto.

When Elimelekh saw what had happened to his brother, he made Zusya trade places with him so that he too might receive his share of blows should the wedding guests attack them again.

Sure enough, the guests continued to drink and soon became even rowdier. They eyed the two brothers sleeping in the corner and decided to have some more fun with them. But when one of them grabbed Elimelekh, the others shouted, "No, it's not fair that one receive more than his fellow. Let's give the other one his fair share!" So they grabbed Zusya and beat him up a second time.

Seeing how distressed Elimelekh was by what had happened, Zusya laughed and said to him, "You see, my brother, if blows are destined for you, they will find you no matter where you are."

248
Ransoming the Birds

Once Zusya went on a journey to collect money to ransom Jewish captives. He came to an inn, but no one answered his knock. So he went through the rooms searching for the innkeeper. In one room he came upon a cage filled with birds. At the sight of the poor, confined creatures, his heart filled with pity.

"Here I am trying to ransom captives," he said, "and you are prisoners in this cage!"

So he unlatched the door of the cage and let the birds go free.

When the innkeeper returned from his business in town, he was furious to discover that his birds had all flown away.

"How dare you make me lose all this good money?" he yelled at Zusya.

"Do we not read in the Psalms that God's mercies are over all his works?" replied Zusya calmly.

Enraged, the innkeeper beat Zusya until his hand was sore. Then Zusya continued on his way, content.

249

The Final Question

"In the World to Come," taught Rabbi Zusya of Hanipol, "they will not ask me: 'Why were you not more like Moses our teacher?' They will ask me: 'Why were you not more like Zusya?'"

250

The Sin of Pride

Rabbi David of Lelov fasted and afflicted himself for his sins. For six years he fasted, and then for another six. Yet he was still not satisfied that he had achieved perfect atonement, but he did not know what else to do. So he traveled to Lizhensk to ask the holy Elimelekh what he still lacked.

He arrived just before the Sabbath. That evening he went before the rabbi with all the other disciples and reached out his hand for the rabbi's handshake. To his dismay, Elimelekh shook everyone's hand but his.

"Surely he mistakes me for somebody else," he thought.

When the prayers were over, he approached the rabbi again, but again the rabbi snubbed him.

All that night he wept. In the morning he decided to leave Lizhensk as soon as the Sabbath had ended. But when the Third Meal came, the time when Elimelekh spoke words of Torah, he could not resist peeking in at the window of the rabbi's house and listening in.

"Some people think," he heard the rabbi say, "that by fasting six years and then another six years, they achieve perfection of the soul. Then they come to me so that I can supply the little they still lack. What they fail to see is that all their sacrifices and devotion only serve the idol of their own pride, not heaven. If they want to serve God truly, they must turn away from the path they are now on and serve God with a truthful heart."

When Rabbi David heard Elimelekh's words, his heart trembled within his breast and he began to cry. At the conclusion of *havdalah*, he opened the door to Elimelekh's house and stood there, shaking with fear.

Elimelekh ran up to him, embraced him and cried, "Welcome! A blessing upon your head!"

When he saw this, Eleazar, Elimelekh's son, burst out, "Father, isn't this the same man whom you snubbed twice because you couldn't even stand the sight of him?"

"Oh, no!" replied Elimelekh with a broad smile. "That was somebody completely different. Don't you see that this is our own dear Rabbi David?"

251
The Radish

Rabbi Zev Wolf of Zbarazh always kept his door open to strangers, and many came to sit at his table and learn from his holy teachings.

The Third Meal of the Sabbath was a favorite time for his followers, but they were careful to speak only in low voices at that time, so as not to disturb their master, who was always deep in thought.

Once a poor, unlearned man came in at the beginning of the Third Meal and sat down at the table. He took out a large radish, cut it into pieces, and began eating the pieces with loud, crunching noises.

"Boor! Glutton!" Zev Wolf's disciples yelled at him. "How can you bring such bad manners to such a holy table?"

And the man blushed with shame.

Just then the rabbi stirred himself from his contemplation and said, "Oh, how I would love a delicious radish right now! Does anyone have one?"

Filled with joy, the stranger ran up to the rabbi and offered him a piece of his radish, which Zev Wolf ate with unabashed delight.

252

The Servant Girl's Defender

Once Rabbi Zev Wolf's wife accused a servant girl of breaking a dish. The girl denied the deed. They continued to argue about it until the rabbi's wife decided to bring the matter to court.

Dressed in her Sabbath finery, the rabbi's wife prepared to leave the house. Just then her husband appeared, likewise dressed in his Sabbath best.

"I will go with you," he announced to his wife.

"It is not becoming for you to go there," said his wife. "Besides, I know exactly what I wish to say."

"I know you do," said the rabbi with a smile, "but our poor servant girl does not. Who else but I will defend her?"

253
The Impostor Rebbe

Once a *Hasid* of the Bobover Rebbe came to him on the eve of Yom Kippur to ask the rebbe to bless him so that he and his wife might have a child. The rebbe told him the following story:

"Once a group of *Hasidim* started off to see the Seer of Lublin. Having no horses, wagons, or money, they were forced to journey on foot, and they were soon hungry, thirsty, and tired. So they decided to cast lots and choose one among them as their rebbe so that they would be guaranteed hospitality along the way. Although none of them wanted this honor, they all agreed that it was necessary, so they cast lots and ended up with Motel, a poor shoemaker, as their rebbe.

"When they reached the first town, the news spread rapidly that a great rebbe had arrived with his *Hasidim*. Soon an innkeeper ran up to them and invited them to stay at his inn, explaining that he had a very sick child whom he wished the rebbe to bless. He first served them a sumptuous banquet and then asked the rebbe to bless his sick child.

"Motel approached the boy, placed his hand upon his head, and blessed him. The innkeeper thanked him profusely and handed him a bag of money. Then the *Hasidim* left the town and proceeded on to Lublin. The Seer received them with his customary hospitality, but to their surprise he did not reprimand them about their deception along the way.

"On their way back home, they stopped in the same town. The innkeeper came running out to meet them, his face shining with joy.

" 'As soon as you left, holy master,' he said to Motel, 'my son recovered completely!'

"Amazed, the other *Hasidim* turned to their friend and asked, 'What did you say, Motel, when you blessed the child?'

" 'I asked God not to punish the innkeeper or his son for my own imposture,' replied Motel. 'I thought: "He thinks I'm a rebbe so why not help him? Otherwise he might think that all rebbes are impostors." So God listened and helped the child.' "

Now the Bobover turned to his *Hasidim* seated before him and said, "This man has come to me thinking I'm the rebbe, so why shouldn't he be helped by God, even if I'm an impostor?"

So the *Hasid* returned home, and a year later, his wife gave birth to a child.

254
The Unpaid Pledge

A follower of the Lemberger Rav was rich but stingy. Because of this, he and his wife quarreled all the time. One day he decided to ask the Rav to curse his wife so that she would die.

"Make a pledge for charity," advised the Rav, "but don't pay it. Then as a punishment, as the Talmud says, your wife will die."

So the next *Shabbat* the man went to synagogue and made a generous pledge for charity. As soon as *havdalah* was over, everyone ran up to him, astonished, since he had never given before, and demanded that he pay his pledge. He refused.

But from that moment on, his wife grew stronger every day.

So he went to the Rav and told him what had happened.

"The reason she didn't die was because that would not seem a punishment to you," explained the Rav. "Now go buy her a gift and be kind to her so that you begin to love one another. Then she will die."

So he bought her a beautiful gift and began to treat

her kindly. And for the first time, he realized what a wonderful wife she was and fell in love with her. But then his wife became ill, and the doctors feared for her life.

Desperate, the man ran back to the Rav. "Now I don't want her to die!" he cried. "I love her!"

"Then pay!" ordered the Rav.

255
The Tailor's Sleeve

Once a woman came to Rabbi Israel Hapstein of Kozenitz with her brother and said, "Holy master, my husband abandoned me several years ago. Now I cannot remarry unless I find him and obtain a divorce from him. Please help me!"

The rabbi called for a large bowl of water and then said to the woman, "Look in the water. What do you see?"

The woman gazed down into the water. "I see a big city with many houses," she said.

"Look at the street near the market," said the rabbi. "What do you see?"

"I see many shops."

"Look in the windows," said the rabbi.

The woman peered down into the water. Suddenly she cried out, "There is my husband! He is a tailor with many workers sewing suits. He holds a sleeve in one hand."

"Snatch the sleeve from his hand!" ordered the rabbi.

The woman plunged her hand into the water, seized the sleeve, and drew it out, astonished to find it still hot from the iron.

"Take this sleeve," said the rabbi, "and go to the city you saw in the water. With God's help, you shall soon have your divorce."

"But holy Rabbi," cried the woman's brother, "which way should we go?"

"Whichever way you like," answered the rabbi.

"But what shall we tell the driver when he asks us where we are going?"

"God willing, everything will be well," answered the rabbi.

So they went outside and found a wagon. To their surprise, the wagon driver did not ask them where they were going nor did he mention his fare. They traveled half an hour until they reached a forest. Suddenly sleep overcame them, and the driver toppled out of the wagon. When the woman and her brother awoke, the driver and wagon were gone, and they were alone in the forest. Fear filled their hearts, for they had no idea where they were. They walked for half an hour until they saw a clearing through the trees. When they stepped into the light, the woman let out a cry of joy: There was the city she had seen in the water!

They entered the city and soon found themselves at the market. They walked down a street, and the woman recognized her husband's tailor shop. But instead of going in, they obtained directions to the rabbi's house and went there.

"Where are you from?" the rabbi asked them.

"We came from Kozenitz," they replied.

"But that's a journey of several days!" the rabbi exclaimed.

So they told him why they had come and about the miraculous vision in the water. Then the woman showed him the sleeve she had snatched from the water.

"I know your husband," said the rabbi. "He is married and has several children. But do not worry. God will help you."

He put the woman and her brother in another room, and then sent for the tailor.

"Do you have a wife?" the rabbi asked the tailor when he entered the house.

"Of course, I do!" said the tailor. "Everybody knows my wife and children."

"But do you have a wife from a previous marriage?" asked the rabbi.

"Of course not!" said the tailor. "I was a bachelor when I came to this city."

"What kind of suit were you sewing today?" the rabbi asked.

"What strange questions!" exclaimed the tailor. "But no stranger than what just happened in my tailor shop. I had just finished making a suit for a prince and was about to press the sleeve when it flew out of my hand like a bird and disappeared. We searched everywhere for it, but it was gone. A miracle!"

"What if I were to return this sleeve to you?" asked the rabbi.

"Impossible!" said the tailor. "It vanished into thin air!"

Then the rabbi went into the next room and brought back the sleeve. "Is this the sleeve that disappeared?"

The tailor's mouth dropped open. "Why, yes!"

Then the rabbi called for the woman to come out. "And is this your first wife?"

When he recognized who it was, the tailor fainted. When he regained his senses, he confessed everything and gave his first wife a divorce.

Then she and her brother returned home to Kozenitz.

256

The Broken Betrothal

In a village near Kozenitz there once lived a pious couple who had no children. One day the husband went to Rabbi Israel Hapstein and asked him to pray to God to end their childlessness.

"Would you still want this child if I told you that you and your wife would have to remain poor for the rest of your lives?" asked the rabbi.

"Is there any greater poverty than a house without children?" replied the man.

"Such a thing can only come from God," cautioned the rabbi, "but I will pray on your behalf."

"Rabbi, how can I repay you for this favor?" asked the man.

"It is not me you must repay but another," answered the rabbi. "Your wish for a child will only be granted after you have repaid a debt."

"Tell me what I must do," said the man.

"Go home and gather all your money," said Rabbi Israel. "Then go to the Seer of Lublin and do whatever he asks of you."

So the man returned home, put all his money in a purse, bade farewell to his wife, and set off for Lublin.

He came to Rabbi Jacob Isaac, the Seer, and asked him what he should do.

"In your youth," the Seer told him, "you were betrothed to a certain bride, but when you grew up, you married another. It is because you betrayed your betrothed that you are childless. If you are to have children, you must go to her now and make peace with her. But she has moved far away from the city of her birth, and it will be difficult to find her. Because I feel sorry for you, I will tell you that two months from now there will be a fair at a certain town, and there you will find her if you do not find her before this time."

The man thanked the Seer and set off to find the woman to whom he had been betrothed in his youth. Although the Seer had warned him it would be difficult to find her, he nonetheless hoped that he might find her before the fair opened, thereby saving much time and money. But his search proved fruitless.

So he went to the fair and took lodgings at an inn. Every day he walked through the streets, searching for the woman, but during the whole time he saw no one he recognized. Had it not been for the Seer's promise that he would find her there, he would have despaired and returned home.

On the last day of the fair, he went out walking as usual and was surprised by a sudden rainstorm. When he ran to take cover under an awning, he found himself standing next to a beautiful woman dressed in the finest silks and jewelry. Quickly he stepped aside to avoid being close to her.

"So he still runs from me!" declared the woman to the other bystanders. "When I was young, I was betrothed to this man, but then he broke the betrothal and married another. Yet God did not abandon me, for now I am richer than he is!"

The man started at her words. "Who are you?" he demanded.

"Do you not recognize me? I am she who was once destined to be your bride. And what about you? Where do you now live? Have you any children?

"Alas," sighed the man, "I have no children. A holy rabbi has told me that my wife and I will have no children until I have made peace with you for the sin of my youth. Tell me what I must do, and I will do it."

"God has been kind to me," answered the woman. "I have everything I need. But I have a brother who has a daughter to marry off, and he has no money for her dowry. Go to him and give him two hundred gold coins for the dowry. Then you will certainly have your children."

"I will give you the money and let you give it to him, for I have already been away for several months and I am ready to return home."

"I cannot go," answered the woman. "You yourself must go and hand him the money. As soon as you do, I will forgive you completely, and your house will be blessed with learned children. Now I must leave you, for my journey is urgent and I must depart at once. Do not try to find me again, for it will be impossible."

And then she was gone. The man looked for her all the rest of that day, but she had vanished without a trace.

He traveled to the town where her brother lived and knocked on his door.

"What is it you want?" demanded the distraught brother when he saw the stranger on his doorstep.

"Why are you so upset?" asked the man.

"What business is it of yours?" cried the brother. "Go away and leave me in peace!"

"Just tell me what your trouble is. Perhaps I can help."

"How can you help?" wailed the brother. "I have a young daughter who cannot marry her betrothed because my landlord has raised the rent I owe him and has demanded a year's payment in advance, so I can no longer pay the dowry I promised. And my daughter's future father-in-law has given me only three more days to procure the money before he cancels the match. I am a stranger here and have no family or friends who can lend me the money. So all is lost!"

"I shall give you the money you need," said the man, and he handed the brother his purse. The brother opened the purse and gasped when he saw the two hundred gold coins.

"Why should you give me this?" he demanded. "You do not even know me!"

"Once I was betrothed to your sister," explained the man, "but I broke the betrothal and married another. Three weeks ago I met your sister at a fair and tried to appease her for the wrong I once did her, but she insisted that I travel here and give you this. She said that only this act would atone for my earlier sin."

"You are mocking me!" cried the man, flinging the purse back at the giver. "My sister died fifteen years ago!"

"I do not believe you!" replied the man.

"Then I will prove it!" And the brother took the man to his sister's grave and showed him the inscription with the date of her death.

"Surely she was sent from heaven!" cried the man, and he handed the purse back to the brother. "Take this, for it was certainly meant for you." And he told him the whole story of his visit to the holy rabbis and his journey to the fair.

"Then may you be blessed with learned children," said the brother, "for you have done a righteous deed today and restored my soul."

Then the man returned home and came to Rabbi Israel of Kozenitz to tell him what happened.

"Blessed be the Holy One and blessed be His Name!" said the rabbi. "I prayed that she would appear to you and accept your offering of appeasement. For it was decreed that you would have no children because you broke your betrothal. And now you will indeed have learned children as your betrothed promised you."

Therefore, beware of betraying matches, for they are as hard to achieve as splitting the Red Sea, and they are even harder to break.

257
The Cape

Once a woman came to Rabbi Israel, the Maggid of Kozenitz, lamenting that she still had no child after twelve years of marriage.

"What are you willing to do about it?" asked the Maggid.

The woman was astonished. "What can I do about it?"

"When my mother came to the Baal Shem Tov with a similar problem," said the Maggid, "he asked her the same question."

" 'I am a poor woman,' my mother told him, 'but I do have a beautiful cape, my *katinka*.'

" 'Bring it to me,' said the Besht.

"She went home to fetch the cape, but when she returned to the inn where the Besht was staying, he was gone. She traveled from town to town with her *katinka* until she reached Medzibozh.

"When she reached the Besht's house, she handed him the cape. He hung it on the wall and said, 'It is well.'

"Then she walked all the way home. A year later I was born."

"I too have a cape!" cried the woman. "I will bring it to you at once!"

"No, that will not do," replied the Maggid, "for you have heard the story. My mother had no story to go by."

258
Good Purim, Good Purim!!

Moshele the water carrier was a meek, downtrodden man who barely earned enough from his labors to feed his large family. One Purim he went to the home of his rebbe, Rabbi Israel, the Maggid of Kozenitz, to wish him a Good Purim. Head bowed, he slunk into the house and mumbled, "Good Purim," in a dispirited voice.

The Maggid upbraided him sharply, saying, "Moshele, how can you greet me with such a feeble 'Good Purim'? And where are your *shalakh manos* for today?"

"Rabbi," protested Moshele, "I owe the grocer money. I owe the baker money, and the tailor and the shoemaker. Where could I get enough money to buy *shalakh manos* for you?"

"Moshele," smiled the rabbi. "When you learn to say 'Good Purim,' everything will come your way. Then you will return here with proper *shalakh manos*."

Moshele left the rabbi's house more dejected than before. Not only did he have a mountain of debts he could not pay, but even his rebbe had turned him away because of his poverty.

Hoping to beg one more ruble of credit, Moshele went to the grocery store. But as soon as he walked in the door, the grocer said to him, "Ah, Moshele, maybe you've come to pay me some of the money you owe me?"

Moshele's heart sank. Then he remembered the Maggid's words. With his head held high, he said cheerfully,

"Today is Purim, grocer! Today there is no evil in the world. Good Purim!"

The astonished grocer forgot all about Moshele's overdue bills and gave him enough cakes, honey, and wine for his *shalakh manos* basket. Overjoyed, Moshele ran to the Maggid's house and gave him the basket.

"Good, Moshele!" smiled the Maggid. "I see that you are learning to say 'Good Purim!' Don't you know that today is a wonderful day? Haman and Amalek have been defeated!"

Moshele returned to the grocer and greeted him with another confident "Good Purim!" Then he asked for groceries to provide for his family's Purim *seudah*. The grocer filled his basket with fish, *hallah*, honey, cakes, and wine.

"Thank you!" shouted Moshele as he left the store. "Just put it on my bill. Today is a wonderful day! Our enemies have been defeated! Good Purim!!"

Next he went to the tailor, whose shop he had not entered in ten years.

"Good Purim, tailor!" he cried joyfully as he walked through the door. The tailor dropped his needle and thread in surprise. What was Moshele doing here? Had he suddenly inherited a fortune?

"I want you to make clothes for my entire family," said Moshele. "A new dress for my beloved wife, a new coat for me, and pretty things for all the children."

"Moshele," said the astonished tailor, "the last time you came in here—ten years ago—you bought a suit, and you still owe me money for it!"

"But today is Purim!" said Moshele. "Let's rejoice, for wicked Haman has been defeated! Good Purim!"

"Good Purim to you, Moshele!" answered the bewildered tailor, and he set to work measuring Moshele for a new coat. Then he went to the back of his shop and brought back a tower of boxes. "For your wife and children," he said, handing the boxes to Moshele.

"Just put it on my bill," said Moshele, walking out the door. "Good Purim!"

Then Moshele went home and handed his astonished wife all the packages he was carrying. "Good Purim, dear wife!" he cried. "Stand tall and proud, children! For today is Purim! There is no more evil in the world, for our enemies have been defeated. Say 'Good Purim' with joy in your hearts!"

"Good Purim, Papa!" the children cried, and their hearts did indeed dance with joy.

Then Moshele went to the bank. He marched up to the window and, in a confident voice, said to the teller, "I wish to speak to the manager!"

The startled teller scurried off and soon returned with the manager.

"What seems to be the problem?" asked the manager.

"I am Moshele the water carrier," said Moshele, "but I do not wish to remain a water carrier all my life. I want a loan so that I can start my own business. Today is Purim! We have triumphed over our enemies. Good Purim!"

Impressed by Moshele's confidence, the banker lent him the money he needed to start a business. In a short time, Moshele became a successful merchant and repaid all his debts. The wealthier he became, the more he gave to the poor and oppressed in Kozenitz.

And every Purim the Maggid sent all his followers to Moshele's house to learn how to say "Good Purim! Good Purim!"

259
A Crying Baby

On the eve of Yom Kippur, the entire congregation of Rabbi Moses Leib of Sassov gathered together in the synagogue to pray. But when the time came for *Kol Nidre*, the rabbi had still not arrived. They waited and waited, and finally decided to begin the *Kol Nidre* prayers without him.

Just then the rabbi rushed in, out of breath.

"Forgive me, good people," he said, "but on my way to synagogue tonight, I passed a house where I heard a baby crying. Her mother had already gone to synagogue, so I picked up the child and comforted her and then came here as fast as I could."

Then he began chanting *Kol Nidre,* and the angels rejoiced.

3. REB NAHMAN AND THE LATER MASTERS

260
The Lost Princess

Once a king had six sons and one daughter. The king loved his daughter very much, but one day, in a fit of anger, he shouted at her, "May the Not-Good take you!"

The next day his daughter vanished. They looked everywhere for her but could not find her. The viceroy, seeing the king's great distress, offered to go in search of the missing princess. He traveled for a very long time, through wild and barren places, until he came to a beautiful castle guarded by many troops. He walked up to the front gate, and they let him enter without challenge.

He passed through many rooms and finally came to the throne room, where he saw a king with many attendants and guards. Beautiful music filled the air, and fantastic delicacies were heaped upon the tables. The viceroy entered the room, but no one seemed to notice him. He went to a corner of the vast room, ate and drank his fill, and then lay down to observe the events unfolding before him.

Suddenly the king cried, "Let the queen be brought here!"

When they brought her into the room, the viceroy immediately recognized the lost princess for whom he had searched so long. And when she glanced around the room and saw him lying in the corner, she too recognized him, her father's viceroy.

She rose from her throne and came over to him.

"Do you recognize me?" she asked.

"Yes," he replied. "You are the lost princess. But how did you get here?"

"When my father cursed me, he sent me here. This is the place of the Not-Good."

"Your father is brokenhearted," he told her. "For many years he has searched for you. How can I bring you home?"

"The only way you can free me from here," she said, "is to choose a place and stay there for an entire year. The whole time you must long for me, thinking of nothing else but your desire to free me. And you must fast. On the last day of the year, you must fast and remain awake from sunset to sunset."

The viceroy did so. On the last day of the year, he started off toward the castle, but along the way he saw an apple tree whose boughs hung heavy with beautiful fruit. Desire suddenly seized him, and he ate one of the apples. Instantly he fell to the ground, and a deep sleep overcame him. His servant tried in vain to wake him, but he remained asleep for many years. At last he woke up and asked his servant, "Where in the world am I?"

"You have been sleeping for a long time," the servant told him, "and I have kept myself alive by eating this fruit."

Heartbroken, the viceroy went to the castle and found the princess.

"If only you had come on that day, you would have freed me!" she cried. "Because of one day, you have lost everything! True, it is difficult not to eat, especially on the final day when the evil inclination shows its greatest strength. Choose now a new place and stay there for a year, but this time on the final day, you are permitted to eat. Only refrain from sleeping and do not drink wine, which may make you sleep, for the essential thing is to stay awake."

And he did as the princess had instructed. On the last day he passed by a spring whose waters looked red and smelled like wine. He said to his servant, "Look at this spring! Instead of water, it looks and smells like wine!"

He tasted it and immediately fell asleep, and he slept for seventy years. Soldiers came by, and the viceroy's servant hid from them. Then a carriage came by carrying the princess, and she recognized the viceroy sleeping by the spring. She tried to wake him but could not. Then she began to cry, "How many years have you labored to free me, and you have forfeited everything because of one day! And what a pity for me, too, for I have been here so many years and cannot escape!"

Then she removed her kerchief from her head and wrote on it with her tears and left it beside the sleeping viceroy. Then she got back into her carriage and rode off.

Then the viceroy woke up and asked his servant, "Where in the world am I?"

"You have been sleeping here for seventy years," the servant told him. "During that time many soldiers passed by, and the princess, too, came by in her carriage and wept over you and cried, 'What a pity for us both!'"

Then the viceroy noticed the kerchief.

"Where did this come from?" he asked.

"The princess left it, and she wrote something on it with her tears."

The viceroy held the kerchief up to the sun and read the tearstained words: "No longer am I in the castle, but now you must search for me in a castle of pearls on a golden mountain."

So the viceroy left his servant and went in search of the princess. For several years he traveled across deserts, for he was certain that the golden mountain could only be found far from human settlements. At last he saw a towering giant carrying a tree so huge it dwarfed all trees the viceroy had ever seen.

"Who are you?" asked the giant.

"A human being," answered the viceroy.

"I have been in the desert for a very long time," said the giant, "but never have I seen a human being."

"I am searching for a lost princess," explained the viceroy. "She is in a castle of pearls on a golden mountain."

"What nonsense they told you!" laughed the giant. "No such place exists!"

But the viceroy refused to be discouraged. "I know such a place exists and I shall find it!"

"Very well," said the giant. "If you insist on believing this nonsense, I will summon all the animals and ask them, for I am their master. Perhaps one of them has heard of such a place."

So he summoned all the animals, great and small, and asked them, but none had ever heard of a golden mountain or a castle of pearls.

"What did I tell you?" said the giant. "If you want my advice, go home and forget this crazy idea. You will never find what you seek."

"You are wrong," answered the viceroy. "I will yet find it, for it surely exists."

"Then perhaps my brother can help you, for he is master of all the birds, and they fly high over the earth. Perhaps one of them has seen your golden mountain and castle of pearls. Go to him and tell him that I have sent you."

So the viceroy traveled many years through the wilderness until he met a giant as huge as the first, also carrying an immense tree under one arm. He told him his story and this giant too mocked him, claiming that such a place did not exist anywhere in the world. But the viceroy refused to be dissuaded, so the giant summoned all the birds, great and small, and asked them if they had seen a golden mountain and a castle of pearls. None of them had.

"You see?" said the second giant. "It is all nonsense. Listen to me and return home."

"But I know such a place exists!" insisted the viceroy.

"Then perhaps my brother who is master of the winds knows where it is, for the winds blow throughout the earth. Surely they will know of it if it exists at all."

So the viceroy traveled many more years until he met a third giant as huge as the other two, who like his brothers, carried a large tree. And when the viceroy told the giant why he had come, the giant scoffed and mocked him. But the viceroy insisted that such a place existed, so the giant summoned the winds and asked them if they had ever seen a golden mountain and a castle of pearls. And none of them had.

"Didn't I tell you it was all nonsense?" said the giant.

Then the viceroy began to weep, but he still refused to give up his search.

Just then the last wind arrived and presented itself before the giant.

"Why are you late?" demanded the giant in anger. "Did I not summon all the winds? Why did you not come with the others?"

"I was delayed because I had to carry a princess to a castle of pearls on a golden mountain."

How overjoyed the viceroy was to hear the wind's words!

Then the giant asked the wind, "What things are costly there?"

"All is costly in that place," answered the wind.

Then the giant said to the viceroy, "You have been searching long and have undergone many trials. Perhaps you will now need money to complete your task. Take this purse. Whenever you need money, put your hand inside and take from it whatever you need."

The giant ordered the wind to carry the viceroy to the golden mountain. But the soldiers standing guard at the gate would not let him in. So he reached into the purse and drew forth gold to bribe them, and they let him in. And he saw that it was a beautiful city. He went to a rich man and arranged for his board, for he knew that he must spend much time there, using his wits to free the princess.

And finally he did.

261
The Rabbi's Son

Once a rabbi had an only son whose study, prayer, and pious deeds raised him to such heights that he became the Lesser Light of his generation. Yet he sensed within himself an imperfection and wished to overcome it.

His friends advised him to seek out a certain *tzaddik* in a distant village. But when he told his father of his wish to visit this *tzaddik*, his father at first refused, saying, "You are a greater scholar than he, from a nobler family!"

Still the son continued to plead with him until at last he relented. But his father insisted on accompanying him, saying, "I will show you that he is not what you think."

Before leaving, he made his son agree to a test: "If no accident happens to us on our way, then heaven favors our journey. If, however, we meet with an obstacle, then our quest is not from heaven, and we must return home."

And the son agreed.

So they set out. As they were crossing a bridge over a swollen stream, their horse stumbled, almost plunging them to their deaths.

"You see?" cried the father. "It was not meant to be!" So they returned home.

But the son began to pine away with longing to meet the great *tzaddik*, until the father agreed to try the journey once more. But again they met with an accident. This time both wagon axles broke as they mounted a hill.

"Surely this is a sign for us to abandon our journey!" cried the father. And so they did.

The son begged to try one more time, and at last the

father, stricken with pity for his only son, agreed to a last attempt. This time they proceeded without mishap to an inn.

There they met a merchant. When the man learned of their destination, he warned them that the *tzaddik* they sought was a charlatan, a frivolous man, a sinner.

"You see?" the father told his son. "I knew it!" And he made his son return home. A short time after that, the boy sickened and died.

On the night of his funeral, the son came to the father in a dream. His pale face blazed with anger.

"Why are you so angry?" asked the father.

"Go to the *tzaddik* and he will tell you."

The father awoke, terrified, but quickly dismissed the dream as a phantom of his grief-stricken brain. Later that night, the same dream returned. Again he paid it no heed. But when it happened a third time, the father knew he must go to the *tzaddik*.

On the way he stopped at the inn to rest. There he met the same merchant who had earlier warned them to stay away from the *tzaddik*. When the father greeted the man this time, he noted that he seemed less friendly now, even menacing.

"This time you may complete your journey," laughed the merchant, seeming to grow larger and more menacing even as the father looked on. "Your son no longer threatens to undo me."

"What are you talking about?" cried the father, fear suddenly piercing his heart.

"Surely you recall how your horse stumbled and your axles broke when you tried to reach the *tzaddik*? That was all my doing!" cried the merchant, his ugly body now swelling to fill the room. His face lost its human cast and became terrible. Huge black wings sprouted from his back. With horror, the father recognized Samael, the Evil One.

"Had your son reached the *tzaddik*," said Samael, hovering over the terrified father like a black cloud, "the Lesser Light and the Greater Light would have become one and brought on the Redemption. But now the danger is averted!" And with an earsplitting howl, he flew up to the skies and disappeared.

The father, brokenhearted, traveled on to the *tzaddik*'s house. The holy man was waiting for him.

"What a pity!" cried the *tzaddik*. "What a pity on those who are lost and will never be found! May the Lord soon end our exile!"

262
The Clever Man and the
Simple Man

Once there were two wealthy men who each had a son. One son was clever and the other simple. In their youth the two boys studied together and became fast friends. But after a time the fathers' fortunes declined, and they were forced to send their sons into the world to make their own way.

The simple son was content to become a shoemaker. But the clever son had more ambition, so he apprenticed himself to some traveling merchants and came to the great city of Warsaw. There he apprenticed himself to a new master and learned the ways of business. But in time he wearied of that and began to travel throughout the world. When he came to Italy, he became a goldsmith and soon surpassed his teacher and his teacher's teacher in his artistry. But in time he tired of that, too, and so became a jeweler and then a doctor. At last, surfeited with riches and honor, he decided to return to the place of his birth and take a wife, for he wished to show the friends of his youth how great he had become.

Meanwhile the simple son had become a middling shoemaker, barely eking out a living for himself and his wife. Yet he was content with his lot. Each day he would say to his wife: "Please give me some broth or some kasha or some meat," and each day she gave him only a dry crust of bread. But the simple man ate the dry crust as though it were manna from heaven and thanked his wife with a full heart.

Then he would ask her for his kaftan or sheepskin coat or fur cape, and she would hand him the single pelt they shared between them. And he would put on the pelt and glow with pride at being so finely dressed.

Despite his poverty he was always happy. To the rest of the townspeople he was a laughingstock, for his shoes were poorly made and fetched less than any other shoemaker's. And they would all make fun of him, calling him a fool. But he never became angry with them, for in his heart of hearts he knew that his was the best lot of all.

When his rich friend returned to town, the poor cobbler ran to greet him and invited him to stay in his home, since the other's house had fallen into disrepair after so many years of neglect.

"I will gather all that I own into a bag and leave you the rest of my house for your needs," he said, embracing his friend.

So the clever man moved into his friend's humble quarters, but he was miserable there, for he had returned wanting to impress the townspeople with his wealth and attainments.

Then a rich man came to the clever man and asked him to make him a ring. The clever man used all his art to make an exquisite ring unlike any other. Engraved on it was a wonderful tree with many intricate paths winding around its base. But despite the ring's rare beauty, the buyer was dissatisfied with it, so the clever man's pride in his work turned to ashes in his mouth.

Then a second customer came to the clever man and ordered a ring made to display a certain precious gem. Again the clever man used all his knowledge of precious stones and gold to fashion an extraordinary ring, but when cutting the gem, he made a single mistake discernible only to himself. The customer was delighted with the ring, but the clever man felt only disgust.

And he suffered in his medical art as well, for those he healed attributed their cure to accident, and those he failed to heal blamed him.

And he received no satisfaction from the tailor in the town, for he always found fault with the garments he ordered—a missing stitch here, a crooked lapel there.

Whenever the simple cobbler visited him, he was always surprised to find his friend's brow furrowed and his spirit vexed. "How is it that you are so clever, yet you are always so unhappy, while I am so simple and always content? Perhaps it would be better for you to have less understanding and be more like me."

"You are mad!" scoffed the clever man.

"May the Lord bring you up to my level some day," replied the simple man.

"Only if my reason should flee or I should become ill," said the clever man. "For you are nothing but a madman and a fool."

"We shall see who is the greater fool," replied the simple man.

"You shall never attain my wisdom as long as you live," said the clever man.

"All things are possible with God's help," said the simple man. "It is even possible that I should acquire your wisdom in the twinkling of an eye."

The clever man laughed heartily at his friend's words.

One night the king of the country was looking through his record books, and he discovered that in a certain town there lived two men, friends from childhood, who were known simply as the Simple Man and the Clever Man.

"I should like to meet this pair," said the king, so he sent a messenger to the town, a clever messenger to summon the clever man, and a simple messenger, the royal treasurer, to summon the simple man.

A short while later, the king learned that the governor of this region was dealing dishonestly and unfairly with the people in his charge. So he removed the governor from office and decided to appoint the simple man in his place. "For," thought the king, "what better ruler is there than a simple man who does not use his cleverness to deceive the people."

The simple man was overjoyed to receive a summons from the king. As he set out, he received the news that he had been appointed governor. So the simple man began to rule the region, bringing to his new position the same simple honesty and love of truth that had always guided his actions. And his people loved him and praised his wisdom.

One day one of his advisors said, "It is time for you to appear before the king, for that is what governors must do. And since the king is wise in the ways of science and languages, it is only fitting that you should learn them, too, so that you can talk to him."

So the simple man learned science and languages, but he still ruled his people with a pure and simple heart. And it occurred to him that his words to his clever friend had indeed come true, for he had now acquired the other's worldy wisdom.

Meanwhile the clever man received his summons to the king, but he said to the royal messenger, "Why should the king want to see an unimportant man like me?"

And the more he thought about it, the more convinced he became that there was no king at all. For wouldn't a king have his own wise men? Why should he send for someone in a distant town?

"There is no king!" he told the messenger. "You have been deceived."

"But I have a letter from the king!" protested the messenger.

"Did you receive it from the king's own hand?" asked the clever man.

"No," admitted the messenger, "one of the royal servants gave it to me."

"Have you ever seen the king with your own eyes?" asked the clever man.

"No," said the messenger. "But if there is no king, who rules the country?"

"When I was in Italy," answered the clever man, "I saw that seventy counselors governed there together. After they had governed for some time, others came to take their place."

And his wise words impressed the royal messenger.

"I will prove to you that what I say is true," continued the clever man. "Tomorrow we will journey together and discover whether this king of yours exists."

The next day they came to the marketplace and asked a soldier there, "Whom do you serve?"

"The king," replied the soldier.

"Have you ever seen him with your own eyes?"

"No," replied the soldier, "but surely my officer has."

But the officer had never seen the king, either.

From town to town the two wandered, everywhere seeking someone who had seen the king, but never did they come upon such a person. At last their money ran out, so they sold their horses, and when that money was gone, they became beggars. No longer did people answer their questions about the king, but instead threw stones at them and called them fools.

Meanwhile, the king heard about the wisdom of his new governor, the simple man. He promoted him to prime minister and built him a magnificent palace in the capital.

One day the two beggars reached the capital and passed by the house of a wonder-worker, a *baal shem*. Outside the house a crowd of afflicted people gathered, waiting to be healed. When the two beggars came to an inn, the clever man made fun of this wonder-worker.

"His healing is all a fraud," he jeered, "an even greater lie than the claim that there is a king!"

When the innkeeper heard his words, he beat him

soundly, for the wonder-worker was well respected in the city.

So the clever man came to a judge to protest his harsh treatment at the hands of the innkeeper. The judge, too, beat him, but the clever man continued to take his case to higher and higher courts until he reached the palace of the prime minister.

When the guard brought him before the prime minister, the simple man recognized his friend immediately, but the clever man failed to recognize him, for the simple man was dressed in court clothes and bore himself with great dignity.

"Why are you here?" the simple man asked his friend.

"Because I claimed that the *baal shem* was a fraud, and they beat me," replied the clever man.

"So you still have faith in your cleverness," sighed the simple man. "You see that I have already reached your level, but you have yet to reach mine."

Out of compassion, the simple man ordered new clothes for his destitute friend and had fine food and drink brought before him. While they were eating, the clever man boasted that he had discovered that there really was no king governing the country.

"What do you mean?" cried the simple man. "I see his face daily!"

"Did you know his father and his grandfather?" challenged the clever man. "They just told you he was the king, and you believed their lies."

"How long will you cling to your cleverness and not see life?" cried the simple man. "You shall never merit the grace of simplicity."

Then a messenger came and summoned them to the devil. The simple man became frightened and ran to the *baal shem* for an amulet to protect him. And the *baal shem* gave him the amulet, and he returned home in peace.

But the clever man and his companion scoffed at the idea of a devil and boldly followed the messenger. When they reached the devil's kingdom, they found themselves suddenly mired in clay, and there they remained for several years, suffering torments. Yet all that time, they mistook their tormentors for men, not demons.

Then the simple man went to the *baal shem* and asked him to take him to the devil's kingdom so that he might see what had become of his friend. And they traveled there and found them mired in clay.

"See what these scoundrels are doing to us for no reason!" cried the clever man.

"So you still believe in your wisdom," replied the simple man, "and think these are human beings. Despite your faithlessness, the *baal shem* will redeem you and set you free."

And the *baal shem* did. Only then did the clever man admit his folly and acknowledge that there was a king and servants who did his will.

263

Why Naftali of Ropshitz Wore White Trousers

A young disciple of Naftali of Ropshitz once came to him and asked, "Holy master, why do you always wear white trousers?"

"I cannot tell you," replied the rabbi. "It's a secret."

The rabbi's answer only served to pique the young man's curiosity. Again and again he came to Naftali and begged to know the secret of his white trousers.

Finally Naftali said to him, "Very well, I will tell you. But first you must fast for six days."

So the young man fasted for six days. Then he came to the rabbi and said, "I have done what you requested. Now, holy master, tell me the secret."

"First swear to me that you will tell no one as long as you live."

And the young man swore.

Naftali led him into a room, then a second room, and finally a third, locking all the doors behind him as they passed from one room into the next. All the while, the young man held his breath, certain that the rabbi was about to unveil one of the holiest mysteries.

After checking the locks one last time, the rabbi beckoned to the young man to come close and then bent down to whisper into his ear, "The reason I wear white trousers is that they are the cheapest."

"For this I had to fast for six days!" the young man cried. "Why make such a secret of something so trivial?"

The rabbi smiled. "Because if people found out, they would all want to wear white trousers, and then the price would go up. Now don't forget your promise—don't tell anyone as long as you live!"

264

Reb Eisik's Treasure

A young man once came to Reb Simcha Bunem to study. Before he accepted him as a student, the rabbi told him the following story:

"In Cracow there once lived a poor Jew named Eisik son of Yekl. One night he had a dream that there was a treasure buried under a bridge at the Vltava River in Prague. When he awoke the next morning, he quickly dismissed the dream, but when it returned twice more, he decided that it had been sent from heaven. So he left Cracow and traveled on foot to Prague.

"After many days he saw a palace and a stone bridge that he recognized from his dream. But the bridge was guarded by the king's soldiers, and when Eisik began nosing about on the river bank, they arrested him and brought him to the officer in charge.

"'What were you doing under the bridge?' de-

manded the officer. 'Tell me why I should not have you
executed as a spy!'

" 'Please do not be angry with me,' pleaded Eisik. 'I
mean no harm to the king. I have only come here because
I had a dream that there was a treasure buried under this
bridge.'

"The officer threw back his head and laughed. 'What
a fool you are! How can you believe in dreams? Only old
women believe in such things! Just last night I myself had
a dream that in Cracow, buried under the fireplace of a
poor Jew named Eisik son of Yekl, I would find a fabulous
treasure. Do you see me running off to Cracow to chase
phantoms?'

"Still laughing, the officer ordered his men to let Eisik
go. Eisik thanked him, returned home, and found the
treasure just where the officer said it would be.

"And so," Reb Simcha Bunem said to the young man
standing before him, "we all spend our lives searching for
something of great value, always expecting to find it
elsewhere, perhaps in the heart of a *tzaddik*. But we may
never find what we seek. Yet know that it may be found."

265
The Cost of an Etrog

Nothing meant more to Nahum of Chernobyl than celebrating Sukkot with great joy. And nothing enhanced his
joy like a lovely *etrog* from the Holy Land. But one year
there was a drought in Israel, and there were very few
etrogim available for the holiday. Only one man in Chernobyl had an *etrog*—Moshe Haim, the wealthiest man in
town.

Desolate to be without an *etrog* for the holiday,
Nahum decided that he must buy Moshe Haim's *etrog*.
But he was a very poor man. What could he possibly offer
Moshe Haim, the richest man in Chernobyl? The only
things of value that Nahum owned were the Baal Shem

Tov's *tefillin* that he had inherited from the Master. Surely he could not part with those! But how could he welcome the Festival of Joy without an *etrog*?

Then Nahum reached a decision. Seizing the *tefillin*, he ran to Moshe Haim's house and said to him, "I would like to buy your *etrog*!"

"You!" scoffed the rich man. "You could never afford it!"

Then Nahum held out the *tefillin*. "Would you accept these in exchange? They once belonged to the Baal Shem Tov."

Moshe Haim gasped when he saw what was in Nahum's hand. The holy Besht's *tefillin*!

"Very well," he said, trying to conceal his excitement. "I will sell you my *etrog*," and he placed the gleaming yellow fruit in Nahum's outstretched hand.

Overjoyed, Nahum ran home to show the *etrog* to his wife.

"Where did you get that?" cried his wife when she saw the *etrog*. "We don't even have enough food for the holiday!"

"I traded the Baal Shem Tov's *tefillin* for it," announced Nahum.

Enraged, his wife grabbed the *etrog* out of Nahum's hand and flung it to the ground, breaking off the *pittum* and thus making it unusable for the holiday.

Nahum's face flushed with anger, then suddenly grew calm. "Yesterday," he said, "we owned a priceless treasure—the Besht's *tefillin*. Today we owned another priceless treasure—a beautiful *etrog*. Now we have neither. But we still have each other. Let's not fight. Good *yontov*!"

266

The Alphabet

An ignorant villager, knowing that it was a *mitzvah* to feast well before Yom Kippur, drank himself into such a stupor that he missed *Kol Nidre* services. When he awoke late at night, he wanted to pray, but he didn't know any of the prayers by heart. So he began to recite the alphabet over and over again.

"Dear God!" he cried. "I am giving You all the letters. You arrange them in the right order!"

The next day he went to the Kotsker Rebbe's *shul* for services. As soon as *Neilah* was over, the Kotsker summoned him and asked him to explain his absence at *Kol Nidre* the night before.

"Holy master!" he cried. "So eager was I to welcome the holy day with joy that I overdid it a bit and slept through the service. When I awoke late at night, I tried to pray, but I did not know the proper words. For, you see, all I know by heart is the *aleph-bet*. So I just recited the letters and asked God to make words out of them. Were my prayers acceptable?"

The Kotsker smiled. "More acceptable than mine," he said, "for you spoke them with your whole heart."

267
A Matter of Faith

Once a poor man came to the Kotsker Rebbe and said, "Holy Master, my oldest daughter has reached the age of marriage, but I have no money for a dowry. Please write to one of your wealthy disciples and ask him to give me the money."

So the Kotsker wrote the letter and gave it to the poor man, who traveled on foot to the wealthy man's town a great distance away. But when he reached the wealthy man's house and gave him the Kotsker's letter, the man gave him only a single coin and sent him on his way. Heartbroken, the poor man turned around and began his long journey home.

But before he had taken twenty steps, the wealthy man came running after him and filled his arms with fine foods and wedding garments that had been prepared for his own daughter's upcoming wedding.

"Why didn't you give me all this when I first presented the letter to you?" asked the startled poor man.

"Because I wanted to teach you not to put your trust in any person, even a great rabbi," answered the wealthy man. "You seem to have forgotten that there is a God in Israel."

268
The Goat's Horns and the Snuffbox

Once Rabbi Yitzhak of Vorki went to visit Menahem Mendel of Kotsk when the latter was already in seclusion from the world. He knocked and entered the Kotsker's room.

"Peace be with you, Rabbi!" said Yitzhak.

"Why do you call me 'rabbi'?" asked Menahem Mendel. "I am no rabbi! Don't you recognize me? I'm the goat, the sacred goat!"

And he told this story: Once an old Jew lost his snuffbox made out of horn and went out walking, bemoaning his loss. In a short while he met the sacred goat who was pacing the earth with the tips of his black horns touching the stars. When the goat heard the old Jew crying, he leaned down and said, "Cut a piece of my horn for your snuffbox."

Overjoyed, the man cut off a piece of horn and made a new snuffbox for himself, which he filled with tobacco. When he went to the House of Study later that day, he offered some of the tobacco to his friends.

"What wonderful tobacco!" they cried. "Where did you get that snuffbox?"

So he told them about the sacred goat whose horns reached to the stars. They went in search of the goat, and when they found it, asked for a bit of horn out of which to make snuffboxes. Again and again, the goat leaned down and let them cut off pieces of its horns. From all over they came, and always the goat reached down its horns.

Now the sacred goat still paces the earth, but it has no horns.

269
The More Mud, the Better

Once Israel of Riszhyn, the "Riszhner," was traveling with a group of students on a cold night, and he came to a town. One of his students mentioned that in this town lived a rich man who offered hospitality to great men but not to poor ones.

"Since you are such a great rabbi," said the student, "this miser will surely take us in."

So they went to the home of the rich man and knocked on the door, but the man did not open it. Then the Riszhner went around to the side and knocked on the window. When the rich man saw who it was, he rushed to let the great rabbi in.

"My students, too, wish to come in," said the Riszhner when the man opened the front door.

"But look at their shoes!" cried the rich man. "They're covered with mud. They'll dirty up the whole house!"

To which the Riszhner replied, "Let me tell you a story: Once there was a rich man who was very stingy. Never would he allow poor people into his house. Once when he was on a journey, he passed a poor family whose wagon had turned over in the mud. He took them into his carriage and brought them to their destination.

"When the rich man died, the angels began counting up all his acts of stinginess, and they were almost beyond measure. But one angel came and testified that once the rich man had helped a poor family on their way. Then a second angel came and placed mud from these people's shoes on the scale and it outweighed all his sins.

" 'Send him down to earth again,' the second angel said. 'If he still holds that mud dear, we should let him into Paradise.' "

"When the rich man heard this, he began to tremble.

'Come in! Come in!' he cried. 'All of you, come in and welcome! The more mud, the better!' "

270
Only the Story Remains

Whenever the Jews were threatened with disaster, the Baal Shem Tov would go to a certain place in the forest, light a fire, and say a special prayer. Always a miracle would occur, and the disaster would be averted.

In later times when disaster threatened, the Maggid of Mezritch, his disciple, would go to the same place in the forest and say, "Master of the Universe, I do not know how to light the fire, but I can say the prayer." And again the disaster would be averted.

Still later, his disciple, Moshe Leib of Sasov, would go to the same place in the forest and say, "Lord of the World, I do not know how to light the fire or say the prayer, but I know the place and that must suffice." And it always did.

When Israel of Riszhyn needed intervention from heaven, he would say to God, "I no longer know the place, nor how to light the fire, nor how to say the prayer, but I can tell the story and that must suffice."

And it did.

271
Two Slaps

The Stanislaver liked to arrive at synagogue punctually every morning. One morning the *shammes* did not call him, and he was therefore late. Always quick to anger, the rabbi slapped the man twice to punish him. Immediately he regretted his action, and he vowed to wander as a beggar for a year to make atonement for his sin.

At the end of the year he returned to Stanislav still disguised as a beggar and went to the synagogue for the evening service. The synagogue president invited him home for a meal and then offered him a bed for the night.

The next morning the *shammes* came to call the president for morning prayers but found him still asleep. On tiptoe he crept into the dining room and stole the two silver candlesticks on the mantel, which he hid under his coat. Then he knocked on the president's door.

When the president emerged from his bedroom, he immediately noticed that the silver candlesticks were gone.

"Have you seen any vagabonds roaming about?" he asked the *shammes*.

"If you ask me," said the *shammes*, "it was your beggar who stole the candlesticks."

But the disguised rabbi firmly protested his innocence. He turned to the *shammes* and said, "Will you swear an oath that you saw me take them?"

Enraged at his impudence, the *shammes* struck the Stanislaver twice across the cheek. But when he raised his hand to strike a third blow, the rabbi said, "You only owe me two. I wish no interest. Now return the candlesticks to their place and announce to the congregation that their rabbi has come home."

272
The Mirror and the Glass

Once Rabbi Eisig of Ziditzov traveled to a village where only one poor Jew lived. The poor man took him in, fed him, and prepared a bed for him. But all the while he sighed.

"Why do you sigh?" Rabbi Eisig asked him.

"Because I cannot show you the honor you deserve," replied the poor man.

Touched by the man's generosity of heart, the rabbi gave him his blessing and departed the next day.

From that moment on, the poor man's fortunes began to rise until he became the wealthiest man in the area. So many beggars came to his door that he hired a guard to keep them away. He gained a reputation as a heartless miser.

After a time Rabbi Eisig returned to the village and called at the Jew's house, but the guard turned him away.

"My master is meeting with a very important person," announced the guard gruffly.

"Tell your master," replied Rabbi Eisig, "that I am the one responsible for all his wealth."

The guard went inside and soon returned with permission for Rabbi Eisig to enter. He led the rabbi into a magnificent parlor and told him to wait there. After a long time, his host entered the room and spoke a few curt words to him. It was obvious that he was eager for the rabbi to leave.

"Look through that window," Rabbi Eisig said to him. "What do you see?"

"People going about their business," replied his host.

Then the rabbi said, "Look in the mirror. Now what do you see?"

"Only myself," answered the rich man.

"Both the window and the mirror are made of glass," said Rabbi Eisig, "but through one you can see others and through the other, only yourself. The only difference between them is a gilt coating. It is time to scratch off the gilt."

Immediately grasping the rabbi's meaning, the rich man cried, "Only leave me my wealth, and I promise to change my ways!"

And true to his word, he made true repentance and never again turned away a needy soul from his door.

273
Begin with Yourself

When Hayyim of Zanz was a young man, he set about trying to reform his country from its evil ways. But when he reached the age of thirty, he looked around and saw that evil remained in the world. So he said, "Perhaps I was too ambitious. I will begin with my province." But at the age of forty his province too remained mired in evil. So he said, "I was still too ambitious. From now on I will only try to lift up my community." But at fifty he saw that his community had still not changed. So he decided only to reform his own family. But when he looked around, he saw that his family had grown and moved away, and that he now remained alone.

"Now I understand that I needed to begin with myself."

So he spent the rest of his life perfecting his own soul.

274
Moshele's Gift

When the Sokolover was still a youth, he learned from his grandfather, the Kotsker, that God only loves what is real. So he went into the synagogue looking for a real Jew. Inside he found scholars and rich men, workers and poor men, but he sensed that something was missing from each of their prayers.

Then he noticed in the back of the room someone standing behind the oven. When he drew closer, he heard a man reciting Psalms, and he could see that a soft radiance shone from the man's face. Here at last was a real Jew.

"Who are you?" the Sokolover asked him.

"I am Moshele the water carrier," the man replied.

From that day on, the young man tried to befriend Moshele, but the water carrier was so humble that he never said anything but "I'm fine, thank God," whenever the other tried to start a conversation.

One cold winter night the Sokolover was walking through the poorer section of the city, when he heard singing coming from one of the houses. He peered through the broken window and saw Moshele surrounded by a circle of shoemakers, tailors, and water carriers. Moshele, his face radiant like a full moon, held up a glass of wine while the others danced around him.

When the Sokolover knocked on the door, Moshele said, "Rabbi, what an honor!"

"The honor is mine," answered his guest. "Tell me, Moshele, what *simchah* are you celebrating?"

"Rabbi," began Moshele, "I have always been a poor man. I was orphaned by the time I was five and had to make my living in the street. I married the most beautiful woman in the world, but through all the years of hardship she lost all her beauty. Each of my children was born an angel, but they cry so much for food that they stop being angels and become poor beasts. Every night at three I awake and go to the synagogue to deliver water for people to wash their hands at the morning prayers. While I'm there alone, I pray to God to please give me one thousand rubles so that I can feed my children and start my life over. But all these years God has not heard my prayers.

"Two nights ago I came into the synagogue and found one thousand rubles lying on the floor. I opened the ark and thanked God for answering my prayers. When I came home, I saw that my wife was once again a beauty and my children once more angels. My water buckets became as light as feathers, and I blessed everyone I met.

"But when I returned to synagogue last night, I saw a great crowd gathered in front. I asked someone what had happened.

" 'A catastrophe!' the man told me. 'The whole community collected one thousand rubles for the widow Chaneleh and her eleven orphans, and now the money is lost!'

"Brokenhearted, I went back behind the oven, but I could not pray. 'Holy God!' I cried. 'You will never see my face here again! If You wanted to give me a thousand rubles, why did You have to take them away from Chaneleh? Such a cruel God You are! I don't want to talk to You anymore!'

"I went home feeling miserable. My wife was no longer beautiful nor my children angels. All night I could not sleep. Then suddenly I came to my senses. 'Moshele,' I told myself, 'all your life you trusted in God. Now you need Him more than ever. Pray!' So I prayed to God with all my heart.

"Then I heard a voice speaking to me, saying, 'Moshele the water carrier! Get up and bring the money to Chaneleh. It's not yours. It's hers.'

"Quickly I got up, pulled on my clothes, and ran to Chaneleh's house. When I knocked on the door and handed her the money, her face lit up like a thousand candles. I was in heaven."

"But now you are poor again, Moshele," said the Sokolover.

"No, Rabbi, you are wrong. God gave me the strength to return the money, so my heart is whole again. Praise be to God! *L'chayim!*"

4. FOLKTALES

275
Yes, but Where Am I?

Hanokh of Alexander taught:
Once there was a stupid man who each morning had a difficult time remembering where he had left his clothes the night before. So one day he got a pencil and a piece of paper and wrote down where he was placing each article of clothing. He placed the note next to his bed and thought to himself, "Tomorrow I will have no trouble finding my clothes!"

He awoke the next morning, quite pleased with himself, took the note, and followed it to the letter, finding each piece of clothing exactly where he had set it down. Within a short period of time he was fully dressed.

Suddenly he was seized with a terrible thought: "But where am I?" he cried. "Where in the world am I?"

He looked everywhere but could not find himself.

"And so," taught Hanokh of Alexander, "so it is with us."

276
Yossele the Holy Miser

Many years ago in the Jewish ghetto of Cracow there lived a rich miser named Yossele. Of all the Jews crowded into that small section of the city, only Yossele had enough money to give charity, but he refused to part with even a penny of his wealth. Everywhere he went, people jeered at him and cursed him. Children threw stones at him when he walked down the street. He was not only the richest man in the ghetto; he was also the most despised.

One day word spread that Yossele was dying. The holy burial society came to him and said, "Yossele, you can't take all your money with you. Give us a thousand rubles, and we'll bury you and distribute the money among the poor whom you have neglected all your life."

But Yossele shook his head. "No more than fifty rubles will I give you!"

"Then we refuse to bury you!"

"I don't mind," said Yossele. "I'll bury myself."

Then Yossele recited the *Sh'ma* and died.

It was on a Sunday that Yossele died. For four days his corpse lay upon his bed, until one man took pity on Yossele's wife and children and decided to bury Yossele secretly. So Thursday night he loaded the body onto his wagon and brought it to a lonely tree outside the Jewish cemetery. Quickly he dug a grave and threw Yossele's body in, certain that the miser would soon be forgotten by everyone.

That same night a poor man knocked on the door of Rabbi Kalman, the Chief Rabbi of Cracow, and said, "Rabbi, please give me money to buy food for *Shabbes*."

"Of course," said the Rabbi. "But tell me—where did you get enough for last *Shabbes*? I have never seen you at my door before."

"For the past twenty years," the man answered, "I have made barely enough money to keep my family from starvation. But every Thursday morning, an envelope appeared on my doorstep with five rubles in it so that we can enjoy a beautiful *Shabbes*. But this morning the envelope wasn't there."

So the rabbi gave him five rubles.

A few minutes later, there was another knock at the door. Another poor man stood before the rabbi and said, "Rabbi, please give me money so that I can buy food for *Shabbes*."

"Gladly," said Rabbi Kalman, "but where did you find the money last week since you didn't come to me for it?"

"For the past ten years," the man said, "I have found two rubles under my door every Thursday, but not this morning."

Over the next few hours, all the poor Jews of Cracow came to Rabbi Kalman's door with the same story.

"My friends," cried Rabbi Kalman, "all these years Yossele supported this whole community and nobody knew of it! But how did he know what each family needed?"

Then they all told him the same story: Just once, each of them had approached Yossele for charity, hoping that he would be the one finally to melt the miser's iron heart. At first Yossele would listen to the poor man's story with great compassion, writing down his name, address, and request in a little book. Then, all of a sudden, his manner would change. His face would turn cruel, and he would pick up the petitioner in his strong arms and toss him out into the street, shouting after him, "Do you think I'm crazy enough to give my precious money to the likes of you? Get out of my sight and never come back again!"

The next Thursday an envelope had appeared on the poor man's doorstep, but of course, he never suspected Yossele as the donor.

When Rabbi Kalman heard these stories, he was heartbroken. Yossele, the holiest man in Cracow, the one who had given charity as God gives, secretly, unacknowledged, was now lying in a lonely grave outside the Jewish cemetery, forgotten, unmourned. He declared the following day a public fast day and called the community together to pray to Yossele for forgiveness.

As the sun began to decline, Rabbi Kalman cried out, "Yossele, Yossele, give us a sign that you have forgiven us!"

At that moment, the rabbi fell to the floor as if dead. He began to dream: There was Yossele in the Garden of Eden, surrounded by all the righteous souls.

Yossele said to him, "Tell all my brothers and sisters in Cracow to go home. I have no reason to forgive them.

This was what I chose for myself: to have the privilege of giving as God gives, without anyone knowing. Here I am in heaven, and I lack for nothing. Only one thing do I miss: giving out envelopes of rubles on Thursday mornings."

Rabbi Kalman said to him, "But Yossele, weren't you lonely there in a grave with no others beside you?"

Yossele smiled and said, "But I was not alone, Rabbi! Abraham and Sarah, Isaac and Rebecca, Jacob, Rachel and Leah were all there with me. So were Moses and Aaron, David and Elijah."

Then Rabbi Kalman awoke from his dream and said to the worried faces surrounding him, "Go home and prepare for the Sabbath. Yossele has given us his blessing."

277

A Mother's Prayerbook

It once happened that the Gentile lord of a village took a liking to a Jewish couple within his domain. When the old couple passed away, the lord adopted their only son, making the boy heir to all he possessed. In time the lord told the boy that his parents had been Jews, and he gave him the few poor possessions his parents had owned, among them his mother's prayerbook.

One year at the beginning of the Days of Awe, the boy saw all the Jews of the village walking to synagogue, and he asked them where they were going.

"We are going to ask God to inscribe us in the Book of Life," they told him. "For our fate will soon be decided for the coming year. God will certainly not reject our prayers."

From that moment on, the boy's heart began to turn toward God.

That night, his parents appeared to him in a dream, urging him to return to the faith of his people. Every night during the Ten Days of Penitence, the dream returned, and the boy's soul began to thirst for repentance. He told all this to the lord, but the lord only dismissed it as a phantom of the boy's imagination.

On the eve of Yom Kippur, the boy saw all the Jews of the village again making their way toward the synagogue, dressed in white, prayerbooks in their hands. He asked them what they were doing.

"We are seeking pardon for our sins," they told him. "On this day the Gates of Forgiveness are opened and God grants atonement."

Ignited by their words, the boy seized his mother's prayerbook and hurried to the synagogue, where he found all the people praying and confessing their sins. But he did not know how to pray, and he wept bitterly. And his cries stirred the heavens.

Brokenhearted, he rushed up to the *bimah* and placed his mother's prayerbook on the lectern. Then he gazed up toward heaven and declared, "Holy God! I do not know how to pray. I do not even know what to say. So here is the whole prayerbook!"

And his heart opened itself up to the spirit of repentance, and his prayer was accepted as that of a righteous soul. From that day on, he lived a life of perfect faith.

278
The King and the Tavern-Keeper

Once a war broke out between the Poles and the Russians. When the Polish king saw that the war had turned against him, he ran away from the palace, seeking a place to hide. He came to a Jewish tavern and begged the tavern-keeper to hide him. When the Russian soldiers came to question him, the Jew denied that the king was there, even when they beat him.

When the tide of war turned and the Poles drove away the enemy, the king wished to repay the Jew for his loyalty, but the Jew claimed that he needed nothing. So the king gave him a letter and told him to bring it to the palace if he ever needed something.

Years later, the mayor of the city became drunk and threatened to close down the Jew's tavern unless the tavern-keeper paid him a thousand rubles. The Jew went to the palace and showed the letter to the king, who asked him to come back the next day. When the Jew returned, a general met him and told him that the king wished to honor him by making him second only to the throne. But in order to accept that supreme honor, he would have to convert to Christianity. And if he didn't convert, he would be killed to cover up the king's disgrace at not having rewarded the man who had once saved the king's life.

The Jew refused to convert and was brought into the execution room. As soon as he laid his head upon the block and saw the executioner's raised sword, he fainted. When he regained consciousness, he thought he was in Paradise.

Then the king came in, smiled at him, and said, "No, you are not in heaven, my friend, but safe and well in my palace! Let me explain my actions to you. It has long troubled me that I have been unable to reward you for saving my life. What reward could I possibly give you? A city? Money? To you such things are all vanities that pass away. But I know that for a Jew the greatest honor is to die for the sanctification of God's name. So I have given you this gift and your life as well. Now ask what you wish and I will gladly give it to you."

And the king gave the Jew all the money he needed to save his tavern, and he returned home with a thankful heart.

279

The Gentile's Impatience

Two beggars, one a Gentile and one a Jew, were good friends. One Passover, the Jew advised his Gentile friend to pretend to be a Jew in order to receive an invitation to a *seder* meal.

"But I won't know what to do!" protested the Gentile.

"Just follow the example of your host," the Jew told him.

So the Gentile beggar procured an invitation to a *seder* and arrived just before sundown. When he smelled the delicious foods and saw the many bottles of wine set out on the table, he was filled with delight.

But after he had been sitting for some time, all he received was a glass of wine, which only whetted his appetite further. Then he was given celery soaked in salt water, followed by more wine, and then a dry piece of unleavened bread.

When he next received a sliver of raw horseradish, his patience finally gave out. He leapt up from the table and stormed out of the house. Enraged, he came to his friend and told him of the host's shameful hospitality.

"If you had only waited a little longer," said the Jew, "you would have been treated to a most delicious feast."

"But who can wait that long?" complained the Gentile.

"If you are going to pretend to be a Jew," smiled his friend, "then you must learn the first requirement of being a Jew: Be patient and trust that the future will be better."

280

The Thankful Thief

A thief in his old age was no longer able to make a living at his trade. Hearing of his distress, a rich man sent him food. Not long after this, both the rich man and the thief died on the same day.

They both came before the Heavenly Court. The rich man was tried and sentenced to Gehinnom. But just before he entered the gate, an angel rushed forward to recall him to Paradise, explaining that the Court had had to reverse its verdict. For the thief whom he had helped on earth had stolen the list of his sins.

281

Two She-Goats from Shebreshin

Near the Polish village of Shebreshin there once lived a poor *Hasid* and his wife. On the Sabbath the *Hasid* would go into the village to pray and study, but during the rest of the week he and his wife would eke out a meager living by selling the milk, butter, and cheese produced by their two goats.

One day the wife went out to milk the goats, but she could not find them. She and her husband searched the woods, but the goats were nowhere to be found.

"It is all my fault!" cried the wife. "I forgot to tether them this morning. Now we shall surely starve!"

"Do not worry," her husband reassured her. "Everything God does is for the best."

And his words comforted her.

At sunset the goats returned, heavy with milk. And such sweet milk the *Hasid* and his wife had never before tasted. The next morning the wife again did not tether the goats, and again they returned with their udders bursting with sweet milk.

When they sold the milk in the village, they discovered that the milk had miraculous properties. The sick were instantly healed, the crippled and maimed made whole again. Soon everyone in the village boasted full health.

Six days passed, and on the seventh day the *Hasid* decided to find out where the goats were going each day. Quietly he followed them into the woods, but when they came to a certain place, the goats suddenly vanished. The

Hasid ran up to the spot and saw that there was a hole in the ground between two trees. Not hesitating, he went down into the hole and found himself walking in a dark tunnel toward a light shining in the distance. Far ahead he could see the bobbing tails of the goats.

As he made his way toward the light, leering demons suddenly appeared on his right and left, thrusting their serpents' tongues at him and prodding him with their claws. Naked women cavorted and beckoned to him, and gold coins rained down from above.

But the *Hasid* did not swerve to the left or right, but only pushed resolutely on toward the light. At last he emerged into the sun and saw before him a young shepherd tending his flock.

The shepherd greeted him in Hebrew: "*Shalom aleikhem,* friend! You have reached the holy city of Safed."

When the *Hasid* realized that he was now in the Holy Land, he fell to the ground and kissed the soil. With a full heart he gave thanks to God. Then he wrote a letter to the Jews of Shebreshin and to all the Jews in the Diaspora, telling them to follow the goats to the land of Israel, and instructing them to pay no attention to the devils and other phantoms they might meet along the way, for they were only things of vanity.

Then he rolled up the letter and put it in the ear of one of the goats.

When the goats returned that evening without her husband, the *Hasid's* wife began to weep and pull out her hair. For three days she waited for him, but always the goats returned alone. So she concluded that he had been killed by robbers and that she was now a widow. She sold her house and moved into the village to be among Jews. And she sold the goats to a *shokhet,* for what good would they do her in town?

When the *shokhet* slaughtered the goats, he found the *Hasid's* letter in one of the goat's ears. He showed it to the rabbi of the town, who cried, "The goats can never be returned to life! And thus we are forever exiled from the Promised Land!"

For many years the rabbi kept the letter in the synagogue, and later, when Shebreshin went up in flames, the letter from the Holy Land went up with it.

5. THE WISDOM OF CHELM

282
The Chief Sage's Golden Shoes

One day the citizens of Chelm, a town renowned for its wisdom, decided that they needed a Chief Sage. So they met in council and chose one among them for the position. But when this man walked through the streets of the town, no one treated him any differently than any other citizen.

"Is this why you elected me?" he protested. "To remain unrecognized and unacclaimed?"

So they decided to buy him a pair of golden shoes to distinguish him from ordinary Chelmites. But on the next rainy day, the mud in the streets blackened the golden shoes, so that no one knew that he was the Chief Sage and so paid no attention to him.

Enraged, he stormed into the council room.

"If I do not get more respect immediately, I'll resign as Chief Sage!" he cried.

"You're right!" agreed the council members. "We must protect the dignity of our Chief Sage."

So they ordered for him a pair of fine leather shoes to protect his golden shoes from the mud. The new shoes did keep the mud out, but they also kept the gold in, so that nobody could see that he was wearing special shoes befitting a Chief Sage. And so still no one paid attention to him.

Then they ordered the shoemaker to make new shoes for the Chief Sage, this time cutting holes in the leather.

"This way the leather will keep the mud out, but the holes will reveal the golden shoes underneath," they reasoned. "Now nobody will fail to recognize the Chief Sage!"

But when the Chief Sage walked through the streets, the mud oozed in through the holes and covered up the gold. So they stuffed straw into the holes to keep out the mud, but now the gold was covered up again.

"This is an outrage!" cried the Chief Sage. "A scandal! A disgrace! I demand that you do something!"

So the council members consulted all that day and long into the night, until at last they discovered a solution. They called the Chief Sage and said to him, "From now on, you will wear ordinary leather shoes when you walk in the street, but you will wear a pair of golden shoes on your hands. That way everyone will know that you are the Chief Sage of Chelm!"

283
The Columbus of Chelm

In Chelm there once lived a man named Selig. More than any other citizen in the town, Selig longed to travel and see the world. One day a merchant came to town full of tales about the wonders of Warsaw. From that moment on, Selig could think of nothing else but going to the capital to see for himself.

After thinking the matter over for some time, Selig one day announced to his wife Leah that he was leaving the next morning for Warsaw.

"But you have no money, Selig!" she cried.

"I'll walk," replied her husband.

"But your shoes will wear out! Warsaw is so far away!"

"I'll carry my shoes until I get there," answered Selig.

"You're mad!" said his wife.

"I must see Warsaw!" said Selig.

So Leah threw up her hands and went back to her soup pot.

The next day Selig packed bread and cheese in a sack and set out. At midday he came to a crossroads and sat down to eat his lunch. But when he was about to lie down for a nap, he was suddenly struck by a troubling thought: "Here is a fork in the road. One road leads to Warsaw, and the other back to Chelm. When I wake up, I might make a mistake and return home instead of going to Warsaw."

Then he had an idea. "What a sage I am!" he declared. He placed his shoes in the middle of the road, the toes pointing toward Warsaw. "Now I can't go wrong," thought Selig. "When I wake up, I'll just look at my shoes and know which way to go."

Quite pleased with himself, he stretched out under a tree and was soon sound asleep.

While he was asleep a peasant came by in a wagon. He was delighted to find an unclaimed pair of shoes lying in the road.

"I could use a new pair of shoes," he said.

But when he picked up Selig's shoes, he discovered that they were worn and full of holes. Annoyed, he dropped them in the dust and continued on his way. What did it matter to him that the shoes now pointed back toward Chelm, not Warsaw?

When Selig awoke refreshed from his nap, he jumped up and ran to his shoes.

"How clever I am!" he cried. "Now I can continue on my journey with peace of mind."

And off he went down the road to Chelm.

As he approached the town, he noticed that the streets and houses seemed very familiar to him.

"So Warsaw is not as wonderful as the merchant said," he thought to himself. "Our little Chelm looks quite like it!"

When he neared the marketplace, a man greeted him with a friendly "*Shalom aleikhem*, Reb Selig!"

"Amazing!" thought Selig. "That man looks just like Haim the tailor. And there must be someone here in Warsaw who looks much like me!"

He continued on and came to the synagogue. "How strange!" thought Selig. "I imagined that synagogues in Warsaw would be grander than this. Why, our synagogue in Chelm is built precisely like this one."

Inside, he found to his astonishment that the rabbi looked exactly like his rabbi back in Chelm, with the same straggly beard, watery eyes, and rasping voice. And all the others looked familiar, too, even the *shammes* who treated Selig with the same gruffness that his own *shammes* always did.

He left the synagogue and walked a little further, until he found himself on a street that looked exactly like his own street back home.

"I had to walk all this way just to discover that Warsaw is no different from Chelm," thought Selig, disappointed. "When I return home, I will be content to stay there, for why go exploring if everything elsewhere is just the same?"

Then he noticed a little boy playing in the street. "I cannot believe my eyes!" cried Selig. "Here is a boy in Warsaw who is a twin to my own son Moishele!"

Just then a woman's head thrust itself out of a nearby window. "Nu, Selig, are you going to eat dinner tonight or not?"

"She must mistake me for the Warsaw Selig," thought Selig, who could not get over how much like his own Leah this woman looked and sounded.

Not wishing to disappoint her, he went inside and sat down at the table. How surprised he was to find the same chipped dishes, the same stained tablecloth, even the same oversalted soup before him on the table. But he ate his dinner without saying a word, wondering when the other Selig would return home to set the matter straight.

But the other Selig never did return. And so Selig

from Chelm remained in Warsaw, wondering how things were going on without him back home and hoping that one day he might return there to tell them all the shocking truth: that going all the way to Warsaw was simply not worth the trip.

284
Chelm Captures the Moon

Once the people of Chelm found themselves in desperate straits. After spending all their money to build a watermill on top of the highest mountain, they discovered that the mill did not work, and now they had no money left to buy food.

Then Gimpel, the wisest man in town, came up with a plan: "Let us capture the moon and rent it out! People will of course need the moon to say the Blessing over the New Month, and in the big cities they will want it to light their streets."

"But Gimpel, how can we capture the moon?" they asked him. "It's so far away!"

Gimpel stroked his beard, thinking hard. Suddenly his eyes lit up. "Bring a big barrel of borscht to the marketplace!"

So they brought a big barrel of beet soup to the marketplace and waited eagerly for Gimpel to reveal his clever scheme.

"Now look into the barrel," ordered Gimpel. "What do you see?"

"The moon!" they all cried.

And sure enough, there in the red soup floated the shimmering moon, like a thick slice of onion. Quickly they threw a sack over the barrel, tied the neck with strong rope, and sealed the knots with sealing wax. Finally, they locked the barrel away in the goldsmith's safe.

Then they waited for the old moon to disappear from the sky. It was pitch dark when they carefully carried the heavy barrel of borscht back to the marketplace. Only the stars glistened against the black curtain of the sky. With great anticipation they broke the seals and untied the knots. But when they peered into the barrel, they discovered to their chagrin that the moon was gone!

"What has happened, Gimpel?" they cried. "No one could possibly have stolen it, since the seals were unbroken."

"Alas!" cried Gimpel. "It has melted in the borscht!"

Brokenhearted, they emptied the barrel into the street. And sure enough, there in the thousand puddles of red soup dotting the ground glistened tiny bits of melted moon.

Later that night, when the thin crescent of the new moon rose in the sky, the people of Chelm blessed it with heavy hearts.

285
The Great Power of Psalms

Once Teltza, the beautiful only daughter of Shmuel the Shingle-Maker and Dvarshe the Midwife, was sweeping the floor of their poor house when she began to imagine her future.

"Here I am," she thought, "fifteen years old and beloved of everybody. I'm young and pretty and happy as a lark. In a year or two Papa will find me a fine young scholar, and we'll be married with song, dance, and a delicious feast to which the whole town will be invited. A year later I'll give birth to a fine, healthy son, and what a grand party we'll have at his *bris*! And then will come his *bar mitzvah*—but oh, no! What if he cries: 'My head, my head!' and dies like the son of the Shunnamite in the Bible?"

Teltza dropped her broom and began to weep bitterly. "If he dies, I will surely die of sorrow! Imagine— dead at thirty!"

Her mother heard her crying and came running. "My daughter, what is the matter?"

"Oh, Mama!" cried Teltza. "I was imagining my son's *bar mitzvah* and then I thought: 'What if he dies? I will surely die of sorrow!' "

When she heard this, her mother raised her hands to heaven and began to wail even louder than her daughter.

Her father heard them crying and came running. When they told him why they were crying, he too joined in, and the three of them made so much noise that even the grandmother, who was hard of hearing, came to investigate. Soon she, too, was weeping and wringing her hands.

In a short time word spread throughout Chelm that a great disaster had befallen Teltza and her family. Soon all the people of the town came running to express their sympathy, and they began crying together with the grieving family. Along came the rabbi and asked them why they were all crying.

"Some great calamity has struck the family," they told him.

"There is only one thing to do," declared the rabbi. "We must all chant Psalms to avert the disaster."

So they all began to chant Psalms, beseeching the heavens to have mercy on these poor people.

Then along came the miller, the only person in town who had not been born in Chelm, and asked them why they were crying.

"Some terrible disaster has struck these poor people!" they replied.

"What has happened?" the miller asked.

But nobody could say exactly what had happened. So the miller sought out Teltza and asked her.

With a voice choked with sobs, she told him her sad tale.

The miller threw back his head and laughed. "What a

silly girl you are! Your sorrow is based on four great 'ifs' —
if you marry, and if you have a son, and if he gets sick on
his *bar mitzvah*, and if he dies. But none of these things has
happened!"

Instantly Teltza stopped crying and smiled. When the
others saw this, they too stopped their tears and broke
into smiles. Soon everyone was laughing and slapping
each other on the back.

"You see, my fellow Jews," beamed the rabbi,
"nothing helps in a time of trouble like chanting Psalms.
It never fails!"

PART X

TALES OF ELIJAH THE PROPHET

No figure in Jewish history has captured the storyteller's imagination as much as Elijah the Prophet. Although he is portrayed as a stern agent of divine justice and retribution in the Tanakh, he metamorphoses into quite a different character in the tales of an exiled people. He becomes the redeemer of orphans and widows, the champion of the poor and the oppressed, and most significantly, the herald of the Messiah. Always he travels in disguise, to test us, to teach us that we should treat each stranger as though he were a messenger from heaven.

286
Elijah in Heaven

When it was time for Elijah to depart from the earth, the Angel of Death complained to God that it was not right that this man should escape death and ascend to heaven with the breath of life still within him.

"For if he escapes my grasp, then others will protest their fates," the Angel said, "and so my power will wither away!"

"Be still!" ordered God. "For at the beginning of the world I decreed that you would have no power over this soul. He is none other than the angel Sandalfon who chose to descend to earth in human form to intercede in the affairs of Israel during the reign of the evil Ahab. Now he is returning to My service in the heavens. Beware of his power, for if you do not, he will vanquish you."

But the Angel of Death paid no attention to God's warning and tried to defeat Elijah. And in the fierce battle that took place, Elijah conquered the Angel of Death and would have destroyed him had not God intervened to spare the Angel's life. For Death has its rightful place in the affairs of humankind. But Elijah ascended to heaven with the Destroying Angel pinioned under his feet.

Then God seated him under the Tree of Life and directed him to record all the deeds performed on earth. And so he has done throughout the ages.

When souls ascend to heaven, Elijah greets them at the crossroads of Paradise, directing the righteous toward the path of Love and the sinners toward the path of Justice.

At the beginning of each Sabbath, he brings the souls of the sinners up to heaven to enjoy the pleasures of the holy day, and at sunset he leads them back, sorrowing, to Gehinnom. And after they have atoned for their evil deeds, he leads them heavenward to everlasting bliss.

And from the prayers of those still on earth, Elijah weaves garlands for the Holy One and offers sacrifices in the heavenly Sanctuary, for the Temple was never really destroyed, but only hidden in heaven until the End of Days.

And from time to time, Elijah leaves heaven and descends to earth to do God's will among the living.

287

The Pious Man and the Tax Collector

Once a righteous man and a wicked man died on the same day in the same city. The people of the city buried the wicked man with great pomp and ceremony, but they ignored the funeral of the righteous man.

After the funeral, the righteous man's son-in-law had a dream. In the dream Elijah appeared to him and asked, "Why are you crying?"

"I am crying because they honor the sinner and turn their backs on my pious father!" answered the son-in-law.

Elijah took him to Gehinnom. There he saw a soul

crying, "Water! Water!" There was water near him, but he could not reach it.

"Here is the soul of that wicked man," Elijah told him.

Then they went to Paradise, where the dreamer saw his righteous father-in-law being honored by the angels.

"How can this be?" asked the son-in-law. "Why was the sinner honored on earth and my father-in-law punished if these are their true rewards?"

"During his lifetime," replied Elijah, "the tax collector did only one good deed—once he collected radishes for a tax and accidentally dropped one, which a poor man picked up. The tax collector saw this but pretended not to notice. This one radish satisfied the poor man's hunger and restored his soul. For that one act of kindness, the tax collector received his entire reward in this life. Now he will receive payment for all his sins in the next."

"But what sin could my righteous father-in-law have committed to merit such a punishment in this life?" cried the son-in-law.

"Your father-in-law was a true saint, doing good all his life," answered Elijah. "Only once did he commit a sin. A scholar once visited him and after the man left, his wife spoke ill of the man. Your father-in-law said nothing. He has now been punished for this one sin in this life. Now he can enjoy eternal rest in the next."

Then the son-in-law awoke from his dream.

That morning the community came to his door to honor his departed father-in-law. As for the sinner, his name was soon forgotten in the town.

288
Rabbi Akiva's Daughter, or the
Jewish Snow White

Rachel, Rabbi Akiva's wife, was a righteous and kind woman. She had a daughter named Miriam whom she taught to follow her ways. When she died, Miriam continued her custom of always keeping an extra loaf of bread at her table for travelers and the poor.

Time passed and Rabbi Akiva grew old. One day he said to Miriam, "My daughter, I have chills. The only remedy is for me to marry again."

He married a wicked woman who every day schemed to kill her stepdaughter. But the pious girl did not raise her voice against the woman.

One Thursday the washerman came to Rabbi Akiva's house to wash their Sabbath clothes. The wicked wife said to him, "Take my stepdaughter with you to wash clothes, and kill her in a remote place. Swear to me that you will reveal my secret to no one."

So the washerman swore to kill the girl and to tell no one of the wicked wife's part in her death. The two journeyed to a faraway place. Then the washerman said to Miriam, "I have only brought you here to kill you."

But when he raised his hand to strike the girl, he felt pity for her and, instead of killing her, cut off her hand and foot and left her there to die. All that night she wept, and in the morning she crawled to a sheltered spot where she remained all day.

As the evening approached, a Jewish traveler arrived near the place where she lay, and he tethered his donkey, since it was time for the Sabbath to begin. He laid out his simple meal upon a stone and recited the Sabbath prayers. When he finished, a voice called out, "Amen!"

"Who said that?" cried the startled man.

He searched and found the wounded girl. "Are you a human being or a demon?" he asked her. "There has never been a Jew here!"

"I am human," she replied, and she told him what had befallen her, but she withheld the name of her father from him.

The man wept at her tale, and together they spent the Sabbath, sharing the simple food and reciting prayers. When the Sabbath ended, he placed her upon his donkey and brought her to his home. There he ordered an artisan to make her a hand of gold and a foot of silver, and he gave her servants to attend to her every need. In time they were married, and he set her in charge of his entire household.

A year later Miriam bore a child. Her husband rejoiced in the child, and said to her, "I wish now to go to Rabbi Akiva to study Torah."

"Go in peace," said Miriam, "and may God watch over you."

So he came to Rabbi Akiva and studied Torah. One day he told his teacher about his wife and all that happened to her, and Rabbi Akiva understood that it was his own daughter Miriam of whom he spoke. He wept bitterly to hear of her sufferings, but thanked God that she had married such a good man.

When the wicked stepmother heard the story, she feared that her husband would discover her part in the matter and send her away. So she forged a letter in the name of Miriam's husband and sent it to the man's relatives.

"I have discovered that my wife's family is unworthy," said the letter. "Therefore take from her the golden hand and the silver foot I had made for her, and send her away with the child."

And his kinsmen did what the letter asked.

Now when they told Miriam about the letter, she knew at once that the letter was false, for the daughter of a sage is also a sage. And she protested to God, "Lord of the Universe, how can You permit such a thing to happen? Please help me and my child!"

The two journeyed for a long time, until the boy cried out, "Mother, I shall die of hunger and thirst!"

And Miriam wept, for she had nothing to give the boy.

Then Elijah appeared to her and said, "Fear not, my daughter, for I have come to help you."

Then Elijah caused a great stream to appear before them, and he told Miriam to put her wounded arm in the water. She did and it grew back. Then she put her wounded foot in the stream and it, too, grew back. Then the mother and child drank from the stream, and their spirits revived.

Miriam recited the blessing, "Blessed be God who brings the dead back to life!"

Then Elijah said to her, "Go to the source of this stream and there you will find a great city. In the city you will meet a man with a large piece of land to sell."

"But I am penniless!" protested Miriam.

"A second man will give you the keys to a large house," said Elijah. "Take the keys and go inside. There you will find a great treasure. Buy the land and honor your benefactor with fine gifts. On the land build a synagogue and an inn for travelers."

Miriam did as Elijah had instructed. She built a fine synagogue with many Torah scrolls and hired ten elders to teach her son Torah.

After six years her husband returned home and discovered what had happened to his wife. Heartbroken, he vowed to wander the earth until he found her. He traveled from city to city until at last he reached the place where his wife and son now lived. He went to the inn and there met his son, whose face shone with wisdom even though he was only seven years old. But they did not recognize each other.

The boy ran to his mother and told her that a great scholar had arrived at their inn. Miriam told the boy to bring food and drink to the traveler, but the man refused them, for he had taken a vow to fast until he had found his wife and son. And the boy came back crying to his mother.

"Go to your teachers," Miriam instructed her son, "and ask them to tell the traveler all the sufferings that have befallen them in their lives."

So the ten elders told the traveler all that had happened to them, and he in turn told of his own misfortunes. When the boy repeated the stranger's tale to his mother, she knew at once that this traveler must be her husband. So she went to him and fell at his feet, for his face shone with wisdom. And the child rejoiced to know his father.

Then the people of the city held a great banquet to celebrate the couple's reunion, for Miriam was beloved in the city. And they made Miriam's husband their leader, because of his great wisdom. Then he sent word to Rabbi Akiva to punish his wicked wife and come live with them. And he also sent for his own parents, and they, too, joined their household.

Then they all lived happily ever after.

289
Soft Like a Reed, Not Hard Like a Cedar

Once Eleazar ben Simeon, returning from his teacher in Migdal Gedor, was riding his ass along the shore. As he rode, he said to himself, "What a great scholar am I! How much Torah have I acquired!"

Soon he met a tall black man who greeted him, saying, "Peace to you, O master!"

Eleazar did not return his greeting but instead insulted the man: "Tell me, wretch, are all the people in your town as black as you?"

"I don't know," replied the man. "Why don't you ask the artisan who fashioned me why he made such a shoddy piece of work?"

The man's strange reply pierced Eleazar's heart, and he realized that he had sinned in speaking this way to him. At once he dismounted from the ass and asked the man's forgiveness.

"I cannot forgive you until you go to the artisan and ask him to explain why he made me this way," replied the man, and he turned around and began walking toward the town. Eleazar followed him.

When the people saw that it was Rabbi Eleazar who had arrived in their midst, they cried, "Peace unto you, master and teacher!" For Eleazar was known throughout the land as a great sage.

"Whom are you calling master and teacher?" demanded the black man.

"Don't you know that this man is a great rabbi?" said the people.

"May there be no more such great men in Israel!" said the black man, and he told them what had happened between them on the road into town.

"We beg you to forgive him," the people pleaded with him, "for he is indeed a revered teacher of Torah."

"For your sakes, I will forgive him" answered the black man, "but in the future let him be warned not to behave this way toward his fellow man."

Then Rabbi Eleazar went to the House of Study and taught, "One should always be soft like a reed, not hard like a cedar." For he realized that pride could harden a man's heart and make of his learning a worthless thing.

Then he went to find the stranger to beg his forgiveness once again, but the man had vanished. Only then did he realize that the man had been none other than Elijah the Prophet.

290
The Slave Elijah

Once a poor man, the father of a large family, prayed to God for help. God sent Elijah, who appeared before the man as a slave.

"Sell me in the marketplace, and you shall have more than enough for your needs," said Elijah.

"How can I sell another man into bondage?" protested the poor man.

"Do not fear for my welfare," Elijah reassured him. "God will watch over me."

At last the man agreed to sell Elijah in the market. A rich buyer paid him eighty dinars, enough to sustain his family for a long time. After offering a prayer of thanksgiving to God, the man returned home with full pockets, although his heart grieved for the fate of the slave.

The prince who bought Elijah soon discovered that his new slave was a skilled architect. He offered to give him his freedom if he would build his new master a palace in six months. The next morning when the prince awoke, he was astonished to see before him a magnificent palace, but when he sent for his new slave to praise him, he was told that the man had mysteriously disappeared.

"Surely he was an angel!" marveled the prince.

Meanwhile Elijah returned to the poor man's house. But when the man saw his former slave, he became alarmed, for he thought that Elijah had escaped from his new master.

"It is not right that you do this thing," said the poor man, "for then I have cheated the buyer of his money."

"Not only has the buyer not been cheated," replied Elijah, "but he is now one hundred times richer than before, for I have built him a magnificent palace worth many times my price."

And he told the poor man all that he had done and all that he was. Then he disappeared.

In time the poor man's eighty dinars grew to eight hundred, and he and his family lacked for nothing for the rest of their lives.

291
The Gift of Seven Years

Once a rich man fell upon hard times and lost all his wealth. In order to support his family, he took a job as a manual laborer.

One day Elijah appeared to him disguised as an Arab and said to him, "You are destined to enjoy seven good years of prosperity. Do you want them now or at the end of your life?"

"You are a devil!" cried the man, and chased Elijah away.

Again Elijah appeared and repeated his offer.

"You are a wizard!" cried the man, and chased him away.

A third time he appeared, and this time the man said, "I shall ask my wife for advice."

She told him, "Ask for the good years now. For if we ask for them at the end of our lives, we will know our days are numbered as soon as good fortune comes to us."

So he went back and told Elijah what his wife had said.

When he returned home that day, his children greeted him trembling with excitement and said, "Father, see what we found while we were digging under the large stone in our yard! A treasure!"

His wife said to him, "Let us use this gift wisely. If we share what we have with those less fortunate, perhaps God may grant us more good years."

And so for the next seven years, they opened their hands generously to the poor and performed many acts of charity.

At the end of seven years, Elijah once again appeared to the man. "I have come to take back my pledge," he said.

"I asked my wife's advice the first time you appeared," the man told him. "Let me consult with her again."

So he ran home and told his wife that the messenger had come to reclaim their fortune.

"Tell him," said his wife, "that if he can find two people who have used such a pledge more wisely than we, he can have it back."

Elijah searched the world over, but nowhere did he find two people with more generous hearts. So he never returned to reclaim his pledge. And they enjoyed prosperity and good health until a ripe old age.

292
Elijah and the Three Wishes

There once lived a man who owned a beautiful spice garden. When the time came for him to die, he called his three sons and said to them, "Promise me that you will never quarrel but will always love one another. And promise to guard our spice garden from thieves, for it is my most precious possession."

And the sons swore to do what their father had asked.

After the father died, the sons agreed to take turns watching over the garden. On the first night Elijah appeared before the oldest son and asked him, "Would you rather have wealth, learning, or a virtuous wife?"

The son replied, "I would rather have wealth."

So Elijah gave him a gold coin, and he became rich.

The next night Elijah appeared before the second son. "Would you rather have wealth, learning, or a virtuous wife?" he asked.

The second son said, "I would rather have learning."

So Elijah handed him a book, and at once he knew the whole Torah.

On the third night Elijah appeared before the youngest son. "Would you rather have wealth, learning, or a virtuous wife?" he asked him.

"I would rather marry a virtuous woman," replied the youngest son, "for her price is above rubies."

"Then you must come with me," said Elijah.

The next day they journeyed to a town and stayed at an inn. That night Elijah overheard the geese and the chickens saying, "What a sinner this young man must be to deserve such a wicked wife! For the people here are evildoers and idolaters."

The next day they traveled to a second inn. Again Elijah overheard the geese and chickens saying, "How sinful this young man must be to deserve such a wretch for a wife, for the people here are heartless and without faith."

The third day they traveled to another inn. That night Elijah overheard the geese and chickens saying, "He must be a virtuous young man to merit such a worthy bride! For the family here is pious and full of kind deeds."

So Elijah became the *shadkhan* and arranged for the two young people to be married.

Years later Elijah disguised himself as a beggar and returned to see what had happened to the three sons. When he came to the house of the oldest son, he was not admitted, for the son had become a heartless miser and shared none of his wealth with the poor.

Elijah appeared before him and said, "I gave you wealth, but you have proved unworthy of it." And he took back the gold coin, and the man lost all he had.

He next went to the house of the second son to whom he had given learning. But this son had grown arrogant because of his great knowledge and held himself above all others. Elijah took back the book, and he forgot all he knew.

Then he came to the house of the youngest son. His wife welcomed him graciously into the house and fed him the finest foods on her best dishes. When her husband returned, Elijah said to him, "Because of the merits of your wife, I am giving you wealth and learning, for the two of you will make good use of them."

And so the youngest son's wish for a virtuous wife proved a true blessing.

293

The Ugly Wise Girl

Long ago in the city of Constantinople there lived a girl, the only child of a great rabbi, whose face resembled that of a wild beast. But even though she was very ugly, she was also very wise, the wisest person in all of Constantinople. Yet because of her great ugliness, her parents kept her locked away in the attic above the House of Study. She received her food through a small opening in the door, and she passed through that same opening whatever she wished to send away. But her face was never seen.

Once a youth from a distant country came to Constantinople to study. He first went to the House of Study and there heard the rabbi present a question that none of the students could answer. All day the youth pondered the rabbi's question, but he was unable to discover the answer. Finally, exhausted from his efforts, he left the House of Study to walk about the city.

When he returned a few hours later, he found a slip of paper lying on his open book. When he read the words written on the slip, he knew at once that here was the answer to the rabbi's question. But when he asked the other students which of them had put the slip of paper there, they only laughed at him.

"Why are you laughing?" he asked them.

"The person who wrote the answer to the rabbi's question is his daughter," they replied. "She lives in the attic above this room. Whenever her father asks a question that is too difficult for us, she always writes it down on a slip of paper and drops it through the floorboards. There is no one wiser in the whole city."

When the youth heard of this extraordinary girl, he wished to make her his wife. But the others warned him not to pursue the matter further.

"For she is a cursed creature whom no one may look upon because of her ugliness. Her father will never give his consent."

Yet the youth would not be dissuaded. "Such wisdom cannot live in an ugly vessel!" he insisted.

As the other students had predicted, the girl's father at first refused to give his consent to the marriage. The youth persisted, however, until finally the rabbi relented and agreed to permit his only daughter to marry.

The girl came to the marriage canopy wearing a large mask that covered the entire upper part of her body. Still the bridegroom was not daunted, for he told himself that this was a custom of the land. But that night, when the bride removed her mask and the youth saw that she was indeed hideous to look upon, her face like that of some monstrous beast, he shrank back in terror.

"Do not flee from me," pleaded the girl, "for did not my father warn you of my blemish? Yet still you desired to wed me. Has not God made me this way? Therefore have pity on me and do not abandon me!"

But the youth felt only disgust for his ugly bride and wished to be rid of her.

"If your heart is indeed set upon leaving me," said his wife, "at least sleep with me this one night as my husband, and fulfill the commandment you have undertaken. Then I shall let you go and demand nothing more of you."

And she cried so piteously that the youth had pity on her and did as she asked.

When he was about to depart, the bride seized him by the arm and said, "Only one more favor do I ask of you. If I should become pregnant, people may doubt that you are the child's father since you have abandoned me on my wedding night. Give me a sign that the child is yours."

"What shall I give you?" asked the youth.

"Your ring and your *tallit*," she replied, and he gave them to her. Then he left Constantinople to return to his country.

Nine months later the abandoned bride gave birth to a son, who was as beautiful as she was ugly. Not wishing him to suffer on her account, the mother wrapped the child in a blanket and left him on the doorstep of her parents' house. The old couple found the child and took him in, raising him as their own son. As for the child's mother, she returned to her lonely room in the attic of the House of Study.

The boy grew up and became a great scholar, for he

had inherited his mother's intelligence and his father's beauty. One day when he was engaged in a dispute with another boy, the other began to tease him, saying, "You are nothing but a fatherless and motherless bastard! Do not pride yourself so much on your learning, for I am much better than you!"

Distressed by these harsh words, the boy returned home and asked his grandparents to explain the accusation. At first, they advised him to disregard the other boy's scornful words, insisting that he had only spoken out of envy. But the boy pressed them until they admitted that they were not his true parents but his grandparents.

"And is my mother then dead?" he cried.

"No," they said, "your mother lives above the House of Study."

So the boy ran to the House of Study and burst into the attic room where his mother lived. The startled woman had no time to cover her face, but turned away in shame when she saw that it was her own son who had come to her.

"Do not hide your face from me, Mother!" cried the boy, and he ran to her and embraced her. His mother wept tears of joy to hold her son in her arms, for she had not seen him face to face since the day of his birth, but had only glimpsed him through the floorboards.

Then the boy noticed books piled upon the table in the center of the room.

"Who comes here to read these books?" he asked her.

"No one but me has ever set foot in this room," answered his mother. "But God in his mercy has granted me a small measure of wisdom to console me, and I have been able to endure my loneliness by filling my days with the light of Torah."

And the boy was astonished by his mother's words, and he began to ask her questions about the holy books. He soon saw that her wisdom surpassed that of all his teachers, and so the two began studying together each day.

One day the boy asked her about his father. "For I

fear my birth was without honor," he said. "Hide nothing from me, dearest Mother, for I wish to know the truth."

"It grieves me to speak of your father," replied his mother, "but I wish to set your mind at ease." And she showed him the *ketubah* with his father's name upon it and told him all that had happened before his birth.

"Did he leave nothing with you when he departed?" asked the boy.

"He left me his ring and his *tallit*," his mother said.

"I must go in search of my father," declared the boy, "for I will have no peace until I have met him."

Then he took his father's ring and *tallit* and enough provisions for a long journey and left Constantinople. After traveling for many months, he came at last to his father's city.

He first went to the synagogue to recite the morning prayers. The rabbi noticed the strange youth and approached him. But when he came near, he saw embroidered on the corners of the boy's *tallit* the name of his own son.

"Where did you get this *tallit*?" he asked the boy.

"It belongs to my father," replied the boy, and he told the rabbi the purpose of his journey.

The rabbi was astonished, for when his son had returned home many years before from his long journey to Constantinople, he had told his father that his *tallit* had been lost in his travels.

Then he noticed a ring on the boy's finger and recognized it as the ring he had given his son in his youth. But his son had told him that this too had been lost on his journey home.

"I believe that your father still lives in this city," said the rabbi, "and with God's help I shall bring him to you. Please give me your *tallit* and ring so that I may be sure."

Then the rabbi went to his son and asked him again to explain what had happened to his *tallit* and ring. And again the son insisted that he had lost them in his travels.

"Would you recognize them if you saw them again?" his father asked him.

"Certainly!" answered the son.

Then the rabbi showed his son the *tallit* and ring, and the son's face became ashen, for it was impossible to deny that these things were his.

"How did you get them?" he asked his father.

"Your son gave them to me," replied the rabbi.

"Forgive me, Father!" cried the son. "And please bring my son to me."

So the rabbi brought the boy to his father, and the two embraced and wept many tears. And the grandparents also rejoiced to see what a wise and handsome grandson they had.

Then the boy said, "Let us return home to my mother."

But the boy's father did not wish to return home to his ugly wife.

"Why don't you wish to return with me?" asked the boy. "For my mother is the wisest and most beautiful woman in the world!"

Then the father thought that some miracle had occurred since he had been gone, and he said to his son, "You go first, and I shall soon follow."

So the boy set out on his journey home, and on the way he met an old man who said to him, "I see how greatly you love your father and mother. Take this bottle and give it to your mother. When your mother washes her face with the water inside this bottle, she will be cured and will become as beautiful as the sun and moon."

The boy thanked the old man and hurried home with the bottle for his mother.

"Mother!" he cried when he reached her room. "My father is coming to see you."

"He will reject me as he did in the past!" lamented the mother. "For have I changed? Am I not as ugly as before?"

"You must wash your face and hair," insisted the boy, giving her the bottle, "and prepare yourself as a bride."

So the mother washed her face and hair in the water from the bottle, and behold! Her ugliness departed, and she became as beautiful as the sun and moon.

"Look in the mirror, Mother," urged the boy.

"Why should I look in the mirror?" said the mother. "I have not done so since my earliest youth."

But the boy insisted, so she gazed into the glass and was astonished to see herself transformed into a beautiful woman. Then the boy told her about the old man he had met on the journey home.

"Surely it was Elijah the Prophet whom you met," said the mother, and she thanked God for performing such a miracle.

Shortly after this, the father arrived. When he beheld his beautiful wife, he too thanked God for the miracle that had come to pass. And the two once again stood together under the wedding canopy and rededicated themselves to each other.

Thus a wise son brought peace and happiness to his parents' house.

294
God Works in Mysterious Ways

Once Joshua ben Levi fasted and prayed to God that he might be allowed to meet Elijah. One day Elijah appeared to him and said, "Whatever you wish, I shall do."

Joshua replied, "I wish to follow you and learn your ways so that I might become wise."

Elijah said, "This is a difficult thing you desire, for you will not be able to bear all that you see me do, nor will you understand it."

"I promise not to bother you with questions, but to watch your deeds in silence and to learn from them."

"Very well," said Elijah. "I will take you along with me on one condition: If you should ask me to explain anything I do, I shall explain it to you, but then I shall depart at once."

So they set out upon their journey. First they came to the home of a poor couple whose only possession was a cow. Despite their great poverty, the old man and woman welcomed Elijah and Joshua graciously, fed them, and gave them their own bed for the night. In the morning when Joshua and Elijah were about to leave, Elijah said a prayer over the cow, and it died.

"Why did you kill the cow of these poor people after they showed us such kindness?" exclaimed Joshua.

"Remember our agreement," warned Elijah. "If you wish me to explain, I will, but then I will leave you." So Joshua fell silent.

Next they came to the house of a rich man. This time they were given no food or drink, and they had to spend the night in the man's stable with the animals. Yet the next morning before leaving, Elijah prayed that the man's broken stone wall be repaired and it was. With great effort, Joshua fought back the urge to ask Elijah the reason for his curious actions.

Then they came to a city. There they entered a synagogue that was more splendid than any Joshua had ever seen. The benches were made of silver and gold, and from the ceiling hung crystal chandeliers. Yet none of the wealthy people inside invited the two strangers to their homes nor did they show them any warmth. So Joshua and Elijah had to content themselves with dry bread and water, and they had to spend the night on the hard benches. Before leaving the next morning, Elijah said to them, "May God make you all leaders." Once again Joshua controlled his desire to ask Elijah about his actions.

The next day they reached a synagogue in another city. This time the people welcomed them warmly. One of the most prominent members of the congregation invited them home for a sumptuous feast and gave them the largest featherbed in the house. Upon departing Elijah said to the congregation, "May God give you only one leader!"

When he heard this, Joshua could no longer contain himself but burst out, "I must know why you have done these things!"

"Very well," said Elijah, "I will explain, but then I

must leave you. In the case of the cow who died, it had been decreed by heaven that the old woman die that day, so I prayed to God that the cow be taken in her place. As for the stone wall at the house of the rich man, there was a vast treasure buried under that wall. If he had repaired it as he was planning to, he would have found it. So I prayed that the wall be repaired so as to conceal the treasure from him.

"In the case of the congregation that treated us so ungraciously, I wished for them all to be leaders, for where there are too many leaders, there are arguments and dissension. But where there is only one leader, there is peace and a common purpose. As the proverb says: 'Too many captains sink the ship.'

"Now before I leave you, let me give you one last piece of wisdom," Elijah told Joshua. "As you travel through this world, you will see much that will strike you as unjust. You will see the wicked prosper and the righteous suffer. You will see the rich acquire even more wealth and the poor sink lower in their misery. But remember what you saw with me these past few days, and understand that God often works in mysterious ways."

And before Joshua could reply, Elijah vanished.

295

The Jewel of the Torah

Rabbi Isaac, the father of Rashi, owned a jewel worth thousands upon thousands of gold pieces. Once the eye of one of the emperor's statues, a jewel of similar worth, was lost. The emperor sent for Rabbi Isaac and asked him to bring his jewel to the palace so that the emperor might buy it.

En route to the capital, Rabbi Isaac contrived to lose the jewel so that it might not be used to adorn an idol. He took out the jewel to show to another passenger, but as he was reaching to place the jewel in the man's hand, he let it fall into the sea.

"Alas!" cried Rabbi Isaac. "All my fortune has just been swallowed up by the sea!" And he fell to the deck and wept bitterly.

The people on board all felt sorry for the rabbi and accompanied him to the emperor to explain his misfortune. The emperor, too, had pity on him and did not punish him for failing to provide him with the jewel.

"For his loss is far greater than mine!" said the emperor.

When Rabbi Isaac returned home, he was greeted by Elijah, who said to him, "Because you gave up your jewel to fulfill the will of your Master, your wife will give birth to a son, who will be a jewel without equal in the world."

And a year later Solomon the son of Isaac of Troyes was born, later known as Rashi, whose commentaries on the Torah, Mishnah, and Talmud have lifted up all succeeding generations. Indeed, there has never been a jewel like him.

296

The Boy Who Was Saved from Hanging

Once there was a pious man to whom people came to cure their illness or to end their childlessness. But he was powerless to act on his own behalf, so he and his saintly wife remained childless.

His wife pleaded with him to pray for a child in their old age, but he said to her, "It is the will of heaven that we remain alone."

Still his wife's heart ached for a child, and at last her husband agreed to fast and beseech the heavens on their behalf. That night he had a dream. "In a year's time you shall have a son," the dream told him. "But on his thirteenth birthday, he will die by hanging. All these years God has left you childless to spare you this suffering. But since you have prayed for a child, God has heard your prayers and answered them."

The next morning, the pious man told his wife about his dream.

"Even so, I wish to have a son," said the wife. "Let us continue to give charity and perform good deeds. Perhaps God will have mercy upon us and avert the severe decree."

A year later, the couple had a son. The boy brought great joy to his old parents' hearts and honor to their name. Each night they laid him between them in their bed, for they feared for his safety and wished to keep him close to them. But their happiness was not complete, for they knew that he soon must leave them.

On the night of the boy's twelfth birthday, the father began to sigh.

"Why are you sighing?" asked his wife.

"Our son is perfect and wise and pious, yet in a short time he is going to be hanged! How should I not sigh?" cried the father. And they both began to weep.

His father's sighs woke the boy and he overheard everything his parents said.

"Why must I die by hanging?" he asked. "Who told you this?"

So his father told his son of the dream he had had before he was born, and of the tragic misfortune it had foretold.

"Then I must leave you and go to a distant place," said the boy, "for a change of place may also change my fate. Perhaps God will have mercy on me and avert the decree."

His father gave him three apples and said to him, "You shall travel to your uncle's house and stay with him until the danger is past. The journey will take three days. Each night a man will greet you. Give him one of the apples and then eat it together with him. If he gives you the better half and keeps the peel and core for himself, you must leave him and proceed on your way alone. But if he keeps the better half for himself and gives you the peel and core, travel with him until you reach your uncle's house."

Then his parents blessed and kissed him and sent him on his way.

The first day the boy met a man and gave him the first apple. The man gave him the better half and ate the peel and core. So the boy left him and went on his way alone. The next day he met a second man who did the same thing. So he parted from this man, too, and traveled on alone.

But on the third day he met an old man who kept the better half for himself and gave his young companion the peel and core. So the boy said to him, "Let us travel together to my uncle's house."

"Gladly," replied the stranger. "But you must do whatever I tell you."

The boy agreed to the old man's conditions.

"Do not be afraid," the old man assured him, "for God will watch over you and annul all harsh decrees against you."

Soon they arrived at the uncle's house.

"I will now leave you," the old man told the boy, "but I will not abandon you." And then he was gone.

The boy's uncle, who was a very rich man, greeted the boy warmly and built him a small house in the garden where he could study Torah. He ordered books for him and supplied his every need.

On the night of his thirteenth birthday, the boy sat studying Torah in the garden. Suddenly he looked up and saw a rope hanging down from the ceiling above him. Then the rope lowered itself and coiled around his throat. The boy reached up and grabbed hold of the rope, but it began to move, dragging him from room to room until it reached the middle of the house.

Suddenly the old man appeared before him. "Have

no fear," he told the boy. He reached up, cut the rope, and gently lowered the boy to the floor.

"This end was decreed for you before you were born," said the old man, "but the Torah that you have studied all your life came before the Throne of Glory dressed in black and pleaded on your behalf, and God granted her request and sent me to save you. For although I have appeared before you in human form, know that I am Elijah the Prophet."

And the next day the boy told his uncle how he had been saved from death by Elijah, and the entire household rejoiced with him. Soon after this, the boy married his uncle's daughter, and they lived together in peace and happiness all the days of their lives.

297

The Bride Who Saved Her Husband from the Angel of Death

Once the Angel of Death appeared to Rabbi Reuben and told him that he had come to take his only son. Rabbi Reuben, a pious man, rebuked the Angel and asked to be allowed at least to see his only son wed before he claimed his soul. The Angel granted his wish.

The next day the father betrothed his son and arranged for the wedding to take place in four weeks. Then he sent his son to invite the wedding guests.

On his way, the son met the Prophet Elijah.

"Where are you going?" Elijah asked him.

"To invite guests to my wedding," replied the young man.

"You are destined to die on your wedding day," Elijah told him.

"If such is God's will," replied the young man, "then I shall accept it as my forefathers did."

"I shall give you good advice that you should follow," said Elijah. "On the day of your wedding, a beggar will appear dressed in rags and with an uncovered head. Welcome him kindly and show him great respect. Invite him to sit at the head table among the honored guests, and if he refuses, sit down beside him wherever he chooses to sit. Take care to honor him. Remember to do what I have told you."

The young man promised to follow Elijah's instructions, and then the prophet departed.

At last the day of the wedding arrived. All the guests arrived in merry spirits, but the bridegroom's face was overcast with gloom. In the middle of the·dinner, an uninvited guest arrived who caused a great commotion among the other guests. The bridegroom looked up and saw an old man dressed in tatters with an uncovered head. Instantly he recalled the prophet's words. He ran over to the man, bowed before him, and invited him to sit at the head table. When the man refused, the bridegroom sat down beside him and ordered the choicest foods brought to their table. The other guests were amazed to see the bridegroom paying such honor to the poor old man, and they also marveled at the young man's pale, frightened face.

Then the old man said to the bridegroom, "My son, let me ask you a question. If you are building a house and need straw to mix with the clay, where do you get the straw?"

"I buy it from a farmer," replied the young man, "for he makes straw."

"And what if the farmer comes and asks for his straw back?"

"I would pay him for the straw or give him other straw," said the bridegroom.

"And what if he insists that you return to him the very same straw he first sold you? What would you do then?"

"I would have no choice but to break up the clay, take out the straw, and give it back to him," said the bridegroom.

"God is the farmer," said the old man, "and the straw is a man's soul. I am the Angel of Death come to take back the straw that God once gave you. God will accept no other."

Then the young man said, "If such is God's will, so be it. But before you take my life, let me first bid farewell to my father and mother and my new bride."

"Very well," said the Angel of Death. "You may do so."

When Rabbi Reuben heard the Angel's words, he rushed forward to offer his life in place of his son's. But when he looked upon the Angel's terrible face, he was so frightened that he drew back and could not face him. The bridegroom's mother, too, came forward to save her son, but she was too terrified even to speak.

Then the bride came forward and said, "Does it not say in the holy Torah that a man who takes a wife shall be free to rejoice with her for a whole year? And does it not also say 'a soul for a soul'? Take me then and let my husband live!"

Then the Angel of Death clothed himself in the four robes of cruelty and placed his foot upon her neck, brandishing his sword before her. But she only cried, "Finish the work of the King of Kings!"

Then the Angel of Death felt pity for her, and a tear of mercy fell from his eye. And he flew to heaven and pleaded on her behalf before the Throne of Glory. God accepted his plea and granted the bridegroom an additional seventy years.

298

Two Brothers and Their Wish

In Jerusalem there once lived two brothers, one rich and the other poor. One day Elijah, disguised as a beggar, appeared at the door of the rich brother and asked for some food. But the man was a hardhearted miser, and he sent the beggar away empty-handed.

Then Elijah went to the home of the poor brother, who welcomed him gladly and shared his meager food with him.

When he was about to leave, Elijah said to the poor man, "Because of your kindness, I will grant you one wish that shall continue until you cry: 'Enough!' "

The poor brother thanked him, and then Elijah departed.

When his guest was gone, the poor man wished for a coin in his empty purse. And when he opened up the purse, there was a shiny gold piece inside! He took the coin out and put it on the table. Then remembering the stranger's promise, he looked in the purse again, and found another coin in place of the one he had removed. For several hours he continued taking gold coins from the purse until he was exhausted. Then he cried out, "Enough!" And this time when he looked inside the purse, it was empty.

The poor brother stared at the mountain of gold coins heaped upon the table and suddenly realized that he was now wealthy beyond his wildest dreams.

The next morning his rich brother came to visit him and was astonished to see the mountain of gold piled upon his brother's table.

"Where did all this come from?" he asked.

Then his brother told him about the wonderful wish the beggar had granted him.

"Describe this beggar to me," said the rich brother.

And when he heard the description of the beggar, he realized to his dismay that it was the same man he had so rudely turned away from his own door.

At once the rich brother ran to the marketplace. He was overjoyed to find the beggar still there.

"Please accept my apologies," he said to him. "It is not like me to turn away someone in need. My wife and I would be glad to welcome you into our house and satisfy your needs."

So the beggar accompanied the rich brother home. This time the rich man and his wife treated their poor guest like a king.

When he was finished eating, Elijah said to his hosts, "Because of your kindness, I will grant you one wish that shall continue until you cry: 'Enough!' "

As soon as he was gone, the rich brother and his wife wished for gold. How excited they were to find gold coins spilling out of their purses in an endless stream! They continued pulling coins out until the entire floor of their house was carpeted in gold. But though they were exhausted, they were not yet ready to stop. Slowly the gold mounted up to their knees, then to their waists, and then their necks, but still they could not stop. Their hands ached and their bellies pleaded for food, but the sight of gold dazzled them so much that they were powerless to resist it.

The next day when the other brother came to call, he found his rich brother and his wife lifeless, buried under a mountain of gold.

299
The Tramp

When Rabbi Meir Primishlaner was young, he pleaded with his father to teach him how he might meet Elijah. His father said to him, "If you study Torah with your whole heart, you will."

He studied for four weeks, but still he did not meet him. So he returned to his father and complained.

"How impatient you are!" his father scolded him. "Continue studying and you will certainly meet him."

One night a tramp came to the House of Study while Meir was there. Meir looked at the man in disgust, for he was dusty and dressed in tatters, with a battered pack upon his back. And never in his life had Meir seen an uglier face. Angry to be disturbed by such an unsavory character, Meir chased the man away.

The next day his father came to the House of Study and asked Meir, "Have you seen Elijah yet?"

"No," replied Meir.

"Did no one come here last night?"

"Yes," replied Meir. "An old tramp."

"Did you wish him *'shalom aleikhem'?*" asked his father.

"No," said Meir.

"You fool!" cried his father. "Didn't you know that that was Elijah the Prophet? But now it's too late."

From that day on, Meir wished every stranger *"shalom aleikhem"* and treated him with kindness.

300

Elijah's Cup

Once there was a wealthy couple named Elkana and Penina. They were generous to the poor, and their large house was always open to strangers. Their most valued possession was a beautiful Elijah's cup that graced their *seder* table each year.

In time the wheel of fortune turned, and they were forced to pawn all their possessions to buy food. All that remained to them was the Elijah's cup that they agreed never to sell, no matter how desperate their circumstances became.

As the holiday of Passover approached, they discovered that they did not have enough money to buy the necessary food and wine for the *seder*.

"Dearest Penina," said Elkana with a heavy heart, "I'm afraid we have no choice but to sell Elijah's cup."

"Never!" replied Penina, and nothing Elkana could say would change her mind.

On the day before Passover, Elkana went off to the

House of Study. It pained him too much to remain at home and see the empty Elijah's cup sitting in the middle of a bare table. How sad the holiday would be for them this year! How could they possibly celebrate Israel's liberation from bondage?

While Elkana was gone, there was a knock on the door. Penina opened the door to find an elderly, well-dressed stranger standing before her.

"I am a stranger in this town," said the man. "May I spend the *seders* with you?"

"I am afraid that we have no money for a *seder* this year," said Penina sadly.

The stranger handed her a heavy purse. "Take these coins and with them buy what you need," he told her. "Tonight I shall return for the *seder*."

With a joyful heart, Penina hurried to the market and bought what she needed for the *seders*. Then she ran home and prepared a great feast. When Elkana returned, Penina told him what had happened and instructed him to bring the man home with him from synagogue that evening.

But Elkana returned from synagogue alone.

"I looked everywhere," he explained to his wife, "but there was no well-dressed stranger there."

They decided not to begin the *seder* until their benefactor arrived. But it began to grow late, and still there was no sign of him. At eleven o'clock, they could wait no longer. They recited all the blessings and passages in the *haggadah* and then began the meal. Right after they finished the *afikomen,* Elkana fell asleep.

But Penina stayed awake, still hoping that the stranger would appear. And a short while later, when she opened the door for Elijah the Prophet, the elderly man walked in.

She ran to wake Elkana, but by the time she succeeded in rousing him from his heavy sleep, the stranger was gone. Elkana fell back to sleep, and Penina finished the *haggadah* by herself.

Shortly after this, Elkana died. When he ascended to

Paradise, the Heavenly Court wished to admit him at once, but the elderly man appeared and said, "This man wanted to sell the Elijah's Cup. He must remain outside!"

So for several years he waited outside the gates.

Then Penina died, and Paradise welcomed her soul gladly. But as she came forward to enter the gates, she noticed something blocking the way. It was the soul of her beloved Elkana.

"I will not enter without him!" she cried.

The Heavenly Court tried to persuade her to change her mind, but she stood firm. So they were forced to admit them both.

List of Sources

References for each tale include the source or sources of the original tale as well as one or more English language sources. In some cases, the source of the original is unknown or has been modified sufficiently so that it bears little resemblance to the original. In a few cases, the tales have only oral sources. Following are the most frequently cited English language sources; I have referred to them by author in the list below:

Ausubel, Nathan. *Treasury of Jewish Folklore*. New York: Crown, 1948.
Bialik, Hayyim Naham. *And It Came to Pass*. Brooklyn: Hebrew Publishing Company, 1938.
Bin Gorion, Micha. *Mimekor Yisrael: Classical Jewish Folktales*. Indiana: Indiana University Press, 1976.
Buber, Martin. *Tales of the Hasidim, Early Masters* (EM). New York: Schocken, 1947.
_____ *Tales of the Hasidim, Later Masters* (LM). New York: Schocken, 1948.
_____ *Legends of the Baal Shem Tov* (LBST). New York: Schocken, 1955.
Field, Claud. *Jewish Legends of the Middle Ages*. Darby, PA: Folcroft Library Editions, 1976.
Gaster, Moses. *The Maaseh Book: Book of Jewish Tales and Legends*. Philadelphia: Jewish Publication Society, 1981.

Ginzberg, Louis. *Legends of the Jews*. 7 vols. Philadelphia: Jewish Publication Society, 1909–1938.

Hanakdan, Berechiah ben Natronai, *Fables of the Jewish Aesop*. Translated by Moses Hadas. New York: Columbia University Press, 1967.

Ish-Kishor, Judith. *Tales from the Wise Men of Israel*. Philadelphia: Lippincott, 1962.

Labovitz, Annette and Eugene. *Time for My Soul*. Northvale, NJ: Jason Aronson, 1987.

Mintz, Jerome. *Legends of the Hasidim*. Chicago: University of Chicago, 1968.

Nadich, Judah. *Jewish Legends of the Second Commonwealth*. Philadelphia: Jewish Publication Society, 1983.

Newman, Louis. *Hasidic Anthology*. Northvale, NJ: Jason Aronson, 1987.

Noy, Dov. *Folktales of Israel*. Chicago: University of Chicago Press, 1963.

Patai, Raphael. *Gates to the Old City*. Northvale, NJ: Jason Aronson, 1988.

Rappaport, Angelo. *Ancient Israel: Myths and Legends*. 3 Vols. Bonanza Books, 1987.

Tale #:

1. *The Beginning:* Genesis 28:4; Midrash Tehillim (ed. Buber), 90:31, 34:245; Midrash Bereshit Rabbah 3:7, 9:2, 28:4; Midrash Kohellet Rabbah 3:11; Midrash Kohellet 1:15, 4:3; Konen (Beit HaMidrash, ed. Jellinek), 37–38; Midrash Behokhmah (Beit HaMidrash, ed. Jellinek), V, 64–66, 63–66; Pesikta Hadta (Beit HaMidrash, ed. Jellinek), 48–49
   English language sources: Ginzberg I, 3–5; Bin Gorion I, 4–5

2. *The Alephbet:* Genesis 1:1; Exodus 20:2; 2 Alephbet of Rabbi Akiva 50–55; Midrash HaGadol Sefer Bereshit I, 10–11; Zohar (Schechter) I, 2b–3a
   English language sources: Ginzberg I, 5–8; V, 6–7, n. 10–12

3. *The Sun and the Moon:* Genesis 1: 14–19; Midrash Bereshit Rabbah 6:3; Konen (Beit HaMidrash, ed. Jellinek), 25–26; B. Hullin 60b
   English language sources: Ginzberg I, 23–24

4. *Ziz-Shaddai:* Genesis 1:20–23; Midrash Vayikra Rabbah 22:10; Midrash Tehillim 80:363; Konen (Beit HaMidrash, ed. Jellinek), 26; Targum on Psalms 50:11; B. Baba Batra 25b, 73b; Midrash Bereshit Rabbah 19:4; B. Gittin 31b
   English language sources: Ginzberg I, 28–9

5. *Leviathan:* Genesis 1:20–23; Midrash Jonah 98; B. Baba Batra 74b–75a; Midrash Bereshit Rabbah 7:4; Konen (Beit HaMidrash, ed. Jellinek), 26; Zohar II, 108b; Targum Yerushalmi Genesis 1:20; B. Shabbat 27b; Pesikta deRav Kahana (ed. Buber), 188a–189b; Midrash Alphabetot 98 (ed. Wertheimer); B. Avodah Zarah 3b; Pirke de Rebbe Eliezer 9
   English language sources: Ginzberg I, 27–28

6. *Leviathan and the Fox:* Alphabet of Ben Sira 27–29
   English language sources: Bin Gorion I, 10–12

7. *The Re'em:* Genesis 1:24–25; Aggadat Karne Re'emim in Agudot I, 37–39
   English language sources: Bin Gorion I, 5–6

8. *Milham, the Phoenix-Bird:* Genesis 3:28–29; 2 Alphabet of Ben Sira 27a,

28b, 29a–b; Midrash Bereshit Rabbah 19:5; Midrash Shmuel 12:81
English language sources: Ginzberg I, 32–33; V, 51, n. 151; Bin Gorion
I, 9

9. *The Creation of Souls:* Genesis 1:26–27; Midrash Bereshit Rabbah 8:1;
   Tanhuma Pikude 3; Yezirat ha-Valad in Abkat Rokel (Beit HaMidrash,
   ed. Jellinek) I, 153–155; B. Ketubot 30a; B. Niddah 39a
   English language sources: Ginzberg I, 55–9

10. *The Creation of Adam:* Genesis 1:26–27; Midrash Bereshit Rabbah 8:1–9,
    14:7, 18:4, 21:3, 24:2,7; Tanhuma, Introduction (ed. Buber), 154; Mi-
    drash Tehillim I: 23; Midrash Pesikta Rabbati 40: 166b; Pirke de Rebbe
    Eliezer 11; Tanhuma Pekude 3; Targum Yerushalmi, Gen. 2:7; B.
    Sanhedrin 38a–b; Midrash HaGadol Sefer Bereshit (ed. Schechter), I, 74;
    Pesikta Rabbati 4:34a; Tanhuma Hukkat 6; Midrash Bamidbar Rabbah
    12:8, 19:3; Midrash Kohellet 7:23; Midrash Tehillim 8:73–74; Midrash
    Shir HaShirim 3:11; B. Hullin 60a; B. Hagiga B. Berakhot 61a; B. Eruvin
    18a; Midrash VaYikra Rabbah 14; Tanhuma Tazria 2
    English language sources: Ginzberg I, 52–62; V, 79–84

11. *Adam's Gift to King David:* Genesis 5:5; Midrash BaMidbar Rabbah 14:12;
    Pirke de Rebbe Eliezer 9; Midrash Tehillim 95:408
    English language sources: Ginzberg I, 61

12. *Lilith:* Genesis 1:27; 2:18–23; 2 Alphabet of Ben Sira 23a–b, 33a–b
    English language sources: Ginzberg I, 65

13. *The First Wedding:* Genesis 2:18–25; Midrash Bereshit Rabbah 8:1; B.
    Berakhot 61a; B. Eruvin 18a; Midrash VaYikra Rabbah 14; Tanhuma B.
    III, 33; Tanhuma Tazria 2; Midrash Tehillim 139:529; Pirke de Rebbe
    Eliezer 12; 2 Alphabet de Rabbi Akiva 60; B. Sotah 17a
    English language sources: Ginzberg I, 66–69

14. *The Shamir:* Pirke Avot 5:6; Sifre Deuteronomy (ed. Friedmann), 355;
    Midrash Tannaim 219; B. Pesahim 54a; Avot de Rabbi Natan 37,95; Pirke
    de Rebbe Eliezer 19; Tosefta Sotah 15:1–Bavli 48b; Yerushalmi 9, 20d
    English language sources: Ginzberg I, 34

15. *The Fall of Satan:* Genesis 2:19–20; Avot de Rabbi Natan 1:8; Midrash
    Bereshit Rabbati 24 (from Eldad HaDani 66:7, ed. Epstein)
    English language sources: Ginzberg I, 62–64; Bin Gorion I, 6–7

16. *The Fall of Adam and Eve:* Genesis 3; Midrash Bereshit Rabbah 4, 5, 15:7,
    17:4, 19:19, 20:6–7, 21:5–9; Midrash Kohellet 1:18; Midrash Shmuel 7:66;
    B. Sanhedrin 59b; Avot de Rabbi Natan 1:4, 5; 8:23; 2 Avot de Rabbi
    Natan 1:6, 14, 42:116–117; Pirke de Rebbe Eliezer 11, 14; 2 Alphabet of
    Ben Sira 28b, 29a–b, 36a; Targum Yerushalmi, Genesis 3:7, 21; B. Eruvin
    100b; Midrash HaGadol Sefer Bereshit I, 106; Seder Eliyahu Rabbah I;
    Targum Yerushalmi Genesis 3:24; Pesikta de Rav Kahana 23:150b;
    Midrash Pesikta Rabbati 46:177b; B. Sanhedrin 38b
    English language sources: Ginzberg I, 71–83

17. *Adam and Eve's Repentance:* Genesis 2:23–24; Pirke de Rebbe Eliezer 20,
    23, 31; B. Avodah Zarah 8a; Avot de Rabbi Natan 1:7; Midrash Bereshit

Rabbah 24:9; Targum Yerushalmi Genesis 8:20
English language sources: Ginzberg I, 86–89, V, 114–117

18. *The Cat and the Dog:* 2 Alphabet of Ben Sira 25a–b
English language sources: Ginzberg I, 35–36; Bin Gorion I, 12–13

19. *Cain and Abel:* Genesis 4:1–24; Sefer HaYashar 8–9; Pirke de Rebbe Eliezer 21; B. Shabbat 146a; B. Yebamot 103b; B. Avodah Zarah 22b; Targum Yerushalmi Genesis 4:1, 5:3; Midrash Bereshit Rabbah 19, 22:6–13; Zohar I, 31a, 54b; Tanhuma Bereshit 9; Aggadat Shir 7,43, 91–92
English language sources: Ginzberg I, 106–113; Bin Gorion I, 13–15

20. *Enoch, the Man Who Never Died:* Genesis 5:18–24; Sefer Yashar Bereshit 11a–13a; Beit HaMidrash (ed. Jellinek), IV, 129–132
English language sources: Ginzberg I, 127–140; Bin Gorion I, 16–20

21. *The Cat and the Mouse:* 2 Alphabet of Ben Sira 25a–26; Iggeret Ba'ale Hayyim 2:6
English language sources: Ginzberg I, 35

22. *Nimrod and the Tower of Babel:* Genesis 10:8–10, 11:1–9; Sefer Yashar Noah 17–21
English language sources: Bin Gorion I, 24–26

23. *The Birth of Abraham:* Genesis 11:26–28; B. Baba Batra 91a; Sefer Yashar Noah 18a–19a, 23–27; Ma'aseh Abraham (Beit HaMidrash, ed. Jellinek), I, 25–28, 30–32; II, 18; Midrash Aseret HaDibrot 2
English language sources: Ginzberg I, 186–193, 207–209; Bin Gorion I, 26–29, 37–41

24. *Abraham and the Idols:* Genesis 11:28, 12:5; Seder Eliayahu Rabbah (ed. Friedmann), 5: 27; Yerahmeel 71–72; Zohar I, 77; Midrash Bereshit Rabbah 38:13; Sefer Yashar Noah 23b–26b
English language sources: Ginzberg I, 195–198, 209–215; Bin Gorion I, 29–32, 41–42

25. *Abraham in Nimrod's Furnace:* Genesis 11:31; Ma'aseh Abraham (Beit HaMidrash, ed. Jellinek), I, 25–34; Sefer Yashar Noah 27
English language sources: Ginzberg I, 198–203; Bin Gorion I, 32–36, 43–46

26. *Nimrod's Dream:* Sefer Yashar Noah 27b–28a
English language sources: Ginzberg I, 204–205

27. *Abraham and Sarah in Egypt:* Genesis 13:10–14:2; Midrash Bereshit Rabbah 25:3; 40:3–5, 41:2, 45:1, 52:13; Tanhuma Lekh Lekha 5; Sefer Yashar Lekh Lekha 31a–32b; Zohar I, 81b–82a; Midrash Tanhuma (ed. Buber) I, 65–66; Pirke de Rebbe Eliezer 26
English language sources: Ginzberg I, 220–225

28. *The Cruel Customs of Sodom:* Genesis 13:13; Tosefta Sotah 3:12; Sifre Deuteronomy 43; Mekilta Shira 2:35b; B. Sanhedrin 109a; Midrash Vayikra Rabbah 4, 5:2; Pesikta de Rav Kahana 19:187b, 27:170; Pirke de Rebbe Eliezer 25; Sefer Yashar Va-Yera 35b–38a
English language sources: Ginzberg I, 245–250; Bin Gorion I, 54–56

29. *Lot's Wife:* Genesis 19:1–29; Midrash Bereshit Rabbah 50, 51; B. Baba

Metzia 87a; Tanhuma Va-Yera 11, 12
English language sources: Ginzberg I, 253–255

30. *Abraham's Impatience with the Old Man:* Botser Ollelot, (Shimon Shanto, 1806), on Genesis 12
English language sources: Bin Gorion I, 63–64

31. *The Birth of Isaac:* Genesis 18:1–15, 21:1–8; Pesikta Rabbati 42:177a–178a; Tanhuma Va-Yera 13–17; Aggadat Bereshit 28:57–58; Tanhuma Toledot 1; Midrash Bereshit Rabbah 46:2, 53:6,9, 84:8; B. Baba Metzia 87a; Pirke de Rebbe Eliezer 29; Pesikta de Rav Kahana 22:1
English language sources: Ginzberg I, 261–263

32. *The Akedah:* Genesis 22:1–9, 23:1–20; Sefer Yashar 43–47; Zohar I, 10a–11b, 128a–b; Midrash Bereshit Rabbah 55:4,7, 56:2,4,10, 58:6; B. Sanhedrin 89b; Pirke de Rebbe Eliezer 31; Sifre Deuteronomy 352
English language sources: Ginzberg I, 271–291; Bin Gorion I, 56–63

33. *Eliezer's Mission to Seek Rebecca:* Genesis 24:1–67; Sefer Yashar Hayye Sarah 48b; Midrash Bereshit Rabbah 59:9–10, 60:5–16; Pirke de Rebbe Eliezer 16, 32; B. Sanhedrin 95a; Tanhuma Ya-Yera 3, Yalkuit Reubeni I, 109; Zohar I, 133a; 2 Alphabet of Ben Sira 28b
English language sources: Ginzberg I, 291–299

34. *The Birth of Jacob and Esau:* Genesis 25:20–27; Sefer Yashar Toledot 50; Pirke de Rebbe Eliezer 32; Bereshit Rabbah 62:6, 63:5–8, 67:6; Seder Eliyahu Zuta, 19, 26–27; Midrash HaGadol Sefer Bereshit I, 390–395; Yalkut Reubeni I, 110; Midrash Tehillim 9:83–84; Targum Yerushalmi, Genesis 25:25; Sefer Hadar Zekanim on Genesis 25:25; Avot de Rabbi Natan 2:2
English language sources: Ginzberg I, 311–15

35. *Jacob's Flight from Esau:* Genesis 25:29–34, 27:41–45, 28:10–22, 29:1–28; Pirke de Rebbe Eliezer 35–36; Midrash Bereshit Rabbah 68:10–12, 69:4–5, 70:11, 73:12–14; B. Hullin 91a; B. Shabbat 118a; Targum Yerushalmi, Exodus 28:30
English language sources: Ginzberg I, 349–354

36. *Jacob Wrestles with Samael:* Genesis 32:2–33; Midrash Bereshit Rabbah 77:2–3; 78:3; Midrash Shir HaShirim Rabbah 3:5; Tanhuma Vayishlach 4:8; Zohar I, 146a; Yalkut Reubeni, Genesis 32:25–33
English language sources: Ginzberg I, 384–388; V, 309–310, n. 273

37. *Asnat:* Genesis 34:1–1, 26, 46:10; Pirke de Rebbe Eliezer 38; Midrash Aggadah, Genesis 41:45; Abkir (Yalkut Reubeni), I, 146; Tokpo shel Yosef (Y. S. Farhi), 28–29; Midrash Bereshit Rabbah 80:11
English language sources: Ginzberg II, 38, 76, 170–174, 172–174; Bin Gorion I, 71–72

38. *Kimtas the Physician:* Genesis 40:1–8; Tokpo shel Yosef (Y. S. Farhi)
English language sources: Rappaport, II, 65–69

39. *Joseph and Benjamin:* Genesis 43:29–34; Tokpo shel Yosef (Y. S. Farhi), 39; Sefer Yashar 104–105; Midrash Bereshit Rabbah 74:10, 92:5
English language sources: Ginzberg V, 351, n. 244–252; Bin Gorion I, 72–74

40. *The Birth of Moses:* Exodus 1:8–22, 2:1–3; Divrei HaYamim le'Moshe Rabbeinu (Beit HaMidrash, ed. Jellinek), II, 1–4; Sefer Yashar 128–129, 131–132; B. Sotah 12a; B. Baba Batra 120a; Zohar II, 11b; Midrash Devarim Rabbah 9, 11
    English language sources: Ginzberg II, 254–265; V, 393–394, 407–410; Bin Gorion I, 76–78

41. *Moses in the Bulrushes:* Exodus 2:3–10; B. Sotah 12a–13a; Midrash Shir HaShirim Rabbah 1:21–25; Targum Yerushalmi, Exodus 2:5; Pirke de Rebbe Eliezer 48; Sefer Yashar Shemot 130b–131a; Midrash Hagadol Sefer Bereshit II, 14; Midrash VaYikra Rabbah 1, 3; Midrash Mishle 31:111; 2 Alphabet of Ben Sira 28b
    English language sources: Ginzberg II, 265–269

42. *The Coal and the Crown:* Exodus 2:10; Sefer Yashar Shemot 131b–132b; Divrei HaYamim le'Moshe Rabbeinu (Beit HaMidrash, ed. Jellinek II), 1–4; Midrash Shemot Rabbah 1:26
    English language sources: Ginzberg II, 272–276; Bin Gorion I, 76–78

43. *Moses, King of Ethiopia:* Exodus 2:15; Divrei HaYamim le'Moshe Rabbeinu (Beit HaMidrash, ed. Jellinek II), 5–7; Sefer Yashar Shemot 132–136, 138; Midrash Shemot Rabbah 1:27, 31; Midrash Devarim Rabbah 2:29
    English language sources: Ginzberg II, 277–279; Bin Gorion I, 78–80; Rappaport, II, 244–249

44. *Moses Marries Zipporah:* Exodus 2:15–22, 4:18–26; Midrash VaYosha (Beit HaMidrash, ed. Jellinek I), 42–44; Divrei HaYamim le'Moshe Rabbeinu; Sefer Yashar 140–141; Midrash Shemot Rabbah 1:32–34; Tanhuma Shemot 11; Mekilta Yitro 1:57b, 59a; Midrash Devarim Rabbah 2:8
    English language sources: Ginzberg II, 289–291; Bin Gorion I, 80–81

45. *The Thornbush:* Exodus 3:1–22, 4:1–17; Zohar II, 21a; Midrash Shemot Rabbah 2:5; Tanhuma Shemot 14–15; B. Yoma 21b; Aggadat Bereshit 32:64; B. Shabbat 67a; B. Sotah 5a
    English language sources: Ginzberg II, 303–304

46. *The Ten Plagues:* Exodus 5:1–12:36; Tanhuma Va'Era 13–14; Tanhuma Bo 4; Midrash Shemot Rabbah 9–15; Pesikta de Rav Kahana 7:64a, 66b–67a; Pesikta Rabbati 17:87b, 89b, 197a–b; Midrash VaYosha (Beit HaMidrash, ed. Jellinek), I, 44–45, 49–51; Seder Eliyahu Rabbah 7, 40–43; Mekilta Beshallah 6, 32; Mekilta Bo 13; Midrash Tehillim 27:299, 78:355
    English language sources: Ginzberg II, 341–367

47. *The Crossing of the Sea of Reeds:* Exodus 13:17–22, 18:1–31; Mekilta Beshallah 2:28b, 3:29–30a, 4:30b–31a, 5:31a–32, 6:33; Midrash Shemot Rabbah 21–24, 27; Zohar II, 33a, 34a, 181b; Midrash Tehillim 18:147; Pirke de Rebbe Eliezer 42–43; B. Sotah 36b–37a; Midrash VaYosha (Beit HaMidrash, ed. Jellinek), I, 39–40, 45–47, 51–53; Avot de Rabbi Natan 27:83, 38:10; Targum Yerushalmi, Exodus 14:22; Abkir (Yalkut Reubeni), I, 241; Divrei HaYamim le'Moshe Rabbeinu 11
    English language sources: Ginzberg III, 9–31; Rappaport, II, 286–296

48. *Manna from Heaven:* Exodus 16:1–36; Pirke de Rebbe Eliezer 3; B.

Haggigah 12b; Midrash Tehillim 76: 346, 78:345; Mekilta Va'Yassa 4:50b, 3:48b–49a, 5:51b; Midrash Shemot Rabbah 25:3, 10; B. Yoma 75a
English language sources: Ginzberg III, 41–50

49. *Miriam's Well:* Exodus 17:1–7; Numbers 20:1–2; Mekilta Va'Yassa 6:52; Midrash Shemot Rabbah 26:2; Tanhuma Beshallah 22; Seder Olam 5; Pirke de Rebbe Eliezer 3; Tosefta Sukkah 3:11–13; Yalkut Reubeni I, 426; Midrash BaMidbar Rabbah 1:2, 19:26; Midrash Tehillim 23:200; Midrash Shir HaShirim 36–37
English language sources: Ginzberg III, 50–54

50. *We Will Obey and We Will Hear:* Exodus 19:3–9; Sifre Deuteronomy 343, 142b; Midrash Tannaim 210; Mekilta BaHodesh 1:62a, 5:67a; B. Avodah Zarah 2b; B. Baba Kammah 38a; Sohar II, 91b
English language sources: Ginzberg III, 80–82

51. *The Contest of the Mountains:* Exodus 19:20; Midrash Bereshit Rabbah 99:1; Midrash Tehillim 68:318; Targum Tehillim 68:16–17; Tosefta Targum Judges 5:5; Mekilta BaHodesh 5:66b
English language sources: Ginzberg III, 82–85; VI, 32, n. 185

52. *Our Children Shall Be Our Guarantors:* Exodus 19:21–25, 20:1–22; Midrash Shir HaShirim 1:4; Midrash Tehillim 8:76–77; Midrash Aseret Ha-Dibrot 68
English language sources: Ginzberg III, 89–90

53. *Divine Blackmail at Sinai:* Exodus 19:7–8; Mekilta BaHodesh 3:65a; B. Shabbat 88a, 129b; B. Avodah Zarah 2b; Pesikta Rabbati 10:37a, 21:103b, 28:154a
English language sources: Ginzberg III, 92–94

54. *The Revelation at Sinai:* Exodus 20:16–22, 24:3–18; Mekilta Yitro 1:57a; Mekilta BaHodesh 3:64b–65a, 4, 5:67, 9:71–2; Pesikta Rabbati 20:95a, 21:99–106, 21:203b; Pirke de Rebbe Eliezer 41; Pesikta de Rav Kahana 12:108a, 110; Midrash Aseret HaDibrot 69–70; Midrash Shemot Rabbah 5:9, 28:6, 29:9; B. Shabbat 88b; Midrash Tehillim 68:317, 92:403; Tanhuma Yitro 11; Midrash Shir HaShirim 1:2
English language sources: Ginzberg III, 90–94, 94–98, 106–109

55. *Moses and the Angels Wrestle Over the Torah:* Exodus 24:12–18, 31:18; Pirke de Rebbe Eliezer 41; Ma'ayan HaHokhmah 58–61; Pesikta Rabbati 20:96a–98a, 25:128a; B. Shabbat 88b; Avot de Rabbi Natan 2:10
English language sources: Ginzberg III, 109–114; Gaster #3

56. *Moses Visits Akiva's Classroom:* B. Shabbat 89a; B. Menahot 29b
English language sources: Ginzberg III, 114–115

57. *The Golden Calf:* Exodus 32:1–35; Seder Eliyahu Zuta 4:179–180; Y. Taanit 4:68c; B. Sanhedrin 102a; Midrash Shemot Rabbah 19:3, 41:1,5,7, 42–44, 46:3; B. Shabbat 87a, 89a; Tanhuma Ke-Tissa 19, 21–24, 26; Tanhuma Beha'alotekha 14; Pirke de Rebbe Eliezer 45; Midrash VaYikra Rabbah 2:1, 7:1, 10:3; Midrash Shir HaShirim 13; Midrash Tehillim 3:37; Avot de Rabbi Natan 2, 11; Zohar II, 113b; B. Yoma 66b; Avodah Zarah 44a
English language sources: Ginzberg III, 119–124; VI, 51, n. 266

58. *The Pouch of Gold:* Exodus 33:13; Derashot al-ah-Torah (Ibn Shu'aib), Devarim, 98c; Seder Eliyahu Zuta 6:182-183; Pirke de Rebbe Eliezer 46
   English language sources: Ginzberg III, 135-136; Bin Gorion I, 85

59. *The Twelve Spies:* Numbers 13:1-33, 14:1-45; Sifre Deuteronomy 20, 24; Midrash Tannaim 11-12; Zohar III, 158a, 160b; Likkutim II, 20c; Midrash Bereshit Rabbah 46:1; Midrash Shemot Rabbah 6:1; B. Baba Batra 15a-b, 121a-b; B. Sotah 34a-35b; Midrash BaMidbar Rabbah 16:3, 11-13, 17:21, 26:25; Tanhuma Shelah 6-9, 12; Midrash Shir HaShirim Rabbah 4:13; Yelammedenu (Yalkut Reubeni), I, 743, Numbers 14:1; Midrash Tehillim 106:455; Midrash Devarim Rabbah 5:13; B. Taanit 30b
   English language sources: Ginzberg III, 261-264, 267-282; VI 94, n. 513

60. *The Rebellion of Korakh:* Numbers 16:1-35; B. Sanhedrin 110a-b; Midrash Mishle 11:70-71; Midrash BaMidbar Rabbah 18; Tanhuma Korakh 1, 2, 5, 6, 10; B. Nedarim 39b; Midrash Shmuel 5:61-62; Targum Yerushalmi, Numbers 16:22-34; Sifre Numbers 117; B. Baba Batra 74a
   English language sources: Ginzberg III, 286-307

61. *The Waters of Meribah:* Numbers 20:2-13; Yelammedenu (Batte Midrashot, ed. Wertheimer) III, 8-10, Yelammedenu (Yalkut Reubeni), I, 763, II, 879; Targum Yerushalmi, Numbers 20:8; Tanhuma Hukkat 9-10; Midrash BaMidbar Rabbah 19:12; Pesikta de Rav Kahana 14:118b; Midrash Bereshit Rabbah 4:6
   English language sources: Ginzberg III, 307-314

62. *The Death of Aaron:* Numbers 20:23-29; Petirat Aharan 92-95; Yelammedenu (Yalkut Reubeni), I, 764; Seder Eliyahu Rabbah 13:63,68, 20:112, 25:128; Sifra Milluim 8:7; B. Baba Batra 17a
   English language sources: Ginzberg III, 320-327

63. *The Giant Og:* Numbers 21:33-35; B. Niddah 24b, 61a; Midrash Devarim Rabbah 1:24; Likkutim, Midrash Eleh HaDevarim 27; Soferim 21; Tanhuma Hukkat 25; Midrash BaMidbar Rabbah 19:32; Zohar III, 181a; Yelammedenu (Yalkut Reubeni), I, 810; B. Berakhot 54b
   English language sources: Ginzberg I, 160; III, 343-348; V. 215, n. 41; VI, 118-119, n. 684

64. *Balak and Balaam:* Numbers 22:2-24:25; Zohar III, 184b, 194; Tanhuma Balak 3-13, 17; Midrash BaMidbar Rabbah 19-23; B. Sanhedrin 105a-106a; B. Sotah 10a; Midrash Aggadah Numbers 22:21; B. Berakhot 7a; B. Avodah Zarah 4; Yelammedenu (Yalkut Reubeni), I, 765, 771, 785; Targum Yerushalmi, Numbers 31:8
   English language sources: Ginzberg III, 351-382, 410-411

65. *Moses Resists His Fate:* Deuteronomy 31:3; Midrash Tannaim 14-16, 18; Mekilta BeShallakh 2:55a; Midrash Devarim Rabbah 11:9-10; Petirat Moshe 117-126; 2 Petirat Moshe 375-380; Sifre Deuteronomy 27; Tanhuma VaEthanan 6
   English language sources: Ginzberg III, 417-436

66. *Only a Glimpse of the Promised Land:* Deuteronomy 31:1-9, 14-30, 32:48-52, 34:1-4; Petirat Moshe 122-123; 2 Petirat Moshe 378-379; Midrash Devarim Rabbah 9:9; Sifre Numbers 135-1336; Beit HaMidrash

(ed. Jellinek), VI, Introduction 22
English language sources: Ginzberg III, 439–448; Bin Gorion I, 92–93

67. *The Kiss of the Shekhinah:* Deuteronomy 34:1–6; Petirat Moshe 127–129; 2 Petirat Moshe 381:2–3; Midrash Deuteronomy Rabbah 11:5,10; B. Baba Batra 17a; Sifre Deuteronomy 357; B. Sotah 14a
English language sources: Ginzberg III, 466–473

68. *The Death of Moses—An Ethiopian Tale:* Genesis 34:6; Mota Musa (Faitlovitch, 1906), 9–20
English language sources: Ginzberg VI, 162–163

69. *The Birth of Joshua:* Rav Pe'alim (Avraham ben Eliyahu), 12a; Otsar Midrashim I, 209 (ed. Eisenstein)
English language sources: Ginzberg IV, 3; Bin Gorion I, 94–95

70. *The Battle of Jericho:* Joshua 2–4, 6; Tanhuma Shelakh 1; Midrash BaMidbar Rabbah 14:1, 16:1; Kinat Setarim 31c, 44d; Sifre Numbers 78; B. Sotah Tosefta 8:1–4; Tanhuma Naso 28
English language sources: Ginzberg IV, 4–8; VI, 174–175, n. 22

71. *Joshua's Last War:* Yalkut Reubeni, Deuteronomy (end); The Samaritan Book of Joshua (Ed. Gaster); Karme Shomron, 68–74 (ed. Carmoly)
English language sources: Ginzberg IV, 13–15; Bin Gorion I, 95–100

72. *Yael and Sisera:* Judges 4:1–24, 5:24–31; Pseudo-Philo 33–5; Aggudat Aggadot 77–78; Seder Eliyahu Rabbah 10:48–49; B. Megillah 14a, 15a
English language sources: Ginzberg IV, 34–39

73. *Gideon:* Judges 6–7; Midrash Tehillim 106 (end); Pseudo-Philo 34–37; Yelammedenu (Yalkut Reubeni II, 62); Midrash HaGadol I, 722–723; Pesikta de Rav Kahana 8:71a; Pesikta Rabbati 18:92b
English language sources: Ginzberg IV, 39–43

74. *Jephthah's Daughter:* Judges 11; Yerahme'el 211–215; Pseudo-Philo 39–42; Midrash VaYikra Rabbah 37:4; Tanhuma Behukkotai 5; B. Taanit 4a
English language sources: Ginzberg IV, 43–47; Bin Gorion I 102–103

75. *Samson:* Judges 13–16; B. Baba Batra 91a; Midrash BaMidbar Rabbah 9:24, 10:5; Midrash Bereshit Rabbah 98:13, 99:11; B. Sotah 9a–10a; Tosefta Targum Judges 15:15
English language sources: Ginzberg IV, 47–49, VI, 208–209, n. 121, 124

76. *The Birth of Samuel:* I Samuel 1–2; Aggadat Bereshit 49:100–101; Seder Eliyahu Rabbah 7:47–48; Midrash Kohellet 5:19; B. Megillah 13a; Pirke de Rav Kahana 43:179b, 181a; B. Berakhot 31b; Midrash Shmuel 1:48–49, 3:52; B. Rosh Hashanah 11a
English language sources: Ginzberg IV, 57–60; VI 218–219, n. 17

77. *The Selection of David:* I Samuel 16; Yalkut HaMakhir, Psalm 118:28; Midrash Shmuel 19:102; Yelammedenu (Yalkut Reubeni II, 124)
English language sources: Ginzberg IV, 82–84; Bin Gorion I, 104–105

78. *Goliath:* I Samuel 17; B. Sotah 42b; Midrash Ruth Rabbah 1:4, 14; Midrash Shmuel 20:106–108, 21:108–109; Tanhuma V, 1:207–208; Tanhuma Emor 4; Zohar III, 272a; Midrash VaYikra Rabbah 10:7, 21:2; Kimhi on I Samuel 17:49; Midrash Tehillim 18:160
English language sources: Ginzberg IV, 85–89

79. *The Spider:* I Samuel 22:1, 23:25–26; 2 Alphabet of Ben Sira 24b
   English language sources: Ginzberg IV, 89–91; Bin Gorion I, 106–107
80. *The Hornet:* I Samuel 26; 2 Alphabet of Ben Sira 24b
   English language sources: Ginzberg IV, 89–91; Bin Gorion I, 106–107
81. *The Jars of Honey:* Meshalim shel Shlomo (Beit HaMidrash, ed. Jellinek),
   IV, 150–151, Gaster #5
   English language sources: Ginzberg IV, 85; Bin Gorion I, 105–106;
   Gaster #199
82. *The Witch of Endor:* I Samuel 28:3–25, 31:1–6; Pirke de Rebbe Eliezer 33;
   Midrash VaYikra Rabbah 26:7; Tanhuma Emor 2,7; B. Hagigah 4b
   English language sources: Ginzberg IV, 70–72
83. *Bathsheba:* II Samuel 11; B. Baba Batra 16a; B. Avodah Zarah 4b–5a; B.
   Sanhedrin 107a; R. Moses Al-Sheikh on II Samuel 12; Midrash Tehillim
   18:157, 26:216; Seder Eliyahu Rabbah 2:7; B. Yoma 22b; Midrash Shmuel
   26:127
   English language sources: Ginzberg IV, 103–104
84. *Absalom's Rebellion:* II Samuel 14:25–33, 15:1–6, 18:1–18; Midrash Ba-
   Midbar Rabbah 9:24; Tosefta Sotah 3:16; B. Nazir 4a; Midrash Shmuel
   27; B. Sanhedrin 103b, 107a; Midrash Devarim Rabbah 4:4; Zohar III 24a;
   B. Sotah 10b–11a; Pirke de Rebbe Eliezer 53; Ma'aseh de R. Joshua ben
   Levi (Beit HaMidrash, ed. Jellinek), II, 50–51
   English language sources: Ginzberg IV, 104–107
85. *The Brave Avishai:* II Samuel 21:15–22; B. Sanhedrin 95a; Midrash
   Bereshit Rabbah 59:11; Tanhuma VaYetze; B. Hullin 91b; Midrash
   Tehillim 18:157–159; Midrash Al-Yithallel (Beit HaMidrash, ed. Jellinek,
   VI, 107; Midrash Goliyat HaPelishti (Beit HaMidrash ed. Jellinek) IV,
   140–141
   English language sources: Ginzberg IV, 107–109; Bin Gorion I, 108–110
86. *The Egg and the Boiled Beans:* Psalms 72:1–2; Un recueil des contes Juifs
   inedits, #9, (Otsar Midrashim, ed. Eisenstein) I, 347–348
   English language sources: Ginzberg VI, 285, n. 27; Bin Gorion I, 120–121
87. *The Sack of Flour and the Wind:* Ma'asim Tovim, #13, 18–19; Even Sappir,
   I, 18–19
   English language sources: Ginzberg VI, 285, n. 27; Bin Gorion I, 125–128
88. *The Death of David:* I Kings 2:1–11; I Chronicles 29:26–28; B. Shabbat
   30a–b; Midrash Ruth Rabbah 1:17; Midrash Kohellet 5:10
   English language sources: Ginzberg IV, 113–114; Gaster #17
89. *Solomon's Gift of Wisdom:* I Kings 3:5–15; II Chronicles 1:7–13; Pesikta
   Rabbati 14:59a; Midrash Shir HaShirim 1:1; Ibn Sabba on VaYetze 33b
   (Perush al Ha'Torah); 10th C. Muslim legend
   English language sources: Ginzberg IV, 130; Bialik, 75–80
90. *The White Lion:* English language source: Bialik, 81–86
91. *The Two-Headed Cainite:* I Kings 4:31; Zohar I, 9b; II, 80a; Hibbur
   ha-Ma'asiyot, #11; Beit HaMidrash (ed. Jellinek), IV, 151–152
   English language sources: Ginzberg IV, 131–132; Bin Gorion I, 147–149
92. *The Maid, the Youth and the Thief:* I Kings 3:28; Rabbenu Nissim 38 (Sefer

Ma'asiyot); Midrash Aseret HaDibrot, Eighth Commandment (Beit HaMidrash, ed. Jellinek), I, 86–87; Sefer Ha-Ma'siyot (Eliezar Araki), #46
English language sources: Ginzberg IV, 132–134; Bin Gorion I, 157–158

93. *The Three Brothers Who Went to King Solomon to Learn Wisdom:* Proverbs 16:16; Meshalim shel Shlomo, #4 (Beit HaMidrash, ed. Jellinek), IV, 148–150; Divre ha-Yamim le'Moshe Rabbeinu, 62–63
English language sources: Bin Gorion I, 158–161; Gaster #198

94. *Buried Treasure:* Meshalim shel Shlomo; Midrash Aseret HaDibrot, Third Commandment (Beit HaMidrash, ed. Jellinek), I, 87–88
English language sources: Ginzberg VI, 286, n. 30; Gaster, #215

95. *The Game of Chess:* German Folktale; Beit HaMidrash (ed. Jellinek), VI, 124–126
English language sources: Bin Gorion I, 151–153; Gaster #230

96. *The Jug of Milk and the Serpent:* Genesis 3:15; Deuteronomy 19:17; Psalms 145:9; Midrash Tanhuma, 79
English language sources: Ginzberg IV, 134–135; Bin Gorion I, 122–125; Gaster #144

97. *Life and Death in the Power of the Tongue:* II Samuel 23:20; Proverbs 18:21; Midrash Tehillim 39:2; Yalkut Shimoni II, #721
English language sources: Bin Gorion I, 149–151

98. *The Circle of Death:* English language source: Bialik, 95–96

99. *Ziz-Shaddai and the Queen of Sheba:* I Kings 10:1–2; II Chronicles 9:1–2; Midrash Shir HaShirim 1:1; Midrash Mishle 20:88, 30:104; 2 Alphabet of Ben Sira 21b; Patshegen haKetav, Targum Sheni, Esther 1:2 (ed. M. David)
English language sources: Ginzberg IV, 142–145; VI, 289, n. 41; Bin Gorion I, 128–131

100. *Sheba's Riddles:* I Kings 10:1–13; II Chronicles 9:1–12; Targum Sheni 1:3, 8–10 (ed. M. David); MS. Midrash HaHefetz (Folklore I, 349–358, ed. Schechter); Midrash Mishle I, 20–21, 40–41; Yalkut Shimoni II, #1085
English language sources: Ginzberg IV, 145–149; Bin Gorion I, 131–132

101. *The Bee and the Queen of Sheba:* Arab Legend
English language sources: Bialik, 87–92; Rappaport, III, 202

102. *How the Hoopoe Got Its Crest:* Arab Folktale
English language sources: Bialik, 97–101

103. *How the Temple Site Was Chosen:* II Chronicles 3:1; Psalms 133:1; Midrash Vayikra Rabbah 13; Mikveh Israel (Israel Kosta, 1851), #89
English language sources: Ginzberg IV, 154; VI, 293–294, n. 57

104. *Asmodeus and the Shamir:* I Kings 5:17, 6:7; B. Gittin 68a–b; B. Sotah 48b; Tosefta Sotah 15:1; Pesikta Rabbati 33:155a; B. Berakhot 6a; Ma'aseh HaGedolim #330; Midrash Tehillim 78:12
English language sources: Ginzberg IV, 165–169; Bin Gorion I, 138–141

105. *The Craftsman's Wife and the Vial:* Likkute Ma'asiyot (Yisrael Ben Sasson), 11–15
English language sources: Bin Gorion I, 164–169

106. *Solomon and Naamah:* I Kings 14:21; II Chronicles 12:13; Ecclesiastes 1:12;

B. Gittin 68a–b; Midrash Tehillim 78:351–353; Midrash Al-Yithallel (Sefer ah-Likkutim I, 20–22, ed. Gruenhut); Midrash Shir HaShirim 29a–30a; B. Berakhot 6a; Zohar III, 309a; Emek HaMelekh, 12
English language sources: Ginzberg IV, 169–172; Bin Gorion I, 141–146

107. *The Mysterious Palace:* Ma'aseh HaNemalah (Beit HaMidrash, ed. Jellinek), V, 22–26
English language sources: Ginzberg IV, 163–165

108. *The Ruby Serpent:* Psalms 68:7; Tanhuma, Introduction, 136
English language sources: Ginzberg IV, 175–176; Bin Gorion I, 170–171

109. *This Too Shall Pass:* English language source: Ish-Kishor, 19–26; Noy #63

110. *The Tale of Tobit:* The Book of Tobit (Apocrypha)
English language sources: Bin Gorion I, 179–187; Nadich, 87–90

111. *Shadrach, Mishach and Abednego:* Daniel 2:49–3:33; Tanhuma, 1:38–41
English language sources: Ginzberg IV, 328–331

112. *Suzannah and the Elders:* The Story of Suzannah (Apocrypha); Yerahme'el 267–270; Beit HaMidrash (ed. Jellinek), VI, 126–128
English language sources: Bin Gorion I, 202–206

113. *Bel and the Dragon:* The Story of Bel and the Dragon (Apocrypha); Yossifon (ed. Ginzburg/Kahana), 29–31
English language sources: Bin Gorion I, 206–208

114. *The Strongest Thing in the World:* I Chronicles 3:17; I Esdras 3–4 (Apocrypha); B. Sanhedrin 38a; Yossifon (ed. Ginzburg/Kahana) 3:10a–11a; Josephus, Antiquities, II, 3–9
English language sources: Nadich 24–25

115. *The Capture and Release of the Evil Urge:* B. Yoma 69b
English language sources: Nadich 21–22, 163–164

116. *Alexander Enters Jerusalem:* Yossifon (ed. Ginzburg/Kahana), 60–3; Sefer Aleksander HaMokedoni, IV, 99–102; Josephus, Antiquities, XI, 5:5
English language sources: Bin Gorion I, 223–230

117. *The Fair Judgment:* Sefer Aleksander Mokedon (Tehillah le'Moshe), 149; Sefer Ha-Ma'asiyot (Eleazar Araki), #8; B. Tamid 32b; Midrash Tanhuma, Emor 9; Yalkut Shimoni I, #727
English language sources: Bin Gorion I, 244–245

118. *Alexander and the Eyeball:* B. Tamid 32b; Sefer Aleksander Mokedon (Tehillah le'Moshe), 155–156
English language sources: Bin Gorion I, 248–249

119. *Alexander Has Horns:* Iraqui Jewish Legend; Edoth I: 184–185 (A. Ben-Ya'akov)
English language sources: Patai, 664

120. *Judith and Holofernes:* The Book of Judith (Apocrypha); Hibbur Yafeh min ha-Yeshu'ah (Sefer Ha-Ma'asiyot, Nissim ben Yaakov), 22–23; Beit HaMidrash (ed. Jellinek), I, 130–131, 133–134
English language sources: Bin Gorion I, 258–262

121. *The Legend of the Septuagint:* B. Megillah 9a–b
English language sources: Nadich, 45–46

122. *The Death of Nicanor:* I Maccabees 7; 2 Maccabees 15 (Apocrypha); B.

Taanit 18b; Hemdat Ha-Yamim II, 55; Midrash aher le-Hanukkah (Beit HaMidrash, ed. Jellinek), I, 137–141
English language sources: Bin Gorion I, 262–268; Nadich 64–70

123. *Shame Destroys Jerusalem:* B. Gittin 55b–57a
English language sources: Nadich 339–340

124. *Beyond the River Sambatyon:* Eldad ha-Dani, 42–43; Haggadot Ketu'ot (Ha-Goren, ed. Horodezky), IX, 43–45
English language sources: Bin Gorion I, 322–7, 335–337

125. *Honi the Circle Maker:* Mishnah Taanit 3:8; B. Taanit 23a
English language sources: Patai, 224–226

126. *Honi and the Carob Tree:* Mishnah Taanit 3:8; B. Taanit 23a
English language sources: Patai, 226–227

127. *The Hidden Jewel of Shimon ben Shetakh:* Y. Baba Metzia II, 8b; Midrash Deuteronomy Rabbah III, 3; Ha-Ma'arikh (Menahem di Lonzano), 123–124
English language sources: Bin Gorion II, 589–590

128. *The Witches of Ashkelon:* Y. Hagigah 77d–78a
English language sources: Patai, 253–256

129. *Hillel the Snow Scholar:* B. Yoma 35b; Hibbur Yafeh min ha'Yeshu'ah (Sefer Ha-Ma'asiyot, Nissim ben Yaakov), 17
English language sources: Bin Gorion II, 549

130. *Hillel and Shammai:* B. Shabbat 31a
English language sources: Patai, 222

131. *The Patience of Hillel:* B. Shabbat 30b–31a; Yafeh min ha'Yeshu'ah (Sefer Ha-Ma'asiyot, Nissim ben Yaakov), 18–19; Avot de Rabbi Natan (2nd version), 29
English language sources: Bin Gorion II, 559–561; Patai, 223–224

132. *Yohanan and Vespasian:* B. Gittin 56a–b; Midrash Lamentations Rabbah 1:5,15; Midrash Ecclesiastes Rabbah 7:12; Avot de Rabbi Natan 4:5
English language sources: Patai, 211–212; Nadich 272–275

133. *Titus and the Gnat:* B. Gittin 56b–57a; Midrash VaYikra Rabbah 22:3
English language sources: Patai, 213–214; Nadich 350–351

134. *Hanina ben Dosa's Heel:* B. Berakhot 33a
English language sources: Nadich 256

135. *Bread from Twigs:* B. Taanit 24b–25a
English language sources: Nadich 256

136. *The Missing Table Leg:* B. Taanit 25a; Hibbur Yafeh min ha'Yeshu'ah (Sefer Ha-Ma'asiyot, Nissim ben Yaakov), 11–12
English language sources: Bin Gorion II, 563–564; Nadich 256–257

137. *The Law Is Not In Heaven:* B. Baba Metzia 59b
English language sources: Patai, 244–245

138. *The Conversion of the Onkelos:* B. Avodah Zarah 11a–b; Hibbur Yafeh min ha'Yeshu'ah (Sefer Ha-Ma'asiyot, Nissim ben Yaakov), 17–18
English language sources: Bin Gorion II, 585; Gaster #38

139. *A Box of Dust:* B. Taanit 21a; Hibbur Yafeh min ha'Yeshu'ah (Sefer

Ha-Ma'asiyot, Nissim ben Yaakov), 8–9
English language sources: Patai, 242–243
140. *Ugly Vessels:* B. Taanit 7a–b
English language sources: Patai, 219–220
141. *God is Everywhere:* B. Sanhedrin 39a
English language sources: Gaster #50
142. *The Pious Cow:* Hibbur Ma'asiyot (Pesikta Rabbati XIV, 56–57), 34–35;
Beit HaMidrash (ed. Jellinek), 74–75; Yalkut Sippurim II, 21
English language sources: Bin Gorion II, 617–618
143. *How Akiva Became a Scholar:* B. Nedarim 50a; B. Ketubot 62–63; Avot de
Rabbi Natan (1st version, supplement 2), 163; Midrash HaGadol,
Exodus 36–37
English language sources: Bin Gorion II, 552–558; Patai, 233–235
144. *Everything God Does is for the Best:* B. Berakhot 60b–61a
English language sources: Patai, 233
145. *Charity Saves from Death:* Proverbs 10:2; B. Shabbat 156b
English language sources: Patai, 235
146. *The Debt Paid By the Sea:* B. Nedarim 50a
English language sources: Gaster #70
147. *The Doctor and the Farmer:* Midrash Temura (Beit HaMidrash, ed.
Jellinek), I, 107
English language sources: Patai, 375
148. *The Four Who Entered Paradise:* B. Hagigah 14b
English language sources: Patai, 171–172
149. *The Death of Rabbi Akiva:* B. Berakhot 61b; Eleh Ezkerah (Beit HaMidrash,
ed. Jellinek), II, 64–72; Midrash Shir HaShirim, 3–7
English language sources: Bin Gorion I, 382–383; Patai, 235–236
150. *The Martyrdom of Hanina Ben Teradyon:* B. Avodah Zarah 17b; Eleh
Ezkera (Beit HaMidras, ed. Jellinek), II, 64–72
English language sources: Bin Gorion I, 383–384; Patai, 364–365
151. *Spitting in the Rabbi's Eye:* Y. Sotah I, 16d; Ma'aseh Rabbi Meir (Manzur
al-Dhamari, 4, ed. H.Y. Kohut)
English language sources: Bin Gorion II, 562–563
152. *Rabbi Meir and His Sister-in-Law:* B. Avodah Zarah 18a–b; Hibbur Yafeh
min ha'Yeshu'ah (Sefer ha-Ma'asiyot, Nissim ben Yaakov), 13–14
English language sources: Bin Gorion II, 576–577; Gaster #47
153. *The Two Jewels:* Midrash Mishle 31:10
English language sources: Bin Gorion II, 592
154. *Beruriah:* B. Avodah Zarah 18a–b; B. Pesahim 62b; B. Eruvim 53b; B.
Berakhot 10a
English language sources: Sondra Henry and Emily Taitz, *Written Out of
History* (Biblio, 1983), 54–58
155. *The Punishment of Rabbi Meir:* Midrash Aseret HaDibrot (Beit HaMidrash,
ed. Jellinek), I, 81–83; Batte Midrashot II, 26–28; Hibbur Yafeh min
ha'Yeshu'ah (Sefer ha-Ma'asiyot, Nissim ben Yaakov), 28
English language sources: Bin Gorion II, 577–82; Patai, 530–533

156. *Shimon bar Yohai and the Cave:* B. Shabbat 33b
     English language sources: Patai, 216–218
157. *The Most Precious Thing in the World:* Midrash Shir HaShirim Rabbah 1:31
     English language sources: Rappaport, Folklore of the Jews (Gale, reprint
     of 1937 edition), 31–32
158. *The Exchange of Sons:* Tossafot Avodah Zarah 10b; Menorat Ha-Ma'or 34
     English language sources: Bin Gorion II, 542–543
159. *Miriam Bat Tanhum and Her Seven Sons:* Psalms 113:9; B. Gittin 27b; Seder
     Eliyahu Rabbah 151–153; Hibbur Ma'asiyot veha-Midrashot, #2
     English language sources: Bin Gorion I, 272–273; Patai, 355–358
160. *The Inheritance of a Fool:* Midrash Tehillim 92:14
     English language sources: Montefiore, C. G. and Loewe, H. *Rabbinic
     Anthology.* New York: Schocken, 1974, p. 521, #1472
161. *Joseph the Sabbath-Lover:* B. Shabbat 119a
     English language sources: Bin Gorion II, 618; Patai, 220
162. *The Suffering of Animals:* Psalms 145:9; B. Baba Metzia 85a; Hibbur Yafeh
     min ha'Yeshu'ah (Sefer Ha-Ma'asiyot, Nissim ben Yaakov), 9
     English language sources: Bin Gorion II, 584
163. *Rabbi Hiyya and the Pomegranate:* B. Kiddushin 81b (MS in Vatican
     Library)
     English language sources: Levine, H. Three talmudic tales of seduction,
     Judaism, 36 (Fall 1987), 466–468
164. *How Resh Lakish the Robber Became a Jew:* B. Baba Metziah 84a
     English language sources: Gaster #66
165. *Abaye's Suspicions:* B. Shabbat 31a
     English language sources: Gaster #15
166. *The Tithe:* Tanhuma Re'eh 10; Tosafot Taanit 9a; Sefer haManhig
     (Abraham ibn Yarhi), 3
     English language sources: Bin Gorion II, 632–634
167. *The Weasel and the Well:* B. Taanit 8a, Rashi's commentary; Midrash
     HaGadol, Genesis 15:9
     English language sources: Bin Gorion II, 612–614
168. *The Birthday of the Messiah:* Y. Berakhot 2:4; Midrash Lamentations
     Rabbah 1:16; Midrash Ekhah Zuta, 133
     English language sources: Nadich 369–370
169. *Ariel, or the Pious Man and the Lion:* Ma'aseh Nissim, #11; Edoth
     2:205–206 (Abraham Elmaleh, Morocco, 15th C.); Ma'asiyot Mora'im
     Ve'Nifla'im, 14–15
     English language sources: Bin Gorion I, 513–515; Patai, 642–643
170. *The Wooden Sword:* Afghan Jewish Folktale
     English language sources: Patai, 631–634
171. *The Sabbath Loaves:* Shivhai he-Ari (Safed, 16th C.), 24
     English language sources: Bin Gorion I, 524–527
172. *The Man Who Kept the Sabbath and the Bear Who Kept Him:* MS. Oxford,
     Exempla (Gaster), 1.c.
     English language sources: Gaster #138

173. *Only the Dead Lose Hope:* Hibbur Yafeh min ha'Yeshu'ah (Sefer Ha-Ma'a-siyot, Nissim ben Yaakov, Italy 16th C.), 138–139; Kad Ha-Kemah #1, 6–7 (Bahya ben Asher)
     English language sources: Bin Gorion III, 1178–1179; Gaster #189
174. *The King's Loaves:* Afghanistani Jewish Folktale
     English language sources: Noy, #34
175. *Sincere Friendship:* Beit HaMidrash (ed. Jellinek), VI, 135–137; Sefer Hanokh, 49–52
     English language sources: Bin Gorion III, 1272–1275
176. *The Bail:* Beit HaMidrash (ed. Jellinek), IV, 143–144
     English language sources: Patai, 552–555
177. *The Bird that Sang to a Bridegroom:* Eastern European (Lithuanian, Estonian, Russian) folktale
     English language sources: Field, 3–5
178. *The Clever Wife:* Iraqi Jewish Folktale
     English language sources: Noy, #47
179. *The Revival of the Dead:* Osseh Pele II, 37–44, (Y.S. Farhi)
     English language sources: Bin Gorion III, 1067–1075
180. *The Will of Heaven:* Iraqi Jewish Folktale
     English language sources: Noy, #49
181. *The Kamzan (The Tongs):* Otzar Midrashim (Y.D. Eisenstein), II, 338–339; Beit HaMidrash (ed. Jellinek), VI, 143–146
     English language sources: Patai, 552–554
182. *The Three Sons in the Orchard:* Aqedat Yitzhak (Isaac Arama), 5:112b–114a (Salonika 16th C.)
     English language sources: Patai, 542–548
183. *The Jar of Tears:* Syrian Jewish Folktale
     English language sources: Patai, 648–650
184. *The Rich Beggar and the Wonderful Purse:* Bulgarian Jewish Folktale
     English language source: Noy, #19
185. *Have Mercy on Animals, Not Men:* Kalila and Dimnah I, #14; Iraqi Jewish Folktale
     English language sources: Noy, #29
186. *The Hunter and the Bird:* Haggadot Ketu'ot #3 (Ha-Goren, ed. Horodesky, IX, 41–42); Ben HaMelekh ve-ha-Nazir, XXI, 65–67
     English language sources: Bin Gorion III, 1284–1287
187. *The Three Friends:* Tossefta Atika II-III, 34; Pirke de Rebbe Eliezer 34; Kad HaKemah #1, 6–7; Ben HaMelekh ve-ha-Nazir XIII, 44–46; Menorat Ha-Ma'or II, #278, 90
     English language sources: Bin Gorion III, 1321–13226
188. *Abraham the Carpenter and the Money Hidden in the Tree:* No known Hebrew source
     English language sources: Gaster #203
189. *Slander Slays Three:* Hibbur Ma'asiyot, XXVI, 2; Beit HaMidrash (ed. Jellinek), V, 145–146
     English language sources: Bin Gorion II, 616–617

190. *The Man Who Never Took an Oath:* Midrash Aseret HaDibrot, Third Commandment (Beit HaMidrash, ed. Jellinek), I, 72–73
English language sources: Gaster #222

191. *Cast Your Bread Upon the Waters:* Alphabet of Ben Sira #7; Tanhuma Hukkat 1
English language sources: Bin Gorion III, 1280–1282

192. *Had Gadya:* Based on 16th C. German Folksong, first appeared in haggadah, Prague, 1590

193. *Rashi's Companion:* Tanhuma, 68; Hibbur Yafeh min ha'Yeshu'ah (Sefer ha-Ma'asiyot, Nissim ben Yaakov, Italy 16th C.), 20–21
English language sources: Bin Gorion II, 648–652

194. *Maimonides and the Lime-Kiln:* Sippurim, Vol I, 135–142, Wolff Pascheles (German, 1853)
English language sources: Field, 37–50

195. *Ibn Ezra's Bad Luck:* Iraqi Jewish Folktale
English language sources: Noy, #10, Penguin Book of Hebrew Verse, 353

196. *Pope Elhanan:* Beit HaMidrash (ed. Jellinek), V, 148–152; Beit HaMidrash (ed. Jellinek), VI, 137–138
English language sources: Bin Gorion I, 408–413

197. *Rabbi Amnon of Mayence:* Shalshelet HaKabbalah (Gedalyah ibn Yahiya), 44
English language sources: Bin Gorion I, 416–418

198. *The Pound of Flesh:* Based on *Vita di Sixto Quinto,* Gregorio Leti (Venice, 1587)
English language sources: Field, 81–96

199. *The Pasha's Lance:* Ma'aseh Nissim (ed. S.B. Hotsin), #2; Mora'im Gedolim (Y.S. Farhi), 74–75
English language sources: Bin Gorion I, 496–498

200. *The Bullet in the Mirror:* Likkute Ma'asiyot, #1, 3–8
English language sources: Bin Gorion II, 905–911

201. *In Pursuit of the White Gazelle:* English language sources: Ish-Kishor, 112–125

202. *A Box of Bones:* Polish Jewish Folktale
English language sources: Noy, #50

203. *The Two Husbands:* Iraqi Jewish Folktale
English language sources: Noy, #69

204. *The Voice from the Tree:* Kalilah and Dimnah II, 356–357
English language sources: Bin Gorion III, 1313–1315

205. *The Story of Kunz and the Shepherd:* German Folktale
English language sources: Gaster #227

206. *Joseph de la Reina:* Sippur Rabbi Yossef della Reina; Eder HaYekar (Samuel Abba Horodezsky), 107–108
English language sources: Bin Gorion II, 837–852

207. *The Grateful Dead:* Ma'aseh Nissim, #5 (ed. Hotsin); Mora'im Gedolim,

77–79 (Y. S. Farhi); Sha'arei Yerushalayim, 42
English language sources: Bin Gorion I, 508–511

208. *Soothsaying Dogs:* Lithuanian Jewish Folktale
English language sources: Noy, #25

209. *The Demon Wife and the Broken Oath:* Ma'aseh shel Yerushalmi (ed. Y.C. Zlotnik); Divre HaYamim shel Moshe Rabbeinu; Sefer ha-Ma'asiyot (Eleazar Araki), #110
English language sources: Bin Gorion III, 1079–1094

210. *The Scorpion in the Goblet:* Un recueil des contes Juifs inedits (Israel Levi) in Otsar Midrashim (Y.D. Eisenstein), II, 344–347
English language sources: Bin Gorion, III, 1112–1122

211. *The Serpent Prince:* Bukharan Jewish Folktale
English language sources: Noy, #58

212. *The Werewolf and the Ring:* German Folktale
English language sources: Gaster #228

213. *The Golem of Prague:* Nifle'ot Maharal (ed. Y.Y. Rosenberg)
English language sources: Bin Gorion I, 472–477; Patai, 636–642

214. *The Dog, the Cheese, and the Water:* Mishle Shualim (Berechiah HaNakdan), #5
English language sources: Hanakdan, 14–15

215. *The Wolf and the Crane:* Mishle Shualim (Berechiah HaNakdan), #8
English language sources: Hanakdan, 20–21

216. *The City Mouse and the Country Mouse:* Mishle Shualim (Berechiah HaNakdan), #10
English language sources: Hanakdan, 25–27

217. *The Crow and the Fox:* Mishle Shualim (Berechiah HaNakdan), #13
English language sources: Hanakdan, 31–32

218. *The Lion, the Mouse, and the Snare:* Mishle Shualim (Berechiah HaNakdan), #15
English language sources: Hanakdan, 34–36

219. *The Cicada and the Ant:* Mishle Shualim (Berechiah HaNakdan), #17
English language sources: Hanakdan, 38–39

220. *The Mouse Seeks a Wife:* Mishle Shualim (Berechiah HaNakdan), #28
English language sources: Hanakdan, 58–60

221. *The Sun, the Wind, and the Man:* Mishle Shualim (Berechiah HaNakdan), #53
English language sources: Hanakdan, 97–98

222. *Two Apes and a Lion:* Mishle Shualim (Berechiah HaNakdan), #67
English language sources: Hanakdan, 118–120

223. *The Lion, The Man, the Pit and the Snake:* Mishle Shualim (Berechiah HaNakdan), #68
English language sources: Hanakdan, 120–123

224. *The Stag and the Dogs:* Mishle Shualim (Berechiah HaNakdan), #74
English language sources: Hanakdan, 134–135

225. *The Ape and the Leopard:* Mishle Shualim (Berechiah HaNakdan), #61
English language sources: Hanakdan, 592–593

226. *The Starling and the Princess:* Mishle Shualim (Berechiah HaNakdan), #71
     English language sources: Hanakdan, 128–130
227. *The Werewolf:* Shivhei HaBesht, 7
     English language sources: Bin Gorion II, 928; Buber, LBST, 51–55
228. *The Yom Kippur Flute:* Emunat Tzaddikim, 6; K'hal Hasidim heHadash,
     11–12
     English language sources: Bin Gorion II, 939–940; Patai, 671–672
229. *The Baal Shem Tov and the Professor of Pozna:* Sefer Sippurim Nora'im
     (Kadaner), 8b–11a
     English language sources: Bin Gorion II, 938–939; Patai, 676–686
230. *Two Socks on One Foot:* Shivhei HaBesht, 94–95
     English language sources: Bin Gorion II, 954–955
231. *The Vengeful Widow:* English language sources: Buber, LBST, 98–106
232. *The Forgotten Story:* Adat Tzaddikim (M.L. Frumkin, 1877)
     English language sources: Buber, LBST, 107–120; Patai, 687–695
233. *The Disturbed Sabbath:* Peer Israel (publ. S. Freund, 1925), 4–7
     English language sources: Buber, LBST, 139–148; Newman, 407
234. *The Second Chance:* Sefer Maasiyot, II, 231–237
     English language sources: Buber, LBST, 162–171; Meyer Levin, Classic
     Hassidic Tales, 101–108
235. *The Gold Buttons:* Niflaot HaMaggid Koznitz, (publ. Kleiman, 1925), 25
     English language sources: Buber, LBST, 179–184; Newman, 151
236. *The Bird's Nest:* Midrash Ribesh Tov, (L. Abraham, 1927), 42
     English language sources: Buber, EM, 54–55; Newman, 247
237. *Slacken the Reins:* Shivhei HaBesht (1908)
     English language sources: Buber, EM, 56–59
238. *Paying God's Wages:* Peer Israel (publ. S. Freund, 1925), 21
     English language sources: Buber, EM, 58; Newman, 60
239. *The Happy Drunkard:* Yeshuat Yisrael, ed. Mordechai Rabinowitz
     English language sources: Labovitz, 136–145
240. *The Rabbi Who Thought Friday Was Shabbat:* Sippurei HaGedolim (M. Z.
     Slodovnik, 1925), 38
     English language sources: Newman, 410–411
241. *The Return of the Rich Man's Soul:* Sifron Shel Tzaddikim
     English language sources: Buber, EM, 273–275
242. *Let Them Eat Stones:* Priester der Liebe (Chaim Bloch, 1930), 70
     English language sources: Newman, 467–468
243. *Reb Haim and the Three Lawsuits:* Oral tale—Klausenberg Hasidim
     English language sources: Mintz, 339–342
244. *The Shofar Blower:* Ozroth Idisher Humor (I. Ashkenazy, 1929), 15
     English language sources: Newman, 400
245. *The Missing Ruble:* Tiferet HaTzaddikim (S.G. Rosenthal, 1928), 51–53
     English language sources: Labovitz, 107–114; Newman, 174–175
246. *Two Kinds of Gifts:* Sikhot Yikkarim
     English language sources: Buber, EM, 238–239

247. *Blows:* Ohel Elimelekh (1911)
     English language sources: Buber, EM, 239–240
248. *Ransoming the Birds:* Tiferet ha-Achim (publ. A. Kahan, 1924), 10–11
     English language sources: Buber, EM, 245; Newman, 74
249. *The Final Question:* Oral Tale, transmitted by Yehuda Ya'eri
     English language sources: Buber, EM, 251
250. *The Sin of Pride:* Ohel Elimelekh (1911), #170, 35–36
     English language sources: Buber, EM, 255–256; Bin Gorion II, 988–989
251. *The Radish:* Sefer Ha-Dorot he-Hadash (publ. E. I. Stand, 1865), Ch. 4
     English language sources: Buber, EM, 159–160; Newman, 439–440
252. *The Servant Girl's Defender:* Tiferet ha-Zaddikim (publ. A. Kahan, 1924),
     321
     English language sources: Buber, EM, 161; Newman, 206
253. *The Impostor Rebbe:* Oral Tale – Bobover Hasidim
     English language sources: Mintz, 285–287
254. *The Unpaid Pledge:* Oral Tale – Klausenberg Hasidim
     English language sources: Mintz, 381–383
255. *The Tailor's Sleeve:* Sippurim Nora'im (Kadaner), 36–38
     English language sources: Buber, EM, 165–166; Patai, 740–743
256. *The Broken Betrothal:* Adat Tzaddikim, 45–50
     English language sources: Bin Gorion II, 1001–1006
257. *The Cape:* Likkutim Hadashim
     English language sources: Buber, EM, 286
258. *Good Purim, Good Purim!!:* Shlomo Carlebach (oral tale); Yom Tov
     Ehrtzellungen, Menahem Mendel (Admon Press, 1980)
     English language sources: Labovitz, 294–297
259. *A Crying Baby:* Menorah HaTehorah, 28
     English language sources: Bin Gorion, II, 995–996
260. *The Lost Princess:* Sefer Sippurei Maasiyot shel Nahman Mi Bratzlav
     (1815), #1
     English language sources: Band, A. *Nahman of Bratslav: The Tales.*
     Mahwah, NJ: Paulist Press, 1978, 55–61
261. *The Rabbi's Son:* Sefer Sippurei Maasiyot shel Nahman Mi Bratzlav
     (1815), #8
     English language sources: Band, A. *Nahman of Bratslav: The Tales.*
     Mahwah, NJ: Paulist Press, 1978, 5–8
262. *The Clever Man and the Simple Man:* Sefer Sippurei Maasiyot shel
     Nahman Mi Bratzlav (1815), #9
     English language sources: Band, A. *Nahman of Bratslav: The Tales.*
     Mahwah, NJ: Paulist Press, 1978, 143–161
263. *Why Naftali of Ropshitz Wore White Trousers:* English language sources:
     Langer, J. *Nine Gates.* James Clark and Co., 1961, 76–77
264. *Reb Eisik's Treasure:* Classic Hasidic tale – many variants
     English language sources: Buber, LM, 245–246; Mintz, 431; Langer, J.
     Nine Gates. James Clark and Co., 1961, 247–249

265. *The Cost of an Etrog:* Admorei Tchernobyl, 24 (variant)
English language sources: Labovitz, 188–190
266. *The Alphabet:* Kotsker Maasiyot (E. Bergman, 1924), 70
English language sources: Newman, 212
267. *A Matter of Faith:* Siach Sarfei Kodesh (J.K.K. Rokotz 1929), IV, 22
English language sources: Newman, 103
268. *The Goat's Horns and the Snuffbox:* Oral Tale, transmitted by A. M. Hoberman
English language sources: Buber, LM, 288
269. *The More Mud, the Better:* Sichot Hayyim (S.Z. Breistein), 36–37
English language sources: Newman, 169–170
270. *Only the Story Remains:* Kenesset Yisrael (Reuven Zak, 1900)
English language sources: Buber, LM, 92–93
271. *Two Slaps:* Tiferet Menachem (publ. A. Kahan, 1924), 24
English language sources: Newman, 10
272. *The Mirror and the Glass:* Gemeinde der Chassidim (Chaim Bloch, 1920), 337
English language sources: Newman, 425–426
273. *Begin with Yourself:* English language sources: Buber, LM 214
274. *Moshele's Gift:* Oral Tale, Rabbi Shlomo Carlebach
275. *Yes, But Where Am I?:* English language sources: Buber, LM, 314
276. *Yossele the Holy Miser:* MiDor Dor, II, #1664 (variant)
English language sources: Rabbi Shlomo Carlebach (oral tale)
277. *A Mother's Prayerbook:* Devarim 'arevim I, #26
English language sources: Bin Gorion, II, 940–941
278. *The King and the Tavern-keeper:* Oral Tale—Bobover Hasidim
English language sources: Mintz, 428–430
279. *The Gentile's Impatience:* Kotsker Ma'asiyot (E. Bergman, 1924), 108
English language sources: Newman, 417–418
280. *The Thankful Thief:* Kotsker Ma'asiyot (E. Bergman, 1924), 57
English language sources: Newman, 473–474
281. *Two She-Goats from Shebreshin:* Polish Jewish Folktale
English language sources: Noy, #2
282. *The Chief Sage's Golden Shoes:* Yiddish Folktale
English language sources: Ausubel, 326; Simon, S. *More Wise Men of Chelm.* New York: Behrman House, 1965, 44–49
283. *The Columbus of Chelm:* Yiddish Folktale
English language sources: Ausubel, 334–336; Simon, S. *Wise Men of Chelm.* New York: Behrman House, 1961, 89–102
284. *Chelm Captures the Moon:* Yiddish Folktale
English language sources: Simon, S. *Wise Men of Chelm.* New York: Behrman House, 1961, 35–42
285. *The Great Power of Psalms:* Yiddish Folktale
English language sources: Simon, S. *More Wise Men of Chelm.* New York: Behrman House, 1965, 54–62
286. *Elijah in Heaven:* II Kings 2; B. Eruvim 45a; Pirke de Rav Kahana 9; Zohar

Hadash Ruth 1:1; Seder Olam 1, 7; B. Baba Batra 121b; Midrash VaYikra Rabbah 34:8; Pirke de Rebe Eliezer 15; Yalkut Reubeni (addenda); Emek ha-Melek, 65, 175c; Zohar II, 58a
English language sources: Ginzberg, IV, 201

287. *The Pious Man and the Tax-Collector:* Tosefta 'atika V, 71–72
English language sources: Bin Gorion II, 642–643; Gaster #88

288. *Rabbi Akiva's Daughter, or the Jewish Snow White:* Haggadot Ketu'ot (HaGoren, ed. S. A. Horodezky, 1922), 34–38
English language sources: Bin Gorion, II, 659–663

289. *Soft Like a Reed, Not Hard Like a Cedar:* B. Taanit 20a
English language sources: Gaster #101

290. *The Slave Elijah:* Hibbur Yafeh min ha-Yeshu'ah (Sefer HaMa'asiyot, Nissim ben Yaakov, 1557), 57–59
English language sources: Ginzberg, IV, 205–206

291. *The Gift of Seven Years:* Midrash Zuta Ruth 4:11; Yalkut Shim'oni II, #607
English language sources: Bin Gorion III, 1220–1223

292. *Elijah and the Three Wishes:* English language sources: Gaster #157; Ginzberg IV, 209–210

293. *The Ugly Wise Girl:* Osseh Pele (Y.S. Farhi), II, 32–37
English language sources: Bin Gorion III, 1056–1057

294. *God Works in Mysterious Ways:* Hibbur Yafeh min ha-Yeshu'ah (Sefer HaMa;asiyot, Nissim ben Yaakov, 1557), 4–6; Hibbur Ma'asiyot, 22–24; Beit HaMidrash (ed. Jellinek), V, 133–135
English language sources: Bin Gorion II, 644–646

295. *The Jewel of the Torah:* Haggadot Ketu'ot #9 (HaGoren, ed. S. A. Horodezsky, 1922)
English language sources: Bin Gorion, II, 759–760

296. *The Boy Who Was Saved From Hanging:* Osseh Pele (Y.S. Farhi) II, 21–23
English language sources: Bin Gorion, III, 1232–1235

297. *The Bride Who Saved Her Husband from the Angel of Death:* English language sources: Bin Gorion II, 692–697; Gaster #195

298. *Two Brothers and Their Wish:* German Jewish Folktale
English language sources: Ginzberg, IV, 211–212

299. *The Tramp:* Sefer Gevurat Yisrael, 1925
English language sources: Ausubel, 193–194

300. *Elijah's Cup:* Sippurei Beit Din Shel Ma'alah, Yisrael Klapholtz
English language sources: Labovitz, 350–352

Glossary

Note: Words or phrases marked with an asterisk can be found in separate entries.

Adonai: "Lord" (Hebrew). One of the names of God.*

Afikomen: "Dessert" (Greek). The middle of the three portions of *matzah* on the *seder** plate. One cannot complete the *seder* meal without eating a piece of the *afikomen.* It is traditional for the leader of the *seder* or the children to hide the *afikomen* and bargain for its return.

Aggadah: Nonlegal sections of the Talmud* and *midrash,** including stories, legends, animal fables, folklore, proverbs, wordplay, medicine, astronomy, astrology, etc.

Agunah: "Grass widow" (Hebrew). A woman who cannot remarry under Jewish law because her husband has either deserted her or because his death cannot be verified by witnesses.

Akedah: "Binding" (Hebrew). The traditional name for the story of the Binding (also called "Sacrifice") of Isaac.

Amalek: Descendants of Esau who attacked the Israelites from the rear as they crossed the wilderness. In legend, Amalek is a symbol of Israel's most treacherous enemies. Haman, mastermind of the plot to destroy the Jews in the Book of Esther, was a descendant of Amalek.

Amoraim: "Spokesmen" (Aramaic. Singular—*Amora).* Rabbis of the post-mish-

631

naic period (200–500 C.E.) who interpreted the Mishnah.* Their interpretations comprise the bulk of the Babylonian and Jerusalem Talmuds.*

Ark: (*Aron*–Hebrew). Cabinet housing the Torah* scrolls. In the wilderness and in the Temple* in Jerusalem, the Ark of the Covenant housed the Ten Commandments.

B.C.E.: "Before the Common or Christian Era." Traditional Jewish term designating the centuries before the birth of Jesus.

Baal Shem: "Master of the (Divine) Name" (Hebrew). A wonderworker or kabbalist* from the Middle Ages through the hasidic* period who used his secret knowledge of God's sacred names to heal or perform miracles. The most famous of these *baalei shem* was Rabbi Israel ben Eliezer, known as the Baal Shem Tov (Master of the Good Name), who founded the hasidic movement in Eastern Europe in the 18th century.

Bar Mitzvah/Bat Mitzvah: "Son/Daughter of the Commandment" (Hebrew). The occasion marking a Jewish child's attainment of religious maturity and responsibility. Also used to designate the child on that occasion. For a boy the age of *bar mitzvah* is thirteen; for a girl, twelve.

Bat: "Daughter of" (Hebrew).

Beit HaMidrash: "House of Study" (Hebrew). Part of the traditional synagogue where men gather to study Torah* and Talmud.*

Ben: "Son of" (Hebrew).

Besht: Abbreviation for "Baal Shem Tov," the popular name of Rabbi Israel ben Eliezer, founder of Hasidism.* See also "Baal Shem."

Bimah: "Raised Place" (Hebrew). The platform in the synagogue upon which the reader stands to read the Torah* and conduct the service. Often translated as "pulpit."

Blood Libel: Allegation that Jews murder Christians to obtain their blood for Passover* rituals. Such false accusations often led to pogroms in the Middle Ages. Cases of blood libel have been reported up until modern times.

Brit: "Covenant" (Hebrew. *Bris*–Yiddish). The ceremony of circumcision *(brit milah)* performed on a male Jewish child on the eighth day after birth.

C.E.: "Common or Christian Era." Traditional Jewish term designating the centuries after the birth of Jesus.

Cherubim: (Hebrew). Winged celestial creatures that guard the Tree of Life in the Garden of Eden. Wooden cherubim adorned the Ark* of the Covenant in the Tabernacle* *(Mishkan**–Hebrew) and Solomon's Temple* in Jerusalem.

Daven: To pray (Yiddish).

Days of Awe: (*Yamim Nora'im*–Hebrew). Period extending from the Hebrew month of Elul,* which precedes Rosh Hashanah,* through Yom Kippur.* A time of soul-searching and repentance.

Diaspora: "Dispersion" (Greek. *Galut*–Hebrew; *Galus*–Yiddish). Exile. Jews living outside the land of Israel.

D'rash: "Seeking" (Hebrew. Root of midrash*). A deciphering and presentation of the latent meanings of a sacred text, usually the Bible.

Eden: (Hebrew). The Garden of Eden, described in Genesis 2–3. Also refers to Paradise,* where souls go after death. See also "World to Come."

Elul: (Hebrew). Sixth month of Hebrew calendar, preceding Rosh Hashanah.* A time of spiritual preparation and repentance.

End of Days: The Messianic Era. *(Aharit Ha-Yamim–*Hebrew). The end of human history and the beginning of the reign of the Messiah, a descendant of King David. Generally viewed as a time of political and religious reconciliation. Traditional Jewish sources also speak of the resurrection of the dead and a universal return to Jerusalem.

Etrog: "Citron" (Hebrew). A sweet-smelling lemon-like fruit grown in Israel, used during the holiday of Sukkot.* If the pistil *(pittum*–*Hebrew), the stem-like protuberance at one end of the *etrog,* is broken off, the fruit is unusable for ritual purposes.

Even Shetiyah: "Foundation Stone" (Hebrew). According to legend, the rock at the center of the world upon which the Temple* in Jerusalem was built.

Gehinnom: "Valley of Hinnom" (Hebrew. Also called "Gehenna"). Hell. At the time of the Israelite monarchy, this valley south of Jerusalem was the site of child sacrifice to the pagan god Moloch. In later Jewish tradition, Gehinnom came to signify the place where the wicked suffer torments after death.

Good Yontov!: "Happy Holiday!" (Yiddish).

Haggadah: "Telling" (Hebrew). A compilation of songs, prayers, stories, biblical excerpts, and rituals that together comprise the text for the Passover* *seder.* *

Hakham: "Sage" (Hebrew). Honorary title of the religious head of a Sephardic (north African or Middle Eastern) Jewish community.

Halakhah: "The Way" (Hebrew). Jewish law as articulated in the Bible, Talmud,* codes, and subsequent rabbinic rulings.

Hallel: "Praise" (Hebrew. Root of "hallelujah"). A special section of liturgy, composed of Psalms 113–118, recited in synagogue on most holidays.

Hanukkah: "Dedication" (Hebrew). An eight-day festival beginning on the 25th day of Kislev, commemorating the Maccabean victory over the Greeks in the second century B.C.E. and the rededication of the Temple* in Jerusalem.

Hasidism: Religious movement founded by Rabbi Israel ben Eliezer, also known as the Baal Shem Tov, in the eighteenth century. Members of this movement are known as *hasidim* (singular—*hasid).*

Havdalah: "Separation" (Hebrew). Ceremony with a braided candle, spice-box, and wine, marking the end of the Sabbath.*

Hazzan: (Hebrew). Cantor.

Heder: "Room" (Hebrew). Elementary school for Jewish boys in Eastern Europe.

Holy of Holies: *(Devir–*Hebrew). The innermost chamber in the Temple,* where the Ark* of the Covenant resided. The only time anyone entered this chamber was on Yom Kippur,* when the High Priest went in alone and pronounced the Awesome Name of God.*

Huppah: "Canopy" (Hebrew). Wedding canopy under which the bride, groom, and rabbi stand during the wedding ceremony.

Judah: The fourth son of Jacob and one of the twelve tribes of Israel. After the defeat of the northern kingdom of Israel in 722 B.C.E. by Assyria, Judah, together with the tribe of Benjamin and the landless Levites, were all that remained of the Jewish people. From this tribe comes the Hebrew word *Yehudi*—Jew.

Kabbalah: "That which is received" (Hebrew). The Jewish esoteric tradition, based on a cosmology of Divine emanations and secret names of God.* Although the kabbalistic tradition stretches back two millennia, it received its fullest elaboration in the thirteenth century mystical work called the *Zohar* ("Book of Splendor") and in the writings of the fifteenth-century Jewish mystics of Safed.

Kabbalist: One who studies and practices *Kabbalah.**

Kavanah: "Directed intention" (Hebrew). The act of focusing one's thoughts and feelings during prayer or the performance of a commandment.

Ketubah: "Marriage contract" (Hebrew). Document stating husband's obligations to his wife. These legal documents are often lavishly ornamented and displayed in homes as works of art.

Kiddush: "Sanctification" (Hebrew). The prayer over wine recited at the beginning of Sabbath* and holiday meals.

Kiddush HaShem: "Sanctification of (the Divine) Name" (Hebrew). Religious martyrdom.

Kol Nidre: "All vows" (Aramaic). Prayer opening the Yom Kippur* evening service at the start of the holy day.

Kosher: "Ritually acceptable" (Hebrew).

L'Chayim!: "To Life!" (Hebrew). A popular toast.

Maariv: Evening Prayer (from root *erev*—evening. Hebrew). Recited every evening at sundown. See also "Prayer."

Maggid: "Teller" (Hebrew). An itinerant preacher who teaches Torah* through stories.

Marrano: "Swine" (Spanish). Deprecating term for Jews who converted to Christianity rather than leave Spain and Portugal when the Jews were expelled from these countries in 1492 and 1496. These "New Christians," as they were also called, practiced their faith in secret to escape detection by the Inquisition.

Matzah: "Unleavened bread" (Hebrew). Flat bread containing no yeast, eaten during the eight days of Passover,* in commemoration of the hasty exodus of the Children of Israel from Egyptian bondage.

Messianic Era: See "End of Days."

Mezuzah: "Doorpost" (Hebrew). Parchment scroll attached to the doorposts of rooms in Jewish homes. Often enclosed in decorative boxes inscribed with the name of God. It is customary to kiss the *mezuzah* when entering or leaving a house.

Midrash: "That which is sought out" (Hebrew). The genre of rabbinic literature deriving meaning out of biblical texts or embroidering traditional teachings. The term refers both to the method of interpretation and to the literature itself.

Minhah: "Offering" (Hebrew). The afternoon prayer service, recited between midday and nightfall. See also "Prayer."

Minyan: "Number" (Hebrew). A quorum of ten adult Jews necessary to recite certain prayers and perform certain ceremonies.

Mishkan: "Dwelling" (Hebrew). The portable Tabernacle or Tent of Meeting housing the Ark* of the Covenant when the Israelites traveled through the wilderness.

Mishnah: "Study by Repetition" (Hebrew). Earliest code of Jewish oral law, arranged by Judah the Prince in 200 C.E.

Mitzvah: "Commandment" (Hebrew. Plural—*mitzvot*). One of the 613 divinely ordained commandments articulated in the Torah. *Mitzvah* also means "good deed."

Mohel: "Circumciser" (Hebrew). The person who performs a ritual circumcision.

Musaf: "That which is added" (Hebrew). The additional service on Sabbath* and Festivals. See also "Prayer."

Name of God: Also called the "Awesome Name," the "Divine Name," or the "Tetragrammaton."* Refers to the four-letter divine name, spelled *yud, heh, vav, heh* (YHVH), pronounced in ancient times only on Yom Kippur* by the High Priest. After the Destruction of the Temple,* the pronunciation was lost; since then the name has been vocalized and pronounced as *Adonai**—"Lord," as a substitute for the now unpronounceable name. Some English translators have incorrectly transliterated the word as Jehovah. In legend, holy rabbis and kabbalists sometimes use the Name to perform miracles or to ward off evil spirits.

Nasi: "Prince" (Hebrew). Talmudic* term for president of the Sanhedrin;* also the spiritual and political leader of the Jewish people.

Neilah: "Closing" (Hebrew). Concluding service of Yom Kippur.*

Nisan: First month of Hebrew calendar. Passover* occurs on the fifteenth of this month.

Paradise: (Greek). The Garden of Eden.* Also the heavenly realm where the righteous receive their eternal reward after death. See also "World to Come."

Passover: (*Pesah*—Hebrew). Seven-day (eight-day in the Diaspora*) spring festival commemorating the Exodus from Egypt. The holiday begins with an elaborate festive meal called a *seder** and requires abstention from all leavened foods during its duration. See also *Haggadah*, "Blood Libel."

Pilgrimage Festivals: (*Shalosh Regalim*—Hebrew). The holidays of Passover,* Shavuot,* and Sukkot,* when it was customary, in ancient times, for Jews to bring agricultural offerings to the Temple* in Jerusalem.

Pittum: "Protuberance" (Hebrew. Also *pitma*). The pistil of the *etrog.**

Without this stem, the *etrog* is not ritually acceptable for use on Sukkot.*

Prayer: Jewish tradition requires that a Jew pray three times a day: *shaharit** in the morning, *minhah** in the afternoon, and *maariv** in the evening. On Sabbaths* and Festivals there is an additional service called *Musaf.** On *Yom Kippur,** there is a fifth service, *Neilah,* which concludes the holy day. Prayers recited with proper *kavanah** can effect great changes in the world. The three main functions of prayer are petition, praise, and thanksgiving.

Purim: "Lots" (Hebrew). A holiday commemorating the Jews' delivery from the Persian villain Haman through the intercession of Esther and Mordecai. It is customary on this holiday to dress in costume, read the Book of Esther, and deliver *shalakh manos,** gifts of food.

Rabban: "Master" (Hebrew). Honorary title higher than rabbi, used for the head of the Sanhedrin.*

Rabbi(s): "Master" or "Teacher" (Hebrew). In the singular, a Jewish teacher, leader, or decisor of Jewish law. In the plural, the term usually refers to the talmudic sages of the Mishnah* and Talmud* whose legal judgments and interpretations of Jewish tradition shaped mainstream (also called "rabbinic") Judaism as it is practiced today. See also *"Amoraim," "Tannaim."*

Rebbe: "Rabbi" (Yiddish). The leader of a hasidic community. A rebbe's followers are called his *hasidim.*

Rosh Hashanah: "Head of the Year" (Hebrew). Jewish New Year occurring on the first of Tishrei* (in September). The major symbols of this holiday are the Book of Life, in which God inscribes each Jew's fate for the coming year, and the *shofar,** the ram's horn, which summons worshippers to take stock of their sins and return to the right path.

Rosh Hodesh: "Head of the Month" (Hebrew). The first day of a Hebrew month, celebrated as a minor holiday.

Rosh Yeshivah: "Head of the Academy" (Hebrew). The principal of a talmudic* college.

Sanhedrin: "Council" (Greek). An assembly of seventy-one sages who served as the supreme religious, legislative, and political body in Jerusalem during the Roman period.

Seder: "Order" (Hebrew). The religious home service celebrated on the first (and second, in the Diaspora*) nights of Passover,* during which the *haggadah** is read.

Seudah: "Meal" (Hebrew). Festive meal. See *"Shalas Sheudas."*

Shabbat: "Sabbath" (Hebrew. *Shabbos*—Yiddish). The seventh day of the week, beginning sundown Friday and lasting until sundown Saturday, during which a Jew refrains from work. Jewish law specifically defines what is permitted and forbidden on this day. Traditionally, the day is filled with study, prayer, and festive meals enhanced by singing and words of Torah.*

Shadkhan: "Matchmaker" (Hebrew). A person who arranges marriages.

Shaharit: "Morning" (Hebrew). The morning prayer service. See also "Prayer."

Shalakh Manos: "Sending Gifts" (Yiddish. *Mishlo'akh Manot*—Hebrew). On Purim,* it is traditional to send plates of fruits, nuts, and three-cornered pastries called *hamentaschen* (Haman's pockets) to friends and family in honor of the holiday.

Shalas Sheudas: "Third Meal" (Yiddish. *Seudah Shelishit*—Hebrew). The final Sabbath* meal preceding the concluding ceremony of *havdalah** during which it is customary for the rabbi to speak words of Torah* to his students.

Shalom Aleikhem: "Peace unto you" (Hebrew). A traditional greeting, answered with *Aleikhem Shalom.*

Shammash: "Attendant" (Hebrew. *Shammes*—Yiddish). Often translated as "sexton" or "beadle." A salaried employee who supervised the daily operations of the synagogue, such as attending the eternal light over the ark,* checking the supply of *kiddush** wine, awakening congregants for morning prayers, and delivering messages for the rabbi.

Shavuot: "Weeks" (Hebrew). Festival of Weeks, also called Pentecost. A holiday occurring exactly seven weeks and one day after Passover,* commemorating the Receiving of the Torah.* It is also an agricultural festival, marking the end of the barley and beginning of the wheat harvest.

Shekhinah: "Presence" (Hebrew). A feminine designation for God, characterized by compassion, watchfulness, and immanence. Especially popular among kabbalists.* The *Shekhinah* is often described as having wings that shelter the people of Israel.

Sh'ma: "Hear!" (Hebrew). The first word of the Hebrew prayer called by the same name: *"Sh'ma Yisrael, Adonai** Elohaynu, Adonai Ekhad"*—"Hear O Israel! *Adonai* is our God. *Adonai* is One." The Sh'ma is one of the central prayers of the liturgy and is traditionally recited at the moment of death.

Shemini Atzeret: "Eighth Day of Assembly" (Hebrew). Final day (two days in Diaspora*) of Sukkot,* during which time the congregation recites a special prayer for rain.

Shofar: "Ram's Horn" (Hebrew). Blown in biblical times to call the people to war, to proclaim the Jubilee Year, and to call the people to repentance on Rosh Hashanah.* Only the last practice is still observed today. According to tradition, the *shofar* will also be blown to announce the coming of the Messiah at the End of Days.*

Shokhet: "Slaughterer" (Hebrew). A ritual slaughterer. Animals not butchered by a *shokhet* are not considered kosher.*

Shul: "Synagogue" (Yiddish).

Siddur: "Prayer Book" (Hebrew).

Simchah: "Happiness" (Hebrew). A happy occasion such as a wedding, *bar mitzvah*, or birth.

Simchat Torah: "Joy of the Torah" (Hebrew). The final day of Sukkot,* during which time the annual reading of the Torah* is completed and begun again. In synagogue, the congregation sings and dances with the Torah scrolls.

Sparks: A kabbalistic* notion that fragments of the Divine permeate all matter and can be "lifted up" or "redeemed" through prayer and *mitzvot.* * Evil creates "shells" *(klipot*—Hebrew), around the sparks, that must be shattered to effect *tikkun* (repair) of our imperfect world.

Sukkot: "Booths" (Hebrew). Holiday occurring on the fifteenth day of Tishrei,* following Yom Kippur.* On this holiday, Jews build temporary shelters, called *sukkot* (singular—*sukkah*), commemorating the shelters used by the Children of Israel in the wilderness. During the eight days of this festival, Jews "dwell" in the *sukkah,* eating and even sleeping there. Sukkot is also a fall harvest festival.

Tabernacle: (Hebrew—*Mishkan*). The portable sanctuary housing the Ark* of the Covenant and the altar in the wilderness.

Tallit: "Prayer Shawl" (Hebrew. *Talles*—Yiddish. Plural—*Tallesim*). Fringed garment traditionally worn by Jewish men during prayer. Orthodox boys and men also wear a *tallit katan* (little *tallit*) under their shirts during the day.

Talmud: "Teaching" (Hebrew). Collection of discussions on the Mishnah* by generations of scholars in Babylonia and Palestine, redacted in 500 C.E.* "Gemara" refers to the post-Mishnaic portion of the Talmud. A "Y" in front of a Talmudic tractate refers to the "Yerushalmi" (Jerusalem) Talmud; a "B," to the Babylonian edition.

Tanakh: Abbreviation for *Torah** (Pentateuch), *Nevi'im* (Prophets), and *Ketuvim* (Writings). The traditional Jewish term for the Hebrew Bible; called by Christians "the Old Testament."

Tannaim: "Teachers" (Aramaic. Singular—*Tanna*). Rabbinic teacher of the Mishnaic* period. Followed by Amoraim.* See also "Rabbis."

Tashlikh: "Casting Out" (Hebrew). Ceremony performed on the first day of Rosh Hashanah,* during which time Jews toss crumbs into a stream to symbolize the casting off of their sins.

Tefillin: (From *Tefilah*—prayer. Hebrew). Small leather boxes containing passages from the Bible, attached to the forehead and arm by male Jews during morning weekday prayers.

Temple: (*Beit HaMikdash*—Hebrew). The first Temple was built by Solomon in Jerusalem to house the Ark* of the Covenant and the altar; it was later destroyed by the Babylonians in 586 B.C.E. The Second Temple was rebuilt under Ezra and Nehemiah and renovated by Herod; it was destroyed by the Romans in 70 C.E. In Jewish tradition, the Temple was considered the holiest site in the land and its destruction the greatest tragedy ever to strike the Jewish people. In Messianic times, the Temple will be rebuilt on its former site.

Ten Lost Tribes: When Assyria conquered the northern kingdom of Israel in 722 B.C.E., the ten tribes living there were exiled to foreign lands and subsequently lost their national identity. Many legends have arisen about their fates.

Teshuvah: "Returning" (Hebrew). Repentance.

Tetragrammaton: "Four-letter Word" (Greek). The Sacred Name of God* consisting of the letters *yod, heh, vav, heh* (YHVH), often mistakenly translated as Jehovah.

Third Meal: See "*Shalas Sheudas.*"

Tisha B'Av: "Ninth Day of Av" (Hebrew). Fast day during the summer month of Av, commemorating the destruction of the Temples* in Jerusalem.

Tishrei: Seventh Hebrew month (corresponding to September/October) during which the holidays of Rosh Hashanah,* Yom Kippur,* and Sukkot* occur.

Torah: "Teaching" (Hebrew). The five books of Moses, also called the Pentateuch or *Humash* ("five" in Hebrew), read in synagogue every Monday, Thursday, Sabbath, and Festival. The Torah is the foundation of all Jewish law and practice. The term is very elastic, referring sometimes to the Pentateuch, sometimes to the entire body of Jewish teaching and literature, and occasionally to an individual's teachings based upon traditional texts.

Tu B'Shevat: "Fifteenth day of Shevat" (Hebrew). Mid-winter holiday celebrating the New Year of the Trees in Israel.

Tzaddik: "Righteous One" (Hebrew. Sometimes written "*Zaddik*"). An especially pious individual. In more recent times, the term refers to the leader of a hasidic* community.

Tzedakah: "Righteousness" (Hebrew). Charity.

Tzitzit: "Fringes" (Hebrew). Threads attached to the four corners of the *tallit** as commanded in the Torah.*

World to Come: (*Olam Ha'Ba*—Hebrew). The heavenly realm where righteous souls go after death. A person's deeds earn him or her a "portion in the World to Come." See also "Paradise," "Eden."

Yasher koach: "May you be strengthened" (Hebrew). Traditional Hebrew expression of congratulations.

Yeshivah: "Sitting" (Hebrew). Traditional talmudic* academy.

Yom Kippur: "Day of Atonement" (Hebrew). Fast day observed on the tenth of Tishrei,* during which a Jew makes atonement for his sins.

INDEXES

Note: The numbers listed after the entries in these indexes are tale numbers, not page numbers.

I. HOLIDAYS (in chronological order)

II. TORAH AND HAFTORAH READINGS

III. CHARACTER TYPES

IV. SYMBOLS

V. TOPICS

648

VI. GENERAL INDEX OF NAMES AND PLACES